Lecture Notes in Artificial Intelligence   3194

Edited by J. G. Carbonell and J. Siekmann

Subseries of Lecture Notes in Computer Science

Rui Camacho   Ross King
Ashwin Srinivasan (Eds.)

Inductive
Logic Programming

14th International Conference, ILP 2004
Porto, Portugal, September 6-8, 2004
Proceedings

 Springer

Series Editors

Jaime G. Carbonell, Carnegie Mellon University, Pittsburgh, PA, USA
Jörg Siekmann, University of Saarland, Saarbrücken, Germany

Volume Editors

Rui Camacho
Faculty of Engineering of the University of Porto (FEUP)
Department of Electrical Engineering and Computing
Rua Dr Roberto Frias, s/n, 4200-465 Porto, Portugal
E-mail: rcamacho@fe.up.pt

Ross King
University of Wales, Department of Computer Science
Penglais, Aberystwyth, Ceredigion, SY23 3DB, Wales, UK
E-mail: rdk@aber.ac.uk

Ashwin Srinivasan
IBM India Research Laboratory, Indian Institute of Technology
Hauz Khas, New Delhi 110 016, India
E-mail: ashwin.srinivasan@in.ibm.com

Library of Congress Control Number: 2004095629

CR Subject Classification (1998): I.2.3, I.2.6, I.2, D.1.6, F.4.1

ISSN 0302-9743
ISBN 3-540-22941-8 Springer Berlin Heidelberg New York

Springer is a part of Springer Science+Business Media

springeronline.com

© Springer-Verlag Berlin Heidelberg 2004
Printed in Germany

Typesetting: Camera-ready by author, data conversion by PTP-Berlin, Protago-TeX-Production GmbH
Printed on acid-free paper   SPIN: 11315803   06/3142   5 4 3 2 1 0 .

Preface

"How often we recall, with regret", wrote Mark Twain about editors, "that Napoleon once shot at a magazine editor and missed him and killed a publisher. But we remember with charity, that his intentions were good." Fortunately, we live in more forgiving times, and are openly able to express our pleasure at being the editors of this volume containing the papers selected for presentation at the 14th International Conference on Inductive Logic Programming.

ILP 2004 was held in Porto from the 6th to the 8th of September, under the auspices of the Department of Electrical Engineering and Computing of the Faculty of Engineering of the University of Porto (FEUP), and the Laboratório de Inteligência Artificial e Ciências da Computação (LIACC). This annual meeting of ILP practitioners and curious outsiders is intended to act as the premier forum for presenting the most recent and exciting work in the field. Six invited talks—three from fields outside ILP, but nevertheless highly relevant to it— and 20 full presentations formed the nucleus of the conference. It is the full-length papers of these 20 presentations that comprise the bulk of this volume. As is now common with the ILP conference, presentations made to a "Work-in-Progress" track will, hopefully, be available elsewhere.

We gratefully acknowledge the continued support of Kluwer Academic Publishers for the "Best Student Paper" award on behalf of the journal; and Springer-Verlag for continuing to publish the proceedings of these conferences. The Fundação para a Ciência e a Tecnologia, Fundação Luso-Americana para o Desenvolvimento, Fundação Oriente, Departamento de Engenharia Electrotécnica e de Computadores, and KDNet, the European Knowledge Discovery Network of Excellence have all been extremely generous, and we are thankful. Special mention too must be made of João Correia Lopes, who orchestrated the electronic components of the conference most beautifully.

Porto, June 2004

Rui Camacho
Ross King
Ashwin Srinivasan

Program Committee Chairs

Ashwin Srinivasan	IBM India Research Laboratory, India
Ross King	University of Wales, United Kingdom

Program Committee

Michael Bain	University of New South Wales, Australia
Hendrik Blockeel	Katholieke Universiteit Leuven, Belgium
Luc De Raedt	Albert-Ludwigs-University Freiburg, Germany
Sašo Džeroski	Jozef Stefan Institute, Slovenia
Peter Flach	University of Bristol, United Kingdom
Lawrence Holder	University of Texas at Arlington, USA
Tamas Horvath	University of Bonn and Fraunhofer Inst. for AIS, Germany
Katsumi Inoue	National Institute of Informatics, Japan
Roni Khardon	Tufts University, USA
Jorg-Uwe Kietz	Switzerland
Ross King	University of Wales, United Kingdom
Stefan Kramer	TU München, Germany
Nicolas Lachiche	LSIIT, Pôle API, France
Nada Lavrač	Jozef Stefan Institute, Slovenia
Francesca Lisi	Università degli Studi di Bari, Italy
John Lloyd	Australian National University, Australia
Donato Malerba	University of Bari, Italy
Eric McCreath	Australian National University, Australia
Tetsuhiro Miyahara	Hiroshima City University, Japan
Stephen Muggleton	Imperial College London, United Kingdom
Ramon Otero	University of Corunna, Spain
Tomonobu Ozaki	Graduate School of Media and Governance, Japan
David Page	University of Wisconsin, USA
Jan Ramon	K.U.Leuven, Belgium
Dan Roth	University of Illinois at Urbana-Champaign, USA
Michele Sebag	Université Paris-Sud Orsay, France
Jude Shavlik	University of Wisconsin, USA
Takayoshi Shoudai	Kyushu University, Japan
Ashwin Srinivasan	IBM India Research Laboratory, India
Tomoyuki Uchida	Hiroshima City University, Japan
Christel Vrain	Université d'Orléans, France
Stefan Wrobel	Fraunhofer AIS and University of Bonn, Germany
Akihiro Yamamoto	Kyoto University, Japan
Gerson Zaverucha	Universidade Federal do Rio de Janeiro, Brazil
Filip Železný	Czech Institute of Technology in Prague, Czech Republic
Jean-Daniel Žucker	University of Paris XIII, France

Organizing Committee

Rui Camacho   Universidade do Porto, Portugal
João Correia Lopes   Universidade do Porto, Portugal

Sponsoring Institutions

FCT, Fundação para a Ciência e a Tecnologia (Portugal)
DEEC, Departamento de Engenharia Electrotécnica e de Computadores
(FEUP, Portugal)
FEUP, Faculdade de Engenharia da Universidade do Porto (Portugal)
FLAD, Fundação Luso-Americana para o Desenvolvimento (Portugal)
Fundação Oriente (Portugal)
KDNet, The European Knowledge Discovery Network of Excellence
"Machine Learning" journal of Kluwer Academic Publishers

Additional Referees

Annalisa Appice
Teresa Basile
Margherita Berardi
Michelangelo Ceci
Yann Chevaleyre
Vítor Santos Costa
Damjan Demšar
Frank DiMaio
Nicola Fanizzi
Stefano Ferilli
Daan Fierens

Murdoch J. Gabbay
Kristian Kersting
Nicola Di Mauro
Richard Maclin
Martijn van Otterlo
Aloisio Carlos de Pina
Philip Reiser
Kate Revoredo
Taisuke Sato
Antonio Varlaro
Joost Vennekens

Invited Speakers

James Cussens   University of York, United Kingdom
Luc Dehaspe   Katholieke Universiteit Leuven, Belgium
Jude Shavlik   University of Wisconsin-Madison, USA
Wray Buntine   Helsinki Institute of Information Technology,
    Finland
Pedro Domingos   University of Washington, USA
Steve Oliver   University of Manchester, United Kingdom

Table of Contents

Addendum

Author Index

Automated Synthesis of Data Analysis
Programs: Learning in Logic

Wray Buntine

Complex Systems Computation Group
Helsinki Institute for Information Technology
P.O. Box 9800, FIN-02015 HUT, Finland
Wray.Buntine@HIIT.FI

Program synthesis is the systematic, usually automatic construction of correct and efficient executable code from declarative statements. Program synthesis is routinely used in industry to generate GUIs and for database support.

I contend that program synthesis can be applied as a rapid prototyping method to the data mining phase of knowledge discovery. Rapid prototyping of statistical data analysis algorithms would allow experienced analysts to experiment with different statistical models before choosing one, but without requiring prohibitively expensive programming efforts. It would also smooth the steep learning curve often faced by novice users of data mining tools and libraries. Finally, it would accelerate dissemination of essential research results. For the synthesis task, development on such a system has used a specification language that generalizes Bayesian networks, a dependency model on variables. With decomposition methods and algorithm templates, the system transforms the network through several levels of representation into pseudo-code which can be translated into the implementation language of choice. The system applies computational logic to make learning work.

In this talk, I will present the AutoBayes system developed through a long program of research and development primarily by Bernd Fischer, Johann Schumann and others [1,2] at NASA Ames Research Center, starting from a program of research by Wray Buntine [3] and Mike Lowry. I will explain the framework on a mixture of Gaussians model used in some commercial clustering tools, and present some more realistic examples.

References

1. Bernd Fischer and Johann Schumann. Autobayes: a system for generating data analysis programs from statistical models. *J. Funct. Program.*, 13(3):483–508, 2003.
2. Bernd Fischer and Johann Schumann. Applying Autobayes to the analysis of planetary nebulae images. In *ASE 2003*, pages 337–342, 2003.
3. W. Buntine, B. Fischer, and T. Pressburger. Towards automated synthesis of data mining programs. In *Proceedings of the fifth ACM SIGKDD international conference on Knowledge discovery and data mining*, pages 372–376. ACM Press, 1999.

R. Camacho, R. King, A. Srinivasan (Eds.): ILP 2004, LNAI 3194, p. 1, 2004.
© Springer-Verlag Berlin Heidelberg 2004

At the Interface of Inductive Logic Programming and Statistics

James Cussens

Department of Computer Science
University of York
Heslington, York, YO10 5DD, United Kingdom
http://www-users.cs.york.ac.uk/~jc/

Inductive logic programming can be viewed as a style of statistical inference where the model that is inferred to explain the observed data happens to be a logic program. In general, logic programs have important differences to other models (such as linear models, tree-based models, etc) found in the statistical literature. This why we have ILP conferences!

However, the burden of this talk is that there is much to be gained by situating ILP inside the general problem of statistical inference. I will argue that this can be most readily achieved within a Bayesian framework. Compared to other models a striking characteristic of logic programs is their non-probabilistic nature: a query either fails, succeeds (possibly instantiating output variables) or does not terminate. Defining a particular probability distribution over possible outputs—the hallmark of a statistical model—is not easy to implement with 'vanilla' logic programs.

Recently, there has been a surge of interest in addressing this lacuna: with a number of formalisms proposed (and developed) which explicitly incorporate probability distributions within a logic programming framework. Bayesian logic programs (BLPs), stochastic logic programs (SLPs), PRISM programs and CLP($\mathcal{BN}$) programs are just four such proposals. These logic-based developments are contemporaneous with the growth of "Statistical Relational Learning" (SRL). In SRL the basic goal is to develop learning techniques for data composed of a set of independent and identically distributed (iid) datapoints sitting in a single data table. In other words there is some relationship between the data; or, equivalently, there is some structure in the data which it would be misleading to ignore. Existing SRL models (PRMs are probably the best-known) are not always logical—it remains to be seen how influential statistical ILP will be on this area.

Interestingly, there are related developments emanating from the statistical community. Benefitting from more powerful computers and theoretical advances concerning conditional independence and Bayesian methods, statisticians can now model   —this is the title of a recent book (and European project) in this area. The ILP community has been dealing with "highly structured" learning problems for well over a decade now,

R. Camacho, R. King, A. Srinivasan (Eds.): ILP 2004, LNAI 3194, pp. 2–3, 2004.
© Springer-Verlag Berlin Heidelberg 2004

so this is potentially an area to which statistical ILP can contribute (and benefit from).

My own efforts (together with Nicos Angelopoulos) at the intersection of logic programming and statistics have centred on combining SLPs with a Markov chain Monte Carlo (MCMC) algorithm (the Metropolis-Hastings algorithm, in fact) to effect Bayesian inference. We use SLPs to define prior distributions, so given a non-SLP prior it would be nice to be able to automatically construct an equivalent SLP prior. Since the structure of an SLP is nothing other than a logic program this boils down to an ILP problem. So it's not only that ILP can benefit from statistical thinking, statistics can sometimes benefit from ILP.

From Promising to Profitable Applications of ILP: A Case Study in Drug Discovery

Luc Dehaspe

PharmaDM and Department of Computer Science
Katholieke Universiteit Leuven, Belgium
http://www.cs.kuleuven.ac.be/~ldh/

PharmaDM was founded end 2000 as a spin-off from three European universities (Oxford, Aberystwyth, and Leuven) that participated in two subsequent EC projects on Inductive Logic Programming (ILP I-II, 1992-1998). Amongst the projects highlights was a series of publications that demonstrated the added-value of ILP in applications related to the drug discovery process. The mission of PharmaDM is to build on those promising results, including software modules developed at the founding universities (i.e., Aleph, Tilde, Warmr, ILProlog), and develop a profitable ILP based data mining product customised to the needs of drug discovery researchers. Technology development at PharmaDM is mostly based on "demand pull", i.e., driven by user requirements. In this presentation I will look at the way ILP technology at PharmaDM has evolved over the past four years and the user feedback that has stimulated this evolution.

In the first part of the presentation I will start from the general technology needs in the drug discovery industry and zoom in on the data analysis requirements of some categories of drug discovery researchers. One of the conclusions will be that ILP—via its ability to handle background knowledge and link multiple data sources—offers fundamental solutions to central data analysis problems in drug discovery, but is only perceived by the user as a solution after is has been complemented with (and hidden behind) more mundane technologies.

In the second part of the presentation I will discuss some research topics that we encountered in the zone between promising prototype and profitable product. I will use those examples to argue that ILP research would benefit from very close collaborations, in a "demand-pull" rather than "technology push" mode, with drug discovery researchers. This will however require an initial investment of the ILP team to address the immediate software needs of the user, which are often not related to ILP.

R. Camacho, R. King, A. Srinivasan (Eds.): ILP 2004, LNAI 3194, p. 4, 2004.
© Springer-Verlag Berlin Heidelberg 2004

Systems Biology: A New Challenge for ILP

Steve Oliver

School of Biological Sciences
University of Manchester
United Kingdom

The generation and testing of hypotheses is widely considered to be the primary method by which Science progresses. So much so, that it is still common to find a scientific proposal or an intellectual argument damned on the grounds that "it has no hypothesis being tested", "it is merely a fishing expedition", and so on. Extreme versions run "if there is no hypothesis, it is not Science", the clear implication being that hypothesis-driven programmes (as opposed to data-driven studies) are the only contributor to the scientific endeavour. This misrepresents how knowledge and understanding are actually generated from the study of natural phenomena and laboratory experiments. Hypothesis-driven and inductive modes of reasoning are not competitive, but complementary, and both are required in post-genomic biology.

Thus, post-genomic biology aims to reverse the reductionist trend that has dominated the life sciences for the last 50 years, and adopt a more holistic or integrative approach to the study of cells and organisms. Systems Biology is central to the post-genomic agenda and there are plans to construct complete mathematical models of unicellular organisms, with talk of the 'virtual   ', the '   yeast' etc. In truth, such grand syntheses are a long way off— not least because much of the quantitative data that will be required, if such models are to have predictive value and explanatory power, simply does not exist. Therefore, we will have to approach such comprehensive models in an incremental fashion, first constructing models of smaller sub-systems (e.g. energy generation, cell division etc.) and then integrating these component modules into a single construct, representing the entire cell.

The problem, then, is to ensure that the modules can be joined up in a seamless manner to make a complete working model of a living cell that makes experimentally testable predictions and can be used to explain empirical data. In other words, we do not want to be in a situation, in a five or ten years time, where we attempt to join all the sub-system models together, only to find that we 'can't get there from here'. Preventing such a debacle is partly a mechanical problem—we must ensure that the sub-system models are encoded in a truly modular fashion and that the individual modules are fully interoperable. However, we need something beyond these operational precautions: we require an overarching framework within which the models for the different sub-systems may be constructed. There is a general awareness of this problem and there is much debate about the relative merits of 'bottom-up' and 'top-down' approaches

R. Camacho, R. King, A. Srinivasan (Eds.): ILP 2004, LNAI 3194, pp. 5–6, 2004.
© Springer-Verlag Berlin Heidelberg 2004

in Systems Biology. In fact, both will be needed—but the foregoing discussion demonstrates that the 'top-down' approach faces the larger conceptual problems.

It is difficult to construct an overarching framework for a model of, say, a yeast cell when one has no idea what the final model will look like. There are two kinds of solution to this problem. One is to build a structure that is simply a data model, where different kinds of genomic, functional genomic, genetic, and phenotypic data can be stored. We have already done this (in part) for yeast and have constructed a data warehouse containing all of these data types. However, although the schema for this warehouse looks a bit like a model of a yeast cell, this is an illusion—there is no dynamics and the structure is a hierarchical one, which (while convenient) is far too simplistic a view of the cell. While it would be possible to attach the Systems Biology Modules to the objects in this schema, this would be a cumbersome device, and not sufficiently integrative or realistic. The second kind of solution is to build a very coarse-grained model of the yeast cell based on our current knowledge. This is dangerous since our current knowledge is very incomplete, with much relevant data being unavailable at present. Such a construct would very likely lead to us being in a 'can't get there from here' situation a few years down the road.

A coarse-grained model is certainly desirable, it would be best to get the yeast cell to construct it for us, rather than make an imperfect attempt ourselves. How might this be achieved? First, we need a general mathematical framework in which to build the coarse-grained model. We have chosen to use the formalism of Metabolic Control Analysis, which was developed in part as a shorthand way of modelling biochemical genetic systems and metabolism, but is more widely applicable since, in effect, it represents a sensitivity analysis of the degree of control that different components of a system have over the system as a whole. As such, it seems eminently suitable for our purposes. What we now need to do is to identify those components of the system that exert the greatest degree of control over the pathways in which they participate (or which they regulate). In this initial model, we will not concern ourselves with the complications of the yeast life cycle (i.e. sex!), but will confine our coarse-grained model to a representation of cell growth and mitotic division. Thus, we need to identify those components of a yeast cell that exert the greatest degree of control over its rate of growth and division. In the parlance of Metabolic Control Analysis, these components would be said to have high Flux-Control Coefficients. I will describe the sorts of experiments that might be used for such an approach to Systems Biology, and discuss the role that ILP could play in both the design of these experiments and the derivation of novel insights into biology from the data that they produce.

Scaling Up ILP: Experiences with Extracting Relations from Biomedical Text

Jude Shavlik

Departments of Computer Sciences and
Biostatistics and Medical Informatics
University of Wisconsin-Madison, USA
http://www.cs.wisc.edu/~shavlik/

We have been applying Inductive Logic Programming (ILP) to the task of learning how to extract relations from biomedical text (specifically, Medline abstracts). Our primary focus has been learning to recognize instances of "this protein is localized in this part of the cell" from labeled training examples. ILP allows one to naturally make use of substantial background knowledge (e. g., biomedical ontologies such as the Gene Ontology - GO - and MEdical Subject Headings - MESH) and rich representations of the examples (e. g., parse trees). We discuss how we formulated this task for ILP and describe our methods for scaling ILP to this large task. We conclude with a discussion of some of the major challenges that ILP needs to address in order to scale to large tasks.

Our dataset can be found at ftp://ftp.cs.wisc.edu/machine-learning/ shavlik-group/datasets/IE-protein-location/, and two technical publications on our research can be found in these proceedings. This research was supported by United States National Library of Medicine (NLM) Grant R01 LM07050-01, DARPA Grant F30602-01-2-0571, and United States Air Force Grant F30602-01-2-0571.

R. Camacho, R. King, A. Srinivasan (Eds.): ILP 2004, LNAI 3194, p. 7, 2004.
© Springer-Verlag Berlin Heidelberg 2004

Macro-Operators Revisited in Inductive Logic Programming

Érick Alphonse

MIG - INRA/UR1077
F-78352 Jouy en Josas Cedex France
ealphons@jouy.inra.fr

Abstract. For the last ten years a lot of work has been devoted to propositionalization techniques in relational learning. These techniques change the representation of relational problems to attribute-value problems in order to use well-known learning algorithms to solve them. Propositionalization approaches have been successively applied to various problems but are still considered as ad hoc techniques. In this paper, we study these techniques in the larger context of macro-operators as techniques to improve the heuristic search. The macro-operator paradigm enables us to propose a unified view of propositionalization and to discuss its current limitations. We show that a whole new class of approaches can be developed in relational learning which extends the idea of changes of representation to more suited learning languages. As a first step, we propose different languages that provide a better compromise than current propositionalization techniques between the cost of building macro-operators and the cost of learning. It is known that ILP problems can be reformulated either into attribute-value or multi-instance problems. With the macro-operator approach, we see that we can target a new representation language we name multi-table. This new language is more expressive than attribute-value but is simpler than multi-instance. Moreover, it is PAC-learnable under weak constraints. Finally, we suggest that relational learning can benefit from both the problem solving and the attribute-value learning community by focusing on the design of effective macro-operator approaches.

1 Introduction

After [1], concept learning is defined as search : given a hypothesis space defined a priori, identified by its representation language, find a hypothesis consistent with the learning data. This paper, relating concept learning to search in a space state, has enabled machine learning to integrate techniques from problem solving, operational research and combinatorics. The search is NP-complete for a large variety of languages of interest (e.g. [2,3,4]) and heuristic search is crucial for efficiency. If heuristic search has been showed effective in attribute-value languages, it appeared early that learning in relational languages, known for more than a decade as Inductive Logic Programming (ILP), had to face important

R. Camacho, R. King, A. Srinivasan (Eds.): ILP 2004, LNAI 3194, pp. 8–25, 2004.

[5,6,7] : the evaluation function, used to prioritize nodes in the refinement graph is constant in parts of the search space, and the search goes blind. These plateau phenomenas are the pathological case of heuristic search.

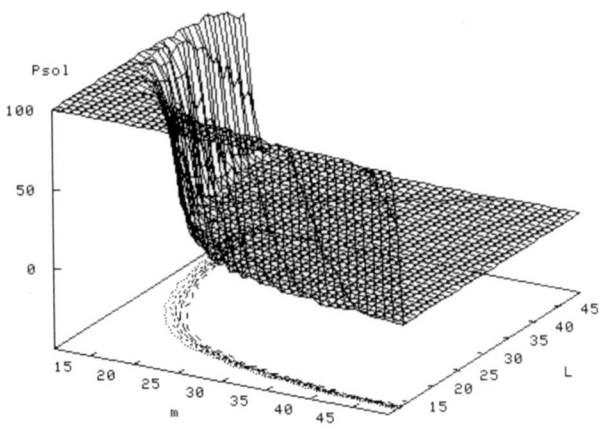

Fig. 1. (from [8]) Coverage probability P_{sol} of an example with L constants by a hypothesis with m literals (built from 10 variables). The contour level plots, projected onto the plane (m, L), correspond to the region where P_{sol} is between 0.99 and 0.01

An explanation can be given after the seminal work of [8], who studied the ILP coverage test within the phase transition framework. As illustrated in figure 1, the covering test is NP-complete and therefore exhibits a sharp phase transition in its coverage probability [9]. If one studies the probability of covering an example of a fixed size by a hypothesis given the hypothesis' size, one distinguishes three well-identified regions: a region, named "yes", where the probability of covering an example is close to 1, a region, named "no", where the probability is close to 0, and finally the phase transition where an example may or may not be covered. As the heuristic value of a hypothesis depends on the number of examples covered (positive or negative), we see that the two regions "yes" and "no" represent plateaus that need to be crossed during search without an informative heuristic value.

The state of the art on evaluation functions used in learning (see for example [10]) shows that all of them are based on two main parameters that are the rate of positive and negative examples covered. As these two parameters are inherited from the definition of the learning task, it is unlikely that a solution for solving the plateau problem consists in designing new evaluations functions. This problem has been well studied in the problem solving community [11] and the solution proposed is based on macro-operators. Macro-operators (macros, for short) are refinement operators defined by composition of elementary refinement operators. They are able to apply several elementary operators at a time (adding or removing several literals in a hypothesis in the case of relational learning) and therefore are likely to cross non informative plateaus. The application of macros in relational learning is not new and has been investigated in e.g. [5,6,7,12]. In these systems, macros   to the list of initial refinement operators and are then classically exploited to search in the refinement graph. In general, this type of technique is known in Machine Learning as Constructive Induction [13], or Predicate Invention in ILP. However, in practice the induced growth of the hypothesis space leads to a decrease of performances [14].

As opposed to these approaches, we view macros as a means to the search space by considering only macros as elementary operators. In other words, our focus is only on the sub-graph generated by the macros. We propose to study a macro-operator approach with respect to the complexity of the new representation language of the hypothesis space associated with this sub-graph. Our approach is similar to abstraction by means of macro-operators [15,11].

We are going to show that a large set of ILP approaches, named   after [16], implicitly use macros to select a sub-graph whose representation language is equivalent to attribute-value (AV). In doing so, they can delegate the simplified learning problems to well-known AV algorithms [17,18, 16,19,20,21,22,23]. The advantage of formalizing theses approaches in terms of macro-operators is threefold. Firstly, it allows to clarify and motivate the propositionalization approaches, which are still considered as ad hoc techniques in literature, as techniques to improve the heuristic search. Secondly, by drawing a parallel with macro-operators, it allows ILP to benefit from techniques formalized and developed in this framework by the Problem Solving community (see e.g. [24,11]). Finally and most importantly, this formalization, by showing propositionalization as a two-stage process (creation of macros and delegation of the simplified search space to simpler learning algorithms), points to promising extensions. Propositionalization as proposed in literature appears to be a special case of resolution by macro-operators. If targeting AV languages is interesting because of the subsequent use of efficient learning algorithms, the cost of building macro-operators for this language is prohibitive and equivalent to the cost of "classical" ILP systems[1] on very simple cases, as we will show it. We propose to relax the constraint on the hypothesis space induced by the definition of macros, by allowing more expressive languages, to offer a better trade-off between the cost of building macros and the cost of learning.

In the next section, before describing the use of macro-operators to solve ILP problems, we are going to recall the different works of various researchers to delegate the resolution of ILP problems to simpler learning algorithms, namely AV and multi-instance ones, without loss of information [25,26,3,27,28,29,30]. We will use this section to introduce the notations used in the rest of the paper. In section 3, we will illustrate the macro-operator approach and we will show how we can associate a language to the hypothesis sub-space selected by macros. A set of languages that can be chosen by means of macros will be presented. We will

---

[1] We refer here to "classical" ILP systems as learning systems not built on macro-operators.

then show in section 5 that the language used by current propositionalization approaches, which is a determinate language, cannot efficiently delegate learning to AV algorithms. In section 6, we will discuss the k-locale language [3] that appears to be the first promising relaxation of the hypothesis space language. We will show that this language allows to reformulate the initial ILP problem into a new representation language we name   . This language is simpler than the multi-instance language [31]. Moreover, in a more constraint form of the language, we will see that a monomial is PAC-learnable, which suggests that efficient algorithms exist. In section 7, we generalize further the hypothesis subspace language to the k-free and k-indeterminate languages and discuss shortly the properties of propositionalization in these languages. Finally, we will conclude and argue that the important effort put in propositionalization techniques can be pursued in richer languages that lift their current shortcomings.

2   Propositionalization

[25,26,32] showed that the ij-determinate language (determinate for short), restricting both the hypothesis space, $\mathcal{L}_h$, and the instance space, was the stronger language bias that could be applied to ILP. Indeed, they proved that it was as expressive as an AV language and that it could be compiled in polynomial time into it. This language has been used as learning language in LINUS and DINUS [33]. Their strategy is to change the representation of the determinate ILP problem to AV, then to delegate learning to AV algorithms and finally to write the learnt theory back into the determinate language. The work of Lavrač and Džeroski has been fruitful to ILP because it suggested that the AV expertise could be reused by change of representation of the initial learning problem.

Extensions of this approach have been proposed in more expressive languages that introduce indeterminism [3,27,28,29,30]. In this case, the reformulated ILP problem is not an AV problem but a multi-instance one. We now give a general description of this change of representation. It is often termed propositionalization in the literature, in a more specific way than [16], as it refers only to the change of representation, independently of the use of macro-operators. We will use this more specific meaning in the rest of the paper in order to better distinguish the different techniques presented in the next section.

A prerequisite to delegate the resolution of an ILP problem to AV or multi-instance algorithms is that the hypothesis spaces in both languages must be isomorphic. In the following, we represent such a bias as a hypothesis base (by analogy with a vectorial base), noted $\mathcal{B}$.

Definition 1 (hypothesis base). $\mathcal{B}$

$$\mathcal{B} = (tc \leftarrow < l_1, \ldots, l_n, v_1, \ldots, v_m >)$$

$l_1, \ldots, l_n$ $v_1, \ldots, v_m$
$l_1, \ldots, l_n$
$\mathcal{B}$

Table 1. A train problem and its propositionalization given $\mathcal{B}$

Examples	Background Knowledge
e^+ $west(t1)$	$car(t1,c11). \; roof(c11). \; \#loads(c11,2).$
e^- $west(t2)$	$car(t1,c12). \; short(c12). \; \#loads(c12,2).$
	$car(t2,c21). \; short(c21). \; \#loads(c21,4).$
	$car(t2,c22). \; rect(c22). \;\; \#loads(c22,2).$

	Variables		Attributes					
	$C1$	$C2$	$car(T,C1)$	$roof(C1)$	$\#loads(C1,2)$	$car(T,C2)$	$\#loads(C2,N)$	N
e^+	$c11$	$c11$	T	T	T	T	T	2
	$c11$	$c12$	T	T	T	T	T	2
	$c12$	$c11$	T	F	T	T	T	2
	$c12$	$c12$	T	F	T	T	T	2
e^-	$c21$	$c21$	T	T	F	T	T	4
	$c21$	$c22$	T	T	F	T	T	2
	$c22$	$c21$	T	F	T	T	T	4
	$c22$	$c22$	T	F	T	T	T	2

By construction, there is a one-to-one mapping between a hypothesis in the clausal space and a hypothesis in the AV space. To perform the search in the AV search space, the ILP instance space needs to be reformulated to emulate the covering test. In other words, the change of representation hard-codes the covering test between the hypotheses and the examples by computing all matchings between $\mathcal{B}$ and the ILP examples for subsequent use by the AV or multi-instance algorithms. If the language is determinate, there will only be one matching and therefore an example will be reformulated into one AV vector, and in the case where the language is indeterminate, an example will be reformulated into a bag of vectors. The fact that the new instance space in the latter case is a multi-instance space is due to the definition of the covering test in ILP: to cover an ILP positive example, we need to find one matching substitution, and to reject an ILP negative example, we need not find any matching substitutions.

An example of propositionalization of a toy problem a la Michalski's trains under θ-subsumption is given in table 1 with the base:

$$\mathcal{B} = (west(T) \leftarrow< car(T,C1), roof(C1), \#loads(C1,2), car(T,C2),$$
$$\#loads(C2,N), N >)$$

For lack of space, we assume the reader is familiar with ILP (see e.g. [34]). The semantic is classical and for example the first positive example reads : the train goes west, its first car has a roof and carries two loads, and its second car is short and has two loads as well. As the train representation is indeterminate, the new representation obtained by propositionalization is a multi-instance one. For a better reading, we omit the instantiation of the head variables of $\mathcal{B}$, as they are determinate.

As noted in [35], the propositionalization is not tractable in the general case: the covering test being NP-complete, the reformulation of a single relational example e can yield an exponential number of AV vectors with respect to the size of $\mathcal{B}$ and e. However, propositionalization has been used successfully in numerical learning. As we can see in the example above, $\mathcal{B}$ introduces the constraint variable N and constraints can be learnt by a multi-instance algorithm. This propositionalization dedicated to numerical learning, which can be traced back to INDUCE [36], has been developed in [27,37,38,39]. In the rest of the paper, we are going to show that this is one of the advantages that motivates the definition of macro-operators in richer languages than determinate languages.

3 Solving ILP Problems by Means of Macro-Operators

As mentioned previously, macro-operators have already been used in ILP [5,6, 7,12]. We illustrate their approach in an example showing a plateau at the first refinement step.

Example 1.

Examples	Background Knowledge
e_1^+ $west(t1)$	$car\_1(t1, c11)$. $short(c11)$. $car\_2(t1, c12)$.
e_2^+ $west(t2)$	$roof(c12)$. $car\_1(t2, c21)$. $short(c21)$.
e_1^- $west(t3)$	$car\_2(t2, c22)$. $short(c22)$. $car\_1(t3, c31)$.
	$roof(c31)$. $car\_2(t3, c32)$. $roof(c32)$.

$$west(T) \leftarrow car\_1(T, C), short(C)$$

fi
$$car\_1(T, C) \qquad car\_2(T, C)$$

$$car\_2(T, C)$$
$$car\_1(T, C), short(C)$$

fi

One solution we adopt to define the macro-operators, which is also discussed in [6], is to create a new literal whose definition corresponds to the composition of the elementary refinement operators. By adding this literal to the background knowledge by saturation (see e.g. [40]), the initial refinement operators can use this literal to refine a hypothesis. Classically, we define a macro-operator with respect to the hypothesis language, its definition corresponding to a valid sequence of refinement operators.

Definition 2 (macro-operator).

m $\{D_i\}$ m m

$\mathcal{L}_h$

$$\forall i, \exists h \in \mathcal{L}_h \qquad body(D_i) = body(h)$$

Example 2.   fi   fi

$$car\_1\_short(T) : - \; car\_1(T, C), short(C).$$
$$car\_2\_roof(T) \;\; : - \; car\_2(T, C), roof(C).$$

fi

Examples	Background Knowledge			
e_1^+ $west(t1)$	$car\_1(t1, c11).$	$short(c11).$	$car\_2(t1, c12).$	$roof(c12).$
e_2^+ $west(t2)$	$car\_1(t2, c21).$	$short(c21).$	$car\_2(t2, c22).$	$short(c22).$
e_1^- $west(t3)$	$car\_1(t3, c31).$	$roof(c31).$	$car\_2(t3, c32).$	$roof(c32).$
	car_1_short(t1). car_2_roof(t1). car_1_short(t2). car_2_roof(t3).			

Here, we propose to simplify the representation by using only the newly defined literals. In other words, we are not interested in the refinement graph augmented with the macros, but only by the sub-graph generated by the macros. If we consider again the above example with this approach, we have the new representation:

Examples	Background knowledge
e_1^+ $west(t1)$	$car\_1\_short(t1). \; car\_2\_roof(t1).$
e_2^+ $west(t2)$	$car\_1\_short(t2). \; car\_2\_roof(t3).$
e_1^- $west(t3)$	

We can notice now that only the constants of the examples ($t1$, $t2$, $t3$) are in the background knowledge. This language is remarkable because it is a determinate language and is known to be as expressive as the attribute-value language, as explained in the previous section. The search can then be delegated to an AV algorithm by propositionalizing the learning examples. This reformulation is shown in table 2.

Table 2. Reformulation of a determinate ILP problem into an AV problem

	Variables	Attributes	
	T	$car\_1\_short(T)$	$car\_2\_roof(T)$
e_1^+	$t1$	T	T
e_2^+	$t2$	T	F
e_1^-	$t3$	F	T

This example is representative of ILP problem solving by macro-operators that we propose and we are going to later give a general algorithm (section 4).

As far as we know, the first works on this approach, even if they do not refer to macros, are due to [17,18]. A lot of subsequent work has been done [16,19, 20,21,22,23] with the same principle of defining macros to simplify the problem into a determinate language, then propositionalizing to delegate learning to AV algorithms. We do not discuss the different techniques that they propose to build what we refer to as macros as it is out of the scope of the paper.

Viewing these approaches as a two-stage process points out interesting directions. On the one hand, it unifies all the above-mentioned approaches focusing on the way they build the macro-operators. Moreover, it proposes a motivation for them, as they are still viewed in literature as ad hoc techniques, as a way to improve heuristic search in ILP. On the other hand, these approaches appear to be a   . They define macros to target the particular determinate language, but we can develop new approaches that define macros to target more expressive languages. By doing so, we argue that we are going to yield different trade-offs between the cost of building macros and the cost of learning. For instance, we are going to show in the next section that building macros for a determinate language is as expensive as "classical" ILP on simple cases.

Even though all languages from determinate languages, actually used, to restrictions of first-order logic can be used, we restrict ourselves to relational languages where propositionalization was proposed. The restriction to these particular languages is motivated by the fact that learning algorithms for these languages are well-known and efficient and we can hope for better trade-offs. We consider all above-mentioned approaches , which have been shown competitive with respect to "classical" ILP systems, as an empirical validation.

4   The General Macro-Operator Approach

We now give the general algorithm for solving ILP problems by means of macro-operators:

1. Choose $\mathcal{L}_\mathcal{B}$, the language in which the hypothesis base $\mathcal{B}$ will be expressed
2. Build a set of macro-operators with respect to $\mathcal{L}_\mathcal{B}$ to define $\mathcal{B}$ in $\mathcal{L}_\mathcal{B}$.
3. Propositionalize the learning data
4. Apply a learning algorithm tailored to the representation of the new learning problem
5. Write the learnt theory back into the initial ILP language[2]

Note that we mix up the saturation and propositionalization stages (step 3) as it is done in the systems proposed in the literature; the cost of saturation, which is NP-complete in the general case, is added to the cost of propositionalization. The size of the reformulated problem can be straightforwardly deduced from the

---

[2] This is not always possible depending on the learning algorithm, like neural networks for example. Classification of future instances must be done in the propositionalized space.

hypothesis base. The size is exponential in the number of variables in the base, the variables appearing in the head excepted.

The gain that more expressive languages than determinate languages can provide to the macro-operator approach is compensated by the cost of reformulation of an ILP problem by propositionalization. Indeed, propositionalization of indeterminate languages yields multi-instance problems of exponential size as the covering test is NP-complete in these languages (section 2). A control of the cost of propositionalization must be done by using languages with bounded indeterminism. Some of these languages have been well studied by [3] and we propose to use them as a basis for new languages for the macro-operator approach. The resulting expected trade-offs between the cost of building macros and the cost of learning is presented in figure 2. The cost of building macro-operators has to be understood as the complexity of defining macros in order to obtain a consistent representation of the new problem.

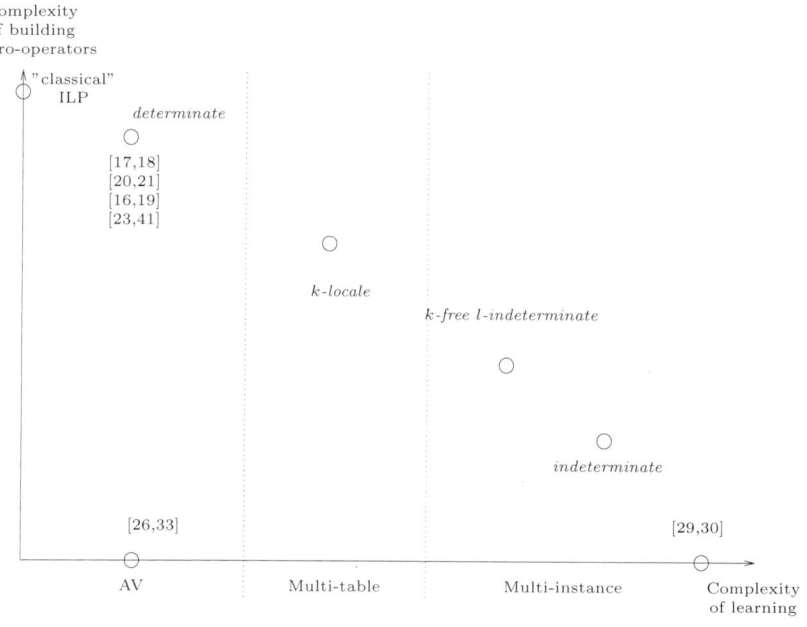

Fig. 2. Trade-offs between cost of building macros and cost of learning

On one side of the range of possible trade-offs, we have "classical" ILP systems. Indeed, we can see a clausal theory as a set of macro-operators[3] and a propositionalization can be performed. Learning is straightforward, classifying a new example as positive if one of its attributes is true, and negative otherwise,

---

[3] This approach has been used early in ILP and has been refined recently in the "repeat learning framework" [14].

that is to say if at least one of the clauses covers the example[4]. This example illustrates the cost of building the macros necessary to obtain a trivial representation of the examples.

On the opposite side, we have the approaches of [29,30] that do not build any macros, or more precisely in our framework, define directly a macro as a literal. The cost of learning is then entirely delegated to a multi-instance algorithm which has to deal with data of exponential size in the general case.

In between these two extreme sides, we see the different classes of approaches which depend on the expressivity of the representation language of the hypothesis base. In the next section, we discuss the limitations of the first class that targets the determinate language to delegate some cost to AV algorithms [17,18,16,19,20, 21,22,23]. We then evaluate the interest of the languages we propose, focusing on the k-locale language which is the first promising relaxation of the determinate language.

5 Limitations of the Determinate Language

Intuitively, the cost of building macros in order to get a consistent representation of the learning problem in a determinate language is very high. It comes from the fact that the new representation describes the example as a whole, as a unique entity, what [20] named an individual-centered representation. That is to say, the macros must define global properties of the learning example. If we have a look at a macro for the determinate language :

$$short\_car\_w/roof(T) : -car(T, C1), short(C1), roof(C1)$$

We see that it describes a property of the train, of the example as a whole: the train has the property of having a short car with a roof. This impacts the cost in two ways.

5.1 Complexity of Numerical Learning

The numerical learning capacity is very limited. We can have a macro describing the total number of loads that the train carries, but not the number of loads carried by a car of the train for example. In other words, the numerical learning part delegated to the learning algorithm is limited only to the properties of the example as a whole. For example, as a workaround, the RELAGGS system [21] computes statistics like the average and the maximum of numerical values appearing in the example. To do numerical learning on parts of the example, the ILP system must generate macro-operators such as:

$$car\_2 + \_loads(T) : -car(T, C1), \#loads(C1, N), N \geq 3$$

to learn that a car must carry more than 2 loads.

---

[4] This is very similar to the table of macro-operators defined by [11] who notes that once the table is computed, no search has to be done to solve the problem.

A solution to this problem is to delegate the complexity of numerical learning to multi-instance algorithms as in [27,28] for example. Numerical variables are then introduced in the hypothesis base (introducing indeterminism) and the set of all their matchings is gathered under a tabular format. As an example, learning constraints on the number of car loads is allowed by the definition of the macro:

$$\#car\_loads(T, N) : -car(T, C1), \#loads(C1, N)$$

The associated hypothesis base $\mathcal{B} = (west(T) \leftarrow< \#car\_loads(T, N), N >)$ would give the following reformulation on a hypothetic ILP problem:

	Variables	Attributes	
	T	$\#car\_loads(T, N)$	N
e^+	$t1$	T	1
	$t1$	T	3
	$t1$	T	2
e^-	$t2$	T	1
	$t2$	T	2
	$t2$	T	2

A multi-instance algorithm could then induce the concept definition:

$$west(T) \leftarrow \#car\_loads(T, N), N \geq 3$$

5.2 Size of Macro-Operators

A second limitation is that some concepts cannot be learnt by AV algorithms and therefore must be represented by a single macro. The cost of building the macros is then   the cost of a classical ILP algorithm. We show this case in a simple example. Let us assume that we have to learn the following concept:

$$west(T) \leftarrow car(T, C1), rect(C1), car(T, C2), rect(C2), C1 \neq C2$$

The concept is that a train has two different rectangular cars. We can see that it cannot be learned by building macros defined with a subset of the concept's literals. The only way to prevent the instantiations of the two cars on a same car is to form a unique macro equivalent to the definition of the concept:

$$2\_rect\_cars(T) : -car(T, C1), rect(C1), car(T, C2), rect(C1), C1 \neq C2$$

By relaxing the constraint of determinism, one can build two macros less complex, defining a rectangular car each, and obtain a multi-intance problem.

We see that in both cases the use of a richer representation language allows to better use the learning algorithms. The first promising language that we consider is the k-locale language.

6   The *k*-locale Language

The *k*-locale language has been proposed by [3] to introduce a bounded indeterminism in each locale of a clause. A locale is defined as a maximal set of
literals where their free variables do not appear in other locales. By bounding
the maximum number of literals in a locale by k, the covering test complexity
of a *k*-locale clause is exponential in k, the covering test of each locale being
independent. In this language, the hypothesis base is a k-locale of the form
$\mathcal{B} = (cc \leftarrow < LOC_1, \ldots, LOC_n >)$, where each LOC_i, a conjunction of macros,
is a locale. However, as opposed to the definition of [3], the number of matching
substitutions of a locale depends here on its number of variables (the saturation
process being implicit). We therefore redefine the notion of locality as follows:

Definition 3 (*k*-locale base). k

$$\mathcal{B} = (tc \leftarrow < LOC_1, \ldots, LOC_n >)$$

$$\forall i \in \{1, \ldots, n\}, LOC_i \qquad\qquad k \geq (vars(LOC_i) \backslash vars(tc))$$

This language allows to define macros that introduce a bounded indeterminism
at the level of each locale of $\mathcal{B}$. For example, $\mathcal{B}$ is a 2-locale with its 2-locales
underlined:

$$\mathcal{B} = (west(T) \leftarrow \quad < \underline{short\_car(T, C1), roof(C1),}$$
$$\underline{short\_car(T, C2), \#loads(C2, N), N} >)$$

This definition of locality is similar to [42], who used the principle of locality
as a decomposition technique to improve the covering test. This decomposition
technique is classical to decompose a problem into a set of sub-problems (see
e.g. [43]), and we will see the additional benefit of *k*-locale bases on propositionalization.

By definition of the locality, while propositionalizing an ILP problem with
$\mathcal{B}$, the instantiation of variable $C1$ does not constraint the instantiations of
variable $C2$. Therefore, it is more efficient to represent the new instance space
by a product representation.

Let us consider the following train problem example:

Examples	Background knowledge
e^+ $west(t1)$	$car(t1, c11)$. $roof(c11)$. $rect(c11)$.
e^- $west(t2)$	$car(t1, c12)$. $short(c12)$. $\#loads(c12, 2)$.
	$car(t2, c21)$. $short(c21)$. $roof(c21)$.
	$car(t2, c22)$. $rect(c22)$. $\#loads(c22, 3)$.

The propositionalization must take into account the locales to generate for each
of them a multi-instance problem as we show in figure 3. This representation of
the problem has only two lines at the maximum per example, instead of four
in its developed representation, which would be obtained by naive propositionalization. This representation, obtained by decomposition of a multi-instance

adapted from [3]: the k-free and the l-indeterminate languages. These languages are complementary in the way they bound the indeterminism. The first language, bounding the number of free variables in $\mathcal{B}$, bounds theoretically the size of the multi-instance problem by an exponential in k. The second one directly bounds the size of the multi-instance problem by l, which is the number of matchings between $\mathcal{B}$ and the examples. As opposed to the former, it takes into account the background knowledge and the type of the variables, and therefore allows for a tighter upper bound.

As an example, one simple and efficient use of these languages is to introduce indeterminism only with the numerical variables to delegate numerical learning to multi-instance algorithms.

8 Conclusion

It is known that ILP is prone to plateau phenomenas during heuristic search and macro-operators are well motivated to reduce these problems. We have proposed a paradigm to solve ILP problems by means of macro-operators. As opposed to previous approaches, the macros are not used to extend the refinement graph but only to select a relevant sub-graph. We have shown that we can associate a representation language to the sub-graph and study a macro-operator approach in terms of the expressivity of this representation language. We have shown that a large set of ILP techniques [17,18,16,19,20,21,22,23] are a particular case of the paradigm. They define macros to reformulate ILP problems in a determinate language and delegate learning by propositionalization to AV learning algorithms, suitable for determinate languages. However, their cost of building macros is in the worst case as expensive as "classical" ILP. Notably, numerical learning has to be done in the ILP search space and cannot be delegated to AV algorithms. We have then proposed a range of different languages adapted from [3] that allows better trade-offs between the cost of building macros and the cost of learning.

The first promising trade-off is the k-locale language that reformulates ILP problems to a new representation language we have named   . It is a product representation of a multi-instance problem and can represent the same amount of information in a more compact way. Moreover, we have shown that monomials was PAC-learnable if the number of attributes per table was fixed, which suggests that efficient learning algorithms are available. Such a restriction appears naturally in the propositionalization framework if we limit the size of each locale in the hypothesis space. We think that the definition of the multi-table representation goes beyond its use in ILP and may be used as learning language as well.

From our point of view, the important effort put in designing macro-operators for the determinate language for the last ten years can be pursued in richer languages that lift their current shortcomings. ILP can benefit from the problem solving community by reusing techniques to build macro-operators and then delegate learning to simpler learning algorithms like AV, multi-table and multi-instance algorithms. To start experimenting with the different classes of approach, we will work on a multi-table algorithm and develop techniques to build macro-operators for the k-locale language.

Acknowledgments. We would like to thank Céline Rouveirol and all the reviewers for their valuable comments. We would also like to acknowledge Claire Nédellec for her support in the writing of this article.

References

1. Mitchell, T.M.: Generalization as search. Artificial Intelligence **18** (1982) 203–226
2. Haussler, D.: Learning conjunctive concepts in structural domains. Machine Learning **4** (1989) 7–40
3. Cohen, W.W.: Learnability of restricted logic programs. In Muggleton, S., ed.: Proceedings of the 3rd International Workshop on Inductive Logic Programming, J. Stefan Institute (1993) 41–72
4. Kearns, M.J., Vazirani, U.V.: An Introduction to Computational Learning Theory. The MIT Press, Cambridge, Massachusetts (1994)
5. Quinlan, J.R.: Determining literals in inductive logic programming. In: Proceedings of the 12th International Joint Conference on Artificial Intelligence, Sydney, Austalia (1991) 746–750
6. Silverstein, G., Pazzani, M.J.: Relational cliches: Constraining constructive induction during relational learning. In Birnbaum, L., Collins, G., eds.: Proceedings of the 8th International Workshop on Machine Learning, Morgan Kaufmann (1991) 203–207
7. Richards, B., Mooney, R.: Learning relations by pathfinding. In: Proceedings of the Tenth National Conference on Artificial Intelligence. (1992) 723–738
8. Giordana, A., Saitta, L.: Phase transitions in learning relations. Machine Learning **41** (2000) 217–25
9. Cheeseman, P., Kanefsky, B., Taylor, W.M.: Where the really hard problems are. In Myopoulos, John; Reiter, R., ed.: Proceedings of the 12th International Joint Conference on Artificial Intelligence, Sydney, Australia, Morgan Kaufmann (1991) 331–340
10. Fürnkranz, J., Flach, P.: An analysis of rule learning heuristics. Technical Report CSTR-03-002, Department of Computer Science, University of Bristol (2003)
11. Korf, R.E.: Macro-operators: a weak method for learning. Artificial Intelligence, 1985 **26** (1985) 35–77
12. Peña Castillo, L., Wrobel, S.: Macro-operators in multirelational learning: a search-space reduction technique. In: Proceedings of the 13th European Conference on Machine Learning. Volume 2430 of Lecture Notes in Artificial Intelligence., Springer-Verlag (2002) 357–368
13. Michalski, R.S.: Pattern recognition as knowledge-guided computer induction. Technical Report 927, Department of Computer Science, University of Illinois at Urbana-Champaign, Urbana, Illinois (1978)
14. Khan, K., Muggleton, S., Parson, R.: Repeat learning using predicate invention. In Page, C., ed.: Proc. of the 8th International Workshop on Inductive Logic Programming (ILP-98). LNAI 1446, Berlin, Springer-Verlag (1998) 165–174
15. Amarel, S. In: On Representations of Problems of Reasoning about Actions. American Elsevier, New York, NY (1968) 131–171

16. Kramer, S., Pfahringer, B., Helma, C.: Stochastic propositionalization of non-determinate background knowledge. In Page, D., ed.: Proc. of the 8th International Workshop on Inductive Logic Programming, Springer Verlag (1998) 80–94

17. Turney, P.: Low size-complexity inductive logic programming: The East-West challenge considered as a problem in cost-sensitive classification. In: Proceedings of the 5th International Workshop on Inductive Logic Programming. (1995) 247–263

18. Geibel, P., Wysotzki, F.: Learning context dependent concepts. In Raedt, L.D., ed.: Proceedings of the 5th International Workshop on Inductive Logic Programming, Department of Computer Science, Katholieke Universiteit Leuven (1995) 323–337

19. Cumby, C., Roth, D.: Relational representations that facilitate learning. In Cohn, A.G., Giunchiglia, F., Selman, B., eds.: Proceedings of the Conference on Principles of Knowledge Representation and Reasoning (KR-00), S.F., Morgan Kaufman Publishers (2000) 425–434

20. Lavrač, N., Flach, P.A.: An extended transformation approach to inductive logic programming. ACM Transactions on Computational Logic **2** (2001) 458–494

21. Krogel, M.A., Wrobel, S.: Transformation-based learning using multirelational aggregation. In: Proceedings of the 11th International Conference on Inductive Logic Programming. Volume 2157 of LNAI., Springer-Verlag (2001) 142–155

22. Roth, D., Yih, W.: Relational learning via propositional algorithms: An information extraction case study. In Nebel, B., ed.: Proceedings of the seventeenth International Conference on Artificial Intelligence (IJCAI-01), San Francisco, CA, Morgan Kaufmann Publishers, Inc. (2001) 1257–1263

23. Kramer, S., de Raedt, L.: Feature construction with version spaces for biochemical applications. In: Proc. 18th International Conf. on Machine Learning, Morgan Kaufmann, San Francisco, CA (2001) 258–265

24. Hernádvölgyi, I.T.: Searching for macro operators with automatically generated heuristics. Lecture Notes in Computer Science **2056** (2001) 194–??

25. Lavrac, N., Dzeroski, S., Grobelnik, M.: Learning nonrecursive definitions of relations with LINUS. In Kodratoff, Y., ed.: Proceedings of the European Working Session on Learning : Machine Learning (EWSL-91). Volume 482 of LNAI., Porto, Portugal, Springer Verlag (1991) 265–281

26. Dzeroski, S., Muggleton, S., Russell, S.J.: PAC-learnability of determinate logic programs. In: Proceedings of the Fifth Annual ACM Workshop on Computational Learning Theory (COLT-92), Pittsburgh, Pennsylvania, ACM Press (1992)

27. Zucker, J.D., Ganascia, J.G.: Selective reformulation of examples in concept learning. In: Proc. 11th International Conference on Machine Learning, Morgan Kaufmann (1994) 352–360

28. Sebag, M., Rouveirol, C.: Induction of maximally general clauses consistent with integrity constraints. In Wrobel, S., ed.: Proceedings of the 4th International Workshop on Inductive Logic Programming. Volume 237 of GMD-Studien., Gesellschaft für Mathematik und Datenverarbeitung MBH (1994) 195–216

29. Fensel, D., Zickwolff, M., Wiese, M.: Are substitutions the better examples? Learning complete sets of clauses with Frog. In: Proceedings of the 5th International Workshop on Inductive Logic Programming. (1995) 453–474

30. Sebag, M., Rouveirol, C.: Resource-bounded relational reasoning: Induction and deduction through stochastic matching. Machine Learning **38** (2000) 41–62

31. Dietterich, T.G., Lathrop, R.H., Lozano-Pérez, T.: Solving the multiple instance problem with axis-parallel rectangles. Artificial Intelligence **89** (1997) 31–71

32. Kietz, J.U., Dzeroski, S.: Inductive logic programming and learnability. SIGART Bulletin **5** (1994) 22–32

33. Lavrač, N., Džeroski, S.: Inductive Logic Programming : techniques and Applications. Ellis Horwood (1994)

34. Nienhuys-Cheng, S.H., de Wolf, R.: Foundations of Inductive Logic Programming. Volume 1228 of Lecture Notes in Artificial Intelligence. Springer-Verlag (1997)

35. Sebag, M., Rouveirol, C.: Tractable induction and classification in first order logic via stochastic matching. In: 15th Int. Join Conf. on Artificial Intelligence (IJCAI'97), Morgan Kaufmann (1997) 888–893

36. Dietterich, T.G., Michalski, R.S.: A comparative review of selected methods for learning from examples. In Michalski, R.S., Carbonell, J.G., Mitchell, T.M., eds.: Machine Learning, an Artificial Intelligence approach. Volume 1. Morgan Kaufmann, San Mateo, California (1983) 41–81

37. Sebag, M., Rouveirol, C.: Constraint inductive logic programming. In Raedt, L.D., ed.: Proceedings of the 5th International Workshop on Inductive Logic Programming, Department of Computer Science, Katholieke Universiteit Leuven (1995) 181–198

38. Anthony, S., Frisch, A.M.: Generating numerical literals during refinement. In Lavrač, N., Džeroski, S., eds.: Proceedings of the 7th International Workshop on Inductive Logic Programming. Volume 1297 of LNAI., Berlin, Springer (1997) 61–76

39. Botta, M., Piola, R.: Refining numerical constants in first order logic theories. Machine Learning **38** (2000) 109–131

40. Rouveirol, C.: Flattening and saturation: Two representation changes for generalization. Machine Learning **14** (1994) 219–232

41. Liquière, M.: Du structurel au propositionnel, une approche formelle. In: CAP, Grenoble (2001)

42. Kietz, J.U., Lübbe, M.: An efficient subsumption algorithm for inductive logic programming. In Cohen, W.W., Hirsh, H., eds.: Proc. 11th International Conference on Machine Learning, Morgan Kaufmann (1994) 130–138

43. Gottlob, G., Leone, N., Scarello, F.: A comparison of structural CSP decomposition methods. Artificial Intelligence **124** (2000) 243–282

44. de Raedt, L.: Attribute-value learning versus inductive logic programming : The missing link. In Page, D., ed.: Proc. of the 8th International Workshop on Inductive Logic Programming, Springer Verlag (1998) 1–8 Extended abstract.

45. Chevaleyre, Y., Zucker, J.D.: A framework for learning rules from multiple instance data. In: Machine Learning: ECML 2001, 12th European Conference on Machine Learning, Freiburg, Germany, September 5-7, 2001, Proceedings. Volume 2167 of Lecture Notes in Artificial Intelligence., Springer (2001) 49–60

46. Pitt, L., Warmuth, M.K.: Prediction preserving reducibility. J. of Comput. Syst. Sci. **41** (1990) 430–467 Special issue of the for the *Third Annual Conference of Structure in Complexity Theory* (Washington, DC., June 88).

problem, is simpler and exponentially more compact than the developed multi-instance problem. We name this new representation the   representation, each table being a multi-instance problem. Note that we do not see the multi-table representation as a generalization of the multi-instance representation, but as a representation in between AV and multi-instance, as a result of a product representation of a multi-instance problem, like other decomposition techniques (see [42,43]). We present some learnability result in this language.

	Variables	Attributes	
	$C1$	$sh\_c(T,C1)$	$roof(C1)$
e^+	c11	F	T
	c12	T	F
e^-	c21	T	T
	c22	F	F

$\times$

	Variables	Attributes		
	$C2$	$sh\_c(T,C2)$	$\#loads(C2,N)$	N
e^+	c11	F	F	-
	c12	T	T	2
e^-	c21	T	F	-
	c22	F	T	3

	Variables		Attributes				
	$C1$	$C2$	$short\_car(T,C1)$	$roof(C1)$	$short\_car(T,C2)$	$\#loads(C2,N)$	N
e^+	c11	c11	F	T	F	F	-
	c11	c12	F	T	T	T	2
	c12	c11	T	F	F	F	-
	c12	c12	T	F	T	T	2
e^-	c21	c21	T	T	T	F	-
	c21	c22	T	T	F	T	3
	c22	c21	F	F	T	F	-
	c22	c22	F	F	F	T	3

Fig. 3. A multi-table representation and its developed multi-instance one

6.1 On Learnability of Multi-table Problems

A multi-table representation is a vector $< T_1, \ldots, T_n >$ where each coordinate is a multi-instance problem. An example is of the form $e =< b_1, \ldots, b_n >$ with b_i a bag of AV instances defined in the instance space of T_i. The number of instances in each bag is variable and depends on the table.

No learning algorithms are devoted to this representation yet, but it is easy to extrapolate with the expertise gained from the design of multi-instance algorithms from AV algorithms. As with the multi-instance representation, it is easy to adapt top-down generate-and-test algorithms as noted in [44,45] : these algorithms search the same hypothesis space but adapt the covering test to the multi-table representation.

Much in line with Cohen's work on PAC-learnability of single clause in the k-locale language, an interesting restriction of the multi-table representation is to bound the number of attributes by a constant l, for any number of tables. In the macro-operator approach, this restriction corresponds to bounding the size of the locales in the hypothesis base, but not its size. In this language, we show that monomials are PAC-learnable and then efficient algorithms exist. We give the proof for completeness as we work with the multi-table representation and that we do not have the same parameters as Cohen (l and k). Following, [3], this concept language is noted $\mathcal{L}^1_{l-MULTI-TABLE}$.

Theorem 1. fi l $\mathcal{L}^1_{l-MULTI-TABLE}$

Proof 1.
    $\mathcal{L}^1_{l-MULTI-TABLE}$

Lemma 1 (from [46]). $\mathcal{L}_{h1}$ $\mathcal{L}_{h2}$ $\mathcal{L}_{e1}$
$\mathcal{L}_{e2}$ $C \in \mathcal{L}_{h1}$
$f_i : \mathcal{L}_{e1} \to \mathcal{L}_{e2}$ $f_c : \mathcal{L}_{h1} \to \mathcal{L}_{h2}$
      $\mathcal{L}_{h1}$ $\mathcal{L}_{h2}$ $\mathcal{L}_{h2}$ $f_c^{-1}(C)$
          $\mathcal{L}_{h1}$

         l

        $n \times 2^{2l}$
     T_i l $\{t_{i1}, \ldots, t_{il}\}$ fi
$2l$ $A_i = \{t_{i1}, \ldots, t_{il}, \neg t_{i1}, \ldots, \neg t_{il}\}$ A_i fi
   B_i 2^{2l} T_i
  A_i

f_i $n \times 2^{2l}$ $(B_1, \ldots, B_n)$

f_c $< c_1, \ldots, c_n >$ c_i
      $b \in B_i$ c_i $ff\ b$ f_c

7 Discussion

Besides the k-locale language, all languages with bounded indeterminism (i.e. yielding bounded multi-instance problems through propositionalization) are candidate for the language of the hypothesis space targeted by the macro-operators. The relative benefit of these different languages with respect to the trade-off between the cost of building macros and the cost of learning is still an open question and a good amount of future works will be to experiment with them. In figure 2, we extrapolate on the trade-offs we can expect from two other languages

Bottom-Up ILP Using Large Refinement Steps*

Marta Arias and Roni Khardon

Department of Computer Science, Tufts University
Medford, MA 02155, USA
{marias,roni}@cs.tufts.edu

Abstract. The LOGAN-H system is a bottom up ILP system for learning multi-clause and multi-predicate function free Horn expressions in the framework of learning from interpretations. The paper introduces a new implementation of the same base algorithm which gives several orders of magnitude speedup as well as extending the capabilities of the system. New tools include several fast engines for subsumption tests, handling real valued features, and pruning. We also discuss using data from the standard ILP setting in our framework, which in some cases allows for further speedup. The efficacy of the system is demonstrated on several ILP datasets.

1 Introduction

Inductive Logic Programming (ILP) has established a core set of methods and systems that proved useful in a variety of applications [20,4]. Early work in the Golem system [21] (see also [19]) used Plotkin's [24] least general generalization (LGG) within a bottom up search to find a hypothesis consistent with the data. On the other hand, much of the research following this (e.g. [25,18,7,3]) has used top down search methods to find useful hypotheses. However, several exceptions exist. STILL [26] uses a disjunctive version space approach which means that it has clauses based on examples but it does not generalize them explicitly. The system of [1] uses bottom up search with some ad hoc heuristics to solve the challenge problems of [11]. The LOGAN-H system [13] is based on an algorithm developed in the setting of learning with queries [12] but uses heuristics to avoid asking queries and instead uses a dataset as input. This system uses a bottom up search, based on inner products of examples which are closely related to LGG. Another important feature of LOGAN-H is that it does a refinement search but, unlike other approaches, it takes large refinement steps instead of minimal ones.

In previous work [13] LOGAN-H was shown to be useful in a few small domains. However, it was hard to use the system in larger applications mainly due to high run time. One of the major factors in this is the cost of subsumption. Like other bottom up approaches, LOGAN-H may use very long clauses early on in the search and the cost of subsumption tests for these is high. This is in contrast to top down approaches that start with short clauses for which subsumption is

---

* This work has been partly supported by NSF Grant IIS-0099446

R. Camacho, R. King, A. Srinivasan (Eds.): ILP 2004, LNAI 3194, pp. 26–43, 2004.
© Springer-Verlag Berlin Heidelberg 2004

easy. A related difficulty observed in Golem [21] is that LGG can lead to very large hypotheses. In LOGAN-H this is avoided by using 1-1 object mappings. This helps reduce the size of the hypothesis but gives an increase in complexity in terms of the size of the search.

The current paper explores a few new heuristics and extensions to LOGAN-H that make it more widely applicable both in terms of speed and range of applications. The paper describes a new implementation that includes several improved subsumption tests. In particular, for LOGAN-H we need a subsumption procedure that finds all substitutions between a given clause and an example. This suggests a memory based approach that collects all substitutions simultaneously instead of using backtracking search. Our system includes such a procedure which is based on viewing partial substitutions as tables and performing "joins" of such tables to grow complete substitutions. A similar table-based method was developed in [8]. This approach can be slow or even run out of memory if there are too many partial substitutions in any intermediate step. Our system implements heuristics to tackle this, including lookahead search and randomized heuristics. The latter uses informed sampling from partial substitution tables if memory requirements are too large. In addition, for some applications it is sufficient to test for existence of substitutions between a given clause and an example (i.e. we do not need all substitutions). In these applications we are able to use the fast subsumption test engine DJANGO [16] in our system. The paper shows that different engines can give better performance in different applications, and gives some paradigmatic cases where such differences occur.

In addition the system includes new heuristics and facilities including discretization of real valued arguments and pruning of rules. Both introduce interesting issues for bottom up learning which do not exist for top down systems. These are explored experimentally and discussed in the body of the paper.

The performance of the system is demonstrated in three domains: the Bongard domain [7,13], the KRK-illegal domain [25], and the Mutagenesis domain [29]. All these have been used before with other ILP systems. The results show that our system is competitive with previous approaches while applying a completely different algorithmic approach. This suggests that bottom up approaches can indeed be used in large applications. The results and directions for future work are further discussed in the concluding section of the paper.

2 Learning from Interpretations

We briefly recall the setup in Learning from Interpretations [6] and introduce a running example which will help explain the algorithm. The task is to learn a universally quantified function-free Horn expression, that is, a conjunction of Horn clauses. The learning problem involves a finite set of predicates whose signature, i.e. names and arities, are fixed in advance. In the examples that follow we assume two predicates $p()$ and $q()$ both of arity 2. For example, $c_1 = \forall x_1, \forall x_2, \forall x_3, [p(x_1, x_2) \wedge p(x_2, x_3) \rightarrow p(x_1, x_3)]$ is a clause in the language. An example is an •• •••••••••••• listing a domain of elements and the extension of predicates over them. The example $e_1 = ([1, 2, 3], [[p(1, 2), p(2, 3), p(3, 1), q(1, 3)]])$ describes an interpretation with domain $[1, 2, 3]$ and where the four atoms listed are true in the interpretation and other atoms are false. The size of an example is the number of atoms true in it, so that $size(e_1) = 4$. The example e_1 falsifies the clause above (substitute $\{1/x_1, 2/x_2, 3/x_3\}$), so it is a negative example. On the other hand $e_2 = ([a, b, c, d], [[p(a, b), p(b, c), p(a, c), p(a, d), q(a, c)]])$ is a positive example. We use standard notation $e_1 \not\models c_1$ and $e_2 \models c_1$ for these facts. The system (the batch algorithm of [13]) performs the standard supervised learning task: given a set of positive and negative examples it produces a Horn expression as its output.

3 The Base System

We first review the basic features of the algorithm and system as described in [13]. The algorithm works by constructing an intermediate hypothesis and repeatedly refining it until the hypothesis is consistent with the data. The algorithm's starting point is the most specific •••••• ••• that "covers" a particular negative example. A clause set is a set of Horn clauses that have the same antecedent but different conclusions. In this paper, we use $[s, c]$ and variations of it to denote a clause set, where s is a set of atoms (the antecedent) and c is a set of atoms (each being a consequent of a clause in the clause set). Once the system has some such clauses it searches the dataset for a misclassified example. Upon finding one (it is guaranteed to be a negative example) the system tries to refine one of its clause sets using a generalization operation which we call •••••• •. Pairing is an operation akin to LGG [24] but it controls the size of the hypothesis by using a restriction imposed by a one to one object correspondence. If pairing succeeds, that is, the refinement is found to be good, the algorithm restarts the search for misclassified examples. If pairing did not produce a good clause, the system adds a new most specific clause set to the hypothesis. This process of refinements continues until no more examples are misclassified.

To perform the above the system needs to refer to the dataset in order to evaluate whether the result of refinements, a proposed clause set, is useful or not. This is performed by an operation we call ••• •••••••. In addition the algorithm uses an initial "minimization" stage where candidate clause sets are reduced in size. The high level structure of the algorithm is given in Figure 3. We proceed with details of the various operations as required by the algorithm.

Candidate clauses: For an interpretation I, $rel\text{-}ant(I)$ is a conjunction of positive literals obtained by listing all atoms true in I and replacing each object in I with a distinct variable. So $rel\text{-}ant(e_1) = p(x_1, x_2) \wedge p(x_2, x_3) \wedge p(x_3, x_1) \wedge q(x_1, x_3)$. Let X be the set of variables corresponding to the domain of I in this transformation. The set of candidate clauses $rel\text{-}cands(I)$ includes clauses of the form $(rel\text{-}ant(I) \rightarrow p(Y))$, where p is a predicate, Y is a tuple of variables from X of the appropriate arity and $p(Y)$ is not in $rel\text{-}ant(I)$. For example, $rel\text{-}cands(e_1)$ includes among others the clauses $[p(x_1, x_2) \wedge p(x_2, x_3) \wedge p(x_3, x_1) \wedge q(x_1, x_3) \rightarrow p(x_2, x_2)]$, and $[p(x_1, x_2) \wedge p(x_2, x_3) \wedge p(x_3, x_1) \wedge q(x_1, x_3) \rightarrow q(x_3, x_1)]$, where

1. Initialize S to be the empty sequence.
2. Repeat until H is correct on all examples in E.
    a) Let $H = variabilize(S)$.
    b) If H misclassifies I (I is negative but $I \models H$):
        i. $[s, c] = one\text{-}pass(rel\text{-}cands(I))$.
        ii. $[s, c] = minimize\text{-}objects([s, c])$.
        iii. For $i = 1$ to m (where $S = ([s_1, c_1], \ldots, [s_m, c_m])$))
            For every pairing J of s_i and s
            If J's size is smaller than s_i's size then
                let $[s, c] = one\text{-}pass([J, c_i \cup (s_i \setminus J)])$.
            If c is not empty then
                A. Replace $[s_i, c_i]$ with $[s, c]$.
                B. Quit loop (Go to Step 2a)
        iv. If no s_i was replaced then add $[s, c]$ as the last element of S.

Fig. 1. The Learning Algorithm (Input: example set E)

all variables are universally quantified. Note that there is a 1-1 correspondence between a ground clause set $[s, c]$ and its variabilized versions. We refer to the variabilization using $variabilize(\cdot)$. In the following we just use $[s, c]$ with the implicit understanding that the appropriate version is used.

As described above, any predicate in the signature can be used as a consequent by the system. However, in specific domains the user often knows which predicates should appear as consequents. To match this, the system allows the user to specify which predicates are allowed as consequents of clauses. Naturally, this improves run time by avoiding the generation, validation and deletion of useless clauses.

The one-pass procedure: Given a clause set $[s, c]$ •••••••• tests clauses in $[s, c]$ against all positive examples in E. The basic observation is that if a positive example can be matched to the antecedent but one of the consequents is false in the example under this matching then this consequent is wrong. For each example e, the procedure •••••••• removes ••• wrong consequents identified by e from c. If c is empty at any point then the process stops and $[s, \emptyset]$ is returned. At the end of ••••••••, each consequent is correct w.r.t. the dataset.

This operation is at the heart of the algorithm since the hypothesis and candidate clause sets are repeatedly evaluated against the dataset. Two points are worth noting here. First, once we match the antecedent we can test all the consequents simultaneously so it is better to keep clause sets together rather than split them into individual clauses. Second, notice that since we must verify that consequents are correct, it is not enough to find just one substitution from an example to the antecedent. Rather we must check all such substitutions before declaring that some consequents are not contradicted. This is an issue that affects the implementation and will be discussed further below.

Minimization: Minimization takes a clause set $[s, c]$ and reduces its size so that it includes as few objects as possible while still having at least one correct consequent. This is done by "dropping objects". For example, for $[s, c] = [[p(1, 2), p(2, 3), p(3, 1), q(1, 3)], [p(2, 2), q(3, 1)]]$, we can drop object 1 and all atoms using it to get $[s, c] = [[p(2, 3)], [p(2, 2)]]$. The system iteratively tries to drop each domain element. In each iteration it drops an object to get $[s', c']$, runs •••••••• on $[s', c']$ to get $[s'', c'']$. If c'' is not empty it continues with it to the next iteration (assigning $[s, c] \leftarrow [s'', c'']$); otherwise it continues with $[s, c]$.

Pairing: The pairing operation combines two clause sets $[s_a, c_a]$ and $[s_b, c_b]$ to create a new clause set $[s_p, c_p]$. When pairing we utilize an injective mapping from the smaller domain to the larger one. The system first pairs the antecedents by taking the intersection under the injective mapping (using names from $[s_a, c_a]$) to produce a new antecedent J. The resulting clause set is $[s_p, c_p] = [J, (c_a \cap c_b) \cup (s_a \setminus J)]$. To illustrate this, the following example shows the two original clauses, a mapping and the resulting values of J and $[s_p, c_p]$.

- $[s_a, c_a] = [[p(1, 2), p(2, 3), p(3, 1), q(1, 3)], [p(2, 2), q(3, 1)]]$
- $[s_b, c_b] = [[p(a, b), p(b, c), p(a, c), p(a, d), q(a, c)], [q(c, a)]]$
- The mapping $\{1/a, 2/b, 3/c\}$
- $J = [p(1, 2), p(2, 3), q(1, 3)]$
- $[s_p, c_p] = [[p(1, 2), p(2, 3), q(1, 3)], [q(3, 1), p(3, 1)]]$

The clause set $[s_p, c_p]$ obtained by the pairing can be more general than the original clause sets $[s_a, c_a]$ and $[s_b, c_b]$ since s_p is contained in both s_a and s_b (under the injective mapping). Hence, the pairing operation can be intuitively viewed as a generalization of both participating clause sets. However since we modify the consequent, by dropping some atoms and adding other atoms (from $s_a \setminus J$), this is not a pure generalization operation.

Clearly, any two examples have a pairing for each injective mapping of domain elements. The system reduces the number of pairings that are tested by using only "live pairings" where each object appears in the extension of at least one atom in J. The details are described in [13].

Caching: The operation of the algorithm may produce repeated calls to ••••••• with the same antecedent since pairings of one clause set with several others may result in the same clause set. Thus it makes sense to cache the results of •••••••. We cache ground versions of the s part of the clause set if •••••• determined that no consequents are true for it. So in such a case we get an immediate answer in future calls. The details are similar to [13].

4   Performance Issues and Applicability

While the results reported in [13] were encouraging several aspects precluded immediate application to real world data sets.

The Subsumption Test: Perhaps the most important issue is run time which is dominated by the cost of subsumption tests and the •••••••• procedure. It is well known that testing subsumption is NP-Hard [14] and therefore we do not expect a solution in the general case. However it is useful to look at the crucial parameters. In general subsumption scales exponentially in the number of variables in the clauses but polynomially with the number of predicates [23]. The problem is made worse in our system because of the bottom-up nature of the learning process[1]. When we generate the most specific clause for an example, the number of variables in the clause is the same as the number of objects in the example and this can be quite large in some domains. In some sense the minimization process tries to overcome this problem by removing as many objects as possible (this fact is used in [12] to prove good complexity bounds). However the minimization process itself runs •••••••• and therefore forms a bottleneck. In addition, for •••••••• it is important to find all substitutions between a clause and an example. Therefore, a normal subsumption test that checks for the existence of a substitution is not sufficient. For problems with highly redundant structure the number of substitutions can grow exponentially with the number of predicates so this can be prohibitively expensive. Thus an efficient solution for •••••••• is crucial in applications with large examples.

Suitability of Datasets and Overfitting: The system starts with the most specific clauses and then removes parts of them in the process of generalization. In this process, a subset of an interpretation that was a negative example becomes the s in the input to ••••••••. If examples matching s exist in the dataset then we may get a correct answer from ••••••••. In fact if a dataset is "downward closed", that is all such subsets exist as examples in the dataset, the system will find the correct expression. Note that we only need such subsets which are positive examples to exist in the dataset and that it is also sufficient to have isomorphic embeddings of such subsets in other positive examples as long as wrong consequents are missing. Under these conditions all calls to •••••••• correctly identify all consequents of the clause. Of course, this is a pretty strong requirement but as demonstrated by experiments in [13] having a sample from interpretations of different sizes can work very well.

If this is not the case, e.g. in the challenge problems of [11] where there is a small number of large examples, then we are not likely to find positive examples matching subsets of the negative ones (at least in the initial stages of minimization) and this can lead to overfitting. This has been observed systematically in experiments in this domain.

Using Examples from Normal ILP setting: In the normal ILP setting [20] one is given a database as background knowledge and examples are simple atoms. We transform these into a set of interpretations as follows (see also [5, 12]). The background knowledge in the normal ILP setting can be typically partitioned into different subsets such that each subset affects a single example only. A similar effect is achieved for intensional background knowledge in the Progol system [18] by using mode declarations to limit antecedent structure. Given example b, we will denote $BK(b)$ as the set of atoms in the background knowledge that is relevant to b. In the normal ILP setting we have to find a theory T s.t. $BK(b) \cup T \models b$ if b is a positive example, and $BK(b) \cup T \not\models b$ if b is negative. Equivalently, T must be such that $T \models BK(b) \rightarrow b$ if b is positive and $T \not\models BK(b) \rightarrow b$ if b is negative.

---

[1] The same is true for other bottom up systems; see for example the discussion in [26].

Space limitations preclude discussion of the general case so we consider only the following special case: Several ILP domains are formalized using a consequent of arity 1 where the argument is an object that identifies the example in the background knowledge. Since we separate the examples into interpretations this yields a consequent of arity 0 for LOGAN-H . In this case, if b is a positive example in the standard ILP setting then we can construct an interpretation $I = ([V], [BK(b)])$ where V is the set of objects appearing in $BK(b)$, and label I as negative. If b is a negative example, we construct an interpretation $I = ([V], [BG(b)])$ and label it positive. For a single possible consequent of arity 0 this captures exactly the same information. As an example, suppose that in the normal ILP setting, the clause $p(a, b) \land p(b, c) \to q()$ is labeled positive and the clause $p(a, b) \to q()$ is labeled negative. Then, the transformed dataset contains: $([a, b, c], [p(a, b), p(b, c)])-$ and $([a, b], [p(a, b)])+$.

In the case of zero arity consequents, the check whether a given clause C is satisfied by some interpretation I can be considerably simplified. Instead of checking all substitutions it suffices to check for existence of some substitution, since any such substitution will remove the single nullary consequent. This has important implications for the implementation. In addition, note that the pairing operation never moves new atoms into the consequent and is therefore a pure generalization operation in this case.

5 Further Improvements

5.1 The Subsumption Test

Table Based Subsumption: While backtracking search (as done in Prolog) can find all substitutions without substantial space overhead, the time overhead can be large. Our system implements an alternative approach that constructs all substitutions simultaneously and stores them in memory. The system maintains a table of instantiations for each predicate in the examples. To compute all substitutions between an example and a clause the system repeatedly performs joins of these tables (in the database sense) to get a table of all substitutions. We first initialize to an empty table of substitutions. Then for each predicate in the clause we pull the appropriate table from the example, and perform a join which matches the variables already instantiated in our intermediate table. Thus if the predicate in the clause does not introduce new variables the table size cannot grow. Otherwise the table can grow and repeated joins can lead to large tables. To illustrate this consider evaluating the clause $p(x_1, x_2), p(x_2, x_1), p(x_1, x_3), p(x_3, x_4)$ on an example with extension $[p(a, b), p(a, c), p(a, d), p(b, a), p(d, c)]$. Then applying the join from left to right we get partial substitution tables (from left to right):

x_1	x_2	x_3	x_4
a	b		
a	c		
a	d		
b	a		
d	c		

x_1	x_2	x_3	x_4
a	b		
b	a		

x_1	x_2	x_3	x_4
a	b	b	
a	b	c	
a	b	d	
b	a	a	

x_1	x_2	x_3	x_4
a	b	b	a
a	b	d	c
b	a	a	b
b	a	a	c
b	a	a	d

Notice how the first application simply copies the table from the extension of the predicate in the example. The first join reduces the size of the intermediate table. The next join expands both lines. The last join drops the row with a b c but expands other rows so that overall the table expands.

One can easily construct examples where the table in intermediate steps is larger than the memory capacity of the computer, sometimes even if the final table is small. In this case the matching procedure will fail. If it does not fail, however, the procedure can be fast since we have no backtracking overhead and we consider many constraints simultaneously.

Nonetheless this is not something we can ignore. We have observed such large table sizes in the mutagenesis domain [29] as well as the artificial challenge problems of [11]. Note that a backtracking search will not crash in this case but on the other hand it may just take too long computationally so it is not necessarily a good approach (this was observed in the implementation of [13]).

Lookahead: As in the case of database queries one can try to order the joins in order to optimize the computation time and space requirements. Our system can perform a form of one step lookahead by estimating the size of the table when using a join with each of the atoms on the clause and choosing the minimal one. This introduces a tradeoff in run time. On one hand the resulting tables in intermediate steps tend to be smaller and therefore there is less information to process and the test is quicker. On the other hand the cost of one step lookahead is not negligible so it can slow down the program. The behavior depends on the dataset in question. In general however it can allow us to solve problems which are otherwise unsolvable with the basic approach.

Randomized Table Based Subsumption: If the greedy solution is still not sufficient or too slow we can resort to randomized subsumption tests. Instead of finding all substitutions we try to sample from the set of legal substitutions. This is done in the following manner: if the size of the intermediate table grows beyond a threshold parameter 'TH' (controlled by the user), then we throw away a random subset of the rows before continuing with the join operations. The maximum size of intermediate tables is TH×16. In this way we are not performing a completely random choice over possible substitutions. Instead we are informing the choice by our intermediate table. In addition the system uses random restarts to improve confidence as well as allowing more substitutions to be found, this can be controlled by the user through a parameter 'R'.

Using DJANGO: The system DJANGO [16] uses ideas from constraint satisfaction to solve the subsumption problem. DJANGO only solves the existence question and does not give all substitutions, but as discussed above this is sufficient for certain applications coming from the standard ILP setting. We have integrated the DJANGO code, generously provided by Jérome Maloberti, as a module in our system.

5.2 Discretization

The system includes a capability for handling numerical data by means of discretization. Several approaches to discretization have been proposed in the literature [10,9,2]. We have implemented the simple "equal frequency" approach that generates a given number of bins (specified by the user) and assigns the boundaries by giving each bin the same number of occurrences of values.

To do this for relational data we first divide the numerical attributes into "logical groups". For example the rows of a chess board will belong to the same group regardless of the predicate and argument in which they appear. This generalizes the basic setup where each argument of each predicate is discretized separately. The dataset is annotated to reflect this grouping and the preferred number of thresholds is specified by the user. The system then determines the threshold values, allocates the same name to all objects in each range, and adds predicates reflecting the relation of the value to the thresholds. For example, discretizing the `logp` attribute in the mutagenesis domain with 4 thresholds (5 ranges), a value between threshold 1 and threshold 2 will yield: [`logp(logp_val.02)`, `logp_val>00(logp_val.02)`, `logp_val>01(logp_val.02)`, `logp_val<02(logp_val.02)`, `logp_val<03(logp_val.02)`, ...].

Notice that we are using both $\geq$ and $\leq$ predicates so that the hypothesis can encode intervals of values.

An interesting aspect arises when using discretization which highlights the way our system works. Recall that the system starts with an example and essentially turns objects into variables in the maximally specific clause set. It then evaluates this clause on other examples. Since we do not expect examples to be identical or very close, the above relies on the universal quantification to allow matching one structure into another. However, the effect of discretization is to ground the value of the discretized object. For example, if we discretized the `logp` attribute from above and variabilize we get `logp(X) logp_val>00(X) logp_val>01(X) logp_val<02(X) logp_val<03(X)`. Thus unless we drop some of the boundary constraints this limits matching examples to have a value in the same bin. We are therefore losing the power of universal quantification. As a result fewer positive examples will match in the early stages of the minimization process, fewer consequents will be removed, and the system may be led to overfitting by dropping the wrong objects. This is discussed further in the experimental section.

5.3 Pruning

The system performs bottom-up search and may stop with relatively long rules if the data is not sufficiently rich (i.e. we do not have enough negative examples) to warrant further refinement of the rules. Pruning allows us to drop additional parts of rules. The system can perform a greedy reduced error pruning [17] using a validation dataset. For each atom in the rule (in some order) the system evaluates whether the removal of the atom increases the error on the validation set. If not the atom can be removed. While it is natural to allow an increase in error using a tradeoff against the length of the hypothesis in an MDL fashion, we have not yet experimented with this possibility.

Notice that unlike top down systems we can perform this pruning on the training set and do not necessarily need a separate validation set. In a top down system one grows the rules until they are consistent with the data. Thus, any pruning will lead to an increase in training set error. On the other hand in a bottom up system, pruning is similar to the main stage of the algorithm in that it further generalizes the rules. In some sense, pruning on the training set allows us to move from a most specific hypothesis to a most general hypothesis that matches the data. Both training set pruning and validation set pruning are possible with our system.

5.4 Consistency Checks

If the input dataset is inconsistent, step (i) of the algorithm may produce an initial version of the most specific clauses set with an empty list of consequents. Similar problems may arise with the randomized subsumption tests. The system includes simple mechanisms for ignoring such examples once a problem is detected.

6 Experiments

The LogAn-H system of [13] implements the algorithm in Section 3 using Prolog and its backtracking search engine. Our new system includes a C implementation of the ideas described above.

6.1 Bongard Problems

To illustrate the improvement in efficiency of the new system w.r.t. the previous implementation, we re-ran experiments done with artificial data akin to Bongard problems [13]. This domain was introduced previously in the ICL system [7]. In this domain an example is a "picture" composed of objects of various shapes (triangle, circle or square), triangles have a configuration (up or down) and each object has a color (black or white). Each picture has several objects (the number is not fixed) and some objects are inside other objects. For these experiments we generated random examples, where each parameter in each example was chosen uniformly at random. In particular we used between 2 and 6 objects, the shape color and configuration were chosen randomly, and each object is inside some other object with probability 0.5 where the target was chosen randomly among "previous" objects to avoid cycles. Note that since we use a "flattened" function free representation the domain size in examples is larger than the number of objects (to include: *up, down, black, white*). We generated (by hand) a target Horn expression of 10 clauses, with 9 atoms and 6 variables each. We used this Horn expression to label the examples. For example, one of the clauses generated in the target expression is

$circle(X) \ in(X,Y) \ in(Y,Z) \ colour(Y,B)$
$colour(Z,W) \ black(B) \ white(W) \ in(Z,U) \rightarrow triangle(Y)$

Work in [13] showed that LogAn-H gives good performance on this domain and that it outperforms ICL. Running the experiments with the new system we obtain exactly the same accuracy as before[2] and the speedup observed is between one and three orders of magnitude over the `Prolog` system in compiled Sicstus Prolog (which is a fast implementation) when run on the same hardware.

6.2 Illegal Positions in Chess

Our next experiment is in the domain of the chess endgame White King and Rook versus Black King. The task is to predict whether a given board configuration represented by the 6 coordinates of the three chess pieces is illegal or not. This learning problem has been studied by several authors [22,25]. The dataset includes a training set of 10000 examples and a test set of the same size.

We use the predicate `position(a,b,c,d,e,f)` to denote that the White King is in position (a, b) on the chess board, the White Rook is in position (c, d), and the Black King in position (e, f). Additionally, the predicates "less-than" `lt(x,y)` and "adjacent" `adj(x,y)` denote the relative positions of rows and columns on the board. Note that there is an interesting question as how best to capture examples in interpretations. In the "all background mode" we include all `lt` and `adj` predicates in the interpretation. In the "relevant background mode" we only include those atoms directly relating objects appearing in the head.

We illustrate the difference with the following example. Consider the configuration "White King is in position (7,6), White Rook is in position (5,0), Black King is in position (4,1)" which is illegal. In "all background mode" we use the following interpretation:
```
[position(7, 6, 5, 0, 4, 1),
lt(0,1), lt(0,2), .. ,lt(0,7),
lt(1,2), lt(1,3), .. ,lt(1,7),
⋮
lt(5,6),lt(5,7),
lt(6,7),
adj(0,1),adj(1,2), .. ,adj(6,7),
adj(7,6),adj(6,5), .. ,adj(1,0)]-
```
When considering the "relevant background mode", we include in the examples instantiations of `lt` and `adj` whose arguments appear in the position atom directly:
```
[position(7, 6, 5, 0, 4, 1),
lt(4,5),lt(4,7),lt(5,7),adj(4,5),adj(5,4),
lt(0,1),lt(0,6),lt(1,6),adj(0,1),adj(1,0)]-
```
Table 1 includes results of running our system in both modes. We trained LOGAN-H on samples with various sizes chosen randomly among the 10000 available. We report accuracies that result from averaging among 10 runs over an independent test set of 10000 examples. Results are reported before and after pruning where pruning is done using the training set. Several facts can be

---

[2] Note that the hypothesis may depend on the order of pairings produced so in principle the results are not guaranteed to be identical.

Table 1. Performance summary for KRK illegal dataset

	25	50	75	100	200	500	1000	2000	3000
w/o disc., rel. back. mode:									
LOGAN-H before pruning	75.49	88.43	93.01	94.08	97.18	99.54	99.79	99.92	99.96
LOGAN-H after pruning	86.52	90.92	94.19	95.52	98.41	99.65	99.79	99.87	99.96
w/o disc., all back. mode:									
LOGAN-H before pruning	67.18	71.08	75.71	78.94	85.56	94.06	98.10	99.38	99.56
LOGAN-H after pruning	79.01	81.65	83.17	82.82	86.02	93.67	96.24	98.10	98.66
with disc., rel. back. mode:									
LOGAN-H before pruning	43.32	43.70	45.05	44.60	52.39	72.26	84.80	90.30	92.17
LOGAN-H after pruning	38.93	42.77	46.46	47.51	56.59	74.29	85.02	90.73	92.59
with disc., all back. mode:									
LOGAN-H before pruning	67.27	72.69	75.15	78.00	82.68	88.60	91.03	91.81	92.01
LOGAN-H after pruning	80.62	86.14	87.42	89.10	90.67	92.25	92.62	92.66	92.74
FOIL [25]					92.50		99.40		

observed in the table. First, we get good learning curves with accuracies improving with training set size. Second, the results obtained are competitive with the results reported for FOIL [25]. Third, relevant background knowledge seems to make the task easier. Fourth, pruning considerably improves performance on this dataset especially for small training sets.

Our second set of experiments in this domain illustrates the effect of discretization. We have run the same experiments as above but this time with the discretization option turned on. Concretely, given an example's predicate position(x1,x2,y1,y2,z1,z2), we consider the three values corresponding to columns (x1,y1,z1) as the same logical attribute and therefore we discretize them together. Similarly, we discretize the values of (x2,y2,z2) together. Versions of adj() for both column and row values are used. We do not include lt() predicates since these are essentially now represented by the threshold predicates produced by the discretization. As can be seen in Table 1 good accuracy is maintained with discretization. However, an interesting point is that now "relevant background mode" performs much worse than "all background mode". In hindsight one can see that this is a result of the grounding effect of discretizing as discussed above. With "relevant background mode" the discretization threshold predicates and the adjacent predicates are different in every example. Since, as explained above, the examples are essentially ground we expect less matches between different examples and thus the system is likely to overfit. With "all background mode" these predicates do not constrain the matching of examples.

This domain is also a good case to illustrate the various subsumption tests in our system. Note that since we put the position predicate in the antecedent the consequent is nullary. Therefore we can use DJANGO as well as the table based subsumption and randomized tables. The comparison is given for the non-discretized "all background mode" with 1000 training examples. Table 2 gives accuracy and run time (on Linux running with Pentium IV 2.80 GHz) for various subsumption settings averaged over 10 independent runs. For randomized

Table 2. Runtime comparison for subsumption tests on KRK-illegal dataset

Subsumption Engine	runtime in s.	accuracy	actual table size
DJANGO	431.6	98.11%	
Tables	19.2	98.11%	130928
Lookahead	25.4	98.11%	33530
No cache	49.4	98.11%	
Rand. TH=1	741.7	33.61%	16
Rand. TH=10	30.7	33.61%	160
Rand. TH=100	12.4	72.05%	1600
Rand. TH=1000	20.3	98.11%	16000

runs TH is the threshold of table size after which sampling is used. As can be seen, the table based method is faster than DJANGO (both are deterministic and thus give identical hypotheses and accuracy results). The lookahead table method incurs some overhead and results in slower execution on this domain, however it saves space considerably (see third column of Table 2). Caching gives a reduction of about 60% in run time. Running the randomized test with very small tables (TH=1) clearly leads to overfitting, and in this case increases run time considerably mainly due do the large number of rules induced. On the other hand with fairly small tables sizes (TH=1000) the randomized method does very well and reproduces the deterministic results.

6.3 Mutagenesis

The Mutagenesis dataset is a structure-activity prediction task for molecules introduced by [29]. The dataset consists of 188 compounds, labeled as active or inactive depending on their level of mutagenic activity. The task is to predict whether a given molecule is active or not based on the first-order description of the molecule. This dataset has been partitioned into 10 subsets for 10-fold cross validation estimates and has been used in this form in many studies (e.g. [29,26, 7]). We therefore use the same partitions as well. Each example is represented as a set of first-order atoms that reflect the atom-bond relation of the compounds as well as some interesting global chemical properties. Concretely, we use all the information corresponding to the background level B3 of [28]. Notice that the original data is given in the normal ILP setting and hence we transformed it as described above using a single nullary consequent. In addition, since constants are meaningful in this dataset (for example whether an atom is a carbon or oxygen) we use a flattened version of the data where we add a predicate for each such constant.

This example representation uses continuous attributes (`atom-charge`, `lumo` and `logp` in particular), hence discretization is needed. Although the discretization process is fully automated it requires the number of discrete categories to be specified by the user. Here, we use a method that allows us to determine this number automatically and without any use of the test set: for each partition of the cross validation, we split the training data into two random sets,

Table 3. Runtime comparison for subsumption tests on mutagenesis dataset

Subsumption Engine	runtime in s.	accuracy
DJANGO	1162	87.96%
Rand. TH=1	3	85.52%
Rand. TH=10	15	86.46%
Rand. TH=100	19	89.47%

one which we call `disc-train` and consists of 80% of the training data, and another called `disc-test` which consists of the remaining training data. Then, for each of the possible values (`atom-charge`= 5, 15, 25, 35, 45; `lumo`= 4, 6, 8, 10; `logp`= 4, 6, 8, 10) we train and test over the sets `disc-train` and `disc-test`. This procedure is repeated 5 times and we choose the discretization values that obtain the best average accuracy on this partition. Note that these values might be different for different partitions of the global cross validation and indeed we did not get a stable choice. Once a set of values is chosen for a particular partition of the data, the learning process is performed over the entire training set and then it is tested on the corresponding independent test set.

For this domain deterministic table-based subsumption was not possible, not even with the lookahead heuristic since the table size grew beyond memory capacity of our computer. However, here the DJANGO subsumption engine yields good run times. The average training time per fold, after the discretization values have been determined, is 14 min. (on Linux running with Pentium IV 2.80 GHz). Prediction accuracies obtained for each partition in this fashion are (in order from 1 to 10): 73.68%, 89.47%, 78.95%, 84.21%, 84.21%, 89.47%, 89.47%, 73.68%, 73.68%, 88.24%, which results in a final average of 82.5%. Additionally, we ran a regular 10-fold cross-validation for each combination of discretization values. The values `atom-charge`= 45, `lumo`= 10 and `logp`= 4 obtained the best average accuracy of 87.96%. Our results compare well to other ILP systems: PROGOL [29] reports a total accuracy of 83% with B3 and 88% with B4; STILL [26] reports results in the range 85%–88% on B3 depending on the values of various tuning parameters, ICL [7] reports an accuracy of 84% and finally [15] report that FOIL [25] achieves an accuracy of 83%.

Here again we ran further experiments with the randomized subsumption tests. We used the discretization values `atom-charge`= 45, `lumo`= 10 and `logp`= 4. Table 3 gives run time (on Linux running with Pentium IV 2.80 GHz) per fold and the 10 fold cross validation accuracy with various parameters. One can observe that even with small parameters the randomized methods do very well. An inspection of the hypothesis to the deterministic runs with DJANGO shows that they are very similar.

6.4 Evaluating Randomized Subsumption Tests

The experiments above already show that there are cases where the table based method is fast and faster than DJANGO even though it searches for all substitutions compared to just one in DJANGO. On the other hand the table based

Table 4. Subsumption run time in linear chain family

	Django	Tables	Lookahead	TH=1	TH=10	TH=100
	100.0% 296s	100.0% 242s (14161)	100.0% 318s (118)			
R=1				6.9% 13s	18.6% 49s	100.0% 240s
R=10				32.2% 60s	66.6% 181s	100.0% 243s
R=100				96.9% 185s	100.0% 280s	100.0% 241s

Table 5. Subsumption run time in subgraph isomorphism family

	Django	TH=1	TH=10	TH=100	TH=1000
	100.00% 7.1s				
R=1		0.01% 0.8s	3.21% 1.7s	31.71% 8.9s	85.46% 52.4s
R=10		0.03% 2.6s	15.29% 7.0s	78.95% 26.8s	95.12% 76.1s
R=100		0.22% 23.6s	67.88% 38.9s	99.92% 39.1s	99.97% 103.1s

method can be slow in other cases and even run out of memory and fail. The following experiments give simple synthetic examples where we compare the subsumption tests on their own, without reference to the learning system, showing similar behavior. In each case we generate a family of problems parametrized by size, each having a single example and single clause. We run the subsumption test 1000 times to observe run time differences as well as accuracies for the randomized methods.

For the first family both example and clause are chains of length n built using a binary predicate as in $p(x_1, x_2), p(x_2, x_3), \ldots, p(x_{n-1}, x_n)$. Thus there is exactly one matching substitution. Results for $n = 120$ are given in Table 4. As can be seen, in this case tables are faster than Django, randomized tables work well with small parameters, and both table size and repeats (controlled by TH and R in Table 4) are effective in increasing the performance of the randomized tests. This behavior was observed consistently for different values of n. The numbers in parentheses are the actual table sizes needed by the table-based methods; the lookahead heuristic saves considerable space.

The second family is motivated by the mutagenesis domain and essentially checks for subgraph isomorphism. The clause is a randomly generated graph with n nodes and $3n$ edges, and the example is the same set plus $3n$ extra edges. The results for $n = 10$ are given in Table 5. Deterministic tables fail for values of

n larger than 8 and are omitted. As can be seen DJANGO works very well in this case and randomized tables work well even with small parameters, and both table size and repeats (contolled by TH and R in Table 5) are effective in increasing the performance of the randomized tests. Similar results were obtained for different values of n where randomized tables sometimes achieve high accuracy with lower run times than DJANGO though in general DJANGO is faster.

7 Discussion

The paper presents a new implementation of the LOGAN-H system including new subsumption engines, discretization and pruning. Interesting aspects of discretization and pruning which are specific to bottom up search are discussed in the paper. The system is sufficiently strong to handle large ILP datasets and is shown to be competitive with other approaches while using a completely different algorithmic approach. The paper also demonstrates the merits of having several subsumption engines at hand to fit properties of particular domains, and gives paradigmatic cases where different engines do better than others.

As illustrated in [13] using the Bongard domain, LOGAN-H is particularly suited to domains where substructures of examples in the dataset are likely to be in the dataset as well. On the other hand, for problems with a small number of examples where each example has a large number of objects and dramatically different structure our system is likely to overfit since there is little evidence for useful minimization steps. Indeed we found this to be the case for the the artificial challenge problems of [11] where our system outputs a large number of rules and gets low accuracy. Interestingly, a similar effect can result from discretization since it results in a form of grounding of the initial clauses and thus counteracts the fact that they are universally quantified and thus likely to be contradicted by the dataset if wrong. This suggests that skipping the minimization step may lead to improved performance in such cases if pairings reduce clause size considerably. Initial experiments with this are as yet inconclusive.

Our experiments demonstrated the utility of informed randomized subsumption tests. Another interesting possibility is to follow ideas from the successful randomized propositional satisfiability tester WalkSat [27]. Here one can abandon the table structure completely and search for a single substitution using a random walk over substitutions where in each step we modify an unsuccessful substitution to satisfy at least one more atom. Repeating the above can improve performance as well as find multiple substitutions when needed. Initial experiments suggest that this indeed can be useful albeit our current implementation is slow. It would be interesting to explore this further in LOGAN-H and other systems.

Our system also demonstrates that using large refinement steps with a bottom up search can be an effective inference method. As discussed above, bottom up search suffers from two aspects: subsumption tests are more costly than in top down approaches, and overfitting may occur in small datasets with large examples. On the other hand, it is not clear how large refinement steps or insights gained by using LGG can be used in a top down system. One interesting idea in this direction is given in the system of [1]. Here repeated pairing-like operations are performed without evaluating the accuracy until a syntactic condition is met (this is specialized for the challenge problems of [11]) to produce a short clause. This clause is then used as a seed for a small step refinement search that evaluates clauses as usual. Finding similar ideas that work without using special properties of the domain is an interesting direction for future work.

Acknowledgments. Much of the code for LOGAN-H was written by Constantine Ashminov as part of his MS work at Tufts. We are grateful to Jérome Maloberti for providing the code for the DJANGO system. Some of the experiments were performed on a Linux cluster provided by Tufts Central Computing Services.

References

[1] Jacques Alès Bianchetti, Céline Rouveirol, and Michèle Sebag. Constraint-based learning of long relational concepts. In *Proceedings of the International Conference on Machine Learning*, pages 35–42. Morgan Kaufmann, 2002.

[2] H. Blockeel and L. De Raedt. Lookahead and discretization in ilp. In S. Džeroski and N. Lavrač, editors, *Proceedings of the 7th International Workshop on Inductive Logic Programming*, volume 1297 of *Lecture Notes in Artificial Intelligence*, pages 77–84. Springer-Verlag, 1997.

[3] H. Blockeel and L. De Raedt. Top down induction of first order logical decision trees. *Artificial Intelligence*, 101:285–297, 1998.

[4] I. Bratko and S. Muggleton. Applications of inductive logic programming. *Communications of the ACM*, 38(11):65–70, November 1995.

[5] L. De Raedt. Logical settings for concept learning. *Artificial Intelligence*, 95(1):187–201, 1997. See also relevant Errata (forthcoming).

[6] L. De Raedt and S. Dzeroski. First order jk-clausal theories are PAC-learnable. *Artificial Intelligence*, 70:375–392, 1994.

[7] L. De Raedt and W. Van Laer. Inductive constraint logic. In *Proceedings of the 6th Conference on Algorithmic Learning Theory*, volume 997. Springer-Verlag, 1995.

[8] N. Di Mauro, T.M.A. Basile, S. Ferilli, F. Esposito, and N. Fanizzi. An exhaustive matching procedure for the improvement of learning efficiency. In T. Horváth and A. Yamamoto, editors, *Proceedings of the 13th International Conference on Inductive Logic Programming*, volume 2835 of *Lecture Notes in Artificial Intelligence*, pages 112–129. Springer-Verlag, 2003.

[9] James Dougherty, Ron Kohavi, and Mehran Sahami. Supervised and unsupervised discretization of continuous features. In *International Conference on Machine Learning*, pages 194–202, 1995.

[10] U.M. Fayyad and K. B. Irani. Multi-interval discretization of continuous-valued attributes for classification learning. In *Proceedings of the International Conference on Machine Learning*, pages 1022–1027, Amherst, MA, 1993.

[11] Attilio Giordana, Lorenza Saitta, Michèle Sebag, and Marco Botta. Relational learning as search in a critical region. *Journal of Machine Learning Research*, 4:431–463, 2003.

[12] R. Khardon. Learning function free Horn expressions. *Machine Learning*, 37:241–275, 1999.

[13] Roni Khardon. Learning horn expressions with LogAn-H. In *Proceedings of the International Conference on Machine Learning*, pages 471–478. Morgan Kaufmann, 2000.

[14] J-U. Kietz and M. Lübbe. An efficient subsumption algorithm for inductive logic programming. In S. Wrobel, editor, *Proceedings of the 4th International Workshop on Inductive Logic Programming*, volume 237, pages 97–106. Gesellschaft für Mathematik und Datenverarbeitung MBH, 1994.

[15] W. Van Laer, H. Blockeel, and L. De Raedt. Inductive constraint logic and the mutagenesis problem. In *Proceedings of the Eighth Dutch Conference on Artificial Intelligence*, pages 265–276, November 1996.

[16] J. Maloberti and Sebag M. Theta-subsumption in a constraint satisfaction perspective. In *Proceedings of the 11th International Conference on Inductive Logic Programming*, pages 164–178. Springer Verlag LNAI 2157, 2001.

[17] T. Mitchell. *Machine Learning*. McGraw-Hill, 1997.

[18] S. Muggleton. Inverse entailment and Progol. *New Generation Computing, Special issue on Inductive Logic Programming*, 13(3-4):245–286, 1995.

[19] S. Muggleton and W. Buntine. Machine invention of first order predicates by inverting resolution. In S. Muggleton, editor, *Inductive Logic Programming*. Academic Press, 1992.

[20] S. Muggleton and L. DeRaedt. Inductive logic programming: Theory and methods. *The Journal of Logic Programming*, 19 & 20:629–680, May 1994.

[21] S. Muggleton and C. Feng. Efficient induction of logic programs. In S. Muggleton, editor, *Inductive Logic Programming*, pages 281–298. Academic Press, 1992.

[22] S. H. Muggleton, M. Bain, J. Hayes-Michie, and D. Michie. An experimental comparison of human and machine learning formalisms. In *Proc. Sixth International Workshop on Machine Learning*, pages 113–118, San Mateo, CA, 1989. Morgan Kaufmann.

[23] Christos H. Papadimitriou and Mihalis Yannakakis. On the complexity of database queries (extended abstract). In *Proceedings of the 16th Annual ACM Symposium on Principles of Database Systems*, pages 12–19. ACM Press, 1997.

[24] G. D. Plotkin. A note on inductive generalization. *Machine Intelligence*, 5:153–163, 1970.

[25] J. R. Quinlan. Learning logical definitions from relations. *Machine Learning*, 5:239–266, 1990.

[26] Michele Sebag and Celine Rouveirol. Resource-bounded relational reasoning: Induction and deduction through stochastic matching. *Machine Learning*, 38:41–62, 2000.

[27] Bart Selman, Henry Kautz, and Bram Cohen. Local search strategies for satisfiability testing. In *Cliques, Coloring, and Satisfiability: the Second DIMACS Implementation Challenge*, volume 26, pages 521–532. American Mathematical Society, 1996.

[28] A. Srinivasan, S. Muggleton, and R.D. King. Comparing the use of background knowledge by inductive logic programming systems. In *Proceedings of the 5th International Workshop on Inductive Logic Programming*, pages 199–230, 1995.

[29] A. Srinivasan, S. H. Muggleton, R. D. King, and M. J. E. Sternberg. Mutagenesis: ILP experiments in a non-determinate biological domain. In S. Wrobel, editor, *Proc. 4th Int. Workshop on Inductive Logic Programming*, pages 217–232, September 1994.

On the Effect of Caching in Recursive Theory Learning

Margherita Berardi, Antonio Varlaro, and Donato Malerba

Dipartimento di Informatica – Università degli Studi di Bari
via Orabona 4 - 70126 Bari
{berardi, varlaro, malerba}@di.uniba.it

Abstract. This paper focuses on inductive learning of recursive logical theories from a set of examples. This is a complex task where the learning of one predicate definition should be interleaved with the learning of the other ones in order to discover predicate dependencies. To overcome this problem we propose a variant of the separate-and-conquer strategy based on parallel learning of different predicate definitions. In order to improve its efficiency, optimization techniques are investigated and adopted solutions are described. In particular, two caching strategies have been implemented and tested on document processing datasets. Experimental results are discussed and conclusions are drawn.

1 Introduction

Learning a single predicate definition from a set of positive and negative examples is a classical problem in ILP. In this paper we are interested into the more complex case of learning multiple predicate definitions, provided that both positive and negative examples of each concept/predicate to be learned are available. Complexity stems from the fact that the learned predicates may also occur in the antecedents of the learned clauses, that is, the learned predicate definitions may be interrelated and depend on one another, either hierarchically or involving some kind of mutual recursion. For instance, to learn the definitions of odd and even numbers, a multiple predicate learning system will be provided with positive and negative examples of both odd and even numbers, and may generate the following recursive logical theory:

$$odd(X) \leftarrow succ(Y,X), even(Y)$$
$$even(X) \leftarrow succ(Y,X), odd(Y)$$
$$even(X) \leftarrow zero(X)$$

where the definitions of *odd* and *even* are interdependent. This example shows that the problem of learning multiple predicate definitions is equivalent, in its most general formulation, to the problem of learning recursive logical theories.

There has been considerable debate on the actual usefulness of learning recursive logical theories in knowledge acquisition and discovery applications. It is a common opinion that very few real life concepts seem to have recursive definitions, rare examples being "ancestor" and natural language [4, 14]. Despite this scepticism, in

R. Camacho, R. King, A. Srinivasan (Eds.): ILP 2004, LNAI 3194, pp. 44-62, 2004.

the literature it is possible to find several ILP applications in which recursion has proved helpful [10]. Moreover, many ILP researchers have shown some interest in multiple predicate learning [9], which presents the same difficulty of recursive theory learning in its most general formulation.

To formulate the recursive theory learning problem and then to explain its main theoretical issues, some basic definitions are given below.

Generally, every logical theory T can be associated with a directed graph $\gamma(T)=<N,E>$, called the *dependency graph* of T, in which (i) each predicate of T is a node in N and (ii) there is an arc in E directed from a node a to a node b, iff there exists a clause C in T, such that a and b are the predicates of a literal occurring in the head and in the body of C, respectively.

A dependency graph allows representing the predicate dependencies of T, where a *predicate dependency* is defined as follows:

Definition 1 (predicate dependency). A predicate p depends on a predicate q in a theory T iff (i) there exists a clause C for p in T such that q occurs in the body of C; or (ii) there exists a clause C for p in T with some predicate r in the body of C that depends on q.

Definition 2 (recursive theory). A logical theory T is *recursive* if the dependency graph $\gamma(T)$ contains at least one cycle.

In *simple* recursive theories all cycles in the dependency graph go from a predicate p into p itself, that is, simple recursive theories may contain recursive clauses, but cannot express mutual recursion.

Definition 3 (predicate definition). Let T be a logical theory and p a predicate symbol. Then the *definition* of p in T is the set of clauses in T that have p in their head. Henceforth, $\delta(T)$ will denote the set of predicates defined in T and $\pi(T)$ will denote the set of predicates occurring in T, then $\delta(T) \subseteq \pi(T)$.

In a quite general formulation, the recursive theory learning task can be defined as follows:

Given
- A set of *target* predicates $p_1, p_2, \ldots, p_r$ to be learned
- A set of positive (negative) examples E_i^+ (E_i^-) for each predicate p_i, $1 \le i \le r$
- A background theory BK
- A language of hypotheses L_H that defines the space of hypotheses S_H

Find

a (possibly recursive) logical theory $T \in S_H$ defining the predicates $p_1, p_2, \ldots, p_r$ (that is, $\delta(T)=\{p_1, p_2, \ldots, p_r\}$) such that for each i, $1 \le i \le r$, $BK \cup T \models E_i^+$ (*completeness* property) and $BK \cup T \not\models E_i^-$ (*consistency* property).

Three important issues characterize recursive theory learning. First, the generality order typically used in ILP, namely θ-subsumption [17], is not sufficient to guarantee the completeness and consistency of learned definitions, with respect to logical entailment [16]. Therefore, it is necessary to consider a stronger generality order, which is consistent with the logical entailment for the class of recursive logical theories we take into account.

Second, whenever two individual clauses are consistent in the data, their conjunction need not be consistent in the same data [8]. This is called the non-monotonicity property of the normal ILP setting, since it states that adding new clauses to a theory T does not preserve consistency. Indeed, adding definite clauses to a definite program enlarges its least Herbrand model (LHM), which may then cover negative examples as well. Because of this non-monotonicity property, learning a recursive theory one clause at a time is not straightforward.

Third, when multiple predicate definitions have to be learned, it is crucial to discover dependencies between predicates. Therefore, the classical learning strategy that focuses on a predicate definition at a time is not appropriate.

To overcome these problems some solutions have been proposed in [12] and implemented in the learning system ATRE (www.di.uniba.it/~malerba/software/atre). This approach differs from related works for at least one of the following three aspects: the learning strategy, the generalization model, and the strategy to recover the consistency property of the learned theory when a new clause is added.

In this paper we focus on the main problem of the interleaving of the learning of one (possible recursive) predicate definition with the learning of the other ones. In particular, different aspects of the adopted strategy for the automated discovery of predicate dependencies, namely the separate-and-parallel-conquer strategy, are presented. Efficiency problems due to the computational complexity of the search space are also discussed and some solutions implemented in a new version of the system ATRE are described.

The paper is organized as follows. Section 2 illustrates details on the learning strategy. Section 3 introduces efficiency problems and related works. Section 4 presents optimization approaches adopted in ATRE. The application of ATRE on real-world documents and results on efficiency gain are reported in Section 5. Finally, some conclusions are drawn.

2 The Learning Strategy

2.1 The Separate-and-Parallel-Conquer Search

The high-level learning algorithm in ATRE belongs to the family of *sequential covering* (or *separate-and-conquer*) algorithms [13] since it is based on the strategy of learning one clause at a time, removing the covered examples and iterating the process on the remaining examples. Indeed, a recursive theory T is built step by step, starting from an empty theory T_0, and adding a new clause at each step. In this way we get a sequence of theories

$$T_0 = \varnothing, T_1, \ldots, T_i, T_{i+1}, \ldots, T_n = T,$$

such that $T_{i+1} = T_i \cup \{C\}$ for some clause C. If we denote by LHM(T_i) the least Herbrand model of a theory T_i, the stepwise construction of theories entails that LHM(T_i) $\subseteq$ LHM(T_{i+1}), for each $i \in \{0, 1, \ldots, n-1\}$, since the addition of a clause to a theory can only augment the LHM. Henceforth, we will assume that both positive and negative examples of predicates to be learned are represented as *ground atoms* with a + or - label. Therefore, examples may or may not be elements of the models LHM(T_i). Let $pos(LHM(T_i))$ and $neg(LHM(T_i))$ be the number of positive and negative examples in LHM(T_i), respectively. If we guarantee the following two conditions:

1. $pos(LHM(T_i)) < pos(LHM(T_{i+1}))$ for each $i \in \{0, 1, ..., n-1\}$, and
2. $neg(LHM(T_i)) = 0$ for each $i \in \{0, 1, ..., n\}$,

then after a finite number of steps a theory T, which is complete and consistent, is built.

In order to guarantee the first of the two conditions it is possible to proceed as follows. First, a positive example e^+ of a predicate p to be learned is selected, such that e^+ is not in LHM(T_i). The example e^+ is called *seed*. Then the space of definite clauses more general than e^+ is explored, looking for a clause C, if any, such that $neg(LHM(T_i \cup \{C\})) = \varnothing$. In this way we guarantee that the second condition above holds as well. When found, C is added to T_i giving T_{i+1}. If some positive examples are not included in LHM(T_{i+1}) then a new seed is selected and the process is repeated.

The second condition is more difficult to guarantee because of the second issue presented in the introduction, namely, the non-monotonicity property. The approach followed in ATRE to remove inconsistency due to the addition of a clause to the theory consists of simple syntactic changes in the theory, which eventually creates new *layers*, just as the stratification of a normal program creates new strata [1]. Details on the layering approach and on the computation method are reported in [12]. The layering of a theory introduces a first variation of the classical separate-and-conquer strategy sketched above, since the addition of a locally consistent clause generated in the conquer stage is preceded by a global consistency check.

As explained above, in recursive theory learning it is necessary to consider a generality order that is consistent with the logical entailment for the class of recursive logical theories. The main problem with the well-known θ-subsumption is that the objects of comparison are two clauses and no additional source of knowledge (e.g., a theory T) is considered. Instead, we are only interested in those relative generality orders that compare two clauses relatively to a given theory T. In ATRE, a new generalization order named *generalized implication* is adopted [12], since both Buntine's *generalized subsumption* [5] and Plotkin's [17,18] notion of *relative generalization* are not appropriate (they are either too strong or too weak).

A solution to the problem of automated discovery of dependencies between target predicates $p_1, p_2, ..., p_r$ is based on another variant of the separate-and-conquer learning strategy. Traditionally, this strategy is adopted by single predicate learning systems that generate clauses with the same predicate in the head at each step. In multiple/recursive predicate learning, clauses generated at each step may have different predicates in their heads. In addition, the body of the clause generated at the i-th step may include all target predicates $p_1, p_2, ..., p_r$ for which at least a clause has been added to the partially learned theory in previous steps. In this way, dependencies between target predicates can be generated.

Obviously, the order in which clauses of distinct predicate definitions have to be generated is not known in advance. This means that it is necessary to generate clauses with different predicates in the head and then to pick one of them at the end of each step of the separate-and-conquer strategy. Since the generation of a clause depends on the chosen seed, several seeds have to be chosen such that at least one seed per incomplete predicate definition is kept. Therefore, the search space is actually a forest of as many search-trees (called *specialization hierarchies*) as the number of chosen seeds. A directed arc from a node C to a node C' exists if C' is obtained from C by a single refinement step. Operatively, the (downward) refinement operator considered in this work adds a new literal to a clause.[1]

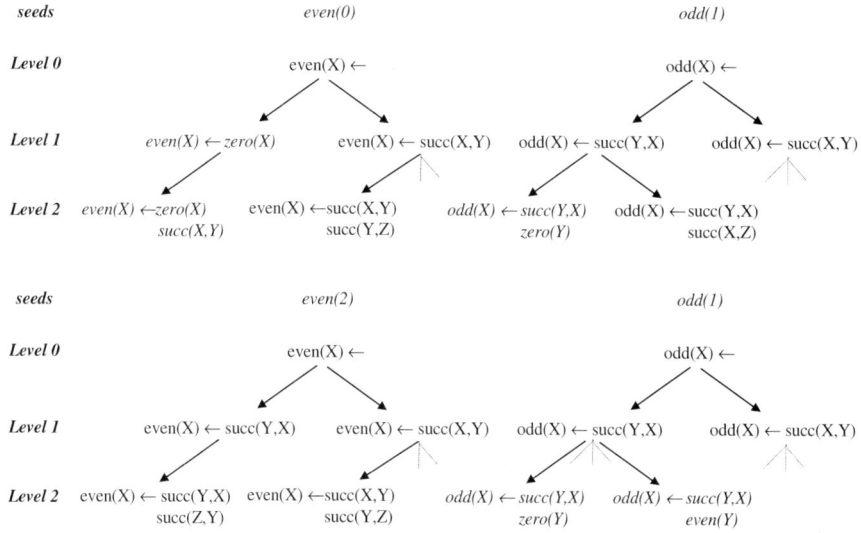

Fig. 1. Two steps (up and down) of the parallel search for the predicates *odd* and *even*. Consistent clauses are reported in italics.

The forest can be processed in parallel by as many concurrent tasks as the number of search-trees (hence the name of separate-and-parallel-conquer for this search strategy). Each task traverses the specialization hierarchy top-down (or general-to-specific), but synchronizes traversal with the other tasks at each level. Initially, some clauses at depth one in the forest are examined concurrently. Each task is actually free to adopt its own search strategy, and to decide which clauses are worth to be tested. If none of the tested clauses is consistent, clauses at depth two are considered. Search proceeds towards deeper and deeper levels of the specialization hierarchies until at least a user-defined number of consistent clauses is found. Task synchronization is performed after that all "relevant" clauses at the same depth have been examined. A supervisor task decides whether the search should carry on or not on the basis of the results returned by the concurrent tasks. When the search is stopped, the supervisor selects the "best" consistent clause according to the user's preference criterion. This strategy has the advantage that simpler consistent clauses

---

[1] A discussion on properties of this operator is beyond the scope of this paper. A thorough description of upward and downward refinement operators can be found in [16].

are found first, independently of the predicates to be learned.[2] Moreover, the synchronization allows tasks to save much computational effort when the distribution of consistent clauses in the levels of the different search-trees is uneven. The parallel exploration of the specialization hierarchies for *odd* and *even* is shown in Fig. 1.

2.2 Some Refinements

The learning strategy reported in the previous section is quite general and there is room for several distinct implementations. In particular, the following some points have been left unspecified: 1) how seeds are selected; 2) what is the search strategy adopted by each task. In this section, solutions adopted in the last release of the learning system ATRE are illustrated.

Seed selection is a critical point. In the example of Fig. 1, if the search had started from *even(2)* and *odd(1)*, the first clause added to the theory would have been $odd(X) \leftarrow succ(Y,X), zero(Y)$, thus resulting in a less compact, though still correct, theory for odd and even numbers. Therefore, it is important to explore the specialization hierarchies of several seeds for each predicate. According to the classical ILP learning setting, the set of training examples is a set of ground atoms. In this case, the choice of seeds should be stochastic because of the large number of candidate seeds. However, a random choice does not guarantee that the right seeds are chosen for the generation of the base clauses of the recursive definition. For this reason ATRE adopts a variant of the learning interpretation setting, where training examples of target predicates $p_1, p_2, ..., p_r$ are partitioned into training objects, each of which also includes a set of ground facts from the extensional BK. As observed by [3] within the setting of learning from interpretations, it is possible to develop more efficient learning algorithms than the classical ILP setting. This is especially true for recursive theory learning. Indeed, the object-centered representation adopted by ATRE has the advantage of reducing the number of candidate seeds. The main assumption made in this approach is that *each object contains examples explained by some base clauses of the underlying recursive theory.*[3] Therefore, by choosing as seeds *all* examples of different concepts represented in one training object, it is possible to induce some of the correct base clauses. Since in many learning problems the number of positive examples in an object is not very high, a parallel exploration of all candidate seeds is feasible. Mutually recursive concept definitions will be generated only after some base clauses have been added to the theory.

Seeds are chosen according to the textual order in which objects are input to ATRE. If a complete definition of the predicate p_j is not available yet at the *i*-th step

---

[2] Apparently, some problems might occur for those recursive definitions where the recursive clause is syntactically simpler than the base clause. However, the proposed strategy does not allow the discovery of the recursive clause until the base clause has been found, whatever its complexity is.

[3] Problems caused by incomplete object descriptions violating the above assumption are not investigated in this work, since they require the application of *abductive* operators, which are not available in the current version of the system.

of the separate-and-conquer search strategy, then there are still some uncovered positive examples of p_j. The first (seed) object O_k in the object list that contains uncovered examples of p_j is selected to generate seeds for p_j.

The second undefined point of the search strategy concerns the search strategy adopted by each task. ATRE applies a variant of the beam-search strategy. The system generates all candidate clauses at level $l+1$ starting from those filtered at level l in the specialization hierarchy. During task synchronization, which occurs level-by-level, the best m clauses are selected from those generated by all tasks. The user specifies the beam of the search, that is m, and a set of preference criteria for the selection of the best m clauses.

3 Improving Efficiency in ATRE

Considering the separate-and-parallel-conquer search sketched in Section 2.1, it presents some efficiency problems and leaves a large margin for optimization. One of the reasons is that every time a clause is added to the partially learned theory, the specialization hierarchies are reconstructed for a new set of seeds, which may intersect the set of seeds explored in the previous step. Therefore, it is possible that the system explores the same specialization hierarchies several times, since it has no memory of the work done in previous steps. This is particularly evident when concepts to learn are neither recursively definable nor mutually dependent. Intuitively, caching the specialization hierarchies explored at a certain step of the separate-and-conquer strategy and reusing part of them at the following step, seems to be a good strategy to decrease the learning time while keeping memory usage under acceptable limits. Furthermore, clause evaluation requires a number of generalized implication tests, one for each positive or negative example. Although the generalized implication test is optimized in ATRE, when the number of tests to perform is high, the clause evaluation leads to efficiency problems anyway. To reduce the number of tests, a caching method on the list of positive and negative examples of each clause has been investigated.

In this section we present the novel caching strategy implemented in ATRE to solve efficiency problems above. Generally speaking, caching aims to save useful information that would be repeatedly recomputed otherwise, with a clear waste of time. In particular, the proposed strategy affects the two most computationally expensive phases of the learning process, namely the clause generation step and the clause evaluation step.

3.1 Caching for Clause Generation

To prevent the exploration of the same specialization hierarchies several times, we propose a caching mechanism that aims to save the specialization hierarchies explored at the i-th step of the separate-and-conquer strategy so to reuse part of them at the $(i+1)$-th step.

First of all, we observe that a necessary condition for reusing a specialization hierarchy between two subsequent learning steps is that the associated seed remains the same. This means that if the seed of a specialization hierarchy is no longer considered at the $(i+1)$-th step, then the corresponding clauses cached at the i-th step can be discarded.

However, even in the case of same seed, not all the clauses of the specialization hierarchy will be actually useful. For instance, the cached copies of a clause C added to Ti can be removed from all specialization hierarchies including it. Moreover, all clauses that cover only positive examples already covered by C can be dropped, according to the separate-and-conquer learning strategy. These examples explain why a cached specialization hierarchy has to be pruned before considering it at the $(i+1)$-th step of the learning strategy.

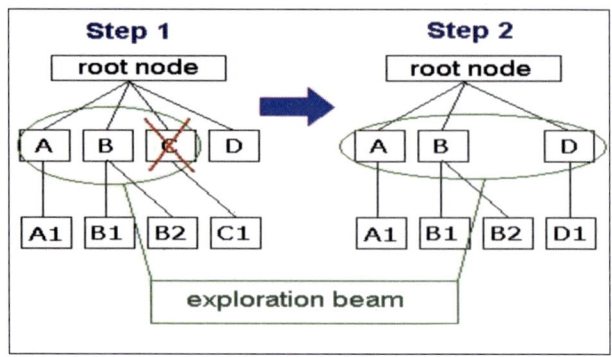

Fig. 2. An example of search-tree pruning effect on beam search width.

In order to maintain unchanged the width of the search beam, some grafting operations are necessary after pruning. Indeed, by removing the clauses that will be no more examined, the exploration beam decreases. Grafting operations aim to consider previous unspecialized clauses in order to restore the beam width, as shown in Fig.2.

Grafting operations are also necessary to preserve the generation of recursive clauses. For instance, by looking at the two specialization hierarchies of the predicate *odd* in Fig. 1, it is clear that once the clause $even(X) \leftarrow zero(X)$ has been added to the empty theory (step 1), the consistent clause $odd(X) \leftarrow succ(Y,X)$, $even(Y)$ can be a proper node of the specialization hierarchy, since a base clause for the recursive definition of the predicate *even* is already available. Therefore, the grafting operations also aim to complete the pruned specialization hierarchy with new clauses that take predicate dependencies into account.

3.2 Caching for Clause Evaluation

To clarify the caching technique proposed for the clause evaluation phase, we need to distinguish between *dependent* clauses, that is, clauses with at least one literal in the body whose predicate symbol is a target predicate p_i, and *independent* clauses (all the others).

In independent clauses, the lists of negative examples remain unchanged between two subsequent learning steps. Indeed, the addition of a clause C to a partially learned theory T_i does not change the set of consequences of an independent clause, whose set of negative examples can neither increase nor decrease. Therefore, by caching the list of negative examples, the learning system can prevent its computation.

A different observation concerns the list of positive examples to be covered by the partially learned theory. For the same reason reported above it cannot increase, while it can decrease since some of the positive examples might have been covered by the added clause C. Actually, the set of positive examples of a clause C' generated at the $(i+1)$-th step can be calculated as intersection of the cached set computed at the i-th step of the learning strategy and the set of positive examples covered by the parent clause of C' in the specialization hierarchy computed at the $(i+1)$-th step (see Fig. 3). In the case of dependent clauses, both lists of the positive and negative examples can increase, decrease or remain unchanged, since the addition of a clause C to a partially learned theory T_i might change the set of consequences of a dependent clause. Therefore, caching the set of positive/negative examples covered by a dependent clause is useless.

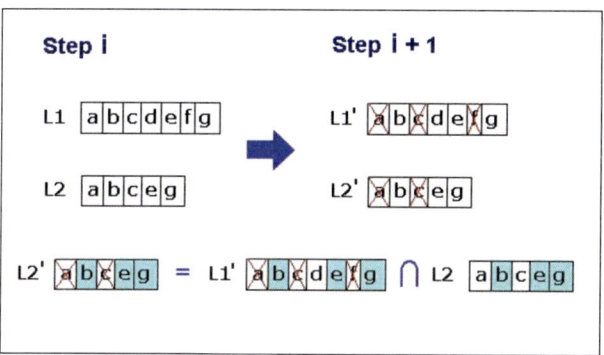

Fig. 3. An example of the positive examples list computation as intersection of the positive examples list of the same clause in the previous learning, step (i), and the positive examples list of the parent clause in the current learning, step (i+1).

It is noteworthy that, differently from the caching technique for clause generation, caching for clause evaluation does not require additional memory resources since all requested information are kept from the current learning step (see Section 5.1.3).

4 Related Work

Efficiency of ILP systems is strongly dependent on the strategy adopted while searching the space of candidate hypotheses. Different techniques have been investigated to improve efficiency. A common approach is to reduce the number of hypotheses to evaluate during the search. Language bias specification to constraint the number of hypotheses [15] and branch-and-bound as well as heuristic searches have been widely employed in this perspective.

The caching of information on clauses coverage seems instead to be a convenient solution when exhaustive search is carried out. Indeed, [7] implements in Progol the caching of positive and negative cover of clauses during the search. Results show an improvement expressed by a 15.75 speed up factor. This approach is very similar to the caching strategy adopted in the clause evaluation phase of ATRE. Nevertheless, it presents some differences due to the additional difficulties raised by recursive theory learning. Indeed, as explained in Section 3.2, ATRE has to take into account the distinction between dependent/independent clauses in order to decide whether caching strategy should be applied or not. In addition, Progol implements a *prune cache* method that aims to cache clauses representing points of the hypothesis space where the search should be pruned.

Other approaches focusing on clause evaluation phase have been investigated by [6] whose work has been later extended by [2] in the particular ILP setting that considers examples of predicate definition to be learned as composing a database to repeatedly query. In this context, a query (clause) is a conjunction of goals (literals) to refine in order to generate a predicate definition. In particular, [6] propose a method to reduce the number of literals in clause bodies in order to optimize the number of predicate calls. The method is based on redundant literal reduction by means of a subsumption relation test. They also propose an optimisation of the number of clause coverage tests by grouping dependent body literals in equivalence classes and adding a cut predicate between literals of different equivalence classes. This method based on the cut introduction has been generalized by [2], which also implement a strategy to remove literals whose success is known and that will not influence the success of the examined clause.

[19] propose a method to minimize clause evaluation costs that is based on the reordering of dependent literals. In particular, they look for clause transformations with the shortest execution time. The idea is inspired by relational database management systems area and it is based on the observation that first order clauses are more efficient if "selective" literals are placed first.

All these last approaches address the goal of minimizing the number of theorem-proving for clauses to evaluate. In ATRE, the problem of managing redundancy or ordering of literals has never been tackled but it suggests interesting directions for further improvement.

5 Experimental Results

To evaluate the efficacy of the implemented caching strategies we performed extensive comparisons on the document understanding domain which is a source of interesting data sets for multiple predicate learning [11]. For this purpose, release of ATRE with caching has been also integrated in WISDOM++

(www.di.uniba.it/~malerba/wisdom++), an intelligent document processing system that uses logical theories learned by ATRE to perform automatic classification and understanding of document images. We show experimental results for the document image understanding task alone.

A document is characterized by two different structures representing both its internal organization and its content: the layout structure and the logical structure. The former associates the content of a document with a hierarchy of layout components, while the latter associates the content of a document with a hierarchy of logical components. Here, the term document understanding denotes the process of mapping the layout structure of a document into the corresponding logical structure. The document understanding process is based on the assumption that documents can be understood by means of their layout structures alone. The mapping of the layout structure into the logical structure can be performed by means of a set of rules which can be automatically learned from a set of training objects. Each training object describes the layout of a document image and the logical components associated to layout components.

In our empirical study on the effect of the proposed caching strategies, we selected twenty-one papers, published as either regular or short, in the IEEE Transactions on Pattern Analysis and Machine Intelligence (*tpami*), in the January and February issues of 1996. Each paper is a multi-page document; therefore, the dataset is composed by 197 document images in all. Since in the particular application domain, it generally happens that the presence of some logical components depends on the order page (e.g. *author* is in the first page), we have decomposed the document understanding problem into three learning subtasks, one for the first pages of scientific papers, another for intermediate pages and the third for the last pages. Target predicates are only unary and concern the following logical components of a typical scientific paper published in a journal: *abstract, affiliation, author, biography, caption, figure, formulae, index_term, page_number, references, running_head, table, title*.

By running ATRE on a document understanding dataset obtained from scientific papers, a set of theories is learned. Some examples of learned clauses follow:

```
author(X1)  ← alignment(X1,X2)=only_middle_col, abstract(X2),
              height(X1)∈[7..13]
figure(X1)  ← type_of(X1)= image, width(X1)∈[12..227],
              x_pos_centre(X1)∈[335..570]
references(X1)  ← to_right(X1,X2), biography(X2),
                 width(X2)∈[261..265]
```

They can be easily interpreted. For instance, the first clause states that if a quite short layout component (X1), whose height is between 7 and 13, is centrally aligned with another layout component (X2) labelled as the abstract of the scientific paper, then it can be classified as the author of the paper. These clauses show that ATRE can automatically discover meaningful dependencies between target predicates.

5.1 Settings and Results

Experiments have been conducted in order to compare running time of the standard version of the system (*ATRE*) against the running time of ATRE with caching (*ATRE-cache*). Three different experiments have been performed to investigate different factors affecting the use of caching varying the dataset setting. In particular, we evaluate the caching effect in the following settings: the set of 21 documents are divided into 5 folds according to a 5-fold cross-validation; the training set is incrementally built by adding 3 documents each time until all the 21 documents are taken into account; the learning parameters that affect the size of the search space are set to different values.

5.1.1 Experiment 1
In the first experiment, the 21 *tpami* documents have been divided in five folds removing some documents in turn (Table 1).

Table 1. Distribution of pages and examples per document grouped by 5 folds.

Fold number	List of documents	Number of pages	Number of positive examples	
			First pages	Last pages
1	Tpami1	13	27	13
	Tpami13	3	12	5
	Tpami14	10	26	14
	Tpami 16	14	34	19
2	Tpami8	5	16	6
	Tpami15	15	35	20
	Tpami18	10	24	12
	Tpami24	6	16	7
3	Tpami3	15	34	17
	Tpami7	6	16	6
	Tpami12	6	14	6
	Tpami20	14	34	16
4	Tpami9	5	15	7
	Tpami11	6	15	7
	Tpami19	20	45	24
	Tpami21	11	25	16
5	Tpami4	14	31	15
	Tpami6	1	6	2
	Tpami10	3	11	3
	Tpami17	13	31	17
	Tpami23	7	18	9

For each fold, the two versions of ATRE have been run on the four remaining folds. Besides, only the two learning tasks of first and last document pages have been examined. Execution time of each learning task, efficiency gain rates and caching rates are reported in Table 2 and Table 3. The caching rate is computed as the average on the percentages of cached clauses over the total number of clauses at each learning step. In particular, the caching rate estimates the caching effort in the clause generation phase. Running times refer to executions performed on a 1.4 Ghz IBM Centrino notebook equipped with 512 Mb of RAM.

Table 2. Running times, efficiency gain rates and caching rates for the first page learning task.

First pages	ATRE	ATRE-cache		
Fold No	Execution time	Execution time	Caching rate	Time gain rate
1	3095,470	1203,706	65,240%	61,114%
2	3096,785	1282,777	68,888%	58,577%
3	2545,410	1156,807	70,292%	54,553%
4	2790,321	1206,513	73,645%	56,761%
5	2851,612	1238,228	68,286%	56,578%
Mean values	2875,920	1217,606	69,270%	57,662%

Table 3. Running times, efficiency gain rates and caching rates for the last page learning task.

Last pages	ATRE	ATRE-cache		
Fold No	Execution time	Execution time	Caching rate	Time gain rate
1	2199,972	1381,098	31,726%	37,222%
2	1681,480	1317,043	34,102%	21,674%
3	1817,711	1254,341	35,878%	30,993%
4	1641,837	1117,979	44,403%	31,907%
5	2016,882	1299,936	35,286%	35,547%
Mean values	1871,576	1274,079	36,279%	31,925%

Results reported in the Table 2 and 3 show that the running time gain as well as the caching rates vary with respect to the training fold because it may happen that some folds are composed by more complex training objects than others. Moreover, the above tables show that the two rates are not so proportional as one can expect. This is because the caching rate is only related to the clause generation phase, while the time gain rate is related to both the clause generation and evaluation phases. Interesting observations can arise relating trends on caching and time gain rates.

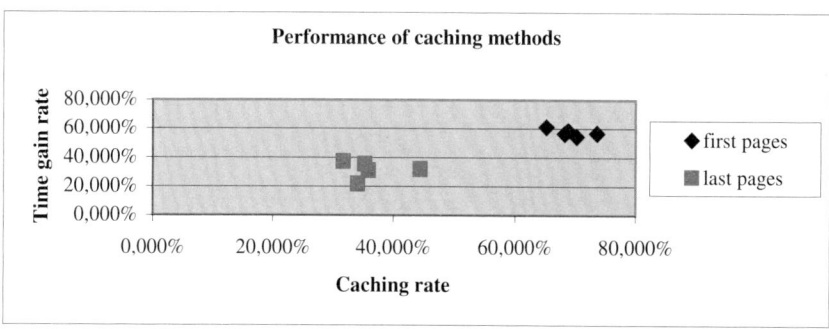

Fig. 4. Time gain rates on the varying of the caching rate.

Fig. 4 shows that the two tasks generate two distinct clusters. No definite relationship seems to characterize the use of caching with respect to the efficiency gain inside each cluster. In addition, we observe that the cluster generated for the last pages task is further down positioned with respect to the cluster generated for the first pages task. This means that the employment of caching strongly improves the running time in first pages task while does not significantly affect the last pages task. This is because in the case of first page documents, the system has more target predicate definitions to learn than in the case of last pages documents. Consequently, the search space in last pages task is composed by few specialization hierarchies. Hence, every seed change (i.e. a search-tree to remove) more heavily affects the search space portion to be re-explored. Obviously, this is because the caching rate is computed as the average of rates at each learning step. A more significant information could be   provided by also evaluating   the caching rate standard deviation. Indeed, for the last pages task, the standard deviation varies between 27 and 44, while for the first pages task it varies between 68 and 73. This suggests that on the first pages task, the effect of caching is more uniform than in the other task. The higher efficiency gain as well as the more uniform variation of caching rate for the first pages task are due to a more homogeneous distribution of examples in the training set. From a more general point of view, the dataset peculiarities affect both the caching rate and the time gain rate since whenever one of the two measures is high, the other one is high too.

5.1.2   Experiment 2

In this experiment we progressively increase the size of the dataset. The two versions of the system have been run on a set of 3, 6, 9, 12, 15, 18 and 21 *tpami* documents. For each dataset trends of the efficiency gain rate and the caching rate for first and last pages tasks are shown in Fig. 5 and Fig. 6, respectively.

Graphs in Fig. 5 and 6 show that both the measures tend to approximately follow the same trend. In the first pages task, both the caching rate and the time gain rate are quite constant, that is the effect of caching has no influence on performances while the dataset grows. In the last pages task, both the rates decrease starting from the dataset with 12 documents.

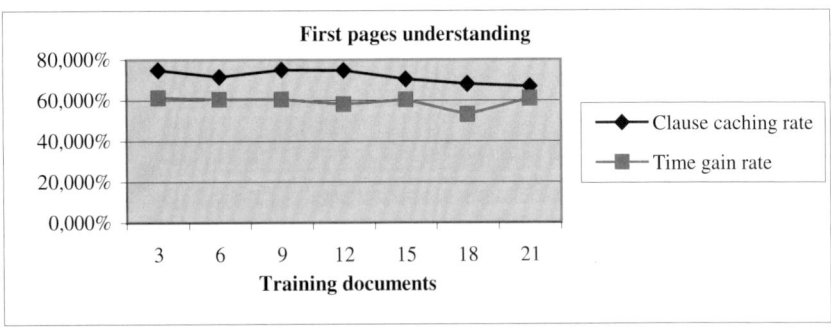

Fig. 5. Time gain rate and caching rate in first page document task varying the complexity of datasets in terms of examples number.

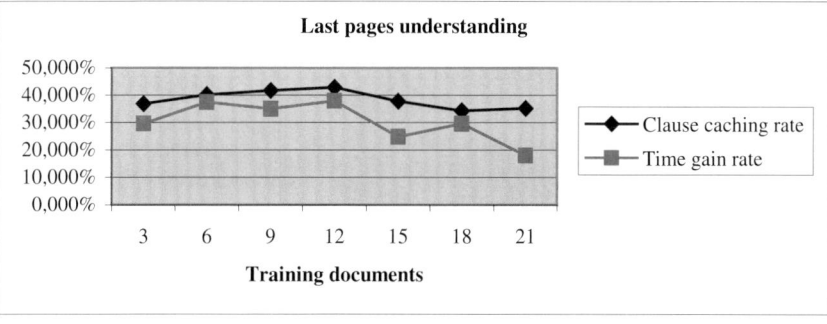

Fig. 6. Time gain rate and caching rate in last page document task varying the complexity of datasets in terms of examples number.

When we relate the two measures (Fig. 7), we can observe that in the case of last pages task there is a fairly good dependence between the caching and the time gain rates because when the caching rate raises, the time gain tends to raise too. Moreover, both the measures are affected by peculiarities of each task, because as in the first experiment, when one of the two rates is high, the other one tends to be high too, and vice versa.

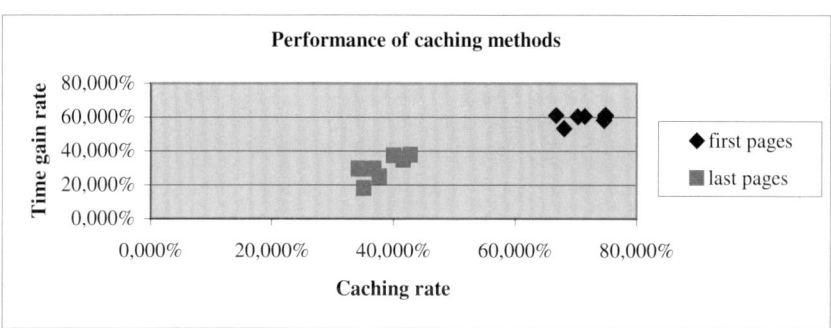

Fig. 7. Distribution of time gain and caching rates for first and last pages tasks varying the complexity of datasets in terms of examples number.

5.1.3 Experiment 3

In this experiment the effect of the caching is investigated with respect to two system parameters, the minimum number of *consistent* clauses found at each learning step before selecting the best one and the beam of the search. The former affects the depth of specialization hierarchies, because the higher the number of consistent clauses is, the deeper the hierarchies are. The latter affects the width of the search-tree.

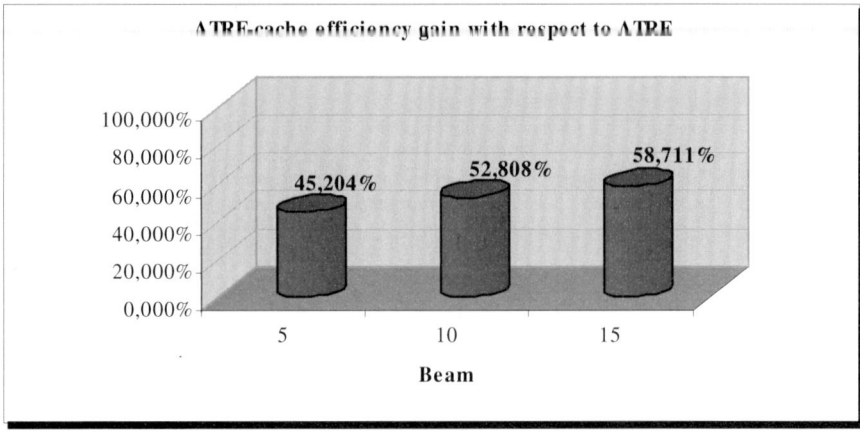

Fig. 8. Efficiency gain on first pages task on beam value variation.

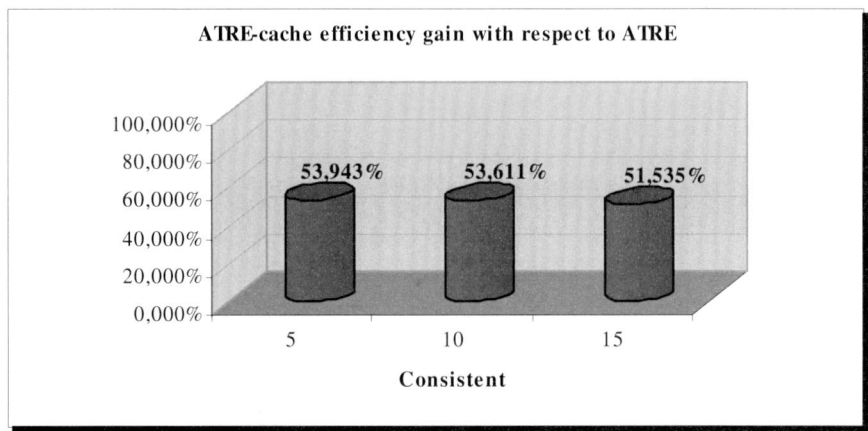

Fig. 9. Efficiency gain on first pages task on *consistent* variation.

Results for the first page learning task are shown in Fig. 8 and 9. Percentages refer to efficiency gain in time of *ATRE-cache* with respect to *ATRE*. Results show a positive dependence between the size of the beam and the efficiency gain rate. On the contrary, slight increases in the number of consistent clauses do not seem to significantly affect the efficiency gain due to caching.

From the memory use point of view, the application of caching leads to additional memory requirements. As an example, the memory use of *ATRE-cache* with respect to *ATRE* for the last pages learning task is reported in Fig. 10. Results show that the additional memory need is directly affected by the size of the beam. Results computed with respect to *consistent* variation do not point out any dependency between further memory requirements and the parameter variation.

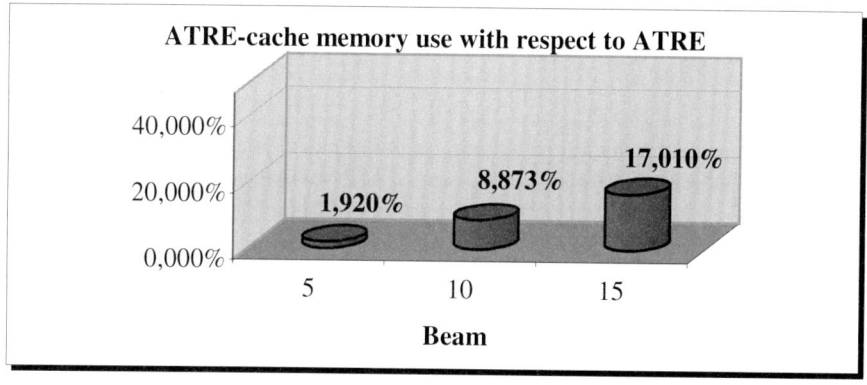

Fig. 10. Memory use on last pages task on beam value variation.

5.1.4 Accuracy and Structure of Induced Theories

Concerning the induced theories, we can observe that sometimes slight differences occur both in the number of learned clauses and in the order in which they have been learned. Considering that the clause generation caching implies the storage of the sequence of clauses to be explored, this can influence the order that the learning strategy "naturally" follows. Indeed, generally it may happen that going down from a learning step to the following step, the learning strategy generates the same clauses by following a different sequence. To evaluate the effect of caching on the accuracy of the learning problem, we compare results of a 5-fold cross-validation test performed on both the versions of the system. In particular, the set of 21 documents is firstly divided as reported in Table 1, and then, for every fold, *ATRE* and *ATRE-cache* are trained on the remaining folds and tested on the hold-out fold. For each learning problem, the number of omission/commission errors is recorded. O*mission* errors occur when logical labelling of layout components are missed, while *commission* errors occur when wrong logical labelling are "recommended" by a rule. Experimental results are reported in Table 4 for each trial, and the average number of omission and commission errors is also given. We can conclude that the caching does not significantly affect the accuracy.

Table 4. Accuracy of induced theories in the first page documents task.

Fold	ATRE		ATRE-cache	
	Omissions	**Commissions**	**Omissions**	**Commissions**
1	21/99	15/4080	20/99	12/4080
2	13/91	16/4697	12/91	11/4697
3	17/98	15/4781	18/98	17/4781
4	19/100	14/5318	19/100	14/5318
5	31/97	8/3746	30/97	9/3746
Average %	20,76	0,30	20,34	0,28
Std Dev. %	6,75	0,06	6,50	0,05

6 Conclusions

In this paper evolutions on a search strategy for recursive theory learning to tackle efficiency problems are proposed. They have been implemented in ATRE and tested in the document understanding domain. Initial experimental results show that the learning task benefits from the caching strategy. As future work we plan to perform more extensive experiments to investigate the real efficiency gain in other real-word domains. As future work, further improvements concerning the quality of induced theories are worth to be investigated. The complexity and comprehensibility of learned theories are affected by the application of the layering technique and an optimisation on the number of layering operations can be profitably feasible.

References

1. Apt, K.R.: Logic programming. In: van Leeuwen, J. (ed.): Handbook of Theoretical Computer Science, Vol. B. Elsevier, Amsterdam (1990) 493-574.
2. Blockeel H., Demoen B., Jansseens G., Vandecasteele H., Van Laer W.: Two Advanced Transformations for Improving the Efficiency of an ILP System, In J. Cussens and A. Frisch (ed.), Proceedings of the Work-in-Progress Track at the 10th International Conference on Inductive Logic Programming (2000) 43-59.
3. Blockeel H., De Raedt L., Jacobs N., and Demoen B.: Scaling up inductive logic programming by learning from interpretations. Data Mining and Knowledge Discovery, 3(1) 59-93 (1999).
4. Boström H.: Induction of Recursive Transfer Rules. In J. Cussens (ed.), Proceedings of the Language Logic and Learning Workshop (1999) 52-62.
5. Buntine, W.: Generalised subsumption and its applications to induction and redundancy. Artificial Intelligence, Vol. 36 (1988) 149-176.
6. Costa V. S., Srinivasan A., Camacho R.: A note on two simple trasformations for improving the efficiency of an ILP system, Proceedings of the 10th International Conference on Inductive Logic Programming, Lecture Notes in Artificial Intelligence, Springer-Verlag (2000).
7. Cussens J.: Part-of-speech tagging using Progol. In Inductive Logic Programming: Proceedings of the 7th Int. Workshop. Lecture Notes in Artificial Intelligence, vol.1297 93–108 Springer-Verlag (1997).
8. De Raedt, L., Dehaspe, L.: Clausal discovery. Machine Learning Journal, 26(2/3) (1997) 99-146.
9. De Raedt, L., and N. Lavrac: Multiple predicate learning in two Inductive Logic Programming settings. Journal on Pure and Applied Logic, 4(2) (1996) 227-254.
10. Khardon, R.: Learning to take Actions. Machine Learning, 35(1) (1999) 57-90.
11. Malerba D., Esposito F., Lisi F.A. and Altamura O.: Automated Discovery of Dependencies Between Logical Components in Document Image Understanding. Proceedings of the 6th International Conference on Document Analysis and Recognition, Seattle (WA), (2001) 174-178.
12. Malerba D.: Learning Recursive Theories in the Normal ILP Setting, Fundamenta Informaticae, 57(1) (2003) 39-77.
13. Mitchell, T.M.: Machine Learning. McGraw-Hill (1997).

14. Muggleton, S. and C.H. Bryant: Theory completion using inverse entailment. In: J. Cussens and A. Frisch (eds.): Inductive Logic Programming, Proceedings of the 10th Int. Conference ILP 2000, LNAI 1866, Springer, Berlin, Germany (2000) 130-146.
15. Nedellec C., Ad H., Bergadano F., and Tausend B.: Declarative bias in ILP. In L. De Raedt (ed.), Advances in Inductive Logic Programming, volume 32 of Frontiers in Artificial Intelligence and Applications (1996) 82-103, IOS Press.
16. Nienhuys-Cheng, S.-W., de Wolf, R.: The Subsumption theorem in inductive logic programming: Facts and fallacies. In: De Raedt, L. (ed.): Advances in Inductive Logic Programming. IOS Press, Amsterdam (1996) 265-276.
17. Plotkin, G.D.: A note on inductive generalization. In: Meltzer, B., Michie, D. (eds.): Machine Intelligence 5. Edinburgh University Press, Edinburgh (1970) 153-163.
18. Plotkin, G.D.: A further note on inductive generalization. In: Meltzer, B., Michie, D. (eds.): Machine Intelligence 6. Edinburgh University Press, Edinburgh (1971) 101-124.
19. Struyf J. and Blockeel H.: Query optimisation in Inductive Logic Programming by Reordering Literals. In T. Horváth and A. Yamamoto (ed.), Proceedings of the 13th International Conference on Inductive Logic Programming, Lecture Notes in Artificial Intelligence, vol. 2835 (329-346). Springer-Verlag, 2003.

FOIL-D: Efficiently Scaling FOIL for Multi-relational Data Mining of Large Datasets

Joseph Bockhorst° and Irene Ong°

Department of Computer Sciences
University of Wisconsin, Madison WI 53706
{joebock,ong}@cs.wisc.edu

Abstract. Multi-relational rule mining is important for knowledge discovery in relational databases as it allows for discovery of patterns involving multiple relational tables. Inductive logic programming (ILP) techniques have had considerable success on a variety of multi-relational rule mining tasks, however, most ILP systems do not scale to very large datasets. In this paper we present two extensions to a popular ILP system, FOIL, that improve its scalability. (i) We show how to interface FOIL directly to a relational database management system. This enables FOIL to run on data sets that previously had been out of its scope. (ii) We describe estimation methods, based on histograms, that significantly decrease the computational cost of learning a set of rules. We present experimental results that indicate that on a set of standard ILP datasets, the rule sets learned using our extensions are equivalent to those learned with standard FOIL but at considerably less cost.

1 Introduction

Traditional data mining techniques aim to extract patterns from data sets that may be naturally represented in flat files. Conversely, relational databases represent data as a set of interconnected relational tables. Many useful patterns involve multiple tables, and since data in this format often cannot naturally be represented in flat files, traditional propositional data mining methods have difficulties learning such patterns.

Inductive Logic Programming (ILP) [1] algorithms aim to learn a set of first-order logical rules from multi-relational data and thus are well suited to multi-relational data mining tasks. There are however, two practical barriers that must be overcome before ILP systems may be applied to mining of large datasets. (i) ILP systems must deal with a limited amount of physical memory. Most ILP implementations, such as FOIL [2], tacitly assume the whole database fits into main memory. If it does not fit, these programs either crash or grind to an effective halt as they rely on the operating system to manage moving

---

° Both authors contributed equally to this work

R. Camacho, R. King, A. Srinivasan (Eds.): ILP 2004, LNAI 3194, pp. 63–79, 2004.

data between physical memory and disk. (ii) ILP systems must be faster. The search space of ILP systems is very large and even heuristic methods are slow. Moreover, since the time needed to score an operator typically depends on the database size, direct application of most ILP systems to very large datasets is impractical.

In this paper, we describe extensions to the ILP algorithm FOIL that address both of these barriers. To deal with limited physical memory we leverage off the considerable effort that has been addressed to this issue in the design of relational database management systems (RDBMSs). We show how to succinctly express FOIL's operations in terms of SQL statements that RDBMSs have been optimized to execute. To deal with time cost we describe probabilistic models that we use to estimate the gain of FOIL's operators. We show how to use these models to significantly speed up learning. Finally, we present experimental results that indicate that with our estimation method we are able to learn the same rules as standard FOIL on several standard ILP datasets, but in significantly less time.

The interest in scaling up ILP for relational data mining on large datasets has been growing as Dimaio and Shavlik [3], Tang et. al [4] and Mooney et. al [5] have recently published research in this direction. Further, Stonebraker et. al [6], Fu and Han [7], Brockhausen and Morik [8] and recently Lisi and Malerba [9] have directly interfaced relational data-mining algorithms with RDBMSs. Although the idea of incorporating the ability to learn first order rules from RDBMSs is not new, the use of probabilistic models to estimate scores for learning rules has, to the best of our knowledge, not been done before. Similar estimation methods have been used in the area of query-optimization in databases [10,11].

2 FOIL

Quinlan's first-order inductive learner [2,12] (FOIL) is a popular ILP algorithm that learns function-free first order rules for a target relation. FOIL requires as input a set of •••• •• •••• defined relations. That is, each input relation is defined by a listing of its tuples rather than •• ••• ••• • •• as a set of logical rules. This parallels closely the organization of data in relational databases where we can think of the tuples of a table as defining a relation. One of the input relations, which we refer to as POS, is designated as the target relation. Another input relation, which we refer to as NEG, is of the same arity as POS and contains tuples that do not belong to the target relation. These two relations define FOIL's •• ••••• positive and negative tuple set. The other relations $B1, ..., BN$ serve as background knowledge.

Given its input, FOIL learns rules of the form

$$POS(X_1, ..., X_m) \leftarrow L_1 \wedge L_2 \wedge ...$$

where each L_i is a (possibly negated) literal and $X_1, ..., X_m$ are distinct variables. The goal of FOIL is to discover a set of rules that entails all of the tuples in POS and none of the tuples in NEG.

Table 1. The FOIL algorithm. Given a set of tuples, POS, in the target relation, a set of tuples, NEG, not in the target relation and sets for tuples $B_1, ..., B_M$ that define M background relations, FOIL returns a set of first-order rules for the target relation. The symbol $\Leftarrow$ indicates variable assignment and the symbol $\leftarrow$ indicates logical implication.

```
 1: procedure FOIL(POS, NEG, B₁, ···, B_N)
 2:    learnedRules ⇐ {}
 3:    POS_unc ⇐ POS                              ▷ start with all positive tuples uncovered
 4:    repeat                                                    ▷ begin FOIL's outer loop
 5:       newRule ⇐ LEARNONERULE()                          ▷ POS is head of newRule
 6:       update POS_unc              ▷ remove tuples in POS_unc covered by newRule
 7:       add newRule to learnedRules
 8:    until |POS_unc| == 0
 9:    return learnedRules
10: end procedure

11: procedure LEARNONERULE()
12:    newRuleBody ⇐ {}                              ▷ start with general rule POS ← true
13:    POS_curr ⇐ POS_unc                ▷ all positive tuples are covered by newRule
14:    NEG_curr ⇐ NEG                    ▷ all negative tuples are covered by newRule
15:    repeat                                                    ▷ begin FOIL's inner loop
16:       bestLit ⇐ getBestLiteral(candidateLiterals())
17:       conjoin bestLit to newRuleBody                   ▷ add literal to growing rule
18:       update POS_curr                            ▷ arity of POS_curr may increase
19:       update NEG_curr                            ▷ arity of NEG_curr may increase
20:    until |NEG_curr| == 0
21:    return POS ← newRuleBody
22: end procedure

23: procedure GETBESTLITERAL(C)                            ▷ C is set of candidate literals
24:    maxGain ⇐ −∞
25:    for all candLit ∈ C do
26:       p' ⇐ |POS_curr| if candLit is added to newRule
27:       n' ⇐ |NEG_curr| if candLit is added to newRule
28:       p⁺⁺ ⇐ number of tuples in POS_curr covered by candLit
29:       gain ⇐ GAIN(p', n', p⁺⁺)
30:       if gain > maxGain then
31:          bestLiteral ⇐ candLit
32:          maxGain ⇐ gain
33:       end if
34:    end for
35:    return bestLiteral
36: end procedure
```

Table 1 presents a high level outline of FOIL. FOIL is a covering algorithm that on each iteration of its outer loop, which starts at Line 4[1], adds a single clause to its learned rule set that logically entails (covers) some of the previously uncovered tuples in POS and none of the tuples in NEG. FOIL's method of building a single rule, shown in the LEARNONERULE procedure of Table 1, begins with the general rule $POS \leftarrow$ true, which covers all positive and negative tuples. This rule is then specialized by greedily conjoining literals one at a time to the body until the new rule covers no negative tuples.

One trait of FOIL that distinguishes it from most propositional supervised learning algorithms is the dynamic nature of the positive and negative example training sets. When deciding which literal to append to the body of the new rule, FOIL considers only the •••••• positive and negative tuple sets, POS_{curr} and NEG_{curr} in Table 1. From one iteration to the next, these sets may shrink, grow, increase in arity or some combination thereof.

At the start of the LEARNONERULE procedure POS_{curr} is initialized to the tuples of POS that are not covered by any rule learned so far, POS_{unc}, and NEG_{curr} is set to all the tuples in NEG. Following the addition of the chosen literal (Line 17), FOIL updates POS_{curr} and NEG_{curr}. Let $L(N_1, ..., N_a, O_1, ..., O_b)$ be the chosen literal where N_i is a ••• variable that does not appear anywhere else in the new rule and O_i is an •• variable that appears either in the head or a previously introduced literal. If L is unnegated, the arity of tuples in the updated POS_{curr} and NEG_{curr} sets increases by a, the number of new variables. A tuple t in POS_{curr} (or NEG_{curr}) gives rise to a (possibly expanded) tuple in the updated set for each tuple in the relation associated with the chosen literal that matches t on the arguments indicated by the old variables.

FOIL uses an information theoretic heuristic to determine which literal to append to the body of a growing rule. On each iteration of its inner loop, which starts on Line 15, FOIL chooses the literal that has maximum gain where it defines the gain of literal L_i as

$$GAIN(L_i) = p^{++} \times \left\{ \log(\frac{p'}{p'+n'}) - \log(\frac{p}{p+n}) \right\}.$$

Here p and n are the sizes of POS_{curr} and NEG_{curr}, p' and n' are the sizes of the updated POS_{curr} and NEG_{curr} if L_i were added and p^{++} is the number of tuples in POS_{curr} that are covered by L_i.

The main computational cost of FOIL comes from the evaluation of all the candidate literals every time a new literal is added to a growing clause. If the input data set cannot fit in main memory, management of the current positive and negative tuple becomes more complicated. In the next section we show how, if our data is stored in relational database tables, these tasks can be concisely expressed by a small number of SQL statements.

---

[1] This and all subsequent references to line numbers refer to those in Table 1.

3 FOIL-D

In this section we present FOIL-D, our implementation of FOIL that interfaces directly with relational databases. FOIL-D assumes operations that involve manipulation of the relational data may not fit in main memory and thus provides database operations, in terms of SQL statements, for them. FOIL-D does however, assume that other operations, such as generating and storing the candidate literals, fit in main memory.

One difference between FOIL and our current implementation of FOIL-D is that for simplicity FOIL-D only considers unnegated literals while FOIL considers both unnegated and negated literals. There is nothing fundamental that prevents FOIL-D from considering negated literals though, and we plan to add support for them in the future.

3.1 Database Organization and Operations

Let the tuples defining the input relations be in database tables named POS, NEG, B1, ..., BN where the mapping between tables and the relations in Table 1 is the obvious one. If the data is not in such a format, temporary tables can be constructed. We store the uncovered positive tuples and the current positive and negative examples in database tables named POS_UNC, POS_CURR and NEG_CURR respectively. Due to the dynamics of the training sets, the number of columns of POS_CURR and NEG_CURR may change during the course of the algorithm. At any time though there is a one-to-one correspondence between the columns of POS_CURR (and NEG_CURR) and the distinct variables that have been introduced by either the head or a literal in the body of the growing clause.

The left-hand column of Table 2 lists the line numbers from Table 1 where FOIL-D issues database queries. The right-hand column gives the SQL statements[2] for the corresponding line. We now discuss each of these operations in turn.

Line 3. Here we initialize POS_UNC to all the tuples in POS. SQL statements of the from CREATE • • • •••••••••• • LIKE •••••• ••••••••• • create a new empty table that has the same column names and types as the existing table indicated.

Line 6. Here we remove from POS_UNC those tuples covered by the rule just learned. We first save the tuples of POS_UNC into the temporary table OLD_POS_UNC and recreate an empty POS_UNC. The INSERT INTO statement fills POS_UNC with those tuples of OLD_POS_UNC that do not have any matching tuple in POS_CURR, the expanded tuples covered by the new rule. The semantics of LEFT JOIN is to include at least one tuple from the "left" table (OLD_POS_UNC in this case) even if none of them are selected

---

[2] These statements are compatible with version 4.1 of MySQL (http://www.mysql.com) and they can be adapted to other RDBMSs

Table 2. SQL statements used by FOIL-D. The left-hand-column indicates line numbers from Table 1 where FOIL-D issues database queries. The right-hand-column lists the corresponding SQL statements.

Line 3	`CREATE TABLE POS_UNC LIKE POS`
	`INSERT INTO POS_UNC SELECT * FROM POS`
Line 6	`ALTER TABLE POS_UNC RENAME OLD_POS_UNC`
	`CREATE TABLE POS_UNC LIKE POS`
	`INSERT INTO POS_UNC SELECT` *cols* `FROM OLD_POS_UNC`
	`LEFT JOIN POS_CURR ON` *cond* `WHERE` *cond′*
	`DROP TABLE OLD_POS_UNC`
Line 13	`CREATE TABLE POS_CURR LIKE POS`
	`INSERT INTO POS_CURR SELECT * FROM POS_UNC`
Line 14	`CREATE TABLE NEG_CURR LIKE NEG`
	`INSERT INTO NEG_CURR SELECT * FROM NEG`
Line 18	`ALTER TABLE POS_CURR RENAME OLD_POS_CURR`
	`CREATE TABLE POS_CURR (...)`
	`INSERT INTO POS_CURR SELECT` *cols* `FROM OLD_POS_CURR,` *rel(bestLit)* `WHERE` *cond*
	`DROP TABLE OLD_POS_CURR`
Line 19	`ALTER TABLE NEG_CURR RENAME OLD_NEG_CURR`
	`CREATE TABLE NEG_CURR (...)`
	`INSERT INTO NEG_CURR SELECT` *cols* `FROM OLD_NEG_CURR,` *rel(bestLit)* `WHERE` *cond*
	`DROP TABLE OLD_NEG_CURR`
Line 26	`SELECT COUNT (*) FROM POS_CURR,` *rel(candLit)* `WHERE` *cond*
Line 27	`SELECT COUNT (*) FROM NEG_CURR,` *rel(candLit)* `WHERE` *cond*
Line 28	`SELECT DISTINCT COUNT (*) FROM POS_CURR,` *rel(candLit)* `WHERE` *cond*

with the condition in the ON clause, provided they pass the condition in the WHERE clause. These tuples have null values for any columns that come from the "right" table (POS_CURR). The statement FOIL-D issues selects only those tuples of OLD_POS_UNC that do not match any in POS_CURR by setting *cond′* to *col* = null where *col* is a column in POS_CURR. The condition *cond* in the ON clause is a set of equality constraints between columns in OLD_POS_UNC and columns in POS_CURR that correspond to variables in the target relation.

Lines 13 and 14. Here we initialize POS_CURR and NEG_CURR, the current positive and negative example set.

Lines 18 and 19. Here we update POS_CURR and NEG_CURR after we add the highest scoring literal *bestLit* to the growing rule. The statements for updating POS_CURR are analogous to those for updating NEG_CURR. For simplicity, we only describe those for updating POS_CURR. Before getting the tuples with the INSERT INTO statement, we save the old tuples in a temporary table OLD_POS_CURR and create a new POS_CURR table that will hold the updated examples. The new POS_CURR table will have a column for each column in OLD_POS_CURR and each new variable in *bestLit*. The INSERT INTO statement joins OLD_POS_CURR with the relation of *bestLit*, *rel(bestLit)*. The condition •••• in the WHERE clause is a conjunction of equalities, one for each old variable in *bestLit*, between columns in OLD_POS_CURR and the corresponding columns in *rel(bestLit)*. The projection *cols* lists the columns in OLD_POS_CURR along with the columns in *rel(bestLit)* that correspond to the new variables in *bestLit*.

Lines 26-27. Here we compute counts p' and n' that, along with p^{++}, we need for computing the gain of the candidate literal *candLit*. The conditions *cond* in the WHERE clauses are conjunctions of equalities, one for each new variable in *candLit*, and are the same for both statements. If *candLit* becomes *bestLit*, *cond* will also be used in the INSERT INTO SELECT statements issued when updating POS_CURR and NEG_CURR on Lines 18 and 19.

Line 28. Here we compute p^{++}. The DISTINCT keyword assures that tuples in POS_CURR are counted at most once. The condition *cond* is the same as the one used on Line 26 to compute p.

3.2 Computational Cost of FOIL-D

The primary computational cost of running FOIL-D on large databases comes from the database •• •• operations used to execute the six conditional SELECT statements (Lines 6, 18, 19, 26, 27 and 28). A join operation ($r \bowtie s$) between tables r and s selects a subset of the tuples in the cross product $r \times s$ that matches a specified set of constraints. The implementation of the join operation is a heavily studied topic in database research. See for example, Ramakrishnan's textbook [13]. The cost of a join depends on a number of properties of the join such as the number and types of constraints (••, $>, <, =$), the presence of any database indexes on the join columns, and the number of tables. In FOIL-D all joins involve only equality constraints (••• •••• ••) between two tables. FOIL-D does perform joins with $k > 1$ equality constraints (k-column joins). In this paper, we are agnostic about the implementation of join but measure the computational cost by the total number of joins performed to learn a theory.

Inspection of Tables 1 and 2 reveals that the number of joins needed to learn a rule set of R rules with L total literals where C total candidates are considered is

$$\# \text{ of join operations} = R + 2L + 3C$$

The number of rules in a learned theory R is typically small, often less than five, and the number of literals L is also manageable, in the ten's at most. The number of candidates C, however, is often much larger and thus C dominates the others. The number of candidate literals considered at •••• step depends most strongly on the arity of the maximum arity relation and the number of old variables introduced so far [14]. For example, the number of candidate literals considered to append to a rule with 5 old variables and max arity of 3 is 136 [14]. FOIL-D uses type constraints on the arguments of the relations (or the columns in the database) which reduces the total number of candidate literals somewhat but not so much that it does not dominate in the above expression. Next, we describe extensions to FOIL-D that reduce the total number of join operations needed to learn a theory.

4 FOIL-DH

To get the counts p', n' and p^{++} needed to compute the gain of a candidate literal we only need the ••• ••• of tuples in the result sets of the SQL statements listed in Table 2 that we execute on Lines 26-28. Thus, one way to reduce the total number of joins is to compute p', n' and p^{++} by more efficient means. The approach we consider here is, using histograms, to construct probabilistic models of the tuples in each table and to use these models to estimate the counts. We call this system "FOIL-D with histograms" or simply FOIL-DH.

We maintain a histogram for each column of POS_UNC, NEG, B1, ..., BN, POS_CURR and NEG_CURR. Let $h^{r.c}$ be the histogram for the column $r.c$ of table r. The domain of $h^{r.c}$ is the same as the domain of the type of column $r.c$. The count $h^{r.c}(v)$ for value v is the number of tuples in r for which the value of column $r.c = v$.

4.1 Estimating p' and n'

Now we show how, given the column histograms and an independence assumption, to estimate quickly the size of any k-column equi-join, such as the ones to get p' and n'.

The probability $p^{r.c}(v)$ that a randomly selected tuple in table r has value v in column c is

$$p^{r.c}(v) = h^{r.c}(v)/|r|.$$

For an equi-join between columns c of table r and c' of table s the probability that a randomly selected tuple from the cross product $r \times s$ satisfies the equality constraint, and thus is included in the result set, is

$$p(r.c, s.c') = \sum_v p^{r.c}(v) \times p^{s.c'}(v)$$

where the sum is over all values in the type of column $r.c$ (and $s.c$). The number of tuples in the result set is exactly given by

$$size(r \bowtie_1 s) = |r||s| \times p(r.c, s.c')$$

where $\bowtie_1$ indicates a 1-column join between r and s.

This is an exact calculation because the nature of the cross product guarantees that for a randomly selected tuple in $r \times s$, the value in a column from r is statistically independent of the value of a column from s. For multi-column joins the summary statistics in the histograms are not sufficient to exactly compute the size of the result set. If we assume, however, that the values of all columns in the join from the ••• • table are statistically independent, we can estimate the size of a $k-$column join as

$$\hat{size}(r \bowtie_k s) = |r||s| \prod_{i=1}^{k} p(r.i, s.i) \tag{1}$$

where without loss of generality we assume column $r.i$ is joined with $s.i$ for $1 \leq i \leq k$.

Our estimates of p' and n' for candidate literal $candLit$ then are

$$\hat{p}' = si\hat{z}e(\text{POS\_CURR} \bowtie_b rel(candLit))$$

and

$$\hat{n}' = si\hat{z}e(\text{NEG\_CURR} \bowtie_b rel(candLit))$$

where $rel(candLit)$ is the relation of $candLit$ and b is the number of old variables in $candLit$.

4.2 Estimating p^{++}

In order to compute the gain of $candLit$, in addition to p' and n', we need p^{++}, the number of tuples in POS_CURR (pre-update) still covered by the new rule if we accept $candLit$. Thus, we need to estimate the number of tuples in $r = $ POS_CURR that give rise to at least one tuple in $r \bowtie_k s$ where s is $rel(candLit)$.

To estimate p^{++}, we first compute q, the probability a randomly selected tuple in $r \times s$ matches on join columns 2 through k given the independence assumptions as

$$q = \prod_{i=2}^{k} p(r.i, s.i)$$

where again we assume column $r.i$ is joined with $s.i$ for $1 \leq i \leq k$. If $k = 1$ we set q to 1.0. If we randomly pick with replacement j tuples from $r \times s$, the probability that at least one matches on join columns 2 through k is

$$m(j) = (1.0 - (1.0 - q)^j).$$

A tuple in r with value v in the first join column has $h^{s.1}(v)$ tuples in the cross product that match in the first column and this many "chances" to match on the remaining $k - 1$ columns. So, we estimate the probability that the tuple will have at least one match in the result set as $m(h^{s.1}(v))$. Summing over all values and multiplying by $h^{r.1}(v)$ gives our estimation of p^{++}:

$$\hat{p}^{++} = \sum_v h^{r.1}(v) * m(h^{s.1}(v)).$$

Our choice of doing this final sum over values of the first join column is arbitrary. We could have chosen any i of the k join columns as the one to do the final sum over; however, we would then calculate q as the probability of a match on the $k - 1$ columns excluding join column i. Due to errors introduced by the sampling with replacement assumption of $m(j)$, in general the estimate $\hat{p}^{++}$ will be different for each choice of final join column i. In practice however, we have found $\hat{p}^{++}$ to be close for any choice of i.

As with the expression for estimating p' and n', our estimation $\hat{p}^{++}$ is exact for 1-column joins. Thus, we can exactly compute the gain for candidate literals with exactly 1 old variable given the column histograms.

4.3 Estimating the Highest Gain Literal

We speed up FOIL-D by using estimations of p', n' and p^{++} to estimate the highest scoring candidate literal in two ways. The first method simply estimates the gain of every candidate literal directly with $\hat{p}'$, $\hat{n}'$ and $\hat{p}^{++}$ and chooses the one with highest estimated gain to append to the growing clause. This method eliminates the $3C$ joins needed to estimate the gain of the C candidate literals thereby reducing the number of joins performed to learn a theory with R rules and L literals to

$$\text{\# of join operations} = R + 2L.$$

A problem with this method is that the independence assumption often causes the estimated gains of the highest-scoring candidate literals with 2 or more old variables to be less than their true gains. In cases where the candidate literal with highest gain has multiple old variables, this procedure often erroneously estimates the highest scoring literal to be one with only 1 old variable.

We find, however, the relative ranks of the candidate literals with multiple old variables, especially the highest scoring ones, is relatively stable following the estimation procedure. This leads to our other use of $\hat{p}'$, $\hat{n}'$ and $\hat{p}^{++}$.

We also use the estimates of the candidate literal gains as a filter to reduce the number of candidate literals whose gains are computed exactly. Given filter size F we pick a candidate literal to conjoin to the growing clause with this method as follows. First, we compute the estimated gains of the entire candidate set using our histograms as described above. Next, we rank the candidate literals with two or more old variables by estimated gain and compute the exact gain for the top F. Finally, we choose that the literal with the highest true gain among these F and the top scoring candidate literal with a single old variable. We call this method FOIL-DH(F).

The number of joins performed to learn a theory with FOIL-DH(F) is

$$\text{\# of join operations} = R + 2L + 3FL$$

which is still much smaller than $R + 2L + 3C$ for small F.

4.4 Richer Probabilistic Models

As just described, the current implementation of FOIL-DH estimates the size of a multi-column join by assuming that, for a randomly selected tuple from either of the tables in the join, the values for the join columns are independent of one another. If the join columns are highly correlated, this assumption is likely to lead to inaccurate gain estimates and could result in poor rules.

One way to address this pitfall is to explicitly represent the dependencies between columns with a more complex probability model, such as a • •••••••
••• •••[15], for each table's tuples. Using Bayesian networks, the product on

---

[3] The current version of FOIL-DH corresponds to a Bayesian network for each table that has one vertex for each column and no edges.

the right-hand-side of Equation 1 would be replaced with the probability, as given by the Bayesian networks for the two tables, that a randomly selected tuple from the cross-product would match on the join columns.

5 Experimental Results

This section describes experiments conducted and results obtained by FOIL-D, FOIL-DH and FOIL-DH(F) on three learning tasks taken from machine learning literature, which were used by Quinlan [2] to illustrate the power of FOIL. Descriptions of the domains are also taken from Quinlan [2]. The aim of the experiments performed is to determine whether the cost of obtaining accurate hypotheses, with respect to FOIL, can be significantly reduced by using probabilistic models (FOIL-DH) and filtering (FOIL-DH(F)) to estimate the scores of literals.

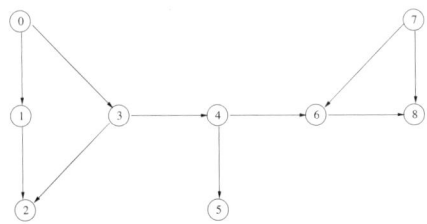

Fig. 1. A small network, where ⟵ indicates linked-to, from Quinlan [2]

Table 3. Rules learned for *can-reach*

FOIL-D, FOIL-DH(1-6)	can-reach(X0, X1) ← linked-to(X0, X1)
	can-reach(X0, X1) ← linked-to(X0, X2), can-reach(X2, X1)
FOIL-DH(0)	can-reach(X0, X1) ← linked-to(X0, X2), linked-to(X3, X1), linked-to(X2, X4), can-reach(X2, X1)
	can-reach(X0, X1) ← linked-to(X0, X2), linked-to(X3, X1), linked-to(X2, X4), linked-to(X4, X5), linked-to(X6, X3)

5.1 Learning Connectivity of a Network

Our first learning task involved learning the definition of can-reach in the network [2] shown in Figure 1. Extensional definitions of can-reach(N,N), not-can-reach(N,N) as well as linked-to(N,N) were given as positive examples, negative examples and background knowledge respectively. Variables in this relation consists of one type, N (Node). The goal is to learn a general definition for can-reach. Table 3 shows the rules learned by FOIL-D and FOIL-DH(0-6), which are using filter sizes set to 0 through 6.

5.2 Learning Eastbound Trains

The second learning task is from the INDUCE system by Michalski et. al [16]. Trains in Figure 2 have different numbers of cars, with various shapes and tops, carrying loads of various number and shape. The task is to distinguish between eastbound and westbound trains. The target relation eastbound(T) is to be defined in terms of the following relations has_car(T,C), not_has_car(T,C), in_front(C,C), behind(C,C), long(C), short(C), open_rectangle(C), not_open_rectangle(C), hexagon(C), not_hexagon(C), bucket(C), not_bucket(C), ellipse(C), not_ellipse(C) rectangle(C), not_rectangle(C), u_shaped(C), not_u_shaped(C), jagged_top(C), not_jagged_top(C), peaked_top(C), not_peaked_top(C), flat_top(C), not_flat_top(C), arc_top(C), not_arc_top(C), open_top(C), closed_top(C), contains_no_load(C), contains_load(C,LS), one_load(C), two_load(C), three_load(C), two_wheels(C), three_wheels(C), double(C), and not_double(C).

The variables are of three types: T (train_type), C (car_type) and LS (load_shape_type). Clauses learned by FOIL-D and FOIL-DH(0-6) are shown in Table 4.

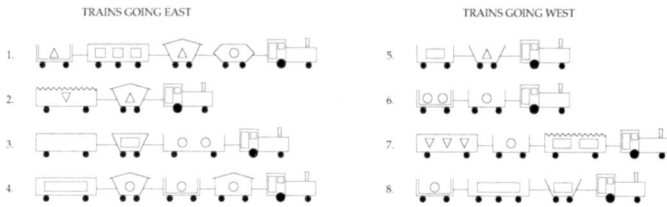

Fig. 2. Eastbound and westbound trains from Michalski et. al [16]

Table 4. Rules learned for *eastbound*

FOIL-D, FOIL-DH(0-6)	eastbound(X0) ← has-car(X0, X1), closed-top(X1), short(X1)

5.3 Learning Family Relationships

The third and final task we consider is that of learning family relationships from Hinton [17]. Figure 3 shows two isomorphic families of twelve members each. There are twelve relationship types to be learned: mother, father, wife, husband, son, daughter, sister, brother, aunt, uncle, niece and nephew. Each target relation to be learned are to be defined in terms of the following background relations: mother(P,P), father(P,P), wife(P,P), husband(P,P), son(P,P), daughter(P,P), sister(P,P), brother(P,P), aunt(P,P), uncle(P,P), niece(P,P), nephew(P,P), and their negations. The variables are all of type P (People).

The rules learned by FOIL-DH(1) for this task are identical to those learned by FOIL-D on all twelve relations. Table 5 and Table 6 show the definitions learned by FOIL-D and FOIL-DH(0-6) for uncle and mother respectively. Since all uncles happen to also be married in these families, the second literal in both uncle clauses serves the purpose of asserting that person X0 is a man. The rules learned by FOIL-D and FOIL-DH(1-6) for other relations are similar in structure. FOIL-DH(0) fails to learn any rules[4]

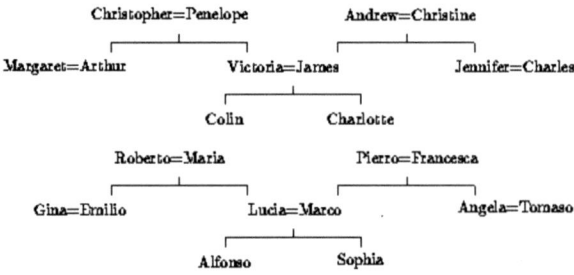

Fig. 3. Two family trees, where = means married-to, from [17] and [2]

Table 5. Rules learned for uncle

FOIL-D, FOIL-DH(1-6)	uncle(X0, X1) ← niece(X1, X0), husband(X0, X2)
	uncle(X0, X1) ← nephew(X1, X0), husband(X0, X2)
FOIL-DH(0)	No rules learned

Table 6. Rules learned for mother

FOIL-D, FOIL-DH(1-6)	mother(X0, X1) ← daughter(X1, X0), husband(X2, X0)
	mother(X0, X1) ← son(X1, X0), husband(X2, X0)
FOIL-DH(0)	No rules learned

When learning the relations can-reach and the twelve familial relationships, FOIL-D as well as FOIL-DH(1-6) constructs accurate, compact rules. However, for the can-reach relation, FOIL-DH(0) generates long, convoluted clauses that consist of only literals with ••• old variable. Furthermore, FOIL-DH(0) does not generate any rules for any of the twelve family relationships. The reason for this can be seen in Figure 4. Whenever FOIL-DH(0) makes an estimation of the gain for literals with • •••• •• old variables, it always under estimates the actual gain of the highest scoring literals, whereas it always estimates the ••••• actual

---

[4] FOIL-DH(0) learns no rules in cases where the first rule it "learns" covers zero positive examples and is discarded.

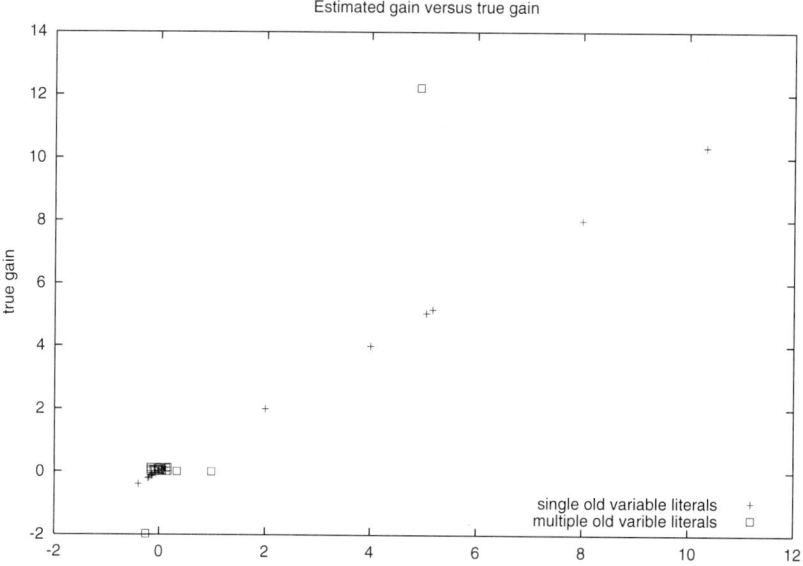

Fig. 4. Estimated gain versus actual gain calculations for adding the first literal in the relation uncle. The literal with the highest scoring true gain, niece(X1,X0), has true gain of near 12 and estimated gain of near 5. This literal is not chosen by FOIL-DH(0), but since this literal has the highest estimated score of the literals with multiple old variables it is correctly chosen by FOIL-DH(1).

gain for literals with exactly one old variable. Hence, literals with exactly one old variable will score higher than literals with multiple old variables, resulting in the unique property of the rules learned by FOIL-DH(0) for the relation can-reach. This reasoning also supports the results of FOIL-DH(0) on the relationships of the family dataset because the definitions of those relations require literals with two old variables to be added first to the body of the clause.

How then was FOIL-DH(1), with a filter size of just 1, able to learn the correct definitions for can-reach and the twelve familial relationships? One possible explanation is that even though the estimations for literals with multiple old variables are lower, the order of the estimated gain for these literals is maintained. This would allow FOIL-DH(1), which specifically considers the highest estimated literal with multiple old variables, to accurately select the best literal.

Surprisingly, all the different FOIL types in our experiments were able to learn the exact rule for eastbound trains as shown in Table 4. It is interesting to note that FOIL-DH(0) was able to learn the exact rule for eastbound trains, in accordance with our reasoning above, because the rule is comprised of literals with exactly one old variable.

Figure 5 shows the total number of JOINs performed for the different FOIL types. FOIL-DH(0) to FOIL-DH(6) grows linearly in the number of JOINs per-

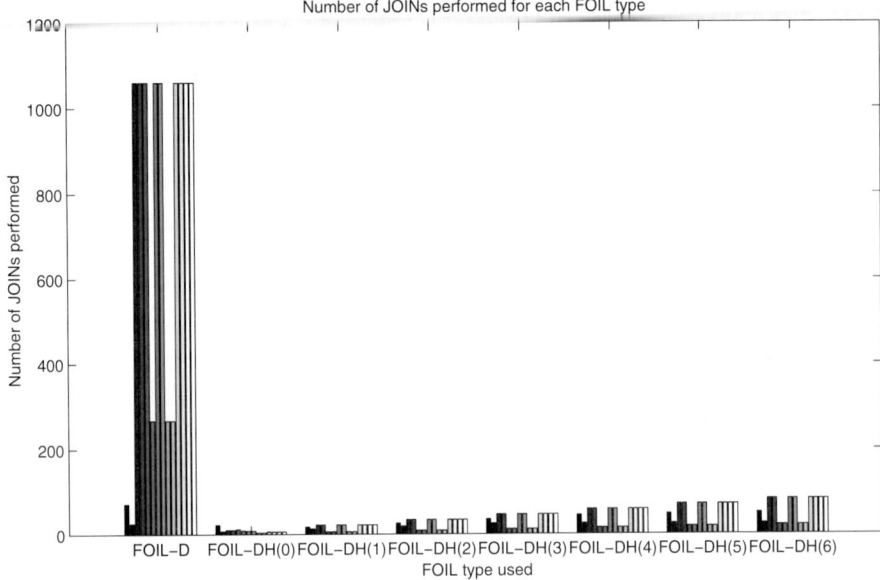

Fig. 5. Total number of JOINs performed for the different FOIL types when learning the following relations (in order from left to right in the histogram): can-reach, east-bound, mother, father, wife, husband, son, daughter, sister, brother, aunt, uncle, niece, nephew

formed. Hence, the use of FOIL-DH(F), with a resonable filter size, would still provide significantly more savings than FOIL-D.

6   Conclusion

We have presented preliminary methods towards enabling the ILP system FOIL to be applied to multi-relational data mining tasks on large data sets. Our methods address both the space and time hurdles that prohibit standard ILP implementations from being applied to these problems.

To deal with insufficient physical memory we leverage off relational database management systems. We have described FOIL-D, a system that mimics the operation of FOIL but that performs the memory intensive FOIL operations using SQL queries to a relational database.

To deal with the slowness of FOIL on very large datasets we have described FOIL-DH, an extension of FOIL-D that uses histograms to quickly estimate the gains of candidate literals without performing expensive database join operations. We also showed how we use the estimation procedure as a filter to select a small number of candidate literals whose gain we compute exactly.

Our experimental results show that while FOIL-DH dramatically reduces the numbers of joins it sometimes fails to learn the correct theories on a set of standard ILP problems because of erroneous estimates. If, however, we use the estimates as a filter we are able to learn the same correct theories as FOIL-D on the datasets we looked at while performing significantly fewer joins.

The experiments we present in this paper all involve small datasets on standard but contrived problems. Our plans for the future involve evaluating FOIL-D and FOIL-DH in terms of accuracy and efficiency on a number of large real-world datasets. In addition, we plan on investigating more complex probability models based on Bayesian networks.

In closing we note that although this paper has dealt exclusively with extending FOIL, some of the concepts developed here are applicable to other ILP systems. For example, systems that score whole clauses (as opposed to FOIL's scoring of literals) as a function of the number of positive and negative examples covered may benefit from similar estimation methods.

Acknowledgments. We gratefully acknowledge support for this research from U.S. Air Force grant F30602-01-2-0571 and NIH grant T15-LM07359-01. Thanks to David Page, Vítor Santos Costa and Inês Dutra who helped and encouraged us to present the ideas in this paper. Thanks also to Rich Maclin for help with graph formatting.

References

1. Lavrac, N., Dzeroski, S.: Inductive Logic Programming: Techniques and Applications. Ellis Horwood (1994)
2. Quinlan, J.R.: Learning logical definitions from relations. Machine Learning **5** (1990) 239–2666
3. Dimaio, F., Shavlik, J.: Speeding up relational data mining by learning to estimate candidate hypothesis scores. In: Proceedings of the ICDM Workshop on Foundations and New Directions of Data Mining. (2003)
4. Tang, L.R., Mooney, R.J., Melville, P.: Scaling up ilp to large examples: Results on link discovery for counter-terrorism. In: Proceedings of the KDD-2003 Workshop on Multi-Relational Data Mining, Washington, DC (2003) 107–121
5. Mooney, R.J., Melville, P., Tang, L.R., Shavlik, J., Dutra, I., Page, D., Santos Costa, V.: Relational data mining with inductive logic programming for link discovery. In Kargupta, H., Joshi, A., Sivakumar, K., Yesha, Y., eds.: Data Mining: Next Generation Challenges and Future Directions. Volume To appear. AAAI Press (2004)
6. Stonebraker, M., Kemnitz, G.: The postgres next-generation database management system. Communications of the ACM **34** (1991) 78–92
7. Fu, Y., Han, J.: Meta-rule-guided mining of association rules in relational databases. In: Proc. 1995 Int'l Workshop. on Knowledge Discovery and Deductive and Object-Oriented Databases. (1995) 39–46
8. Brockhausen, P., Morik, K.: Directaccess of an ilp algorithm to a database management system. In: Proceedings of the MLnet Familiarization Workshop. (1996) 95–110

9. Lisi, F.A., Malerba, D.: Inducing multi-level association rules from multiple relation. Machine Learning **55** (2004) 175–210
10. Ioannidis, Y.E., Poosala, V.: Histogram-based solutions to diverse database estimation problems. IEEE Data Eng. Bull. **18** (1995) 10–18
11. Ioannidis, Y.E., Poosala, V.: Balancing histogram optimality and practicality for query result size estimation. In: SIGMOD Conference. (1995) 233–244
12. Quinlan, J.R., Cameron-Jones, R.M.: FOIL: A midterm report. In: Proceedings of the European Conference on Machine Learning, Vienna, Austria (1993) 3–20
13. Ramakrishnan, R.: Database Management Systems. McGraw-Hill, New York (1998)
14. Pazzani, M., Kibler, D.: The utility of knowledge in inductive learning. Machine Learning **9** (1992) 57–94
15. Pearl, J.: Probabalistic Reasoning in Intelligent Systems: Networks of Plausible Inference. Morgan Kaufmann, San Mateo, CA (1988)
16. Michalski, R.S., Mozetič, I., Hong, J., Lavrač, N.: The multipurpose incremental learning system AQ15 and its testing application to three medical domains. In: Proceedings of the Fifth National Conference on Artificial Intelligence, Philadelphia, PA, Morgan Kaufmann (1986) 1041–1045
17. Hinton, G.E.: Learning distributed representations of concepts. In: Proceedings of the Eighth Annual Conference of the Fifth International Joint Conference on Artificial Intelligence, Amherst, MA, Lawrence Erlbaum (1986) 356–362

Learning an Approximation to Inductive Logic Programming Clause Evaluation

Frank DiMaio and Jude Shavlik

Computer Sciences Department, University of Wisconsin - Madison,
1210 W. Dayton St., Madison, WI 53706
{dimaio,shavlik}@wisc.edu

Abstract. One challenge faced by many Inductive Logic Programming (ILP) systems is poor scalability to problems with large search spaces and many examples. Randomized search methods such as stochastic clause selection (SCS) and rapid random restarts (RRR) have proven somewhat successful at addressing this weakness. However, on datasets where hypothesis evaluation is computationally expensive, even these algorithms may take unreasonably long to discover a good solution. We attempt to improve the performance of these algorithms on datasets by learning an approximation to ILP hypothesis evaluation. We generate a small set of hypotheses, uniformly sampled from the space of candidate hypotheses, and evaluate this set on actual data. These hypotheses and their corresponding evaluation scores serve as training data for learning an approximate hypothesis evaluator. We outline three techniques that make use of the trained evaluation-function approximator in order to reduce the computation required during an ILP hypothesis search. We test our approximate clause evaluation algorithm using the popular ILP system Aleph. Empirical results are provided on several benchmark datasets. We show that the clause evaluation function can be accurately approximated.

1 Introduction

Inductive Logic Programming (ILP) systems [1] have been widely used in classification, data mining, and information extraction tasks. Their natural treatment of relational data, harnessing the expressive power of first-order logic, makes them useful for working with databases containing multiple relational tables. ILP systems combine background domain knowledge and categorized training data in constructing a set of rules in the form of first-order logic clauses. Formally, given a training set of positive examples E^+, negative examples E^-, and background knowledge B, all as sets of clauses in first-order logic, ILP's goal is to find a hypothesis (a set of clauses in first-order logic) h, such that

$$B \cup h \Rightarrow E^+ \qquad B \cup h \not\Rightarrow E^- \qquad (1)$$

That is, given the background knowledge and the hypothesis, one can *deduce* all of the positive examples, and none of the negative examples. In real world applications, these constraints are typically relaxed, allowing h to explain *most* positive examples and *few* negative examples. ILP systems have been successfully employed in a

R. Camacho, R. King, A. Srinivasan (Eds.): ILP 2004, LNAI 3194, pp. 80–97, 2004.

number of varied domains including molecular biology [2, 3], engineering design [4], natural language processing [5], and software analysis [6].

One challenge many ILP systems face is scalability to large datasets with large hypothesis spaces. We define a general framework for learning a function that *estimates* the goodness of a hypothesis without looking at actual data. We suggest a number of ways in which such an approximation may be employed. One possible application eliminates poor hypotheses without wasting time evaluating them. Another uses the approximate hypothesis evaluator to guide the generation of promising new candidate hypotheses. Yet another application mines the estimator function itself for rules that can be used to invent useful predicates.

The remainder of the paper is structured as follows. Section 2 provides a background and related work on scaling up ILP. Section 3 describes construction of the hypothesis evaluation estimator. Section 4 describes in detail possible uses of such an estimator function. Section 5 shows some results of estimator learning on benchmark datasets, and Section 6 presents future research directions.

2 ILP Background and Related Work

The algorithm underlying most ILP systems is basically the same – it treats hypothesis generation as a local search in the *subsumption lattice* [7]. The subsumption lattice is constructed based on the idea of specificity of clauses. Specificity here refers to implication; a clause C is more specific than a clause S if $S \Rightarrow C$. In general, it is undecidable whether or not one clause in first-order logic *implies* another [8], so ILP systems use the weaker notion of *Plotkin's θ-subsumption*. Subsumption of candidate clauses puts a partial ordering on all clauses in hypothesis space. With this partial ordering, a lattice of clauses can be built, as in Figure 1. ILP implementations perform some type of local search over this lattice when considering candidate hypotheses.

The major distinction separating various ILP implementations is the strategy used in exploring the subsumption lattice. Algorithms fall into two main categories (with

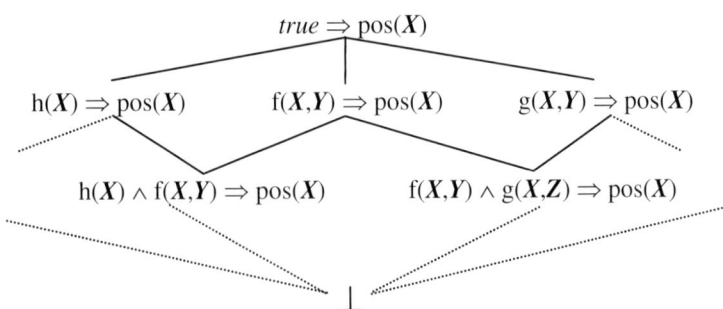

Fig. 1. This illustrates an example of the subsumption lattice over which many ILP implementations search. The lattice is bounded above by *true*, and below by the bottom clause. Many ILP systems treat clause discovery as local search, moving along lattice edges.

some exceptions): general-to-specific ("top-down") [9] and specific-to-general ("bottom-up") exploration of the subsumption lattice [10]. Within these two frameworks, a variety of common local search strategies have been employed, including breadth-first search [11], depth-first search, heuristic-guided hill-climbing variants [10,11], uniform random sampling [12], rapid random restarts [13], and genetic algorithms [14]. Our work provides a general framework for increasing the speed of any ILP algorithm, regardless of the order candidate clauses are evaluated.

One challenge ILP systems face is that they scale poorly to large datasets. Srinivasan [12] investigated the performance of various ILP algorithms, and found that the running-time depends on two factors: (1) the size of the subsumption lattice and (2) the time required for clause evaluation, which in turns depends on the number of examples in the background corpus.

The first factor – the size of the subsumption lattice – mainly depends on the number of terms in a specific example's *saturation*. Saturation is used to put a lower bound on the subsumption lattice. The process is performed on a *single positive example*. Using the background knowledge, saturation constructs the *most specific, fully-ground* clause that entails the chosen example. It is constructed by applying *all possible substitutions* for variables in the background knowledge B with ground terms in B. This clause is called the chosen example's *bottom clause*, and it serves as the bottom element ($\perp$) in the subsumption lattice (Figure 1) over which ILP searches. That is, all clauses considered by ILP (in the subsumption lattice) subsume $\perp$.

As a simple example, suppose we are given background knowledge (using Prolog notation where ground atoms are denoted with an initial lowercase letter and variables are denoted with an initial uppercase letter):

```
f(e,b)     g(b,c)
∀X,Y,Z f(X,Y) ∧ g(Y,Z) ⇒ h(Y)
```

We are also given the current positive example, e.

We first begin saturation by letting all ground atoms in H imply e:

```
f(e,b) ∧ g(b,c) ⇒ positive(e)
```

Then we apply all possible consistent substitutions, i.e., if we make the substitutions {e/X, b/Y, c/Z} (using the notation {*atom/Variable*} to indicate 'atom' is being substituted for 'Variable'), we can apply the rule given in the third line of our background knowledge, that is:

```
f(e,b) ∧ g(b,c) ⇒ h(b)
```

Finally, combining gives us the saturation of e:

```
f(e,b) ∧ g(b,c) ∧ h(b) ⇒ positive(e)
```

Clearly, the size of the subsumption lattice is directly related to the size of $\perp$. If we ignore multiple variablizations of a single ground literal and consider only hypotheses that contain less than c terms, then the size of the subsumption lattice – given a bottom clause $\perp$ – is at most $O(|\perp|^c)$ [12]. Taking into account multiple variablizations introduces an additional factor, exponential in the number of constants in the bottom clause.

The second factor – the evaluation time of a clause – is more complicated to analyze. Srinivasan simplifies the analysis by assuming that every clause can be evaluated on an example in constant time β; thus, the evaluation of a clause against the entire training set occurs in time $\beta|E| = O(|E|)$ where E is the set of training examples. An exhaustive search of the subsumption lattice for a single clause, then, takes worst-case running time $O(|\perp|^c|E|)$.

However, for most datasets clause evaluation is even worse than $O(|E|)$. Srinivasan's work assumed that deducing each candidate hypothesis takes constant time. However, even with just one recursive rule and one background fact, deduction can be undecidable [15]. Restricting ourselves to the simpler case where function symbols are not considered (i.e., Datalog) and not allowing recursive clauses, evaluating a candidate clause against a set of ground background facts is NP-complete [16]. Most ILP datasets fall into this simpler, function-free category, where evaluation time is exponential (unless P=NP) in the number of variables, which relates to the length of the expression. In other words, a long hypothesis will take significantly longer to test against the examples in the background knowledge than will a shorter hypothesis. For many large datasets, it is precisely these long hypotheses that are most interesting. As a result, approaches to scaling up ILP [9,10] have focused upon one of these two factors: reducing the number of clauses considered, or decreasing the time spent on clause evaluations.

In reducing the number of clauses considered, the simplest techniques employ general AI search strategies, such as **A***, iterative deepening, or beam search, to reduce the number of clauses in the subsumption lattice considered. For example, using a beam reduces the worst-case running time to $O(|\perp||E|)$. However, for extremely large datasets where $|\perp|$ may be in the thousands and $|E|$ in the hundred thousands, even this may take prohibitively long.

A novel approach at reducing the number of clauses in the subsumption lattice considered has been successfully employed by Srinivasan. It uses a random sampling strategy that considers sampling n clauses from the subsumption lattice, where the value of n chosen is independent of the size of the subsumption lattice. This gives worst-case running time of $O(|E|)$ for finding a single clause. However, Srinivasan's idea only works for domains where there are a sizable number of "sufficiently good" solutions. Recent work by Zelezny et al. [13] has coupled random clause generation method with heuristic search using the idea of *rapid random restarts* (RRR) to explore the subsumption lattice. They repeatedly generates random clauses followed by a short local search. Rückert and Kramer [17] have also had success using stochastic search for bottom-up rule learning, outperforming GSAT and WalkSAT.

Other ILP optimizations focus instead on decreasing the time spent on clause evaluations: the $|E|$ term in ILP's running time. Several improvements to Prolog's clause evaluation function have been developed. Blockeel et al. [18] consider reordering candidate clauses to reduce the number of redundant queries. Santos Costa et al. [19] developed several techniques for intelligently reordering terms within clauses to reduce backtracking. Srinivasan [20] developed a set of techniques for working with a large number of examples that only considers using a fraction of all available examples in the learning process. Sebag and Rouveirol [21] use stochastic matching to perform approximate inference in polynomial (as opposed to exponential) time. Maloberti and Sebag [22] provide an alternative to Prolog's SLD resolution for θ-subsumption. They instead treat θ-subsumption as a constraint satisfaction problem (CSP), then use a combination of CSP heuristics to quickly perform θ-subsumption.

Our work is distinct from all of these techniques. We describe a method for learning a function that *estimates* the clause evaluation function, which can be used in several different ways. It can reduce the evaluation time of a clause by quickly approximating the goodness of a clause, in an amount of time *independent of the number of training examples*. We can couple it with Zelezny *et al.*'s rapid random restart method in order to bias restarts toward better regions in the search space. We can use it in a manner similar to Boyan and Moore's STAGE algorithm [23] to escape local maxima in a heuristic search. Finally, we can extract hypotheses and perform predicate invention using the estimator itself.

3 Learning the Clause Evaluation Function

Heuristic approaches to exploring the subsumption lattice all make use of a scoring function to represent the *goodness* of a hypothesis at explaining the training data. Given a hypothesis (a candidate clause in first-order logic) h, a set of categorized training examples $E = \{E^+, E^-\}$, π^E_{evalfn} maps clause h to h's score on training set E under scoring metric *evalfn*:

$$\pi^E_{evalfn} : h \to \Re \tag{2}$$

We use a multilayer, feed-forward neural network described in Section 3.1 to learn an approximate scoring function $\hat{\pi}^E_{evalfn}$. Some preliminary testing revealed that other machine learning algorithms (e.g. naïve Bayes, linear regression, C4.5) were significantly less accurate at approximating the clause evaluation function. Furthermore, a neural network with a single hidden layer is capable of approximating any bounded continuous function with arbitrarily small error [24]. We use an online training algorithm detailed in the Section 3.2 to train the neural network.

3.1 Neural Network Topology

Before constructing our clause evaluation function approximator, we need a method for encoding clauses as neural network inputs. Our encoding is based on the top-down lattice exploration used by a number of popular ILP implementations. In such implementations, a positive example is chosen at random from the training set. The chosen example is then saturated, building a bottom clause ($\perp$). Recall that this bottom clause consists of only fully ground literals. An ILP system constructs candidate hypotheses by choosing a subset of these fully-ground literals and "variablizing," replacing ground atoms with variables in a manner that replaces multiple instances of a single ground atom with a single variable (our approach does *not* consider multiple – or *split* - variablizations of a single set of fully-ground literals). Approaches differ in how they select ground literals from the bottom clause.

Our neural-network inputs are comprised of a set of features derived from the candidate clause both *before* and *after* variablization. When saturating an example, each literal in that example's bottom clause is associated with an input in the neural network. This input is set to **1** if the corresponding literal in the bottom clause was used in constructing the clause, and set to **0** otherwise. Notice that there may be multiple sets of literals from the bottom clause that, when variablized, yield the same clause. This means there may be many different input representations for a single clause. However, we only use the input representation corresponding to the specific literals that *were actually chosen* when constructing the candidate clause.

Formally, let candidate clause C be chosen by selecting some subset of literals from the most-specific bottom clause $\perp_i$ for current example e_i. We treat this clause as a vector $\bar{x} = \{x_1, \ldots, x_{|\perp_i|}\}$ in $|\perp_i|$-dimensional space, with:

$$x_k = \begin{cases} 1 & \text{if ground literal } k \text{ chosen in constructing } C \\ 0 & \text{otherwise} \end{cases} \tag{3}$$

This vector $\bar{x}$ is a subset of the inputs to our neural network. One important aspect of the input vector is that every possible candidate clause – that is, every clause in the subsumption lattice – has a unique input vector representation. However, the mapping does not work in the other direction: not every possible bit vector corresponds to a legal clause. In many cases, the majority of bit vectors correspond to *illegal* clauses, which contain unbound input variables. (Algorithms using the neural network to search the space of bit vectors, as in Section 4.2, need to be aware of this).

Additionally, we give each *predicate* a specific input in the network, as well. Here, we consider a vector $\bar{y}$, in which each dimension corresponds to a predicate appearing in $\perp_i$. Construction of $\bar{y}$ is based upon the number of times a particular predicate is used in a candidate clause, that is:

$$y_j = \text{\# of ground literals in } C \text{ of predicate } j \tag{4}$$

Finally, a third set of inputs to the neural network comes from features extracted from the variablized clause C'. These features include

- **length** - number of literals in C'.
- **nvars** - number of *distinct* variables in C'.
- **nshared_vars** - number of distinct variables appearing more than once in C'.
- **avg_var_freq** - average number of times each variable appears in C'.
- **max_var_chain** - longest variable chain appearing in C', i.e., the clause
  f(A):-g(A,B),h(B,C) has max chain 3 (A→B→C).

The neural network consists of one (fully-connected) hidden layer and a two output units. The output units correspond to P and N, the predicted positive and negative coverage of a clause (that is, the number of examples from E^+ and E, respectively, deduced from the hypothesis). Given these predicted values and a scoring function, computation of the predicted output $\hat{\pi}^E_{evalfn}$ is trivial. For example, commonly used evaluation functions include *coverage* ($P-N$) and *accuracy* ($P/P+N$). Thus, we can evaluate a clause on the neural network by converting it to the vector notation specified in Equations (3) and (4), forward-propagating it on a trained neural network to estimate $\hat{P}$ and $\hat{N}$, and calculating $\hat{\pi}^{E}_{evalfn}$ from $\hat{P}$ and $\hat{N}$. Figure 2 presents this network topology graphically.

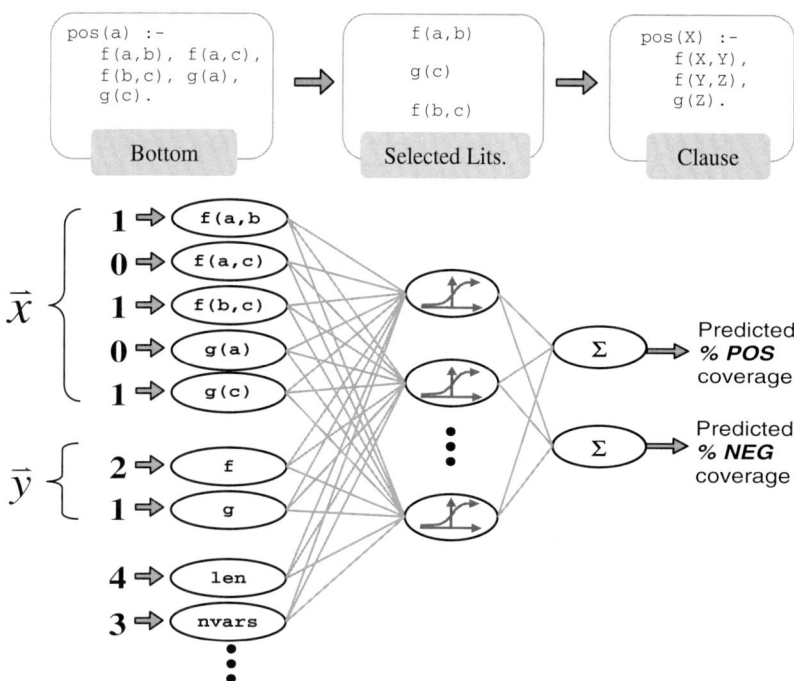

Fig. 2. An overview showing the neural network's topology, and an example of input vector construction. Notice that the vector $\vec{x}$ is constructed by the literals chosen from the fully-ground bottom clause, not the candidate clause. It is quite possible for several different sets of selected literals to correspond to the same candidate clause; we only consider the set that was *actually chosen* in the clause's construction.

3.2 Online Training

The neural network's initial training makes use of Srinivasan's random uniform sampling [12]. The user specifies a burn-in length b, and the algorithm uniformly randomly selects b clauses from the space of legal clauses (up to a given maximum clause length). We evaluate these clauses on the training data, thereby creating input/output pairs for training. Using uniform sampling to generate I/O pairs ensures that the neural network approximation is reasonably accurate over the entire search space. Using other local search methods tends to bias the neural network's approximation toward some local region in the search space. Table 1a contains an overview of the algorithm used to initially train the neural network.

The methods we present in the Section 4 – that use our approximation to explore the subsumption lattice – continue to evaluate clauses (on actual data) once the relatively short burn-in period is concluded. It seems wasteful to just throw this potential training data for the network approximation away. Our algorithm uses an *online learning algorithm* to make use of these clause evaluations – that occur as part of ILP's regular search – to improve the accuracy of the approximation. This allows us to generate a virtually unlimited number of I/O pairs for our network by simply scoring clauses on actual data.

Our online training algorithm is shown in Table 1b. When a clause is evaluated by ILP, generating an I/O pair for training our neural network, our online learning algorithm adds the pair to a cache of recently evaluated clauses. The cache typically stores 1000 to 10000 recently evaluated clauses, and, once full, elements in the cache are randomly removed to make room for incoming elements. At regular intervals (typically every 50-100 insertions) the neural network is updated by backpropagation, using the entire cache for a fixed number of epochs (typically 10). The continually changing training set, relatively short training intervals, and small number of hidden units (typically 5-10) prevent overtraining.

While the goal of our approximation is to learn an approximation of the clause evaluation function over the entire subsumption lattice, we are *especially* concerned with high accuracy of this approximation in high-scoring regions of the subsumption lattice. To ensure this accuracy, we also maintain a cache of the *best* clauses seen so

Table 1. The Neural Network burn-in training and online training algorithms. **(a)** The burn-in training algorithm. Given bottom clause $\perp_i$, a set of training examples E, and the size of the training set *trainset_size*, train a neural network to learn the clause evaluation function π^E_{evalfn}. We use early stopping to avoid overtraining, returning the learned network. **(b)** The online training algorithm, called for each I/O pair $<C,\{pos,neg\}>$ that ILP generates. The algorithm keeps a cache of recent and best-scoring clauses. At some regular interval (every *arrivals_between_updates* arrivals), the algorithm updates trained network *NN* for a preset number of epochs (*epochs_per_update*). When a new arrival overflows the cache, it removes old items at random.

(a)	(b)
BurninTraining($\perp_i$, E, *burnin*)	**OnlineTrainingArrival**(*NN*, $<C,\{pos,neg\}>$)
IOPairs ← ∅	if full(**recent_cache**)
NN ← new NeuralNetwork	delete_random(**recent_cache**)
minError ← +inf	insert $<C,\{pos,neg\}>$ into **recent_cache**
for $i = 1$ to *burnin*	if score(*pos,neg*) > min(**best_cache**)
C ← rand. clause built from $\perp_i$	insert $<C,\{pos,neg\}>$ sorted into **best_cache**
$\{pos,neg\}$ ← evaluate(*evalfn*, C, E)	
add $<C,\{pos,neg\}>$ to *IOPairs*	*num_arrivals* ← *num_arrivals* + 1
	if (*num_arrivals* = *arrivals_between_updates*)
Split *IOPairs* into **TrainSet** and **TuneSet**	*num_arrivals* ← 0
for $j = 1$ to *MAX_EPOCHS*	for $j = 1$ to *epochs_per_arrival*
foreach $<ex,\{pos,neg\}>$ in **TrainSet**	foreach $<ex,\{p,n\}>$ in **recent_cache**
run backprop on *NN* using $<ex,\{pos,neg\}>$	run backprop on *NN* using $<ex,\{p,n\}>$
error ← SSE of *NN* on **TuneSet**	foreach $<ex,\{p,n\}>$ in **best_cache**
if (*error* < *minError*)	run backprop on *NN* using $<ex,\{p,n\}>$
minError ← *error*	
bestNN ← *NN*	return *NN*
return *bestNN*	

far. This cache is typically 10% of the size of the recent-clauses cache, and when this cache is full, the lowest-scoring element is always removed to make room for incoming, higher-scoring clauses. When the neural network is updated, clauses in the best-scoring cache are also added to the training set and used to update the neural network as well.

4 Using the Clause Evaluation Approximation

This section describes three methods for using our clause approximator to scale ILP to larger datasets, and speed discovery of high-scoring hypotheses. These methods are:

(1) approximately evaluating clauses during the search of the subsumption lattice
(2) using the *evalfn* surface defined by the neural network to escape local maxima and to bias random restarts
(3) extracting hypotheses and performing predicate invention using the approximator function

4.1 Rapidly Exploring the Subsumption Lattice Using the Clause Approximator

This first method allows us to piggyback on just about any other local search method (though not stochastic methods). We perform our search in the usual manner; however, when we expand a node, instead of evaluating successor clauses on the complete set of examples, we use the neural network to compute the *approximate* clause evaluation score $\hat{\pi}^E_{evalfn}$. We then choose the next node to expand depending on our search strategy and the approximate scores. If this next node was approximately scored on the network, we then score it on actual data (and cache it for future training). We expand this new node and repeat the process. Recall that approximate evaluation takes O(1) running time, not the $O(|E|)$ running time required to perform the actual evaluation on the training data.

Interestingly enough, the behavior of this technique varies quite a bit depending on the search strategy employed. For a branch-and-bound search, this method serves to optimize the order in which clauses are evaluated – coupled with pruning, this could significantly reduce the total number of $O(|E|)$ real evaluations required. With **A*** search, this instead lets one "throw away" clauses that don't seem promising without wasting time evaluating them on actual data. Clauses that the neural network predicts to score poorly will never reach the font of the open list and will never be evaluated on the actual data (Note that this does break the guaranteed optimality of **A***).

Nix and Weigend have developed a technique for using a neural network to predict not only a regression value, but also to place an error bar on its prediction [25]. Using their technique, we can instead approximately score clauses, storing them in the open list with a 95% confidence bound instead of simply their predicted score. This tends to favor evaluation of clauses that the neural network cannot accurately predict – areas that should probably be thoroughly explored (but still seem promising!).

Additionally, we can use the surface defined by the trained neural network to guide our search. *The function encoded by a neural network with fixed weights* defines a smooth surface in the space of network inputs. We can employ this neural-network designed surface in a stochastic search. For example, we can use this surface to perform "biased" rapid random restarts (hereafter referred to as biased-RRR): instead of randomly selecting literals, we perform stochastic gradient ascent on the neural-network defined surface. That is, starting from a random clause, we perform stochastic gradient ascent on this surface. The endpoint is our "random restart": the point from which we begin evaluating clauses on the actual training examples. These "guided" restarts bias search toward better regions of the search space.

One issue that arises is that the neural network contains two separate output units – one that predicts positive coverage and one that predicts negative coverage – and we want to perform gradient ascent over the surface of some scoring function that is a (possibly nonlinear) combination of the two. Fortunately, for all of the common scoring functions we can derive a simple expression relating the derivative of the scoring function to the derivative of the two output units. The derivatives of each output unit with respect to the input – $\partial P / \partial x_i$ and $\partial N / \partial x_i$ – are easily computed with a backpropagation variant (backprop computes $\partial Err_P / \partial w_{ij}$ and $\partial Err_N / \partial w_{ij}$). Table 2 summarizes these expressions for commonly used scoring functions.

An interesting variant of this approach uses the network-defined surface to escape local maxima while performing a standard ILP best-first search. We can think of this as equivalent to the biased rapid random restart above; however, instead of some ran-

Table 2. This table expresses the gradient of several common scoring functions π_{evalfn} in terms of the gradients of the two network output units – predicted positive and predicted negative coverage. Stochastic gradient ascent uses one of these equations to compute the network-surface gradient under some scoring function. In the equations below, P denotes positive coverage, N denotes negative coverage, and L denotes clause length.

Scoring Function	π	Gradient Ascent Equation
compression	$P - N$	$\dfrac{\partial \pi}{\partial x_i} = \dfrac{\partial P}{\partial x_i} - \dfrac{\partial N}{\partial x_i}$
coverage	$P - N - L + 1$	$\dfrac{\partial \pi}{\partial x_i} = \dfrac{\partial P}{\partial x_i} - \dfrac{\partial N}{\partial x_i}$
accuracy	$\dfrac{P}{P+N}$	$\dfrac{\partial \pi}{\partial x_i} = \dfrac{1}{(P+N)^2}\left(N \cdot \dfrac{\partial P}{\partial x_i} - P \cdot \dfrac{\partial N}{\partial x_i} \right)$
Laplace	$\dfrac{P+1}{P+N+2}$	$\dfrac{\partial \pi}{\partial x_i} = \dfrac{1}{(P+N+2)^2}\left((N+1) \dfrac{\partial P}{\partial x_i} - (P+1) \cdot \dfrac{\partial N}{\partial x_i} \right)$
entropy	$-\dfrac{P}{P+N}\log\left(\dfrac{P}{P+N}\right) - \dfrac{N}{P+N}\log\left(\dfrac{N}{P+N}\right)$	$\dfrac{\partial \pi}{\partial x_i} = \dfrac{1}{(P+N)^2}\left(N \cdot \dfrac{\partial P}{\partial x_i} - P \cdot \dfrac{\partial N}{\partial x_i} \right) \cdot \left(\ln \dfrac{N}{N+P} - \ln \dfrac{P}{N+P} \right)$
GINI	$2 \cdot \dfrac{P}{P+N}\left(1 - \dfrac{P}{P+N}\right)$	$\dfrac{\partial \pi}{\partial x_i} = \dfrac{2(P-N)}{(P+N)^3}\left(P \cdot \dfrac{\partial N}{\partial x_i} - N \cdot \dfrac{\partial P}{\partial x_i} \right)$

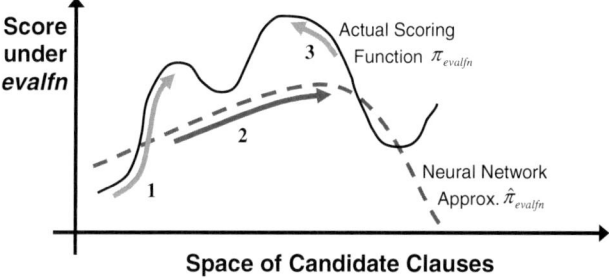

Fig. 3. This graphic illustrates our algorithm using stochastic gradient ascent on the surface defined by the neural network to escaping a local minima in ILP's standard best-first search. The search alternates between periods of ILP's best-first search (1 and 3), and stochastic gradient ascent on the network-defined surface (2). The only difference between this variant and our biased-RRR search is the *starting point* of the stochastic gradient ascent. Biased-RRR begins each period of stochastic gradient ascent at a *random* point in search space.

dom point, the *starting* point for our network-guided gradient ascent is the *ending* point from the previous period of ILP's standard search (on real data). That is, in this variation we rapidly alternate between brief periods of ILP's standard (best-first) search and stochastic gradient ascent on the neural-network-defined surface. This variation is illustrated in Figure 3.

This idea of intelligent rapid random restarts to escape local maxima is not a new one. Though not in the domain of ILP, Boyan and Moore's STAGE algorithm [23] use quadratic regression to approximate search "trajectories." That is, they learn a function mapping points in feature space to the endpoint of a local search starting at that point. They use this approximation to escape local maxima in a heuristic search. Their algorithm ran in less time, and reported better test-set accuracy than solutions discovered using local search alone.

4.3   Extracting Concepts from the Function Approximation

Finally, we can extract concepts from the neural network itself. Craven and Shavlik [26] have developed a method to extract a decision tree from a trained neural network. Running their algorithm on the (thresholded) trained clause-evaluation approximator would produce a theory – a set of clauses – that we could variablize and score on the actual data set.

The neural network, in fitting a nonlinear surface to the scoring function, will hopefully find pairs and triplets of terms that – while individually not helpful – lead to a highly accurate rule when combined. Two terms that share one or more variables and are connected to the same single hidden unit via a highly-weighted edge that possibly have an impact on the accuracy of the rule when taken together. Such a pair of terms is a likely candidate for terms of an invented predicate. The neural network approximation could be used to find such predicates using only one or a few seeds; then the invented predicates could be added to the background knowledge for the search over the remaining seeds' subsumption lattices.

5 Results and Discussion

This section presents our results on several benchmark datasets. We first show that the neural network is indeed capable of learning an approximation to the clause evaluation function. We then use the network in a rapid-random-restart search to bias restarts towards more promising regions of search space, as described in Section 4.2.

5.1 Benchmark Dataset Overview

We tested clause evaluation function approximation on four standard ILP benchmark datasets. The tasks included predicting mutagenic activity [27] and carcinogenic activity [28] in compounds, predicting the smuggling of nuclear and radioactive materials, and predicting metabolic activity of proteins. A brief description of the four datasets follows.

Mutagenesis. This task is concerned with predicting the *mutagenicity* of certain compounds. The ILP learner is provided background knowledge consisting of the chemical properties of 188 compounds, as well as general chemical knowledge in the form of first-order logic relations. The dataset is a popular benchmark, and explores a reasonably large search space.

Carcinogenesis. Similar to the mutagenesis task, but an inherently more difficult problem, this task's main concern is predicting *carcinogenic* activity compounds from potential carcinogenic compounds. The database for this problem consists of 332 labeled examples, of which about half are carcinogenic.

Nuclear Smuggling. This dataset, based on reports of Russian nuclear materials smuggling, is interesting in its highly-relational nature, with over 40 relational tables. The task is concerned with predicting when two smuggling events are *linked*. The dataset we use is a subset of the complete dataset, 192 examples split evenly into positive and negative examples.

Protein Metabolism. This task is taken from the gene-function prediction task of the 2001 KDD Cup challenge (www.cs.wisc.edu/~dpage/kddcup2001/). While the challenge involves learning 14 different protein functions, our sub-task is only concerned with predicting which proteins are responsible for *metabolism*. Here we also use a subset of the complete dataset, 230 examples split evenly between positives and negatives.

5.2 Learning the Clause Evaluation Function

This section details empirical evaluation of the neural network learning task. Our goal is to ascertain whether a neural network can learn the ILP clause evaluation function. To simplifying the task, in our experiments we only consider a batch learning process, not the online learning process outlined in Section 3.2.

We use the ILP system *Aleph* (web.comlab.ox.ac.uk/oucl/research/areas/machlearn/Aleph/aleph_toc.html) to generate 10 sets of 1000 randomly sampled clauses for each of the four datasets, corresponding to 10 different positive examples that were used in construction of the bottom clause. These 10 "seed examples" were chosen randomly. We considered a maximum clauselength $c=6$ for all but the Nuclear Smuggling task; we considered a larger value of $c=10$ for this task. Clauses were scored using a standard scoring metric, a *variant of Aleph's compression* heuristic; that is, a clause's score is given by

$$\text{score} = \frac{(\text{pos. exs. covered}) + (\text{neg. exs. covered}) - (\text{clauselength}) + 1}{(\text{total pos. exs.})} \quad (6)$$

Unlike Aleph's compression (which does not include the term in the denominator), we convert scores into a good range for neural networks by dividing by the total number of positive examples. This also allows comparison of scores across datasets.

For each dataset, these clauses and their corresponding scores were used to train the neural network. Using the machine learning package WEKA [29], we generated learning curves using 10-fold cross-validation. For all datasets, the neural network was constructed with 10 hidden units. The learning rate was fixed at 0.2. We added *early stopping* to WEKA to avoid overtraining. For each cross-validation fold, we set aside 33% of each training set as a tuning set. Then, after 200 epochs, we *kept the neural network that performed best on the tuning set*. WEKA's numeric feature normalization was enabled for all numeric features.

The learning curves for each of the four datasets appear in Figure 4. The "All Data" curves show the *mean* root-mean-squared (RMS) error over the 10 different sets of examples. (Section 3.4 explains the other two curves in each of these graphs.)

For all four datasets, the hypothesis evaluation function π_{evalfn}^{E} was learned with reasonable accuracy. In all four datasets, as more data is added to the training set, the neural network more accurately learns the evaluation function. It is interesting to note, however, that the number of examples required to accurately learn the approximator, and the accuracy of the final classifier varies amongst the datasets.

The absolute accuracy of the approximator varies across the datasets as well. For *protein metabolism*, the fully-trained network averages 0.005 RMS error; for *mutagenesis*, the results are an order of magnitude worse, at 0.05. Still, it seems promising that the worst performing approximator saw an RMS error of just 0.05.

So far, we have assumed no transfer of knowledge between seed examples, i.e., we learn a new neural network from scratch for *each* saturated example. However, several of the features we employ are independent of the example selected for saturation. In particular, every feature *except* the ground literals selected (the vector $\bar{x}$ described in Section 3) is instance-independent (or at least has an instance independent representation). These features can be shared when generating different rules from different seed examples, and, for all rules after the first, this allows us to bootstrap an initial classifier based on knowledge garnered from previous rules.

Consequently, we looked at the contribution of each subset of features on each of the four datasets. In particular, we wanted to see how instance-independent features contributed to the learning task. As before, we used WEKA to construct two learning curves for each dataset. These two learning curves correspond to training the network on (1) only instance-independent features, and (2) only instance-dependent features.

As Figure 4 illustrates, with the exception of *protein metabolism*, training on the instance-independent features alone did not produce as accurate a classifier as training on the instance-dependent features alone, or on the complete set of features. Furthermore, *on all four datasets*, using the complete set of features did not produce a significantly more accurate network approximator than using the instance-dependent features alone did. This suggests that the instance-independent features are unlikely to help transfer learning for one seed example to the next seed example, and that better approaches need to be developed.

Although these graphs illustrate that we are capable of *learning* the clause evaluation function, they do not show the degree to which the function is learned. Figure 5 compares the RMS error of the network approximation to the RMS error obtained by using a random sampling of *training examples* to approximately score clauses. This provides an alternate method for computation reduction against which we compare our method. It also allows us to determine the number of evaluations the neural network is "worth." This number varies significantly across the four datasets, ranging from between 25% and 50% sampling to well beyond 90% sampling. As these are all fairly small benchmark datasets, it remains an open question how our method will compare to sampling the training examples in larger problems (with both larger hypothesis spaces as well as datasets). This includes large problems that often arise in the biological sciences and text extraction [30].

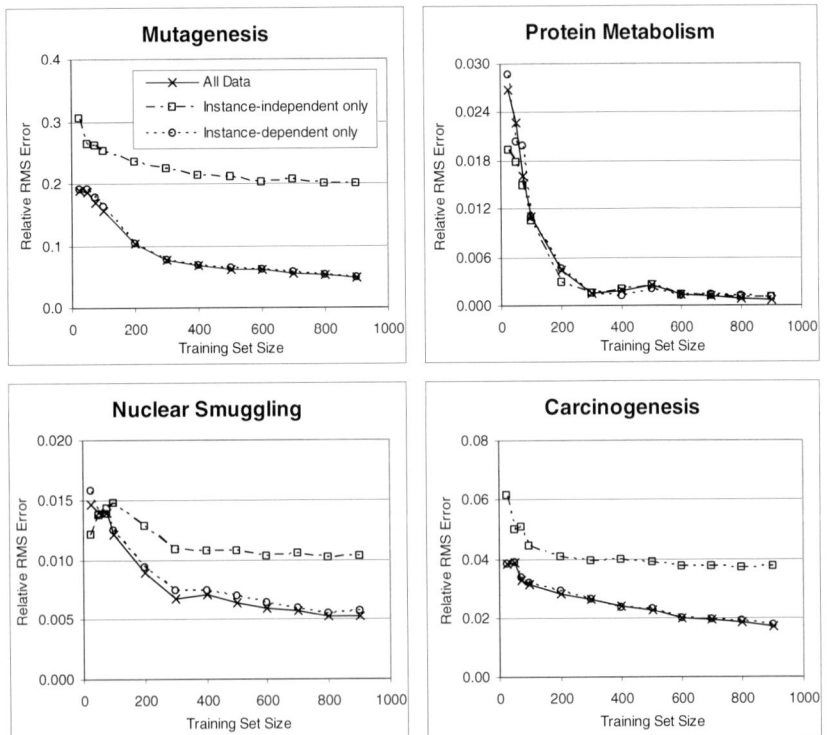

Fig. 4. Learning curves showing *test-set* accuracy over four domains comparing the roles of instance-dependent versus instance-independent features. Learning curves were generated only using a subset of the complete set of features, and the results were compared to the case where all features were used to train the network.

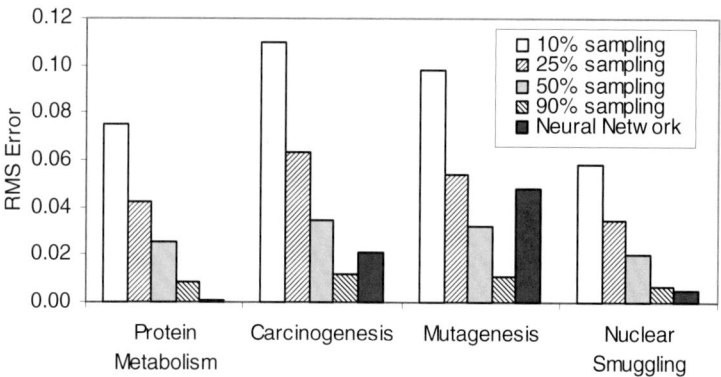

Fig. 5. Comparing the RMS error of the neural-network approximation with that obtained by using a random sampling of *training examples* to approximate clauses. The error of the neural-network approximation varies widely, but in all cases does better than a 25% sampling of examples, and for two of the four datasets, does better than a 90% sampling.

5.3 Using the Evaluation Function Approximator to Guide Random Search

This section details the use of trained neural network to bias the random restarts in a rapid random restart search. Our goal here is to find the best-scoring clause in the subsumption lattice using as few clause evaluations as possible. Thus, results in this section are only concerned with maximizing some evaluation function over the *training data*. Assuming a well-designed evaluation function, this corresponds with good test-set performance.

We implemented the previous-described online learning algorithm in *Aleph*. To enable biased random restarts, we also implemented a stochastic gradient ascent algorithm. Our gradient ascent implementation, at each step, only considered flipping an input bit on or off, and did not allow flipping a bit on if the clause length was already at its maximum. The probability of a bit flip of input x_i is given by:

$$P(\text{flip } x_i) = \frac{1}{Z} \exp\left(\frac{1}{\sigma_x^2} \cdot \frac{\partial \hat{\pi}_{evalfn}^E}{\partial x_i} \right) \cdot (-1)^{x_i} \tag{7}$$

In this formula, σ^2 determines the "softness" of the gradient ascent. For our results, it was set such that we were 100 times more likely to flip the "best" literal than the "worst." The $(-1)^x$ term simply flips the sign of the gradient when we consider flipping a bit *off* (since this is a move in the negative direction).

In order to test the performance of our algorithm, we attempt to find the clause that maximizes the *coverage* scoring function, defined as the number of positive examples covered minus the number of negative examples covered. We used stochastic gradient ascent to bias RRR search towards with 1000 restarts and 10 steps per restart, and compare the biased-RRR versus normal RRR with the same parameters. For the biased-RRR, the "burn-in period" consisted of a single random restart and the local moves following. We report results on three of the four datasets from the previous

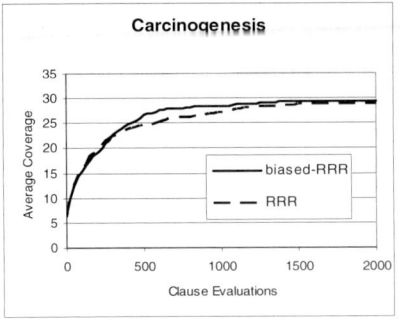

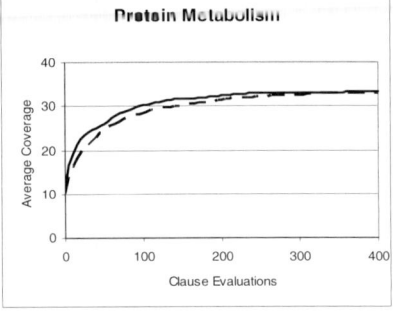

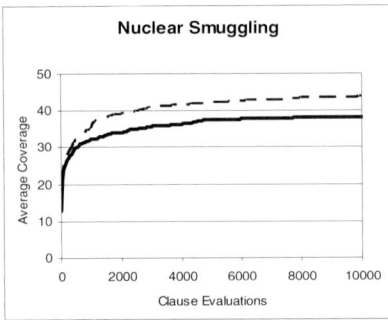

Fig. 6. Performance of the biased-RRR search versus a traditional RRR search. The x-axis shows the number of clauses evaluated, and the y-axis displays the average coverage of the best clause found at that x value. For carcinogenesis and protein metabolism, the biased-RRR performs better, but for nuclear smuggling it is clearly outperformed.

section, omitting mutagenesis as it too quickly converges: over 80% of seeds found their best clause in the very first restart. For each dataset we explored the subsumption lattices of 100 different seed examples. Our neural network consisted of 10 hidden units. Finally, each rapid random restart began at the endpoint of the previous local search and finished after a fixed number of random steps. *Aleph* search parameters are left at default whenever possible.

Figure 6 shows the results for each of the three datasets. In each of the three graphs, the x-axis shows the number of clauses evaluated, and the y-axis shows the average coverage over all seeds of the best example found thus far. As the plots show, for two of the datasets – carcinogenesis and protein metabolism – biased-RRR found a better clause quicker than did traditional RRR. However, in the third task, nuclear smuggling, biased-RRR did worse than the default implementation. The reasons for this are unclear, as the neural network was clearly able to learn the evaluation function approximator in this domain.

6 Conclusion and Future Work

We demonstrated that the use of a neural network for clause evaluation is a useful tool for improving runtime efficiency when handling large search spaces in ILP. As ILP is confronted with increasingly larger problems, the need for methods like the ones we present grows. So far, we have treated the network learning and evaluation tasks as computationally "free" operations, which is not entirely true. However, it is true that the running time of neural network evaluation (and training) is independent of the number of ILP examples in the dataset. This means that *given enough examples in the ILP training set*, neural-network evaluation can be made virtually free. This strategy can be used to decrease the runtime of ILP systems on large tasks.

The most pressing work that remains is implementing and evaluating the other strategies for taking advantage of the clause-evaluation approximator outlined in Sections 4.1 and 4.3. Clearly accuracy is lost in approximating the clause-evaluation function, but it is difficult to determine how it affects solutions generated by using it to quickly evaluate clauses in a typical ILP search. Another open question is whether useful information can be extracted from the trained neural network itself [26].

Also, Botta *et al.* [31] have characterized hypothesis space, discovering a critical region they have named the *phase transition*. In this critical region, the computational complexity of inference increases, and clauses generated in this region tend to have poor generalization to unseen test examples. This phase transition is a difficult region for ILP algorithms; our algorithm's performance here specifically needs exploration.

Finally, we have discussed learning the evaluation approximation in a least-squared-error sense. However, what may be more important for ILP is the relative *ranking* of candidate clauses. Thus, an approach like Caruana and Baluja's *Rankprop* algorithm [32] – an alternative to backprop concerned with correctly predicting the ranking of the output variables – may be more natural.

Acknowledgments. This work was supported by National Library of Medicine (NLM) grant 1T15 LM007359-01, DARPA Grant F30602-01-2-0571, United States Air Force Grant F30602-01-2-0571, and NLM grant 1R01 LM07050-01. The authors would also like to thank the UW Condor Team and the anonymous reviewers.

References

1. N. Lavrac & S. Dzeroski (1994). *Inductive Logic Programming*. Ellis Horwood.
2. R. King, S. Muggleton & M. Sternberg (1992). Predicting protein secondary structure using inductive logic programming. *Protein Engineering*, 5:647-657.
3. A. Srinivasan, R. King, S. Muggleton & M. Sternberg (1997). The predictive toxicology evaluation challenge. *Proc. 15th Intl. Joint Conf. on Artificial Intelligence*, 1-6.
4. B. Dolsak & S. Muggleton (1991). The application of ILP to finite element mesh design. *Proc. 1st Intl. Workshop on ILP*, 225-242.
5. J. Zelle & R. Mooney (1993). Learning semantic grammars with constructive inductive logic programming. *Proc. 11th Natl. Conf. on Artificial Intelligence*, 817-822.
6. I. Bratko & M. Grobelnik (1993). Inductive learning applied to program construction and verification. *Proc. 3rd Intl. Workshop on Inductive Logic Programming*, 169-182.
7. S. Nienhuys-Cheng & R. de Wolf (1997). *Foundations of Inductive Logic Programming*. Springer-Verlag.
8. M. Schmidt-Schauss (1988). Implication of clauses is undecidable. *Theoretical Computer Science*, 59:287-296.
9. J. Quinlan (1990). Learning logical definitions from relations. *Machine Learning*, 239-266.
10. S. Muggleton & C. Feng (1990). Efficient induction of logic programs. *Proc. 1st Conf. on Algorithmic Learning Theory*, 368-381.

11. S. Muggleton (1995). Inverse Entailment and Progol. *New Generation Computing*, 13:245-286.
12. A. Srinivasan (2000). A study of two probabilistic methods for searching large spaces with ILP. *Tech. Report PRG-TR-16-00*. Oxford Univ. Computing Lab.
13. F. Zelezny, A. Srinivasan & D. Page (2002). Lattice-search runtime distributions may be heavy-tailed. *Proc. 12th Intl. Conf. on Inductive Logic Programming*, 333-345.
14. A. Giordana, L. Saitta & F. Zini (1994). Learning disjunctive concepts by means of genetic algorithms. *Proc. 11th Intl. Conf. on Machine Learning*, 96-104.
15. P. Hanschke & J. Wurtz (1993). Satisfiability of the smallest binary program. *Info. Proc. Letters*, 496:237-241.
16. E. Dantsin, T. Eiter, G. Gottlob & A. Voronkov (2001). Complexity and expressive power of logic programming. *ACM Computing Surveys*, 33:374-425.
17. U. Rückert & S. Kramer (2003). Stochastic local search in k-term DNF learning. *Proc. 20th Intl. Conf. on Machine Learning*, 648-655.
18. H. Blockeel, L. Dehasp, B. Demoen, G. Janssens, J. Ramon & H. Vandecasteele (2002). Improving the efficiency of inductive logic programming through the use of query packs. *J. AI Research*, 16:135-166.
19. V. Santos Costa, A. Srinivasan, R. Camacho, H. Blockeel, B. Demoen, G. Janssens, J. Struyf, H. Vandecasteele & W. Van Laer (2003). Query transformations for improving the efficiency of ILP systems, *J. Machine Learning Research,* 4:465-491.
20. A. Srinivasan (1999). A study of two sampling methods for analysing large datasets with ILP. *Data Mining and Knowledge Discovery*, 3:95-123.
21. M. Sebag & C. Rouveirol (2000). Resource-bounded relational reasoning: induction and deduction through stochastic matching. *Machine Learning*, 38:41-62.
22. J. Maloberti & M. Sebag (2001). Theta-subsumption in a constraint satisfaction perspective. *Proc. 11th Intl. Conf. on Inductive Logic Programming*, 164-178.
23. J. Boyan & A. Moore (2000). Learning evaluation functions to improve optimization by local search. *J. Machine Learning Research*, 1:77-112.
24. K. Hornik, M. Stinchcombe & H. White (1989). Multilayer feedforward networks are universal approximators. *Neural Networks*, 2:359-366.
25. D. Nix & A. Weigend (1995). Learning local error bars for nonlinear regression. *Advances in Neural Information Processing Systems*. MIT Press.
26. M. Craven & J. Shavlik (1995). Extracting tree-structured representations of trained networks. *Advances in Neural Information Processing Systems*. MIT Press.
27. R. King, S. Muggleton, A. Srinivasan & M. Sternberg (1996). Structure-activity relationships derived by machine learning. *PNAS*, 93:438-442.
28. A. Srinivasan, R. King, S. Muggleton & M. Sternberg (1997). Carcinogenesis predictions using ILP. *Proc. 7th Intl. Workshop on Inductive Logic Programming*, 273-287.
29. I. Witten & E. Frank (1999). *Data Mining*. Morgan Kaufmann Publishers.
30. M. Goadrich, L. Oliphant & J. Shavlik (2004). Learning ensembles of first-order clauses for recall-precision curves: a case study in biomedical information extraction. *Proc. 14th Intl. Conf. on Inductive Logic Programming*.
31. M. Botta, A. Giordana, L. Saitta & M. Sebag (2003). Relational learning as search in a critical region. *J. Machine Learning Research*, 4:431-463.
32. R. Caruana & S. Baluja (1996). Using the future to 'sort out' the present. *Advances in Neural Information Processing Systems*. MIT Press.

Learning Ensembles of First-Order Clauses for Recall-Precision Curves: A Case Study in Biomedical Information Extraction

Mark Goadrich, Louis Oliphant, and Jude Shavlik

Department of Biostatistics and Medical Informatics and
Department of Computer Sciences,
University of Wisconsin-Madison, USA

Abstract. Many domains in the field of Inductive Logic Programming (ILP) involve highly unbalanced data. Our research has focused on Information Extraction (IE), a task that typically involves many more negative examples than positive examples. IE is the process of finding facts in unstructured text, such as biomedical journals, and putting those facts in an organized system. In particular, we have focused on learning to recognize instances of the protein-localization relationship in Medline abstracts. We view the problem as a machine-learning task: given positive and negative extractions from a training corpus of abstracts, learn a logical theory that performs well on a held-aside testing set. A common way to measure performance in these domains is to use *precision* and *recall* instead of simply using accuracy. We propose Gleaner, a randomized search method which collects good clauses from a broad spectrum of points along the recall dimension in recall-precision curves and employs an "at least N of these M clauses" thresholding method to combine the selected clauses. We compare Gleaner to ensembles of standard Aleph theories and find that Gleaner produces comparable testset results in a fraction of the training time needed for ensembles.

1 Introduction

Domains suitable for Inductive Logic Programming (ILP) can be roughly divided into two main groups. In one group, there are tasks in which each example has some inherent relational structure. One classic example of this domain is the trains dataset [20], where the goal is to discriminate between two types of trains, and the trains themselves are relational objects, having varying length and types of objects carried by each car. A more realistic example is the mutagenesis dataset [29], where the goal is to classify a chemical compound as mutagenic or not using the relational nature of the atomic structure of each chemical. ILP has proven successful in these domains by bringing the inherently relational attributes into the hypothesis space. The other group contains tasks where examples, in addition to having a relational structure, have relations to

R. Camacho, R. King, A. Srinivasan (Eds.): ILP 2004, LNAI 3194, pp. 98–115, 2004.

other examples. One such domain is the learning of friendship in social networks [2], where instead of classifying people, we try to determine the structural relationships of people based on a combination of their personal attributes and the attributes of their known friends. Another domain of this type is learning to suggest citations for scientific publications [21], where a correct citation can be a combination of data in this particular paper as well as the currently listed citations. The overall goal in these domains is to classify ••• •• between objects instead of the objects themselves.

Our research has focused on Information extraction (IE), the process of finding facts from unstructured text such as biomedical journals and putting those facts in an organized system. In particular, we have focused on learning multi-slot protein localization from Medline[1] abstracts, where the task is to identify ••• •• between phrases which correspond to a protein and the location of that particular protein in a cell. When seen as a relational data task, multi-slot IE clearly falls into the link-learning category described above.

Link-learning tasks present a number of problems to an ILP system. First, these domains tend to have a large number of objects and relations, causing a large explosion in the search space of clauses. A first approach is to sample these objects and bring the space down to a reasonable size. However, even a moderate number of objects brings about the second problem, a large skew of the data toward negative examples. Suppose in the social network domain we have 500 people, each of whom have 10 friends amongst these 500 people. This gives us 5000 positive examples, assuming that the friendship relationship is not necessarily symmetric. Our negative examples must include all other possible friendships, for $500 \times 500 - 5000 = 245,000$ negative examples, a skew of 1:49.

Information extraction is a domain that typically has unbalanced data; for example, only a very small number of phrases are protein names. Learning the relation between two entities, such as protein and location, only increases this imbalance, as the number of positive examples is now a subset of the cross-product of the entities, and the negative examples are every other pairing in the dataset.

These issues lead us away from using the standard performance measure of accuracy. Letting TP stand for true positives, FP for false positives, TN for true negatives and FN for false negatives, accuracy can be defined as $\frac{TP+TN}{TP+FP+TN+FN}$. With the positive class so small relative to the negative class, it is trivial to achieve high accuracy by labeling all test examples negative. To concentrate on the positive examples, more appropriate performance measures are ••• •••• • , defined as $\frac{TP}{TP+FP}$, and ••••• ••, defined as $\frac{TP}{TP+FN}$. Precision can be seen as a measure of how accurate we are at predicting the positive class, while recall is a measure of how many of the total positives we are able to identify.

We chose to pursue IE from a machine-learning perspective. Given a set of journal abstracts manually tagged with protein-localization relationships, our goal is to learn a theory that extracts only these relations from a set of abstracts and performs well on unseen abstracts. We use five-fold cross validation, with

---

[1] http://www.ncbi.nlm.nih.gov/pubmed

approximately 250 positive and 120,000 negative examples in each fold. Our division of examples is not uniform because we chose to split our data into folds at the journal-abstract level (so that all the sentences in a given abstract are in the same fold), and the number of examples per abstract is variable.

We believe that ILP can be applied successfully for Information Extraction in biomedical domains as well as other link-learning tasks. ILP offers us the advantages of a straight-forward way to incorporate domain knowledge and expert advice and will produce logical clauses suitable for analysis and revision by humans to improve performance. We use Aleph [27], a mature ILP system, to learn first-order clauses.

The standard approach to ILP is to learn clauses sequentially until almost all of the positive examples are covered by at least one clause, thus creating a theory. By itself, an individual theory will produce one value for precision and recall, at least if one uses the standard logical approach of disjunction to combine the clauses in a theory. A more useful evaluation would be to create a recall-precision curve, which illustrates the trade-off between these two measurements. One way to create a recall-precision curve from a theory containing M clauses is to require that •• •••• N of the clauses are satisfied. By varying N from 1 to M, one can obtain a variety of points in the recall-precision curve [10]. However, ILP systems have not traditionally been designed to produce recall-precision curves, and it is likely that specially designed algorithms will do better than simply counting the number of clauses that are satisfied by a given example.

To address the goal of efficiently producing good recall-precision curves with ILP, we propose the Gleaner algorithm. Gleaner is a randomized search method that collects good clauses from a broad spectrum of points along the recall dimension in recall-precision curves and employs an "at least N of these M clauses" thresholding method to combine the selected clauses. We compare Gleaner to ensembles of standard Aleph theories [11]. We find that Gleaner produces comparable results in a fraction of the training time needed for Aleph ensembles. These smaller theories will also reduce classification time, an important consideration when working with large domains.

2 Biomedical Information Extraction

Information Extraction (IE) is the process of scanning plain text files for objects of interest and facts about these objects. As a learning task, IE is defined as: given information in unstructured text documents, extract the relevant objects and relationships between them. There are two main IE tasks, Named Entity Recognition (NER) and Multi-Slot Extractions. NER can be seen as identifying a single type of object, for example the name of an individual, corporation, gene, or weapon. Successful rule-based approaches for named-entity IE include Rapier [8], a system which learns clauses with the format •••• •• •••••• ••••• •• •••••• •, and Boosted Wrapper Induction (BWI) [14], a method for boosting weak rule-based classifiers of extraction boundaries into a powerful extraction method. BWI has been further examined by Kauchak et al. [17] showing results with high recall

> "We suggest that SMF1 and SMF2 are mitochondrial membrane proteins that
> influence PEP-dependent protein import, possibly at the step of protein
> translocation."
>
> ```
> protein_location(SMF1, mitochondrial)
> protein_location(SMF2, mitochondrial)
> ```

Fig. 1. Sample Sentence with its Correct Extractions

and high precision on a wide variety of tasks. Multi-slot extraction builds upon
the objects found in NER, and looks for a relationship between these items in the
text, some examples being a parent-child relationship between individuals, the
CEO of a particular company, or the interaction of two proteins in a cell. Multi-
slot extraction is typically much harder; not only must the objects of the relation
be identified, but also the semantic relationship between these two objects.

Recently, biomedical journal articles have been a major source of interest in
the IE community for a number of reasons: the amount of data available is enor-
mous, the objects, proteins and genes, do not have standard naming conventions,
and there is a definite interest from biomedical practitioners to quickly find relevant information [3,26]. Biomedical journals also contain highly domain-specific
language, as seen in Figure 1.

Previous machine-learning work in the biomedical multi-slot domain includes
a number of different approaches. Ray and Craven [23] use a Hidden Markov
Model (HMM) modified to include part of speech tagging, and analyze their
method on protein localization, genetic disorder and protein-protein interaction
tasks. For the same datasets, Eliassi-Rad and Shavlik [13] implemented a neural
network for IE primed with domain-specific prior knowledge. Aitken [1] uses
FOIL to perform ILP, working with a closed ontology of entities, while Brunescu
et al. [7] propose the use of ELCS, a bottom up approach to finding protein
interactions with rule templates for sentences. Brunescu et al. have also extended
Rapier and BWI to handle multi-slot extractions.

2.1 Data Labeling

In this paper, we focus on one particular dataset, learning the location of yeast
proteins in a cell as illustrated in Figure 1. Our testbed comes from Ray and
Craven [23]. The data consist of 7,245 sentences from 871 abstracts found in
the Medline database, and contains 1,200 relations. In the original dataset, the
labeling was performed semi-automatically, in order to avoid the laborious task of
labeling by a human. Protein localizations were gathered from the Yeast Protein
Database (YPD), and sentences which contained instances of both a protein and
location pair were marked as positive by a computer program.

In our early exploration of the dataset, we found that there were a significant number of false positives that looked like true positives but were apparently

missed by the automated labeling algorithm. Also, some of the labelings were ambiguous at best, finding both parts of a positive protein localization, whereas the human-judged semantics of the sentence did not involve localization. In addition, by using this labeling scheme, we did not have data on all yeast proteins in the corpus, only those listed in YPD. Because of these issues, we decided to relabel the dataset by hand. We were assisted in this effort by Soumya Ray.

To label the positive examples, we manually performed both protein and location named-entity labeling and relational labeling. Our labeling standards differ from those used by other groups [16], as our task is to extract the locations of yeast proteins. If there was any disagreement among the labelers, we did not tag the protein or location, to make sure our training set was as precise as possible at the expense of some recall.

For the protein labeling, we strove to be specific rather than general, and only labeled those words that directly refered to a protein or gene molecule. This included gene names such as "SMF1", protein names like "fet3p" and full chemical names of enzymes, such as "qh2-cytochome c reductase". Therefore, while we would label SEC53 from "SEC53 mutant", we did not label "isp4delta" or "rrp1-1" as these gene products are defective and would not give rise to a functioning protein molecule. We did not label protein families such as "hsp70" unless it was an adjective to a protein, as in "hsp70 dnaK". Fusion proteins, such as when a gene is combined with a fluorescent tag, were labeled as proteins. Protein complexes, antibodies and open reading frames were never labeled as positive protein examples. Also, only proteins that are known to exist in yeast were labeled, not those which were found in other species, since our dataset dealt with the localization of yeast proteins.

Labeling the location words was much more direct. We used a list of known cellular locations listed in an introductory cellular biology text book, including locations and abbreviations such as "cytoskeleton", "membrane", "lumen", "ER", "npc", "bud", etc. Also labeled were location adjectives, such as "nucleoporin" and "ribosomal".

To determine if there was a relationship between any tagged proteins and tagged locations, we used three classifications: clear, ambiguous, or co-occurrence. Relationships directly implied by the text, as in protein_location(YRB1p, cytosol) from the sentence "YRB1p is located in the cytosol," were classified as ••••, while those relationships where the protein location was implied rather than stated, such as protein_location(LIP5, mitochondrial) from the sentence "LIP5 mutants undergo a high frequency of mitochondrial DNA deletions," were labeled as •• •••••. The correct classification was agreed upon by all three labelers. For our experiments, we used the •••• category as positive examples, and all other phrase pairings as negative examples. A future goal is to improve our manual-labeling interface.

2.2 Background Knowledge

Instead of the standard feature-vector machine learning setup, ILP uses logical relations to describe the data. Algorithms attempt to construct logical clauses

Sentence Fragment						
Phrase Type	NP	VP	NP	VP	PP	NP
Part Of Speech	N	V	V	N	V	P	N
Text	... we	haved	named	YFH1,	localizes	to	mitochondria ...

Fig. 2. Sample Sentence Parse from Sundance Sentence Analyzer (N=noun, V=verb, P=preposition or phrase)

based on this background structure that will separate positive and negative examples. For our information extraction task, we construct background knowledge from sentence structure, statistical word frequency, lexical properties, and biomedical dictionaries.

Our first set of relations comes from the sentence structure. We use the Sundance sentence parser [24] to automatically derive a parse tree for all sentences in our dataset and the part-of-speech for all words and phrases of the tree. This tree is then flattened to some degree, so that there are no nested phrases; all phrases have the sentence as the root, and therefore all words are only members of one phrase. Figure 2 shows an example sentence parse.

Each word, phrase, and sentence is given a unique identifier based on its ordering within the given abstract. This allows us to create relations between sentences, phrases and words not based on the actual text of the document but on its structure, such as `sentence_child`, `phrase_previous` and `word_next` about the tree structure and sequence of words, and relations like `nounPhrase`, `article`, and `verb` to describe the sentence structure. To include the actual text of the sentence in our background knowledge, the predicate `word_ID_to_string` maps these identifiers to the words. In addition, the words of the sentence are stemmed using the Porter stemmer [22], and currently we only use the stemmed version of words.

Another group of background relations comes from looking at the frequency of words appearing in the target phrases in the training set. This is done on a per-fold basis to prevent learning from the test set. For example, the words "body", "npc", and "membrane" are at least 10 times more likely to appear in location phrases than in phrases in general in training set 1. We created predicates for several gradations from 2 times to 10 times the general word frequency across all abstracts in a given training set. These gradations are calculated for both arguments–protein and location–as well as for words that appear more frequently in between the two arguments or before or after them. We create semantic classes, consisting of these high frequency words. These semantic classes are then used to mark up all occurrences of these words in a given training and testing set.

A third source of background knowledge is derived from the lexical properties of each word. `Alphanumeric` words contain both numbers and alphabetic characters, whereas `alphabetic` words have only alphabetic characters. Other lexical and morphological features include `singleChar`, `hyphenated` and `capitalized`.

```
Sentence Structure Predicates
phrase_after(Phrase1,Phrase2)
phrase_contains_specific_word(Phrase,Word,WordString)

Statistical Word Frequency Predicates
phrase_contains_2x_word(Phrase,Argument)
phrase_contains_no_between_halfX_word(Phrase,Argument,PartOfSpeech)

Lexical Properties Predicates
alphabetic(Word)
few_wordPOS_in_sentence(Sentence,PartOfSpeech)

Biomedical Dictionaries Predicates
phrase_contains_mesh_term(Phrase,Term,StemmedTerm)
phrase_contains_go_term(Phrase,Term,StemmedTerm)
```

Fig. 3. Sample Predicates used in our Information Extraction Task

Also, words are classified as `novelWord` if they do not appear in the standard `/usr/dict/words` dictionary in UNIX.

Finally, we incorporate semantic knowledge about biology and medicine into our background relations, such as the Medical Subject Headings (MeSH)[2], the Gene Ontology (GO)[3], and the Online Medical Dictionary[4]. As in sentence structure, we have simplified these hierarchies to only be one level. We have picked three categories from MeSH (protein, peptide and cellular structure), the cellular-localization category from GO, and the cellular-biology category from the Online Medical Dictionary, and have labeled phrases with these predicates if any of the words in the given phrase match any words in the category.

Sentence structure predicates like `word_before` and `phrase_after` are added allowing navigation around the parse tree. Phrases are also tagged as being the first or last phrase in the sentence, likewise for words. The length of phrases is calculated and explicitly turned into a predicate, as well as the length (by words and phrases) of sentences. Also, phrases are classified as short, medium or long. An additional piece of useful information is the predicate `different_phrases`, which is true when its arguments are distinct phrases.

Lexical predicates are augmented to make them more applicable to the phrase level. If a phrase contains an alphabetic word, the phrase is given the predicate `phrase_contains_alphabetic_word(A)`. Similarly phrases with specific words are marked with `phrase_contains_specific_word(A, ''lumen'')`. This is the equivalent of adding both `phrase_child(A,B)`, `word_ID_to_string(B, ''lumen'')` at once. These predicates are also created for pairs and triplets of

[2] http://www.nlm.nih.gov/mesh/meshhome.html
[3] http://www.geneontology.org/
[4] http://cancerweb.ncl.ac.uk/omd/

words, so we can assert that a phrase has the word "golgi" labeled as a noun all in one search step.

Finally, predicates are added to denote the ordering between the phrases. `Target_arg1_before_target_arg2` asserts that the protein phrase occurs before the location phrase, similarly for `target_arg2_before_target_arg1`. Also created are `adjacent_target_args` (which is true when the protein and location phrases are adjacent to each other in the sentence), and `identical_target_args` (which says the same noun phrase contains both the protein and its location), as well as the count of phrases before and after the target arguments. A list of our predicate categories and some sample predicates are found in Figure 3. Overall, we have defined 251 predicates for use in describing the training examples.

2.3 Unbalanced Data Filtering

As previously mentioned, one of the difficulties we face with this domain is the large number of possible examples we must consider. Within each sentence, we need to examine each pair of phrases. With only a few positive examples, our positive:negative ratio is 1:600, leading to severely unbalanced data.

For this domain, we use prior knowledge to help reduce the number of false positive examples. We observe that 95% of our positive relations contain only noun phrases, while the overall ratio is 26%, and use this to limit the size of our training data to only those candidate extractions where both arguments are noun phrases. This reduces the positive:negative ratio in our data to 1:158. We must necessarily keep track of all missed positive in the testing set, those that have at most one non-noun phrase, and record them as false negatives in our recall-precision results.

To further reduce the positive:negative ratio we randomly under-sample the negatives, retaining only a fourth during training. This allows for faster clause learning. Future work includes selecting the "close" negative examples to use during training rather than randomly selecting them.

3 Aleph

Aleph [27], is a top-down ILP covering algorithm developed at Oxford University, UK. It is written completely in Prolog and is open source. As input, Aleph takes background information in the form of predicates, a list of modes declaring how these predicates can be chained together, and a designation of one predicate as the "head" predicate to be learned. Also required are lists of positive and negative examples of the head predicate. As a high-level overview, Aleph generates clauses for the positive examples by picking a random example to be a seed. This example is saturated to create the bottom clause, i.e. every relation in the background knowledge that can be reached from this example. The bottom clause becomes the possible search space for clauses. Aleph heuristically searches through the space of possible clauses until the "best" clause is found or time runs out. The standard way to use Aleph is to combine these learned clauses into a theory when enough clauses are learned to cover almost all positive training examples.

Aleph is a very flexible ILP system with a wide variety of learning parameters available for modification. Some of the parameters we utilized were:

minimum accuracy. We can place a lower bound on the accuracy of all clauses learned by our system. This is only the accuracy of the clause on the examples covered by it, in other words, precision.

minimum positives. To prevent Aleph from learning narrow clauses, ones which only cover a few examples, we can specify that each acceptable clause must cover at least a certain number of positives.

clause length. The size of a particular clause can be constrained using clause length. By limiting the length, we can explore a wider breadth of clauses and prevent clauses from becoming too specific.

search strategy. As Aleph uses search to find good clauses, the type of search is a parameter. These include the standard search methods of breadth-first search, depth-first search, iterative beam search, iterative deepening, as well as heuristic methods requiring an evaluation function.

evaluation function. There are many ways to calculate the value of a node for further exploration. The most common heuristic used in ILP is •••••••. This is defined as the number of positives covered by the clause minus the number of negatives $(TP - FP)$. A very similar heuristic is ••• •••••••, which is coverage minus the length of the clause $(TP - FP - L)$. Since we are working within domains to generate precision/recall curves, we also explored as our heuristic-search's evaluation function (a) $precision \times recall$, and (b) the F1 measure, which is $\left(\frac{2 \cdot Precision \cdot Recall}{Precision + Recall}\right)$. To improve clause quality and correct accuracy estimates for clauses that cover a small number of examples, one can also use the Laplace estimate, $\left(\frac{TP+1}{TP+FP+2}\right)$.

coverage in tune set. To encourage our clauses to be more general, we added a parameter to Aleph requiring each recorded clause to have some small positive coverage in the tuneset. We believe this will help our clauses on the unseen examples in the test set.

4   Gleaner

Since our biomedical IE task is a link-learning task, we need to evaluate the success of our methods using precision and recall. In order to rapidly produce good recall-precision curves, we have developed Gleaner, a two-stage algorithm to (1) learn a broad spectrum of clauses and (2) then combine them into a thresholded disjunctive clause aimed at maximizing precision for a particular choice of recall. Our algorithm is summarized in Figure 4.

Our first stage of Gleaner learns a wide spectrum of clauses. We have Aleph search for clauses using K seed examples. We diversify the search by first uniformly dividing the recall dimension into B equal sized bins, for example, $[0, 0.05], [0.05, 0.10], \ldots, [0.95, 1]$. For each seed, we consider up to N possible

Create B recall bins, uniformly dividing the range [0,1]
For $i = 1$ to K
    Pick a seed example to generate bottom clause
    Use Random Local Search to find clauses
    After each generation of a new clause r
        Find the recall bin b_k for r
        If the $Precision \times Recall$ of r is best yet
            Store r in b_k
For each bin b
    Find $L_b \in [1, K]$ on trainset such that
        recall of "At least L of K clauses match examples" $\approx$ recall for this bin
Find precision and recall of testset using each bin's "at least L of K" decision process

Fig. 4. Gleaner Algorithm

clauses using a random local-search method. As these clauses are generated, we compute the recall of each clause and determine into which bin the clause falls. Each bin keep tracks of the highest precision clause learned in that bin so far and will be replaced when a more precise clause is found (actually, rather than finding the highest precision clause within each bin, we save the clause whose product of precision and recall is highest among those clauses falling into this recall bin). At the end of this search process, there will be B clauses collected for each seed and K seed examples for a total of $B \times K$ clauses (assuming a clause is found that falls into each bin for each seed).

To perform random local search, we considered four search methods, Rapid Random Restart (RRR), Stochastic Clause Selection (SCS), GSAT, and Walk-SAT. SCS randomly picks clauses which are subsets of the bottom clause according to the distribution of clauses based on length. SCS has a hard time finding high quality clauses and is biased to select long clauses due to the heavy-tailed distribution of clause lengths. GSAT selects an initial clause at random and then chooses to either add or remove a randomly selected literal if the new clause is "better" according to the evaluation function; WalkSAT modifies GSAT by allowing a certain percent of "bad" moves. RRR works similarly to GSAT and WalkSAT in the initial clause selection, but only refines clauses by adding predicates (using best first search), restarting with a new clause after a specified number of evaluations. GSAT and WalkSAT occasionally make "downhill" moves in the search space, while RRR does not, and due to the interal workings of Aleph, adding predicates to a clause is much more efficient than removing them. We found that RRR both takes less time and produces higher quality clauses than the other methods, and we use it as Gleaner's search method in the remainder of this article.

The second stage takes place once we have gathered our clauses using random search. We need a way to combine these clauses into a single precision/recall point for each bin. We could choose the best clause collected from each bin, however this is likely to have poor generalization to the test set, especially for the low-recall bins. If we classify an example as positive only if it matches $\bullet \bullet \bullet$ K

clauses collected for a bin, we obtain high precision, but our recall will be drastically reduced. Alternatively, if we classify an example as positive if it matches ••• of our K clauses, we will probably have a theory with high recall but low precision. Instead, we need to find a balance between these two extremes, and classify examples to be positive if they are covered by a large enough subset of clauses. • •• •••••••••• •• •••• •••• • ••••• • ••• •••••••• • ••••••• • ••• •••••• ••• ••• • •••••••• ••• • ••• •••••••• •••• ••••••• •••••••••• ••••• ••• ••• ••••••• ••• •• • •••••• ••• •••••• •••• • •• •••••••• • •••••• •• ••••••• ••••••• ••• • $L > 1$••

Gleaner combines the clauses in each bin to create one large thresholded disjunctive clause, of the form "At least L of these K clauses must cover an example in order to classify it as a positive." We want this clause to have about the same recall as as that of the clauses in the bin (so that we cover the full range of possible recalls), thus we need to find the best threshold L for each bin. We can find this L on the training set for each bin by starting with $L = K$ and incrementally lowering the threshold to increase recall. We stop when any lower L would increase the distance between the recall of the best L of K clause and our desired recall. With this L, we now evaluate our disjunctive clause on the testset and record the precision and recall. We will end up with B precision/recall points, one for each bin, that span the recall-precision curve.

5 Ensembles in ILP

Bagging [6] is a popular ensemble approach to machine learning where multiple classifiers are trained using different subsamples of the training data. These classifiers then vote on the classification of testset examples, usually with the majority class being selected as the output classification. How they vote is user-dependent, with some common schemes being equal voting or weighted according to the tuneset accuracy of each voter. The main idea of bagging is that it will produce diverse classifiers that make their mistakes in different regions of the input space; when their votes are combined, prediction errors will be reduced. The use of bagging for ILP has been previously investigated by Dutra et al. [11] where they demonstrate bagging to be helpful for modest improvements in accuracy as well as a straight-forward way to calculate the confidence of a particular example. We use their "random seeds" approach for creating ensembles. This approach, which Dutra et al. showed to have essentially equivalent predictive accuracy as bagging, produces diversity in its learned models by starting each run of its underlying ILP system with a different "seed" example.

We compare our Gleaner approach to that of using "random seeds" in Aleph. In this experimental control, we call Aleph N times and have it create N theories (i.e., sets of clauses that cover most of the positive training examples and few of the negative ones). To create a recall-precision curve from these N theories, we simply classify an example as positive if at least K of the theories classify it as positive; varying L from 1 to N produces a family of ensembles, and each of these ensembles produces a point on a recall-precision curve.

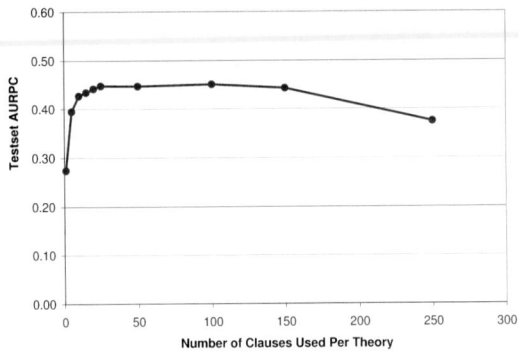

Fig. 5. Area Under the Recall-Precision Curve for 100 Aleph Ensembles With Varying Number of Clauses

Aleph involves a large number of parameters, and we use the train and test sets to choose a good set (since this is the experimental control against which we compare our Gleaner system, it is "fair" to use the testset to tune parameters). We compare several different evaluation functions for judging clauses: Laplace (which essentially measures accuracy, but corrects for small coverage), coverage (the number of positive examples covered minus the number of negatives covered), *precision* × *recall*, and $F1$ (the harmonic mean of precision and recall; $F1$ is the most commonly used performance measure in information extraction). We consider two settings for minimum accuracy for learned clauses: 0.75 and 0.90. We require all clauses to at least cover seven positive examples and to be no longer than ten terms (the same settings we use for random sampling of the hypothesis space in our Gleaner approach). We limit the number of clauses considered to 100 thousand and we also limit the number of reductions to 100 million (using the `call_counting` predicate available in YAP Prolog[5]).

We obtained our best area under the recall-precision curve using Laplace as the evaluation function and a minimum clause accuracy of 0.75. (Under this setting, the average number of clauses considered per constructed theory is approximately 35,000.)

One new finding we encountered that was not reported by Dutra et al. is that it is better to limit the size of theories. Figure 5 plots the area under the recall-precision curve (AURPC) as a function of the maximum number of clauses we allow in the learned theories. Running Aleph to its normal completion given the above parameters leads to theories containing 295 clauses on average. However, if we limit this to the first C clauses, the AURPC can be drastically better. The likely reason for this is that larger theories have less diversity amongst themselves than do smaller ones, and diversity is the key to ensembles [12]. A nice side-effect of limiting theory size is that the runtime of individual Aleph executions is substantially reduced.

---

[5] http://www.ncc.up.pt/~vsc/Yap/yap.html

In the next section, where we evaluate our Gleaner algorithm, we limit theory size in our "ensemble of Aleph theories" approach to 50 clauses, since as seen in Figure 5, testset AURPC has essentially peaked by then. In that section's experiments we do vary the size of the ensemble (i.e., number of theories) and the number of clauses in each theory, in order to see the impact on AURPC as a function of the amount of time spent training.

While we are from having considered all possible parameters settings and algorithm designs with which one could use Aleph to create an ensemble of theories, we have evaluated a substantial number of variants and feel that our chosen settings provide a satisfactory experiment control against which to compare our new algorithm, Gleaner.

6 Results

For our experiments, we divided the protein localization data into five folds, equally divided at the journal-abstract level. Each training set consisted of three folds, with one fold held aside for tuning and another for testing. For our current experiments we only use the tuning set minimally, requiring each clause learned on the training set to cover at least two positive examples in the tuning set. To evaluate the performance of our algorithms, we use recall-precision curves [19], or more precisely, we use the Area Under the Recall-Precision Curve (AURPC) to gather a single score for each algorithm. AUC has traditionally been used to analyze ROC curves [5], which plot the true positive rate versus the false positive rate. To calculate the AURPC, we first standardize our recall-precision curves to always cover the full range of recall values and then interpolate between the threshold points. From the first threshold point, which we designate (R_{first}, P_{first}), the curve is extended horizontally to the point $(0, P_{first})$, since we could randomly discard a fraction, f, of the extracted relations and expect the same precision on the remaining examples; the setting of f would determine the recall. An ending point of $(1, \frac{Pos}{Neg})$ can always be found by calling everything a positive example. This will give us a closed curve extending from 0 to 1 along the recall dimension.

For any two points A and B in a recall-precision curve, we must interpolate between their true positive (TP) and false positive (FP) counts in order to calculate the area. To do this, we create new points for each of $TP_A + 1, TP_A + 2, ..., TP_B - 1$, increasing the false positives for each new point by $\frac{FP_B - FP_A}{TP_B - TP_A}$. Interpolation for the recall-precision curve is different than for an ROC curve; whereas the ROC interpolation would be a linear connection between the two points, in recall-precision space the connection can be curved, depending the actual number of positive and negative examples covered by each point. The curve is especially pronounced when two points are far away in recall and precision. Consider a curve constructed from a single point of $(0.02, 1)$, and extended to the endpoints of $(0, 1)$ and $(1, 0.008)$ as described above (for this example, our dataset contains 433 positives and 56,164 negatives). Interpolating as we have described, would produce an AURPC of 0.031; a linear connection would overestimate with an AURPC of 0.50 (Figure 8 shows this graphically).

```
protein_location(P,L,S) :-
    first_word_in_phrase(L,A),
    phrase_after(L,_),
    target_arg1_before_target_arg2(P,L,S),
    after_both_target_phrases(S,B),
    phrase_contains_some_marked_up_location(L,_),
    few_POS_in_phrase(P,alphanumeric),
    few_wordPOS_in_sentence(S,alphanumeric),
    phrase_contains_no_between_halfX_word(B,between_arg1_and_arg2,verb),
    phrase_contains_some_art(L,A).
```

where P is the protein phrase, L is the location phrase, S is the sentence, and '_' indicates variables that only appear once in the clause.

Positive Extraction
"NPL3 encodes a nuclear protein with an RNA recognition motif and similarities to a family of proteins involved in RNA metabolism."
```
protein_location('NPL3', 'a nuclear protein')
```

Negative Extraction (i.e., a false positive)
"Subcellular fractionation studies further demonstrate that the 1455 amino acid Vps15p is peripherally associated with the cytoplasmic face of a late Golgi or vesicle compartment."
```
protein_location('the 1455 amino acid Vps15p', 'the cytoplasmic face')
```

Fig. 6. Sample Clause with 29% Recall and 34% Precision on Testset 1

A sample clause found by Gleaner is shown in Figure 6. We can see for our dataset that it is important to require the protein phrase to contain alphanumeric words. Also important for this clause is the sentence structure, requiring that the protein phrase comes before the location phrase, and that the location phrase is not the last phrase in the sentence.

Our Aleph-based method for producing ensembles has two parameters that we vary: N, the number of theories (i.e., the size of the ensemble), and C, the number of clauses per ensemble. To produce ensemble points in Figure 7, we choose N from $\{10, 25, 50, 75, 100\}$ and C from $\{1, 5, 10, 15, 20, 25, 50\}$, producing 20 combinations for each fold.

For the parameters of Gleaner, we used 20 recall bins and 100 seed examples to collect 2,000 clauses total. We told RRR to construct 1,000 clauses before restarting with a new random clause. We generate AURPC data points for Gleaner by choosing the number of seed examples from $\{25, 50, 75, 100\}$, and using the intervals of $\{1K, 10K, 25K, 50K, 100K, 250K, 500K\}$ for the number of candidate clauses generated per seed.

The results of our comparison are found in Figure 7; the points are averaged over all five folds. Note this graph has a logarithmic scale in the number of

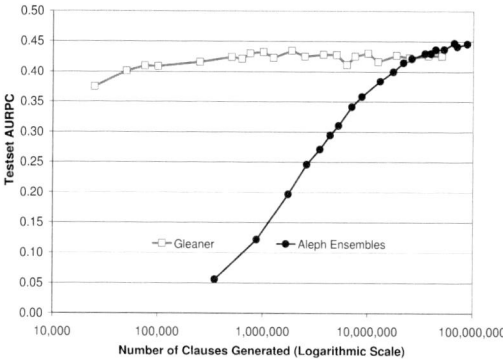

Fig. 7. Comparison of AURPC from Gleaner and Aleph Ensembles by Varying Number of Clauses Generated

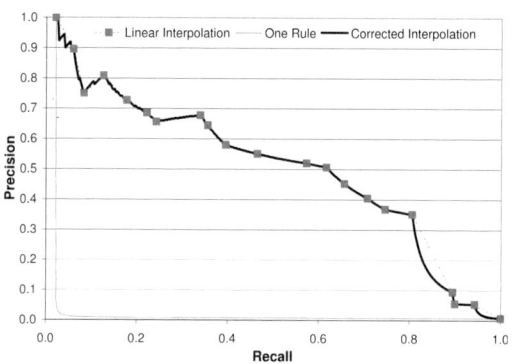

Fig. 8. A Sample Gleaner Recall-Precision Curve From Fold 5

clauses generated. We see that Gleaner can find comparable AURPC numbers using two orders of magnitude fewer clauses. It is interesting to note that the Gleaner curve is very consistent across the number of clauses allowed, while the ensemble method increases when more clauses are considered. It is a topic of future work to devise a new version of Gleaner that is able to better utilize additional candidate clauses.

In Figure 8, we show one of the better recall-precision curve produced by Gleaner using 10,000 candidate clauses per seed and 100 seed examples (on fold 5). For comparison, we also show the one-point interpolation curve mentioned above. Gleaner's "L of K" clauses theoretically should produce higher precision than individual rules with the same recall, as long as coverage of positives is greater than coverage of negatives. In practice, our clauses are not as independent as we would like, especially in the high-recall bins, with many of the learned clauses being identical. This overlap degrades the performance.

7   Conclusions and Future Work

Multi-Slot Information Extraction is a an appealing challenge task for ILP, due to its large amount of examples and background knowledge, as well as the substantial skew of examples. We have developed a method called Gleaner, which gathers a wide spectrum of clauses and combines them within bins based on recall using an "at least N of these M clauses" thresholding method. We find that Aleph ensembles can perform well when using early stopping (i.e., only learning a dozen or two rules); however, Aleph ensembles suffer when allotted a limited amount of time to create multiple theories. Our method of Gleaner results in similar curves to Aleph ensembles, and outperforms ensembles when both are only allowed to evaluate a limited number of clauses. There are not many large, heavily skewed datasets available for ILP research, and we believe this information-extraction task will provide a useful testbed for further ILP research. To aid in ILP research this dataset is being made available at our website (see Acknowledgements).

There are a number of approaches relating to the combination of learned clauses to produce a confidence measure, as opposed to combining multiple theories as in bagging or Gleaner. Propositionalization of the feature space has been examined by Lavrac et al. [18], which allows for any propositional learner that generates confidence measures to be used. Similarly, Srinivasan [28] investigated using ILP as a feature construction tool for propositional learners, namely linear regression. Craven and Slatterly [10] use a logical setup combined with Naive Bayes classifiers for IE and generate recall-precision curves with their resulting theories. We plan to compare these within-theory ensemble methods to the multiple theory ensemble methods and to Gleaner.

In this same vein, we see the use of boosting in ILP [15] as another alternative method to searching for clauses and learning how to combine them in one single step. Recent work has shown that a RankBoost, a variant of boosting, directly optimizes the area under the ROC curve [9]. We believe that a similar optimization of the area under the recall-precision curve can be achieved, and plan to implement this algorithm in Aleph for comparison to Gleaner.

We noticed that many of our learned clauses are focused on learning the individual entities of the relation, in our case, creating logical clauses for protein and location, and little of the clause is relevant to the relation •••• ••• these two entities. We believe that using a named-entity classifier to identify promising pieces of our relation first could both reduce the number of examples as well as produce high quality clauses due to their direct focus on the relation. Blaschke et al. [4,3] and Rindflesh et al. [25] have found success in biomedical information extraction using domain expert rules, and Temkin and Gilder [31] use hand-crafted context-free grammars to similar ends. Another step in this direction is taking these clauses from a domain expert and learning to revise their advice, similar to work by Eliassi-Rad and Shavlik [13].

Finally, there are many more datasets in Information Extraction where we are planning to test our method for comparison, namely the genetic disorder and protein interaction from Ray and Craven [23] and a protein interaction dataset from Brunescu et al. [7]. Other datasets outside of IE where we believe Gleaner will be useful include the nuclear smuggling dataset from Tang et al. [30], the social network dataset from Taskar et al. [2], and the CiteSeer citation dataset from Popescul et al. [21]

Acknowledgements. Our dataset can be found at ftp://ftp.cs.wisc.edu/ machine-learning/shavlik-group/datasets/IE-protein-location

This work was supported by National Library of Medicine (NLM) Grant 5T15 LM007359-02, NLM Grant 1R01 LM07050-01, DARPA EELD Grant F30602-01-2-0571, and United States Air Force Grant F30602-01-2-0571. We would like to thank Ines Dutra and Vitor Santos Costa for their help with Yap, the UW Condor Group for Condor assistance, Soumya Ray and Marios Skounakis for their help with labeling the data, and David Page for his help with Aleph, as well as the anonymous reviewers for their informative comments.

References

1. S. Aitken. Learning Information Extraction Rules: An Inductive Logic Programming Approach. In F. van Harmelen, editor, *Proceedings of the 15th European Conference on Artificial Intelligence*, Amsterdam, 2002.
2. M.-F. W. Ben Taskar, Pieter Abbeel and D. Koller. Label and Link Prediction in Relational Data. In *IJCAI Workshop on Learning Statistical Models from Relational Data*, 2003.
3. C. Blaschke, L. Hirschman, and A. Valencia. Information Extraction in Molecular Biology. *Briefings in Bioinformatics*, 3(2):154–165, 2002.
4. C. Blaschke and A. Valencia. Can Bibliographic Pointers for Known Biological Data be Found Automatically? Protein Interactions as a Case Study. *Comparative and Functional Genomics*, 2:196–206, 2001.
5. A. Bradley. The Use of the Area Under the ROC Curve in the Evaluation of Machine Learning Algorithms. *Pattern Recognition*, 30(7):1145–1159, 1997.
6. L. Breiman. Bagging Predictors. *Machine Learning*, 24(2):123–140, 1996.
7. R. Bunescu, R. Ge, R. Kate, E. Marcotte, R. Mooney, A. Ramani, and Y. Wong. Comparative Experiments on Learning Information Extractors for Proteins and their Interactions. *Journal of Artificial Intelligence in Medicine*, 2004.
8. M. Califf and R. Mooney. Relational Learning of Pattern-Match Rules for Information Extraction. In *Working Notes of AAAI Spring Symposium on Applying Machine Learning to Discourse Processing*, pages 6–11, Menlo Park, CA, 1998. AAAI Press.
9. C. Cortes and M. Mohri. AUC Optimization vs. Error Rate Minimization. In *Neural Information Processing Systems NIPS2003*, 2003.
10. M. Craven and S. Slattery. Relational Learning with Statistical Predicate Invention: Better Models for Hypertext. *Machine Learning*, 43(1/2):97–119, 2001.
11. I. de Castro Dutra, D. Page, V. S. Costa, and J. Shavlik. An Empirical Evaluation of Bagging in Inductive Logic Programming. In *Twelfth International Conference on Inductive Logic Programming*, pages 48–65, Sydney, Australia, 2002.
12. T. Dietterich. Machine-Learning Research: Four Current Directions. *The AI Magazine*, 18(4):97–136, 1998.

13. T. Eliassi-Rad and J. Shavlik. A Theory-Refinement Approach to Information Extraction. In *Proceedings of the 18th International Conference on Machine Learning*, 2001.

14. D. Freitag and N. Kushmerick. Boosted Wrapper Induction. In *AAAI/IAAI*, pages 577–583, 2000.

15. S. Hoche and S. Wrobel. Relational Learning Using Constrained Confidence-Rated Boosting. In *11th International Conference on Inductive Logic Programming*, Strasbourg, France, 2001.

16. Z. Hu. Guidelines for Protein Name Tagging. Technical report, Georgetown University, 2003.

17. D. Kauchak, J. Smarr, and C. Elkan. Sources of Success for Boosted Wrapper Induction. *Journal of Machine Learning Research*, 5:499–527, May 2004.

18. N. Lavrac, F. Zelezny, and P. Flach. RSD: Relational Subgroup Discovery through First-order Feature Construction. In *Proceedings of the 12th International Conference on Inductive Logic Programming (ILP'02)*, Sydney, Australia, 2002.

19. C. Manning and H. Schutze. *Foundations of Statistical Natural Language Processing*. MIT Press, 1999.

20. R. Michalski and J. Larson. Inductive Inference of VL Decision Rules. In *Proceedings of the Workshop in Pattern-Directed Inference Systems*, May 1977.

21. A. Popescul, L. Ungar, S. Lawrence, and D. Pennock. Statistical Relational Learning for Document Mining. In *IEEE International Conference on Data Mining, ICDM-2003*, 2003.

22. M. Porter. An Algorithm for Suffix Stripping. *Program*, 14(3):130–137, 1980.

23. S. Ray and M. Craven. Representing Sentence Structure in Hidden Markov Models for Information Extraction. In *Proceedings of the 17th International Joint Conference on Artificial Intelligence (IJCAI-2001)*, 2001.

24. E. Riloff. The Sundance Sentence Analyzer. *http://www.cs.utah.edu/projects/nlp/*, 1998.

25. T. Rindflesch, T. Tanabe, L. Weinstein, and J. Hunter. Edgar: Extraction of drugs, genes and relations from the biomedical literature. In *Proceedings of the Pacific Symposium on Biocomputing.*, 2000.

26. H. Shatkay and R. Feldman. Mining the Biomedical Literature in the Genomic Era: An Overview. *Journal of Computational Biology*, 10(6):821–55, 2003.

27. A. Srinivasan. The Aleph Manual Version 4. *http://web.comlab.ox.ac.uk/oucl/research/areas/machlearn/Aleph/*, 2003.

28. A. Srinivasan and R. King. Feature Construction with Inductive Logic Programming: A Study of Quantitative Predictions of Biological Activity Aided by Structural Attributes. In S. Muggleton, editor, *Proceedings of the 6th International Workshop on Inductive Logic Programming*, pages 352–367. Stockholm University, Royal Institute of Technology, 1996.

29. A. Srinivasan, S. Muggleton, M. Sternberg, and R. King. Theories for Mutagenicity: A Study in First-Order and Feature-Based Induction. *Artificial Intelligence*, 85(1-2):277–299, 1996.

30. L. Tang, R. Mooney, and P. Melville. Scaling up ILP to Large Examples: Results on Link Discovery for Counter-Terrorism. In *KDD Workshop on Multi-Relational Data Mining*, 2003.

31. J. Temkin and M. Gilder. Extraction of Protein Interaction Information From Unstructured Text Using a Context-Free Grammar. *Bioinformatics*, 19(16):2046–2053, 2003.

Automatic Induction of First-Order Logic Descriptors Type Domains from Observations

Stefano Ferilli, Floriana Esposito, Teresa M.A. Basile, and Nicola Di Mauro

Department of Computer Science, University of Bari, Italy
{ferilli,esposito,basile,nicodimauro}@di.uniba.it

Abstract. Successful application of Machine Learning to certain real-world situations sometimes requires to take into account relations among objects. Inductive Logic Programming, being based on First-Order Logic as a representation language, provides a suitable learning framework to be adopted in these cases. However, the intrinsic complexity of this framework, added to the complexity of the specific application context, often requires pure induction to be supported by various kinds of meta-information on the domain itself and/or on its representation in order to prune the search space of all possible definitions. Indeed, avoiding the exploration of paths that do not lead to any correct solution can greatly reduce computational times, and hence becomes a critical issue for the performance of the whole learning process. In the current practice, providing such information is often in charge of the human expert. It is also a difficult and error-prone activity, in which mistakes are highly probable because of a number of factors. This makes it desirable to develop procedures that can automatically generate such information starting from the same observations that are input to the learning process. This paper focuses on a specific kind of meta-information: the *types* used in the description language and their related *domains*. Indeed, many learning systems known in the literature are able to exploit (and sometimes require) such a kind of knowledge to improve their performance. An algorithm is proposed to automatically identify types from observations, and detailed examples of its behaviour are given. An evaluation of its performance in domains with different characteristics is reported, and its robustness with respect to incomplete observations is studied.

Keywords: Description Languages, Knowledge Acquisition

1 Introduction

Learning in particular contexts, characterized by a high degree of complexity, often requires pure induction to be supported by a variety of techniques that can cope with different aspects of the learning task. A way to overcome such a limitation is the use of other kinds of inferences in support of induction, according to an integrated framework that tries to emulate the human way of reasoning [11]. For instance, some learning systems can take great advantage

R. Camacho, R. King, A. Srinivasan (Eds.): ILP 2004, LNAI 3194, pp. 116–131, 2004.

from meta-information on the domain itself and/or on its representation, in order to prune the search space and focus on the parts of it in which a solution is more likely to be found.

In the current practice, it is in charge of the human expert to specify all the 'added-value' information needed by such techniques for being applicable. It goes without saying that quality, correctness and completeness in the formalization of such meta-information is a critical issue, that can determine the very feasibility of the learning process. Providing it is a very difficult task, also, that requires a deep knowledge of the application domain, and is in any case an error-prone activity, since omissions and errors may take place for a number of reasons. For instance, the domain and/or the language used to represent it might be unknown to the experimenter, because he is just in charge of properly setting and running the learning system on a dataset provided by third parties and/or generated by other people (or even by automatic systems), as in the case of classical machine learning datasets available on the Internet. In any case, it is often not easy for non-experts to single out and formally express such meta-knowledge in the form of parameters or other kinds of representations needed by the automatic systems, just because they are not familiar with the representation language and the related technical issues. Other possible causes include the great number of such parameters to be specified, and the fact that they are sometimes hidden from the normal focus-of-attention when reasoning on the problem.

These considerations would make it highly desirable to develop procedures that can automatically generate such information starting from the same observations that are input to the learning process. Hence, a strong motivation for the research presented in this paper, aimed at proposing algorithms to automatically infer the meta-information required by the techniques referred to above, and at assessing the validity and performance of the corresponding procedures. The challenge in this attempt is that it does not try to learn something the given instances, but instead aims at gathering information on the domain and/or its description . the given instances. This means that we are no more concerned with the description of concepts by proper juxtaposition of literals, but rather with the meaning underlying the language used. Thus, the problem can be seen as a higher-order learning, that deals with semantics rather than with syntax.

The next section presents a technique to automatically infer the description language from the very same data used by the learning procedure, and motivates the interest of researchers for having available this kind of meta-information. Then, Sections 3 and 4 extensively test the proposed approach, even in the case of incomplete input information. Last section concludes the paper and outlines future work.

2 Inducing Descriptors Type Domains

One of the most interesting issues, when dealing with observations in an unknown language, is the identification of what properties are used to describe the available knowledge, and what are the possible values for each property. In other words, there is a need to know what are the ___ used in the description language and their related ___ . These issues are clearly strongly related to work on ontologies, where we are concerned with the representation of concepts along with their interrelationships and properties/domains. However, most of the current research in that field is devoted to devise methodologies and techniques for representing and exploiting ontological information (that in the current practice is tipically entered by human experts), while the issue of automatically learning and refining such information has not yet been takled thoroughly (also due to the inherent complexity of the task).

On the other hand, various learning systems in the literature can exploit meta-information of this kind, if available, to prune the search space and obtain this way more efficiency. Just to cite the major ones, MIS [14], FOIL [3], Progol [13] and Mobal [12] allow the experimenter to specify the type of arguments in the predicates of the description language. A straightforward exploitation of such kind of information is to carry out a pruning of the search space, that eliminates hypotheses that contrast with the descriptor meaning. This would turn out to be particularly useful in the case of incomplete descriptions, where the presence of particular properties can be only abductively guessed and the availability of integrity constraints of this kind may be a valuable help for driving such guesses. For instance, knowing that ___ and . ___ are two different values of one domain, would allow a learning system to avoid generating and testing clauses that refer both values to the same individual. It is clear that, along with the complexity of the representation language and the number of properties and values used, significant amounts of impossible hypotheses could be recognized in this way and discarded in advance.

Some attempts to automatically infer such information have already been carried out: in [10], for instance, the Authors exploit the occurrence, in the available observations, of the same specific value in different positions to identify predicate arguments to be filled with information of the same type. In this case, the domain of a type can be inferred by simply collecting all the constants that appear in the predicate positions associated to that type. However, some issues about type inference still remain unsolved. Indeed, theories learned by many systems are constant-free, and allow only variables as terms. In those cases, the information expressed by constants can be recovered by a process of fi ___ , that (loosely speaking) transforms ___ into predicates, and uses constants as just ___ for specific objects. For instance, the property ___ is translated into ___ , this way being able to express the fact that an object is red as ___ .

This is usual when using First Order Predicate Logic as a representation language: n-ary ($n > 1$) predicates are used to express relationships among different objects. Specifically, binary predicates, in addition to expressing a relationship between two objects, can be exploited to associate objects with the corresponding values for their relevant (atomic) properties. In order to avoid such ambiguity, a process of fi ___ can be carried out on symbolic properties, so that each possible value for them becomes itself a property, and hence can be represented by a unary predicate. This obviously breaks the association of specific values and types to particular predicate arguments, which makes it more difficult to collect them according to the properties they refer to. In such a situation, discovering the type domains for the properties in the language can be cast as the search for groups of unary predicates that semantically refer to the same attribute. Knowing this kind of types could be of great help for limiting the search space in some systems that are not strongly observation-driven: systems like Claudien [4], Primus [7] and Tertius [8], for instance, could avoid generating clauses in which more than two values belonging to the same type are associated to one object, thus dramatically limiting the combinatorial explosion in clause generation.

Given the following examples and descriptions:

$$
\begin{array}{ccccc}
a & \_\_ \cdot a \; a' & a' & a' & a' \\
\_\_ \cdot a \; a'' & a'' & a'' & a'' & \_ \quad a' \; a'' \\
b & \_\_ \cdot b \; b' & b' & b' & b' \\
\_\_ \cdot b \; b'' & b'' & b'' & b'' & \_ \quad b' \; b'' \\
c & \_\_ \cdot c \; c' & c' & c' & c' \\
\_\_ \cdot c \; c'' & c'' & c'' & c'' & \_ \quad c' \; c''
\end{array}
$$

the set of unary predicates in the description language is:
$$
\{ \quad , \quad , \quad , \quad , \quad , \quad , \quad \}
$$
We would like the system to understand that the values they represent define three domains referred to different types, according to the following groups:

- $\{ \quad , \quad , \quad , \quad \}$ (that, being able to catch their semantics, could be recognized as belonging to property),
- $\{ \quad , \quad \}$ (that are related to property), and
- $\{ \quad , \quad \}$ (related to property).

In the rest of this presentation, the following (clearly non restricting) assumptions will be made:

- all non-numeric (symbolic or discretized) properties are reified, so that all of their possible values are expressed by means of unary predicates[1];
- there is no overloading on unary predicates, i.e. no unary predicate expresses a value that belongs to many types (this is a typical feature of strongly typed programming languages, e.g. for enumerative types);
- there are no 'boolean' properties, i.e. properties that are expressed by just the presence or absence of a corresponding predicate (e.g., · , would require an opposite predicate ⌐);
- all properties are applicable to any object that occurs in the descriptions (in case this does not hold, it is sufficient to include an additional ⌐ value to each property that makes sense for some objects only)[2].

---

[1] This is the actual problematic situation, since if the property values were associated to objects as arguments of (e.g., binary) predicates, the predicates themselves would be sufficient to separate and semantically identify the type domains.

The first consideration one can do is that different values for the same attribute are mutually exclusive, since one given object cannot have two of them at the same time (e.g., an object can be black or blue, but not both). Hence, the first problem to be solved is finding all couples of predicates that are mutually exclusive, i.e. never co-occur referred to the same object in the available knowledge of the world (let us call them   [3]). Such information can be obtained as follows: after collecting the set of all unary predicates used in the available example descriptions, all the possible pairs of such predicates (without regard to the order) are generated, associated with the same variable as argument and then tested for occurrence in the observations themselves.

The set of unary predicates identified in the previous example yields 56 possible pairs to be tested. Among these, some occur in the available observations, and hence the corresponding predicates cannot belong to the same type domain. For instance:

$$\langle \quad X \qquad X \rangle, \langle \quad X \qquad X \rangle, \langle \quad X \qquad X \rangle$$

are verified by object a'. Others never occur, some including values that actually belong to the same semantic domain:

$$\langle \quad X \qquad X \rangle, \langle \quad X \qquad X \rangle, \langle \quad X \qquad X \rangle, \dots$$

and others including values that belong to different ones:

$$\langle \quad X \qquad X \rangle, \langle \quad X \qquad X \rangle, \langle \quad X \qquad X \rangle, \dots$$

It goes without saying that finding mutually exclusive couples is not sufficient: More precisely,   value in a given domain cannot co-occur in one object with   other value in the same domain. Thus, the problem becomes identifying groups of unary predicates whose elements are   mutually exclusive. In particular, since for any set of predicates fulfilling such property it holds that all of its subsets fulfill the same property as well, we are interested in maximal sets only, i.e. we discard groups that are subsets of other groups. This can be obtained by mapping the problem onto a corresponding one in the graph context. Specifically, we build an undirected graph G_e whose nodes are unary predicates in the description language, and where an edge connects two nodes if and only if they are mutually exclusive. In such a setting, the maximal sets we are looking for correspond to all the   cliques (i.e., cliques that cannot be further extended) in G_e.

Applying the above technique to the set of unary predicates and mutually exclusive pairs obtained in previous examples, the following cliques (i.e., groups of pairwise mutually exclusive values) are found:

---

[2] For instance, when describing books, properties *weight* and *price* would make sense only for the book as a whole, and not for its layout/content components such as title, foreword, etc. In such a case, the domains of the above properties (e.g., {*weight_light*, *weight_medium*, *weight_heavy*} and {*cheap*, *expensive*}) could be extended by two additional values *weight_not_applicable* and *price_not_applicable*, respectively.

[3] This notion of *constraint* can be extended to the case of n-tuples of predicates that never occur together referred to the same object.

- { , , }
- { , , }
- { , , , }
- { , }
- { , }
- { , }

The groups found this way are still far from being the desired solutions. Indeed, there can be groups of predicates with couplewise mutually exclusive elements even if they do not refer to a same attribute. For instance, it is generally true that a line is never too tall, hence in a paper document domain we might find the group { , , - , } in which it is obvious that value belongs to the domain of type , while the other three values refer to the type . Nevertheless, we expect that two correct (i.e. distinct, or, more precisely,) groups exist, one containing all (and only those) values belonging to property , and the other containing all (and only those) values belonging to property . Here, the clue is that, in the end, the desired solution will include only groups that have no element in common. Hence, since the above group would have elements in common with properties and , it should be discarded. Again, this problem can be solved in the graph context by building an undirected graph G_d in which nodes are groups identified in the previous step as cliques of graph G_e, and an edge connects two nodes if and only if they are disjoint sets. Now, the solution will be made up by only couplewise disjoint subsets, and specifically by maximal groups of disjoint subsets, each of which corresponds to a maximal clique in G_d.

Continuing with the previous examples results, the clique technique returns the following sets of possible mutually disjoint groups of predicates:

- { { , , }, { , }, { , } } (including 7 values)
- { { , , }, { , } } (including 5 values)
- { { , , }, { , } } (including 5 values)
- { { , , , }, { , }, { , } } (including 8 values)

As in the example above, the clique in G_d will probably not be unique, in which case one must have a clue for choosing the right one. The intuition, in this case, is that any 'wrong' clique, in order to fulfill the mutual disjunction requirement, will have overall a number of values that is less than that of the correct solution, since the correct solution should be the only one containing all the possible values for each property (represented by a group), and hence the union of predicates in all of its components should be equal to the whole set of values for all possible attributes. In other words, the solution is actually a of the set of unary predicates. This holds because the description language is assumed not to contain 'boolean' properties; if it does, the union would not be a partition, but should in any case contain more unary predicates than any other candidate partition.

Algorithm 1 Identification of type domains

Require: L: Description language
1: $U := \{p \in L \mid p \text{ unary}\}$
2: $E := \{(p, q) \in U \times U \mid \nexists X : p(X) \wedge q(X)\}$
3: $G_e := (U, E)$
4: $S := \{C \subseteq U \mid C \text{ clique in } G_e\}$
5: $F := \{(p, q) \in S \times S \mid p \cap q = \emptyset\}$
6: $G_d := (S, F)$
7: $T := \{C \subseteq S \mid C \text{ clique in } G_d\}$
Ensure: $argmax_{t \in T}(|\bigcup_{t_i \in t} t_i|)$: type domains

Among the sets of disjoint groups identified in the previous step, the only one containing all 8 unary predicates in the description language is $\{ \{ \quad , \quad , \quad \}, \{ \quad , \quad \}, \{ \quad , \quad \} \}$, that also corresponds to the solution, as expected.

The whole strategy is summarized in Algorithm 1. Given a set of examples along with their descriptions, all unary predicates (corresponding to property values) in the description language are collected, and a graph is built having such predicates as nodes and an edge between two nodes if the corresponding predicates are never referred to the same object in the available observations. Then, the cliques in such a graph are identified, and used as nodes for building another graph, whose edges connect two nodes if they share no predicate. Lastly, for each clique in this latter graph the union of the sets of predicates in the nodes is computed, and the one with the greatest cardinality is chosen as the solution. $argmax_{t \in T}(|\bigcup_{t_i \in t} t_i|)$ corresponds to the clique t in G_d that maximizes the cardinality of (i.e., the number of predicates in) the set union of its composing nodes t_i.

It is presented in a simple and linear fashion, since it includes two clique computations (for which algorithms are known in the literature and often implemented as standard libraries in programming languages compilers) in steps 4 and 7, and other trivial operations: steps 3 and 6 consist of a simple name assignment to graphs, step 1 requires to scan the descriptors used in the given observations just once in order to collect the corresponding unary predicates; steps 2 and 5 collect all couples of graph nodes without regard to the order (which can be done in $\mathcal{O}(m^2)$ steps for m nodes) and test a condition on each of them. Informally speaking, the problem resembles a puzzle, in which more pieces than necessary are provided, such that the additional pieces can partly fit the others, but when added will always prevent reaching a complete solution. A consideration is worth. The feasibility of reaching the target solution requires that the number of values for the domains to be identified and the amount of available knowledge about observations to be strictly proportional. Indeed, the more the values, the more the possible interrelations that can take place between them. If the available observations are not sufficiently significant, i.e. too many existing interrelations are not recognizable in them, then knowledge about the actual biases in the given domain would be too loose for the algorithm to properly separate semantically different values.

Given the following problem setting:

a	$\,\,\,\_\,\cdot\, a\, a'$	a'	a'	a'
$\_\,\cdot\, a\, a''$	a''	a''	a''	$\_\quad a'\, a''$
b	$\_\,\cdot\, b\, b'$	b'	b'	b'
$\_\,\cdot\, b\, b''$	b''	b''	b''	$\_\quad b'\, b''$
c	$\_\,\cdot\, c\, c'$	c'	c'	c'
$\_\,\cdot\, c\, c''$	c''	c''	c''	$\_\quad c'\, c''$

two different partitions, both involving all 9 unary predicates { , , ,
, , , , , } could be found, and specifically:

$-\{\{\quad,\quad,\quad,\quad\},\{\quad,\quad\},\{\quad,\quad\}\}$
$-\{\{\quad,\quad,\quad\},\{\quad,\quad\},\{\quad,\quad\}\}$

which provides no clue for understanding which is the correct one.

As to the practical implementation of the proposed algorithm, some considerations can be made that are useful to restrict the search space of candidate disjoint predicate groups. First, note that when all unary predicates in the description language represent values of only one type, they are all mutually exclusive, thus the graph G_e is completely connected and yields just one candidate group, which coincides with the only element of the singleton partition to be found (thus, there is no need for computing G_d). Let us now face the case in which at least two types are present. Here, a way to restrict the range of possibilities to be checked is inspired to a well-known mathematical trick, that runs more or less as follows. "

n_i

$i = 1, ..., m$

" The answer is, clearly, $m + 1$ (the number of colors plus one), so that the set of socks will contain at least a double. In our case, a procedure (sketched in Algorithm 2) is implemented that progressively returns the pairs $(n_k, m_k)_{k=2,3,...}$, where n_k is the number of unary predicate k-tuples that are new (i.e., constraints that are not a superset of a previous constraint found at a step $j < k$), and m_k is the number of those that are not constraints, according to the available observations, until a $(n_{\bar{k}}, m_{\bar{k}})$ is found such that $(n_{\bar{k}+1}, m_{\bar{k}+1}) = (0, 0)$.

Then, only the cliques of size (greater than or) equal to $\bar{k}$ must be taken into account. Indeed, if the number of types is $\bar{k}$, any group of unary literals of size $\bar{k} + 1$ will contain at least 2 values taken from one type domain. Thus, these two literals have surely appeared previously as binary constraints, and hence no (new) constraint nor non-constraint will be present of size $\bar{k} + 1$, i.e. $(n_{\bar{k}+1}, m_{\bar{k}+1}) = (0, 0)$. Conversely, for $k \leq \bar{k}$ there will surely be a k-tuple of unary predicates, in which each unary predicate is taken from a different domain. Such a k-tuple is either a (superset of a previous) constraint, or it is

Algorithm 2 Identification of the maximum number of domains

Require: U: Unary predicates in the description language, O: Available observations
$NonConstraints_1 \leftarrow \{\{p\}|p \in U\}$
$n_1 \leftarrow 0;\ m_1 \leftarrow |NonConstraints_1|$
$k \leftarrow 1$
while $\neg(n_k = 0 \wedge m_k = 0)$ **do**
  $k \leftarrow k + 1$
  $NonConstraints_k \leftarrow \emptyset$
  $Constraints_k \leftarrow \emptyset$
  for all $N \in NonConstraints_{k-1}$ **do**
    for all $p \in U,\ p \notin N$ **do**
      if $N' = N \cup \{p\}$ is verified by some object in O **then**
        $NonConstraints_k \leftarrow NonConstraints_k \cup \{N'\}$
      else
        if $\not\exists C \in Constraints_j, j < k \ni' C \subset N'$ **then**
          $Constraints_k \leftarrow Constraints_k \cup \{N'\}$
        end if
      end if
    end for
  end for
  $n_k \leftarrow |Constraints_k|;\ m_k \leftarrow |NonConstraints_k|$
end while
Ensure: k: number of domains in O

---

verified by the available observations, in which case it is a non-constraint (and thus $m_k > 0$).

Given the following examples and descriptions:

$$
\begin{array}{cccccccc}
a & & \_\ \bullet\ a\ a' & a' & & \_\ \bullet\ a\ a'' & a'' & \\
b & \_\ \bullet\ b\ b' & & b' & b' & \_\ \bullet\ b\ b'' & b'' & b'' \\
c & \_\ \bullet\ c\ c' & & c' & & \_\ \bullet\ c\ c'' & c'' & c''
\end{array}
$$

the set of unary predicates in the description language is:
$$U = \{ \qquad , \qquad , \qquad , \_ \}$$
We would like the procedure to infer the number $\bar{k}$ of types. We first set:
$NonConstraints_1 = \{\{ \quad \},\{ \quad \},\{ \quad \},\{ \quad \}\},$
$n_1 = 0$ and $m_1 = |NonConstraints_1| = 4.$
Since $m_1 \neq 0$, each singleton in $NonConstraints_1$ must be extended in all possible ways by means of a new unary predicate in the description language, thus the procedure generates the following couples:
$\{large, small\}, \{large, blue\}, \{large, red\},$
$\{small, blue\}, \{small, red\}, \{blue, red\}.$
By testing each of such couples against the available observations, the procedure generates the following sets:
$NonConstraints_2 = \{\{small, blue\}, \{large, red\}\}$
since in the observations object b' is both small and blue, and there are two objects (b'' and c'') that are large and red at the same time.
$Constraints_2 = \{\{large, blue\}, \{small, red\}, \{large, small\}, \{blue, red\}\}.$

since no observed object is at the same time large and blue, nor small and red, nor large and small, nor blue and red. Now, since $n_2 = |Constraints_2| = 4 \neq 0$ and $m_2 = |NonConstraints_2| = 2 \neq 0$ the procedure tries to extend each couple in $NonConstraints_2$ by adding a new unary predicate. But each triple that can be obtained in this way is a superset of an element of $Constraints_2$, thus we will have $NonConstraints_3 = Constraints_3 = \emptyset$ and hence $n_3 = m_3 = 0 \Rightarrow \overline{k} = 2$.

Not only this avoids the computational overhead of handling those with lesser size, since they will not be part of the solution, but can be used also to recognize that the available data are not sufficient to carry out the desired task. Indeed, if no cliques (i.e., partitions) of size (i.e., cardinality) at least $\overline{k}$ exist in the graph, the procedure can warn the user that information in the observations is probably too loose to allow the reconstruction of the types in the representation language used.

3 Experimental Results

The proposed method was implemented in SICStus Prolog, and tested on various domains, suitably chosen in order to cover all the possible cases of available observations and target types to be recognized. Here, we report the results obtained on one sample dataset for each case.

The Scientific Papers dataset [6] is based on a representation language made up of predicates with various arities, of which unary predicates represent values belonging to many different domains (case). It includes 112 scientific papers, belonging to 4 different classes (Springer-Verlag Lecture Notes, Proceedings of the International Conference on Machine Learning, IEEE Transactions, and none of the above) whose layout structure was described in terms of its composing layout blocks features (height, width, horizontal position, vertical position, content type) and relative position (horizontal adjacency, vertical adjacency, horizontal alignment, vertical alignment). The procedure reached $\overline{k} = 5$, and found the following (correct) types:

1.   : {large, medium, medium_large, medium_small, small, very_large, very_small}
2.   : {graphic, hor_line, image, mixed, text,ver_line}
3.   : {lower, middle, upper}
4.   : {center, left, right}
5.   : {large, medium, medium_large, medium_small, small, smallest, very_large, very_small, very_very_large, very_very_small}

The Family Relationships dataset [2] refers to a description language made up of predicates with various arities, of which unary predicates all belong to the same type. It describes a hypothetical family in terms of each person's sex and of the basic relations among persons (parent and married), whose members' pairs are tagged according to the derived relations (father, mother, son, daughter, uncle, aunt, etc.). In this case, all the unary predicates fell in one group (thus there was no need for building G_d), that was also the only type (successfully retrieved by the algorithm):

1.   : {female, male}

The Multiplexer dataset [5] describes 6-bit configurations, with the aim of inducing the definition of a multiplexer such that, among the last four bit positions, the position denoted by the first two bits must be 1. All 64 possible bit configurations are included, which should make significantly easier the type induction task, as confirmed by the algorithm output:

1.   : {bit6at0, bit6at1}
2.   .   : {bit5at0, bit5at1}
3.   : {bit4at0, bit4at1}
4.   : {bit3at0, bit3at1}
5.   : {bit2at0, bit2at1}
6.   : {bit1at0, bit1at1}

The Tic Tac Toe dataset [1] description language is made up of unary predicates only (representing values of different types). It contains all possible instances of final game configurations, each reporting the status (blank, X, or O) of all 9 positions (identified by their horizontal and vertical position on the board). Thus, with respect to the previous dataset, here the complexity is augmented by the greater number of types, the greater number of values per type and the elimination of a significant portion of all possible board configurations (specifically, all non-final ones). In this case, $\overline{k} = 9$ (even if no new constraints of size 7, 8 and 9 were found), just like the number of types (each corresponding to one possible position) correctly recognized by the system:

1.   : {tr_b, tr_o, tr_x}
2.   : {tc_b, tc_o, tc_x}
3.   .   : {tl_b, tl_o, tl_x}
4.   : {mr_b, mr_o, mr_x}
5.   : {mc_b, mc_o, mc_x}
6.   .   : {ml_b, ml_o, ml_x}
7.   : {br_b, br_o, br_x}
8.   : {bc_b, bc_o, bc_x}
9.   .   : {bl_b, bl_o, bl_x}

Lastly, the Congressional Votes [9] dataset describes 435 Congressmen as being democrats or republicans according to their votes on 16 issues. It is made up of 435 examples, described by means of 32 predicates, each representing the favorable ( ) or opposite ( ) vote on one of the above issues. It is particularly interesting because a certain amount of noise is present in the descriptions, in the form of unknown (omitted) votes, as reported in Table 1. Nevertheless, the algorithm is able to correctly infer all the 16 types (corresponding to the issues), each with its 2 descriptors (corresponding to the yes/no options).

Table 1. Noise on Congressmen votes

Issue	No. of Omissions
handicapped infants	0
crime	25
adoption budget resolution	48
mx missile	15
physicians fee freeze	11
el salvador aid	11
religious groups in schools	15
immigration	22
synfuels corporation cutback	7
education spending	21
water project cost sharing	12
duty free exports	17
aid to nicaraguan contrast	14
superfund right to sue	31
export administration act S.A.	28
anti satellites test ban	11

4 Experiments with Incomplete Knowledge

Once assessed the validity of the proposed algorithm in contexts with different characteristics, an interesting issue is evaluating its effectiveness under stress. A preliminary idea about this was given by the Congressional Votes dataset, where a number of observations missed some votes. Specifically, the aim was checking if it works also in presence of a small amount of information, and to what extent it does. To this purpose, we focused on the Scientific Papers dataset, for a number of reasons. First, because it is a real-world one, and is probably the most complex among those considered. Second, the shape of the descriptions is not fixed, differently from the Votes, Multiplexer and Tic Tac Toe ones. Third, it was made up of many different observations, differently from the Family one. Various experiments were run, in which noise was progressively introduced in the dataset descriptions. For each fixed amount of noise to be introduced, 10 random corruptions of the dataset were performed, on which running the proposed algorithm. Then, the learned types were checked and categorized in one of the following categories (listed by decreasing desirability):   ,   (i.e., missing some types or some values in some type domains, but without mixing values belonging to different types),   (when the algorithm autonomously recognized that the available information was too loose for getting to a correct solution), and   (when at least one of the identified types contained in its domain values actually belonging to different types).

A first experiment in this direction aimed at assessing how sensitive the algorithm is to the amount of observations provided to it. In this case, the dataset corruption consisted in progressively eliminating observations (examples) from it (remember that the initial size was 112). The amount of corruption ranged

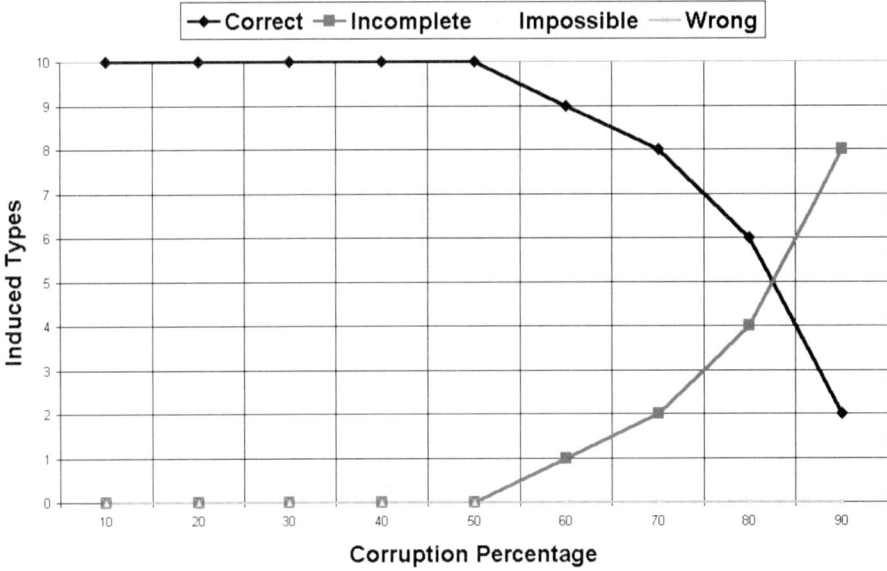

Fig. 1. Performance for Progressively Smaller Datasets

between 10% and 90% of the entire dataset, and the corresponding results are reported in Figure 1. It is interesting to note that the algorithm never generated undesirable (i.e., impossible or wrong) type domains. Actually, up to 50% of the dataset it always gave correct and complete answers. After that threshold, completeness started decreasing, but even when 90% of the observations was dropped (i.e., only 12 paper descriptions were available) in 2 cases it succeeded in finding the correct and complete types. This should allow one to state that the system is effective also when provided with very few observations.

Then, the next question was how much noise could be present in the available knowledge in order for the system not to be misleaded in its task. For this purpose, all the available observations were corrupted by eliminating from them a progressively larger amount of information, ranging from 10% to 60%. The experimental outcomes, graphically represented in Figure 2, suggest that the algorithm is more sensitive to partial descriptions than it was to a small number of observations. Indeed, in this case complete and correct types are induced only up to 20% of corruption, while accepting also incomplete types is ok up to 30%. Anyway, also after that threshold, the sum of desirable cases (i.e., correct and incomplete ones) far outperforms the number of undesirable ones. Only when 60% of each description in the dataset is dropped the number of wrong inductions becomes predominant, but interestingly it does not exceed half of the trials.

This behaviour can be explained because the proposed algorithm heavily relies on co-occurrence of values for inducing the type domains. Thus, eliminating

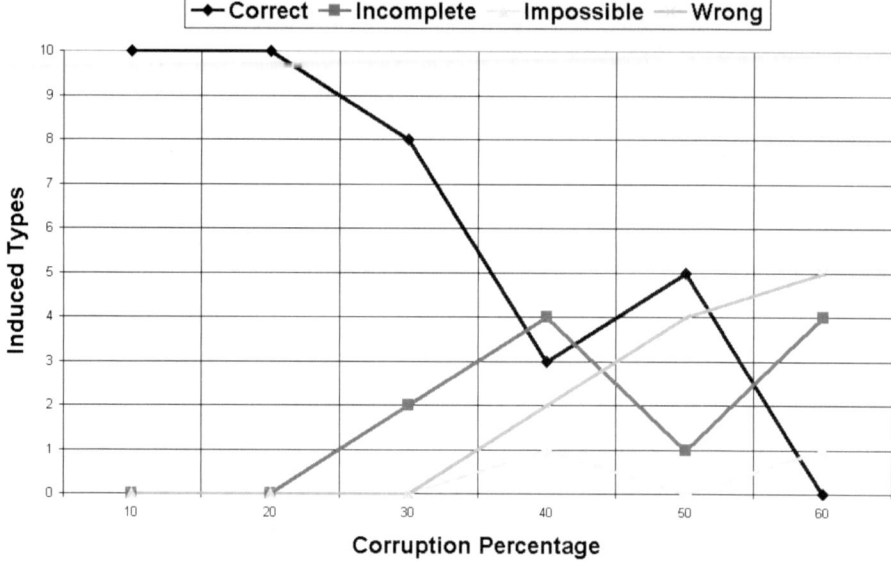

Fig. 2. Performance for Progressively Incomplete Descriptions

whole observations, but leaving complete the remaining ones, potentially still preserves many co-occurrences. On the contrary, dropping portions of each observation is likely to introduce false (supposed) incompatibilities among values that actually belong to different types. As already pointed out, some of these false incompatibilities are already present in the complete dataset (e.g., a line can have any width or height but is never too thick), thus artificially adding more noise of this kind makes an already hard task even harder. However, if the procedure is to be used in a Machine Learning context, incomplete (unknown) information in the available observations is a problem on its own, and experimental results show that abductive operators can cope with it only to some extent, which is in any case far below the threshold after which the proposed algorithm's performance becomes too low to be acceptable (and in general does not deal with datasets in which all descriptions are corrupted).

5 Conclusions

Many learning systems known in the literature are able to exploit and/or require knowledge about the types used in the description language and their related domains to improve their performance by pruning accordingly the search space of all possible hypotheses. This paper proposed an algorithm to automatically identify this kind of meta-information from the same observations that are input to the learning process, providing detailed examples of its behaviour. Experimental evaluation in several domains with characteristics that stress different features of the algorithm reveals encouraging performance. Moreover, being the algorithm dependent on the amount and quality of observations available, specific experiments have been run aimed at assessing its robustness, even when incomplete information is provided.

Given the good performance of the algorithm by itself in identifying type domains from observations, the next step will be exploiting the induced meta-information to support the inductive step of learning algorithms, in order to assess the gain in computational effort and predictive accuracy that it can bring, in particular when the available descriptions are incomplete and abduction is to be used. Additional future work will concern a theoretical study of the algorithm behavior and complexity, in order to develop heuristics that can improve its performance by avoiding unnecessary computations. A comparison with other (e.g., Constraint Satisfaction Problem – CSP) solutions to the same task is also planned. Then, the next objective will be studying the case of structured types, which causes additional interrelations among descriptors to be taken into account.

Acknowledgement. This work was partially funded by the EU project IST-507173 Two Knowledge VIKEF, "Virtual Information and Knowledge Environment Framework".

References

[1] D. W. Aha. Incremental constructive induction: An instance-based approach. *Proceedings of the 8th International Workshop on Machine Learning*, pages 117–121. Morgan Kaufmann, 1991.

[2] H. Blockeel and L. De Raedt. Inductive database design. In *Foundations of Intelligent Systems*, volume 1079 of *Lecture Notes on Artificial Intelligence*, pages 376–385. Springer, 1996.

[3] R.M. Cameron-Jones and J.R. Quinlan. Efficient top-down induction of logic programs. *SIGART bulletin*, 5(1):33–42, 1994.

[4] L. De Raedt and L. Dehaspe. Clausal discovery. *Machine Learning*, 26(2):99–146, 1997.

[5] W. V. de Velde. IDL, or Taming the Multiplexer Problem. *Proceedings of the 4th European Working Session on Learning*. Pittman, 1989.

[6] S. Ferilli, N. Di Mauro, T.M.A. Basile and F. Esposito. Incremental Induction of Rules for Document Image Understanding. In *AI*IA 2003: Advances in Artificial Intelligence*, volume 2829 of *Lecture Notes on Artificial Intelligence*, pages 176–188. Springer, 2003.

[7] P.A. Flach and N. Lachiche. Cooking up integrity constraints with primus. Preliminary Report CSTR-97-009, University of Bristol - Department of Computer Science, December 1997.

[8] P.A. Flach and N. Lachiche. Confirmation-guided discovery of first-order rules with Tertius. *Machine Learning*, 42(1/2):61–95, 2001.

[9] A. Kakas and F. Riguzzi. Abductive concept learning. *New Generation Computing*, 1999.

[10] E. McCreath and A. Sharma. Extraction of meta-knowledge to restrict the hypothesis space for ilp systems. In *Proceedings of the 8th Australian Joint Conference on Artificial Intelligence*, pages 70–82. World Scientific, 1995.

[11] R. S. Michalski. Inferential theory of learning. developing foundations for multistrategy learning. In R. S. Michalski and G. Tecuci, editors, *Machine Learning. A Multistrategy Approach*, volume IV, pages 3–61. Morgan Kaufmann, San Mateo, CA, U.S.A., 1994.

[12] K. Morik. Balanced cooperative modeling. *Machine Learning*, 11:217–235, 1993.

[13] S. Muggleton. Inverse entailment and Progol. *New Generation Computing, Special issue on Inductive Logic Programming*, 13(3/4):245–286, 1995.

[14] E. Shapiro. Inductive inference of theories from facts. Technical Report 192, Computer Science Department, Yale University, 1981.

On Avoiding Redundancy in Inductive Logic Programming

Nuno Fonseca[1], Vítor S. Costa[2], Fernando Silva[1], and Rui Camacho[3]

[1] DCC-FC & LIACC, Universidade do Porto
R. do Campo Alegre 823, 4150-180 Porto, Portugal
{nf, fds}@ncc.up.pt
[2] COPPE/Sistemas, UFRJ Centro de Tecnologia, Bloco H-319, Cx. Postal 68511
Rio de Janeiro,Brasil
vitor@cos.ufrj.br
[3] Faculdade de Engenharia & LIACC, Universidade do Porto
Rua Dr. Roberto Frias, s/n 4200-465 Porto, Portugal
rcamacho@fe.up.pt

Abstract. ILP systems induce first-order clausal theories performing a search through very large hypotheses spaces containing redundant hypotheses. The generation of redundant hypotheses may prevent the systems from finding good models and increases the time to induce them. In this paper we propose a classification of hypotheses redundancy and show how expert knowledge can be provided to an ILP system to avoid it. Experimental results show that the number of hypotheses generated and execution time are reduced when expert knowledge is used to avoid redundancy.

Keywords: Redundancy, Expert-Assistance

1 Introduction

Inductive Logic Programming (ILP) [1] is a form of supervised learning that aims at the induction of logic programs, or theories, from a given set of examples and prior knowledge (   ), also represented as logic programs. Like other Machine Learning approaches, ILP systems have to traverse a potentially infinite search space. At each search node an ILP system generates and then evaluates an   (represented as a clause). The evaluation of an hypothesis usually requires computing its coverage, that is, computing how many examples it explains. ILP systems therefore may have long execution times.

Research in improving the efficiency of ILP systems has thus focused in reducing their sequential execution time, either by reducing the number of generated hypotheses [2,3]; by efficiently testing candidate hypotheses [4,5,6]; or through parallelism [7,8]. Arguably, best results can be achieved through a reduction of the search space. In this work, we start from the well-known observation that the search space for ILP can be highly   . It is known that redundancy cannot be completely eliminated on finite and complete systems [9]. Instead, we

R. Camacho, R. King, A. Srinivasan (Eds.): ILP 2004, LNAI 3194, pp. 132–146, 2004.

identify and classify several common forms of redundancy that are frequently found in ILP applications, and suggest techniques to address them. To the best of our knowledge this is the first time that someone presents a classification of hypotheses redundancy found in ILP systems search spaces.

In order to explain why ILP systems generate redundant hypotheses, we first observe that ILP systems may be seen as using refinement operators [10] to generate hypotheses. According to Van der Laag [9], ideal refinement operators should respect three properties: , i.e., a refinement operator should not generate equivalent (redundant) clauses;   *fi*   ; and   . Van der Laag showed that ideal operators do not exist for unrestricted θ-subsumption ordered set of clauses, as used in most ILP systems. Hence, generic refinement operators for ILP cannot be ideal. Since guaranteeing completeness and local finiteness is fundamental, properness is usually sacrificed. Thus it is usual the generation of redundant hypotheses by ILP systems.

The efficiency of an ILP system may therefore be significantly improved if the number of redundant hypotheses is decreased. A first step to achieve this goal is to identify and classify the types of redundancy actually found in ILP systems search spaces. Based on this information one can envisage ways to avoid the generation of redundant hypotheses. We thus classify several types of redundancy. A second step is to deal with these forms of redundancy. We describe several strategies through which experts can easily provide relevant knowledge to help reduce redundancy. The exploitation of the human expertise is not novel in ILP. Recently, Srinivasan et al. [11] obtained good results by using human expertise to provide a partial ordering on the sets of background predicates.

The remainder of this paper is organized as follows. Section 2 presents a classification of hypotheses redundancy and in Section 3 we describe how to handle the identified types of redundancy. In Section 4 we present and discuss some experimental results. We conclude in Section 5 pointing out future work.

2 Redundancy in Hypotheses

Our goal is to prune the search space by eliminating   hypotheses. Clearly, if an ILP system generates a single hypothesis, the hypothesis can never be redundant. Redundancy is therefore a property of a clause within a search space.

To guarantee completeness, we should prune the search at an hypothesis C_i if C_i is such that (i) C_i itself is redundant, and (ii) and C_i's   will be redundant, too. The first condition says that we want to prune repeated hypotheses. The second condition requires further explanation. Consider a clause obtained in an example run of Aleph [12], a top-down ILP system. In this example we consider the well-known carcinogenesis problem. We first reach a clause saying that a molecule is active if it includes a Carbon 22:

$$\textbf{1.} \quad active(A) \leftarrow atm(A, B, c, 22, C)$$

The derivation eventually generates a clause, where D and B are Carbon 22s (they may refer to the same atom):

2. $active(A) \leftarrow atm(A, B, c, 22, C), atm(A, D, c, 22, C)$

We may say that the second clause is redundant because if the first clause is satisfiable, the second is too, and vice-versa. Should we prune here? Aleph does not prune, and eventually derives a clause saying that the atoms B and D must have a bond:

3. $active(A) \leftarrow atm(A, B, c, 22, C), atm(A, D, c, 22, C), bond(A, D, B, 7)$

This clause is not redundant: pruning an hypothesis is therefore wrong, if we do not consider descendants.

Next we describe the set of prunable hypotheses as $\mathcal{R}*$. Our goal in this work can be phrased as trying to obtain the best possible approximation to $\mathcal{R}*$. The reader may have noticed that whether a new hypothesis C_i is in $\mathcal{R}*$ depends **(a)** on the hypotheses $C_j, j < i$ that have been generated so far, and **(b)** on the hypotheses $C_k, k > i$ that are to be generated. The structure of $\mathcal{R}*$ thus depends on the ordering we use when we build the search space. Here, we shall consider the popular top-down approach where clauses are refined by introducing new substitutions and literals.

Detecting whether a clause is redundant and detecting whether all refinements of a clause are also redundant is hard. We would like an efficient approach, that could detect interesting cases with little computational overhead. Our observation is that we can be confident that two clauses will have the same refinements, if the clauses always generate the same bindings for their variables. More precisely, given a clause C, the set of variables $\mathcal{V} = \{V : V \in Vars(C)\}^1$, and the set of success substitutions θ from all variables in $\mathcal{V}$ to ground terms that satisfy C, we say that two clauses C_1 and C_2 are interchangeable if there is a mapping ω from the variables in $\mathcal{V}_1$ to the variables in $\mathcal{V}_2$ such that if $\forall \theta_1 \exists \theta_2, \theta_1 = \omega \theta_2$.

If the two clauses generate the same set of substitutions for all their variables, they have the same answers for the head variables, and must thus cover the same number of examples. One is therefore   . Refining in top-down approaches consists of introducing extra goals and/or constraints, say C'. But it is straightforward to show that if $(C_1 \wedge C')\sigma$ is satisfiable so must be $(C_2 \wedge C')\omega\sigma$, hence $(C_2 \wedge C')\sigma$. Therefore, all refinements to C_2 would be redundant (if the search for C_1 is complete).

Next, we address how to recognise cases of redundancy that address the conditions discussed above. We will use the following notation: C is a fi   [9], i.e., a sequence of literals, in the form $L_0 \leftarrow L_1, \dots, L_n$ ($n \geq 1$); L_i ($1 \leq i \leq n$) is a literal in the body of the clause and L_0 is the head literal of the clause; each literal L_i can be represented by $p_i(A_1, \dots, A_{ia})$ where p_i is the predicate symbol with arity ia and $A_1, \dots, A_{ia}$ are the arguments; two

---

[1] $Vars(C)$ is the set of variables in a clause C.

literals are _____ if they have the same predicate symbol and sign; two clauses are compatible if they have the same head literal; and S is the multiset of hypotheses of the search space generated by an ILP system. The symbol $\vDash_B$ denotes the logical implication and $\equiv_B$ the logical equivalence considering the background knowledge provided (B). Since there is no doubt of the context of both logical relations we simplify the representation using only $\vDash$ and $\equiv$. For further definitions on logic we refer the reader to [13]. For an introduction to ILP we refer the reader to [14].

2.1 Self-Redundant Clauses

Ideally we would like to verify redundancy _____, that is, just through scanning the literals or clauses. On the other hand, we sometimes require _____ information, that is, prior knowledge on the model, to determine equivalence between clauses or literals. We also distinguish the interesting cases of self-redundant clauses i.e., where by just looking at a clause we know that the clause must repeat a parent in the search tree, naming the remainder cases _____.

The problem of verifying whether a clause h is self-redundant corresponds to the problem of verifying whether the clause is _____, that is, whether it does not subsume any proper subset of itself. Gottlob et al. [15] showed that the problem of verifying whether a clause is condensed is co-NP-complete. They also showed that it is undecidable to verify that a clause does not contain any proper subset that is implied by the clause. We thus can only hope to address specific instances of the problem.

The ILP process refines a clause by adding an extra literal or by binding variables in a clause. It is therefore natural to focus on redundant literals:

Definition 1 (Self-Redundant Literal). L_i _____.
$$C \centerdot (C \setminus L_i) \vDash C$$

Clauses which have a self-redundant literal are clearly _____ : they can be reduced back to a simpler parent. Consider for example the clause $a(X) \leftarrow b(X), b(X)$. All solutions and refinements to $a(X) \leftarrow b(X), b(X)$ are solutions and refinements to $a(X) \leftarrow b(X)$. A case where we can prune clauses through syntactic analysis is therefore the basic case where a literal appears duplicate in a clause.

Semantic Redundancy. Other examples of self-redundant clauses can be found using background knowledge. We may know of some degenerate cases when a literal is always or never satisfiable. We may also have extensional information on a predicate stating whether it is reflexive, associative, or commutative. Last, we generalize this concept through the notion of entailment between sub-goals.

We consider reflexivity as an example of two degenerate cases, a valid literal or an unsatisfiable literal:

Definition 2 (Tautology). L_i _____ $C \centerdot L_i$
_____

Consider for instance the "greater or equal" relation denoted by $\geq$. The literal $X \geq X$ is a tautologically redundant literal in the clause $a(X) \leftarrow X \geq X$.

Definition 3 (Contradiction). L_i $C \cdot C \setminus L_i$
fi C

Consider for instance the "greater than" relation denoted by $>$ and the "less than" relation denoted by $<$. The literal $X > Y$ is a contradiction redundant literal in the clause $a(X) \leftarrow X < Y, X > Y$.

Definition 4 (Commutativity). $L_i = p_i(A_1, \ldots, A_{ia})$
$C \cdot$ $L_j =$
$p_i(B_1, \ldots, B_{ja})$

$L_j \neq L_i$
$\exists \, permutation((B_1, \ldots, B_{ja})) = (A_1, \ldots, A_{ia})$
$L_j \equiv L_i$

Consider the clause $C = r(X, Z) \leftarrow mult(X, 2, Z), mult(2, X, Z)$ where $mult(X, Y, Z)$ is true if $Z = X * Y$. Since multiplication is commutative, it is known that $mult(X, Y, Z) \equiv mult(Y, X, Z)$, thus $mult(2, X, Z)$ is a commutative redundant literal.

Definition 5 (Transitivity). L_i
$C \cdot$ L_j L_k C $L_i \neq L_j \neq L_k$
$L_j \wedge L_k \models L_i$

Consider again the "greater or equal" relation: the literal $X \geq Z$ is transitive redundant in the clause $p(X, Y, Z) \leftarrow X \geq Y, Y \geq Z, X \geq Z$.

The previous declarations are easy to compute and do capture some of the most common cases of redundancy. The price is that we are restricted to some very specific cases. We next move to more general definitions:

Definition 6 (Direct Equivalence). L_i
$C \cdot$ L_j C $L_i \neq L_j$ $L_i \equiv L_j$

Note that in the definition of direct equivalent redundant literal we drop the compatibility constraint on the literals. For instance, the literal $X < 1$ is equivalent redundant in the clause $p(X) \leftarrow 1 > X, X < 1$ since $1 > X \equiv X < 1$. This is another type of semantic redundancy.

We can move one step further and consider entailment.

Definition 7 (Proper Direct Entailment). L_i
$C \cdot$ L_j C $L_i \neq L_j$
$L_j \models L_i$

For instance, the literal $X < 2$ is a proper direct entailed redundant in the clause $p(X) \leftarrow X < 1, X < 2$.

Definition 8 (Direct Entailment). L_i

C . . SC $C \setminus L_i$ $SC \vDash L_i$

For instance, consider the clause $p(X) \leftarrow X \leq 1, X \geq 1, X = 1$. The literal $X = 1$ is direct entailed redundant because there is a sequence of literals ($X \leq 1, X \geq 1$) that imply L_i. In general, verifying whether a set of sub-goals entails another one requires solving a constraint system over some specific domain (the integers in the example).

Our definitions do not guarantee that all the refinements of a redundant clause with a redundant literal L_i are themselves redundant. In the case of equivalence, a sufficient condition to guarantee that the clause belongs to $\mathcal{R}_*$ is that all variables in the right hand of the equivalence also appear in the left-hand side L_i, and vice-versa: if two literals are equivalent, all their instances will also be equivalent. In the case of entailment, it is sufficient that all variables in the left-hand side appear in L_i. Otherwise we could refine the entailing literal to a more specific set of literals which would not entail L_i.

2.2 Context-Derived Redundancy

When considering contextual redundancy we are manipulating the set of clauses (hypotheses) found so far $\mathcal{S}$, instead of sets of literals as in self redundancy:

Definition 9 (Context-Derived Redundant Clause). C

$\mathcal{S} \cup \{C\}$. $\mathcal{S} \vDash C$

The major types of contextual redundancy are obtained by generalizing over the cases of self redundancy:

Definition 10 (Duplicate). C $\mathcal{S} \cup \{C\}$.
$C \in \mathcal{S}$

For instance, consider that $\mathcal{S}$ contains the clause $p(X) \leftarrow a(X,Y)$. Then the clause $C = p(X) \leftarrow a(X,Y)$ is duplicate redundant in $\mathcal{S} \cup \{C\}$.

Definition 11 (Commutativity). C
$\mathcal{S} \cup \{C\}$. $D \in \mathcal{S}$. C
ff $C \equiv D$

For instance, $C = p(X) \leftarrow a(c, X), a(d, X)$ is a commutative redundant clause in $\mathcal{S}$ if $\mathcal{S}$ contains $p(X) \leftarrow a(d, X), a(c, X)$.

Definition 12 (Transitivity). C $\mathcal{S} \cup \{C\}$
. D E $\mathcal{S}$

    . D E ff L_D L_E
    . C D L_C
$L_C \wedge L_D \vDash L_E$

For instance, consider the clause $p(X, Y, Z) \leftarrow X > Y, Y > Z$. Such clause is transitive redundant in a set S containing $p(X, Y, Z) \leftarrow X > Y$ and $p(X, Y, Z) \leftarrow X > Z$.

Definition 13 (Direct Equivalence).

$$S \cup \{C\} \text{ .} \qquad\qquad \begin{array}{c} C \\ D \in S \end{array}$$

$$. C \quad D \quad \text{ff} \qquad\qquad L_C \qquad L_D$$

$$L_C \qquad\qquad\qquad\qquad\qquad D$$

As an example consider $S = \{D = p(X) \leftarrow X > 1\}$. The clause $p(X) \leftarrow 1 < X$ is proper equivalent redundant in S since the clauses differ in one literal ($X > 1$ and $1 < X$) and $1 < X$ is a direct equivalent redundant literal in D.

Definition 14 (Direct Entailment).

$$S \cup \{C\} \text{ .} \qquad L_C \quad C \qquad\qquad\qquad \begin{array}{c} C \\ D \in S \end{array}$$

$$L_C \qquad\qquad\qquad\qquad D \text{ .} \qquad SC$$
$$D \setminus SC = C \setminus L_C$$

Consider $S = \{D = p(X) \leftarrow X \leq 1, X \geq 1\}$. The clause $C = p(X) \leftarrow X = 1$ contains a literal $X = 1$ that is a directly entailed redundant literal in D. Thus C is a directly entailed redundant clause.

The types of redundancy just described, both self and contextual redundancy, form an hierarchy as illustrated in Figure 1, in the Appendix.

3 Handling Redundancy

In this section we describe how and where the redundancy types identified in the previous section can be eliminated in ILP systems that follow a top-down search approach.

In general, the generation of hypotheses in top-down ILP systems can be seen as being composed by the following two steps. First, an hypothesis is selected to be specialized (refined). Then, some literal generation procedure selects, or generates a literal, to be added to the end of the clause's body. We advocate that almost all types of redundancy identified could be efficiently eliminated if an expert provides meta-knowledge to ILP systems about predicates' properties and relations among the predicates in the background knowledge. Such information can be used by the literal generation procedure or by the refinement procedure to avoid the generation of self and contextual redundant hypotheses.

3.1 Possible Approaches

We envisage several approaches to incorporate the information provided by the expert in ILP systems to avoid the generation of redundant hypotheses. In a nutshell, either we can take advantage of user-defined constraint mechanisms, or user-defined pruning, or we can improve the refinement operator.

A first approach could be the extension of user-defined constraint mechanisms available in some systems (e.g., Progol [16], Aleph [12], Indlog [17]). The constraints are added by a user in the form of clauses that define when an hypothesis should not be considered. Integrity constraints are currently used to prevent the generation of self redundant clauses containing contradiction redundant literals. Note that an " ... integrity constraint does not state that a refinement of a clause that violates one or more constraints will also be unacceptable." [12]. Thus the constraint mechanism is not suitable for our needs since we want to discard refinements of redundant clauses.

Another approach to eliminate redundant literals could be through user-defined pruning declarations that some ILP systems accept (e.g., Progol [16], Aleph [12], IndLog [17]). Pruning is used to exclude clauses and their refinements from the search. It is very useful to state which kinds of clauses should not be considered in the search. Some ILP systems allow a user to provide such rules defining when an hypothesis should be discarded (pruned). The use of pruning greatly improves the efficiency of ILP systems since it leads to a reduction of the size of the search space. User-defined pruning declarations to encode meta-knowledge about redundancy has the advantage that they can easily be incorporated into ILP systems that support user-defined pruning. However, in our opinion, one should try to eliminate the redundancy as a built-in procedure of the refinement operator instead of using mechanisms like user-defined pruning since the first option should be more efficient.

A third approach is the modification of the refinement operator and the literal generation procedure to allow the use of information provided by the expert. This is the approach followed and is next described.

3.2 Redundancy Declarations

To eliminate the generation of redundant hypotheses we modified the refinement operator and literal generation procedure to exploit redundancy meta-knowledge provided by an expert. We modified the April [18] ILP system to accept the redundancy declarations that we next describe. The declarations are provided to the system as background knowledge in the form of Prolog rules. We chose the April system due to our knowledge regarding its implementation but we should note that the work described is also applicable to other ILP systems.

We start by describing the declarations that a user may pass to the literal generation procedure. Duplicate, commutative, and direct equivalent redundant literals can be eliminated during literal generation.

The user may inform the April system of literals' properties through declarations such as tautology, commutative, and equiv. For instance, the declaration :- tautology('$\leq$'(X,X)) informs the system that literals of the form '$\leq$'(X,X) are tautological redundant literals. With this information the ILP system avoids the generation of such redundant literals.

The `commutative` declaration indicates that a given predicate is commutative. This information helps the ILP system to avoid the generation of hypotheses with commutative redundant literals. As an example consider that we inform the ILP system that the predicate `adj(X,Y)` is commutative (e.g., `:-commutative(adj(X,Y),adj(Y,X))`). That information can be used to prevent the generation of commutative equivalent literals such as $adj(X,2)$ and $adj(2,X)$.

The `equiv` declaration allows an expert to indicate that two predicates, although possibly different, generate equivalent literals. For instance, the declaration `:-equiv('≤'(X,Y),'≥'(Y,X))` informs that the literals like `'≤'(X,1)` and `'≥'(1,X)` are equivalent.

An ILP system using equivalence declarations needs only to consider one literal of each equivalence class. There is redundancy in having `commutative` and `equiv` declarations, since we can define commutativity using only the `equiv` declaration. The main reason for this is to keep compatibility with other systems (e.g., Aleph). We point out that the described declarations allow the ILP system to avoid the generation of several types of self redundant hypotheses and contextual redundant hypotheses (direct equivalent redundant clauses).

The remaining types of redundancy are handled in the refinement operator. The generation of commutative redundant clauses or clauses containing duplicate literals is automatically avoided by April's refinement operator without the need of extra information provided by the user.

The declaration `contradiction` can be used to avoid the generation of contradiction redundant hypotheses. The declaration has the form of `contradiction([$L_1, \ldots, L_k$])`, where $L_1, \ldots, L_k$ is the conjunction of literals that when appearing together in a clause makes it inconsistent. For instance, $contradiction([X < Y, X > Y])$ states that both literals can not occur in an hypothesis because they would turn it inconsistent.

The generation of transitive redundant literals and clauses can be avoided by providing information indicating which predicates are transitive. For instance, the rule `:- transitive(lt(X,Y),lt(Y,Z),lt(X,Z))` informs that the `lt` (less than) predicate is transitive. With such information, a redundant hypothesis containing the literals `lt(X,Y),lt(Y,Z)` will not be generated by the refinement operator.

Proper direct entailment redundant literals can be avoided with the knowledge that a literal implies another. The knowledge can be provided using declarations such as `semantic_rule(L1,L2):-RuleBody`, meaning that L1 implies L2 if the `RuleBody` is evaluated as true. For instance, the rule `semantic_rule(lt(A,B),lt(A,C)):-C<B` allows the refinement operator to avoid the generation of hypotheses containing a literal like $lt(A,2)$ followed by a literal like `lt(A,1)` (e.g..$p(X)\leftarrow$ `lt(A,2),lt(A,1)`).

Direct entailed redundant literals or clauses can be prevented from being generated if we state that there is a set of literals such that each literal in the set implies the redundant literal. Such information can be provided with the declaration `d_entail([$L_1, \ldots, L_k$],L)`. With such information the refinement

Table 1. Redundancy Declarations

Redundancy Type	Handled	Declaration	Example
Self / Tautological	literal generation	`:-tautology('≥'(X,X)).`	$p(X)\leftarrow X\geq X$
Self / Contradiction	refinement	`:-contradiction(` `['>'(X,Y),'<'(X,Y)]).`	$p(X)\leftarrow X<2,X>2$
Self / Commutative	literal generation	`:-commutative(` `mult(X,Y,R),mult(Y,X,R))`	$p(X)\leftarrow$ mult(X,3,R), mult(3,X,R)
Self & Contextual Transitivity	refinement	`:-transitive('>'(X,Y),` `'>'(Y,Z), '>'(X,Z))`	$p(X)\leftarrow X>Y,Y>Z$
Self / Proper Direct Entailment	refinement	`semantic_rule('<'(A,B),` `'<'(A,C)):- C<B`	$p(X)\leftarrow X<0,X<2$
Self & Contextual Direct Equivalence	literal generation	`:-equiv('<'(X,Y),` `'≥'(Y,X))`	$p(X,Y)\leftarrow X<Y,Y\geq X$
Self & Contextual Direct Entailment	refinement	`:-d_entail(['≤'(X,Y),` `'≥'(X,Y))],'='(X,Y)`	$p(X,Y)\leftarrow X\leq Y,X\geq Y,$ $X=Y$

operator will not generate clauses containing L together with any of the L_i ($1 \leq i \leq k$) and clauses containing all L_i. For instance, the clauses $p(X) \leftarrow X\leq1,X=1$ or $p(X) \leftarrow X\leq1,X\geq1$ would not be generated if the expert provides a declaration like `d_entail([X≤Y,X≥Y],X=Y)`.

The unforeseen types of redundancy can be handled by the declaration `redundant(Literal,HypothesisBody):-Body`, where `Literal` is the literal to be added to the `HypothesisBody` and `Body` is a conjunction of literals that specify the conditions that make an hypothesis redundant. All types of redundancy could be handled by using this generic declaration. There are two main reasons that lead us to provide a set of declarations instead of a single declaration. The first reason is efficiency - ILP system implementors can devise more efficient ways of handling the redundancy described by each declaration than through a generic declaration of redundancy like `redundant`. The second reason is legibility - declarations with names that indicate the type of redundancy simplify the reading and the understanding of the background knowledge.

Table 1 summarizes the types of redundancy supported in our implementation, where redundancy is handled, examples of redundancy declarations and redundant hypotheses.

A final note on the implementation. Most of the declarations described (e.g., `transitive`, `contradiction`, `commutative`, `equiv`, and `d_entail`) are implemented by performing a matching between the literals in a declaration and the ones in a clause. The declaration `semantic_rule` is the only exception to this schema, since it involves the evaluation of the `body` of the semantic rule. The test if a declaration is applicable to a clause involves comparing (matching) the literals in the clause with the ones in the declaration. The cost of such a test is linear on its size (number of literals), thus having a low computational cost.

Table 2. Datasets characteristics and main experiment settings

Dataset	Characterization			April's Settings	
	$\mid E^+ \mid$	$\mid E^- \mid$	$\mid B \mid$/wrd	i	noise
krki I	342	658	1/1	1	10
krki II	3240	6760	1/1	1	10
mutagenesis	114	57	21/7	2	5
multiplication	37	24	3/2	2	0
range	19	14	1/1	1	0
proteins	848	764	24/8	2	90
ackermann	51	119	4/2	2	0

4 Experiments and Results

The utility of the redundancy declarations presented in the previous section is empirically evaluated by determining the impact of their use in the execution time and number of hypotheses generated. Six datasets were used in the experiments. We selected datasets for which our knowledge, regarding the predicates in the background knowledge, enabled us to identify redundancy. The datasets were gathered from the Machine Learning repositories of Oxford[2] and York[3], and from one of the authors' home page[4].

Table 2 characterizes the datasets in terms of number of positive and negative examples as well as background knowledge size (number of predicates) and number of predicates **w**ith **r**edundancy **d**eclarations (   ). Furthermore, it shows the April settings used with each dataset. The -depth corresponds to the maximum depth of a literal with respect to the head literal of the hypothesis [19]. Finally, the parameter   defines the maximum number of negative examples that an hypothesis may cover in order to be accepted. In all datasets the search was constrained to find hypotheses with a body containing a maximum of seven literals. The only exception was the   dataset with a maximum number of literals set to 2. No limit was imposed on the number of hypotheses generated, and thus an exhaustive search within language restrictions was performed. In the appendix, Table 4, we show examples of redundancy declarations used in each dataset. The experiments were made on an AMD Athlon XP 1400+ processor PC with 512MB of memory, running the Linux Fedora (kernel 2.4.25) operating system. The ILP system used was the April [18] system version 0.9 together with the YAP Prolog engine version 4.4.

Table 3 summarizes the performance of the April system using redundancy declarations and not using them. It shows the **p**ercentage of predicates **w**ith **r**edundancy **d**eclarations (   ), the total number of hypotheses generated, execution time, and the impact in the number of generated hypotheses and execution time (given as a ratio between using redundancy declarations and not

---

[2] http://web.comlab.ox.ac.uk/oucl/research/areas/machlearn/
[3] http://www.cs.york.ac.uk/mlg/index.html
[4] http://www.fe.up.pt/~rcamacho/datasets/datasets.html

Table 3. Impact of using redundancy declarations (**red-decl**).*pwrd* is the percentage of predicates in the background knowledge with redundancy declarations.

Dataset	pwrd	| Hypotheses |			Time (sec.)		
		normal	red-decl	(%)	normal	red-decl	(%)
krki I	100	2,671	411	15	4.8	1.39	29
krki II	100	4,999	1,341	27	67.72	28.65	42
mutagenesis	30	3,823	3700	97	31,133	30,975	99
multiplication	66	2,163	1,032	47	2.03	0.96	47
range	100	5,257	303	6	6.3	0.15	2
proteins	33	1,470,742	1,303,351	88	499,638	457,582	91
ackermann	50	38,197	31,656	82	70.69	60,77	85

using them). For the purposes of this study we do not present accuracies of the models generated because they do not differ in both runs for each dataset. However, it is important to remember that the accuracy of the models is not affected negatively since the redundancy information provided is used to eliminate $\mathcal{R}*$ redundant hypotheses. Note that the performance results for the
dataset are very preliminary. In this dataset, due to time limitations, we had to constrain the search to find clauses using only up to two literals in the body. Nevertheless, the results show that even for such small search space we can obtain a slight improvement. For the remaining datasets considered, one can observe that redundancy declarations reduced the execution time and the number of hypotheses generated. The reductions were more substantial in the datasets with greater   .

5   Conclusions

This work contributes to the effort of improving the efficiency of ILP systems. We studied the major forms of redundancy found in the search space of ILP applications and described how to avoid redundancy. In our approach, a domain expert provides meta-knowledge about the redundancy types by describing high-level properties of the relations in the background knowledge. Experimental results show that performance improvements can be obtained by using redundancy declarations.

The major thrust of our work is to make ILP systems able to learn from large datasets. Most ILP systems are configured to generate a limited number of hypotheses. Therefore, avoiding redundant hypotheses may also lead to the generation of better hypotheses that otherwise would be lost due to the search limit. We hope that this may result in an improvement of the quality of the induced models. Further experiments are required to better assess this claim, and to understand what redundancy declarations and how often each contributes to the reduction on the search space. It would be also interesting to see which types of redundancy can be detected automatically, perhaps in a pre-processing stage, in order to automatically generate the redundancy declarations.

Acknowledgments. We thank the anonymous reviewers for their useful comments. The work has been partially supported by project APRIL (Project POSI/SRI/40749/2001) and

and   . Nuno Fonseca is funded by the FCT grant SFRH/BD/7045-/2001.

References

1. S. Muggleton. Inductive logic programming. In *Proceedings of the 1st Conference on Algorithmic Learning Theory*, pages 43–62. Ohmsma, Tokyo, Japan, 1990.
2. M. Sebag and Rouveirol C. Tractable induction and classification in first order logic via stochastic matching. In *15th Int. Join Conf. on Artificial Intelligence (IJCAI'97)*, pages 888–893. Morgan Kaufmann, 1997.
3. Rui Camacho. Improving the efficiency of ilp systems using an incremental language level search. In *Annual Machine Learning Conference of Belgium and the Netherlands*, 2002.
4. H. Blockeel, L. Dehaspe, B. Demoen, G. Janssens, J. Ramon, and H. Vandecasteele. Improving the efficiency of Inductive Logic Programming through the use of query packs. *Journal of Artificial Intelligence Research*, 16:135–166, 2002.
5. V.S. Costa, A. Srinivasan, R. Camacho, H. Blockeel, and W. Van Laer. Query transformations for improving the efficiency of ilp systems. *JMLR*, 2002.
6. Rui Camacho. As lazy as it can be. In P. Doherty B. Tassen, P. Ala-Siuru and B. Mayoh, editors, *The Eighth Scandinavian Conference on Artificial Intelligence (SCAI'03)*, pages 47–58. Bergen, Norway, November 2003.
7. L. Dehaspe and L. De Raedt. Parallel inductive logic programming. In *Proceedings of the MLnet Familiarization Workshop on Statistics, Machine Learning and Knowledge Discovery in Databases*, 1995.
8. T. Matsui, N. Inuzuka, H. Seki, and H. Itoh. Comparison of three parallel implementations of an induction algorithm. In *8th Int. Parallel Computing Workshop*, pages 181–188, Singapore, 1998.
9. P.R.J. van der Laag. *An analysis of refinement operators in inductive logic programming*. PhD thesis, Erasmus Universiteit, Rotterdam, the Netherlands, 1995.
10. E.Y. Shapiro. *Algorithmic Program Debugging*. The MIT Press, 1983.
11. A. Srinivasan, R.D. King, and M.E. Bain. An empirical study of the use of relevance information in inductive logic programming. *JMLR*, 2003.
12. Ashwin Srinivasan. Aleph manual, 2003.
13. C. J. Hogger. *Essentials of Logic Programming*. Oxford University Press, 1990.
14. S.-H. Nienhuys-Cheng and R. de Wolf. *Foundations of Inductive Logic Programming*, volume 1228 of *Lecture Notes in Artificial Intelligence*. Springer-Verlag, 1997.
15. G. Gottlob and C.G. Fermuller. Removing redundancy from a clause. *Artificial Intelligence*, 61(2):263–289, June 1993.
16. Stephen Muggleton and John Firth. Relational rule induction with cprogol4.4: A tutorial introduction. In Saso Dzeroski and Nada Lavrac, editors, *Relational Data Mining*, pages 160–188. Springer-Verlag, September 2001.
17. R. Camacho. *Inducing Models of Human Control Skills using Machine Learning Algorithms*. PhD thesis, Department of Electrical Engineering and Computation, Universidade do Porto, 2000.

18. Nuno Fonseca, Rui Camacho, Fernando Silva, and Vítor S. Costa. Induction with April: A preliminary report. Technical Report DCC-2003-02, DCC-FC, Universidade do Porto, 2003.
19. S. Muggleton and C. Feng. Efficient induction in logic programs. In S. Muggleton, editor, *Inductive Logic Programming*, pages 281–298. Academic Press, 1992.

Appendix

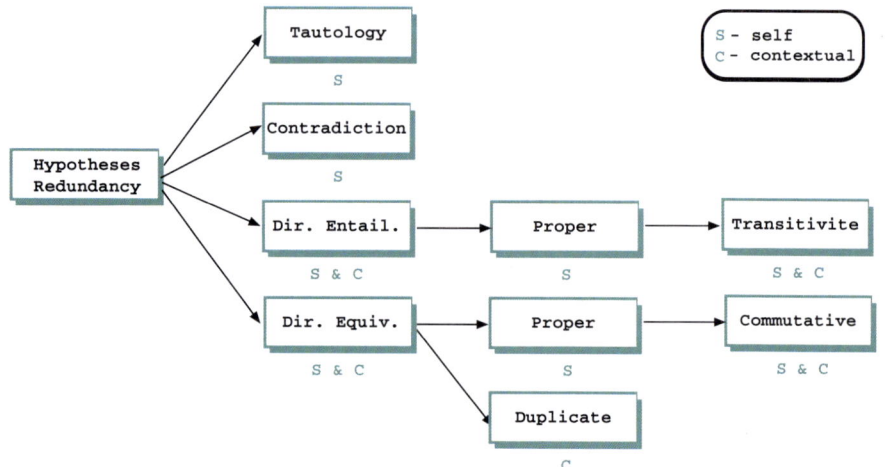

Fig. 1. Redundancy hierarchy

Table 4. Examples of redundancy declarations used on the experiments

Datasets	Declarations
Krki I & II	:-commutative(adj/2). :-tautology(adj(X,X)).
multiplication	:- equiv(mult(A,B,C),mult(B,A,C)). :- equiv(plus(A,B,C),plus(B,A,C)).

range	semantic_rule(lt(A,B),lt(A,C)):-
	    number(B),number(C),
	    C<B.
	semantic_rule(lt(A,B),lt(C,B)):-
	    number(A),number(C),
	    C<A.

proteins	:-transitive(lth). :-transitive(ltv). semantic_rule(lth(A,B),ltv(B,A)). semantic_rule(ltv(A,B),lth(B,A)). :-d_entail([very_hydrophobic(A)],aromatic_or_very_hydrophobic(A)). :-d_entail([aromatic(A)],aromatic_or_very_hydrophobic(A)). :-d_entail([small(A)],small_or_polar(A)). :-d_entail([polar(A)],small_or_polar(A)). :-d_entail([aromatic_or_very_hydrophobic(A),not_very_hydrophobic(A)],aromatic(A)). :-d_entail([small_or_polar(A),large(A)],polar(A)).
ackermann	:-transitive(incr(A,B),decr(B,A),'='(A,B)).

mutagenesis	:-tautology(gteq(X,X)).
	:-tautology(lteq(X,X)).
	semantic_rule(gteq(A,B),gteq(A,C)):-
	    number(B),number(C),
	    B>C.
	semantic_rule(gteq(A,B),gteq(C,B)):-
	    number(A),number(C),
	    A>C.
	:-transitive(lteq).
	:-transitive(gteq).
	:-commutative(connected/2).
	:-d_entail([benzene(X,Y)],ring_size_6(X,Y)).
	:-d_entail([carbon_5_aromatic_ring(X,Y)],ring_size_5(X,Y)).
	:-d_entail([carbon_6_ring(X,Y)],ring_size_6(X,Y)).
	:-d_entail([hetero_aromatic_6_ring(X,Y)],ring_size_6(X,Y)).
	:-d_entail([hetero_aromatic_5_ring(X,Y)],ring_size_5(X,Y)).

Generalization Algorithms for Second-Order Terms *

Kouichi Hirata[1], Takeshi Ogawa[2]**, and Masateru Harao[1]

[1] Department of Artificial Intelligence
{hirata,harao}@ai.kyutech.ac.jp
[2] Graduate School of Computer Science and Systems Engineering
ogawa@dumbo.ai.kyutech.ac.jp
Kyushu Institute of Technology
Kawazu 680-4, Iizuka 820-8502, Japan

Abstract. In this paper, we study the *generalization algorithms* for *second-order terms*, which are treated as first-order terms with *function variables*, under an *instantiation* order denoted by $\succeq$. First, we extend the least generalization algorithm *lg* for a pair of first-order terms under $\succeq$, introduced by Plotkin and Reynolds, to the one for a pair of second-order terms. The extended algorithm *lg*, however, is insufficient to characterize the generalization for a pair of second-order terms, because it computes neither the least generalization under $\succeq$ nor the structure-preserving generalization. Since the *transformation rule* for second-order matching algorithm consists of an *imitation* and a *projection*, in this paper, we introduce the *imitation-free generalization* algorithm *ifg* and the *projection-free generalization* algorithm *pfg*. Then, we show that *ifg* computes the least generalization under $\succeq$ of any pair of second-order terms, whereas *pfg* computes the generalization equivalent to *lg* under $\succeq$. Nevertheless, neither *ifg* nor *pfg* preserves the structural information. Hence, we also introduce the algorithm *spg* and show that it computes a *structure-preserving generalization*. Finally, we show that the algorithms *lg*, *pfg* and *spg* are *associative*, while the algorithm *ifg* is not.

1 Introduction

A   between terms is one of the most basic and powerful tool for concept learning. For given terms t and s, we say that t is
            s if there exists a substitution θ such that $t\theta = s$ and denote it by $t \succeq s$. Plotkin [18] and Reynolds [19] have independently introduced the
            algorithm   for first-order terms and shown that it computes the least generalization under $\succeq$. The generalization algorithms are applied to

---

* This work is partially supported by Grand-in-Aid for Scientific Research 15700137 and 16016275 from the Ministry of Education, Culture, Sports, Science and Technology, Japan, and 13558036 from the Japan Society for the Promotion of Science.
** Current address: Matsushita Electric Industrial Co., Ltd.

R. Camacho, R. King, A. Srinivasan (Eds.): ILP 2004, LNAI 3194, pp. 147–163, 2004.
© Springer-Verlag Berlin Heidelberg 2004

several knowledge processing such as machine learning, inductive logic programming, analogical reasoning, and so on [2,4,6,13,15]. The generalization algorithm has been also developed widely by many researchers (. [16]).

In order to deal with the structural information of terms, formulas, or tree-structural data, it is useful to extend the first-order terms to the with not only individual variables but also . . Note that every function variable takes a function as its value, which causes several computational difficulty stated in [1,3,5,8]. In particular, the problem of determining whether or not $t \succeq s$ is NP-complete for a second-order term t and a first-order ground term s [1] (under several restrictions [8]).

The generalization for or is usually formulated in the framework of λ-calculus. Lu [13] and Pfenning [17] have discussed the generalizations over $\lambda 2$ and Calculus of Constructions, respectively. Feng and Muggleton [4] have investigated the generalizations over M_λ, similar as the basis L_λ of λ-Prolog [14], and Hasker [7] has discussed the second-order generalizations with . However, in λ-calculus, the instantiation order $\succeq$ highly depends on the order of λ-application (. [13]). Furthermore, any λ-abstraction is inessential for tree-structural data.

Hence, we adopt the simple second-order terms according to [3,5,8], which contain no λ operators . The second-order terms in this paper are defined inductively by individual constants, individual variables, function constants and function variables. We also adopt the instantiation order $\succeq$ without the several semantics of function variables.

In this paper, first we extend the least generalization algorithm for a pair of first-order terms under $\succeq$, elegantly designed by Lassez [12], to the one for a pair of second-order terms. Then, we point out that it is insufficient to characterize the generalization for second-order terms, because it computes neither the least generalization under $\succeq$ nor the structure-preserving generalization.

Since the . for second-order matching algorithm consists of an and a [9,10], in this paper, we introduce the . algorithm . and the . algorithm . . The algorithm . , motivated by Feng and Muggleton [4], replaces different terms t and s with a second-order term $F(t, s)$ for a newly introduced function variable F. On the other hand, the algorithm . replaces the same occurrence of function symbols with the same function variable. We show that the algorithm . computes the least generalization under $\succeq$ for a pair of second-order terms, and the algorithm . computes the generalization of t and s such that . $(t, s) \sim$ (t, s), that is, . $(t, s) \succeq$ (t, s) and $(t, s) \succeq$. (t, s).

As stated above, it is the main advantage for the second-order terms to preserve the structural information by using . . However, neither . nor . preserves the structural information for given terms. Hence, in this paper, we also introduce the algorithm and show that it computes the generalization of t and s such that (t, s) contains the structural information for t and s completely.

Finally, we discuss the   of the algorithms   , . , . and   such that $A(A(t_1, t_2), t_3) \sim A(t_1, A(t_2, t_3))$ for $A \in \{ \ , . \ , . \ , \quad \}$. Then, we show that the algorithms   , . and   are associative, while the algorithm . is not. Also we improve . to the generalization algorithm for a finite set of terms.

This paper is organized as follows. In Section 2, we prepare some notions necessary for the later discussion. In Section 3, we introduce three algorithms,   , . and . . Then, we show that $(t, s) \sim$. $(t, s) \succeq$. (t, s) and . (t, s) is the least generalization of t and s under $\succeq$. In Section 4, we introduce the algorithm   and show that $(t, s) \succeq$ $(t, s) \succeq$. (t, s). Furthermore, by formulating the   as a tree structure of a term, we show that the context of (t, s) contains both contexts of t and s. In Section 5, we show that the algorithms   , . and   are associative, while the algorithm . is not.

2 Preliminaries

Instead of considering arbitrary second-order languages, we shall restrict our attention to languages containing only simple terms (i.e., terms without variable-binding operators like the λ operator). Throughout this paper, we deal with the term languages adopted by Goldfarb [3,5,8].

Let a L be a quadruple $(\mathrm{IC}_L, \mathrm{IV}_L, \mathrm{FC}_L, \mathrm{FV}_L)$, where

1. IC_L is a set of   (denoted by $a, b, c, \ldots$);
2. IV_L is a set of   (denoted by $x, y, z, \ldots$);
3. FC_L is a set of .   (denoted by $f, g, h, \ldots$);
4. FV_L is a set of .   (denoted by $F, G, H, \ldots$).

Each element $d \in \mathrm{FC}_L \cup \mathrm{FV}_L$ has a fixed arity ≥ 1. $\mathrm{IC}_L, \mathrm{IV}_L, \mathrm{FC}_L$ and FV_L are mutually disjoint. We call an element of $\mathrm{IV}_L \cup \mathrm{FV}_L$ a   simply, and an element of $\mathrm{FC}_L \cup \mathrm{FV}_L$ a .

Definition 1. The L-   are defined inductively as follows.

1. Each $d \in \mathrm{IC}_L \cup \mathrm{IV}_L$ is an L-term.
2. If $d \in \mathrm{FC}_L \cup \mathrm{FV}_L$ has arity $n \geq 1$ and $t_1, \ldots, t_n$ are L-terms, then $d(t_1, \ldots, t_n)$ is an L-term.

We sometimes call an L-term a   or a   simply. In particular, we call an L-term or a second-order term containing no function variables a fi L or a fi   . A term containing no variables is called   . We denote the set of all L-terms and all first-order terms by $\mathcal{T}_L$ and $\mathcal{T}_L^1$, respectively.

An L-term is a second-order λ-term [4,10,13,14] without λ-abstraction. Hence, in order to formulate substitutions, it is necessary to introduce a similar concept to β-reduction in λ-calculus. In this paper, we use the following L^*-terms, instead of β-reduction.

Definition 2. Let BV_L be an infinite collection $\{w_i\}_{i\geq 1}$ of symbols, called   , not contained in L. Then, the L^*-   are defined inductively as follows.

1. Each $d \in IC_L \cup IV_L \cup BV_L$ is an L^*-term.
2. If $d \in FC_L \cup FV_L$ has arity $n \geq 1$ and $t_1,\ldots,t_n$ are L^*-terms, then $d(t_1,\ldots,t_n)$ is an L^*-term.

The   of an L^*-term t is the largest n such that w_n occurs in t. For $n \geq 1$, L^*-terms of rank n intuitively represent n-ary functions.

Let t be an L^*-term. The   of t, denoted by (t), is the outermost symbol occurring in t. Note that, if $t \in IC_L \cup IV_L$, then $(t) = t$. Furthermore, (t) denotes the set of all variables occurring in t, and (t) (, - (t)) denotes the set of all function (, individual) variables occurring in t.

For L^*-terms $t, t_1,\ldots,t_n$, we write $t[t_1,\ldots,t_n]$ for the L^*-term obtained by replacing each occurrence of w_i in t with t_i for all i $(1 \leq i \leq n)$ simultaneously. This is equivalent to β-reduction in λ-calculus [4,10,13,14].

A   in L is a function σ with a finite domain $\mathrm{dom}(\sigma) \subseteq IV_L \cup FV_L$ which maps individual variables to L-terms and n-ary function variables with $n \geq 1$ to L^*-terms of rank $\leq n$. The substitution with an empty domain is called an   and denoted by ε. The result obtained by applying a substitution σ in L to $v \in \mathrm{dom}(\sigma)$ is denoted by $v\sigma$. We assume that $x\sigma \neq x$ and $F\sigma \neq F(w_1,\ldots,w_n)$ for all substitutions σ and variables $x, F \in \mathrm{dom}(\sigma)$. A substitution σ is denoted as $\{s_1/v_1,\ldots,s_m/v_m\}$, where $\mathrm{dom}(\sigma) = \{v_1,\ldots,v_m\}$ and σ maps v_i to s_i for each i $(1 \leq i \leq m)$. Each s_i/v_i is called a   of σ.

Definition 3. Let σ be a substitution $\{s_1/v_1,\ldots,s_m/v_m\}$ in L. The result $t\sigma$ of applying σ to an L^*-term t is defined inductively as follows.

1. If $t = c$, then $t\sigma = c$.
2. If $t = x$ and $x \in \mathrm{dom}(\sigma)$, then $t\sigma = x\sigma$.
3. If $t = x$ and $x \notin \mathrm{dom}(\sigma)$, then $t\sigma = x$.
4. If $t = f(t_1,\ldots,t_n)$, then $t\sigma = f(t_1\sigma,\ldots,t_n\sigma)$.
5. If $t = F(t_1,\ldots,t_n)$ and $F \notin \mathrm{dom}(\sigma)$, then $t\sigma = F(t_1\sigma,\ldots,t_n\sigma)$.
6. If $t = F(t_1,\ldots,t_n)$ and $F \in \mathrm{dom}(\sigma)$, then $t\sigma = (F\sigma)[t_1\sigma,\ldots,t_n\sigma]$.

The   . σ and θ, denoted by $\sigma\theta$, is the substitution such that $v(\sigma\theta) = (v\sigma)\theta$ for any variable v.

We give some results of applying substitutions to L-terms as follows:

1. For an L-term $t_1 = F(x)$, it holds that $t_1\{w_1/F\} = x$, $t_1\{f(w_1)/F, a/x\} = f(a)$, and $t_1\{a/F, b/x\} = a$.
2. For an L-term t_2 $=$ $F(G(a,b), G(c,d))$, it   holds   that $t_2\{w_1/F, f(w_2,w_1)/G\} = f(b,a)$ and $t_2\{f(w_2,w_1)/F, w_1/G\} = f(c,a)$.
3. For an L-term $t_3 = F(F(F(a_1,a_2), F(a_3,a_4)), F(F(a_5,a_6), F(a_7,a_8)))$, the following statements hold.

$$t_3\{w_1/F\} = a_1,$$
$$t_3\{w_2/F\} = a_8,$$
$$t_3\{f(w_2, w_1)/F\} = f(f(f(u_8, u_7), f(u_6, u_5)), f(f(u_4, u_3), f(u_2, u_1))).$$

Definition 4. Let t and s be L-terms.

1. We say that t s if there exists a substitution θ such that $t\theta = s$, and denote it by $t \succeq s$. Furthermore, we denote it by $t \succ s$ if $t \succeq s$ and $s \not\succeq t$.
2. We say that t and s are   if $t \succeq s$ and $s \succeq t$, and denote it by $t \sim s$.

It is obvious that $\succeq$ is a quasi-order on $\mathcal{T}_L$, and called it an   .
If s is a first-order ground term, then the problem of determining whether or not $t \succeq s$ is equivalent to a   [1,8,10]. Hence, the following theorem holds.

Theorem 1 (. Baxter [1]). $t \succeq s$

     . t *fi* s

Huet and Lang [10] have designed the   based on the following   . $\Rightarrow$.

1. **simplification**:

$$\{\langle f(t_1, \ldots, t_n), f(s_1, \ldots, s_n)\rangle\} \cup E \Rightarrow \{\langle t_1, s_1\rangle, \ldots, \langle t_n, s_n\rangle\} \cup E \quad (n \geq 0).$$

2. **imitation** (on F): if $\langle F(t_1, \ldots, t_n), f(s_1, \ldots, s_m)\rangle \in E$ $(n, m \geq 0)$, then

$$E \Rightarrow E\{f(H_1(w_1, \ldots, w_n), \ldots, H_m(w_1, \ldots, w_n))/F\}.$$

Here, $H_1, \ldots, H_m$ are new function variables not appearing in E.
3. **projection** (on F): if $\langle F(t_1, \ldots, t_n), s\rangle \in E$ $(n \geq 1, 1 \leq i \leq n)$, then

$$E \Rightarrow E\{w_i/F\}.$$

It is known that $t \succeq s$ if and only if $\{\langle t, s\rangle\} \Rightarrow^* \emptyset$ [10], where $\Rightarrow^*$ is the transitive closure of $\Rightarrow$.

Definition 5. Let t be an L-term and θ the following substitution.

$$\theta = \{y_1/x_1, \ldots, y_n/x_n, G_1(w_1, \ldots w_{l_1})/F_1, \ldots, G_m(w_1, \ldots w_{l_m})/F_m\}.$$

Here, the arity of G_i is equal to the one of F_i for each i $(1 \leq i \leq m)$. Then, we say that θ is a   . t if the following statements hold.

1. Each x_i $(1 \leq i \leq n)$ and F_j $(1 \leq j \leq m)$ occurs in t.
2. $y_1, \ldots, y_n$ are distinct individual variables such that each y_i is either identical with $x_{i'}$ $(1 \leq i' \leq n)$ occurring in θ or y_i does not occur in t.
3. $G_1, \ldots, G_m$ are distinct function variables such that each G_j is either identical with $F_{j'}$ $(1 \leq j' \leq m)$ occurring in θ or G_j does not occur in t.

For L-terms t and s, t and s are called   if there exist two renaming substitutions θ and σ for t and s such that $t\theta = s$ and $s\sigma = t$, respectively.

It is well-known that first-order terms t and s are variants if and only if $t \sim s$ [16]. On the other hand, for second-order terms, the following proposition holds.

Proposition 1. . t s
$t \sim s$

. Suppose that t and s are variants. By the definition, there exist renaming substitutions θ for t and σ for s such that $t\theta = s$ and $s\sigma = t$. Hence, it holds that $t \succeq s$ and $s \succeq t$, so it holds that $t \sim s$. Conversely, let t and s be L-terms $F(a)$ and x, respectively. Since $F(a)\{x/F\} = x$ and $x\{F(a)/x\} = F(a)$, it holds that $F(a) \sim x$. However, t and s are not variants.   □

3 Generalization Algorithms Under Subsumption

In this section, we introduce the generalization algorithms , . and . for a pair of L-terms under $\succeq$ in $\mathcal{T}_L$.

Definition 6. Let t, s and r be L-terms. We say that r is a   of t and s $\succeq$ in $\mathcal{T}_L$ if it holds that $r \succeq t$ and $r \succeq s$. A generalization r of t and s under $\succeq$ in $\mathcal{T}_L$ is called   in $\mathcal{T}_L$ if it holds that $q \succeq r$ for each generalization q of t and s under $\succeq$ in $\mathcal{T}_L$.

Plotkin [18] and Reynolds [19] have shown that a quasi-ordered set $\langle \mathcal{T}_L^1, \succeq \rangle$ forms a lattice, and hence there always exists the   of t and s under $\succeq$ in $\mathcal{T}_L^1$ for each $t, s \in \mathcal{T}_L^1$. Also they have presented the algorithm   to compute the least generalization of t and s.

We can apply the algorithm   to L-terms, by extending ψ to a bijection from pairs of L-terms to individual variables. Note that $(t, s) \in \mathcal{T}_L^1$, even if $t, s \in \mathcal{T}_L - \mathcal{T}_L^1$. We describe the extended algorithm   as Figure 1, according to the manner of Lassez   [12].

$lg(t, s)$ /* $t, s \in \mathcal{T}_L$ */
/* ψ: a bijection from pairs of L-terms to individual variables */
$lg(f(t_1, \ldots, t_n), f(s_1, \ldots, s_n)) = f(lg(t_1, s_1), \ldots, lg(t_n, s_n))$ if $f \in \mathrm{IC}_L \cup \mathrm{FC}_L$
$\quad\quad\quad\quad lg(t, s) = \psi(t, s)$ otherwise

Fig. 1. A generalization algorithm lg according to Lassez *et al.* [12]

Concerned with the algorithm , we introduce the concept of   , corresponding to a pair applied to ψ in (t, s).

Definition 7. Let t and s be L-terms. Then, the set $\quad(t,s)$ of all $\quad$ of t and s is defined inductively as follows.

1. If $c \in \mathrm{IC}_L$ and $t = s = c$, then $\quad(t,s) = \emptyset$.
2. If $f \in \mathrm{FC}_L$, $t = f(t_1, \ldots, t_n)$ and $s = f(s_1, \ldots, s_n)$, then

$$(t,s) = \quad(t_1, s_1) \cup \cdots \cup \quad(t_n, s_n).$$

3. Otherwise $\quad(t,s) = \{\langle t, s \rangle\}$.

It arises a question whether or not $\quad(t,s)$ is the least generalization of t and s under $\succeq$ in $\mathcal{T}_L$. The following proposition answers this question negatively, even if t and s are first-order terms.

Proposition 2. $\quad$.

$$
\begin{array}{c}
L \qquad t,s \in \mathcal{T}_L^1 \qquad r \in \mathcal{T}_L \qquad\qquad r \succ t \quad r \succ s \\
(t,s) \succ r \\[4pt]
L \qquad t,s \in \mathcal{T}_L \qquad t \succeq s \qquad (t,s) \succ t \\
\quad L \qquad t \in \mathcal{T}_L \qquad (t,t) \succ t
\end{array}
$$

$\quad$ 1. Let t and s be first-order terms $f(a,b)$ and $f(b,a)$. Then, $\quad(t,s) = f(x,y)$. Consider the second-order term $r = f(F(a,b), F(b,a))$. Since $r\{w_1/F\} = t$ and $r\{w_2/F\} = s$, $f(F(a,b), F(b,a))$ is a generalization of t and s under $\succeq$ in $\mathcal{T}_L$. Furthermore, it holds that $\quad(t,s) \succeq r$, since $\quad(t,s)\{F(a,b)/x, F(b,a)/y\} = r$. However, there exists no substitution θ such that $r\theta = f(x,y)$.
2. Let t and s be $f(F(a), F(b))$ and $f(a,b)$, respectively. Then, it holds that $t \succeq s$, because $f(F(a), F(b))\{w_1/F\} = s$, and $\quad(t,s) = f(x,y)$. However, it also holds that $\quad(t,s) \succ t$.
3. Let t be $f(F(a), F(b))$. Then, it holds that $\quad(t,t) = f(x,y) \succ t$. $\qquad\square$

Instead of the algorithm $\quad$, we introduce the algorithm $\,.\,$ described as Figure 2, which is motivated by Feng and Muggleton [4]. Here, $\,.\,$ is an abbreviation of an $\quad.\quad$, because the two substitutions $\{w_1/F\}$ and $\{w_2/F\}$ such that $.\ (t,s)\{w_1/F\} = t$ and $.\ (t,s)\{w_2/F\} = s$ are corresponding to just $\quad$ but not $\quad.\quad$

$ifg(t,s)$ /* $t, s \in \mathcal{T}_L$ */
/* F: a new function variable not appearing in t and s */
$ifg(f(t_1, \ldots, t_n), f(s_1, \ldots, s_n)) = f(ifg(t_1, s_1), \ldots, ifg(t_n, s_n))$ if $f \in \mathrm{IC}_L \cup \mathrm{FC}_L$
$\qquad\qquad ifg(t,s) = F(t,s) \qquad\qquad\qquad$ otherwise

---

Fig. 2. An imitation-free generalization algorithm ifg

Let t and s be the following first-order terms:

$$s = f(g(a), g(b)), \; t = f(h(b), h(a))$$

Consider the following second-order terms:

$$
\begin{aligned}
g_1 &= f(F(g(a), h(b)), F(g(b), h(a))), \\
g_2 &= f(F(a, b), F(b, a)), \\
g_3 &= f(F(x, y), F(y, x)), \\
g_4 &= f(x, y), \\
g_5 &= f(F(x), F(y)).
\end{aligned}
$$

All g_i's are generalizations of t and s under $\succeq$ in $\mathcal{T}_L$, that is, $g_i \succeq t$ and $g_i \succeq s$ for $1 \le i \le 5$. Furthermore, it holds that $g_5 \sim g_4 \sim g_3 \succ g_2 \succ g_1$, because the following statements hold.

$$
\begin{aligned}
g_5\{w_1/F, F(g(a), g(b))/x, F(h(b), h(a))/y\} &= g_1, \\
g_5\{w_1/F, F(a, b)/x, F(b, a)/y\} &= g_2, \\
g_5\{w_1/F, F(x, y)/x, F(y, x)/y\} &= g_3, \\
g_5\{w_1/F\} &= g_4, \\
g_4\{F(x, y)/x, F(y, x)/y\} &= g_3, \\
g_4\{F(x)/x, F(y)/y\} &= g_5, \\
g_3\{w_1/F\} &= g_4, \\
g_3\{F(w_1)/F\} &= g_5, \\
g_2\{F(g(w_1), h(w_2))/F\} &= g_1.
\end{aligned}
$$

Lemma 1. $t, s \in \mathcal{T}_L$.

- $(t, s) \succeq \; . \; (t, s)$
- . $(t, t) \sim t$
- . $t \succeq s$. $(t, s) \sim t$
- . $t \sim s$. $(t, s) \sim t$. $(t, s) \sim s$

- Suppose that (t, s) is of the form $\{\langle t_1, s_1 \rangle, \ldots, \langle t_n, s_n \rangle\}$.
1. It holds that $(t, s)\{F(t_i, s_i)/\psi(t_i, s_i)\} \; = \; . \; (t, s)$. Hence, $(t, s) \succeq$. (t, s).
2. By the definition of the algorithm . , . (t, t) is obtained from t by replacing an individual variable x in t with $F(x, x)$ and a subterm $G(t_1, \ldots, t_n)$ in t ($G \in \mathrm{FV}_L$) with $F(G(t_1, \ldots, t_n), G(t_1, \ldots, t_n))$. Since . $(t, t)\{w_1/F\} = t$, it holds that . $(t, t) \succeq t$. Conversely, let θ be the following substitution:

$$\{F(x, x)/x \mid x \in \;(t)\} \cup \{F(G(w_1, \ldots, w_n), G(w_1, \ldots, w_n))/G \mid G \in . \;(t)\}.$$

Then, it holds that $t\theta = . \; (t, t)$. Hence, it holds that $t \succeq . \; (t, t)$.
3. It is obvious that . $(t, s) \succeq t$. Conversely, since $t \succeq s$, it holds that $(t_i) \in \;(t)$ for each $1 \le i \le n$. Let θ be a substitution $\{F(t_i, s_i)/ \;(t_i) \mid 1 \le i \le n\}$. Then, it holds that $t\theta = . \; (t, s)$. Hence, it holds that $t \succeq . \; (t, s)$.
4. It is obvious by the statement 3.   □

Theorem 2. $t, s \in \mathcal{T}_L$. (t, s) . t s
$\succeq$ $\mathcal{T}_L$

· It is sufficient to show that every generalization r of t and s subsumes · (t, s). We show this statement by structural induction on t and s.

Suppose that ·(t), ·$(s) \in \mathrm{IC}_L \cup \mathrm{IV}_L$. (In this case, $t, s \in \mathrm{IC}_L \cup \mathrm{IV}_L$.) If $t = s$ and $t, s \in \mathrm{IC}_L$, then ·$(t, s) = t = s$. If $t \neq s$ and $t, s \in \mathrm{IC}_L$, then r is of the form either $x \in \mathrm{IV}_L$ or $G(\bar{r})$ ($G \in \mathrm{FV}_L$). Thus, it holds that $x\{\cdot(t, s)/x\} = \cdot(t, s)$ and $G(\bar{r})\{\cdot(t, s)/G\} = \cdot(t, s)$, respectively. Hence, it holds that $r \succeq \cdot(t, s)$. If $t, s \in \mathrm{IV}_L$, then $t \sim s$, so it holds that ·$(t, s) \sim t$ by Lemma 1.4. If $t \in \mathrm{IV}_L$ and $s \in \mathrm{IC}_L$, then it holds that $t \succ s$, so it holds that ·$(t, s) \sim t$ by Lemma 1.3.

Suppose that ·(t), ·$(s) \in \mathrm{FC}_L \cup \mathrm{FV}_L$. If ·$(t)$, ·$(s) \in \mathrm{FV}_L$, then it holds that $t \sim s$, so it holds that ·$(t, s) \sim t$ by Lemma 1.4. If ·$(t) \in \mathrm{FV}_L$ and ·$(s) \in \mathrm{FC}_L$, then it holds that $t \succ s$, so it holds that ·$(t, s) \sim t$ by Lemma 1.3. If ·(t), ·$(s) \in \mathrm{FC}_L$ and ·$(t) \neq$ ·(s), then r is of the form either $x \in \mathrm{IV}_L$ or $G(\bar{r})$ ($G \in \mathrm{FV}_L$). By using the same discussion to the above case, it holds that $r \succeq \cdot(t, s)$.

Suppose that ·(t), ·$(s) \in \mathrm{FC}_L$ and ·$(t) = $·$(s)$. Let t and s be of the forms $f(t_1, \ldots, t_n)$ and $f(s_1, \ldots, s_n)$. In this case, r is one of the forms $x \in \mathrm{IV}_L$, $G(\bar{r})$ ($G \in \mathrm{FV}_L$) or $f(r_1, \ldots, r_n)$. If r is either x or $G(\bar{r})$, then it holds that $r \succeq \cdot(t, s)$ as above. Otherwise, by the induction hypothesis, it holds that $r_i \succeq \cdot(t_i, s_i)$, that is, there exists a substitution θ_i such that $r_i \theta_i = \cdot(t_i, s_i)$ for each i ($1 \leq i \leq n$). Without loss of generality, the newly introduced variable in ·(t_i, s_i) is uniquely assumed to be F for each i. Since $r \succeq t$ and $r \succeq s$, we can suppose that there exist substitutions τ and σ such that $r\tau = t$ and $r\sigma = s$. By the forms of r, t and s, it holds that $r_i \tau = t_i$ and $r_i \sigma = s_i$ for each i. Since ·$(t_i, s_i)\{w_1/F\} = t_i$ and ·$(t_i, s_i)\{w_2/F\} = s_i$, it holds that $r_i \theta_i\{w_1/F\} = \cdot(t_i, s_i)\{w_1/F\} = t_i$ and $r_i \theta_i\{w_2/F\} = \cdot(t_i, s_i)\{w_2/F\} = s_i$ for each i. Then, we can suppose that $\theta_i\{w_1/F\} = \tau$ and $\theta_i\{w_2/F\} = \sigma$ for each i, which implies that we can let $\theta = \theta_1 = \cdots = \theta_n$. Hence, it holds that $r\theta = f(r_1, \ldots, r_n)\theta = f(r_1\theta, \ldots, r_n\theta) = f(\cdot(t_1, s_1), \ldots, \cdot(t_n, s_n)) = \cdot(t, s)$, that is, $r \succeq \cdot(t, s)$.

Hence, it holds that $r \succeq \cdot(t, s)$ for every generalization r of t and s, that is, ·(t, s) is the least generalization of t and s under $\succeq$ in $\mathcal{T}_L$. □

In contrast to · , we introduce the ·   algorithm · described as Figure 3. Here, ψ is a bijection from pairs of L-terms to individual variables, and φ is a new bijection from function symbols in L to function variables.

Let t and s be first-order terms $f(a, g(a))$ and $f(b, h(b))$, respectively. Then, it holds that ·$(t, s) = f(x, y)$, ·$(t, s) = f(F(a, b), F(g(a), h(b)))$, and ·$(t, s) = f(x, G(x))$.

Furthermore, let t and s be the following first-order terms.

$$s = f(h(a, b), h(b, c)), \; t = g(k(a), k(b), k(c))$$

Then, the following statements hold.

·$(t, s) = x$,

· $(t, s) = F(f(h(a, b), h(b, c)), g(k(a), k(b), k(c)))$,

· $(s, t) = F(G(a, x_1), G(x_2, b), G(x_3, x_4), G(x_1, x_5), G(b, x_6), G(x_7, c))$.

```
pfg(t, s)  /* t, s ∈ T_L */
/* ψ: a bijection from pairs of L-terms to individual variables
   φ: a bijection from pairs of function symbols in L to function variables */
pfg(f(t_1, ..., t_n), f(s_1, ..., s_n)) = f(pfg(t_1, s_1), ..., pfg(t_n, s_n))
          if f ∈ IC_L ∪ FC_L
pfg(d(t_1, ..., t_n), e(s_1, ..., s_m))
      = φ(d, e)(pfg(t_1, s_1), ..., pfg(t_1, s_m), ..., pfg(t_n, s_1), ..., pfg(t_n, s_m))
          if d, e ∈ FC_L ∪ FV_L and d ≠ e
pfg(t, s) = ψ(t, s)
          otherwise
```

Fig. 3. A projection-free generalization algorithm *pfg*

Note that the substitutions θ and σ such that $\centerdot (t, s)\theta = t$ and $\centerdot (t, s)\sigma = s$ are not determined uniquely in general. In this case, it holds that $\centerdot (t, s)\theta = t$ and $\centerdot (t, s)\sigma = s$ for $\theta = \{f(w_1, w_2)/F, h(w_1, w_2)/G, b/x_1, a/x_2\}$ and $\sigma = \{g(w_1, w_2, w_6)/F, k(w_2)/G, a/x_1\}$. Such θ and σ contain no binding of the form w_i/F, so we call $\centerdot (t, s)$ a $\centerdot$ generalization algorithm.

Theorem 3. $\qquad t, s \in T_L \qquad\qquad \centerdot (t, s) \sim (t, s)$

$\centerdot$ In this proof, we denote a bijection ψ in (t, s) by ψ'.
Let θ be the following substitution:

$$\theta = \{\varphi(d, e)(\centerdot (t_1, s_1), \ldots, \centerdot (t_n, s_m))/\psi'(d(t_1, \ldots, t_n), e(s_1, \ldots, s_m)) \mid \langle d(t_1, \ldots, t_n), e(s_1, \ldots, s_m)\rangle \in (t, s) \ (n, m \geq 1, d \neq e)\}.$$

Hence, it holds that $(t, s)\theta = \centerdot (t, s)$, so $(t, s) \succeq \centerdot (t, s)$.
Conversely, we divide (t, s) into $D_\varphi \cup D_\psi$, where:

$$D_\varphi = \{\langle t_i, s_i \rangle \in (t, s) \mid (t_i), (s_i) \in FC_L \cup FV_L\},$$
$$D_\psi = (t, s) - D_\varphi.$$

Note that D_φ is the set of all disagreement pairs to which is applied φ in $\centerdot (t, s)$. Then, let σ be the following substitution:

$$\sigma = \{\psi'(t_i, s_i)/\varphi((t_i), (s_i)) \mid \langle t_i, s_i \rangle \in D_\varphi\}.$$

Hence, it holds that $\centerdot (t, s)\sigma = (t, s)$, so $\centerdot (t, s) \succeq (t, s)$. □

4 Structure-Preserving Generalization Algorithm

It is the main advantage for the second-order terms to preserve the structural information by using $\centerdot$. However, neither $\centerdot$ nor $\centerdot$ preserves the structural information for given terms. Hence, in this section, we introduce the $\qquad\qquad$ algorithm.

An L-term can be described as an
L. Then, in this paper, we formulate the structural information of an L-term
t as the tree   , and we call it a   of t and denote it by (t).
Also the   of t is defined as the length of the longest pass from the root to
a leaf in (t) and denoted by (t).

Definition 8. Let t and s be L-terms. Then, we say that t
s if (s) is an ordered rooted subtree of (s) by identifying the root of (s)
with one of (t), and denote it by $(t) \sqsupseteq$ (s).

We point out that no algorithms   ,   and   preserves the structural
information of given terms as follows.

Proposition 3. $t, s \in \mathcal{T}_L$.

$(t) \sqsupseteq$ ((t, s)) $(s) \sqsupseteq$ ((t, s))
((t, s)) $\leq \min\{$ (t), $(s)\}$

                                                        . (t, s) t s
$\max\{$ (t), $(s)\} \leq$ ($\cdot$ (t, s)) $\leq \max\{$ (t), $(s)\} + 1$
                                                        . (t, s) t s

($\cdot$ (t, s)) $\leq \min\{$ (t), $(s)\}$

. The statements 1 and 2 obviously hold by the application of ψ in   . The
statement 3 holds since . $(f(a, a, a), g(a, a, a)) = F(f(a, a, a), g(a, a, a))$. The
statement 4 holds since, in every branch in   ($\cdot$ (t, s)), .   replaces a subterm
t' of t and a subterm s' of s with $F(t', s')$ at most once. The statement 5 follows
that . $(f(h(h(a)), h(h(b))), g(a, b)) = F(x, y, z, w)$. The statement 6 holds by
the application of ψ in . . The depth does not change by applying φ in . . □

The reason why Proposition 3.5 holds is that . $(t, s) = \psi(t, s) \in IV_L$ for
t such that $(t) \in FC_L \cup FV_L$ and $s \in IC_L \cup IV_L$. By improving . to
introduce function variables into such a case, we design the
            algorithm   described as Figure 4. Here, ψ is a bijection from
pairs of L-terms to individual variables, and φ is a bijection from pairs of symbols
containing at least one function symbol in L to function variables.

For $t = f(h(h(a)), h(h(b)))$ and $s = g(a, b)$ in the proof of Proposition 3.5, it holds that $(s, t) = F(G(G(a)), H(H(x)), G(G(y)), H(H(b)))$.
Furthermore, let t and s be first-order terms $f(h(h(a)), b)$ and $g(a, h(h(b)))$,
respectively. Then, the following statements hold.

$(t, s) = x,$
. $(t, s) = F(f(h(h(a)), b), g(a, h(h(b)))),$
. $(s, t) = F(x, h(h(y)), z, w),$
$(s, t) = F(G(G(a)), h(h(x)), y, H(H(b))).$

Lemma 2. $t, s \in \mathcal{T}_L$ $(t, s) \succeq t$ $(t, s) \succeq s$

$$spg(t, s) \ /^* \ t, s \in \mathcal{T}_L \ ^*/$$

$/^*$ ψ: a bijection from pairs of L-terms to individual variables

φ: a bijection from pairs of symbols containing at least one function symbol in L
to function variables $^*/$

$$spg(f(t_1, \ldots, t_n), f(s_1, \ldots, s_n)) = f(spg(t_1, s_1), \ldots, spg(t_n, s_n))$$
$$\text{if } f \in \mathrm{IC}_L \cup \mathrm{FC}_L$$

$$spg(d(t_1, \ldots, t_n), e(s_1, \ldots, s_m))$$
$$= \varphi(d, e)(spg(t_1, s_1), \ldots, spg(t_1, s_m), \ldots, spg(t_n, s_1), \ldots, spg(t_n, s_m))$$
$$\text{if } d, e \in \mathrm{FC}_L \cup \mathrm{FV}_L$$

$$spg(d(t_1, \ldots, t_n), s) = \varphi(d, s)(spg(t_1, s), \ldots, spg(t_n, s))$$
$$\text{if } d \in \mathrm{FC}_L \cup \mathrm{FV}_L \text{ and } s \in \mathrm{IC}_L \cup \mathrm{IV}_L$$

$$spg(t, e(s_1, \ldots, s_m)) = \varphi(t, e)(spg(t, s_1), \ldots, spg(t, s_m))$$
$$\text{if } e \in \mathrm{FC}_L \cup \mathrm{FV}_L \text{ and } t \in \mathrm{IC}_L \cup \mathrm{IV}_L$$

$$spg(t, s) = \psi(t, s)$$
$$\text{otherwise}$$

Fig. 4. A structure-preserving generalization algorithm spg

First we show the statement $(t, s) \succeq t$. Note that all variables in (t, s) are newly introduced variables by the bijections φ and ψ.

Suppose that $(\ (t, s), t)$ is of the form $\{\langle l_1, t_1 \rangle, \ldots, \langle l_m, t_m \rangle\}$. By the definition of (t, s), it holds that $(l_i) \in \mathrm{IV}_L \cup \mathrm{FV}_L$. For each i, we construct the binding b_i as follows.

If $t_i \in \mathrm{IC}_L \cup \mathrm{IV}_L$, then let b_i be a binding $t_i / (l_i)$. Otherwise, suppose that $(t_i) \in \mathrm{FC}_L \cup \mathrm{FV}_L$ and (t_i) is n-ary. If $(l_i) \in \mathrm{IV}_L$, then let b_i be a binding $t_i / (l_i)$. If $(l_i) \in \mathrm{FV}_L$, then we can suppose that (l_i) is l-ary and there exists a $k (\geq 1)$ such that $nk = l$ by the definition of (t, s). Then, let b_i be a binding $(t_i)(w_1, w_{k+1}, \ldots, w_{(n-1)k+1}) / (l_i)$.

Let θ be a substitution $\{b_1, \ldots, b_m\}$. By the construction of b_i, it is obvious that $(t, s)\theta = t$.

In order to show the statement $(t, s) \succeq s$, suppose that $(\ (t, s), s)$ is of the form $\{\langle l_1, s_1 \rangle, \ldots, \langle l_m, s_m \rangle\}$. Then, we can show this statement as similar as the above case, by replacing the binding

$$(t_i)(w_1, w_{k+1}, \ldots, w_{(n-1)k+1}) / (l_i)$$

with a binding $(s_i)(w_1, w_2, \ldots, w_n) / (l_i)$. □

As similar as , the substitutions θ and σ such that $(t, s)\theta = t$ and $(t, s)\sigma = s$ are not determined uniquely in general.

Theorem 4. $t, s \in \mathcal{T}_L$ $(t, s) \succeq$ $(t, s) \succeq$. (t, s)

In this proof, we denote a bijection ψ in (t, s) by ψ'.
Let θ be the following substitution:

$$\theta = \{\varphi(d,e)(\quad (t_1,s_1),\ldots,\quad (t_n,s_m))/\psi'(d(t_1,\ldots,t_n),e(s_1,\ldots,s_m))$$
$$|\ \langle d(t_1,\ldots,t_n),e(s_1,\ldots,s_m)\rangle \in \quad (t,s)\ (n,m \geq 1, d \neq e)\}$$
$$\cup\ \{\psi(d,s)(\quad (t_1,s),\ldots,\quad (t_n,s))/\psi'(d(t_1,\ldots,t_n),s)$$
$$|\ \langle d(t_1,\ldots,t_n),s\rangle \in \quad (t,s)\ (n \geq 1, s \in \mathrm{IC}_L \cup \mathrm{IV}_L)\}$$
$$\cup\ \{\varphi(t,e)(\quad (t,s_1),\ldots,\quad (t,s_m))/\psi'(t,e(s_1,\ldots,s_m))$$
$$|\ \langle t,e(s_1,\ldots,s_m)\rangle \in \quad (t,s)\ (m \geq 1, t \in \mathrm{IC}_L \cup \mathrm{IV}_L)\}.$$

Hence, it holds that $(t,s)\theta = \quad (t,s)$, so it holds that $(t,s) \succeq \quad (t,s)$. On the other hand, the statement $(t,s) \succeq \ .\ (t,s)$ is obvious by Theorem 2 and Lemma 2. $\qquad\square$

The subsume-equivalence of Theorem 4 does not hold in general: Consider $t = f(a,a,a)$ and $s = f(a,F(a),F(F(a)))$. Then, the following statements hold.

$$(t,s) = f(a,x,y),$$
$$.\ (t,s) = f(a,x,y),$$
$$(t,s) = f(a,G(a),G(G(a))).$$

In this case, there exists no substitution θ such that $(t,s)\theta = \quad (t,s)(\sim$ $.\ (t,s))$. Furthermore, for $t = f(a,g(a))$ and $s = f(b,h(b))$ in Example 3, it holds that $(t,s) = f(x,F(x)) \succ \ .\ (t,s) = f(F(a,b),F(g(a),h(b)))$.

Finally, we show that $\quad$ preserves the structural information as follows.

Theorem 5. $\quad t,s \in \mathcal{T}_L \qquad .$

$$(\quad (t,s)) \sqsupseteq \quad (t) \qquad (\quad (t,s)) \sqsupseteq \quad (s)$$
$$(\quad (t,s)) = \max\{\quad (t),\quad (s)\}$$

$.$ 1. We show the statement $(\quad (t,s)) \sqsupseteq \quad (t)$ by structural induction on t. We can show the statement $(\quad (t,s)) \sqsupseteq \quad (s)$ similarly. Suppose that $t \in \mathrm{IC}_L \cup \mathrm{IV}_L$. Then, it holds that:

$$(t,s) = \begin{cases} \bullet\ t & \text{if } t = s, \\ \bullet\ x & \text{if } t \neq s \text{ and } s \in \mathrm{IC}_L \cup \mathrm{IV}_L, \\ \bullet\ \varphi(t,e)(\quad (t,s_1),\ldots,\quad (t,s_m)) & \text{if } t \neq s \text{ and } s = e(s_1,\ldots,s_m). \end{cases}$$

For all of the above cases, it holds that $(\quad (t,s)) \sqsupseteq \quad (t)$. Suppose that t is of the form $d(t_1,\ldots,t_n)$ $(d \in \mathrm{FC}_L \cup \mathrm{FV}_L)$, and $(\quad (t_i,s)) \sqsupseteq \quad (t_i)$ for each s. Then, it holds that:

$$(t,s) = \begin{cases} \vdots\ f(\quad (t_1,s_1),\ldots,\quad (t_n,s_n)) & \text{if } d = f \in \mathrm{FC}_L \\ & \text{and } s = f(s_1,\ldots,s_n), \\ \vdots\ \varphi(d,s)(\quad (t_1,s),\ldots,\quad (t_n,s)) & \text{if } s \in \mathrm{IC}_L \cup \mathrm{IV}_L, \\ \varphi(d,e)(\quad (t_1,s_1),\ldots,\quad (t_n,s_m)) & \text{if } s = e(s_1,\ldots,s_m). \end{cases}$$

For the first case, by the induction hypothesis, it holds that:

$$(\quad (t,s)) = \quad (f(\quad (t_1,s_1),\ldots,\quad (t_n,s_n))) \sqsupseteq \quad (f(t_1,\ldots,t_n)) = \quad (t).$$

For the second case, by the induction hypothesis, it holds that:

$$(\quad(t,s)) = \quad(\varphi(d,s)(\quad(t_1,s),\ldots,\quad(t_n,s))) \sqsupseteq \quad(\varphi(d,s)(t_1,\ldots,t_n)).$$

By the form of t, it holds that $\quad(\varphi(d,s)(t_1,\ldots,t_n)) = \quad(t)$. Thus, it holds that $(\quad(t,s)) \sqsupseteq \quad(t)$.

For the third case, by the induction hypothesis, it holds that:

$$\begin{aligned}
(\quad(t,s)) = \quad&(\varphi(d,e)(\quad(t_1,s_1),\ldots,\quad(t_1,s_m),\\
&\qquad\ldots,\quad(t_n,s_1),\ldots,\quad(t_n,s_m)))\\
\sqsupseteq \quad&(\varphi(d,e)(\quad(t_1,s_1),\ldots,\quad(t_n,s_1)))\\
\sqsupseteq \quad&(\varphi(d,e)(t_1,\ldots,t_n)).
\end{aligned}$$

By the form of t, it holds that $\quad(\varphi(d,s)(t_1,\ldots,t_n)) = \quad(t)$. Thus, it holds that $(\quad(t,s)) \sqsupseteq \quad(t)$.

2. In the algorithm $\quad$, φ is applied until either t or s achieves to leaves in $\quad(t)$ or $\quad(s)$, i.e., individual constants or individual variables. □

5 Associativity

In this section, we discuss the $\quad$ of the algorithms $\quad$, $\cdot$, $\quad$ and $\quad$ such that $A(A(t_1,t_2),t_3) \sim A(t_1,A(t_2,t_3))$ for $A \in \{\quad,\cdot,\quad,\cdot,\quad\}$.

Plotkin [18] and Reynolds [19] have shown that there exists the $\quad(S)$ of a finite set S of first-order terms under $\succeq$ in $\mathcal{T}_L^1$. Since the algorithm $\quad(t,s)$ is $\quad$, that is, $(\quad(t_1,t_2),t_3) \sim (t_1,\quad(t_2,t_3))$, $\quad(S)$ can be realized as $\quad(t_1,\quad(\cdots\quad(t_{m-1},t_m)\cdots))$ for a finite set $S = \{t_1,\ldots,t_m\}$. Note that, as similar as $\quad(t,s)$, $\quad(S)$ is also applied to a finite set S of L-terms. On the other hand, $\cdot$ is $\quad$ associative as follows.

Proposition 4. $\quad t_1,t_2,t_3 \in \mathcal{T}_L$

$$\cdot\,(\cdot\,(t_1,t_2),t_3) \not\sim \cdot\,(t_1,\cdot\,(t_2,t_3))$$

$\cdot$ Let t_1, t_2 and t_3 be L-terms $f(a,b)$, $f(b,c)$ and $f(c,a)$, respectively. Then:

$$\begin{aligned}
\cdot\,(\cdot\,(t_1,t_2),t_3) &= f(G_1(F_1(a,b),c),G_1(F_1(b,c),a)),\\
\cdot\,(t_1,\cdot\,(t_2,t_3)) &= f(G_2(a,F_2(b,c)),G_2(b,F_2(c,a))).
\end{aligned}$$

However, it holds that $\cdot\,(\cdot\,(t_1,t_2),t_3) \not\sim \cdot\,(t_1,\cdot\,(t_2,t_3))$. □

Since $\quad$ is associative and by Theorem 3, the following corollary holds.

Corollary 1. $\quad t,s,r \in \mathcal{T}_L \qquad \cdot\,(\cdot\,(t,s),r) \sim \cdot\,(t,\cdot\,(s,r))$

Furthermore, the following theorem also holds.

Theorem 6. $\quad t,s,r \in \mathcal{T}_L \qquad (\quad(t,s),r) \sim \quad(t,\quad(s,r))$

By Corollary 1, it is sufficient to show the different case between　.　and that either (1)　　$(t) \in FC_L \cup FV_L$ and $s, r \in IC_L \cup IV_L$ or (2)　　(t),　$(s) \in FC_L \cup FV_L$ and $r \in IC_L \cup IV_L$. We show only the statement (1) by structural induction on t, s and r. We can show the statement (2) similarly.

Suppose that $t = d(t_1, \ldots, t_n)$ and $s, r \in IC_L \cup IV_L$. Also suppose that $(\ (t_i, s), r) \sim (t_i, (s, r))$ for each i $(1 \leq i \leq n)$. Since $(s, r) = \psi(s, r)$, the induction hypothesis is that $(\ (t_i, s), r) \sim (t_i, \psi(s, r))$. Then, there exist substitutions θ_i and σ_i such that $(\ (t_i, s), r)\theta_i = (t_i, \psi(s, r))$ and $(t_i, \psi(s, r))\sigma_i = (\ (t_i, s), r)$. On the other hand, the following statements hold.

$$(\ (t, s), r) = (\varphi(d, s)(\ (t_1, s), \ldots, (t_n, s)), r)$$
$$= \varphi(\varphi(d, s), r)(\ (\ (t_1, s), r), \ldots, (\ (t_n, s), r)),$$
$$(t, (s, r)) = (d(t_1, \ldots, t_n), \psi(s, r))$$
$$= \varphi(d, \psi(s, r))(\ (t_1, \psi(s, r)), \ldots, (t_n, \psi(s, r))).$$

Let θ and σ be the following substitutions.

$$\theta = \theta_1 \cdots \theta_n \{\varphi(d, \psi(s, r))(w_1, \ldots, w_n)/\varphi(\varphi(d, s), r)\},$$
$$\sigma = \sigma_1 \cdots \sigma_n \{\varphi(\varphi(d, s), r)(w_1, \ldots, w_n)/\varphi(d, \psi(s, r))\}.$$

By the induction hypothesis, it holds that $(\ (t, s), r)\theta = (t, (s, r))$ and $(t, (s, r))\sigma = (\ (t, s), r)$. Hence, it holds that $(\ (t, s), r) \sim (t, (s, r))$. □

By using the similar method in [18,19], we can obviously extend the algorithm　.　to the one for a finite set of L-terms as Figure 5. Also we can extend the algorithm　.　to the one for a finite set of L-terms as Figure 6.

$lg(S)$ /* $S = \{t_i \in \mathcal{T}_L \mid 1 \leq i \leq m\}$ */
/* ψ: a bijection from a set of L-terms to individual variable */
$lg(S) = f(lg(S_1), \ldots, lg(S_n))$ if $t_i = f(t_1^i, \ldots, t_n^i)$ for each i $(1 \leq i \leq m)$
$\qquad\qquad\qquad\qquad\qquad$ and $S_j = \{t_j^1, \ldots, t_j^m\}$ for each j $(1 \leq j \leq n)$
$lg(S) = \psi(t_1, \ldots, t_m)$ $\qquad$ otherwise

Fig. 5. A generalization algorithm lg for a finite set of L-terms [18,19]

It is obvious that　(S) and　.　(S) are　　the least generalization of S under $\succeq$ in $\mathcal{T}_L$ by Proposition 4. By Lemma 1, the following corollary also holds.

Corollary 2.　fi　　$S \subseteq \mathcal{T}_L$　　　$(S) \succeq$　.　(S)

6 Conclusion

In this paper, we have introduced the four　　　　　　　　for a pair of second-order terms,　,　.　,　.　and　　. The algorithm　　is a simple extension of the least generalization algorithm for a pair of first-order terms. The

$$ifg(S) \quad /* \ S = \{t_i \in \mathcal{T}_L \mid 1 \le i \le m\} \ */$$
$$/* \ F: \text{a new function variable not appearing in } S \ */$$
$$ifg(S) = f(ifg(S_1), \ldots, ifg(S_n)) \quad \text{if } t_i = f(t_1^i, \ldots, t_n^i) \text{ for each } i \ (1 \le i \le m)$$
$$\qquad\qquad\qquad\qquad \text{and } S_j = \{t_j^1, \ldots, t_j^m\} \text{ for each } j \ (1 \le j \le n)$$
$$ifg(S) = F(t_1, \ldots, t_m) \qquad\quad \text{otherwise}$$

Fig. 6. An imitation-free generalization algorithm *ifg* for a finite set of L-terms

algorithm . computes the   . generalization, which is the least generalization under $\succeq$ for a pair of second-order terms, and the algorithm . computes the   . generalization such that $. \ (t, s) \sim \ (t, s)$. Furthermore, the algorithm   computes the   , that is, $(\quad (t, s)) \sqsupseteq \quad (t)$ and $(\quad (t, s)) \sqsupseteq \quad (s)$. Finally, we have shown that the algorithms   ,   .   and   are associative, while the algorithm . is not. We have also improved the algorithm . to the generalization algorithm for a finite set of terms.

In this paper, we adopt the generality order as a simple instantiation order $\succeq$. As we have seen in this paper, it is not an appropriate order to characterize both the least generalization and the structure-preserving generalization. In particular, under $\succeq$, it holds that $x \sim F(a)$ as shown in the proof of Proposition 1. On the other hand, since F is a function variable and x is an individual variable, it is possible to characterize both the least generalization and the structure-preserving generalization, by introducing some semantics of variables into $\succeq$. It is a future work to study such possibility.

Furthermore, as stated in the last of Section 5, there exists no generalization algorithm that outputs the least generalization for a finite set of L-terms under $\succeq$, by extending our algorithms. Hence, it is also a future work to design the least generalization algorithm for a finite set, by adding some information to $\succeq$ or reformulating $\succeq$.

In this paper, by introducing the context of second-order terms, we have designed the structure-preserving generalization algorithm   . However, the result computed by   is large as a tree description. Hence, it is a future work to improve to obtain the structure-preserving generalization with small size as a tree description.

In order to apply the generalization techniques given by this paper to semistructural data such as HTML or XML documents, it is necessary to relax the usage of function constants as tags that the same function constant have different arities or function constants are associative or commutative. It is a future work to formulate the generalization for second-order terms with such relaxation. and without computational difficulty (. [11]). It is also a future work to incorporate our works with the researches for graph terms (, [20,21]).

Acknowledgment. The authors would like to thank the anonymous referees for valuable comments to revise the preliminary version of this paper.

References

1. L. D. Baxter, *The complexity of unification*, Doctoral Thesis, Department of Computer Science, University of Waterloo, 1977.
2. S. Dietzen, F. Pfenning, *Higher-order and modal logic as a framework for explanation-based generalization*, Mach. Learn. **9**, 23–55, 1992.
3. W. M. Farmer, *Simple second-order languages for which unification is undecidable*, Theor. Comput. Sci. **87**, 25–41, 1991.
4. C. Feng, S. Muggleton, *Towards inductive generalisation in higher order logic*, in: Proc. 9th Internat. Conf. Machine Learning, 154–162, 1992.
5. W. D. Goldfarb, *The undecidability of the second-order unification problem*, Theor. Comput. Sci. **13**, 225–230, 1981.
6. M. Harao, *Proof discovery in LK system by analogy*, in: Proc. 3rd Asian Computing Science Conf., LNCS **1345**, 197–211, 1997.
7. R. Hasker, *The reply of program derivations*, Ph.D. Thesis, Department of Computer Science, University of Illinois at Urbana-Champaign, 1995.
8. K. Hirata, K. Yamada, M. Harao, *Tractable and intractable second-order matching problems*, J. Symb. Comput. **37**, 611-628, 2004.
9. G. P. Huet, *A unification algorithm for typed λ-calculus*, Theor. Comput. Sci. **1**, 27–57, 1975.
10. G. P. Huet, B. Lang, *Proving and applying program transformations expressed with second-order patterns*, Acta Inform. **11**, 31–55, 1978.
11. D. Kapur, P. Narendran, *Complexity of unification problems with associative-commutative operators*, J. Auto. Reason. **9**, 261–288, 1992.
12. J.-L. Lassez, M. J. Maher, L. Marriot, *Unification revisited*, in J. Minker (ed.): Foundations of deductive databases and logic programming, Morgan-Kaufmann, 587–625, 1988.
13. J. Lu, J. Mylopoulos, M. Harao, M. Hagiya, *Higher order generalization and its application in program verification*, Ann. Math. Artif. Intel. **28**, 107–126, 2000.
14. D. Miller, *A logic programming language with lambda-abstraction, function variables, and simple unification*, J. Logic Comput. **1**, 497–536, 1991.
15. S. Muggleton, *Inverse entailment and Progol*, New Generat. Comput. **13**, 245–286, 1995.
16. S.-H. Nienhuys-Cheng, R. de Wolf, *Foundations of inductive logic programming*, LNAI **1228**, 1997.
17. F. Pfenning, *Unification and anti-unification in the calculus of constructions*, in: Proc. 6th Annual Symp. Logic in Computer Science, 74–85, 1991.
18. G. D. Plotkin, *A note on inductive generalization*, Mach. Intel. **5**, 153–163, 1970.
19. J. C. Reynolds, *Transformational systems and the algebraic structure of atomic formulas*, Mach. Intel. **5**, 135–152, 1970.
20. Y. Suzuki, K. Inomae, T. Shoudai, T. Miyahara, T. Uchida, *A polynomial time matching algorithm of structured ordered tree patterns for data mining from semistructural data*, in: Proc. 12th Internat. Conf. Inductive Logic Programming, LNAI **2583**, 270–284, 2002.
21. Y. Suzuki, T. Shoudai, S. Matsumoto, T. Uchida, *Efficient learning of unlabeled term trees with contractible variables from positive data*, in: Proc. 13th Internat. Conf. Inductive Logic Programming, LNAI **2835**, 347–364, 2003.

Circumscription Policies for Induction

Katsumi Inoue[1] and Haruka Saito[2]

[1] National Institute of Informatics
2-1-2 Hitotsubashi, Chiyoda-ku, Tokyo 101-8430, Japan
ki@nii.ac.jp
[2] Internet System Research Laboratories, NEC Corporation
8916-47 Takayama-cho, Ikoma, Nara 630-0101, Japan
h-saitou@ia.jp.nec.com

Abstract. There are two types of formalization for induction in logic. In *descriptive induction*, induced hypotheses describe rules with respect to observations with all predicates minimized. In *explanatory induction*, on the other hand, hypotheses abductively account for observations without any minimization principle. Both inductive methods have strength and weakness, which are complementary to each other. In this work, we unify these two logical approaches. In the proposed framework, not all predicates are minimized but minimality conditions can be flexibly determined as a *circumscription policy*. Constructing appropriate policies, we can intentionally minimize models of an augmented axiom set. As a result, induced hypotheses can have both conservativeness and explainability, which have been considered incompatible with each other in the literature. We also give two procedures to compute inductive hypotheses in the proposed framework.

1   Introduction

In inductive logic programming (ILP), induction has been mainly studied in first-order logic, and learning methods are investigated to induce hypotheses from observations and background knowledge. Logical foundations for induction have been one of the most important research issues in ILP, and several formalizations for induction exist in the literature [9,4,21,7,2,16], still seeking better theories to account for inductive capability by human being. Depending on goals of inductive tasks, there are two main frameworks of logical formalization for ILP: and   . Both inductive methods have strength and weakness, which are complementary to each other.

                is the inference to general rules which explain the given observation [21,7,16]. Given background knowledge B and an observation E, the task of explanatory induction is to find a hypothesis H that accounts for E. This condition is represented by the equation:

$$B \wedge H \models E$$

where $B \wedge H$ is consistent. Explanatory induction is suitable for many inductive tasks including   fi   [21] as well as   [22], and

R. Camacho, R. King, A. Srinivasan (Eds.): ILP 2004, LNAI 3194, pp. 164–179, 2004.
© Springer-Verlag Berlin Heidelberg 2004

hypotheses obtained by explanatory induction are appropriate for justifying observations. However, explanatory induction often realizes an [4], which deduces new facts not stated in given observations. Inductive leaps are often undesirable for databases, because facts not explicitly given in E can often be regarded as false statements rather than unknown observations. In such a situation, the (CWA) [26] is applied to the database. Obviously, inductive leaps are not consistent with the CWA.

, on the other hand, does not primarily intend to learn classification rules but simply points out confirmed by observations. Hence, descriptive induction is also called fi [7]. Expectedly, descriptive induction never realizes an inductive leap. Avoidance of inductive leaps is related to the classical logical notion of of theories [27]. Moreover, a clear distinction between explanatory induction and descriptive induction is important to avoid in the sense of Flach [7].

Descriptive induction is increasingly important in the context of . However, the issue of formalizing descriptive induction has not yet been sufficiently settled although there has been some previous works [9,7,3,16]. One of the most serious problems in the previous formalizations of descriptive induction is that hypotheses obtained by descriptive induction often fail to explain observations. It is not easy to achieve explainability in descriptive induction, as Flach [7] has pointed out that combining explanatory induction and descriptive induction may lead to a contradiction in the process of hypothesis formation. We look deep into this problem in previous approaches as follows.

Both explanatory induction and descriptive induction are related with . Actually, induction is nonmonotonic reasoning because its conclusions, i.e., hypotheses, may become incorrect when new knowledge is added. Originally, nonmonotonic reasoning has been investigated as a method of reasoning under . On the other hand, an induction problem is usually given with incomplete knowledge because of the nature of induction; otherwise, we do not have to learn anything. It has also been argued that induction should be somehow related with , and again nonmonotonic reasoning has its origin in formalizing commonsense reasoning [20]. Thus, it is reasonable that a method for nonmonotonic reasoning is applied to induction problems.

In descriptive induction, nonmonotonicity also appears in closed-world reasoning about positive objects. Unless otherwise stated, objects not mentioned in E or not derived from $B \wedge E$ are assumed to be negative with respect to the predicate to be learned. Thus, the previous approaches to descriptive induction [9,4,3] are based on the , and use Clark's [1] on $B \wedge E$ to minimize individuals in the theory.

However, these previous approaches to descriptive induction have a serious problem that there is no distinction between observations and background knowledge. This distinction is, however, important from practical viewpoints, as the following two main reasons indicate. Firstly, when we already have our current knowledge B and then an observation E is obtained to revise or update B, this

E should be assimilated into our knowledge.[1] As argued in [15], such knowledge assimilation should be realized through   or   : E should change the current theory B into an augmented theory $B \wedge H$ such that $B \wedge H \models E$ holds. Secondly, background knowledge is intrinsic to knowledge evolution. We cannot realize continuous and incremental learning if we merely treat examples without any prior knowledge.

As an introductory example of induction under incomplete knowledge, let us consider the following background knowledge and the observation:

$$B = Bird(Tweety) \wedge Bird(Oliver),$$
$$E = Flies(Tweety).$$

In this case, we do not have any information about Oliver's ability to fly. In explanatory induction, one possible hypothesis to explain E is:

$$H_1 = \forall x\,(Bird(x) \supset Flies(x)).$$

This hypothesis satisfies that $B \wedge H_1 \models E$, but realizes an inductive leap for $Flies(Oliver)$, that is, $B \wedge H_1 \models Flies(Oliver)$. On the other hand, a possible hypothesis by descriptive induction is:

$$H_2 = \forall x\,(Flies(x) \supset Bird(x)).$$

This hypothesis never realizes an inductive leap, but fails to explain E. That is, it holds that $B \wedge H_2 \not\models E$ and $B \wedge H_2 \not\models Flies(Oliver)$.

To overcome the difficulties in previous approaches, we define a new form of induction which integrates explanatory induction with descriptive induction. The new form of induction is called   , which is based on [19] and the idea of explanation in   [15]. By specifying the roles of predicates in circumscription, we can intentionally minimize models of an augmented axiom set, so that no inductive leap is realized. By adopting the idea of explanation in abduction, we can distinguish between background knowledge and observations, so that a resulting hypothesis can explain the observation. Formally, we present that the desired properties of hypotheses can be obtained by circumscriptive induction if the roles of predicates is suitably chosen in computing circumscription. Since we would like to make obtained hypotheses explain the observation, we reflect this intention in the   .
For the above bird example, by minimizing the predicate $Bird$ with the predicate $Flies$ varied, circumscriptive induction can produce the hypothesis:

$$H_3 = \forall x\,(Bird(x) \wedge x \neq Oliver \supset Flies(x)).$$

Then, it holds that $B \wedge H_3 \models E$ and $B \wedge H_3 \not\models Flies(Oliver)$.

---

[1] Note here that E does not need to be a new observation: E can be existing knowledge, e.g., a database of known facts. At least, E has not yet been incorporated into background knowledge B.

Motivated by the above discussion, this paper formally gives the definition of circumscriptive induction, carefully investigates its mathematical properties, and introduces computational procedures. The rest of this paper is organized as follows. In Section 2, we review the framework of ILP and circumscription. In Section 3, we define circumscriptive induction, and investigate its properties. In particular, two sufficient conditions are given to avoid inductive leaps. In Section 4, we give two correct procedures to compute circumscriptive induction. We discuss related work in Section 5, and conclude the paper in Section 6.

2 Preliminaries

2.1 Inductive Logic Programming

In this section, we review the terminology of inductive logic programming. A   is a disjunction of literals:

$$\neg A_1 \vee \cdots \vee \neg A_m \vee A_{m+1} \vee \cdots \vee A_n \quad (n \geq m \geq 0)$$

where each A_i is an atom. Any variable in a clause is assumed to be universally quantified at the front. A clause of the above form is also written as:

$$A_1 \wedge \cdots \wedge A_m \supset A_{m+1} \vee \cdots \vee A_n.$$

The left-hand side of $\supset$ is the *body* and the right-hand side is the *head* of the clause. A   is a finite set of clauses. A clausal theory is identified with the conjunction of the clauses in it, and is also simply called a .   . A predicate p in a formula F if p is a predicate of some atom A_i $(1 \leq i \leq m)$ in the body of a clause in F, and   in F if p appears in some atom A_j $(m + 1 \leq j \leq n)$ in the head of a clause in F.

Let B, E, and H be all clausal theories, where B, E, and H are called   , an   , and a   , respectively. The task of ILP is to construct a hypothesis H when B and E are given. According to the property of inferred hypotheses, there are two types of inductive schemes in ILP: one is   , and the other is   .

Definition 2.1. (explanatory induction [21,16])
Given background knowledge B and an observation E, the task of   is to infer a hypothesis H such that

$$B \wedge H \models E, \tag{1}$$

where $B \wedge H$ is consistent.

Note that the condition (1) in explanatory induction has the same logical form as the definition of   [11,15,16]. Abduction is often used in AI to infer an H for an observation E, given background knowledge B, such that $B \wedge H \models E$. A hypothesis obtained by explanatory induction can thus be regarded as an explanation of the observation. For the relationship between abduction and induction, see [8] and [13] for details.

Definition 2.2. (descriptive induction [9,4,16])
Given background knowledge B and an observation E, the task of
is to infer a hypothesis H such that

$$Comp(B \wedge E) \models H \tag{2}$$

where $Comp(B \wedge E)$ denotes the predicate completion of $B \wedge E$ relative to all predicates [1].

Definition 2.2 shows that hypotheses of descriptive induction are obtained by minimizing models of $B \wedge E$ relative to all predicates.

2.2 Circumscription

Circumscription was introduced by McCarthy [20] to realize nonmonotonic reasoning within classical logic. A general definition of circumscription is given in second-order logic as follows [18,19]. For any two predicates P and Q with the same arity, $(P \leq Q)$ is defined as $\forall x(P(x) \supset Q(x))$, where x is a tuple of distinct variables. Next, let P and Q be tuples of predicates $P_1, \ldots, P_n$ and $Q_1, \ldots, Q_n$, respectively, such that P_i and Q_i have the same arity for $i = 1, \ldots, n$. Then, $(P \leq Q)$ stands for $(P_1 \leq Q_1) \wedge \cdots \wedge (P_n \leq Q_n)$, and $(P < Q)$ stands for $(P \leq Q) \wedge \neg(Q \leq P)$.

Definition 2.3. (parallel circumscription [18,19])
Let $A(P, Z)$ be a formula containing tuples P and Z of predicates $P_1, \ldots, P_n$ and $Z_1, \ldots, Z_m$, respectively. Suppose that p_i and z_j are predicate variables of the same arity as P_i and Z_j, respectively, for $i = 1, \ldots, n$ and $j = 1, \ldots, m$. If we denote the tuple $p_1, \ldots, p_n$ by p and $z_1, \ldots, z_m$ by z, the
$P \quad A \quad Z \qquad$ is defined as:

$$\mathrm{CIRC}[A; P; Z] \equiv A(P, Z) \wedge \neg \exists pz[A(p, z) \wedge (p < P)].$$

When Z is empty, the circumscription is denoted as $\mathrm{CIRC}[A; P]$.

Circumscription is based on the   . That is, any model of $\mathrm{CIRC}[A; P; Z]$ is a model of A in which the extension of P cannot be made smaller without losing the property A even at the price of changing the interpretations of the constants Z. In other words, a structure M is a model of $\mathrm{CIRC}[A; P; Z]$ if and only if M is a model of A which is $\qquad \leq^{P;Z}$ [18,19]. Hence, for a formula F, $\mathrm{CIRC}[A; P; Z] \models F$ if and only if F is satisfied by every $\leq^{P;Z}$-minimal model of A.

Definition 2.4. (solitary formulas [18])
A formula $A(P)$ is   a tuple P of predicates if $A(P)$ can be written in the form of $N(P) \wedge (K \leq P)$, where $N(P)$ is a formula not containing any predicate in P positively, and K is a tuple of predicates not containing any predicate in P.

Definition 2.5. (separable formulas [18])
A formula $A(P)$ is   a tuple P of predicates if $A(P)$ can be constructed from formulas solitary in P using conjunctions and disjunctions. Equivalently, $A(P)$ is P if $A(P)$ can be written in the form of

$$\bigvee_i [N_i(P) \wedge (K_i \leq P)]$$

where each $N_i(P)$ is a formula not containing any predicate in P positively, and each K_i is a tuple of predicates not containing any predicate in P.

Obviously, any formula solitary in P is separable in P. It is known that $\text{CIRC}[A(P, Z); P; Z]$ becomes first-order when $A(P, Z)$ is separable in P and solitary in Z [18]. For example, $\text{CIRC}[\forall x(Q(x) \supset P(x)); P] \equiv \forall x(P(x) \equiv Q(x))$ and $\text{CIRC}[P(A) \wedge P(B); P] \equiv \forall x(P(x) \equiv x = A \vee x = B)$ can be shown using the method by Lifschitz [18]. A more general form of separable formulas is shown in [19], which can also be collapsible to first-order formulas.

3   Circumscriptive Induction

As mentioned in Section 1, both explanatory induction and descriptive induction have strength and weakness, which are complementary to each other. In order to integrate explanatory and descriptive induction by avoiding their demerits but keeping their merits, this section presents a new induction framework called

3.1   Definition

Circumscriptive induction is defined with circumscription and the idea of explanation in abduction as follows.

Definition 3.1. (circumscriptive induction problem)
Let B and E be two clausal theories, and P and Z two disjoint tuples of predicates appearing in B and E. Then, a   is defined as a quadruple $\langle B, E, P, Z \rangle$, where B and E represent background knowledge and an observation, respectively.

Definition 3.2. (circumscriptive induction)
Given a circumscriptive induction problem $\langle B, E, P, Z \rangle$, a formula H is a   if

$$\text{CIRC}[B \wedge E; P; Z] \models H \tag{3}$$

and

$$B \wedge H \models E, \tag{4}$$

where $B \wedge H$ is consistent.

In Definition 3.2, circumscriptive induction is defined with two conditions which inherit from both descriptive and explanatory induction. The first condition (3) is a more general form of (2) in descriptive induction. Here, each hypothesis H is defined with circumscription instead of Clark's predicate completion. The differences between the use of predicate completion and that of circumscription are as follows.

1. A more general class of formulas can be treated by circumscription than by predicate completion.
2. Models of $B \wedge E$ can be minimized more intentionally by partitioning predicates in $B \wedge E$ into P, Q and Z (called a   ), where Q is the predicates other than P and Z (called fi   ).

On the other hand, the second condition (4) of circumscriptive induction is the same as (1) in explanatory induction. This gives us a criterion in deciding which hypotheses should be adopted, so that background knowledge and observations are distinguished in an induction problem.

3.2 Example

Here, we show an elaboration of the introductory example in Section 1.

Example 3.1. Suppose that background knowledge B and observations E are given as follows [4].

$$B = Bird(Jan) \wedge Bird(Eric) \wedge Bird(Louis)$$
$$E = Flies(Jan) \wedge Flies(Eric)$$

A possible hypothesis H_1 obtained by   (Definition 2.1) is:

$$H_1 = (Bird(x) \supset Flies(x)).$$

H_1 involves an inductive leap. That is, the clause $Flies(Louis)$ not occurring in E is one of the consequences of $B \wedge H_1$.

On the other hand, a hypothesis H_2 obtained by   in the previous form (Definition 2.2) is:

$$H_2 = (Flies(x) \supset Bird(x)).$$

H_2 does not realize an inductive leap, but E is not the consequence of $B \wedge H_2$. This hypothesis does not reflect the distinction between B and E. Note that H_1 is not obtained by descriptive induction and that H_2 is not obtained by explanatory induction.

Now, for   , suppose that the circumscription policy is chosen as $P = Bird$ and $Z = Flies$. Then,

$$\mathrm{CIRC}[B \wedge E; Bird; Flies]$$
$$\equiv E \wedge \mathrm{CIRC}[B; Bird]$$
$$\equiv (x = Jan \vee x = Eric \supset Flies(x))$$
$$\wedge (x = Jan \vee x = Eric \vee x = Louis \equiv Bird(x)).$$

A possible hypothesis H_3 satisfying both $CIRC[B \wedge E; Bird; Flies] \models H_3$ and $B \wedge H_3 \models E$ is:

$$H_3 = (Bird(x) \wedge x \neq Louis \supset Flies(x)).$$

In this case, E is the consequence of $B \wedge H_3$, and H_3 does not realize an inductive leap, i.e., $B \wedge H_3 \not\models Flies(Louis)$. Note that neither H_1 nor H_2 is a correct solution in circumscriptive induction but H_3 can also be obtained by descriptive induction using the predicate completion in this case. Hence, circumscriptive induction sometimes restricts the hypotheses obtained by descriptive induction. In general, however, the predicate completion is only applicable to limited classes of clausal theories.

3.3 Properties of Hypotheses

We show properties of hypotheses obtained by circumscriptive induction. For this purpose, we need to formally define the concept of inductive leaps.

Definition 3.3. (inductive leap)
For a clausal theory S and a predicate p, let

$$M(S, p) = \{ A \mid S \models A, \ A \text{ is a ground atom whose predicate is } p \}.$$

Suppose that B, E and H are clausal theories. Then, a hypothesis H
if there is a predicate p occurring positively in E such that

$$M(B \wedge H, p) - M(B \wedge E, p) \neq \emptyset.$$

Definition 3.3 can be used to give the definition of of hypotheses. A hypothesis H is if H does not realize an inductive leap, that is, if

$$M(B \wedge H, p) \subseteq M(B \wedge E, p) \qquad (5)$$

holds for every predicate p occurring positively in E. Note that conservativeness of H implies of H as follows.

Proposition 3.1.

B E H $\qquad$ fi $\qquad$ $M(B \wedge E, p)$
$\qquad$ $p(t)$. $\qquad$ t . B $\qquad$ H
$\qquad$ $B \wedge H$

. Since H does not realize an inductive leap, the Eq. (5) holds. Since the set $M(B \wedge E, p)$ does not contain every $p(t)$ for any term t, nor $M(B \wedge H, p)$ does. This implies that $B \wedge H$ is consistent. $\qquad \square$

Note that an inductive leap derives a property p of an individual t such that (i) t appears in an initial database B, but (ii) $p(t)$ is not mentioned in either B or the observation E. Therefore, the concept of inductive leaps is not applied on unknown (or new) individuals not appearing in the initial database.

For Example 3.1, if the new facts $Bird(John)$ and $John \neq Louis$ enter the database, $Flies(John)$ is derived from $B \wedge Bird(John) \wedge John \neq Louis \wedge H_3$, which is not regarded as an inductive leap. Like other descriptive induction, hypotheses of circumscriptive induction reflect a   [16] such that "unknown individuals behave like the known ones".

On the other hand, the notion of explainability is related to   of hypotheses. That is, a hypothesis H is   if for any predicate p occurring positively in E, it holds that

$$M(B \wedge E, p) \subseteq M(B \wedge H, p). \tag{6}$$

Note that the set inclusion relationship in (6) is converse to that in (5).

Proposition 3.2.

(1)   fi

(2)   fi

▪ (1) For explanatory induction, completeness (6) immediately follows from the Eq. (1). An inductive leap occurs as shown in Example 3.1. That is, $H_1 = (Bird(x) \supset Flies(x))$ is obtained by explanatory induction, but $B \wedge H_1 \models Flies(Louis)$ holds for $Luis$ not occurring in the given $B \wedge E$.
(2) Any hypothesis H obtained by descriptive induction from B and E satisfies the Eq. (2). Since the predicate completion $Comp(B \wedge E)$ is a special case of the circumscription $CIRC(B \wedge E; P; Z)$ where P is the set of all predicates and Z is empty. Then, for any predicate p, $M(B \wedge E, p)$ is minimized by the predicate completion, and thus conservativeness (5) holds. Completeness does not hold as shown in Example 3.1. That is, $H_2 = (Flies(x) \supset Bird(x))$ is obtained by descriptive induction, but $B \wedge H_2 \not\models Flies(Jan)$ for $Flies(Jan) \in E$. □

Now, what about circumscriptive induction? By the condition (3) of explainability for E, completeness (6) immediately holds in circumscriptive induction.

Theorem 3.3.   ▪
B E H H
$$\langle B, E, P, Z \rangle \qquad H$$

▪ For any element m of $M(B \wedge E, p)$, m is an element of $M(CIRC[B \wedge E; P; Z], p)$ because $CIRC[B \wedge E; P; Z] \models B \wedge E$. On the other hand, a hypothesis H is selected from $CIRC[B \wedge E; P; Z]$ under the condition that it satisfies $B \wedge H \models E$ by (4). Therefore, m is an element of $M(B \wedge H, p)$ that is contained in $CIRC[B \wedge E; P; Z]$. □

For conservativeness, we can give sufficient conditions by specifying either restricted classes of clausal theories or suitable circumscription policies.

Theorem 3.4.

B $\quad$ E $\qquad\qquad\qquad\qquad\qquad$ $B \wedge E$ $\qquad\qquad\qquad$ Z

$\qquad\qquad$ H

$\langle B, E, P, Z \rangle$ $\qquad\qquad$ H

. Each predicate p in E belongs to either P, Q or Z.

1. p is in P:
   $M(B \wedge E, p)$ is minimized by $\mathrm{CIRC}[B \wedge E; P; Z]$. This immediately implies that $M(B \wedge H, p) \subseteq M(B \wedge E, p)$.
2. p is in Q:
   The circumscription $\mathrm{CIRC}[B \wedge E; P; Z]$ does not change the extensions of Q. Thus, $M(B \wedge H, p) = M(B \wedge E, p)$.
3. p is in Z:
   Since $B \wedge E$ is solitary in Z, $B \wedge E$ can be written as $(K \leq Z) \wedge N(Z)$, where K is a predicate expression not containing Z and $N(Z)$ is a formula not containing Z positively (Definition 2.4). Then, the following equivalence holds [18]:

   $$\mathrm{CIRC}[B \wedge E; P; Z] \equiv (K \leq Z) \wedge N(Z) \wedge \mathrm{CIRC}[N(K); P].$$

   In this formula, $K \leq Z$ becomes $K \equiv Z$ by the additional formula $Z \leq K$ implied by the circumscription $\mathrm{CIRC}[N(K); P]$. Then, the extension of Z in $B \wedge H$ is not larger than that in $B \wedge E$. Hence, $M(B \wedge H, p) \subseteq M(B \wedge E, p)$ holds.

Therefore, the theorem holds. $\qquad\qquad\qquad\qquad\qquad\qquad\qquad\qquad\qquad\qquad$ $\square$

A sufficient condition for the solitary condition in Theorem 3.4 can be represented by the following syntactical condition.

Theorem 3.5.

$\qquad\qquad\qquad\qquad\qquad\qquad$ B $\qquad\qquad\qquad\qquad$ E

$\quad Z$ $\qquad\qquad\qquad$ *.* $\qquad\qquad\qquad\qquad\qquad\qquad$ *.* $B \wedge E$

$\qquad H$ $\qquad\qquad\qquad\qquad\qquad\qquad\qquad\qquad\qquad$ $\langle B, E, P, Z \rangle$

. Completeness follows from Theorem 3.3. For conservativeness, $B \wedge E$ is solitary in Z since Z appears only in heads of $B \wedge E$, which implies that H does not realize an inductive leap by Theorem 3.4. $\qquad\qquad\qquad\qquad\qquad$ $\square$

In Theorem 3.5, we give a circumscription policy such that Z is a tuple of predicates appearing only in heads of $B \wedge E$. According to [19], one way to decide predicates in Z is to set Z as predicates that we intend to characterize by means of circumscription. From the viewpoint of induction problems, Z corresponds to _____ . Thus, it is reasonable to regard predicates occurring in heads of E as Z.

On the other hand, Theorem 3.4 holds under the condition that $B \wedge E$ is solitary in Z. The introduction of Z makes the models of P more minimized, yet hypothesized formulas are made more generalized, which sometimes allows an inductive leap for predicates Z. Therefore, we could put Z as small as possible if we would like to obtain hypotheses that never realize an inductive leap in general cases. One such an extreme case corresponds to the previous form of descriptive induction, in which Z is set empty and every predicate in $B \wedge E$ is minimized through the predicate completion.

4 Computing Circumscriptive Induction

In this section, we consider procedures to compute circumscriptive induction. We show two versions for this problem, depending on which condition of (3) and (4) is firstly computed in circumscriptive induction.

4.1 Collapsible Case

In the first method, we firstly compute the circumscription, and then check if a consequence of the circumscription explains the observation. In this method, it is necessary that $B \wedge E$ $\qquad$ P $\qquad$ Z. This condition guarantees that the circumscription formula $\mathrm{CIRC}[B \wedge E; P; Z]$ is collapsible to first-order logic.

Procedure 1 (computing circumscriptive induction, I)

1. Divide the predicates of $B \wedge E$ into P, Q, Z as follows.
   a) Z is a tuple of some predicates occurring only in heads of $B \wedge E$;
   b) Q is a tuple of some predicates not occurring in heads of $B \wedge E$;
   c) The rest of predicates are in P.
2. Compute a formula H_C such that $\mathrm{CIRC}[B \wedge E; P; Z] \equiv H_C$.
3. Compute a consequence H_Z of H_C: $H_C \models H_Z$ such that H_Z is a set of clauses each of which has only Z in the head and only P and Q in the body.
4. Select a hypothesis H from $H_C \wedge H_Z$ which satisfies the condition: $B \wedge H \models E$.

Step 1 determines the policy of circumscriptive induction, which implies that $B \wedge E$ is solitary in Z. The justification of this policy has been explained in Section 3.3. In Step 2, $\mathrm{CIRC}[B \wedge E; P; Z]$ can be represented in first-order logic if $B \wedge E$ is separable in P and solitary in Z [19]. The second-order formula in circumscription can also be converted to an equivalent first-order formula using the SCAN algorithm [23].

As a method of computing Step 3, we can use $\qquad$ [11] or $\qquad$ [5], which are sound and complete for $\qquad$ fi $\qquad$. For example, SOL-resolution derives minimal clauses constructed by a sub-vocabulary of the representation language called a $\qquad$ fi . In our case, we would like to get clauses that have Z in the heads as candidate hypotheses. Then, we can set the production field as $Z^+ \cup P^- \cup Q^-$ in SOL, where P^+ (resp. P^-) represent the set of positive (resp. negative) literals whose predicates are in P. By this way, a clause that characterizes the concept of a predicate in Z, that is, a clause which has Z in the head, is preferred as an inductive hypothesis. Thus, a hypothesis H for an inductive problem may contain clauses from H_Z in Step 4. Note that this computation is incomplete in the sense that it fails to find a solution that does not satisfy the above conditions.

In Step 4, we can consider a naive procedure to select a hypothesis H from candidate hypotheses $H_C \wedge H_Z$: for each subset h of $H_C \wedge H_Z$, check whether the condition $B \wedge h \models E$ is satisfied or not. Of course, this is a very simple yet inefficient procedure. A more efficient method for Step 4 is to use a first-order . Given B, E, H_C, and H_Z, we try to prove E from B, H_C, H_Z using a theorem prover. If E is proved, we identify which clauses from H_C and H_Z are used in the proof of E. Each set of such clauses constitutes a hypothesis H. A similar technique can be realized by a first-order   which allows hypotheses in clausal form, e.g., [24,11].

Any hypothesis obtained by Procedure 1 satisfies Definition 3.2. Moreover, each hypothesis does not realize an inductive leap.

Proposition 4.1.   .

$$B$$ $$E$$

$$B \wedge E$$ $$P^2$$ $$P \quad Z$$

$$H$$

$$\langle B, E, P, Z \rangle$$

. The Eq. (3) is satisfied by Steps 2 and 3. On the other hand, the Eq. (4) immediately holds by Step 4.   □

Theorem 4.2.   .

$$B \quad E \quad P \qquad Z$$ $$H$$

. By Proposition 4.1, H is a correct solution to the circumscriptive induction problem $\langle B, E, P, Z \rangle$. By the circumscription policy determined by Step 1 of Procedure 1, $B \wedge E$ is solitary in Z. As a result, the conditions in this theorem imply those in Theorem 3.5. Hence, the theorem holds.   □

4.2 Using Circumscriptive Theorem Provers

In the second method to compute circumscriptive induction, non-separable theories can be accepted unlike the previous procedure. Two well-known inference procedures are used for this purpose: one is a procedure for explanatory induction, and the other is a theorem prover for circumscription.

Procedure 2 (computing circumscriptive induction, II)

1. Generate a candidate hypothesis H^* from B and E such that H^* satisfies the condition: $B \wedge H^* \models E$.

---

[2] The condition that $B \wedge E$ is solitary in Z is not necessary here, and is guaranteed by Step 1 of Procedure 1. By this property and the condition that $B \wedge E$ is separable in P, the circumscription is reducible to a first-order formula.

2. Choose the circumscription policy in the same way as Step 1 in Procedure 1.
3. Check with a circumscriptive theorem prover whether H^* satisfies the condition: $\mathrm{CIRC}[B \wedge E; P; Z] \models H^*$ for each candidate hypothesis H^*.

In Step 1, we can use any procedure for explanatory induction based on , such as Progol [21], residue hypotheses [28], and CF-induction [12,13]. In Step 3, there are some theorem provers for circumscription [25,10]. Note that Procedure 2 is described nondeterministically. In Step 1, there are many candidate hypotheses as outputs of inverse entailment in general. Thus, it must take much computational cost to check for every candidate hypothesis from Step 1 whether the condition is satisfied or not with a circumscriptive theorem prover in Step 3. Hence, integration of Steps 1 and 3 is somehow necessary for practical uses. For example, in selecting H^* from a large amount of candidate hypotheses, we could call a circumscriptive theorem prover in parallel.

By the construction of a hypothesis H in Procedure 2, H never realizes an inductive leap. Thus, the next theorems hold.

Proposition 4.3. .

$$B \qquad\qquad E$$
$$H$$
$$\langle B, E, P, Z \rangle$$

. The Eq. (3) holds by Step 3, while the Eq. (4) holds by Step 1. □

Theorem 4.4. .

$$B \quad E \quad P \qquad Z \qquad\qquad\qquad\qquad\qquad H$$

. By Proposition 4.3, H is a correct solution to the circumscriptive induction problem $\langle B, E, P, Z \rangle$. The circumscription policy by Step 2 of Procedure 2 implies the conditions in Theorem 3.5. Hence, the theorem holds. □

Procedure 2 is more useful than Procedure 1 in the sense that $B \wedge E$ need not be separable in P nor solitary in Z. A demerit of Procedure 2 lies in the fact that no procedure has been developed for deriving hypotheses which contain the equality predicate $=$ in the framework of inverse entailment. Hence, Procedure 2 cannot induce the hypothesis H_3 in Example 3.1, while Procedure 1 can do it.

5 Related Work

Helft [9] firstly investigated descriptive induction with the minimal model semantics. In his method, the conjunction of background knowledge B and the observation E is considered as one database $B \wedge E$, and all clauses that are satisfied by all minimal models in the database are candidate hypotheses. Similarly, CLAUDIEN [4,3] is a descriptive induction system, and is also defined with the minimal model semantics. These two inductive systems do not distinguish between B and E, so that the difference between B and E cannot be reflected to the inferred hypotheses.

Lachiche and Marquis [17] also propose a method for descriptive induction with the minimal model semantics. In particular, they use a completion principle in their definition, which is different from usual one used in nonmonotonic reasoning. Their completion principle corresponds to the similarity assumption which is required for induction. That is, their completion circumscribes known   , while nonmonotonic inference usually circumscribes   of such individuals. On the other hand, the circumscription policy we proposed here for circumscriptive induction is decided from the viewpoint of dividing roles of predicates so that we can distinguish between B and E.

Flach [7] presents rationality postulates for both explanatory induction and descriptive induction. He clearly distinguishes between the processes of hypothesis formation and hypothesis selection in induction, and also discusses that explanatory induction and descriptive induction must not be mixed up in the process of hypothesis formation to avoid Hempel's paradox. In circumscriptive induction using Procedure 1, Steps 1, 2, and 3 are the processes of hypothesis formation and satisfy his rationality postulates for descriptive induction. In Step 4, we incorporate the concept of explanation, so this step is not the process of hypothesis formation but that of hypothesis selection. Therefore, circumscriptive induction does not mix up explanatory induction and descriptive induction, and does not cause a contradiction.

Dimopoulos   [6] propose a learning framework in which explanatory induction and descriptive induction are integrated. In this framework, hypotheses are represented by a triple of general rules, integrity constraints, and the predicates for the concepts to be learned. The general rules are learned by explanatory induction, while integrity constrains are learned by descriptive induction. Integrity constraints are then used to suppress overgeneralization of the general rules. Therefore, induction in this framework can be regarded as a kind of explanatory induction, although an inductive leap can also be avoided if integrity constrains are appropriately settled.

Inoue and Haneda [14] propose the inductive system LAELP to learn   . In LAELP, inductive leaps can be avoided by introducing new abducibles into rules. For example, when $B = Bird(Tweety) \land Bird(Oliver)$ is background knowledge and $E = Flies(Tweety)$ is the observation, LAELP can generate the rule

$$H = \forall x \, (Bird(x) \land Normal(x) \supset Flies(x))$$

where the new abducible predicate $Normal$ is introduced. In this case, the fact $Normal(Tweety)$ must be added to B along with H to explain $Flies(Tweety)$. For $Oliver$, however, if we assume $Normal(Oliver)$ it flies; otherwise, we cannot conclude whether it flies or not. This kind of weak inference is preferable when the three-valued semantics, e.g., the answer set semantics, is considered like [14]. This is because one often wants to conclude that $Flies(Oliver)$ is   instead of $\cdot$ under the situation that the CWA is not appropriate in learning nonmonotonic or abductive programs. On the other hand, our approach in this paper avoids inductive leaps even when classical first-order programs are learned instead of abductive or nonmonotonic logic programs. In fact, we can specify which is   in the above example, i.e., $\forall x(Normal(x) \equiv x \neq Oliver)$. As a result, the normality of $Tweety$ need not be mentioned explicitly, but there is no chance to derive $Flies(Oliver)$ in our setting.

6 Conclusion

In this paper, we have investigated induction regarded as nonmonotonic reasoning. We have firstly pointed out problems in previous approaches to explanatory and descriptive induction. In particular, explanatory induction involves inductive leaps, while descriptive induction fails to satisfy completeness. To solve these problems, we have defined circumscriptive induction, and considered the properties of its hypotheses from the viewpoint of completeness and conservativeness. We have also shown two procedures for computing circumscriptive induction.

In this paper, we have proposed a circumscription policy for induction problems. If the solitary condition in variable predicates is satisfied, any hypothesis obtained by circumscriptive induction does not realize an inductive leap. However, this property is applicable only to some limited classes of induction problems. Thus, the future issue is to investigate the relationship between circumscriptive policies and properties of hypotheses obtained in more general cases.

References

1. Keith L. Clark. Negation as failure. In: Hervé Gallaire and Jack Minker, editors, *Logic and Data Bases*, pages 119–140, Plenum Press, 1978.
2. Luc De Raedt. Logical settings for concept-learning. *Artificial Intelligence*, 95:187–201, 1997.
3. Luc De Raedt and Luc Dehaspe. Clausal discovery. *Machine Learning*, 26(2,3):99–146, 1997.
4. Luc De Raedt and Nada Lavrač. The many faces of inductive logic programming. In *Proceedings of the 7th International Symposium on Methodologies for Intelligent Systems, Lecture Notes in Artificial Intelligence*, 689, pages 435–449, Springer, 1993.
5. Alvaro del Val. A new method for consequence finding and compilation in restricted languages. In *Proceedings of AAAI-99*, pages 259–264, AAAI Press, 1999.
6. Yannis Dimopoulos, Saso Dzeroski, and Antonis Kakas. Integrating explanatory and descriptive learning in ILP. In: *Proceedings of the 15th International Joint Conference on Artificial Intelligence*, pages 900–906, Morgan Kaufmann, 1997.
7. Peter A. Flach. Rationality postulates for induction. In: Yoav Shoham, editor, *Proceeding of the 6th TALK*, pages 267–281, Morgan Kaufmann, 1996.
8. Peter A. Flach and Antonis Kakas, editors. *Abduction and Induction: Essays on their Relation and Integration*. Kluwer Academic, 2000.
9. Nicolas Helft. Induction as nonmonotonic inference. In: *Proceedings of KR '89*, pages 149–156, Morgan Kaufmann, 1989.
10. Nicolas Helft, Katsumi Inoue, and David Poole. Query answering in circumscription. In: *Proceedings of the 12th International Joint Conference on Artificial Intelligence*, pages 426–431, Morgan Kaufmann, 1991.

11. Katsumi Inoue. Linear resolution for consequence finding. *Artificial Intelligence*, 56(2,3):301–353, 1992.

12. Katsumi Inoue. Induction, abduction, and consequence-finding. In: Celine Rouveirol and Michele Sebag, editors, *Proceedings of the 11th International Conference on Inductive Logic Programming, Lecture Notes in Artificial Intelligence*, 2157, pages 65–79, Springer, 2001.

13. Katsumi Inoue. Induction as consequence finding. *Machine Learning*, 55(2):109–135, 2004.

14. Katsumi Inoue and Hiromasa Haneda. Learning abductive and nonmonotonic logic programs. In: [8], pages 213–231, 2000.

15. A. C. Kakas, R. A. Kowalski and F. Toni. The role of abduction in logic programming. In: D. M. Gabbay, C. J. Hogger and J. A. Robinson, editors, *Handbook of Logic in Artificial Intelligence and Logic Programming*, volume 5, pages 235–324, Oxford University Press, 1998.

16. Nicolas Lachiche. Abduction and induction from a non-monotonic reasoning perspective. In [8], pages 107–116, 2000.

17. Nicolas Lachiche and Pierre Marquis. A model for generalization based on confirmatory induction. In: M. van Someren and G. Widmer, editors, *Proceedings of the 9th European Conference on Machine Learning*, pages 154–161, 1997.

18. Vladimir Lifschitz. Computing circumscription. In: *Proceedings of the 9th International Joint Conference on Artificial Intelligence*, pages 122–127, Morgan Kaufmann, 1985.

19. Vladimir Lifschitz. Circumscription. In: D. M. Gabbay, C. J. Hogger and J. A. Robinson, editors, *Handbook of Logic in Artificial Intelligence and Logic Programming*, volume 3, pages 298–352, Oxford University Press, 1994.

20. John McCarthy. Circumscription—a form of nonmonotonic reasoning. *Artificial Intelligence*, 13:27–39, 1980.

21. Stephen Muggleton. Inverse entailment and Progol. *New Generation Computing*, 13(3,4):245–286, 1995.

22. Stephen Muggleton and Christoper Bryant. Theory completion and inverse entailment. In: J. Cussens and A. Frisch, editors, *Proceedings of the 10th International Conference on Inductive Logic Programming*, LNAI 1866, pages 130–146, Springer, 2000.

23. Hans Jürgen Ohlbach. SCAN—elimination of predicate quantifiers. In: *Proceedings of the 13th conference on automated deduction, Lecture Notes in Artificial Intelligence*, 1104, pages 161–165, Springer, 1996.

24. David Poole, Randy Goebel, and Romas Aleliunas. Theorist: a logical reasoning system for defaults and diagnosis. In: Nick Cercone and Gordon McCalla, editors, *The Knowledge Frontier: Essays in the Representation of Knowledge*, pages 331–352, Springer, 1987.

25. Teodor C. Przymusinski. An algorithm to compute circumscription. *Artificial Intelligence*, 38:49–73, 1989.

26. Raymond Reiter. On closed world data bases. In: Hervé Gallaire and Jack Minker, editors, *Logic and Data Bases*, pages 119–140, Plenum Press, 1978.

27. Eiji Takimoto and Akira Maruoka. Conservativeness and monotonicity for learning algorithms. In: *Proceedings of the 6th Annual Conference on Computational Learning Theory*, pages 377–383, ACM Press, 1993.

28. Akihiro Yamamoto. Hypothesis finding based on upward refinement of residue hypotheses. *Theoretical Computer Science*, 298:5–19, 2003.

Logical Markov Decision Programs and the Convergence of Logical TD(λ)

Kristian Kersting and Luc De Raedt

Institute for Computer Science, Machine Learning Lab
Albert-Ludwigs-University, Georges-Köhler-Allee, Gebäude 079,
D-79110 Freiburg i. Brg., Germany
{kersting,deraedt}@informatik.uni-freiburg.de

Abstract. Recent developments in the area of relational reinforcement learning (RRL) have resulted in a number of new algorithms. A theory, however, that explains why RRL works, seems to be lacking. In this paper, we provide some initial results on a theory of RRL. To realize this, we introduce a novel representation formalism, called logical Markov decision programs (LOMDPs), that integrates Markov Decision Processes (MDPs) with Logic Programs. Using LOMDPs one can compactly and declaratively represent complex MDPs. Within this framework we then devise a relational upgrade of TD(λ) called *logical* TD(λ) and prove convergence. Experiments validate our approach.

1 Introduction

In the past few years, there has been a lot of work on extending probabilistic and stochastic frameworks with abilities to handle objects and relations, see [6] for an overview. From an inductive logic programming or relational learning point of view, these approaches are upgrades of propositional representations towards the use of relational or computational logic representations.

The first contribution of the present paper extends this line of research towards decision making. We introduce a novel representation formalism, called (LOMDPs), that combines MDPs with . The result is a flexible and expressive framework for defining MDPs that are able to handle structured objects as well as relations. For MDPs, such a framework, grounded in computational logic, has been missing. Only [4] report on combining MDPs with Reiter's situation calculus. However, it is more complex, and model-free reinforcement techniques have not yet been addressed. LOMDPs share - with the other upgrades of propositional representations - two advantages. First, logical expressions (in the form of clauses, rules or transitions) may contain variables and as such make of many specific transitions. This allows one to compactly represent complex domains. Secondly, because of this abstraction, the number of parameters (such as rewards and probabilities) is significantly reduced. This in turn allows one - in principle - to speed up and simplify the learning because one can learn at the rather than at the level.

R. Camacho, R. King, A. Srinivasan (Eds.): ILP 2004, LNAI 3194, pp. 180–197, 2004.

Many fascinating machine learning techniques have been developed under the name   (RL) in the context of MDPs over the last few decades, cf. [30]. Recently, there has also been an increased attention for dealing with relational representations and objects in RL, see e.g. [10,13]. Many of these works have taken a practical perspective and have developed systems and experiments that operate in relational worlds. At the heart of these systems there is usually a function approximator (often a logical regression tree) that is able to assign values to sets of states and to sets of state–action pairs. So far, however, a theory that explains why this approach works seems to be lacking. The second contribution of the present paper is a first step in the direction of such a theory. The theory is based on a notion of abstract states and abstract policies represented by logical expressions. An abstract state represents a set of concrete states and an abstract policy is then a function from abstract states to actions. All ground states represented by the same abstract state are essentially assigned the same action. This is akin to what happens with   (RRL-RT) [10][1], where each leaf of the regression tree represents an abstract state and where states classified in the same leaf obtain the same value or action. The convergence result presented is, to the best of our knowledge, the first presented in the context of relational reinforcement learning.

We proceed as follows. Mathematical preliminaries are reviewed in Section 2. The LOMDP framework is introduced in Section 3. Section 4 defines abstract policies, and Section 5 introduces the general framework of   to learn abstract policies. In Section 6, we devise LTD(λ) for evaluation abstract policies. LTD(λ) is experimentally validated in Section 7. Before concluding, we discuss related work.

2 Preliminaries

In this section, we introduce some of the basic terminology of relational logic and MDPs, cf. [14] and [30].

Logic: A fi Σ is a set of relation symbols r with arity $m \geq 0$, and a set of functor symbols f with arity $n \geq 0$. If $n = 0$ then f is called a constant, if $m = 0$ then p is called a proposition. An $r(t_1, \dots, t_m)$ is a relation symbol r followed by a bracketed n-tuple of constants or variables. A conjunction is a set of atoms. A substitution $\theta = \{V_1/t_1, \dots, V_n/t_n\} \{X/ \quad \}$, is an assignment of terms t_i to variables V_i. A conjunction A is said to be θ-subsumed by a conjunction B, denoted by $B \leq_\theta A$, if there exists a substitution θ such that $B\theta \subset A$. A term, atom or clause E is called   when it contains no variables, i.e., $(E) = \emptyset$. A substitution θ is the fi $mgu(a, b)$ of atoms a and b iff. $a = b\theta$ and for each substitution θ' s.t. $a = b\theta'$, there exists a substitution γ such that $\theta' = \theta\gamma$. The   of Σ, denoted as hb_Σ, is the set of all ground atoms constructed with the predicate and functor symbols in the alphabet Σ.

---

[1] RRL is sometimes used as short hand for Džeroski *et al.*'s approach. To distinguish it from relational reinforcement learning we will use RRL-RT as short hand.

Notation: Atoms are written in lower case a, sets of atoms in upper case A, and sets of sets of atoms in bold, upper case $\mathbf{A}$. To highlight that a (resp. A, $\mathbf{A}$) may not be ground, we will write $\mathbf{a}$ (resp. $\mathbb{A}$, $\mathbf{A}$).

Markov Decision Processes (MDP): A MDP is a tuple $\mathbf{M} = (S, A, \mathbf{T}, \lambda)$. Here, S is a set of system states. The agent has available a finite set of actions $A(z) \subseteq A$ for each state $z \in S$ which cause stochastic state transitions. For each $z, z' \in S$ and $a \in A(z)$ there is a transition T in $\mathbf{T}$, i.e., $z' \xleftarrow{p:r:a} z$. The transition denotes that with probability $P(z, a, z') := p$ action a causes a transition to state z' when executed in state z. For each $z \in S$ and $a \in A(z)$ it holds $\sum_{z' \in S} P(z, a, z') = 1$. The agent gains an expected next reward $R(z, a, z') := r$ for each transition. If the reward function R is probabilistic (mean value depends on the current state and action only) the MDP is called   , otherwise   . In this paper, we only consider MDPs with stationary transition probabilities and stationary, bounded rewards. A (stationary) deterministic policy $\pi : S \mapsto A$ is a set of expressions of the form $a \leftarrow z$ for each $z \in S$ where $a \in A(z)$. It denotes a particular course of actions to be adopted by an agent, with $\pi(z) := a$ being the action to be executed whenever the agent is in state z. We assume an infinite horizon and also that the agent accumulates the rewards associated with the states it enters. Future rewards are discounted by $0 \leq \lambda < 1$. The value of a policy π is the solution of the following system of linear functions $V_\pi(z) = \sum_{z' \xleftarrow{p:r:a} z \in \mathbf{T}} p \cdot [r + \lambda \cdot V_\pi(z')]$. A policy π is optimal if $V_\pi(z) \geq V_{\pi'}(z)$ for all $z \in S$ and policies π'. A (stationary) nondeterministic policy π maps a state to a distribution over actions. The value of π is then the expectation.

3 Logical Markov Decision Programs

The   of a MDP is essentially a propositional representation because the state and action symbols are flat. The key idea underlying   (LOMDPs) is to replace these flat symbols by abstract symbols.

Definition 1. $\mathbb{Z}$.
                                              $\emptyset$

Abstract states represent sets of states. More formally, a state Z is a (finite) conjunction of ground facts over the alphabet Σ, i.e. a logical interpretation, a subset of the Herbrand base. In the blocks world, one possible state Z is $on(a, b)$, $on(b, fl), bl(a), bl(b), cl(a), cl(fl)$ where $on(a, b)$ denotes that object a is on b, $cl(a)$ states that a is clear, $bl(a)$ denotes that a is a block, and fl refers to the floor. An abstract state $\mathbb{Z}$ is e.g. $on(X, Y), bl(Y), bl(X)$. It represents all states (over the given alphabet Σ) where a block X is on top of another block Y. Formally speaking, an abstract state $\mathbb{Z}$ represents all states Z for which there exists a substitution θ such that $\mathbb{Z}\theta \subseteq Z$. Let $S(\mathbb{Z})$ denote this set of states. The substitution in the previous example is $\{X/a, Y/b\}$. By now we are able to define abstract transitions.

Definition 2. abstract transition T $\qquad$ . . $\mathbb{H} \xleftarrow{p:r:\mathtt{a}} \mathbb{B}$

$P(T) := p \in [0,1]$ $R(T) := r \in \mathbb{R}$ $\mathtt{a} := act(T)$

$body(T) := \mathbb{B}$ $head(T) := \mathbb{H}$

We assume T to be range-restricted, i.e., $vars(\mathbb{H}) \subseteq vars(\mathbb{B})$, and $vars(\mathtt{a}) \subseteq vars(\mathbb{B})$, so that an abstract transition relies on the information encoded in the current state only. The semantics of an abstract transition[2] are:

$$Z' := [Z \setminus \mathbb{B}\theta] \cup \mathbb{H}\theta \qquad\qquad \mathbb{B} \leq_\theta Z \qquad\qquad \mathtt{a}\theta$$

. r $\qquad\qquad p$

For illustration purposes consider the following abstract transition, which moves block $\mathtt{X}$ from $\mathtt{Y}$ to the floor with probability 0.9:

$$on(\mathtt{X}, \mathtt{fl}), cl(\mathtt{X})cl(\mathtt{Y}) \xleftarrow{0.9:-1:mv\_fl(\mathtt{X})} on(\mathtt{X}, \mathtt{Y}), cl(\mathtt{X})$$

Applied to the state **Exp**, which is

$$on(\mathtt{a}, \mathtt{b}), on(\mathtt{b}, \mathtt{fl}), on(\mathtt{c}, \mathtt{fl}), cl(\mathtt{a}), cl(\mathtt{c}), bl(\mathtt{a}), bl(\mathtt{b}), bl(\mathtt{c}),$$

the abstract transition tells us that $mv\_fl(\mathtt{a})$ leads to

$$on(\mathtt{a}, \mathtt{fl}), on(\mathtt{b}, \mathtt{fl}), on(\mathtt{c}, \mathtt{fl}), cl(\mathtt{a}), cl(\mathtt{b}), cl(\mathtt{c}), bl(\mathtt{a}), bl(\mathtt{b}), bl(\mathtt{c})$$

with probability 0.9 gaining a reward of -1. One can see that this implements a kind of first-order variant of probabilistic STRIPS operators.

As LOMDPs typically consist of a set $\mathbb{T}$ of multiple abstract transitions there are two constraints to be imposed in order to obtain meaningful LOMDPs. First, let $\mathbb{B}$ be the set of all bodies of abstract state transitions in the LOMDP (modulo variable renaming). For $\mathbb{B} \in \mathbb{B}$, let $A(\mathbb{B})$ denote the set of all abstract actions $\mathtt{a}$ such that $\mathbb{H} \xleftarrow{p:r:\mathtt{a}} \mathbb{B}$ is in the LOMDP. We require

$$\forall \mathbb{B} \in \mathbb{B}, \forall \mathtt{a} \in A(\mathbb{B}) \qquad \sum_{\substack{T \in \mathbb{T}, \\ body(T)=\mathbb{B}, \\ act(T)=\mathtt{a}}} P(T) = 1.0. \qquad (1)$$

This condition guarantees that all abstract successor states are specified when executing an abstract action in an abstract state and that their probabilities sum to 1. Secondly, we need a way to cope with contradicting transitions and rewards. Indeed, consider the transitions $e \xleftarrow{1:-1:\mathtt{a}} d$, $g \xleftarrow{0.5:-2:\mathtt{a}} f$ and $e \xleftarrow{0.5:-2:\mathtt{a}} f$, and state $Z = \{d, f\}$. The problem with these transitions is that the first transition says that if we execute $\mathtt{a}$ in Z we will go with probability 1 to state $Z' = \{e, f\}$ whereas the last two ones assign a probability of 0.5 to state $Z'' = \{d, g\}$ and state $Z''' = \{d, e\}$. To ensure that only one abstract state is firing (d or f), we assume a total order $\prec$ over all pairs of actions and rules bodies that appear in $\mathbb{T}$ and apply a conflict resolution similar to Prolog. We do a forward search

---

[2] We implicitly assume that an abstract action has some preconditions.

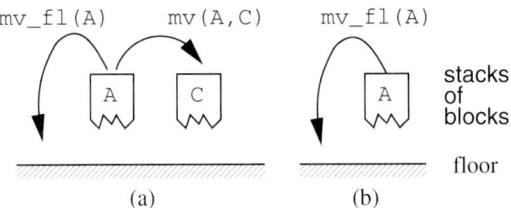

mv_fl(A)   mv(A,C)   mv_fl(A)

Fig. 1. The two underlying patterns of the blocks world for stacking. (a) There are at least two stacks of height > 0. (b) There is only one stack left (the goal state). The serrated cuts indicate that A (resp. C) can be on top of some other block or on the floor.

among the pairs stopping with the first matching one. For instance for $Z = \{d, f\}$ only the first abstract transition fires whereas for state e, f the last two abstract transitions fire.

By now we are able to formally define LOMDPs.

Definition 3. $\mathbb{M} =$
$(\Sigma, \mathbb{A}, \mathbb{T}, \lambda)$ Σ fi $\mathbb{A}$. $\mathbb{T}$
fi . $\mathbb{A}$ $0 \leq \lambda < 1$

.   (1)

Before giving the semantics of LOMDPs, let us also illustrate LOMDPs on the example from the blocks world where the goal is to move all blocks on one single stack. For the sake of simplicity, we assume that all variables denote to different objects[3]:

$$1: \qquad\qquad \text{absorb} \xleftarrow{\;1.0:0.0:\text{absorb}\;} \text{absorb}.$$

$$2: \quad \begin{array}{l} \text{on}(A, fl), \text{cl}(A), \\ \text{on}(C, D), \text{cl}(C), \text{cl}(B) \end{array} \xleftarrow{\;0.9:-1:\text{mv\_fl}(A)\;} \begin{array}{l} \text{on}(A, B), \text{cl}(A), \\ \text{on}(C, D), \text{cl}(C). \end{array}$$

$$3: \quad \begin{array}{l} \text{on}(A, C), \text{cl}(A), \\ \text{on}(C, D), \text{cl}(B) \end{array} \xleftarrow{\;0.9:-1:\text{mv}(A,C)\;} \begin{array}{l} \text{on}(A, B), \text{cl}(A), \\ \text{on}(C, D), \text{cl}(C). \end{array}$$

$$4: \qquad\qquad \text{absorb} \xleftarrow{\;1.0:20:\text{stop}\;} \text{on}(A, B), \text{cl}(A).$$

If the transition probabilities do not sum to 1.0 for an abstract action then there is an additional abstract transition for staying in the current abstract state. In order to understand the LOMDP , one has to understand the abstract states that govern the underlying patterns of the blocks world, cf. Figure 1. Two abstract states (the artificial **absorb** state excluded) together with the order in which they occur cover all possible state action patterns in the blocks world[4]. Furthermore, is an episodic task, i.e., it ends when reaching the goal state. In RL, episodic tasks are encoded using which transition only to themselves and generate only zero rewards. Transition 1 encodes the absorbing

---

[3] This can be achieved by e.g. adding diff(X, Y) to denote that X and Y are different.
[4] We assume that we start in a legal blocks world. Therefore, floor will not be moved.

state. Transitions 2 and 3 cover the cases in which there are (at least) two stacks. Finally, transition 4 encodes the situation that there is only one stack, i.e. our goal state   . Here, $\mathtt{on(A,B)}, \mathtt{cl(A)}, \mathtt{bl(B)}$ are only used to describe the preconditions of $\mathtt{mv(A,B)}$: the floor cannot be moved. When performing action $\mathtt{mv(a,b)}$ in state   (see above) only abstract transition 3 and the omitted abstract transition for staying in the state are firing. Similar, we can easily encode the   goal. Note that we have not specified the number of blocks. The LOMDP represents all possible blocks worlds using only 6 abstract transitions, i.e. 12 probability and reward parameters, whereas the number of parameters of a propositional system explodes, e.g., for 10 blocks there are $58,941,091$ states.

Although, as the following theorem shows, the semantics of LOMDPs are also uniquely specified in the case of functors, we will focus in this paper on functor-free LOMDPs. In this case, the induced MDP $\mathbf{M}(\mathbb{M})$ is finite.

Theorem 1. $\qquad\qquad \mathbb{M} = (\Sigma, \mathbb{A}, \mathbb{T}, \lambda)$ $\qquad$ *fi*
$\mathbf{M}(\mathbb{M}) = (S, A, \mathbf{T}, \lambda)$

Proof sketch: Let $\mathrm{hb}^s_\Sigma \subset \mathrm{hb}_\Sigma$ be the set of all ground atoms built over abstract states predicates, and let $\mathrm{hb}^a_\Sigma \subset \mathrm{hb}_\Sigma$ be the set of all ground atoms built over abstract action names. Now, construct $\mathbf{M}(\mathbb{M})$ from $\mathbb{M}$ as follows. The countable state set S consists of all finite subsets of hb^s_Σ. The set of actions $\mathbf{A}(Z)$ for state $Z \in S$ is given by $\mathbf{A}(Z) = \{\mathbf{a}\theta | \mathbb{H} \xleftarrow{p:r:\mathbf{a}} \mathbb{B} \in \mathbb{T}$ minimal w.r.t. $\prec$, $\mathbb{B} \leq_\theta Z\}$. We have that $|\mathbf{A}(Z)| < \infty$ holds. The probability $P(Z, a, Z')$ of a transition in $\mathbf{T}$ from Z to another state Z' after performing an action a is the probability value p associated to the unique abstract transition matching Z, a, and Z' normalized by the number of transitions of the form $Z'' \xleftarrow{a} Z$ in $\mathbb{T}$. If there is no abstract transition connecting Z and Z', the probability is zero. The bounded rewards $R(Z, a, Z')$ are constructed in a similar way but are not normalized. $\qquad\square$

From Theorem 1 and [27, Theorem 6.2.5] it follows that for every LOMDP, there exists an optimal policy (for ground states). Finally, LOMDPs generalize (finite) MDPs because every (finite) MDP is a propositional LOMDP in which all relation symbols have arity 0.

4   Abstract Policies

Theorem 1 states that every LOMDP $\mathbb{M}$ specifies a discrete MDP $\mathbf{M}(\mathbb{M})$. The existence of an optimal policy π for MDP $\mathbf{M}(\mathbb{M})$ is guaranteed. Of course, this policy is extensional or propositional in the sense that it specifies for each ground state separately which action to execute. Specifying such policies for LOMDPs with large state spaces is cumbersome and learning them will require much effort. Therefore, we introduce π, which intentionally specify the action to take for an abstract state (or sets of states).

Definition 4. $\qquad\qquad\qquad \pi \qquad \Sigma \qquad$ *fi* $\qquad\quad .\qquad\qquad .$
$.\qquad \mathbf{a} \leftarrow \mathbb{L} \qquad\quad \mathbf{a} \qquad\qquad\qquad \mathbb{L} \qquad\qquad\qquad 5$
$\mathrm{vars}(\mathbf{a}) \subseteq \mathit{vars}(\mathbb{L})$

---

[5] We assume that $\mathbf{a}$ is applicable in $\mathbb{L}$.

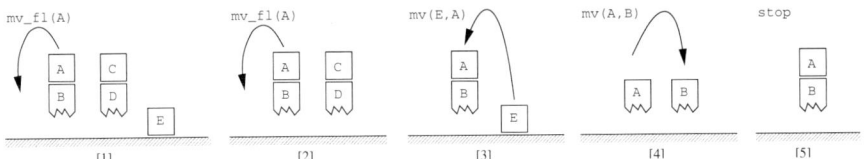

Fig. 2. The decision rules of the *unstack-stack* policy. In the figure, the decision rules are ordered from left to right, i.e., a rule fires only if no rule further to the left fires.

Usually, π consists of multiple decision rules. We apply the same conflict resolution technique as for abstract transitions. This means we assume a total order $\prec^\pi$ among the decision rules in π and do a forward search stopping with the first matching decision rule such as in Prolog. Consider for instance the following abstract policy:

$\langle 1 \rangle \quad \mathtt{mv\_fl(A)} \leftarrow \mathtt{on(A,B), on(C,D), on(E,fl), cl(A), cl(C), cl(E)}.$
$\langle 2 \rangle \quad \mathtt{mv\_fl(A)} \leftarrow \mathtt{on(A,B), on(C,D), cl(A), cl(C)}.$
$\langle 3 \rangle \quad \mathtt{mv(E,A)} \leftarrow \mathtt{on(A,B), on(E,fl), cl(A), cl(E)}.$
$\langle 4 \rangle \quad \mathtt{mv(A,B)} \leftarrow \mathtt{cl(A), cl(B)}.$
$\langle 5 \rangle \quad \mathtt{stop} \leftarrow \mathtt{on(A,B), cl(A)}.$

where we omitted the `absorb` state in front and statements that variables refer to different blocks. For instance in state **Exp** (see before), only decision rule $\langle 3 \rangle$ would fire. The policy, which is graphically depicted in Figure 2, is interesting for several reasons.

1. It is close to the _____ strategy which is well known in the planning community [29]. Basically, the strategy amounts to putting all blocks on the table and then building the goal state by stacking all blocks from the floor onto one single stack. No block is moved more than twice. The number of moves is at most twice the number of blocks.
2. It perfectly generalizes to all other blocks worlds, no matter how many blocks there are.
3. It cannot be learned in a propositional setting because here the optimal , propositional policy would encode the optimal number of moves.

The meaning of a decision rule $\mathtt{a} \leftarrow \mathbb{L}$ is that

$$\pi(Z) \quad \mathtt{a}\theta \quad \quad Z \quad \mathbb{L} \leq_\theta Z \quad \quad 1/ \sum_{\mathtt{a}\leftarrow\mathbb{L}\in\pi} |\{\theta' \mid \mathbb{L} \leq_{\theta'} Z\}|$$

Let $\mathbb{L} = \{\mathbb{L}_1, \ldots, \mathbb{L}_m\}$ be the set of bodies in π (ordered w.r.t. $\prec^\pi$). We call $\mathbb{L}$ the _____ of π and assume that it covers all possible states of the LOMDP. This together with the total order guarantees that $\mathbb{L}$ forms a partition of the states. The equivalence classes $[\mathbb{L}_1], \ldots, [\mathbb{L}_m]$ induced by $\mathbb{L}$ are inductively defined by $[\mathbb{L}_1] = S(\mathbb{L}_1)$, $[\mathbb{L}_i] = S(\mathbb{L}_i) \setminus \bigcup_{j=1}^{i-1}[\mathbb{L}_j]$, for $i \geq 2$. Because $\mathbb{L}$ generally does not coincide with $\mathbb{B}$, the following proposition holds.

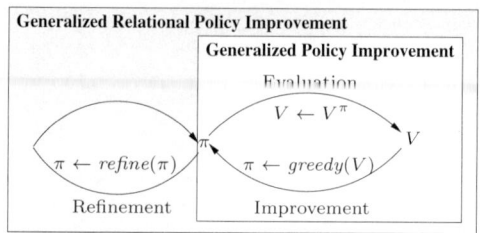

Fig. 3. Generalized relational policy iteration which accounts for different abstraction levels. It is an upgrade of generalized policy iteration for traditional reinforcement learning as illustrated in [30]. *greedy* denotes the greedy policy computed from the current value function, see [30].

Proposition 1. π fi nondeterministic π

5 Generalized Relational Policy Iteration

The crucial question is now, how to learn abstract policies? According to Sutton and Barto [30], almost all reinforcement learning systems follow the so called (GPI) scheme shown in Figure 3. It consists of two interacting processes: and . Here, evaluating a policy refers to computing the value function of the current policy, and policy improvement refers to computing a new policy based on the current value function. Indeed, GPI cannot directly be applied to learn abstract policies. Different abstraction levels have to be explored. Thus, one needs an additional process which we call fi . The resulting (GRPI) scheme is illustrated in Figure 3.

Generally speaking, policy refinement traverses the space of possible abstract policies. To do so, one can apply ILP techniques [24,11]. For instance, we can refine the policy by adding a refined variant of decision rule $\langle 1 \rangle$,

$\langle 0 \rangle$ mv_fl(A) $\leftarrow$ on(A, B), on(C, D), on(D, floor), on(E, fl), cl(A), cl(C), cl(E).

One can, however, do even better. When we have a model of the domain, it can be e.g. used to score different refinements (e.g. measuring the fl of a refinement of one state on the remaining state [25,22]). If we do not have a model of the domain, we can employ the experience we already have, i.e., the states visited. This approach is followed by Džeroski [10] within RRL-RT. To implement the policy refinement, Džeroski employ logical regression trees for (abstract state-action) value function approximations. Starting with some initial abstraction level, RRL then integrates , , and fi in that it uses episodes to build a regression tree. Thus, RRL-RT can be seen as an instance of GRPI.

Empirically, RRL-RT has been proven to work very well on a wide range of domains such as blocks world and Digger. In the present paper, we will provide a

first step in explaining why it works so well. More precisely, we will focus on the
within GRPI approaches and prove convergence
for an upgrade of TD(λ).

6 Logical TD(λ)

The   considers how to compute the state-value function V^{π} for an arbitrary abstract policy π. In this paper, we focus on model-free
approaches. Model-free approaches do not know the reward and the transition
functions in advance when computing the value of an abstract policies from
experiences $\langle X_t, a_t, Y_t, r_t \rangle$. Furthermore, in contrast to traditional model-free
approaches, maintaining values for all states of the underlying MDP $\mathbf{M}(\mathbb{M})$ is
not feasible.

The basic idea to come up with a relational evaluation approach is to de-
fine the expected reward of $\mathbb{L} \in \mathbb{L}$ to be the average expected value for all the
states in $[\mathbb{L}]$. This is a good model because if we examine each state in $[\mathbb{L}_i]$,
we make contradictory observations of rewards and transition probabilities. The
best model is the average of these observations given no prior knowledge of the
model. Unfortunately, it has been experimentally shown that (already model-
based) reinforcement learning with function approximation does not converge in
general, see e.g. [5]. Fortunately, this does not hold for averagers. To prove convergence, we reduce the "abstract" evaluation problem to the evaluation problem
for $\mathbf{M}(\mathbb{M}) = (S, A, \mathbf{T}, \lambda)$ with state aggregation (see e.g. [17,28,22]) with respect
to $[\mathbb{L}_1], \dots, [\mathbb{L}_m]$. For ease of explanation, we will focus on a   (0) approach[6],
see e.g. [30]. Results for general   (λ) can be obtained by applying Tsitsiklis
and Van Roy's results [32].

Algorithm 1 sketches logical   (0). Given some experience following an abstract policy π, LTD(0) updates its estimate V of V. If a nonterminal state is
visited, then it updates its estimate based on what happens after that visit. Instead of updating the estimate at the level of states, LTD(0) updates its estimate
at the abstraction level $\mathbb{L}$ of π.

To show convergence, it is sufficient to reduce   (0) to   (0) with soft
state aggregation [28]. The basic idea of soft state aggregation is to cluster the
state space, i.e., to map the state space S into clusters $c_1, \dots, c_k$. Each state
s belongs to a cluster c_i with a certain probability $P(c_i|s)$. The value function
then is computed at the level of clusters rather than states. Logical TD(0) is
a special case of soft state aggregation. To see this recall that the abstraction
level $\mathbb{L}$ partitions the state space S. Thus, one can view the abstract states
in $\mathbb{L}$ as clusters where each state $Z \in S$ belongs to only one cluster $[\mathbb{L}_i]$, i.e.,
$P([\mathbb{L}_i] \mid Z) = 1$ if $Z \in S([\mathbb{L}])$; otherwise $P([\mathbb{L}_i] \mid Z) = 0$. Furthermore, the
state set S and the action set A of $\mathbf{M}(\mathbb{M})$ are finite, and the agent is following

---

[6] A similar analysis can be done for model-based approaches. Gordon [17] showed
that value iteration with an averager as function approximator converges within a
bounded distance from the optimal value function of the original MDP.

Algorithm 1: Logical TD(0) where α is the learning rate and $\widehat{V}(\mathbb{L})$ is the approximation of $V(\mathbb{L})$.

a nondeterministic policy. Therefore, the assumptions of the following Theorem are fulfilled.

Theorem 2 (adopted from Singh et al. [28], Corollary 2).   (0)
$\cdot$ $\mathbf{M(M)}$ $\cdot$ π
              $\cdot$ $\cdot$ $\cdot$ $\forall \mathbb{L}_i \in \mathbb{L}$:
$V([\mathbb{L}_i]) =$

$$\sum_{Z \in S} P^{\pi}(Z \mid [\mathbb{L}_i])\ R^{\pi}(Z) + \lambda \sum_{\mathbb{L}_j \in \mathbb{L}} P^{\pi}(Z, [\mathbb{L}]_j) V([\mathbb{L}_j]) \tag{2}$$

From this, it follows that $LTD(0)$ converges, i.e.   (0) applied to a LOMDP $\mathbf{M}$ while following an abstract policy π at abstraction level $\mathbb{L}$ converges with probability one to the solutions of the system of equations (2).

   Note that for arbitrary abstraction levels, while Theorem 2 shows that   (0) learning will find solutions, the error in the (ground) state space will not be zero in general. Equation (2) basically states that an abstract policy π induces a process $\mathbf{L}$ over $[\mathbb{L}_1], \dots, [\mathbb{L}_m]$ whose transition probabilities and rewards for a state $[\mathbb{L}_i]$ are averages of the corresponding values of the covered ground states in $\mathbf{M(M)}$, see also [20]. Due to that, the process $\mathbf{L}$ appears to a learner to have a non-Markovian nature. Consider the following LOMDP

$$1: q \xleftarrow{1.0:0.0:a} p, q \qquad 2: \emptyset \xleftarrow{1.0:1.0:a} p \quad \text{and} \quad 3: p \xleftarrow{1.0:0.0:a} \emptyset.$$

and the abstraction level $\mathbb{L} = \{p, q, \emptyset\}$. Here, $\mathbf{L}$ will assign the same probabilities and rewards to the transitions from $[q]$ to $[p]$ and from $[\emptyset]$ to $[p]$, namely the ones of transition 3. Consequently, the values for [q] and [∅] are the same in **L** as the next state is the same, namely [p]. $M(\mathbb{M})$, however, assigns different values to both as the following traces show: $q \xrightarrow{1.0:0.0:a} p, q \xrightarrow{1.0:1.0:a} q \ldots$ and $\emptyset \xrightarrow{1.0:0.0:a} p \xrightarrow{1.0:0.0:a} \emptyset \ldots$ Nevertheless, (0) converges at the level of $\mathbb{L}$ and can generalize well even for unseen ground states due to the abstraction.

To summarize, Theorem 2 shows that temporal-difference evaluation of an abstract policy converges. Different policies, however, will have different errors in the ground state space. In the context of GRPI (see Section 5), this suggests to use refinement operators to heuristically reduce the error in the ground state space. Applied on RRL-RT, this reads as follows.

1. Because each logical regression tree induces a finite abstraction level, temporal-difference evaluation of a fixed regression tree converges.
2. Relational node/state splitting (based on the state sequences encountered so far) is used to heuristically reduce the error in the ground state space.

7 Experiments

Our task was to evaluate abstract policies within the blocks world. This task was motivated by the experiments in relational reinforcement learning (RRL) [10] and by the fact that the blocks world is the prototypical toy domain requiring relational representations. In contrast to the experiments reported by [10] on RRL, we exclusively use the standard predicates `on`, `cl`, and `bl`. [10] also needed to make use of several background knowledge predicates such as `above`, `height` of stacks as well as several directives to the first-order regression tree learner. Another difference to our approach is that RRL induces the relevant abstract states automatically using a regression tree learner. Our goal, however, was not to present an overall GRPI system but to put the following hypotheses to test:

H1 LTD(0) converges for finite abstraction levels.
H2 Using LTD(0), abstract policies can be compared.
H3 LTD(0) works for actions with multiple outcomes.
H4 Relational policy refinement is needed.
H5 Variance can be used as a heuristic state-splitting criterion.

We implemented (0) using the Prolog system YAP-4.4.4. All experiments were run on a 3.1 GHz Linux machine and the discount factor λ was 0.9, and the learning rate α was set to 0.015. We randomly generated 100 blocks world states for 6 blocks, for 8 blocks, and for 10 blocks using the procedure described by [29]. This set of 300 states constituted the set of starting states in all experiments. Note that for 10 blocks a traditional MDP would have to represent $58,941,091$ states of which $3,628,800$ are goal states. The result of each experiment is an average of five runs of 5000 episodes where for each new episode we randomly selected one state from as starting state. For each run, the value function was initialized to zero. Note that in all experiments, the abstract policies and value functions apply no matter how many blocks there are.

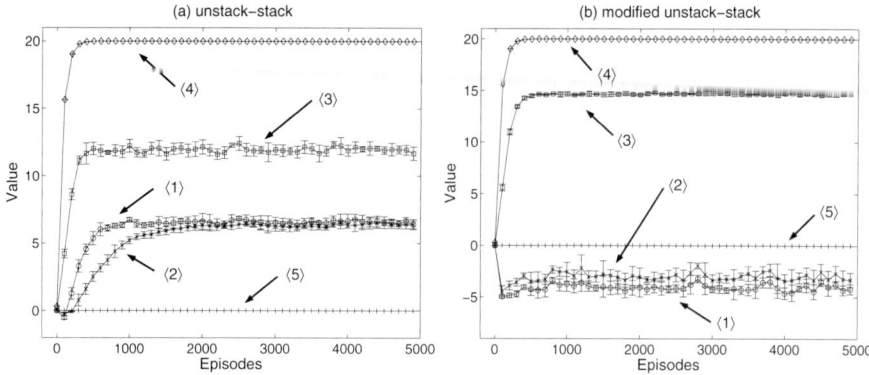

Fig. 4. Learning curves for TD(0) on the evaluation problem **(a)** for the *unstack-stack* policy and **(b)** for the *modified* unstack-stack policy. The predicted values are shown as a function of number of episodes. These data are averages over 5 reruns; the error bars show the standard deviations.

Our task was to evaluate the   abstract policy for the   LOMDP, both introduced above. The results are summarized in Figure 4 **(a)** and clearly show that hypothesis **H1** holds. The learning curves show that the values of the abstract states converged, i.e.,   (0) converged. Note that the value of abstract state ⟨5⟩ remained 0. The reason for this is that, by accident, no state with all blocks on the floor was in   . Furthermore, the values converged to similar values in all runs. The values basically reflect the nature of the policy. It is better to have a single stack than multiple ones. The total running time for all 25000 episodes was 67.5 seconds measured using YAP's build-in `statistics(runtime,_)`.

In reinforcement learning,   refers to computing a new policy based on the current value function. In a relational setting, the success of, e.g., computing the greedy policy given an abstract value function depends on the granularity of the value function. For instance, based on the last value function, it is not possible to distinguish between `mv_fl(A)` and `mv(A, B)` as actions in decision rule ⟨1⟩ because both would get the same expected values. To overcome this, one might refine the abstraction level (see experiment 5) or evaluate different policies at the same abstraction level.

In this experiments, we evaluated a   *fi* "unstack-stack" policy in the same way as in the first experiment. It differed from the "unstack-stack" policy in that we do not perform `mv_fl(A)` but `move(E, A)` in the decision rule ⟨1⟩. The results are summarized in Figure 4 **(b)**. Interestingly, the values of abstract states ⟨1⟩ and ⟨2⟩ dropped from approximately 5 to approximately −4. This shows that   is preferred over this policy. Furthermore, the total running time of all 25000 episodes increased to 97.3 seconds as the average length of an episode increased. This clearly shows that hypothesis **H2** holds.

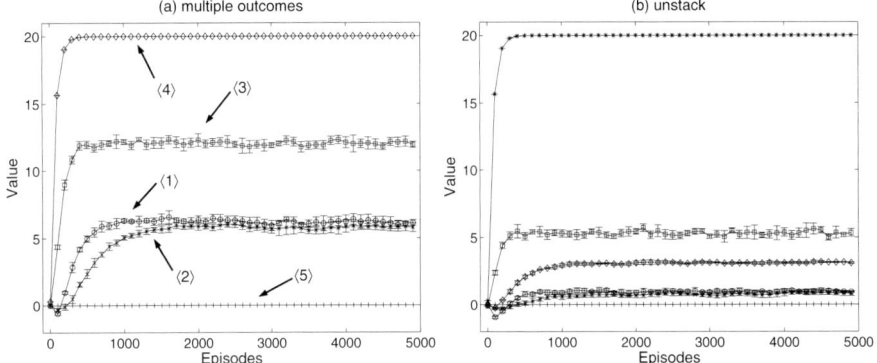

Fig. 5. Learning curves for TD(0) on the evaluation problem for the *unstack-stack* policy where **(a)** the actions of the underlying LOMDP have multiple outcomes and **(b)** the underlying LOMDP encoded the *unstack* problem. The predicted values are shown as a function of number of episodes. These data are averages over 5 reruns; the error bars show the standard deviations.

We reran the first experiment where the underlying LOMDP now encoded that mv_fl and mv have multiple outcomes. For action mv_fl(A, fl), block A may fall on C, and for action mv(A, C) the block A may fall on the floor fl. Again, LTD(0) converged as Figure 5 **(a)** shows. This shows that hypotheses **H3** holds.

We reran the first experiment, i.e., we evaluated the policy, but now the underlying LOMDP encoded the problem. Again, LTD(0) converged as Figure 5 **(b)** shows. The running time over all 25000 episodes, however, increased to 317.7 seconds as the underlying LOMDP was more complex. This shows that hypothesis **H1** holds.

Finally, we investigated on(a, b) as goal. The underlying LOMDP was

$$\text{absorb} \xleftarrow{\ 1.0:20:\texttt{stop}\ } \text{on(a, b)}.$$

$$\text{on(A, fl), cl(A), on(C, D), cl(C), cl(B)} \xleftarrow{\ 0.9:-1:\texttt{mv\_fl(A)}\ } \text{on(A, B), cl(A), on(C, D), cl(C)}.$$

$$\text{on(A, C), cl(A), on(C, D), cl(B)} \xleftarrow{\ 0.9:-1:\texttt{mv(A,C)}\ } \text{on(A, B), cl(A), on(C, D), cl(C)}.$$

$$\text{on(A, floor), cl(A), cl(B)} \xleftarrow{\ 1.0:-1:\texttt{mv(A,floor)}\ } \text{on(A, B), cl(A)}.$$

assuming that all variables denote to different objects and absorb omitted. If the transition probabilities do not sum to 1.0 then there is an additional abstract transition for staying in the current abstract state. Following the same experimental setup as in the first experiment but using a step size $\alpha = 0.5$, we evaluated two different policies, namely $\langle a \rangle - \langle e \rangle, \langle l \rangle$ and $\langle a \rangle - \langle l \rangle$ where

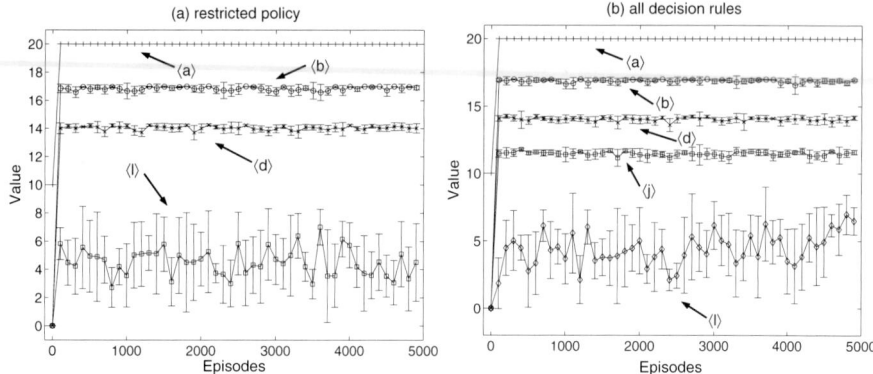

Fig. 6. Learning curves for TD(0) on the evaluation problem for the *on(a,b)* policy where the underlying LOMDP encoded the *on(a,b)* goal. The predicted values are shown as a function of number of episodes. These data are averages over 5 reruns; the error bars show the standard deviations; only state with a non zero value are shown (note that we used a finite set of starting states only). **(a)** Policy restricted to $\langle a \rangle - \langle e \rangle$ and $\langle l \rangle$. **(b)** All decision rules $\langle a \rangle - \langle l \rangle$.

$\langle a \rangle$ $\quad$ stop $\leftarrow$ on(a, b).
$\langle b \rangle$ $\quad$ mv(a, b) $\leftarrow$ cl(a), cl(b), on(a, B).
$\langle c \rangle$ $\quad$ mv_fl(b) $\leftarrow$ cl(b), on(a, C), on(b, a).
$\langle d \rangle$ $\quad$ mv_fl(A) $\leftarrow$ cl(b), cl(A), on(a, C), on(A, a).
$\langle e \rangle$ $\quad$ mv_fl(A) $\leftarrow$ cl(a), cl(A), on(a, C), on(A, b).
$\langle f \rangle$ $\quad$ mv_fl(A) $\leftarrow$ cl(A), on(a, D), on(b, a), on(A, b).
$\langle g \rangle$ $\quad$ mv_fl(b) $\leftarrow$ cl(b), on(a, C), on(b, D), on(D, a).
$\langle h \rangle$ $\quad$ mv_fl(a) $\leftarrow$ cl(a), on(a, C), on(C, b).
$\langle i \rangle$ $\quad$ mv_fl(a) $\leftarrow$ cl(A), on(a, D), on(A, b).
$\langle j \rangle$ $\quad$ mv_fl(A) $\leftarrow$ cl(b), cl(A), on(a, C), on(A, D), on(D, a).
$\langle k \rangle$ $\quad$ mv_fl(A) $\leftarrow$ cl(a), cl(A), on(a, C), on(A, D), on(D, b).
$\langle l \rangle$ $\quad$ mv_fl(A) $\leftarrow$ cl(A), on(A, D).

In both cases, LTD(0) converged as Figure 6 shows. The running time over all 25000 episodes was 4.85 seconds ($\langle a \rangle - \langle e \rangle, \langle l \rangle$) and 6.7 seconds ($\langle a \rangle - \langle l \rangle$). In both experiments, state $\langle l \rangle$ was exceptional. It obeyed a higher variance than the other states. The reason is that it acts as a kind of "container" state for all situations which are not covered by the preceding abstract states. In the refined policy, all added states showed low variances. Thus, we may iterate and refine $\langle l \rangle$ even more. The experiments show that hypotheses **H1**, **H4**, and **H5** hold and supports the variance-based state-splitting approach taken in RRL-RT [10].

8   Related Work

Within reinforcement learning (RL), there is currently a significant interest in using rich representation languages. Kaelbling et al. [19] and Finney et al. [13] investigated propositionalization methods in relational domains, namely (DRs). DRs avoid enumerating the domain by using variables such as *fl*. Although DRs have led to impressive results [23, 34], Finney et al.'s results show that DR may degrade learning performance within relational domains. According to Finney et al. .

such as RRL-RT [10] is one way to effectively learning in domains with objects and relations. The Q-function is approximated using a relational regression tree learner. Although the experimental results are interesting, RRL-RT did not explain, in theoretical terms, why it works. We provide some new insights on this.

Furthermore, the present work complements Kersting and De Raedt's [20] and Van Otterlo's [33] approaches. In [20], Kersting and De Raedt report on experiments with a relational upgrade of Q-learning. Van Otterlo devised a relational prioritized sweeping approach. Both works, however, do not consider convergence proofs.

The LOMDP formalism is related to Poole's independent choice logic [26]. Independent choice logic makes the dependencies among the probabilities explicit, but does not consider the learning problem.

From a more general point of view, our approach is closely related to (DTR) [3]. State spaces are characterized by a number of random variables and the domain is specified using logical representations of actions that capture the regularities in the effects of actions. Because 'existing DTR algorithms are all designed to work with representations of MDPs', Boutilier et al. [4] proposed *fi* which is a probabilistic extension of Reiter's . The language is certainly more expressive than that of LOMDPs. However, it is also much more complex. Furthermore, Boutilier et al. assume that the model is given whereas in the present paper model-free learning methods have been applied.

Using a model-based approach, Yoon et al. [35] introduced a method for generalizing abstract policies from small to large relational MDPs employing description logics. The method has been extended [12] to an approximated policy iteration. Guestrin et al. [18] specify relationally factored MDPs based on probabilistic relational models [15] but not in a reinforcement learning setting. In contrast to LOMDPs, relations do not change over time. This assumption does not hold in many domains such as the blocks world.

The idea of solving large MDP by a reduction to an equivalent, smaller MDP is also discussed e.g. in [7,16]. However there, no relational or first order representations have been investigated. Kim and Dean [22] investigate model-based RL based on non-homogenous partitions of propositional, factored MDPs. Furthermore, there has been great interest in abstraction on other levels than state spaces. Abstraction over time [31] or primitive actions [8,1] are useful ways to abstract from specific sub-actions and time. This research is orthogonal and could be applied to LOMDPs in the future.

Finally, Baum [2] reports on solving blocks worlds with up to 10 blocks using RL related techniques. However, the language is domain-dependent and is not based on logic programming.

9 Conclusions

We have introduced a representation that integrates MDPs with logic programs. This framework allows one to compactly and declaratively represent complex (relationally factored) MDPs. Furthermore, it allows one to gain insights into relational reinforcement learning approaches. More precisely, we introduced abstract policies for LOMDPs and   (GRPI) which is a general scheme for learning abstract policies. Because abstract policies basically introduce state aggregation, they can be evaluated using simple upgrades of (propositional) reinforcement learning methods such as   (λ)-learning. Convergence has been proven and experimentally validated.

Such convergence guarantees are important because recent results on exact relational value iteration (RVI) [21] show that RVI can require an infinite abstraction level, i.e., an infinite logical regression tree in order to converge to exact values. Here, approximative approaches such as   (λ) are useful, as they allow one to cut the regression tree at any level and to estimate the best values one can achieve at that abstraction level (cf. experiment 5). In other words, approximation is not only an interesting feature, but in some cases also a necessity for successful relational reinforcement learning.

The authors hope that the presented framework will be useful as a starting point for further theoretical developments in RRL. Of interest are: real-world applications; extending the language by e.g. negation and $\forall$-quantification; unordered abstract transitions; MDP-specific relational state splitting rules; applying Gordon's convergence results to RRL-RT with k-nearest-neighbour [9] (if possible); and to prove convergence of logical Q-learning [20]. The last point seems to be challenging as it also introduces action aggregation. Nevertheless, initial experiments [20] show that logical Q-learning performs well.

Acknowledgments. The authors are deeply grateful Bob Givan for valuable discussions on the paper and its topic. The authors would also like to thank Martijn Van Otterlo for fruitful discussions on the topic. Also many thanks to the anonymous reviewers whose comments helped to improve the paper. The research was supported by the European Union IST programme, contract no. FP6-508861,   .   .

References

1. D. Andre and S. Russell. Programmable reinforcement learning agents. In *Advances in Neural Information Processing Systems 13*, pages 1019–1025. MIT Press, 2001.

2. E. B. Baum. Towards a Model of Intelligence as an Economy of Agents. *Machine Learning*, 35(2):155–185, 1999.

3. C. Boutilier, T. Deam, and S. Hanks. Decision-Theoretic Planning: Structural Assumptions and Computational Leverage. *JAIR*, 11:1–94, 1999.

4. C. Boutilier, R. Reiter, and B. Price. Symbolic Dynamic Programming for First-order MDPs. In *Seventeenth International Joint Conference on Artificial Intelligence (IJCAI-01)*, pages 690–700, Seattle, USA, 2001.

5. J. A. Boyan and A. W. Moore. Generalization in reinforcement learning: safely approximating the value function. In *Advances in Neural Information Processing Systems*, volume 7, 1995.

6. L. De Raedt and K. Kersting. Probabilistic Logic Learning. *ACM-SIGKDD Explorations: Special issue on Multi-Relational Data Mining*, 5(1):31–48, 2003.

7. R. Dearden and C. Boutilier. Abstraction and approximate decision theoretic planning. *Artificial Intelligence*, 89(1):219–283, 1997.

8. Thomas G. Dietterich. Hierarchical reinforcement learning with the MAXQ value function decomposition. *Journal of Artificial Intelligence Research*, 13:227–303, 2000.

9. K. Driessens and J. Ramon. Relational Instance Based Regression for Relational Reinforcement Learning. In *Proceedings of the Twelfth International Conference on Machine Learning*, pages 123–130, Washington DC, USA, 2003.

10. S. Džeroski, L. De Raedt, and K. Driessens. Relational reinforcement learning. *Machine Learning*, 43(1/2):7–52, 2001.

11. S. Džeroski and N. Lavrač. *Relational Data Mining*. Springer-Verlag, 2001.

12. A. Fern, S. Yoon, and R. Givan. Approximate policy iteration with a policy language bias. In *Proceedings of the Neural Information Processing Conference (NIPS)*, 2003.

13. S. Finney, N. H. Gardiol, L. P. Kaelbling, and T. Oates. The thing that we tried didn't work very well: Deictic representation in reinforcement learning. In *Proceedings of the Eighteenth International Conference on Uncertainty in Artificial Intelligence (UAI-02)*, 2002.

14. P. Flach. *Simply logical: intelligent reasoning by example*. John Wiley and Sons Ltd., 1994.

15. N. Friedman, L. Getoor, D. Koller, and A. Pfeffer. Learning probabilistic relational models. In *Proceedings of the Sixteenth International Joint Conferences on Artificial Intelligence (IJCAI-99)*, pages 1300–1309, Stockholm, Sweden, 1999. Morgan Kaufmann.

16. R. Givan, T. Dean, and M. Greig. Equivalence notions and model minimization in Markov decision processes. *Artificial Intelligence*, 147:163–224, 2003.

17. G. J. Gordon. Stable fitted reinforcement learning. In *Advances in Neural Information Processing*, pages 1052–1058. MIT Press, 1996.

18. C. Guestrin, D. Koller, C. Gearhart, and N. Kanodia. Generalizing Plans to New Environments in Relational MDPs. In *Proceedings of International Joint Conference on Artificial Intelligence (IJCAI-03)*, Acapulco, Mexico, 2003.

19. L. P. Kaelbling, T. Oates, N. H. Gardiol, and S. Finney. Learning in worlds with objects. In *Working Notes of the AAAI Stanford Spring Symposium on Learning Grounded Representations*, 2001.

20. K. Kersting and L. De Raedt. Logical markov decision programs. In *Working Notes of the IJCAI-2003 Workshop on Learning Statistical Models from Relational Data (SRL-03)*, pages pp. 63–70, 2003.

21. K. Kersting, M. Van Otterlo, and L. De Raedt. Bellman goes Relational. In *Proceedings of the Twenty-First International Conference on Machine Learning (ICML-04)*, Banff, Alberta, Canada, July 4-8 2004, (to appear).

22. K.-E. Kim and T. Dean. Solving factored mdps using non-homogeneous partitions. *Artificial Intelligence*, 147:225–251, 2003.

23. A. K. McCallum. *Reinforcement Learning with Selective Perception and Hidden States*. PhD thesis, Department of Computer Science, University of Rochester, 1995.

24. S. Muggleton and L. De Raedt. Inductive logic programming: Theory and methods. *Journal of Logic Programming*, 19(20):629–679, 1994.

25. R. Munos and A. Moore. Influence and Variance of a Markov Chain : Application to Adaptive Discretization in Optimal Control. In *Proceedings of the IEEE Conference on Decision and Control*, 1999.

26. D. Poole. The independent choice logic for modelling multiple agents under uncertainty. *Artificial Intelligence*, 94(1–2):7–56, 1997.

27. M. L. Puterman. *Markov Decision Processes: Discrete Stochastic Dynamic Programming*. John Wiley & Sons, 1994.

28. S. P. Singh, T. Jaakkola, and M. I. Jordan. Reinforcement learning with soft state aggregation. In *Advances in Neural Information Processing 7*, pages 361–268. MIT Press, 1994.

29. J. Slaney and S. Thiébaux. Blocks World revisited. *Artificial Intelligence*, 125:119–153, 2001.

30. R. S. Sutton and A. G. Barto. *Reinforcement Learning: An Introduction*. The MIT Press, 1998.

31. R. S. Sutton, D. Precup, and S. Singh. Between MDPs and semi-MDPs: a framework for temporal abstraction in reinforcement learning. *Artificial Intelligence*, 112:181–211, 1999.

32. J. N. Tsitsiklis and B. Van Roy. An analysis of temporal-difference learning with function approximation. *IEEE Transactions of Automatic Control*, 42:674–690, 1997.

33. M. Van Otterlo. Reinforcement Learning for Relational MDPs. In *Proceedings of the Annual Machine Learning Conference of Belgium and the Netherlands*, 2004.

34. S. D. Whitehead and D. H. Ballard. Learning to perceive and act by trial and error. *Machine Learning*, 7(1):45 – 83, 1991.

35. S. Yoon, A. Fern, and R. Givan. Inductive policy selection for first-order MDPs. In *Proceedings of the International Conference on Uncertainty in Artificial Intelligence (UAI)*, 2002.

Learning Goal Hierarchies from Structured Observations and Expert Annotations

Tolga Könik and John Laird

Artificial Intelligence Lab., University of Michigan
1101 Beal Avenue, MI 48109, USA
{konik, laird}@umich.edu

Abstract. We describe a framework for generating agent programs that model expert task performance in complex dynamic domains, using expert behavior observations and goal annotations as the primary source. We map the problem of learning an agent program on to multiple learning problems that can be represented in a "supervised concept learning" setting. The acquired procedural knowledge is partitioned into a hierarchy of goals and it is represented with first order rules. Using an inductive logic programming (ILP) learning component allows us to use structured goal annotations, structured background knowledge and structured behavior observations. We have developed an efficient mechanism for storing and retrieving structured behavior data. We have tested our system using artificially created examples and behavior observation traces generated by AI agents. We evaluate the learned rules by comparing them to hand-coded rules.

1 Introduction

Developing autonomous agents that behave "intelligently" in complex environments (i.e. large, dynamic, nondeterministic, and with unobservable states) usually presumes costly agent-programmer effort of acquiring knowledge from experts and encoding it into an executable representation. Machine learning can help automate this process. In this paper, we present a framework for automatically creating an agent program using the data obtained by observing experts performing tasks as the primary input. The ultimate goal of this line of research is to reduce the cost and expertise required to build artificial agents.

Learning from expert observations to replicate behavior is often called *behavioral cloning*. Most behavioral cloning research to date has focused on learning subcognitive skills in controlling a dynamic system such as pole balancing [10], controlling a simulated aircraft [11, 16], or operating a crane [20]. In contrast, our focus is capturing deliberate high-level reasoning.

Behavioral cloning was originally formulated as a direct mapping from states to control actions, which produces a reactive agent. Later, using goals was proposed to improved robustness of the learned agents. Camacho's system [2] induced controllers in terms goal parameter so that the execution system can use the same controllers under varying initial conditions and goal settings. It did not however learn how to set the goal parameters. Isaac and Sammut [5] present a two step approach where first a

R. Camacho, R. King, A. Srinivasan (Eds.): ILP 2004, LNAI 3194, pp. 198–215, 2004.
© Springer-Verlag Berlin Heidelberg 2004

mapping from states to goal parameters is learned, then control actions are learned in terms of these goals. Suc and Bratko [19] describe induction of qualitative constraints that model trajectories the expert is trying to follow to achieve goals. These constraints are used in choosing control actions.

In the goal-directed behavioral cloning research mentioned above, goals are predefined parameters of a dynamic system. For example, the learning-to-fly domain has goal parameters such as target turn-rate. In contrast, we want to capture a hierarchy of high-level goals. For example in a building navigation domain, an expert may have a goal of choosing which door it should go through to get to a room containing a particular item. Unlike the above approaches, we don't assume that the system has pre-existing definitions for the goals. Instead in our framework, the meaning of goals are implicitly learned by learning when the experts select them together with the decisions that become relevant once the goals are selected. To facilitate this, we require that the experts annotate the observation traces with the names and parameters of goals (i.e. *select-door(d_i)*). This requirement is feasible in our setting because high-level goals typically change infrequently and the experts are likely to be conscious of them.

Our work is strongly influenced by van Lent's [22] learning by observation framework. His system, KnoMic, also represents and learns an explicit hierarchy of high-level goals. KnoMic uses an attribute-value based representation that would run into difficulties when structured properties of the environment are relevant, for example if there are multiple objects of the same kind (i.e. two enemy planes in a tactical air combat domain), structured domain knowledge (i.e. a building map in a navigation domain), or inferred knowledge (i.e. shortest-path towards a target room) is essential in choosing and executing the right strategy.

Our framework proposes a natural solution for the above limitations by framing the learning problem in the first order setting of Inductive Logic Programming (ILP) while maintaining most of the core features of KnoMic. Unlike KnoMic, our framework allows parametric and structured goal annotations, structured background knowledge, and structured sensors. In addition, KnoMic uses a simple single-pass learning algorithm that cannot deal with noise and assumes that the expert exhibits correct and consistent behavior at all times, while our framework uses an ILP algorithm that is robust in the presence of noise. To be able to use ILP algorithms in domains with large numbers of facts, we have developed an efficient mechanism to store and access structured behavior data.

We use the general agent architecture Soar [8] as the target language for the acquired knowledge. Soar uses a symbolic rule based representation that simplifies the interaction with the ILP learning component. Although Soar influences how knowledge is represented in our framework, we introduce the framework independent of Soar to make our learning assumptions more explicit and to have results that are transferable to other architectures.

The paper is organized as follows. Next, we describe our learning by observation framework. In section 3, we present experimental results. In section 4, we discuss related work. Finally, we conclude with remarks about future directions in section 5.

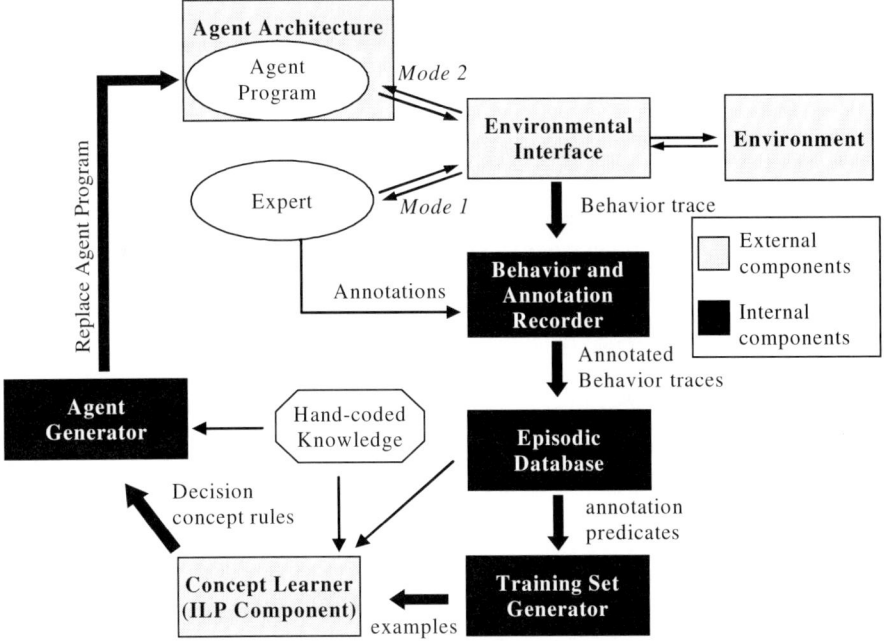

Fig. 1. General overview of our learning by observation framework. In mode 1, the expert generates annotated behavior. In mode 2, an agent program executes behavior and the expert accepts or rejects its annotations

2 Our Learning by Observation Framework

The execution cycle of our framework has two operation modes (Fig. 1). In the first mode, the expert interacts with the environment. In the second mode, the approximately correct agent created during previous learning interacts with the environment. Both of these interactions are recorded to a *behavior trace* structure. In the first mode, the expert annotates the behavior trace with the goals he/she has been pursuing. In the second mode, the agent proposes similar annotations and the expert accepts or rejects them. In both modes, the *annotated behavior traces* are inserted into an *episodic database* that efficiently stores and retrieves the observed situations and the expert annotations. The training set generator component maps the problem of "obtaining an agent program" to multiple problems that can be represented in a "supervised concept-learning" setting. These *decision concepts* are used in the generated agent program. For each decision concept, the training set generator returns positive and negative examples, using the information stored in the episodic database. The concept learner component uses an ILP algorithm that learns rules representing the decision concepts, using the examples in the training set and background knowledge obtained by accessing the episodic database and hand-coded domain theory. The agent generator component converts the decision concept rules to an executable agent program. At each cycle, a new agent program is learned from scratch but since more behavior traces are accumulated, a more accurate agent program is expected to be learned, which can in turn generate new traces when the learned agent program interacts with the environment In the second execution mode. At any time during the agent performance (mode 2), the expert can intervene and take control (mode 1) to generate traces, for example if the agent is doing very poorly at a goal. This may help the learning focus on parts of the task where the agent program is lacking knowledge most.

We have partially implemented this framework to conduct the experiments reported in section 3.2. Our program works in the first mode of the execution cycle, and instead of human expert generated behavior, we use behavior of hand-coded Soar agents. At this stage of the research, cloning artificial agents is a cost-effective way to evaluate our framework - it greatly simplifies data collection and it does not require us to build domain specific components to track expert behavior and annotations. Instead, we built a general interface that can extract annotations and behavior from Soar agents on any environment Soar has been connected to.

2.1 Target Agent Architecture and Environments

We use Soar [8] as our target architecture. A long-term motivation is that Soar is one of the few candidates of unified cognitive architectures [14] and has been successful as the basis for developing knowledge-rich agents for complex environments [6, 9, 24] One practical reason for this choice is that there exist interfaces between Soar and these environments that can be reused in our system. Moreover, the hand-coded agents required significant human effort and they can form a basis of comparison for the agents we create automatically.

In this paper we will use examples from "Haunt 2 game" [9], which is a 3-D first person perspective adventure game built using the Unreal game engine. This environment has a large, structured state space, real time decisions, continues space, external agents and events.

2.2 Representation of the Environment and Task Performance Knowledge

In complex domains, an agent (expert/agent program) may receive vast amounts of raw sensory data and the low level motor interaction the agent has to control may be extremely complicated. Since we focus more on higher level reasoning of a cognitive agent than low-level control, we assume that the agents interact with the environment using an interface that converts the raw data to a *symbolic environmental representation* (*SER*). While the expert makes his decisions using a visualization of the raw data, the agent program will make decisions with corresponding symbolic data. Moreover, both the expert and the agent program execute only symbolic actions provided by SER, which is responsible for implementing these actions in the environment at the control level.

At any given moment, SER maintains a set of facts that symbolically represent the state of the environment as perceived from the expert's perspective. Soar agents represent their beliefs about the external world and internal state using a directed graph of binary predicates. Adapting that style, we will assume that the environment representation maintained by SER contains predicates of the form $p(a, b)$ where p is a relation between the objects in the environment denoted by a and b in SER. In the Haunt domain, a "snapshot" of this time varying representation may be as depicted in Fig. 2. The sensors are represented with a binary predicate where the first argument is a special symbol (i.e. agent) and the second argument is the sensed value. The sensors can be *constant-valued* such as the x-coordinate(agent, 35) or energy-level(agent, high) as well as *object-valued* such as current-room(agent, r_1). The object valued sensors can be used to represent structured relations among perceived objects. For example, when a book on top of a desk enters the visual display of the expert, it is SER's responsibility to build corresponding relations and to bind the sensors to these relations. SER also has the responsibility of associating the directly sensed features of the environment with the hand-coded factual knowledge. For example in Fig. 2, we not only see that the expert is in the room r_1, but we also know that he/she can go towards a room r_3 by following a path that goes through door d_1. During the learning phase both the observed dynamical features and the hand-coded factual knowledge are used in a uniform way.

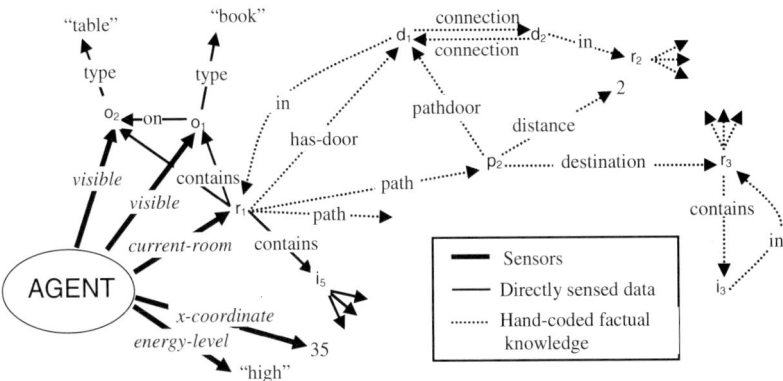

Fig. 2. A snapshot of the data maintained in the symbolic environmental representation (SER) in Haunt domain. SER dynamically updates directly sensed relations and associates factual background knowledge with the sensed objects

We assume that the performance knowledge of the target agent program is decomposed into a hierarchy of operators that represent the goals that the agents pursue and the actions that they take to achieve their goals (Fig. 3). With this assumption, we decompose the "learning an agent program" problem to multiple "learning to maintain an operator" problems. The suboperators correspond to strategies that the agent can use as part of achieving the goal of the parent operator. The agent has to continuously maintain the activity of these operators based on current sensors and internal knowledge. When the agent selects an operator, it must also instantiate the parameters. It then executes the operator by selecting and executing suboperators. The real execution on the environment occurs when *actions*, the lowest level operators, are selected. The names of the selected actions and their parameters are sent to the SER, which applies them in the environment. The actions are continuously applied on the environment as long as the agent keeps them active. We assume that there may be at most one operator active at each level of the hierarchy. This simplifies the learning task because the learner associates the observed behavior only with the active operators and each operator is learned in the context of a single parent operator.

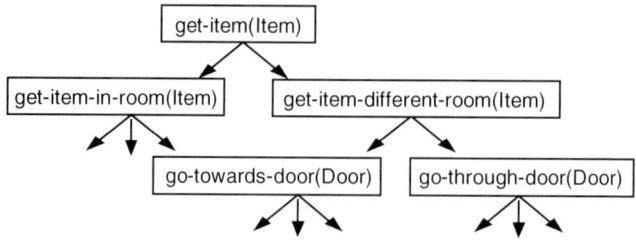

Fig. 3. An Operator Hierarchy in a Building Navigation Domain

For example, if an agent decides to get an item i_1 in a different room by selecting the operator get-item-different-room(Item) with the instantiation Item=i_1, to achieve the task, it could select the suboperator go-towards-door(Door), where Door should be instantiated with the door object on the shortest path from current room to the room where i_1 is in. The real execution occurs with primitive SER actions such as go(forward) or turn(left).

In this representation, information about how the operators are selected implies information about how the operators are executed because execution of an operator at one level is realized by selection of the suboperators at the lower level. Among other more complex possibilities, suboperators may represent alternative or sequential ways of reaching a goal, depending on the learned knowledge of how to maintain the activity of the operators. For example in Fig. 3, get-item-different-room and get-item-in-room are two alternative strategies that may be used to reach the parent goal get-item. Which one of them is preferred depends upon whether the target item is in the current room or not. On the other hand, the operators go-towards-door and go-through-door should be executed sequentially in a loop to achieve their high-level goal. Each time the agent enters a room that does not contain the target item, the agent selects a door and moves towards it (go-towards-door), until the agent is close enough to go through the door to enter a new room (go-through-door). If the item is not in the new room, the agent reselects a door and goes towards it (go-towards-door). If the agent enters a room containing the item, the operator get-item-different-room is immediately retracted with all of its suboperators and get-item-in-room is selected.

The initial knowledge that the system has about the operators consists of their names, the hierarchical relation among them and the scope of their parameters. The final agent obtained as the result of learning should have the capability of maintaining the activity of the operators (i.e. selecting them with correct parameters, stopping them when they achieve their goal, abandoning them in preference of other operators, etc.) and executing them (managing the suboperators).

2.3 Behavior and Annotation Recorder

While the expert or the agent program is performing a task, symbolic state of the environment is recorded into a structure called a *behavior trace*. The symbolic representation that the SER maintains is sampled in small intervals, at consecutively enumerated time points s_i called *situations*. We assume that the domain dependent sampling frequency is sufficiently high so that no significant changes occur between two consecutive situations. We say that the *observed situation predicate* $p(s_i, a, b)$ holds if and only if $p(a, b)$ was in SER at the situation s_i.

If the environment contains static facts (i.e. rooms, doors, etc...) that do not change over different situations, that information can be added to the beginning of the behavior trace manually, even if the expert does not perceive them directly. This corresponds to the assumption that the expert already knows about these features and the learning system will use this information as background knowledge as it creates the model of the expert. If $p(x, y)$ is such a static fact, we say that the *assumed situation predicate* $p(s_i, x, y)$ is true for any s_i.

In the first execution mode, the expert annotates the situations in his/her behavior with the names of the operators and parameters that he/she selects from the operator hierarchy (i.e. Fig. 3). A valid selection that satisfies the semantics of the operator hierarchy must form a connected path of operators starting from the root of the operator hierarchy. Since the actions are executed using SER directly, action annotations can be recorded automatically without any expert effort. In the second execution mode, the expert inspects the annotated behavior traces proposed by the agent program and verifies or rejects the annotations.

We assume that the expert annotates a set of consecutive situations at a time. For a set of consecutive situations R and an operator $op(x)$ where x is an instantiated operator parameter vector, if the expert annotates the situations in R with $op(x)$, we say *accepted-annotation*$(R, op(x))$ where R is called the *annotation region*. Similarly, we say *rejected-annotation*$(R, op(x))$, if the expert has rejected the agent program's annotation of R with $op(x)$.

2.4   Episodic Database

In practice, it is inefficient to store the list of all predicates that hold at each situation explicitly, especially in domains where sampling frequencies are high and there is much sensory input. The *episodic database* efficiently stores and retrieves the information contained in structured behavior traces and expert annotations. In each execution cycle, the training set generator accesses the episodic database while creating positive and negative examples of the decision concepts to be learned. Similarly, the ILP component accesses it to check whether particular situation predicates in the background knowledge hold in the behavior trace. Although the examples are generated only once for each concept, the background situation predicates may be accessed many times during learning. Typically, ILP systems consider many hypotheses before they return a final hypothesis as the result of learning and each time a different hypothesis is considered, the validity of background situation predicates that occur in the hypothesis must be tested. To make learning practical in large domains, it is crucial that the episodic database is an efficient structure.

We assume that for each situation predicate p, the arguments are classified as input or output types. Many ILP systems already require a similar specification for background predicates.[1] The episodic database receives situation predicate queries of the form $p(s, x, y)$ where s is an instantiated situation, x is an instantiated vector of input variables, y is a vector of not instantiated output variables. The result of the query is y vectors that satisfy the query.

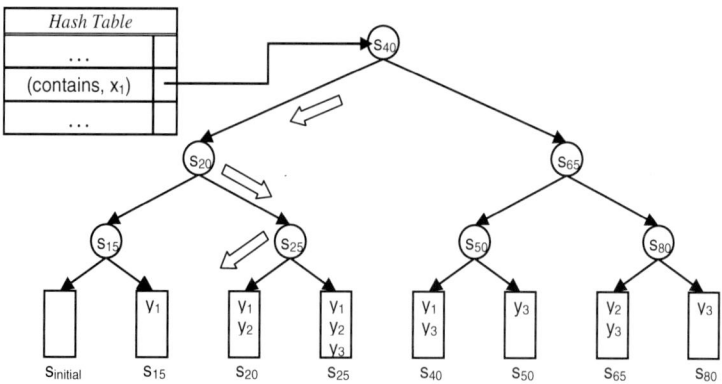

Fig. 4. Search for the query contains(s_{23}, x_1, Y) in the episodic database

In episodic database, each situation predicate is stored using multiple binary trees (Fig. 4). The leaves store the output values explicitly wherever they change and the nodes store the situations where these changes occur. More formally, for each pair (p, x), where p is a situation predicate and x is an input vector, the episodic database explicitly stores the output values Y_s, the set of all y vectors satisfying $p(s, x, y)$ for each situation s, where Y_s has changed compared to previous situation. Moreover, for each (p, x), it contains a binary search tree, where the nodes are these change situations and the leaves are the Y_s vectors. For example in Fig. 4, we have the index structure that represents the predicate contains(+Situation, +Room, -Item). This particular tree shows that room x_1 does not contain any objects in the initial situation. At situation s_{15}, the item y_1 appears in the room x_1. No changes occur, until the situation s_{20} when a new item y_2 is added to the room and so on. For example, to answer the query contains(s_{23}, x_1, Item), first the correct index tree associated with the pair (contains, x_1) is located using a hash table, then by a binary search, the last change before s_{23} is located. In this case, the last change occurs at s_{20} and Item will be instantiated with y_1 and y_2.

In our system, hand-coded static background knowledge is an important special case that is handled very easily by the episodic database. These predicates are added to the behavior trace once and then are never changed. The episodic database stores them very efficiently because their index trees will be reduced to single nodes. The expert annotation predicates are also stored in episodic database by using the operator name as input variable, and the operator arguments as output variables.

The episodic database stores the behavior traces efficiently, unless there are multi-valued predicates (multiple output instantiations at a situation) that change frequently

---

[1] Arguments that are declared constants are treated as input in episodic database representation.

or background predicates that have multiple mode definitions (input/output variable specifications) each requiring a separate set of index trees. In the domains we applied our system to, the first problem is negligible and the second problem does not occur.

Struyf, Ramon and Blockeel [18] describe a general formalization for compactly representing ILP background knowledge in domains that have redundancy between examples, which corresponds to consecutive situations in our case. Their system would represent our situation predicates by storing a list of predicate changes between each pair of consecutive situations. In that representation, to test a particular situation predicate, the behavior trace would have to be traced forward from the initial node, completely generating all facts in all situations until the queried situation is reached. For an ILP system that tests each rule over multiple examples, our approach would be more time efficient in domains having many facts at each situation because we don't need to generate complete states and we don't have to trace all situations. Instead, the episodic database makes binary tree searches only for the predicates that occur in the rule to be tested. In our learning by observation system, the gain from the episodic database is even more dramatic because the examples of the learned concepts are sparsely distributed over situation history.

2.5 Decision Concepts and Generating Examples

In section 2.2, we discuss how the problem of "learning an agent program" is decomposed into multiple "learning to maintain the activity of an operator" problems. In this section, we further decompose it into multiple "decision concept learning" problems that can be framed in an ILP setting.

A decision concept of an operator op is a mapping from the internal state and external observations of an agent to a "decision suggestion" about the activity of op. We currently define four decision concepts: selection-condition (when the operator should be selected if it is not currently selected), overriding-selection-condition (when the operator should be selected even if another operator is selected), maintenance-condition (what must be true for the operator to be maintained during its application), and termination-condition (when the operator has completed and should be terminated). For each decision concept, we have to define how their examples should be constructed from the observation traces and how they are used during execution. In general, for a concept of kind con and an operator $op(x)$, we get a decision concept $con(s, op(x))$ where s is a situation and x a parameter vector of op. For example selection-condition(S, go-to-door(Door)) would describe under which situation S the selection of go-to-door(Door) is advised and with what value Door should be instantiated.

The training set generator constructs the positive and negative examples of decision concepts, using the expert annotation information stored in episodic database. For a decision concept con and expert annotation $op(x_0)$, where x_0 is an instantiated parameter vector, a positive (negative) example is a ground term $con(s, op(x_0))$, where s is an element of a set of situations called *positive (negative) example region* of $op(x_0)$. Fig. 5 depicts the positive and negative example regions of an operator op_A, for different kind of decision concepts. The horizontal direction represents time (situations) in the behavior trace and the boxes represent the accepted annotation regions P, A, and B of three operators $parent(op_A)$, op_A, and op_B such that $parent(op_A)$ is the parent operator of op_A, and op_B is an arbitrary selected operator that shares the same parent with op_A. op_B may be the same kind of operator with op_A, but it should have a different parameter instantiation. The positive example region of the selection condition of op_A is where the expert has started pursuing op_A and its negative example region is where another operator is selected (Fig. 5.b). As an example, if we have op_A = go-towards-door(d_1), $A=s_{20}$-s_{30}, and $B=s_{50}$-s_{60}, we could have the positive example selection-condition(s_{20}, go-towards-door(d_1)) and the negative example selection-condition(s_{50}, go-towards-door(d_1)).

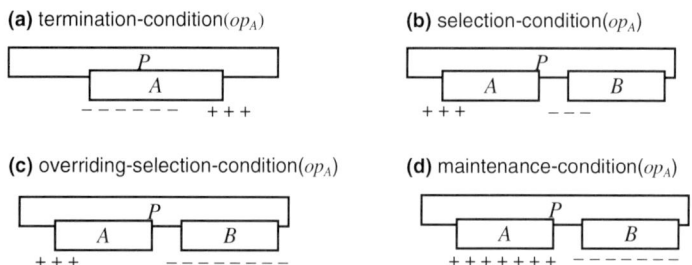

(a) termination-condition(op_A) **(b)** selection-condition(op_A)

(c) overriding-selection-condition(op_A) **(d)** maintenance-condition(op_A)

Fig. 5. The positive and negative example regions of different concepts. A, B, and P are the annotation regions of the operators op_A, op_B, and their parent operator $parent(op_A)$

In general, the examples of decision concepts of an operator op_A are selected only from situations where there is the right context to consider a decision about it. Since the operator hierarchy dictates that $parent(op_A)$ must be active at any situation where op_A is active, all decision concept examples of op_A are obtained only at situations where $parent(op_A)$ is active. Similarly during the execution, the decision concepts of op_A are considered only at situations where $parent(op_A)$ is active.

Different concepts will have different, possibly conflicting suggestions on how the operators should be selected. For example, a situation where termination-condition(op_A) holds suggests that the agent has to terminate op_A, if op_A is active and that op_A should not be selected if it not active. selection-condition(op_A) would be useful to decide whether op_A should be selected, if a previous operator op_B is already terminated (i.e. because of termination-condition(op_B)), it would not be very useful while op_B is still active because such situations are not considered as examples for selection-condition(op_A). On the other hand, overriding-selection-condition(A) could indicate terminating op_B and selecting op_A, even during the situations where op_B is active. Neither selection-condition(op_A) nor overriding-selection-condition(op_A) makes a suggestion while op_A is active, because their examples are not collected in such regions. Finally, like overriding-selection-condition(op_A), maintenance-condition(op_A) suggests that op_A should start even if another operator is still active. Unlike the other selection conditions, absence of maintenance-condition(op_A) suggests that op_A should not be started at situations where it is not active, and that op_A should be terminated, if it is active.

If our goal were programming an agent manually, having only a subset of these concepts could be sufficient. For example, the rules in Soar version 7 are closer to termination/selection conditions while the rules of Soar version 8 are closer to maintenance conditions. Nevertheless, given a representation language, a particular operator may be more compactly represented using a subset of concepts, making it easier to learn inductively.

In general, different decision concepts of an operator may have conflicting suggestions. There are several possibilities for dealing with this problem. One can commit to particular priority between the decision concepts. For example KnoMic [21] learns only selection and termination conditions. In execution, KnoMic assumes that termination conditions have higher priority. Another alternative is to have a dynamic conflict resolution strategy. For example, a second learning step could be used to learn weights for each concept such that the learned weight vector best explains the behavior traces. In this paper, we don't further explore conflict resolution strategies but we concentrate on learning individual decision concepts.

2.6   Learning Concepts

The learning component uses an ILP algorithm, currently inverse entailment [13], to learn a theory that represents decision concepts using the examples received from the training set generator, the situation predicates stored in the episodic database, and hand-coded domain knowledge.

```
selection-condition(S, go-to-door(Door) )    ←
          active-operator(S, get-item(Item) ),
          current-room(S, agent, Room1 ),
          has-door(S, Room1, Door ),
          path(S, Room1, Path),
          pathdoor(S, Path, Door),
          destination(S, Path, Room2),
          contains(S, Room2, Item).
```

Fig. 6. A desired hypothesis for the selection condition of go-to-door operator

Soar stores its binary predicates as a directed graph (Fig. 2), and regular Soar programs take advantage of this property by using only rules that instantiate the first arguments of these predicates before testing them. Fortunately, this structural constraint can be very naturally represented in inverse entailment (and many other ILP algorithms) using mode definitions and it significantly reduces the search space. Fig. 6 depicts a correct rule that is learned during the experiment reported in section 3.1. It reads as: "At any situation S with an active high-level operator get-item(Item), the operator go-to-door(Door) should be selected if Door can be instantiated with the door on the shortest path from the current room to the room where Item is in."

The learning system models the selection decision of go-to-door by checking the high-level goals and retrieving relevant information (active-operator retrieves information about the desired item), by using structured sensors (i.e. current-room), and domain knowledge (i.e. has-door, path)

During evaluation of a hypothesis, the situation predicates, such as current-room or contains, call background predicates that query the episodic database structure. active-operator is a special hand-coded background predicate that generates the parameters of the active parent operator[2] by calling the accepted-annotation predicates stored in the episodic database.

---

[2] The actual syntax of this predicate is slightly more complex to comply with the restrictions of the ILP algorithm used.

The operator hierarchy simplifies the search for a hypothesis in two ways. First, the decisions about an operator are learned in the context of the parent operator. The conditions for maintaining a parent operator are implicit conditions of the child operator; they don't need to be learned and as a result the conditions get simpler and easier to learn. At a level of the hierarchy, learning only the distinctions of selecting between sibling operators may be sufficient. Second, object-valued parameters of a parent operator can provide access to the more relevant parts of the background knowledge (i.e. active-operator), in effect simplifying the learning task. For example in Fig. 6, the conditions for selecting the correct door could be very complex and indirect if the parent operator did not have the Item parameter that guides the search (i.e. the towards the room that contains the item).

We have two mechanisms for encoding domain knowledge to be used in learning. In section 2.2, we described the assumed situation predicates that are added to the behavior trace as factual information the expert may be using. An alternative is to use a hand-coded theory written in Prolog. In our example in Fig. 6, the rule uses assumed knowledge about path structures between each pair of rooms (i.e. path, pathdoor, destination). An alternative would be that the agent infers that information dynamically during learning, for example using knowledge about the connectivity of neighbor rooms. For example we could have a shortest-path(+Situation, +Room1, +Room2, -Door) predicate which infers that Door in Room1 is on the shortest path from Room1 to Room2.

2.7 Agent Generation for a Particular Agent Architecture

At the end of each learning phase, the learned concepts should be compiled to an executable program in an agent architecture, in our case Soar. In general, the conditions at the if-part of the decision concepts should be "testable" by the agent program. The translation of observed situation predicates is trivial. On the other hand, for each hand-coded background predicate, we should have corresponding hand-coded implementations in the agent program. For example, while the active-operator is a prolog program that checks accepted-annotation predicate during learning, it should have an agent architecture specific implementation to be used in execution that checks and returns information about the active high-level operators.

3   Experiments

We have conducted two set of experiments to evaluate our approach. In the first experiment, we generated artificial examples for a selection condition concept in a building navigation problem. We used the inverse entailment implementation Progol [13] for that experiment. For the second experiment, we used behavior data generated by Soar agents with our learning by observation framework (Fig. 1), partially implemented in SWI-Prolog. Our program intercepts the symbolic interaction of Soar agents with the environment, stores the interactions in an episodic database, creates decision concept examples, and declarative bias (such as mode definitions), and calls the ILP engine Aleph [17] that we have embedded in our system. In these more recent experiments, we have used Aleph instead of Prolog because Aleph is more customizable. It was easier to embed Aleph into our system because it also runs on SWI-Prolog. Using behavior of hand-coded Soar agents to create new "clone" agents allows us to easily experiment with and evaluate our framework. Since Soar agents already use hierarchical operators, it is easy to extract the required goal annotations from them. While the intercepted environmental interaction is used to create the behavior trace, the internal reasoning of the agents is only used to extract the goal annotations.

3.1 Learning from Artificially Created Data

In our first experiment the selection condition of go-to-door is learned in the context of get-item using artificially created examples. One possible correct hypothesis in this problem is depicted in Fig. 6. The goal is to learn to select a door such that it is on a path towards an item that the agent wants to get.

In this experiment, we have artificially created situations where go-to-door(Door) operator is selected. First, we generated random map structures consisting of rooms, doors, items, paths, and shortest path distances between rooms. Then, we have generated random situations by choosing different rooms for the current-room sensor, and different items as the parameter of the high-level get-item goal. Finally, we have generated positive examples of our target concept by choosing a situation and the parameter of the go-to-door operator, namely, the correct door objects that leads toward the target item.

Instead of using negative examples, we marked a varying number of positive examples with a "complete selection" tag, indicating that the expert returns all of the best parameter selections for that situation (i.e. there maybe multiple doors that are on a shortest path). We used declarative bias to eliminate hypotheses that satisfy Door variables that are not among the expert selection for these marked examples.

To cover qualitatively different cases, we have generated 6 maps using 2 possibilities for the number of items on the map (1 or 3 items) and 3 possibilities for connectivity of the rooms (0, 3, or 6 extra connections where 0 means a unique path between each pair of rooms.). In these examples, a varying number of examples are marked with the "complete selection" tag (0-5 positive examples are marked). For these 36 combinations, we have conducted 5 experiments each with 5 positive examples. We ran Progol with noise setting turned off, searching for the best hypothesis that cover all positives while satisfying declarative bias.

We measured the learned hypothesis in terms of over-generality, over-specifity and accuracy. For example if for a situation s the doors that satisfy the correct hypothesis are $\{d_1, d_2, d_3\}$ and the doors that satisfy learned hypothesis h are $\{d_1, d_2, d_4, d_5, d_6\}$, then we get: $accuracy(h, s) = 2/6$, $overgenerality(h, s) = 3/6$, and $overspecifity(h, s) = 1/6$.

To evaluate the learned hypothesis, we have created test sets consisting of 6 random maps each with 10 fully connected rooms, choosing from 3 possibilities for connectivity (0, 5, or 10 extra connections) and 2 possibilities for the number of items (1 or 3 items). We have intentionally used test maps larger than training maps to ensure that hypotheses that may be specific to the training map size are not measured as accurate during testing.

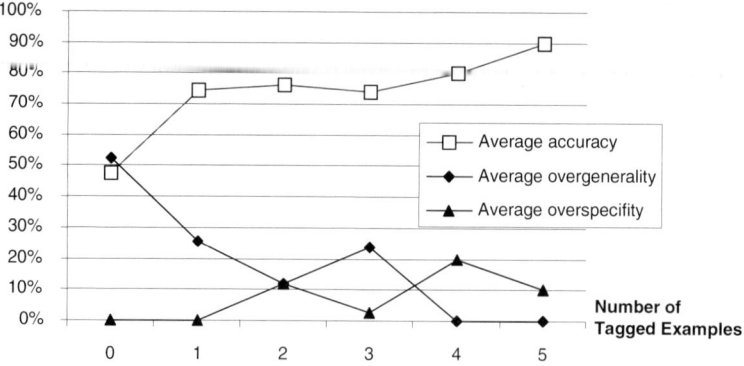

Fig. 7. Average accuracy, overspecifity and overgenerality of learned hypotheses on test data. Each data point is the average of 30 learned hypotheses

For each map, we have tested both the learned hypothesis and the correct hypothesis over all possible situations on these maps. (All possible combinations of current room and target item values.) For each of them, we have compared the output variables the hypotheses generate, namely the instantiations of the door variables. Fig. 7 shows the average *accuracy* is steadily increasing with the number of tagged examples.

3.2 Learning from Agent Program Generated Data

In this experiment, we have used the annotated behavior traces generated by a Soar agent in Haunt domain. All behavior data is created using a single level map consisting of 13 fully connected rooms that are marked with symbolic nodes to help the navigation of the agent. For each door, there are nodes on each side of the door.

The Soar agent controls a virtual character that has previously explored the level and built up an internal map of the rooms and the location of items in the level. In our experiment, we concentrated on the behavior it generates to retrieve items. The Soar agent randomly chooses an item, and selects the goal goto-room(Room) by instantiating Room with the room where the item is in. It then uses goto-node-in-room(Node) and goto-node-next-room(Node) operators to go towards Room. The agent selects goto-node-in-room operator to move to a node in front a door that leads towards Room. To go through the door, the agent chooses goto-node-next-room with a node on the other side of the door and moves towards it. These two operators are used in a loop until the agent is in the target room and the parent operator goto-room is retracted.

In this experiment, our goal is to learn the selection and termination concepts (Fig. 5 a, b) of goto-node-in-room in the context of a given goto-room operator. We have collected 3 minutes of behavior trace of the Soar agent (~30000 situations).

We have recorded several numerical sensors such as x-coordinate, distance to visible objects, and object valued sensors that monitor the last visited node, the nodes the agent can see, the nodes in front of the agent, the nearest visible node, the current room, and the previous room among others. The learning system used background knowledge about the locations of nodes, rooms, doors, and their relation to each other. A typical situation contained over 2000 situation predicates and a typical bottom clause (generated to variable depth 4) has over 500 literals. 600 positive and 200 negatives examples are generated for each concept. We ran Aleph with its default inverse entailment strategy. The numerical sensors are only used in a limited way; only within conditions that test whether sensors are close to constant values.

Although this experiment returned the correct termination condition, we got an overgeneral theory for the selection condition that may select a random node in the current room. Probably this stems from the fact that the negative examples are generated at situations where the learned operator is not selected (Fig. 5.b). These situations do not provide sufficient information about which parameter selections would be incorrect at a situation where the learned operator is selected.

Based on this observation, we have conducted another experiment where the selection condition of goto-node-in-room is learned correctly using a slightly different approach. For each positive example $cond(s, op(x_1))$, we generated negative examples of the form $cond(s, op(x_2))$ using the same situation s but different operator parameters. In our case, x_2 would be a node that the expert has not selected in situation s. This approach resembles the positive-only learning strategy described by Muggleton [13] except that in our case, the negative examples are generated by choosing only the operator parameters randomly not the situations. We have selected these parameters randomly from the set of parameters observed in expert annotations. Using the positive examples in previous experiment and generating 20 random negatives for each, we get the correct rule in Fig. 8.

```
selection-cond( S, goto-node-in-room( TargetNode) ) ←
          active-operator(S, goto-room(TargetRoom) ),
          current-room(S, agent, CurrentRoom),
          path(S, CurrentRoom, Path),
          pathnode(S, Path, TargetNode),
          destination(S, Path, TargetRoom).
```

Fig. 8. Selection condition of goto-node-in-room operator induced using only positive examples

In this experiment, we have demonstrated that general correct concepts for selecting and terminating operators can be learned in structured domains using only correct expert behavior. Our experiment indicates that negative examples obtained at situations where an operator is not selected may not be sufficient in learning operators with parameters. Generating negative examples with random parameters may solve this problem.

4   Related Work

Khardon [7] studied learnability of action selection policies from observed behavior of a planning system and demonstrated results on small planning problems. His framework requires that goals are given to the learner in an explicit representation, while we try to inductively learn the goals.

To learn procedural agent knowledge, there are at least two alternatives to learning by observation. One approach is to learn how the agent actions change the perceived environment and then use that knowledge in a planning algorithm to execute behavior. TRAIL [1] combines expert observations and experimentations to learn STRIPS like teleoperators using ILP. OBSERVER [23] uses expert observations to learn planning operators in a rich representation (not framed in an ILP setting). Moyle [12] describes an ILP system that learns theories in event calculus, while Otero describes an ILP system that learn effects in situation calculus [15]. These systems could have difficulty if changes caused by the actions are difficult to observe, possibly because the actions cause delayed effects that are difficult to attribute to particular actions. In these cases, our approach of trying to replicate expert decisions, without necessarily understanding what changes they will cause, may be easier to learn.

Another alternative to learning by observation is to use reinforcement learning. Relational reinforcement learning [4] uses environmental feedback to first learn utility of actions in a particular state and then compiles them to an action selection policy. Recently, expert behavior traces have been combined with the traces obtained from experimentation on the environment [3]. Expert guidance helps their system to more quickly reach states that return feedback. In this system, the selections of the experts are not treated as positive examples and learning still uses only environmental feedback. In complex domains, our strategy of capturing the expert behavior may be easier than trying to justify actions in terms of future gains, especially when the reward is sparse. Moreover, replicating the problem solving style of an expert, even if he/she makes sub-optimum decisions, is an important requirement for some applications such as creating "believably human-like" artificial characters. Unlike learning by observation, none of the two approaches above are very suitable for that purpose because their decision evaluation criteria is not based on similarity to expert but success in the environment.

5 Conclusions and Future Work

We have described a framework to learn procedural knowledge from structured behavior traces, structured goal annotations and complex background knowledge. We decomposed the learning an agent program problem to the problem of learning individual goals and actions by assuming that they are represented with operators that are arranged hierarchically. We operationalized learning to use these operators by defining decision concepts that can be learned in a supervised learning setting. We have described an episodic database formalism to compactly store structured behavior data. Episodic database was crucial in testing our system in a large domain. We have partially implemented the first cycle of our framework, where the learning system uses only correct behavior data. We have conducted two experiments to evaluate our approach. In the first experiment, we used a small data set of artificially created situations. Here, the target concept is successfully learned, but we required additional expert input in addition to the correct decisions. In the second experiment, we used a large data set generated from the behavior of a hand-coded agent in a complex domain. Learning selection conditions as defined in Fig. 5 generated overgeneral results, because the learning system did not have sufficient information to eliminate incorrect parameter selections. When selection conditions are learned with a "positive examples only" strategy, this problem is overcome and a correct concept is learned.

Our first goal for future work is to implement the second execution cycle of our framework. We predict that the behavior data obtained this way will provide valuable examples and improve learning results. A formal evaluation of our episodic database formalism is also left for future work. We are currently extending this formalism so that it not only compactly represents behavior data, but also test rules more efficiently by testing the rules on a range of situations at once.

Acknowledgements. This work was partially supported by ONR contract N00014-03-10327.

References

1. Benson, S., Nilsson, N.: Inductive Learning of Reactive Action Models. In: Prieditis, A., Russell, S.: Machine Learning: Proceedings of the Twelfth International Conference. Morgan Kaufmann, San Fransisco, CA (1995) 47-54
2. Camacho, R.: Inducing Models of Human Control Skills. In: 10th European Conference on Machine Learning (ECML-1998). Chemnitz, Germany (1998)
3. Driessens, K., Dzeroski, S.: Integrating Experimentation and Guidance in Relational Reinforcement Learning. In: Sammut, C., Hoffmann, C. (eds.): Proceedings of the Nineteenth International Conference on Machine Learning (ICML-2002). Morgan Kaufmann Publishers (2002) 115-122
4. Dzeroski, S., Raedt, L. D., Driessens, K.: Relational Reinforcement Learning. Machine Learning **43** (2001) 5-52
5. Isaac, A., Sammut, C.: Goal-directed Learning to Fly. In: Fawcett, T., Mishra, N. (eds.): Proceedings of the Twentieth International Conference (ICML 2003). AAAI Press (2003)
6. Jones, R. M., Laird, J. E., Nielsen, P. E., Coulter, K. J., Kenny, P. G., Koss, F. V.: Automated Intelligent Pilots for Combat Flight Simulation. AI Magazine **20** (1999) 27-42
7. Khardon, R.: Learning to Take Actions. Machine Learning **35** (1999) 57-90
8. Laird, J. E., Newell, A., Rosenbloom, P. S.: Soar: An Architecture for General Intelligence. Artificial Intelligence **33** (1987) 1-64
9. Magerko, B., Laird, J. E., Assanie, M., Kerfoot, A., Stokes, D.: AI Characters and Directors for Interactive Computer Games. In: The 16th Innovative Applications of Artificial Intelligence (IAAI-2004). San Jose, CA (2004)
10. Michie, D., Bain, M., Hayes-Michie, J.: Cognitive Models from Subcognitive Skills. In: Grimble, M., McGhee, J., Mowforth, P. (eds.): Knowledge-Based Systems in Industrial Control. Peter Peregrinus, Stevenage (1990) 71-90
11. Michie, D., Camacho, R.: Building Symbolic Representations of Intuitive Real-Time Skills From Performance Data. In: Machine Intelligence 13 Workshop (MI-1992). Glasgow, U.K (1992)
12. Moyle, S.: Using Theory Completion to Learn a Robot Navigation Control Program. In: Matwin, S., Sammut, C. (eds.): Inductive Logic Programming, 12th International Conference, Revised Papers. Lecture Notes in Computer Science, Vol. 2583. (2003) 182-97
13. Muggleton, S.: Inverse Entailment and Progol. New Generation Computing **13** (1995) 245-286
14. Newell, A.: Unified Theories of Cognition. Harvard Univ. Press (1990)

15. Otero, R. P.: Induction of the Effects of Actions by Monotonic Methods. In: Horváth, T. (ed.): Inductive Logic Programming, 13th International Conference. Lecture Notes in Computer Science, Vol. 2835. Springer (2003) 299-310

16. Sammut, C., Hurst, S., Kedzier, D., Michie, D.: Learning to fly. In: Sleeman, D., Edwards, P. (eds.): Proceedings of the 9th International Conference on Machine Learning (ICML-1992). Morgan Kaufmann (1992) 385-393

17. Srinivasan, A.: The Aleph 5 Manual. http://web.comlab.ox.ac.uk/oucl/research/areas/machlearn/Aleph (2003)

18. Struyf, J., Ramon, J., Blockeel, H.: Compact Representation of Knowledge Bases in ILP. In: Matwin, S., Sammut, C. (eds.): Inductive Logic Programming, 12th International Conference, Revised Papers. Lecture Notes in Computer Science, Vol. 2583. Springer, Germany (2003)

19. Suc, D., Bratko, I.: Problem decomposition for behavioural cloning. In: 11th European Conference on Machine Learning. Lecture Notes in Computer Science, Vol. 1810. Springer-Verlag, Germany (2000) 382-391

20. Urbancic, T., Bratko, I.: Reconstructing Human Skill with Machine Learning. In: Cohn, A. G. (ed.): Proceedings of the 11th European Conference on Artificial Intelligence (ECAI-94). John Wiley and Sons (1994) 498-502

21. van Lent, M., Laird, J.: Learning procedural knowledge through observation. In: Proceedings of the International Conference on Knowledge Capture (KCAP-2001). ACM Press, New York (2001) 179-186

22. van Lent, M.: Learning Task-Performance Knowledge through Observation. Ph.D. Thesis. Univ. of Michigan (2000)

23. Wang, X.: Learning Planning Operators by Observation and Practice. Ph.D. Thesis (Tech. Report CMU-CS-96-154). Computer Science Department, Carnegie Mellon University (1996)

24. Wray, R. E., Laird, J. E., Nuxoll, A., Stokes, D., Kerfoot, A.: Synthetic Adversaries for Urban Combat Training. In: Proceedings of Innovative Applications of Artificial Intelligence (IAAI-2004). AAAI Press, in press

Efficient Evaluation of Candidate Hypotheses in $\mathcal{AL}$-log

Francesca A. Lisi and Floriana Esposito

Dipartimento di Informatica, University of Bari, Italy
{lisi, esposito}@di.uniba.it

Abstract. In this paper we face the coverage problem in the context of learning in the hybrid language $\mathcal{AL}$-log. Here candidate hypotheses are represented as DATALOG clauses with variables constrained by assertions in the description logic $\mathcal{ALC}$. Regardless of the scope of induction we define coverage relations for $\mathcal{AL}$-log in the two logical settings of learning from implications and learning from interpretations. Also, with reference to the ILP system $\mathcal{AL}$-QUIN, we discuss our solutions to the algorithmic and implementation issues raised by the coverage test for the setting of characteristic induction from interpretations in $\mathcal{AL}$-log.

1 Introduction

When learning in fragments of first-order logic, the most expensive step is the evaluation of candidate hypotheses w.r.t. a set of observations. This step is usually referred to as the coverage test because it checks which observations satisfy (are covered by) the hypothesis. The definition of   is strongly biased by the representation choice for observations. In ILP there are two choices: we can represent an observation as either a ground definite clause or a set of ground unit clauses. The former is peculiar to the normal ILP setting (also called   ) [9], whereas the latter is usual in the logical setting of   .   [6]. The representation choice for observations and the scope of induction are orthogonal dimensions as clearly explained in [5]. Therefore we prefer the term 'observation' to the term 'example' for the sake of generality.

Recently there has been a growing interest in learning in first-order languages other than Horn clausal logic.   such as CARIN [14] and $\mathcal{AL}$-log [8] are particularly interesting because they bridge the gap between Horn clausal logic (or its fragments) and Description Logics (DLs) [1]. Also DL-based hybrid languages have recently found a killer application in the   [2], thus giving rise to the mark-up language ORL [10] for the   of the Semantic Web architecture. There are very few attempts at learning in DL-based hybrid languages [22,12,17]. Among them, only [22] faces the coverage problem more explicitly. Here, the chosen language is CARIN-$\mathcal{ALN}$, the ILP setting is that of discriminant induction from interpretations, and example coverage is based on the existential entailment algorithm of CARIN.

R. Camacho, R. King, A. Srinivasan (Eds.): ILP 2004, LNAI 3194, pp. 216–233, 2004.
© Springer-Verlag Berlin Heidelberg 2004

In this paper we face the coverage problem for hypotheses expressed in tl hybrid language $\mathcal{AL}$-log. This language integrates $\mathcal{ALC}$ [23] and DATALOG [by using $\mathcal{ALC}$ concept assertions essentially as on variables. Re gardless the scope of induction, we define coverage relations for $\mathcal{AL}$-log in th two logical settings of learning from implications and learning from interpreta tions. Here coverage is based on the constrained SLD-resolution algorithm o $\mathcal{AL}$-log. Also, we present our solutions to the algorithmic and implementatior issues raised by the coverage test for the setting of characteristic induction from interpretations in $\mathcal{AL}$-log. These solutions are adopted by the ILP system $\mathcal{AL}$-QUIN and illustrated by means of an example of frequent pattern discovery in data and ontologies extracted from the on-line CIA World Fact Book.

The choice of $\mathcal{AL}$-log as a knowledge representation and reasoning (KR&R) framework in $\mathcal{AL}$-QUIN is driven by a twofold motivation. First, $\mathcal{AL}$-log as op posite to CARIN has several desirable computational properties, e.g. the decid ability of reasoning mechanisms. Second, $\mathcal{AL}$-log is powerful enough to satisfy the actual needs of most application domains that can benefit from learning in hybrid languages, e.g. the aforementioned Semantic Web. Indeed the examples reported throughout the paper refer to an application of $\mathcal{AL}$-QUIN to Seman tic Web Mining. In particular, we propose $\mathcal{AL}$-log as a reasonable substitute of ORL. Indeed ORL extends the standard mark-up language for the , OWL [11], 'to build rules on top of ontologies' in a way that is similar in the spirit to in $\mathcal{AL}$-log. Furthermore the design of OWL has been based on the $\mathcal{SH}$ family of DLs which can be seen as $\mathcal{ALC}$ extended with transitive properties and a property hierarchy.

The paper is organized as follows. Section 2 introduces the basic notions of $\mathcal{AL}$-log. Section 3 defines coverage relations for $\mathcal{AL}$-log. Section 4 presents algo rithmic and implementation solutions adopted in $\mathcal{AL}$-QUIN. Section 5 concludes the paper with final remarks.

2 $\mathcal{AL}$-log in a Nutshell

The system $\mathcal{AL}$-log [8] embodies two subsystems, called and . The former is based on $\mathcal{ALC}$ [23] whereas the latter extends DATALOG [4]. For the sake of brevity we assume the reader to be familiar with DATALOG.

2.1 The Structural Subsystem

The structural subsystem of $\mathcal{AL}$-log allows for the specification of structural knowledge in terms of , , and . Individuals represent ob jects in the domain of interest. Concepts represent classes of these objects, while roles represent binary relations between concepts. Complex concepts can be de fined by means of constructs, such as $\sqcap$ and $\sqcup$. The structural subsystem is itself a two-component system. The component $\mathcal{T}$ consists of concept hier archies spanned by is-a relations between concepts, namely of the form $C \sqsubseteq D$ (read "C is included in D") where C and D are two arbitrary concepts. The ⸻ component $\mathcal{M}$ specifies instance-of relations, e.g. ⸻ of the form $a : C$ (read "the individual a belongs to the concept C") and ⸻ of the form $< a, b >: R$ (read "the individual a is related to the individual b by means of the role R").

In $\mathcal{ALC}$ knowledge bases, an ⸻ $\mathcal{I} = (\Delta^{\mathcal{I}}, \cdot^{\mathcal{I}})$ consists of a set $\Delta^{\mathcal{I}}$ (the ⸻ of $\mathcal{I}$) and a function $\cdot^{\mathcal{I}}$ (the ⸻ . ⸻ of $\mathcal{I}$). E.g., it maps concepts to subsets of $\Delta^{\mathcal{I}}$ and individuals to elements of $\Delta^{\mathcal{I}}$ such that $a^{\mathcal{I}} \neq b^{\mathcal{I}}$ if $a \neq b$ (the ⸻ assumption). We say that $\mathcal{I}$ is a ⸻ for $C \sqsubseteq D$ if $C^{\mathcal{I}} \subseteq D^{\mathcal{I}}$, for $a : C$ if $a^{\mathcal{I}} \in C^{\mathcal{I}}$, and for $< a, b >: R$ if $(a^{\mathcal{I}}, b^{\mathcal{I}}) \in R^{\mathcal{I}}$.

The main reasoning mechanism for the structural component is the satisfiability check. The ⸻ proposed in [8] starts with the tableau branch $S = \mathcal{T} \cup \mathcal{M}$ and adds assertions to S by means of ⸻ such as

- $S \rightarrow_{\sqcup} S \cup \{s : D\}$ if
  1. $s : C_1 \sqcup C_2$ is in S,
  2. $D = C_1$ and $D = C_2$,
  3. neither $s : C_1$ nor $s : C_2$ is in S
- $S \rightarrow_{\forall} S \cup \{t : C\}$ if
  1. $s : \forall R.C$ is in S,
  2. $< s, t >: R$ is in S,
  3. $t : C$ is not in S
- $S \rightarrow_{\sqsubseteq} S \cup \{s : C' \sqcup D\}$ if
  1. $C \sqsubseteq D$ is in S,
  2. s appears in S,
  3. C' is the NNF concept equivalent to $\neg C$
  4. $s : \neg C \sqcup D$ is not in S
- $S \rightarrow_{\bot} \{s : \bot\}$ if
  1. $s : A$ and $s : \neg A$ are in S, or
  2. $s : \neg \top$ is in S,
  3. $s : \bot$ is not in S

until either a contradiction is generated or an interpretation satisfying S can be easily obtained from it.

2.2 The Relational Subsystem

The distinguishing feature of the relational subsystem of $\mathcal{AL}$-log is the so-called DATALOG ⸻, i.e. a clause

$$\alpha_0 \leftarrow \alpha_1, \ldots, \alpha_m \& \gamma_1, \ldots, \gamma_n$$

where $m \geq 0$, $n \geq 0$, α_i are DATALOG atoms and γ_j are ⸻ of the form $s : C$ where s is either a constant or a variable already appearing in the clause, and C is an $\mathcal{ALC}$ concept. The symbol & separates constraints from DATALOG atoms in a clause. A ⸻ DATALOG ⸻ Π is a set of constrained DATALOG clauses. An $\mathcal{AL}$ ⸻ $\mathcal{B}$ is the pair $\langle \Sigma, \Pi \rangle$

where Σ is an $\mathcal{ALC}$ knowledge base and Π is a constrained DATALOG program. For $\mathcal{B}$ to be acceptable, it must satisfy the following conditions: (i) The set of DATALOG predicate symbols appearing in Π is disjoint from the set of concept and role symbols appearing in Σ; (ii) The alphabet of constants used in Π coincides with the alphabet $\mathcal{O}$ of the individuals of Σ; (iii) For each clause in Π, each variable occurring in the constraint part occurs also in the DATALOG part. These properties allows the notion of _____ to be straightforwardly extended from DATALOG to $\mathcal{AL}$-log.

The interaction between the structural and the relational part of an $\mathcal{AL}$-log knowledge base $\mathcal{B}$ is also at the basis of a model-theoretic semantics for $\mathcal{AL}$-log. We call Π_D the set of DATALOG clauses obtained from the clauses of Π by deleting their constraints. We define an _____ $\mathcal{J}$ for $\mathcal{B}$ as the union of an $\mathcal{O}$-interpretation $\mathcal{I}_\mathcal{O}$ for Σ (i.e. an interpretation compliant with the unique names assumption) and an Herbrand interpretation $\mathcal{I}_\mathcal{H}$ for Π_D. An interpretation $\mathcal{J}$ is a _____ of $\mathcal{B}$ if $\mathcal{I}_\mathcal{O}$ is a model of Σ, and for each ground instance $\alpha_0' \leftarrow \alpha_1', \ldots, \alpha_m' \& \gamma_1', \ldots, \gamma_n'$ of each clause $\alpha_0 \leftarrow \alpha_1, \ldots, \alpha_m \& \gamma_1, \ldots, \gamma_n$ in Π, either there exists one γ_i', $i \in \{1, \ldots, n\}$, that is not satisfied by $\mathcal{J}$, or $\alpha_0' \leftarrow \alpha_1', \ldots, \alpha_m'$ is satisfied by $\mathcal{J}$. The notion of _____ paves the way to the definition of answer set for queries. A _____ is a constrained DATALOG clause of the form

$$\leftarrow \beta_1, \ldots, \beta_m \& \gamma_1, \ldots, \gamma_n$$

i.e. without head. An _____ to the query Q is a ground substitution σ for the variables in Q. The answer σ is _____ w.r.t. $\mathcal{B}$ if $Q\sigma$ is a logical consequence of $\mathcal{B}$ ($\mathcal{B} \models Q\sigma$). The _____ of Q in $\mathcal{B}$ contains all the correct answers to Q w.r.t. $\mathcal{B}$.

Reasoning for an $\mathcal{AL}$-log knowledge base $\mathcal{B}$ is based on _____, i.e. an extension of SLD-resolution to deal with constraints. In particular, the constraints of the resolvent of a query Q and a constrained DATALOG clause H are recursively simplified by replacing couples of constraints $t : C$, $t : D$ with the equivalent constraint $t : C \sqcap D$. The one-to-one mapping between constrained SLD-derivations and the SLD-derivations obtained by ignoring the constraints is exploited to extend known results for DATALOG to $\mathcal{AL}$-log. Note that in $\mathcal{AL}$-log a derivation of the empty clause with associated constraints does not represent a refutation. It actually infers that the query is true in those models of $\mathcal{B}$ that satisfy its constraints. Therefore in order to answer a query it is necessary to collect enough derivations ending with a constrained empty clause such that every model of $\mathcal{B}$ satisfies the constraints associated with the final query of at least one derivation. In particular, satisfiability is checked by means of the tableau calculus. _____ is a complete and sound method for answering _____ queries.

Lemma 1. _____ Q _____ $\mathcal{AL}$ _____ $\mathcal{B}$
$\mathcal{B} \vdash Q$. _____ . $\mathcal{B} \models Q$

An answer σ to a query Q is a _____ if there exists a constrained SLD-refutation for $Q\sigma$ in $\mathcal{B}$ ($\mathcal{B} \vdash Q\sigma$). The set of computed answers is called the of Q in $\mathcal{B}$. Furthermore, given   query Q, the success set of Q in $\mathcal{B}$ coincides with the answer set of Q in $\mathcal{B}$. This provides an operational means for answering queries.

3 Coverage Relations for $\mathcal{AL}$-log

In our framework for learning in $\mathcal{AL}$-log the background knowledge is represented as an $\mathcal{AL}$-log knowledge base. Also hypotheses are represented as constrained DATALOG clauses that fulfill the following restrictions. First, we impose constrained DATALOG clauses to be linked and connected (or range-restricted). Linkedness and connectedness have been originally conceived for definite clauses [20]. Second, we impose constrained DATALOG clauses to be compliant with the bias of Object Identity (OI) [24]. This bias can be considered as an extension of the unique names assumption from the semantic level to the syntactic one of $\mathcal{AL}$-log. It can be the starting point for the definition of either an equational theory or a quasi-ordering for constrained DATALOG clauses. The latter option relies on a restricted form of substitution whose bindings avoid the identification of terms: A substitution σ is an   w.r.t. a set of terms T iff $\forall t_1, t_2 \in T : t_1 \neq t_2$ yields that $t_1\sigma \neq t_2\sigma$. From now on, we assume that substitutions are OI-compliant.

We do not make any assumption as regards the scope of induction. Therefore the atom $q(\boldsymbol{X})^1$ in the head of constrained DATALOG clauses can represent a concept to be either discriminated from others (   ) or characterized (   ). Conversely we make assumptions as regards the representation of observations because it impacts the definition of coverage.

From now on we refer to $\mathcal{L}$ as the language of hypotheses, to $\mathcal{K}$ as the background knowledge, to O as the set of observations. We assume $\mathcal{K} \cap O = \emptyset$.

3.1 Observations as Implications

In the logical setting of   .   extended to $\mathcal{AL}$-log, an observation $o_i \in O$ is represented as a ground constrained DATALOG clause having a ground atom $q(\boldsymbol{a}_i)^2$ in the head.

Definition 1. $H \in \mathcal{L}$ $\mathcal{K}$ $o_i \in O$
H covers o_i under entailment $\mathcal{K}$ *ff* $\mathcal{K} \cup H \models o_i$

In order to provide an operational means for testing this coverage relation we resort to the Deduction Theorem for first-order logic formulas [20].

Theorem 1. Σ .. ϕ ψ .
$\Sigma \cup \{\phi\} \models \psi$ *ff* $\Sigma \models (\phi \rightarrow \psi)$

We reduce the coverage test under entailment to query answering.

---

[1] $\boldsymbol{X}$ is a tuple of variables
[2] $\boldsymbol{a}_i$ is a tuple of constants

Theorem 2. $H \in \mathcal{L}$ $\mathcal{K}$ $o_i \in O$ H covers o_i under entailment w.r.t. $\mathcal{K}$ *ff* $\mathcal{K} \cup$ $body(o_i) \cup H \vdash q(\boldsymbol{a}_i)$

- H o_i $\mathcal{K} \leftrightarrow$ *fi*
- $\mathcal{K} \cup H \models q(\boldsymbol{a}_i) \leftarrow body(o_i) \leftrightarrow$
- $\mathcal{K} \cup H \cup body(o_i) \models q(\boldsymbol{a}_i) \leftrightarrow$
- $\mathcal{K} \cup body(o_i) \cup H \vdash q(\boldsymbol{a}_i)$

3.2 Observations as Interpretations

In the logical setting of . extended to $\mathcal{AL}$-log, an observation $o_i \in O$ is represented as a couple $(q(\boldsymbol{a}_i), \mathcal{A}_i)$ where $\mathcal{A}_i$ is a set containing ground DATALOG facts.

Definition 2. $H \in \mathcal{L}$ $\mathcal{K}$ $o_i \in$ O H covers o_i under interpretations w.r.t. $\mathcal{K}$ *ff* $\mathcal{K} \cup \mathcal{A}_i \cup H \models q(\boldsymbol{a}_i)$

We reduce the coverage test under interpretations to query answering.

Theorem 3. $H \in \mathcal{L}$ $\mathcal{K}$ $o_i \in$ O H covers o_i under interpretations w.r.t. $\mathcal{K}$ *ff* $\mathcal{K} \cup \mathcal{A}_i \cup H \vdash q(\boldsymbol{a}_i)$

. $q(\boldsymbol{a}_i)$ $\mathcal{AL}$ $\mathcal{B} = \mathcal{K} \cup \mathcal{A}_i \cup$ H . . *fi*

Recently, the setting of learning from interpretations has been shown to be a promising way of scaling up ILP algorithms in real-world applications [3]. Therefore in the next section we focus on the algorithmic and implementation issues raised by Theorem 3.

4 Evaluating Candidate Hypotheses in $\mathcal{AL}$-QuIn

The system $\mathcal{AL}$-QUIN ($\mathcal{AL}$-log QUERY INDUCTION) learns in $\mathcal{AL}$-log within the setting of characteristic induction from interpretations. In particular, it solves a variant of the frequent pattern discovery problem which takes concept hierarchies into account during the discovery process, thus yielding descriptions of a data set **r** at multiple granularity levels. More formally, given

- a data set **r** including a taxonomy $\mathcal{T}$ where a reference concept and task-relevant concepts are designated,
- a set $\{\mathcal{L}^l\}_{1 \leq l \leq maxG}$ of languages
- a set $\{minsup^l\}_{1 \leq l \leq maxG}$ of support thresholds

the problem of ▪ l ▪ ,
$1 \leq l \leq maxG$, is to find the set $\mathcal{F}$ of all the patterns $P \in \mathcal{L}^l$ frequent in **r**,
namely P's with support s such that (i) $s \geq minsup^l$ and (ii) all ancestors of P
w.r.t. $\mathcal{T}$ are frequent.

In $\mathcal{AL}$-QuIn the data set **r** is represented as an $\mathcal{AL}$-log knowledge base $\mathcal{B}$.

As a running example, we consider an $\mathcal{AL}$-log knowledge base $\mathcal{B}_{\text{CIA}}$
that adds $\mathcal{ALC}$ ontologies to Datalog facts[3] extracted from the on-line 1996
CIA World Fact Book[4]. These ontologies contain concepts such as `Country`,
`EthnicGroup` and `Religion`.

The language $\mathcal{L} = \{\mathcal{L}^l\}_{1 \leq l \leq maxG}$ of **patterns** allows for the generation of
unary conjunctive queries, called $\mathcal{O}$-queries. Given a reference concept $\hat{C}$, an $\mathcal{O}$
Q to an $\mathcal{AL}$-log knowledge base $\mathcal{B}$ is a (linked and connected) constrained
Datalog clause of the form

$$Q = q(X) \leftarrow \alpha_1, \ldots, \alpha_m \& X : \hat{C}, \gamma_2, \ldots, \gamma_n$$

where X is the   and the remaining variables occurring in
the body of Q are the   . We denote by $key(Q)$ the key con-
straint $X : \hat{C}$ of Q. An $\mathcal{O}$-query $q(X) \leftarrow \& X : \hat{C}$ is called   . The language
$\mathcal{L}$ of patterns for a given frequent pattern discovery problem is implicitly defined
by a declarative bias specification. The   of an $\mathcal{O}$-query $Q \in \mathcal{L}^l$ w.r.t an
$\mathcal{AL}$-log knowledge base $\mathcal{B}$ is defined as

$$supp(Q, \mathcal{B}) = | \qquad (Q, \mathcal{B}) | / | \qquad (Q_t, \mathcal{B}) |$$

where Q_t is the trivial $\mathcal{O}$-query for $\mathcal{L}$.

Following Example 1, suppose that we are interested in finding hypotheses that characterize Middle East countries w.r.t. the religions believed and
the languages spoken. An ad-hoc language $\mathcal{L}$ of patterns has been defined. Here
`MiddleEastCountry` is the reference concept, and `Religion` and `Language` are
task-relevant concepts. Examples of $\mathcal{O}$-queries belonging to $\mathcal{L}$ are:

Q_t= q(X) ← & X:MiddleEastCountry
Q= q(X) ← believes(X,Y), believes(X,Z)
       & X:MiddleEastCountry, Y:MonotheisticReligion

In particular, Q_t is the trivial $\mathcal{O}$-query for $\mathcal{L}$.

The **background knowledge** is the portion $\mathcal{K}$ of $\mathcal{B}$ which encompasses the
whole structural subsystem Σ and the intensional part of Π.

The background knowledge $\mathcal{K}_{\text{CIA}}$ of $\mathcal{B}_{\text{CIA}}$ contains axioms such as

---

[3] http://www.dbis.informatik.uni-goettingen.de/Mondial/mondial-rel-facts.flp
[4] http://www.odci.gov/cia/publications/factbook/

```
AsianCountry ⊑ Country.
MiddleEasternEthnicGroup ⊑ EthnicGroup.
MiddleEastCountry=
        AsianCountry⊓∃Hosts.MiddleEasternEthnicGroup.
MonotheisticReligion ⊑ Religion.
ChristianReligion ⊑ MonotheisticReligion.
MuslimReligion ⊑ MonotheisticReligion.
```

and membership assertions such as

```
'ARM':AsianCountry.
'IR':AsianCountry.
'Arab':MiddleEasternEthnicGroup.
'Armenian':MiddleEasternEthnicGroup.
<'ARM','Armenian'>:Hosts.
<'IR','Arab'>:Hosts.
'Armenian Orthodox':ChristianReligion.
'Shia':MuslimReligion.
'Sunni':MuslimReligion.
```

that define taxonomies for the concepts `Country`, `EthnicGroup` and `Religion` respectively. Note that Middle East countries (concept `MiddleEastCountry`) have been defined as Asian countries that host at least one Middle Eastern ethnic group. In particular, Armenia (`'ARM'`) and Iran (`'IR'`) are classified as Middle East countries. Also $\mathcal{K}_{\text{CIA}}$ includes constrained DATALOG clauses such as:

```
believes(CountryID, ReligionName)←
        religion(CountryID,ReligionName,Percent) &
        CountryID:Country, ReligionName:Religion
```

that defines a view on the relation `religion`.

Observations are portions o_i of $\mathcal{B} \setminus \mathcal{K}$, therefore portions of the extensional part of Π. Each observation contains facts related to one and only one individual a_i of the reference concept for the task at hand.

By assuming `MiddleEastCountry` as reference concept, the observation $\mathcal{A}_{\text{IR}}$ contains DATALOG facts such as

```
language('IR','Persian',58).
religion('IR','Shia',89).
religion('IR','Sunni',10).
```

concerning the individual `'IR'` whereas the observation $\mathcal{A}_{\text{ARM}}$ consists of facts like

```
language('ARM','Armenian',96).
religion('ARM','Armenian Orthodox',94).
```

related to the individual `'ARM'`.

The **coverage test** is based on Theorem 3.

Following Example 2 and Example 4, we want to check whether the $\mathcal{O}$-query Q covers the observation $\mathcal{A}_{\mathrm{IR}}$ w.r.t. $\mathcal{K}_{\mathrm{CIA}}$. This is equivalent to answering the query

$$Q^{(0)} = \leftarrow \texttt{q('IR')}$$

w.r.t. $\mathcal{K}_{\mathrm{CIA}} \cup \mathcal{A}_{\mathrm{IR}} \cup Q$. Several refutations can be constructed for $Q^{(0)}$. One of them consists of the following single constrained SLD-derivation. Let $E^{(1)}$ be

```
q(X) ← believes(X,Y), believes(X,Z) &
       X:MiddleEastCountry, Y:MonotheisticReligion
```

A resolvent for $Q^{(0)}$ and $E^{(1)}$ with substitution $\sigma^{(1)} = \{\texttt{X/ 'IR'}\}$ is the query

```
Q^(1) = ← believes('IR',Y), believes('IR',Z) &
        'IR':MiddleEastCountry, Y:MonotheisticReligion
```

Let $E^{(2)}$ be

```
believes(CountryID, ReligionName)←
       religion(CountryID,ReligionName,Percent) &
       CountryID:Country, ReligionName:Religion
```

A resolvent for $Q^{(1)}$ and $E^{(2)}$ is the query

```
Q^(2) = ← religion('IR',Y,Percent), believes('IR',Z) &
        'IR':MiddleEastCountry, Y:MonotheisticReligion
```

with substitution $\sigma^{(2)} = \{\texttt{CountryID/'IR', ReligionName/Y}\}$.

Let $E^{(3)}$ be `religion('IR','Shia',89)`. A resolvent for $Q^{(2)}$ and $E^{(3)}$ with substitution $\sigma^{(3)} = \{\texttt{Y/'Shia', Percent/89}\}$ is the query

```
Q^(3) = ← believes('IR',Z) &
        'IR':MiddleEastCountry, 'Shia':MonotheisticReligion
```

A resolvent for $Q^{(3)}$ and $E^{(4)} = E^{(2)}$ with substitution $\sigma^{(4)} = \{\texttt{CountryID/'IR', ReligionName/Z}\}$ is the query

```
Q^(4) = ← religion('IR',Z,Percent) &
        'IR':MiddleEastCountry, 'Shia':MonotheisticReligion,
        Z:Religion
```

Let $E^{(5)}$ be `religion('IR','Sunni',10)`. Note that $E^{(5)}$ must be different from $E^{(3)}$ because of the OI bias. A resolvent for $Q^{(4)}$ and $E^{(5)}$ with substitution $\sigma^{(5)} = \{\texttt{Z/'Sunni', Percent/10}\}$ is the constrained empty clause

```
Q^(5) = ← & 'IR':MiddleEastCountry, 'Shia':MonotheisticReligion,
        'Sunni':Religion
```

We need now to check the satisfiability of $\Sigma' = \Sigma \cup \{\texttt{'IR':MiddleEastCountry, 'Shia':MonotheisticReligion, 'Sunni':Religion}\}$.

The first check operates on the initial tableau

$$S_1^{(0)} = \Sigma \cup \{\texttt{'IR'}:\neg\texttt{MiddleEastCountry}\} =$$
$$= \Sigma \cup\{\texttt{'IR'}:\neg\texttt{AsianCountry}\sqcup\forall\texttt{Hosts.}(\neg\texttt{MiddleEasternEthnicGroup})\}.$$

By applying $\to_\sqcup$ w.r.t. $\forall\texttt{Hosts.}(\neg\texttt{MiddleEasternEthnicGroup})$ to $S_1^{(0)}$ we obtain $S_1^{(1)}=\Sigma \cup \{\texttt{'IR'} : (\forall\texttt{Hosts.}(\neg\texttt{MiddleEasternEthnicGroup}))\}$. The only propagation rule applicable to $S_1^{(1)}$ is $\to_\forall$ which yields the tableau $S_1^{(2)} = \Sigma \cup \{\texttt{'Arab'}:(\neg\texttt{MiddleEasternEthnicGroup})\}$. It produces the final tableau $S_1^{(3)} = \{\texttt{'Arab'}:\bot\}$ via $\to_\bot$.

The second check operates on the initial tableau

$$S_2^{(0)} = \Sigma \cup\{\texttt{'Shia'}:\neg\texttt{MonotheisticReligion}\}$$

The only propagation rule applicable to $S_2^{(0)}$, i.e. $\to_\sqsubseteq$ w.r.t. $\texttt{MuslimReligion}$ $\sqsubseteq \texttt{MonotheisticReligion}$, returns $S_2^{(1)} = \Sigma \cup \{\texttt{'Shia'}:\neg\texttt{MonotheisticReligion}$, $\texttt{'Shia'}:\neg\texttt{MuslimReligion}\sqcup\texttt{MonotheisticReligion}\}$. We obtain $S_2^{(2)} = \Sigma \cup \{\texttt{'Shia'}:\neg\texttt{MonotheisticReligion}, \texttt{'Shia'}:\texttt{MonotheisticReligion}\}$ by applying $\to_\sqcup$ to $S_2^{(1)}$ w.r.t. $\texttt{MonotheisticReligion}$. Finally $\to_\bot$ yields the final tableau $S_2^{(3)} = \{\texttt{'Shia'}:\bot\}$.

The third check operates on the initial tableau

$$S_3^{(0)} = \Sigma \cup\{\texttt{'Sunni'}:\neg\texttt{Religion}\}$$

and terminates with a clash by working in a way similar to the previous check.

These three results together prove that Σ' is satisfiable, thus that Q covers $\mathcal{A}_{\text{IR}}$ w.r.t. $\mathcal{K}_{\text{CIA}}$.

Note that in $\mathcal{AL}$-QUIN the coverage problem reduces to a query answering problem. Indeed, an ___ to an $\mathcal{O}$-query Q is a ground substitution θ for the distinguished variable of Q. An answer θ to an $\mathcal{O}$-query Q is a ___ w.r.t. an $\mathcal{AL}$-log knowledge base $\mathcal{B}$ if there exists at least one correct (resp. computed) answer to $body(Q)\theta$ w.r.t. $\mathcal{B}$. Therefore proving that an $\mathcal{O}$-query Q covers an observation $(q(a_i), \mathcal{A}_i)$ w.r.t. $\mathcal{K}$ equals to proving that $\theta_i = \{X/a_i\}$ is a correct answer to Q w.r.t. $\mathcal{B}_i = \mathcal{K} \cup \mathcal{A}_i$. In the following subsection we shall use this reformulation of the coverage problem.

4.1 Algorithmic Issues

The system $\mathcal{AL}$-QUIN follows the ___ [19] for frequent pattern discovery. This method is based on the following assumption: If a generality order $\succeq$ for the language $\mathcal{L}$ of patterns can be found such that $\succeq$ is monotonic w.r.t. the evaluation function $supp$, then the resulting space $(\mathcal{L}, \succeq)$ can be searched breadth-first by alternating candidate generation and candidate evaluation phases. In $\mathcal{AL}$-QUIN patterns are ordered according to $\mathcal{B}$-subsumption, a generality relation originally conceived for constrained DATALOG clauses [16] and proved to fulfill the abovementioned condition of monotonicity [18].

Procedure evaluateCandidates($\mathcal{B}$, $\mathcal{C}_k^l$, $minsup^l$, **var** $\mathcal{I}^l$)

1. $\mathcal{F}_k^l \leftarrow \emptyset$;
2. **foreach** pattern Q in $\mathcal{C}_k^l$ **do**
3. $answerset(Q, \mathcal{B}) \leftarrow$ computeAnswerSet(Q, $\mathcal{B}$);
4.   **if** $supp(Q, \mathcal{B}) \geq minsup^l$
5.   **then** $\mathcal{F}_k^l \leftarrow \mathcal{F}_k^l \cup \{Q\}$
6.   **else** $\mathcal{I}^l \leftarrow \mathcal{I}^l \cup \{Q\}$
7.   **endif**
8. **endforeach**
return $\mathcal{F}_k^l$

Fig. 1. Candidate evaluation in $\mathcal{AL}$-QuIN

Definition 3. H Datalog α Datalog
       $\mathcal{J}$ H covers α $\mathcal{J}$.
         θ . H $H\theta$ $body(H)\theta$ $\mathcal{J}$
$head(H)\theta = \alpha$

Definition 4. H_1 H_2 Datalog $\mathcal{B}$ $\mathcal{AL}$
           H_1 $\mathcal{B}$-subsumes H_2 $H_1 \succeq_\mathcal{B} H_2$.
. $\mathcal{J}$. $\mathcal{B}$ Datalog α H_2
α $\mathcal{J}$ H_1 α $\mathcal{J}$

Theorem 4. H_1 H_2 Datalog $\mathcal{B}$ $\mathcal{AL}$
         σ . H_2 $\{H_1\} \cup \mathcal{B}$
      $H_1 \succeq_\mathcal{B} H_2$ ff θ . H_1
$head(H_1)\theta = head(H_2)$ $\mathcal{B} \cup body(H_2)\sigma \vdash body(H_1)\theta\sigma$ $body(H_1)\theta\sigma$

The coverage test procedure plays a key role in the candidate evaluation phases which are responsible for filtering out those candidate patterns with insufficient support. The algorithm for candidate evaluation in $\mathcal{AL}$-QuIN is shown in Figure 1. For a given level l of description granularity and a given level k of search depth, the procedure evaluateCandidates() computes the set $\mathcal{F}_k^l$ of frequent patterns by starting from the set $\mathcal{C}_k^l$ of candidate patterns.

The procedure computeAnswerSet() is reported in Figure 2. Since the computation of each answer hides a coverage test, an open issue is to reduce the number of these tests as much as possible. The procedure computeAnswerSet() benefits from a complementary data structure, called the   .   , that links any candidate Q to the frequent pattern P from which Q has been derived by refinement. This graph is updated during the candidate generation phases [17] and turns out to be useful in candidate evaluation phases because the $\mathcal{B}$-subsumption relations captured in it have the following desirable side effects from the viewpoint of coverage.

Procedure computeAnswerSet$(Q, \mathcal{B})$
1. **if** $intraSpaceEdge(Q) = null$ /* case of trivial pattern */
2.   **then** $answerset(Q, \mathcal{B}) \leftarrow$ listRefIndividuals$(Q, \mathcal{B})$;
3. **else**
4. $P \leftarrow$ getIntraSpaceParent(Q);
5. $answerset(Q, \mathcal{B}) \leftarrow \emptyset$;
6.   **foreach** substitution θ_i in $answerset(P, \mathcal{B})$ **do**
7.   **if** θ_i is a correct answer to Q w.r.t. $\mathcal{B}_i$
8.   **then** $answerset(Q, \mathcal{B}) \leftarrow answerset(Q, \mathcal{B}) \cup \{\theta_i\}$;
9.   **endforeach**
10. **endif**
return $answerset(Q, \mathcal{B})$

Fig. 2. Computation of the answer set of an $\mathcal{O}$-query in $\mathcal{AL}$-QuIn

Lemma 2. $\quad Q \qquad \mathcal{O} \qquad\qquad \mathcal{AL} \qquad\qquad \mathcal{B} \quad . \; \theta \in$
$\quad (Q, \mathcal{B}) \qquad . \qquad\qquad \mathcal{J} \; . \; \mathcal{B} \;\; Q \qquad head(Q)\theta \qquad \mathcal{J}$

$\quad . \quad \theta \qquad\qquad (Q, \mathcal{B}) \qquad . \quad \theta \qquad\qquad\qquad .$
$\qquad\qquad\qquad . \; Q \qquad head(Q)\theta$
$\qquad\qquad\qquad body(Q)\theta \qquad \mathcal{B} \qquad \sigma$
$body(Q)\theta \qquad \sigma \qquad\qquad\qquad . \qquad\qquad body(Q)\theta \qquad \mathcal{B} \models$
$body(Q)\theta\sigma \qquad \theta' \qquad\qquad \theta\sigma \qquad \theta'$
$. \; Q \qquad body(Q)\theta\sigma \qquad \mathcal{J} . \qquad\qquad \mathcal{J} \; . \; \mathcal{B} \qquad head(Q)\theta'$
$\qquad\qquad\qquad head(Q)\theta' = head(Q)\theta \qquad \sigma$
$head(Q)\theta \qquad fi \qquad Q \qquad head(Q)\theta \qquad \mathcal{J}$

Proposition 1. $\quad P \qquad Q \qquad \mathcal{O} \qquad\qquad \mathcal{AL}$
$\mathcal{B} \quad . \; P \succeq_{\mathcal{B}} Q \qquad\qquad (Q, \mathcal{B}) \subseteq \qquad\qquad (P\gamma, \mathcal{B}) \; .$
$\qquad\qquad \gamma \quad . \qquad\qquad\qquad\qquad . \; P$

$\qquad\quad . \qquad \theta \in \qquad (Q, \mathcal{B}) \qquad\qquad . \qquad\qquad \mathcal{J} \; . \; \mathcal{B} \;\; Q$
$head(Q)\theta \qquad \mathcal{J} \qquad P \succeq_{\mathcal{B}} Q$
$\gamma \; . \quad P \qquad\qquad head(P)\gamma = head(Q) \qquad fi \qquad\qquad\qquad \theta \in$
$\qquad (P\gamma, \mathcal{B})$

The following $\mathcal{O}$-query

$P=$ q(A) $\leftarrow$ believes(A,B) &
          A:MiddleEastCountry, B:MonotheisticReligion

covers the observation $\mathcal{A}_{\text{ARM}}$. It can be proved that $P \succeq_{\mathcal{B}} Q$ and Q does not cover $\mathcal{A}_{\text{ARM}}$ w.r.t. $\mathcal{K}_{\text{CIA}}$.

Therefore we store the answer set of frequent patterns and, when evaluating new candidates, we use backward pointers to access this data quickly. This is analogous to a well-known database practice: P is usually a   (i.e. a query whose answers are pre-computed, stored and maintained up-to-date) and the relation of query containment for a query Q in P is exploited to speed up query answering by filtering the answers of P instead of computing the answers of Q from scratch. In particular the procedure computeAnswerSet() uses the intra-space backward pointers, i.e. those edges pointing to the parent node that represents a frequent pattern from $\mathcal{F}^l_{k-1}$. Note that the computation of the answer set of the trivial $\mathcal{O}$-query Q_t for a given language $\mathcal{L}$ needs a special branch in the procedure computeAnswerSet() since the intra-space backward pointer for Q_t is null. In this case the answer set is trivially the list of individuals belonging to the reference concept (returned by the function listRefIndividuals()).

4.2 Implementation Issues

When implementing the coverage test of Theorem 3, the goal has been to reduce constrained SLD-resolution in $\mathcal{AL}$-log to SLD-resolution on DATALOG^{OI}.

We would like to remind the reader that DATALOG^{OI} [24] is a subset of DATALOG$^{\neq}$. In it the equational theory consists of the axioms of Clark's Equality Theory augmented with one rewriting rule that adds $s \neq t$ to any $P \in \mathcal{L}$ for each pair (s, t) of distinct terms occurring in P. Note that $\mathcal{ALC}$ constraints are rendered as , e.g. X:MiddleEastCountry becomes c_MiddleEastCountry(X).

The following unary conjunctive query

$Q^{OI}=$ q(X) ← believes(X,Y), believes(X,Z),
         c_MiddleEastCountry(X), c_MonotheisticReligion(Y),
         X≠Y, X≠Z, Y≠Z

is the DATALOG^{OI} rewriting of the $\mathcal{O}$-query Q reported in Example 2.

Actually the OI bias is only approximated because the definition of the above-mentioned equational theory for DATALOG formulas would make candidate evaluation too costly. In $\mathcal{AL}$-QUIN inequality atoms are added to non-ground clauses any time it is necessary for preserving the semantics of the knowledge base. In particular, the specification of constraints for variables reduces the number of necessary inequality atoms as shown in the following example.

In Q the addition of X≠Y is superfluous because it will never happen that X and Y are instantiated with the same constant. Indeed X and Y appear constrained as individuals of the concepts MiddleEastCountry and MonotheisticReligion respectively, for which it can be proved that the assertion MiddleEastCountry ⊓ MonotheisticReligion = ⊥ holds in $\mathcal{K}_{\text{CIA}}$. Also the addition of X≠Z is superfluous for transitivity. Therefore the following query

$Q'=$ q(X) ← believes(X,Y), believes(X,Z),
         c_MiddleEastCountry(X), c_MonotheisticReligion(Y), Y≠Z

is a simplified yet correct rewriting of Q.

One major drawback of implementing $\mathcal{O}$-queries as DATALOG conjunctive queries with inequalities is the cost of query answering. Indeed, it has been proved that conjunctive queries with inequalities are in general intractable [13] Yet some tractable cases have been investigated. In particular, it has been shown that the class of acyclic conjunctive queries with inequalities is fixed parameter (f.p.) tractable, both with respect to the query size and the number of variables as the parameter [21]. Furthermore, such queries can be evaluated in f.p. polynomial time in the input and the output. Thus we have restricted the language of patterns in $\mathcal{AL}$-QUIN to this tractable class of conjunctive queries with inequalities.

As an illustration, let us consider Q' and the query Q'' obtained from Q' by removing the inequality atom $Y \neq Z$. The hypergraph associated to Q' and reported in Figure 3 shows that the inclusion of edges corresponding to inequality atoms (dashed hyperedges) destroys acyclicity of Q''.

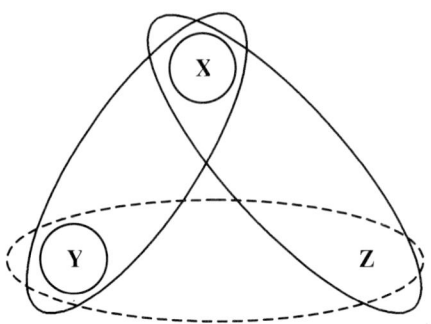

Fig. 3. Hypergraph of the $\mathcal{O}$-query Q'.

Finally note that the order of evaluation of atoms in the query is relevant for the efficiency of query answering. Postponing the evaluation of membership atoms (as done with constraints in constrained SLD-refutations) could cause a waste of computation due to late backtracking, thus affecting the performance significatively. Furthermore inequality atoms need to be fully instantiated before evaluation. This means that it is safe to postpone their evaluation.

The query

```
q(X) ← c_MiddleEastCountry(X), believes(X,Y), c_MonotheisticReligion(Y),
        believes(X,Z), Y≠Z
```

is the actual rewriting of Q in $\mathcal{AL}$-QUIN.

As to the satisfiability tests required by constrained SLD-resolution, they have been replaced by preliminary saturation steps of the background knowledge $\mathcal{K}$. To be more precise, the saturation step involving the reference concept is made only once at the beginning of the whole discovery process because it makes explicit knowledge of interest to all the levels of granularity. Conversely, concept assertions for the task-relevant concepts, if not explicitly represented in $\mathcal{K}$, are obtained by saturating the l-th layer $\mathcal{T}^l$ of $\mathcal{T}$ against $\mathcal{M}$ at the beginning of the search stage in $\mathcal{L}^l$. This makes SLD-refutations of queries in $\mathcal{L}^l$ work only on extensional structural knowledge at the level l of description granularity.

The concept assertions

```
'ARM':MiddleEastCountry.
'IR':MiddleEastCountry.
```

for the reference concept `MiddleEastCountry` are made explicit before the discovery process starts. Conversely the concept assertions

```
'Armenian Orthodox':MonotheisticReligion.
'Shia':MonotheisticReligion.
'Sunni':MonotheisticReligion.
```

for the task-relevant concept `MonotheisticReligion` (belonging to $\mathcal{T}^2$) are derived by saturating the axioms against the assertions of $\mathcal{K}_{\texttt{CIA}}$ at the beginning of the search in $\mathcal{L}^2$.

The intensional relational knowledge is made explicit at the loading of each observation.

When testing the coverage of $\mathcal{A}_{\texttt{IR}}$, the query reported in Example 10 is evaluated w.r.t. the facts

```
believes('IR','Shia').
believes('IR','Sunni').
```

and the assertions reported in Example 11.

4.3 Scalability Tests

The benefits of using the graph of backward pointers in the answer set computation have been empirically verified by comparing the scalability of two versions of $\mathcal{AL}$-QuIn, $\mathcal{AL}$-QuIn 1.0 and $\mathcal{AL}$-QuIn 2.0, w.r.t. the number of observations. The former implements candidate evaluation   graph whereas the latter implements candidate evaluation   graph. The data set considered for these experiments consists of $|O| = 10$ observations and amounts to $5,244$ facts (some of which are obtained by saturation). By bounding the search to the maximum level $maxG = 2$ of description granularity and the maximum level $maxD = 6$ of depth, the discovery process returns 744 patterns out of 3851 candidate patterns. For more details of the task settings see Section 6.1 of [18]. The two versions of $\mathcal{AL}$-QuIn have been first run on the original data set, then on data sets that contain each original observation 2^N times, with N ranging from 1 to 5. The platform for these experiments has been a PC AMD Athlon 2500+ with 512 Mb DDR SRAM running Microsoft Windows XP. Results are reported in Table 1 and show a noteworthy improvement of performance in $\mathcal{AL}$-QuIn 2.0.

Table 1. Scalability of $\mathcal{AL}$-QuIn by varying $|O|$

N	$|O|$	No. facts	$\mathcal{AL}$-QuIn 1.0 (sec)	$\mathcal{AL}$-QuIn 2.0 (sec)
1	10	5,244	5.1	4.7
2	20	16,897	48.5	33.9
3	30	35,508	331.6	217.7
4	40	61,077	1344.7	937.3
5	50	93,604	7010.8	4627.8

Efficiency in ILP depends also on the complexity of candidate hypotheses. Therefore the scalability of $\mathcal{AL}$-QuIn 1.0 and $\mathcal{AL}$-QuIn 2.0 has been compared also w.r.t. the maximum level of search depth. Note that $maxD$ is one of the two factors influencing the complexity measure for $\mathcal{O}$-queries [17]. In particular, it bounds the length of the body of $\mathcal{O}$-queries belonging to a given language. Therefore we have run the two versions of $\mathcal{AL}$-QuIn on the same data set used in the previous experiment by varying $maxD$ from 4 to 9. The results reported in Table 2 show that $\mathcal{AL}$-QuIn 2.0 performs (slightly) better only in a few cases.

Table 2. Scalability of $\mathcal{AL}$-QuIn by varying $maxD$

$maxD$	No. patterns	$\mathcal{AL}$-QuIn 1.0 (sec)	$\mathcal{AL}$-QuIn 2.0 (sec)
4	81/396	0.4	0.4
5	273/1350	1.6	1.5
6	744/3851	5.1	4.7
7	2303/10169	31.0	33.2
8	6203/27920	143.1	140.8
9	17990/67313	1698.0	1993.3

5 Conclusions and Future Work

In this paper we have defined coverage relations for $\mathcal{AL}$-log in the two logical settings of learning from implications and learning from interpretations. Also we have discussed the algorithmic and implementation issues raised by the coverage test under intepretations with reference to the system $\mathcal{AL}$-QuIn. In $\mathcal{AL}$-QuIn, the evaluation of candidate hypotheses is made efficient by:

- the use of the graph of backward pointers to decrease the number of coverage tests per $\mathcal{O}$-query;
- the implementation of $\mathcal{O}$-queries as acyclic conjunctive queries with inequalities to ensure the f.p. tractability of query answering;
- the use of saturation steps to make implicit knowledge (especially the structural one) immediately available when necessary.

This is in addition to the notorious benefits of the setting itself of learning from interpretations. Scalability is particularly important in real-world applications such as Semantic Web Mining.

The efficiency of candidate evaluation in $\mathcal{AL}$-QuIn can be further improved along the following two complementary directions.

First, the levelwise method for frequent pattern discovery evaluates the candidates of each depth level in one single pass through the data set [19]. Currently $\mathcal{AL}$-QuIn does not follow this dictate. Indeed it makes as many passes through the data set as the number of $\mathcal{O}$-queries in $\mathcal{C}_k^l$. A single-pass version of candidate evaluation for $\mathcal{AL}$-QuIn would contain an outer loop on interpretations and an inner loop on candidate patterns. The single-pass principle is extremely important in the case of a tight coupling of $\mathcal{AL}$-QuIn with real-world data sets because it becomes crucial to minimize accesses to the data source. Though it is not generally possible to isolate $\mathcal{B}_i$'s such that $\{\mathcal{B}_i\}$ is a partition on $\mathcal{B}$ because of some overlap, this is not a matter of all or nothing: it is only the information in the intersection between $\mathcal{B}_i$'s which is accessed more than once. If this overlap is minimal, the single-pass principle is virtually upheld. If the overlap is total, one pass through the full data set per $\mathcal{O}$-query cannot be avoided. Between these extreme cases, the single-pass idea is gradually given up.

Second, the implementation of the coverage test in $\mathcal{AL}$-QuIn can take advantage of the theoretical results of both [15] and [7].

As a final remark, we would like to emphasize that in $\mathcal{AL}$-QuIn the pattern languages that can be defined and the coverage relation that has been implemented allow new concepts to be discovered. But these concepts are subconcepts of known concepts. Indeed each $\mathcal{O}$-query can be considered as the description of a cluster of the individuals of the reference concept. From this perspective $\mathcal{B}$-subsumption relations then stand for containment relations between clusters. These links between frequent patterns and clusters are promising and encourage us to carry on working along the direction towards conceptual clustering.

References

1. F. Baader, D. Calvanese, D. McGuinness, D. Nardi, and P.F. Patel-Schneider, editors. *The Description Logic Handbook: Theory, Implementation and Applications*. Cambridge University Press, 2003.
2. T. Berners-Lee. *Weaving the Web*. Harper: San Francisco, 1999.
3. H. Blockeel, L. De Raedt, N. Jacobs, and B. Demoen. Scaling Up Inductive Logic Programming by Learning from Interpretations. *Data Mining and Knowledge Discovery*, 3:59–93, 1999.
4. S. Ceri, G. Gottlob, and L. Tanca. *Logic Programming and Databases*. Springer, 1990.
5. L. De Raedt. Logical Settings for Concept-Learning. *Artificial Intelligence*, 95(1):187–201, 1997.
6. L. De Raedt and S. Džeroski. First order jk-clausal theories are PAC-learnable. *Artificial Intelligence*, 70:375–392, 1994.
7. N. Di Mauro, T.M. Altomare, S. Ferilli, F. Esposito, and N. Fanizzi. An Exhaustive Matching Procedure for the Improvement of Learning Efficiency. In T. Horvath and A. Yamamoto, editors, *Inductive Logic Programming*, volume 2835 of *Lecture Notes in Artificial Intelligence*, pages 112–129. Springer, 2003.

8. F.M. Donini, M. Lenzerini, D. Nardi, and A. Schaerf. $\mathcal{AL}$-log: Integrating Datalog and Description Logics. *Journal of Intelligent Information Systems*, 10(3):227–252, 1998.

9. M. Frazier and C.D. Page. Learnability in inductive logic programming. In *Proceedings of the 10st National Conference on Artificial Intelligence*, pages 93–98. The AAAI Press/The MIT Press, 1993.

10. I. Horrocks and P.F. Patel-Schneider. A Proposal for an OWL Rules Language. In *Proc. of the 13th International World Wide Web Conference*. ACM, 2004. To appear.

11. I. Horrocks, P.F. Patel-Schneider, and F. van Harmelen. From $\mathcal{SHIQ}$ and RDF to OWL: The making of a web ontology language. *Journal of Web Semantics*, 1(1):7–26, 2003.

12. J.-U. Kietz. Learnability of description logic programs. In S. Matwin and C. Sammut, editors, *Inductive Logic Programming*, volume 2583 of *Lecture Notes in Artificial Intelligence*, pages 117–132. Springer, 2003.

13. A.C. Klug. On conjunctive queries containing inequalities. *Journal of ACM*, 35(1):146–160, 1988.

14. A.Y. Levy and M.-C. Rousset. Combining Horn rules and description logics in CARIN. *Artificial Intelligence*, 104:165–209, 1998.

15. F.A. Lisi, S. Ferilli, and N. Fanizzi. Object Identity as Search Bias for Pattern Spaces. In F. van Harmelen, editor, *ECAI 2002. Proceedings of the 15th European Conference on Artificial Intelligence*, pages 375–379, Amsterdam, 2002. IOS Press.

16. F.A. Lisi and D. Malerba. Bridging the Gap between Horn Clausal Logic and Description Logics in Inductive Learning. In A. Cappelli and F. Turini, editors, *AI*IA 2003: Advances in Artificial Intelligence*, volume 2829 of *Lecture Notes in Artificial Intelligence*, pages 49–60. Springer, 2003.

17. F.A. Lisi and D. Malerba. Ideal Refinement of Descriptions in $\mathcal{AL}$-log. In T. Horvath and A. Yamamoto, editors, *Inductive Logic Programming*, volume 2835 of *Lecture Notes in Artificial Intelligence*, pages 215–232. Springer, 2003.

18. F.A. Lisi and D. Malerba. Inducing Multi-Level Association Rules from Multiple Relations. *Machine Learning*, 55:175–210, 2004.

19. H. Mannila and H. Toivonen. Levelwise search and borders of theories in knowledge discovery. *Data Mining and Knowledge Discovery*, 1(3):241–258, 1997.

20. S.-H. Nienhuys-Cheng and R. de Wolf. *Foundations of Inductive Logic Programming*, volume 1228 of *Lecture Notes in Artificial Intelligence*. Springer, 1997.

21. C.H. Papadimitriou and M. Yannakakis. On the complexity of database queries. In *Proceedings of the Sixteenth ACM SIGACT-SIGMOD-SIGART Symposium on Principles of Database Systems, May 12-14, 1997, Tucson, Arizona*, pages 12–19. ACM Press, 1997.

22. C. Rouveirol and V. Ventos. Towards Learning in CARIN-$\mathcal{ALN}$. In J. Cussens and A. Frisch, editors, *Inductive Logic Programming*, volume 1866 of *Lecture Notes in Artificial Intelligence*, pages 191–208. Springer, 2000.

23. M. Schmidt-Schauss and G. Smolka. Attributive concept descriptions with complements. *Artificial Intelligence*, 48(1):1–26, 1991.

24. G. Semeraro, F. Esposito, D. Malerba, N. Fanizzi, and S. Ferilli. A logic framework for the incremental inductive synthesis of Datalog theories. In N.E. Fuchs, editor, *Proceedings of 7th International Workshop on Logic Program Synthesis and Transformation*, volume 1463 of *Lecture Notes in Computer Science*, pages 300–321. Springer, 1998.

An Efficient Algorithm for Reducing Clauses Based on Constraint Satisfaction Techniques

Jérôme Maloberti[1,2] and Einoshin Suzuki[2]

[1] Université Paris-Sud,
Laboratoire de Recherche en Informatique (LRI), Bât. 490,
F-91405 Orsay Cedex, France
malobert@lri.fr
[2] Electrical and Computer Engineering,
Yokohama National University, 79-5 Tokiwadai, Hodogaya,
Yokohama 240-8501, Japan
suzuki@ynu.ac.jp

Abstract. This paper presents a new reduction algorithm which employs Constraint Satisfaction Techniques for removing redundant literals of a clause efficiently. Inductive Logic Programming (ILP) learning algorithms using a generate and test approach produce hypotheses with redundant literals. Since the reduction is known to be a co-NP-complete problem, most algorithms are incomplete approximations. A complete algorithm proposed by Gottlob and Fermüller is optimal in the number of θ-subsumption calls. However, this method is inefficient since it exploits neither the result of the θ-subsumption nor the intermediary results of similar θ-subsumption calls. Recently, Hirata has shown that this problem is equivalent to finding a minimal solution to a θ-subsumption of a clause with itself, and proposed an incomplete algorithm based on a θ-subsumption algorithm of Scheffer. This algorithm has a large memory consumption and performs many unnecessary tests in most cases. In this work, we overcome this problem by transforming the θ-subsumption problem in a Constraint Satisfaction Problem, then we use an exhaustive search algorithm in order to find a minimal solution. The experiments with artificial and real data sets show that our algorithm outperforms the algorithm of Gottlob and Fermüller by several orders of magnitude, particularly in hard cases.

1 Introduction

Relational learning and Inductive Logic Programming (ILP)[16] have been used for building models or mining data [3,14] in complex domains such as chemistry [20], bio-informatics [10], etc. Since these algorithms use the Datalog formalism [23], a hypothesis can be equivalent to a hypothesis with a smaller number of literals because some literals are redundant. For example, two clauses C: $H(X) \leftarrow p(X,Y), p(Y,Z), p(X,W)$ and D: $H(X) \leftarrow p(X,Y), p(Y,Z)$ are equivalent since there exists a substitution $\theta = \{X/X, Y/Y, Z/Z, W/Y\}$ such that

R. Camacho, R. King, A. Srinivasan (Eds.): ILP 2004, LNAI 3194, pp. 234–251, 2004.

$C\theta = D$. Therefore, literal $p(X, W)$ is redundant with $p(X, Y)$, according to θ. Given a clause C, a reduction (also called condensation) algorithm returns a *reduced* clause C'' such that $C' \subseteq C$ and C' is logically equivalent to C. If C has no redundant literal, the algorithm returns C.

Reduction algorithms are used to reduce hypotheses generated by computing a Least General Generalization (LGG) [16,15], to build refinement graphs of reduced clauses [2] and to improve the efficiency of the test of a candidate hypothesis against a data set [18].

Gottlob and Fermüller [6] have shown that reduction is co-NP-complete and they give an optimal algorithm in number of θ-subsumption [16] calls. This algorithm removes one literal at a time, checking with a θ-subsumption test if it is redundant. Since θ-subsumption is an NP-complete problem, this algorithm is intractable and polynomial approximations have been proposed [18,8]. Recently, Hirata [8] has shown that a minimal substitution in the number of literals of a clause C on itself is equivalent to a reduction of C and he describes an algorithm based on a θ-subsumption algorithm of Scheffer et al [19]. This algorithm builds a *substitution* graph in which each node is a possible assignment of a literal and each edge connects two nodes corresponding to assignments of two different literals. If these two literals share a same variable, the variable must not be assigned to different values. Then, it searches for a clique of size $|C|$ which minimizes the number of literals in the substitution. Since it uses a greedy algorithm for exploring the substitution graph, a near optimal solution can be found, therefore it is not suitable for algorithms which need reduced clauses. Furthermore, the substitution graph needs a large amount of memory and is completely computed even if a solution can be found by exploring a small part of the graph.

In this paper, we improve the algorithm of Gottlob and Fermüller with an algorithm able to remove more than one literal at a time by examining the substitution returned by the θ-subsumption. Then we describe Jivaro, a fast algorithm of reduction of clause which searches for a minimal substitution of a clause on itself. Jivaro efficiently explores all the substitutions of a clause using Constraint Satisfaction Techniques and dynamically removes redundant literals from the clause during the search. It significantly improves the algorithm of Gottlob and Fermüller, particularly on hard cases, since it only performs one θ-subsumption test instead of a linear number, in the size of the clause, of θ-subsumption tests. Jivaro is based on a version of Django [12,13], a fast θ-subsumption algorithm using constraint satisfaction techniques, which returns all the substitutions. This version of Django is compared with a new algorithm [4] which finds all the substitutions without backtracks, and experiment shows that Django outperforms it in an order of magnitude. Jivaro has been integrated in a Frequent Query Discovery (FQD) algorithm, Jimi [14], in order to replace the elimination step of redundant candidates and experiment shows a significant improvement of Jimi when the size of each candidate is relatively large.

2 Reduction Problem

2.1 Definitions

We use the Datalog formalism to represent data and concepts. Datalog is a restriction of the first-order logic which does not allow functions in clauses. In Datalog, a *term* is a constant or a variable. In order to distinguish non-numeric constants from variables, the first letter of a variable is written in uppercase.

Let p be an n-ary predicate symbol and each of $t_1, t_2, \cdots, t_n$ a term, then an *atom* is represented by $p(t_1, t_2, \cdots, t_n)$. Let B and A_i be atoms then a formula in the form $B \leftarrow \{A_1, A_2, \cdots, A_n\}$ is called a *clause*.

Definition 1. Substitution
Let $\{V_1, V_2, \cdots, V_n\}$ be a set of variables and $\{t_1, t_2, \cdots, t_n\}$ be a set of terms, then a substitution θ represents a set of bindings $\{V_1/t_1, V_2/t_2, \cdots, V_n/t_n\}$.

Definition 2. θ-subsumption
Let C and D be clauses, then C θ-subsumes D, denoted by $C \succeq D$, if and only if (iff) there exists a substitution θ, such that $C\theta \subseteq D$.

We say that the solution of $C \succeq D$, is $C\theta$. For example, a clause C_1: $H(X) \leftarrow p(X, Y), p(X, b)$ θ-subsumes another clause C_2: $H(a) \leftarrow p(a, b)$ with a substitution $\theta = \{X/a, Y/b\}$.

Definition 3. Logical Equivalence
Let C_1 and C_2 be clauses, then C_1 is logically equivalent to C_2, denoted by $C_1 \sim C_2$, iff $C_1 \succeq C_2$ and $C_2 \succeq C_1$.

For example, a clause C_3: $H(X) \leftarrow p(X, Y), p(X, Z)$ is logically equivalent to another clause C_4: $H(U) \leftarrow p(U, V)$ since $C_3 \succeq C_4$ with $\theta = \{X/U, Y/V, Z/V\}$, and $C_4 \succeq C_3$ with $\theta = \{U/X, V/Y\}$.

Definition 4. Reduction
Let C and D be clauses, then C is a reduction of D, iff $C \subseteq D$ and $C \sim D$. C is reduced if there exists no clause C' such that C' is a reduction of C and $|C'| < |C|$.

Definition 5. Redundant Literal
Let C and D be clauses such that C is a reduction of D, then $\forall lit_i$ such that $lit_i \in D$ and $lit_i \notin C$, lit_i is redundant.

2.2 Conventional Method

The algorithm described in [6] is shown below in the *FAST_CONDENSE* procedure. It computes the reduction C' of a clause C by removing a literal lit from C in line 1 and by testing if C θ-subsumes C' in line 2. If C θ-subsumes C', lit is redundant and can be safely removed from C in line 3. The algorithm checks similarly all the literals of C. It must be noticed that if there is no other literal in the clause with the same predicate symbol than lit, it is not redundant and there is no need to test lit. $A \setminus B$ represents the difference between the sets A and B.

FAST_CONDENSE($\mathcal{C}$)
Input: Clause $\mathcal{C}$
1. **for all** $lit \in \mathcal{C}$ such that (s.t.) the predicate symbol of lit is not unique in $\mathcal{C}$
2. **if** $\mathcal{C} \succeq \mathcal{C} \setminus lit$
3. $\quad | \quad \mathcal{C} \leftarrow \mathcal{C} \setminus lit$

This algorithm is optimal in the number of θ-subsumption calls, however, it performs one θ-subsumption test for each removed literal.

3 Proposed Method

The procedure *FAST_CONDENSE* removes one literal at a time, however, it can be improved by removing all literals that are not in the solution found by the θ-subsumption procedure. Now we prove that this improvement is sound.

Theorem 1. *Let C and D be two clauses such as $C \supset D$ and $C \succeq D$, and a substitution θ such as $C\theta \subseteq D$, then there exists a set $\mathcal{L}$ of literals such as $\mathcal{L} = C \setminus C\theta$ and each literal lit_i such as $lit_i \in \mathcal{L}$ is redundant.*

Proof. Since C θ-subsumes D and $C \supset D$, $\forall lit_i \in C : lit_i\theta \in D$ and transitively $lit_i\theta \in C$. Moreover, $\forall lit_i \in C\theta : lit_i \in D$ and $lit_i\theta \in C$. Obviously, C θ-subsumes $C\theta$ and $C\theta \subseteq D \subset C$. Therefore, according to the definition of redundancy of a literal, each literal lit_i of the set $\mathcal{L}$ such as $\mathcal{L} = C \setminus C\theta$ is redundant. $\square$

Intuitively, if C is a superset of D and C θ-subsumes D, the set of literals $C\theta$ corresponds to a solution of $C \succeq D$. Therefore, any literal of C which is not in $C\theta$ is redundant and can be removed.

For example, a clause C_5: $p(V_0, V_1), p(V_1, V_2), p(V_0, V_3),\ p(V_3, V_4)$ has two equivalent reduced clauses C_5': $p(V_0, V_1), p(V_1, V_2)$ and C_5'': $p(V_0, V_3),\ p(V_3, V_4)$. By applying the substitution $\theta = \{V_0/V_0, V_1/V_1, V_2/V_2, V_3/V_1, V_4/V_2\}$ to C_5, we obtain C_5'. Therefore, if we apply θ to any clause D such as $C_5' \subset D \subset C_5$, we obtain $D\theta = C_5'$. Obviously, $p(V_0, V_3)$, $p(V_3, V_4)$ are redundant and can be removed from C_5.

Consequently, if the θ-subsumption algorithm could return the set of literal $C\theta$, each literal lit_i such as $lit_i \in C$ and $lit_i \notin C\theta$ could be removed safely and more than one literal can be removed for each θ-subsumption test.

The procedure *FAST_REDUCTION* shown below computes the minimal reduction of a clause C by removing a literal lit from C, similarly to the procedure *FAST_CONDENSE*, and by testing if C θ-subsumes $C \setminus lit$ in lines $1 - 2$. However, we use a θ-subsumption procedure, called *ThetaSubsumption*, with two parameters, the clauses C and D, which returns $C\theta$ if C θ-subsumes D, and $\emptyset$ otherwise. Therefore, if the result of *ThetaSubsumption* is not $\emptyset$, all literals of C that are not in the solution are removed in lines 4 and 5. If C has many redundant literals, *FAST_REDUCTION* can perform significantly less θ-subsumption calls than *FAST_CONDENSE* by removing more than one literal for each θ-subsumption call.

FAST_REDUCTION($\mathcal{C}$)

Input: Clause $\mathcal{C}$
  1. **for all** $lit \in \mathcal{C}$ s.t. the predicate symbol of lit is not unique in $\mathcal{C}$
  2. *Solution* $\leftarrow$ *ThetaSubsumption*($\mathcal{C}, \mathcal{C} \setminus lit$)
  3. **if** *Solution* $\neq \emptyset$
  4. $\quad$ | **for all** lit_i s.t. $lit_i \in \mathcal{C}$ **and** $lit_i \notin$ *Solution*
  5. $\quad$ | $\quad$ | $\mathcal{C} \leftarrow \mathcal{C} \setminus lit_i$

If C is reduced, *FAST_REDUCTION* and *FAST_CONDENSE* will perform $|C|$ θ-subsumption calls which returns no solution.

Recently, Hirata [8] has shown that the problem of reduction of clause C is equivalent to a search for a substitution of minimal size in the number of literals for the problem $C \succeq C$. Jivaro uses a similar method, however, it also removes all the redundant literals during the search . The procedure *JIVARO_SIMPLE* shown below is a naive implementation of Jivaro.

JIVARO_SIMPLE($\mathcal{C}$)

Input: Clause $\mathcal{C}$
  1. **for all** θ s. t. $\mathcal{C}\theta \subseteq \mathcal{C}$
  2. **if** $|\mathcal{C}\theta| < |\mathcal{C}|$
  3. $\quad$ | **for all** lit_i s.t. $lit_i \in \mathcal{C}$ **and** $lit_i \notin \mathcal{C}\theta$
  4. $\quad$ | $\quad$ | $\mathcal{C} \leftarrow \mathcal{C} \setminus lit_i$

Now we prove that this algorithm is complete.

Proof. Let C and D be two clauses such that D is a minimal reduction of C. Then, if this algorithm is not complete, there exists at least one redundant literal $lit \in C$ such that *JIVARO_SIMPLE* returns $D \cup lit$. Since lit is redundant, there exists a substitution θ such that for any clause C', $(C' \cup lit)\theta \subseteq C'$, with $(C \setminus lit) \supseteq C' \supseteq D$. Therefore, $(C' \cup lit)\theta \subseteq C' \cup lit$ is also true, and the condition in line 1 is satisfied. Furthermore, $|(C' \cup lit)\theta| \leq |C'|$, since $(C' \cup lit)\theta \subseteq C'$. Then, $|(C' \cup lit)\theta| \leq |C'| < |C' \cup lit|$ is true, and the condition in line 2 is satisfied. The assumption $(C' \cup lit)\theta \subseteq C' \subset C' \cup lit$ satisfies the condition in line 3 for the literal lit. Since the three conditions are satisfied, lit is removed in line 4 and consequently, this algorithm is complete. $\square$

Since we believe that Django [12] is the fastest θ-subsumption algorithm so far, Jivaro extends Django in order to find a minimal solution in an efficient way.

Therefore, Jivaro transforms the problem of reduction in a constraint satisfaction problem similarly to Django.

3.1 Constraint Satisfaction Problem

A Constraint Satisfaction Problem (CSP) [22] is defined by:

$\mathcal{V}$ a set of variables;

$\mathcal{D}$ a set of domains, each of which associates a set of admissible values to a variable;

$\mathcal{C}$ a set of constraints, each of which involves more than one variable, and restricts the simultaneously admissible values of these variables.

A CSP is satisfiable, if it admits a solution which assigns to each variable a value such that all constraints are satisfied. Therefore, given two clauses C: $p(X,Y), p(Y,Z)$ and D: $p(a,b), p(b,c), p(a,c)$, the θ-subsumption problem $C \succeq D$ can be formalized.

$\mathcal{V}$ the literals of C: $\{p(X,Y), p(Y,Z)\}$;

$\mathcal{D}$ a set of domains, each of which associates a set of literals in D with the same predicate symbol to a literal. In this example, all literals have a same domain: $\{p(a,b), p(b,c), p(a,c)\}$;

$\mathcal{C}$ a set of constraints, each of which involves two literals that share a variable. In a θ-subsumption problem, there are only binary constraints. In this example, there is one constraint between $p(X,Y)$ and $p(Y,Z)$. This constraint is satisfied if a literal assigned to $p(X,Y)$ shares its second argument with the first argument of a literal assigned to $p(Y,Z)$. It must be noticed that if a literal l contains more than one occurrence of a variable, a constraint is satisfied if all literals assigned to l have at least the same multiple occurrences of a same term.

There are two kinds of heuristics in CSP algorithms. Reduction heuristics are used to transform a CSP into an equivalent CSP of lower complexity by reducing the variable domains. Search heuristics concern the search strategy.

Reduction proceeds by pruning the candidate values for each variable X. A value a in the domain $dom(X)$ of X is *consistent* if, for all variables Y such that there exists a constraint C which involves X and Y, there exists a candidate value b in $dom(Y)$ such that the pair $\langle a, b \rangle$ satisfies C. Clearly, if a is not consistent, X cannot be mapped onto a, and a can be soundly removed from $dom(X)$.

The reduction heuristic most commonly used is the arc-consistency, which checks for each constraint the consistency of the domains until no value can be removed. The best complexity of arc-consistency algorithms is $\mathcal{O}(|\mathcal{C}||D|^2)$, with $|D|$ being the average domain size.

In the previous example, the initial domains of the literals $p(X,Y)$ and $p(Y,Z)$ are:

− $dom(p(X,Y)) = \{p(a,b), p(b,c), p(a,c)\}$

$$- dom(p(Y, Z)) = \{p(a, b), p(b, c), p(a, c)\}$$

However, the value $p(b, c)$ in $dom(p(X, Y))$ is not consistent, since there is no value in $dom(p(Y, Z))$ such that the first argument is c. Therefore, $p(b, c)$ can be removed from $dom(p(X, Y))$. After the reduction, the domains are:

$$- dom(p(X, Y)) = \{p(a, b)\}$$
$$- dom(p(Y, Z)) = \{p(b, c)\}$$

Arc-consistency is a necessary condition to prove that a CSP has a solution. Furthermore, if the CSP is acyclic, arc-consistency is a sufficient condition.

CSP search algorithms incrementally construct a solution by assigning a value from a domain to its variable through a depth-first exploration of the assignment tree. On each assignment, consistency is checked; on failure, another candidate value for the current node is considered; if no other value is available, the search backtracks.

There are two kinds of search heuristics. Look-back heuristics checks on each assignment if it is consistent with previous assignments. The best look-back algorithms try to prevent the repeated exploration of a same subtree. Look-ahead heuristics remove inconsistent values from the domains connected to the assigned variable. The Forward Checking [7] (FC) algorithm employs a limited propagation, only checking the candidate values for the domains immediately connected, i.e. partial arc-consistency. If a value is removed from a domain D, the Maintaining Arc consistency (MAC) [22] algorithm also checks all the domains connected to D, i.e. full arc-consistency.

In addition, the variable order can be optimized, either statically before the exploration, or dynamically by ordering unassigned variables on each assignment. Dynamic variable ordering is generally more efficient than static variable ordering. One criterion for reordering the variables is based on the First Fail Principle [1], preferring the variable with the smallest domain. Therefore, failures will occur sooner rather than later.

3.2 Jivaro

Jivaro performs a depth-first search using a Forward Checking algorithm [7] which finds a minimal solution that satisfies the constraints and removes all literals in the clause C which are not in the solution. It must be noticed that the algorithm is recursive in order to simplify the description. However, since it removes literals during the search a correct implementation should take care of this fact during the backtracking steps in order to avoid inconsistency or redundant search. Below, we show the procedure *Jivaro* which transforms the problem of reduction of a clause C in a CSP as described previously and in [12,13] by calling the procedures *ComputeConstraints* and *ComputeDomains* in lines 2 and 3. *ComputeConstraints* returns a set C of binary constraints, and *ComputeDomains* returns a set D of domains. Then, Jivaro calls the procedure *ArcConsistency*, line 4, which performs an AC3 algorithm [11] in order to remove for each literal all values in its domain that do not satisfy all its constraints.

Solution is a set, initially empty, which contains pairs of literals that correspond to assignments of a literal by a value. The procedure *Values* is used in order to obtain a set of literals which are used as values in the assignments of *Solution* in line 7. This set corresponds to the set of non-redundant literal of C and is the output of Jivaro. Therefore, Jivaro calls the procedure *Reduction* in line 6 in order to start the search.

Jivaro(C)
Input: Clause C
  1. $\mathcal{L} \leftarrow$ Literals(C)
  2. $\mathcal{C} \leftarrow$ ComputeConstraints($\mathcal{L}$)
  3. $\mathcal{D} \leftarrow$ ComputeDomains($\mathcal{L}$)
  4. ArcConsistency($\mathcal{L}, \mathcal{D}, \mathcal{C}$)
  5. *Solution* $\leftarrow \emptyset$
  6. Reduction($\mathcal{L}, \mathcal{D}, \mathcal{C}, Solution$)
  7. **return** Values(*Solution*)

The procedure *Reduction* recursively builds a partial solution satisfying the constraints to the θ-subsumption problem $C \succeq C$. It adds one literal *Lit* at each recursive call and tries all possible assignments to *Lit*. The search tree is pruned if an assignment does not satisfy the constraints.

At each step, a literal is chosen using the procedure *ChooseBestLiteral*, line 1, with a dynamic variable ordering heuristic based on the First Fail Principle [1]. For each literal, the number of remaining values in its domain is divided by the number of constraints involving this literal. The literal with the highest ratio is selected. This heuristic has been compared in [13] with different heuristics and has shown the best results in the θ-subsumption problem.

Then, the domain of *Lit* is obtained by a call to the procedure *Domain*, and for each value in the domain, a new assignment is added to the solution, lines 2 and 3, before a call to the procedure *Propagation*. *Propagation* checks if all the constraints are satisfied, removes the inconsistent values from the domains and stores them in *RemovedValues*. If all the constraints are satisfied but the solution is not complete, then the search continues by calling recursively *Reduction*. If all the constraints are satisfied and all the literals are assigned, then the procedure *CheckCompleteSolution* is called. *CheckCompleteSolution* removes all literals that are not used in the solution from $\mathcal{L}$ and from all the domains.

The procedure *RestoreDomains*, line 10 puts back in the domains the values removed by *Propagation* and the current assignment is removed from *Solution*, line 11, before the procedure selects the next value in the domain.

Reduction($\mathcal{L}, \mathcal{D}, \mathcal{C}, Solution$)
Input: Set of literals $\mathcal{C}$, Set of domains $\mathcal{D}$, Set of constraints $\mathcal{C}$
        Set of pairs $\langle Literal_i, Literal_j \rangle$ *Solution*
  1. *Lit* $\leftarrow$ ChooseBestLiteral($\mathcal{L}, \mathcal{D}, \mathcal{C}, Solution$)
  2. **for all** $Lit_i \in$ Domain($Lit, \mathcal{D}$)

3. | $Solution \leftarrow Solution \cup \langle Lit, Lit_i \rangle$
4. | $RemovedValues \leftarrow \emptyset$
5. | **if** $\text{Propagation}(\mathcal{L}, \mathcal{D}, \mathcal{C}, RemovedValues, Lit, Lit_i)$
6. | | **if** $|Solution| = |\mathcal{L}|$
7. | | | $\text{CheckCompleteSolution}(\mathcal{L}, \mathcal{D}, Solution)$
8. | | **else**
9. | | | $\text{Reduction}(\mathcal{L}, \mathcal{D}, \mathcal{C}, Solution)$
10. | $\text{RestoreDomains}(\mathcal{D}, RemovedValues)$
11. | $Solution \leftarrow Solution \setminus \langle Lit, Lit_i \rangle$

The procedure *Propagation* checks if the new value $Cand$ assigned to the literal Lit is consistent with the domains of the literals that share a variable with Lit. It selects all the literals Lit_i connected to Lit by a constraint, line 1, and for each literal, it checks whether the values in its domain are consistent with the assignment $Lit = Cand$, lines 2 and 3. If a value does not satisfy a constraint, it is removed from the domain and added to $RemovedValues$, lines $4 - 6$, in order to restore it during the backtrack step. If a domain is empty, the procedure stops and returns $FALSE$, lines 7 and 8. For simplicity, this procedure is written as a simple Forward Checking and only checks the literals connected to Lit. However, Jivaro actually uses the same strategy as the Meta-Django procedure described in [13]. Meta-Django selects a procedure between FCsingleton and MAC according to a probabilistic measure κ [5,13][1]. The procedure FCsingleton can be easily obtained by adding a recursive call to *Propagation* to check the domains with only one value, after the line 8. The MAC (Maintaining Arc Consistency) procedure checks recursively all domains after a removal of a value in line 6.

Propagation$(\mathcal{L}, \mathcal{D}, \mathcal{C}, RemovedValues, Lit, Cand)$
Input: Set of literals $\mathcal{L}$, Set of domains $\mathcal{D}$, Set of constraints $\mathcal{C}$,
 Set of pairs $\langle Literal_i, Literal_j \rangle$ $RemovedValues$,
 Literals $Lit, Cand$
1. **for all** $Lit_i \in \mathcal{L}$ s.t. $\exists c \in \mathcal{C}$ and $\text{Literals}(c) = \{Lit, Lit_i\}$
2. | **for all** $Lit_j \in \text{Domain}(Lit_i, \mathcal{D})$
3. | | **if not** $\text{CheckConstraint}(c, \langle Lit, Cand \rangle, \langle Lit_i, Lit_j \rangle)$
4. | | | $RemovedValues \leftarrow RemovedValues \cup \langle Lit_i, Lit_j \rangle$
5. | | | $\text{Domain}(Lit_i, \mathcal{D}) \leftarrow \text{Domain}(Lit_i, \mathcal{D}) \setminus Lit_j$
6. | | | **if** $\text{Domain}(Lit_i, \mathcal{D}) = \emptyset$
7. | | | | **return FALSE**
8. **return TRUE**

In *CheckCompleteSolution*, the procedure *Values* is used in order to obtain a set of literals which are used as values in the assignments of *Solution* in line 3. In lines $1 - 5$, all literals unused are removed from $\mathcal{L}$, and the variable $found$ is set to $TRUE$ if a literal is removed. Then, if a new minimal solution has been found, the domains are updated in lines $6 - 10$.

---

[1] The relevance of these heuristics has not been evaluated.

CheckCompleteSolution($\mathcal{L}$, $\mathcal{D}$, *Solution*)
Input: Set of literals $\mathcal{L}$, Set of domains $\mathcal{D}$,
      Set of pairs $\langle Literal_i, Literal_j \rangle$ *Solution*
1. literalRemoved $= FALSE$
2. **for all** $Lit_i \in \mathcal{L}$ // *Removes all literals not in the solution*
3.   **if** $Lit_i \notin$ Values(*Solution*)
4. $\mathcal{L} \leftarrow \mathcal{L} \setminus Lit_i$
5.   literalRemoved $= TRUE$
6. **if** literalRemoved // *Removes also these literals from the domains*
7.   **for all** $Dom_i \in \mathcal{D}$
8.   **for all** $Lit_j \in Dom_i$
9.   **if** $Lit_j \notin \mathcal{L}$
10. $Dom_i \leftarrow Dom_i \setminus Lit_j$

4 Related Work

There are few reduction algorithms [6,8,18] and due to the complexity of the problem, most of them are polynomial approximations. The only complete algorithm is [6], described by the procedure *FAST_CONDENSE*, which has been proved to be optimal in number of θ-subsumption calls. The main drawback of this algorithm is that it only considers if a substitution exists or not, therefore, as shown in section 2.2, it does not use the information provided by the substitution. We improved this algorithm in the procedure *FAST_REDUCTION*, shown section 3, with a θ-subsumption procedure which returns the set of literals of a solution. Therefore, if the θ-subsumption has a solution, all literals of the clause that are not in the solution are removed. If C has many redundant literals, *FAST_REDUCTION* can perform a significantly smaller number of θ-subsumption calls than *FAST_CONDENSE* by removing more than one literal for each θ-subsumption call.

    FAST_REDUCTION and *FAST_CONDENSE* have the same worst case complexity, since they will perform $|C|$ θ-subsumption calls which returns no solution, if C is already reduced. However, Jivaro only performs one θ-subsumption call which searches for all substitutions.

    Both algorithms described in [18] and [8] are polynomial approximations, therefore they cannot be used by a learning algorithm which needs completely reduced clauses [2,15,17]. [18] has been proved to be incomplete in [6] because it cannot finds a reduction of a clause such as $p(X,Y,U), p(Y,X,V), p(A,A,A)$. On the other hand, [8] is incomplete because it uses a greedy search in order to find a minimal substitution. Therefore, [8] can be made complete by using an exhaustive search.

    The algorithm described in [18] unifies a literal lit of a clause C with another literal of C and the substitution is applied to C and to $C \setminus lit$. If the clause C is included in $C \setminus lit$, lit is redundant. For example, using the clause C_5: $p(V_0, V_1), p(V_1, V_2), p(V_0, V_3), p(V_3, V_4)$, if we unify $p(V_0, V_1)$ and

$p(V_1, V_2)$, we obtain the substitution $\theta_1 = \{V_0/V_1, V_1/V_2\}$. By applying θ_1 to C_5 and $C_5 \setminus p(V_0, V_1)$, we obtain $C_5\theta_1$: $p(V_1, V_2), p(V_2, V_2), p(V_1, V_3), p(V_3, V_4)$ and $C_5'\theta_1$: $p(V_2, V_2), p(V_1, V_3), p(V_3, V_4)$. Since $C_5\theta_1 \nsubseteq C_5'\theta_1$, $p(V_0, V_1)$ and $p(V_1, V_2)$ cannot be unified. However, if we unify $p(V_0, V_1)$ and $p(V_0, V_3)$, we obtain the substitution $\theta_2 = \{V_1/V_3\}$. By applying θ_2 to C_5 and $C_5 \setminus p(V_0, V_1)$, we obtain $C_5\theta_2$: $p(V_0, V_3), p(V_3, V_2), p(V_0, V_3), p(V_3, V_4)$ and $C_5'\theta_2$: $p(V_3, V_2), p(V_0, V_3), p(V_3, V_4)$.

Since $C_5\theta_2 \subseteq C_5'\theta_2$, $p(V_0, V_1)$ is redundant. This algorithm has a complexity $\mathcal{O}(n^4)$ and can be efficiently used to remove redundant literals as shown in [18].

The reduction algorithm in [8] is an approximation based on a θ-subsumption algorithm described in [19]. This algorithm computes the substitution for the problem $C \succeq C$, and searches for a solution which is minimal in the number of literals, however, since it uses a greedy algorithm, it can return only a near optimal solution. It uses a θ-subsumption algorithm [19] which builds a substitution graph equivalent to the storage of all possible constraint checks between each pair of literals. Therefore it never performs the same constraint check twice. Then it uses a heuristic during the search of a clique of size $|C|$, in order to minimize the size of the substitution. The memory needed to represent the substitution graph can be prohibitive, furthermore, the substitution graph is completely built even if the search only checks a subset of its nodes. This algorithm searches for a clique of size $|C|$ while Jivaro removes dynamically redundant literals from the clause if a smaller solution is found. Since the complexities of the θ-subsumption and the clique problem are exponential, removing literals dramatically reduces the space of the search. The algorithm of Scheffer et al. [19] has been compared with Django in [12,13], and Django has shown better results in an order of magnitude on large scale problems. Django efficiently prunes the search tree with a heuristic based on the First Fail Principle [1]. Moreover, it only checks the constraints associated to the partial solutions. Therefore, even if it can check the same constraint more than once, it does not need to compute all the constraint checks if there is a solution.

Since Jivaro needs a θ-subsumption algorithm which returns all the substitutions instead of a boolean value, the algorithm described in [4] could be used as an alternative implementation. It is a breadth-first algorithm which maintains all the partial substitutions of the variables and tests against these substitutions a new literal of C at each level. The substitutions are compressed in structures termed multi-substitutions. This algorithm has a large memory consumption due to the breadth-first exploration, and a large part of execution time is spent in the compression of the solutions. Django uses a dynamic variable ordering which selects a literal with a minimal domain at each step, therefore it can prune the exploration tree earlier, while [4] must check a same literal at each level. Furthermore, Jivaro removes redundant literals during the search if it finds a solution. Therefore it is not efficient with a breadth-first method, since all the solutions are found in the last level.

5   Experimental Evaluation

There is only one complete algorithm of reduction of clause, therefore the performance of Jivaro has been compared with a version of the algorithm described in the procedure *FAST_CONDENSE* (GOTTLOB) and with the algorithm of the procedure *FAST_REDUCTION* (REDUCTION)[2]. Five experiments have been performed, four experiments compare the performances of the algorithms of reduction, while one experiment compares a version of Django which returns all the substitutions with the algorithm described in [4][3].

Since GOTTLOB and REDUCTION need a θ-subsumption algorithm, we also implemented them with Django in order to fairly compare them with Jivaro. They are first compared in an experiment which corresponds to the worst cases, then in two experiments which correspond to the use of reduction in an ILP learner using an artificial and a real world data sets. A version of Jivaro and GOTTLOB which check if a clause is reduced have been integrated in Jimi [14] and the both versions are compared with the original version of Jimi on a real world data set.

Moreover, since Jivaro uses a version of Django which returns all the solutions, and this problem has been recently addressed in [4] where the authors propose an algorithm without backtracks for this problem, we compare both versions in an experiment defined in [4]. All experiments were performed on a PC with a 3GHz CPU and 1.5GB memory.

5.1   Worst Case Experiment

In this experiment, clauses which represent *cycles* (or rings) of variable sizes are generated using the pattern: $C: \leftarrow p(X_0, X_1), p(X_1, X_2), \cdots, p(X_n, X_{n+1}), p(X_{n+1}, X_0)$. Since these clauses are already reduced, GOTTLOB and REDUCTION will perform $|C|$ calls to a θ-subsumption procedure: these clauses correspond to their worst cases. Jivaro will enumerate all the substitutions in one call to the exhaustive θ-subsumption procedure, but it cannot remove literal since there is no substitution smaller than the clause. Therefore, already reduced clauses are the worst cases for the three algorithms.

Figure 1 shows the results of this test on clauses with 10 to 100 literals, by increasing the size by 10. For each size, 100 clauses are generated and the order of literals is randomized to avoid the influence of the order. For each literal of a clause, GOTTLOB and REDUCTION perform a θ-subsumption test that has no solution, therefore their execution times are exactly the same in this experiment. Since Jivaro only performs one exhaustive θ-subsumption test, it outperforms both algorithms.

---

[2] The algorithm described in [8] can be made complete, but there is no available implementation, as far as we know.

[3] The implementation of this algorithm is available at
http://lacam.di.uniba.it:8000/systems/matching/.

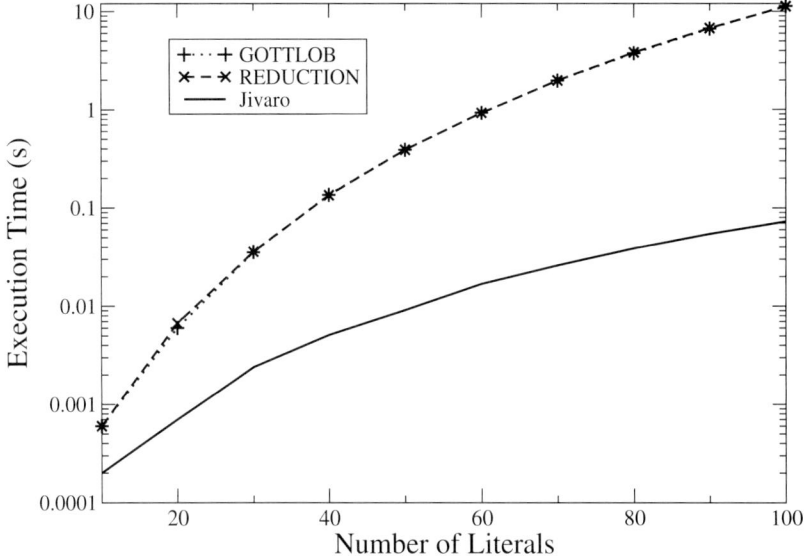

Fig. 1. Execution time for worst cases with [10,100] literals.

5.2 Artificial Data Set

In order to evaluate the use of reduction in an ILP learner, we used an artificial data set which simulates a reduction step of a hypothesis before its covering test as described in [18]. An ILP learner usually generates a large number of hypotheses and each hypothesis must be reduced, therefore a fast reduction algorithm is important. In this data set, each generated clause has 100 literals of predicate symbol p with an arity 2, and 20 to 100 variables. The number of variables is increased by 10, and for each number of variables, 100 clauses are generated. All variables in clauses are first connected in order to avoid the influence of the decomposability of the clauses. Then, the remaining literals are added by randomly selecting pairs of variables. For example, with 4 variables and 4 literals, the generator creates a chain of literals $p(V_1, V_2), p(V_2, V_3), p(V_3, V_4)$, then it adds a random literal $p(V_4, V_2)$. It must be noticed that an average hypothesis in a real ILP learner has usually less than 10 literals and 10 variables and involves more than one predicate symbol, therefore these settings describe very large and hard hypotheses.

Table 1 shows the results of this experiment, the percentage of redundancy corresponds to the percentage of redundant literals removed in the clauses. Jivaro outperforms both algorithms, but the gain is higher, i.e. 80 times faster, when redundancy is low. Since REDUCTION can remove more than one literal at each step, the number of θ-subsumption tests can be significantly reduced when the percentage of redundancy is high and it really improves GOTTLOB. When redundancy is low, the clauses are almost reduced and the complexity is close

Table 1. Comparison of execution times (1/100th second) of GOTTLOB, REDUC-TION and Jivaro on artificial data set with 100 literals and [20, 100] variables. # *Vars* corresponds to the number of variables in a clause, and *Redundancy* corresponds to the percentage of redundant literals in the clauses.

# Vars	GOTTLOB	REDUCTION	Jivaro	Redundancy
20	47.25	46.96	0.72	0.04%
30	41.09	40.36	0.59	1.11%
40	78.87	71.03	0.80	1.63%
50	153.10	149.25	1.76	2.67%
60	221.17	213.67	2.38	1.87%
70	356.85	355.10	3.98	1.49%
80	434.35	429.58	4.54	3.99%
90	845.56	823.11	11.55	6.12%
100	131.20	59.41	8.59	27.31%

to the worst case. In these cases, REDUCTION and GOTTLOB have very close execution time.

5.3   Mutagenesis Data Set

This experiment simulates a learner which uses LGG [16,2,15,17] of a pair of examples in order to create a hypothesis. We use the Mutagenesis data set described in [21]. However, LGG of a pair of clauses of n and m literals can produce a clause with $n \times m$ literals. Therefore we only used the 16 molecules in Mutagenesis with no more than 15 bonds. Furthermore, we used a more restrictive representation than the one described in [21] in order to reduce execution time. All the constants which are not an atom identifier are put in the predicate name. For example, a literal $atm(d59\_1, c, 22, -0.115)$ is transformed to $atm\_c\_22\_ - 0.115(d59\_1)$. Since this transformation increases the number of predicate symbols and reduces the number of variables in the LGG, it reduces the execution time of a reduction algorithm. 120 LGG are computed for each pair of molecules. LGG have 446 to 556 literals, and their reduced clauses have 13 to 204 literals. The total execution time of the reduction 120 clauses for all three algorithms is shown in Table 2.

Table 2. Comparison of execution times (seconds) of GOTTLOB, REDUCTION and Jivaro on Mutagenesis data set.

GOTTLOB	REDUCTION	Jivaro
3672.43	71.20	16.68

In this experiment, the number of redundant literals is very large, therefore REDUCTION removes a large number of redundant literals at each step and is 80 times faster than GOTTLOB which removes one literal at a time. However, REDUCTION still needs to perform more than one θ-subsumption tests while Jivaro only performs one θ-subsumption test. Therefore Jivaro is 4 times faster than REDUCTION. It must be noticed that despite the restrictive representation, no experiment with molecules with more than 15 bonds finished in a reasonable time. The LGG of two cycles of size n and m is a cycle of size l, where l is the least common multiple of n and m. Since there are cycles of size 5 and 6 in the Mutagenesis data set, several LGG contain cycles of size 30. These cycles increase the size of the reduced clauses and the complexity of the reduction. Therefore, ILP learners using LGG to generate hypotheses should be limited to acyclic clauses.

5.4 Experiment in Frequent Query Discovery

Jimi [14] is an FQD algorithm which uses a breadth-first method in order to generate the candidates. At each level, a new literal is added to each frequent query found in the previous step. In order to remove redundant candidates, Jimi needs to check if each candidate is reduced. A reduction algorithm can be easily changed to stop the search as soon as a substitution smaller than the clause is found. Therefore, this check determines if a clause is reduced. In this experiment, we used a version of Jivaro and a version of GOTTLOB which only check if a clause is reduced. Since GOTTLOB stops as soon as a θ-subsumption succeeds, there is no difference with REDUCTION. We integrated these both versions in Jimi, JIMIJIV with Jivaro, JIMIGOT with GOTTLOB, and we compared them with the original version (JIMI) which uses a hash table in order to store the frequent candidates. We used the data set of the Predictive Toxicology Evaluation Challenge [20] with the representation described in [14].

Table 3 shows the results of this test with a support of 20%[4]. From the Table 3, our JIMIJIV outperforms JIMI and JIMIGOT for higher levels. JIMI stores all frequent queries in a hash table and checks for each new candidate if it is equivalent to a frequent query. An equivalence test needs two θ-subsumption tests and the hash table grows exponentially at each level, therefore the elimination of the redundant candidates represents the main part of the execution time at high level. Using a reduction step does not provide any noticeable gain before the level 7. Since the size of the hash table is not very large until the level 7, it does not save a lot of θ-subsumption tests. However, JIMIJIV and JIMIGOT clearly outperforms JIMI at level 9, and JIMIJIV is about 3 times faster than JIMI. JIMIJIV is 10% faster than JIMIGOT at level 5 and the gain increases until 15% at level 9. Therefore, the reduction step improves significantly Jimi, and Jivaro improves GOTTLOB.

---

[4] The differences between the results of JIMI and the results in [14] are due to improvements in the implementation.

Table 3. Comparison of JIMI, JIMIJIV and JIMIGOT on Carcinogenesis data set with a support of 20%. Time is in seconds and # of FQ represents the number of frequent candidates. Level corresponds to the number of literals in the candidates.

Level	# of FQ	JIMI	JIMIJIV	JIMIGOT
2	40	1	1	1
3	164	2	2	2
4	581	4	4	4
5	2118	12	12	13
6	8308	46	45	49
7	34416	228	221	238
8	149356	1531	1077	1211
9	675598	17094	5954	6935

5.5 Exhaustive Subsumption

Since the algorithm described in [4] (*Matching*) could be used instead of Django for computing all the solutions, we compare this algorithm with the version of Django (*DjangoAll*) which enumerates all the solutions used by Jivaro. Both algorithms DjangoAll and Matching are compared using the experiment described in [4].

Hypotheses with 1 to 10 literals and 2 to 10 variables are randomly generated and tested against a real-world data set, Mutagenesis [21]. For each size, we generate 10 hypotheses. The results are summarized in Table 4 and grouped by satisfiability, i.e. the percentage of examples covered in the data set.

DjangoAll outperforms Matching in an order of magnitude, but the differences in execution time are different for each region of satisfiability. At 100% of satisfiability, there are a lot of solutions, because each hypothesis covers all the examples. Since the algorithms find all the solutions, this region is the hardest for both algorithms. Even if DjangoAll explores a large tree, it is 154 times faster in average because Matching spends a lot of time in the compression of the solutions. At 0%, there is no solution therefore this region is easy for both algorithms, but DjangoAll is 57 times faster because the dynamic variable ordering prunes efficiently the search tree in this region. At each level, DjangoAll uses a heuristic which selects the literal with the smallest number of values in its domain. Therefore, failures occur sooner during the exploration. In the Phase Transition region [13], the number of solutions is still large therefore Matching also spends a lot of time in the compression of the solutions. However, since DjangoAll can prune the search tree in this region, it is 333 times faster than Matching.

6 Conclusion

We have presented a new complete algorithm for reduction of clauses, Jivaro, which significantly improves a previous algorithm particularly in the worst cases.

Table 4. Comparison of average execution times of Matching and DjangoAll on Mutagenesis data set. Time is in 1/100th second and **Sat** represents the percentage of examples covered by hypotheses. **P.T.** corresponds to the Phase Transition, i.e. [0.1%, 99.9%].

Sat	Matching	DjangoAll
100%	2308.00	14.90
P.T.	1945.46	5.83
0%	17.36	0.3

Jivaro efficiently explores all the substitutions of a clause in order to find a minimal one using Constraint Satisfaction Techniques. This algorithm has been integrated in an FQD algorithm in order to replace a test of redundancy for the candidates. This test is essential in FQD and is prohibitively expensive in memory and execution time when the size of the candidate increases. The experiments show that using a reduction algorithm improves the FQD algorithm especially for a high level where it is approximately 3 times faster.

Future work includes integration of decomposition of the clause in a preprocessing step and a study of relevant heuristics. Large clauses generated by LGG are probably decomposable in independent components which can be reduced separately [9]. Furthermore, new heuristics have to be tested in order to improve the reduction. For example, a dynamic value ordering heuristic which selects a literal already assigned instead of a static ordering could improve the performance of Jivaro.

Acknowledgments. This work was partially supported by the grant-in-aid for scientific research on priority area "Active Mining" from the Japanese Ministry of Education, Culture, Sports, Science and Technology.

References

1. C. Bessière and J-C Régin. MAC and combined heuristics: Two reasons to forsake FC (and CBJ ?) on hard problems. In *Proc. Second International Conference on Principles and Practice of Constraint Programming*, LNCS 1118, pages 61–75. Springer-Verlag, Berlin, 1996.
2. L. De Raedt and M. Bruynooghe. A theory of clausal discovery. In *Proc. Thirteenth International Joint Conference on Artificial Intelligence*, pages 1058–1063. Morgan-Kaufmann, 1993.
3. L. Dehaspe and L. De Raedt. Mining association rules in multiple relations. In *Proc. Seventh International Workshop on Inductive Logic Programming*, LNCS 1297, pages 125–132. Springer-Verlag, Berlin, 1997.
4. S. Ferilli, N. Di Mauro, T. M. A. Basile, and F. Esposito. A complete subsumption algorithm. In *Advances in Artificial Intelligence*, LNCS 2829, pages 1–13. Springer-Verlag, Berlin, 2003.
5. I.P. Gent, E. MacIntyre, P. Prosser, and T. Walsh. The constrainedness of search. In *AAAI/IAAI, Vol. 1*, pages 246–252, 1996.

6. G. Gottlob and C. G. Fermüller. Removing redundancy from a clause. *Artificial Intelligence*, 61(2):263–289, 1993.

7. R. M. Haralick and G. L. Eliott. Increasing tree search efficiency for constraint satisfaction problems. *Artificial Intelligence*, 14(1):263–313, 1980.

8. K. Hirata. On condensation of a clause. In *Proc. Thirteenth International Conference on Inductive Logic Programming*, LNCS 2835, pages 164–179. Springer-Verlag, Berlin, 2003.

9. J-U. Kietz and M. Lübbe. An efficient subsumption algorithm for inductive logic programming. In W.W. Cohen and H. Hirsh, editors, *Proc. Eleventh International Conference on Machine Learning*, pages 130–138. Morgan-Kaufmann, 1994.

10. R. D. King, A. Karwath, A. Clare, and L. Dephaspe. Genome scale prediction of protein functional class from sequence using data mining. In *Proc. Sixth ACM SIGKDD international conference on Knowledge Discovery and Data mining*, pages 384–389. ACM Press, 2000.

11. A. K. Mackworth. Consistency in networks of relations. *Artificial Intelligence*, 8(1):99–118, 1977.

12. J. Maloberti and M. Sebag. Theta-subsumption in a constraint satisfaction perspective. In *Proc. Eleventh International Conference on Inductive Logic Programming*, LNCS 2157, pages 164–178. Springer-Verlag, Berlin, 2001.

13. J. Maloberti and M. Sebag. Fast theta-subsumption with constraint satisfaction algorithms. *Machine Learning Journal*, 55(2):137–174, 2004.

14. J. Maloberti and E. Suzuki. Improving efficiency of frequent query discovery by eliminating non-relevant candidates. In *Proc. Sixth International Conference on Discovery Science (DS 2003)*, LNAI 2843, pages 219–231, Berlin, Heidelberg, New York, 2003. Springer-Verlag.

15. S. Muggleton and C. Feng. Efficient induction of logic programs. In *Proc. First Conference on Algorithmic Learning Theory*, pages 368–381. Ohmsma, Tokyo, Japan, 1990.

16. G. D. Plotkin. A note on inductive generalization. In *Machine Intelligence*, volume 5, pages 153–163. Edinburgh University Press, Edinburgh, 1970.

17. C. Reddy and P. Tadepalli. Learning first-order acyclic horn programs from entailment. In *Proc. Eighth International Conference on Inductive Logic Programming*, LNAI 1446, pages 23–37. Springer-Verlag, Berlin, 1998.

18. V. Santos Costa, A. Srinivasan, R. Camacho, H. Blockeel, B. Demoen, G. Janssens, J. Struyf, H. Vandecasteele, and W. Van Laer. Query transformations for improving the efficiency of ILP systems. *Journal of Machine Learning Research*, 4:465–491, 2003.

19. T. Scheffer, R. Herbrich, and F. Wysotzki. Efficient θ-subsumption based on graph algorithms. In *Proc. Seventh International Workshop on Inductive Logic Programming*, pages 212–228. Springer-Verlag, Berlin, 1997.

20. A. Srinivasan, R. D. King, S. H. Muggleton, and M. Sternberg. The predictive toxicology evaluation challenge. In *Proc. Fifteenth International Joint Conference on Artificial Intelligence (IJCAI-97)*, pages 1–6. Morgan-Kaufmann, 1997.

21. A. Srinivasan, S. H. Muggleton, M. J. E. Sternberg, and R. D. King. Theories for mutagenicity: a study in first order and feature-based induction. *Artificial Intelligence*, 85(1-2):277–299, 1996.

22. E. Tsang. *Foundations of Constraint Satisfaction*. Academic Press, London, 1993.

23. J. D. Ullman. *Principles of Database and Knowledge-Base Systems*, volume I. Computer Science Press, Rockville, Maryland, 1988.

Improving Rule Evaluation Using Multitask Learning

Mark D. Reid

School of Computer Science and Engineering
University of New South Wales
Sydney, NSW 2052, Australia
mreid@cse.unsw.edu.au

Abstract. This paper introduces DEFT, a new multitask learning approach for rule learning algorithms. Like other multitask learning systems, the one proposed here is able to improve learning performance on a primary task through the use of a bias learnt from similar secondary tasks. What distinguishes DEFT from other approaches is its use of rule descriptions as a basis for task similarity. By translating a rule into a feature vector or "description", the performance of similarly described rules on the secondary tasks can be used to modify the evaluation of the rule for the primary task. This explicitly addresses difficulties with accurately evaluating, and therefore finding, good rules from small datasets. DEFT is implemented on top of an existing ILP system and the approach is tested on a variety of relational learning tasks. Given appropriate secondary tasks, the results show that DEFT is able to compensate for insufficient training examples.

1 Introduction

Obtaining correctly classified examples for a supervised learning problem is a crucial but sometimes costly task, especially if experts are required to classify the examples. This can result in too few training examples for the problem at hand. In some chemical domains for example, small datasets are "not unusual" since "data are often sparse, and bioassays expensive" [1]. The goal of the research presented in this paper is to improve the quality of learning when data is limited by making use of classified examples gathered for other tasks in the same domain. This places the research in the field of multitask learning [2].

The main problem when learning from small amounts of data is that many candidate hypotheses can fit the data equally well. In this situation, a learner must rely heavily on its inductive bias to decide between them [3]. In rule learning, these decisions involve the suitability of individual rules for a hypothesis and the bias of a rule learning algorithm is influenced by several factors. These include choices that determine which rules are admissible, how they are searched and what heuristic is used to evaluate and rank them [4,5]. Making the best choices for a particular learning problem requires expertise in the problem domain as well as a good knowledge of rule learning algorithms and can be more costly than obtaining more classified examples.

R. Camacho, R. King, A. Srinivasan (Eds.): ILP 2004, LNAI 3194, pp. 252–269, 2004.

Multitask learning eases the burden of choosing a bias for a task with limited data by assuming that related, secondary tasks are available. The learner uses these to learn a bias that can improve its performance on the primary task. Existing multitask approaches for rule learning [6,7,8] have focused on learning language or search biases. In contrast, the DEFT system[1] introduced in this paper is concerned exclusively with improving a learner's evaluation of rules on limited data.

The DEFT approach is outlined in Section 2 where *rule descriptions* are introduced to define classes of similar rules. An assessment of a rule on limited primary task data can be augmented using the performance of similar rules on secondary tasks. When the secondary and primary tasks are related the expanded assessment can improve the reliability of an evaluation metric. Section 3 describes an implementation of this approach for ILP that uses ALEPH [9] as the underlying concept learner. This implementation is evaluated on a range of datasets and the results presented in Section 4. Related work from ILP and bias learning is presented in Section 5 and the paper is concluded with a discussion of future directions in Section 6.

2 Description-Based Evaluation

The relative quality of rules according to an evaluation metric can be poorly estimated when only a small number of training examples are available. This section describes a method, called DEFT, that improves these estimates by transforming any evaluation metric into a representation-based one. The transformed metric bases its evaluation of a rule on the training data for the primary task as well as the performance of similar rules on other, secondary, tasks. Rule similarity is defined in Section 2.2 in terms of functions, called *descriptors*, that are used to transform a rule into an attribute vector called a *description*. Section 2.3 shows how classification probabilities can be estimated from a secondary task based on a rule's description. These probabilities can be used to create a *virtual contingency table* for a rule on a secondary task. Section 2.4 explains how these can be combined with a rule's real contingency table for the primary task. The result can then be fed into an evaluation metric to provide an assessment that takes into account a rule's description and its similarity to rules that have been evaluated on the secondary task.

2.1 Preliminaries

For the purposes of this paper, a supervised concept learning task consists of an instance space X, a set of class labels $Y = \{+, -\}$, and training examples $E \subset X \times Y$ for some unknown *target concept* $t : X \to Y$. A *rule* $r = h \leftarrow b$ consists of a label $h \in Y$, called the *head*, and a condition b, called the *body*, that can be tested against instances. A rule is said to *match* an instance $x \in X$ if its

---
[1] Description-based Evaluation Function Transfer

body is true for that instance. In this case, the rule classifies the instance with the label h.

A rule learning algorithm solves a learning task by finding a set of rules that (ideally) classifies every instance in accordance with the target concept. Most existing rule learning algorithms adopt a strategy whereby a set of rules is created by repeatedly finding a single rule that explains some of the training examples and then removing them from the training set. For a comprehensive survey of this "covering" approach to rule learning we refer the reader to [5].

Our primary concern is with the assessment of individual rules on the training examples. In particular, we are interested in "purity-based" evaluation metrics: those that assess a rule based on the type and number of misclassifications it makes on the training examples. These are summarised using a *contingency table*. The contingency table for a rule r and examples E is written in matrix form like so

$$\mathbf{n}_E(r) = \begin{bmatrix} n_{++} & n_{+-} \\ n_{-+} & n_{--} \end{bmatrix}.$$

Each entry n_{ij} is a count of the number of times the rule r assigned the label i to an example $(x, j) \in E$. A matrix containing the relative frequencies of each type of classification can be derived from a contingency table. We call this a *classification probability matrix* (CPM) and define it to be $\mathbf{p}_E(r) = \frac{1}{N}\mathbf{n}_E(r)$ where $N = \sum_{ij} n_{ij}$ is the number of examples in E. The values $p_{ij}(r)$ in a CPM can be viewed as estimates of the true classification probability of a rule, $\Pr_{x \in X}(r(x) = i, t(x) = j)$.

2.2 Rule Descriptions

The key to the DEFT multitask learning approach is to combine the assessment of rule on a primary task with the assessment of the same rule on one or more secondary tasks. The hope is that if the target concepts are similar[2] the combined evaluation will, on the primary task, prefer rules that are similar to those that perform well on the secondary tasks. A straight-forward way to combine task assessments would be to treat examples from a secondary task as extra training examples for the primary task. Caruana's MTL for decision tree learning [2] does exactly this when choosing between splits while building a decision tree. The problem with this approach for evaluating rules is that entire rules are assessed and not the steps in building them. Consider the rules in concepts A and D of Fig. 3. While they are quite similar, the first rule of A will not cover any example covered by the first rule of D. This means the classification probabilities for the two rules will be quite different even though they "look" the same. The problem becomes worse when the same representation language is only partially shared between the tasks. What is required is a looser notion of similarity than "covering the same examples".

---

[2] Concept similarity or relatedness is an important but difficult issue in multitask learning. Space prevents it being discussed here so the reader is referred to [2,10].

We would like to say two rules are similar if they share some salient features such their length, particular conditions or constants. We call these rule features *descriptors* and use them to transform a rule into an attribute-value vector. More formally, a descriptor $d : R \rightarrow V_d$ is a function from the set of rules R to the descriptor values V_d. A collection of descriptors $D = \{d_k\}_{k=1}^n$ is called a *descriptor set* and induces a function $\mathbf{d} : R \rightarrow V_{d_1} \times \ldots \times V_{d_n}$, called a *description*, that maps a rule to a attribute-value vector $\mathbf{d}(r) = (d_1(r), \ldots, d_n(r))$. In general, rules may share the same description or part description. As a shorthand, we will write $r' \in d(r)$ when $d(r') = d(r)$, and write $r' \in \mathbf{d}(r)$ when $r' \in d_k(r)$ for all $k = 1 \ldots n$. Treating descriptions as equivalence classes for rules allows to generalise over them and therefore learn functions of rules based on their description.

2.3 Learning Classification Probabilities

Given a task with target concept t, classification probabilities for this task can be seen as functions $p_{ij}(r)$ that map rules to values in $[0, 1]$. As already discussed, these functions can return very different values for two rules that have a similar description. One way to fix this is to smooth the functions by averaging them over rules that share the same description:

$$q_{ij}(r) = \Pr_{r',x} \left(r'(x) = i, t(x) = j \,|\, r' \in \mathbf{d}(r) \right).$$

The matrix $\mathbf{q}(r) = (q_{ij}(r))$ is analogous to the CPM $\mathbf{p}(r)$ except that the classification probabilities are based on rule descriptions. It is therefore called a *description-based CPM* (DCPM). Using $\Pr(i, j | \mathbf{d}(r))$ as a shorthand, the Bayes' identity and a naïve Bayes' assumption about the independence of the descriptors d_i lets us express

$$q_{ij}(r) = \frac{\Pr(i, j)}{\Pr(\mathbf{d}(r))} \prod_{k=1}^n \Pr(d_k(r) | i, j).$$

If values for $\Pr(d_k(r) | i, j)$ and $\Pr(i, j)$ can be determined, $q_{ij}(r)$ can be computed since the $\Pr(\mathbf{d}(r))$ term just normalises the $q_{ij}(r)$ so that $\sum_{i,j} q_{ij}(r) = 1$. The former terms can be derived from $\Pr(i, j, d_k(r))$ so this is what we now focus on estimating.

The probability we wish to estimate measures the chances of drawing an instance $x \in X$ and rule $r' \in R$ such that r' classifies x with label i, the target concept classifies x with label j and that $d_k(r')$ and $d_k(r)$ have the same value $v \in V_{d_k}$. Given a sample of rules $\overline{R} \subseteq R$ and a set of examples E, the number of times this event occurs in these samples can be counted:

$$\mathbf{s}(d_k, v) = \sum_{\substack{r \in \overline{R} \\ d_k(r) = v}} \mathbf{n}_E(r) \qquad (1)$$

where $\mathbf{n}_E(r)$ is the contingency table for r on the examples E. The collection of matrices $\mathbf{s}_D = \{\mathbf{s}(d_k, v) : d_k \in D, v \in V_k\}$ is called a *descriptor frequency table*

(DFT) for D. By letting $s_{ij} = \sum_{d,v} s_{ij}(d,v)$ and $s = \sum_{i,j} s_{ij}$, a DFT can be used to estimate the probabilities $\Pr(i,j) \approx \frac{s_{ij}}{s}$ and $\Pr(d_k(r)|i,j) \approx \frac{s_{ij}(d_k,d_k(r))}{s_{ij}}$. The functions $q_{ij}(r)$ can therefore be approximated by

$$q_{ij}(r) \approx \frac{s_{ij}}{s} \prod_{k=1}^{n} \frac{s_{ij}(d_k, d_k(r))}{s_{ij}}. \tag{2}$$

In practice, the q_{ij} functions are approximated using rules and examples taken from a secondary task. This requires some way of sampling rules for that task and is discussed in Section 3.3. The quality of the approximation will depend on the size and bias of the rule sample and the examples. It will also depend on the descriptor set used and the validity of the naive Bayes' assumption for those descriptors. While all these factors are important, it must be remembered that the DCPM is only designed to crudely estimate a rule's CPM on a secondary task based on its description. We now introduce a method for combining values in a DCPM with examples from the primary learning task.

2.4 Virtual Contingency Tables

The values $q_{ij}(r)$ in a DCPM $\mathbf{q}(r)$ express the chances that an example with label j will be given label i by r based on its description. If the rule was to classify M examples, the expected number with each type of classification can be summarised in a *virtual contingency table* $\mathbf{m}(r) = M\mathbf{q}(r)$. This can be used to increase the number of examples used to asses a rule as follows. If $\mathbf{n}_E(r)$ is the contingency table for r on some small set of examples E, we can define its *augmented contingency table* $\mathbf{n}^*(r) = \mathbf{n}_E(r) + \mathbf{m}(r)$. The relative size of the number of virtual examples, M, to the number of real examples, N, determines how much emphasis is given to the assessment of the rule on the primary task compared to the secondary task that generated $\mathbf{q}$.

An augmented CPM, $\mathbf{p}^*(r) = \frac{1}{N+M}\mathbf{n}^*(r)$, can be derived from an augmented contingency table. The entries in the resulting matrix are

$$p_{ij}^*(r) = \frac{n_{ij}(r) + m_{ij}(r)}{N + M}$$

and can be seen as "linearly squashing" the values $p_{ij}(r)$ towards the priors $q_{ij}(r)$, or equivalently, assuming that the $n_{ij}^*(r)$ values have a Dirichlet distribution with parameters $m_{ij}(r)$ [11, §4.1].

Any evaluation metric h can be transformed into a description-based metric h^* by using classification probabilities from a rule's augmented CPM. As a special case, this transformation can be used to turn the *precision* metric $prec_E(r) = \frac{pos}{pos+neg}$ into the generalised m-estimate [12] $gm_E(r) = \frac{pos+a}{(pos+a)+(neg+b)}$ where a and b are fixed and $pos = n_{++}(r)$, $neg = n_{+-}(r)$. The transformed metric $prec_E^*(r)$ is equal to $gm_E(r)$ with $a = m_{++}(r)$ and $b = m_{+-}(r)$. Using a description-based precision metric can therefore be seen as using a generalised m-estimate where the costs have been learnt from a secondary task.

3   Implementation

This section briefly outlines an implementation[3] of DEFT for inductive logic programming using ALEPH [9] as the base rule learner. Details of the ALEPH system that are relevant to this paper are provided in Section 3.1 along with the modification that allows it to use description-based evaluations. A discussion of the three main procedures required to implement DEFT make up the remainder of this section. These are procedures to: compute rule descriptions (Section 3.2), build descriptor frequency tables from secondary tasks (Section 3.3), and determine classification priors (Section 3.4). These procedures are applied to an example domain in Section 3.5.

3.1   The Base and Deft Learners

The ILP system ALEPH is designed to replicate the behaviour of many different kinds of rule learning systems. As the base learner for DEFT, however, we are only interested in its implementation of the inverse entailment algorithm PROGOL. Details glossed over in the following summary can be found in [13].

Given a collection of positive and negative ground facts, ALEPH induces a theory as a set of Horn clauses using a covering strategy. Each clause (or rule) in the theory is found by searching a space of *legal* rules. Predicates in the body of a legal rule must come from the *background knowledge* provided to the learner. Exactly how they can be combined in a rule's body is determined by *mode and type constraints*. These restrict the ways variables in the rule can be shared between its conditions. Legal rules are also constrained by an upper limit on their *variable depth*. In ALEPH, this is controlled by the i setting. For any positive example there is a most specific legal clause, called the *bottom clause*, that entails the example given the background knowledge. Any other legal clause that is required to cover the same positive example must also subsume the bottom clause. This fact is used to limit the search to a complete, general-to-specific, breadth-first search of subsets of the bottom clause that meet the legality requirements. The search is further restricted by requiring the subsets' sizes be no larger than the value specified in the clauselength setting. For efficiency reasons, a limit on the total number of rules examined in a single search can be controlled by the nodes setting.

By default, ALEPH uses the *coverage* metric[4] $cov_E(r) = n_{++}(r) - n_{+-}(r)$ to evaluate rules. The rule returned by the search is one that is *acceptable* and maximises this metric on the training data. The acceptability of a rule is controlled by the noise and minacc settings. The noise setting is an upper bound on the number of negative examples covered by a rule while minacc places a lower bound on the accuracy of a rule.

To use the DEFT approach described in the last section, the coverage metric of the base learner is transformed to $cov_E^*(r) = n_{++}^*(r) - n_{+-}^*(r)$, where the

---

[3] The source for the implementation is available from the author upon request.

[4] In [12, Theorem 4.1] this metric is shown to be equivalent to the accuracy metric $acc_E(r) = p_{++} + p_{--}$ and can therefore be defined in terms of a rule's CPM.

$n^*_{ij}(r)$ are the values taken from the rule's augmented contingency table. When the term "DEFT learner" is used in this paper, it refers to the base learner with its coverage metric modified in this way. As well as all the base learner's settings, the DEFT learner is additionally parameterised by the DFT it uses, the number of virtual examples M and the functions used to create rule descriptions.

3.2 Clause Descriptions

This paper will only consider two types of descriptors for clauses. The first type, denoted $pred(P/N)$, tests for the presence of predicate P with arity N in the body of a clause. The second type, $arg(P/N, I, Const)$, tests whether a clause has a predicate P/N with its Ith argument equal to $Const$. Both types of descriptors are Boolean-valued, returning either "true" or "false" when applied to a clause. Defining descriptors in terms of types avoids having to explicitly construct a descriptor set for a task. This is useful when the legal clauses for a search, and hence their predicates and constants, are difficult to determine in advance.

Computing values for descriptors is implemented in Prolog by a `value/3` predicate that asserts a relationship between a clause, a descriptor, and a value. The relation holds if and only if the descriptor would return the specified value when applied to the clause. Each descriptor is also associated with a default value, implemented by the `default/2` predicate. As an example, the implementation of $pred(P/N)$ is shown in Fig. 1.

```
default(pred(P/N), false).
value((Head :- Body), pred(P/N), true) :-
    lit_list(Body,Lits), member(L,Lits), functor(L, P, N).
```

Fig. 1. Prolog code for the $pred(P/N)$ descriptor. The predicate `lit_list/2` takes a goal and turns it into a list of literals.

Due to Prolog's backtracking behaviour, the `value/3` relation can be used to find all descriptors that would return non-default values on a clause. This allows for a sparse representation for clause description s by assuming any descriptor not satisfying `value/3` takes on its default value.

Using a sparse representation has several advantages. Most importantly, the time taken to compute a description for a clause can be made a function of the complexity of clause instead of the description set. This is significant since ALEPH's general-to-specific search will mainly require descriptions for short clauses. Computing descriptions for clauses is also crucial for the construction of descriptor frequency tables from secondary tasks which will be discussed in the next section.

3.3 Descriptor Frequency Tables

As described in Section 2.3, making a DFT for a secondary task requires rules to be sampled from that task and evaluated on its training examples, E. The make_DFT(E) procedure in Fig. 2 shows how this is implemented. The clause sampling procedure scs in line 1 is ALEPH's implementation of the stochastic clause selection algorithm, described in [14]. In a nutshell, scs($\bot$) returns a clause that entails the bottom clause $\bot$ by randomly choosing a subset of its literals. Efficient techniques are used to ensure the procedure only draws legal clauses with uniform probability.

Each drawn clause r has its contingency table n computed against the examples E and added to *total*. The loop at line 2 then finds non-default descriptor-value pairs (d, v) for r using the value/3 predicate described earlier, and for each pair adds the matrix n is added to an accumulation of counts in *counts*$[d, v]$. The whole process is repeated sample_cl times per bottom clause, each generated from one of sample_ex positive examples drawn without replacement from E.

The values collected in the structures *total* and *counts* are sufficient for computing the matrices $\mathbf{s}(d, v)$ described in Section 2.3, and hence represent a DFT. Clearly, for any descriptor d in the DFT and one of its non-default values v, $\mathbf{s}(d, v) = counts[d, v]$. When v_0 is a default value for d, $\mathbf{s}(d, v_0) = total - \sum_{v \neq v_0} counts[d, v]$. This can be seen by observing that the sets of rules $R_{d,v} = \{r \in R \,|\, d(r) = v\}$ partition R for each d. Summing both sides of equation 1 over $v \in V_d$ shows that the matrix $total = \sum_{v \in V_d} \mathbf{s}(d, v)$ for all d.

3.4 Calculating Classification Priors

A DFT constructed using the make_DFT procedure can be used estimate values for the $q_{ij}(r)$ functions of equation 2. The quantities s_{ij} and s in that equation are fixed and can be precomputed once for a DFT since $s_{ij} = total_{ij}$ and $s = \sum_{i,j} s_{ij}$. In the worst case, computing the product term would require iterating through each descriptor d in the DFT, applying it to the rule r and multiplying together the values $\frac{s_{ij}(d, d(r))}{s_{ij}}$. Since most descriptors will take on their default value for any given rule, we can precompute a *base table* $\mathbf{b}$ that contains q_{ij} values for the default description vector (where all descriptors take on their default values) and update it as follows. Letting D denote the descriptors in the DFT, the values in its base table are

$$ b_{ij} = \frac{s_{ij}}{s} \prod_{d \in D} \frac{s_{ij}(d, v_{d,0})}{s_{ij}} $$

where $v_{d,0}$ denotes the default value for d. Given a rule r, $q_{ij}(r)$ can be estimated by multiplying b_{ij} by $u_{ij}(d, v) = \frac{s_{ij}(d,v)}{s_{ij}(d,v_{d,0})}$ for each d and v satisfying value(r,d,v). The matrices $\mathbf{u}(d, v)$ are called the *update tables* and can also be precomputed for a DFT. This means the time taken to calculate a prior for a rule depends only on the time it takes to compute its description and not the size of the DFT.

```
procedure make_DFT(E)
    repeat sample_ex times
        Select new example e ∈ E and saturate to create bottom clause ⊥
        repeat sample_cl times
1           Draw clause r using scs(⊥) and compute matrix n = n_E(r)
            total ← total + n
2           foreach d, v satisfying value(r, d, v) do
                counts[d, v] ← counts[d, v] + n
    return total, counts
```

Fig. 2. Given a set of examples E, make_DFT(E) returns a matrix *total* and a hashtable *counts* with descriptor-value pairs as keys and matrices as values.

3.5 Example Tasks

To clarify the procedures described in the previous sections we introduce four example learning tasks, A, B, C, and D, with target concepts shown in Figure 3. They are all simple attribute-value concepts represented using Horn clauses and instances for the tasks take on the values 0,1 or 2 for each of the four attributes a_0, a_1, a_2 and a_3.

```
A   a(X) :- a1(X,0), a2(X,1).      B   b(X) :- a0(X,0), a1(X,1).
    a(X) :- a2(X,0), a3(X,1).          b(X) :- a0(X,1), a1(X,1).

C   c(X) :- a1(X,0), a2(X,0).      D   d(X) :- a1(X,0), a2(X,0).
    c(X) :- a1(X,1), a2(X,1).          d(X) :- a2(X,1), a3(X,1).
```

Fig. 3. Four example concepts.

Intuitively, rules for concepts A and D are most similar due to their shared predicates and constants while rules from A and B are quite dissimilar. The descriptors $pred(P/N)$ and $arg(P/N, I, Const)$ are able to express these similarities and are used to construct DFTs from training sets containing 50 positive and 50 negative examples of each concept. Figure 4 shows the base tables and some update tables for those DFTs. These can be used to compare the priors given to a description across the four concepts. The ratio $\beta = u_{++} : u_{+-}$ in an update table indicates how the virtual true positive and false positive rates for a concept will shift when a description includes the descriptor-value pair for that table. For $pred(a_0/2) - true$, the values for β on concepts A, B, C and D are 1.2, 11, 1.83 and 1.8 respectively. A rule containing the predicate a_0 will therefore have a much higher true positive count on a virtual contingency table for concept B than for A, C or D. This means an evaluation metric modified by the DFT for B will prefer such a rule more than the same metric modified by the other DFTs. We now look at how this affects the bias of a rule search.

b	A	B	C	D
b	.17 .71 .05 .07	.05 .91 .02 .02	.08 .87 .02 .03	.15 .79 .03 .04
$\mathbf{u}(pred(a_0/2), true)$	.11 .00 .44 .37	?? ?? .37 .39	.11 .06 .45 .38	.09 .05 .47 .38
$\mathbf{u}(pred(a_1/2), true)$	.16 .07 .40 .37	.25 .02 .35 .38	.24 .04 .35 .37	.16 .06 .40 .38
$\mathbf{u}(pred(a_2/2), true)$	.20 .07 .38 .36	.13 .07 .43 .37	.25 .04 .34 .37	.20 .04 .38 .38
$\mathbf{u}(pred(a_3/2), true)$	.25 .09 .33 .33	.14 .17 .37 .32	.12 .13 .40 .35	.20 .16 .33 .32

Fig. 4. The base tables and $pred(P/N)$ update tables for DFTs for concepts A, B, C and D. The update tables have been normalised for easier comparison.

Table 1 lists acceptable rules for task A, in the order in which they were tested, during a search using ALEPH. The training (resp. test) set for the task consisted of 10 (resp. 100) examples with equal number labelled positive and negative. The columns titled "Train" and "Test" show the cov_E score of rules on the respective set. Unsurprisingly, rule f has the highest score (32.0) on the test data as it is one of the target rules for task A. On the training set however, rules a, b, d, e, f and h all share the highest score (3.0). The search policy employed by ALEPH only replaces its current best rule if another one has a strictly greater score. This results in rule a being returned, a sub-optimal choice since its test set score is -8.0.

The last three columns in the table show the score given to the rules by coverage metrics modified using DFTs for tasks B,C and D, all using an M parameter set to 10 (equal to the training set size). When B and C are used as secondary tasks, the rule returned by the search is d. The correct rule, f, is returned when D is the secondary task but is assigned the lowest ranking by B's DFT. Since the ranking of rules in column D are closer to that in the Test column, we would expect a learner to perform better when using an evaluation metric modified by D and worse when modified by B.

4 Empirical Results

To test whether DEFT can improve learning performance on small datasets it needs to be compared to a baseline learner in an *environment* of two or more related learning tasks. This section assesses DEFT on a number tasks of varying size drawn from three different environments.

The first environment, used in Section 4.1, consists of the four concepts A, B, C and D introduced earlier. The results demonstrate that learning performance on tasks for A can be improved when using DFTs from concepts C and D. However, using a DFT from concept B is shown to harm generalisation accuracy.

Section 4.2 tests DEFT on a chess movement environment that has been used by other researchers to test relational multitask learning systems [15,6,7]. The experiments on this domain compare DEFT to the "Repeat Learning" system described in [7]. The results show that DEFT can improve generalisation accuracy

Table 1. Comparison of scores given to acceptable rules for task A.

		Coverage		DEFT Coverage		
ID	Rule	Train	Test	B	C	D
a	t(A) :- a0(A,2)	3.0	-8.0	2.71	1.22	2.05
b	t(A) :- a2(A,0)	3.0	14.0	0.72	3.72	4.69
c	t(A) :- a0(A,2), a1(A,2)	1.0	-4.0	3.21	1.30	0.81
d	t(A) :- a0(A,2), a2(A,0)	3.0	2.0	3.34	3.74	3.99
e	t(A) :- a0(A,2), a3(A,1)	3.0	11.0	1.48	1.86	2.86
f	t(A) :- a2(A,0), a3(A,1)	3.0	32.0	-0.02	3.37	5.12
g	t(A) :- a1(A,2), a2(A,0)	1.0	9.0	1.47	3.29	2.54
h	t(A) :- a0(A,2), a2(A,0), a3(A,1)	3.0	10.0	2.77	3.14	3.60
i	t(A) :- a0(A,2), a1(A,2), a2(A,0)	1.0	2.0	1.88	1.78	1.32
j	t(A) :- a0(A,2), a1(A,2), a3(A,1)	1.0	4.0	1.67	1.05	1.09
k	t(A) :- a1(A,2), a2(A,0), a3(A,1)	1.0	15.0	0.78	1.72	2.07

across these tasks. Furthermore, a combination of DEFT and Repeat Learning is tested and shown to outperform both.

The final environment (Section 4.3) consists of the mutagenesis [16] and carcinogenesis [17] problems from molecular biology. While the results show no significant advantage in using DEFT across these tasks, they do suggest the usefulness of DEFT in this environment.

For reference, a summary of the systems' settings used in each environment is provided in Appendix A.

4.1 Example Environment

The experiment in this section tests whether DEFT can exploit the apparent similarities between concept A and concepts C and D to improve the base learner's generalisation accuracy on small datasets. Concept A was used to generate primary tasks with training sets of size $N = 4, 6, 8, 10, 14, 20, 30$. Twenty tasks were created for each N, each with an equal number of positive and negative examples. Four more tasks with 100 examples and balanced class labels, one for each of concept A, B, C and D, were also created. The task for concept A was used as a test set while the make_DFT procedure was applied to the others to create DFTs using the $pred(P/N)$ and $arg(P/N, I, Const)$ descriptors.

The learner was run on each primary training set E with four different evaluation metrics: the standard coverage metric, cov_E, and cov_E^S for $S \in \{$B,C,D$\}$. Each cov_E^S is a coverage metric modified by DEFT using the DFT for the secondary concept S and DEFT's M parameter set to the size of E. The performance for each evaluation metric on datasets of size N was quantified by averaging the test set accuracies using that metric on all the training sets of size N. The results are summarised in Fig. 5.

The results show that the improvement obtained when using DEFT concurs with our expectations in Section 3.5 regarding the relative similarity of concepts B, C and D to concept A. Using the most similar concept (D) as a secondary

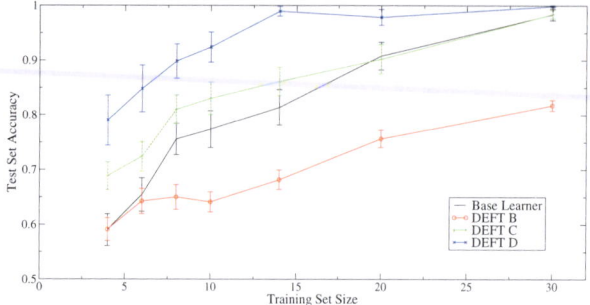

Fig. 5. Average generalisation accuracy on tasks for Concept A using the standard coverage metric and the coverage metric modified by DFTs created by DEFT from tasks for concepts B, C and D. Error bars show the sample standard deviation.

task results in large accuracy gains over the base learner while using the least similar (B) harms its learning performance.

4.2 Chess Environment

The chess movement tasks involve learning rules to describe the legal moves of King and Knight pieces on an empty board. These can be seen as similar concepts since both types of movement are short-range and have an eight-fold symmetry. Each example in a King or Knight task specifies the rank and file for the start and end positions of a move and whether or not it is legal for that piece. Background predicates `rdiff/3` and `fdiff/3` allow rules to determine differences between two ranks or two files.

The background and example sets used in this section are the same as those in [7] and consist of 140 training sets - 20 each of size 10, 20, 30, 40, 60, 80 and 160 - and each with balanced class labels. The supplied test sets, one for each piece, have the 64^2 possible chessboard movements classified according whether they are legal for the piece in question. These datasets were originally used to demonstrate the effectiveness of Repeat Learning (RL) as a bias learning method. The basic idea of RL (details are in [7]) is to invent predicates when learning on a secondary task and then use those predicates as background when learning on the primary task. On the King and Knight problems, the predicates invented by RL allow several file or rank differences (e.g., -1, 0 and 1) to be expressed in a single rule, thus the learner can express the target concept with fewer rules. This change of representation overcomes the small disjunct problem [18] in which rules with small extension do not have any representatives in a small example set.

The effect DEFT and RL have on a learner's bias are more or less independent: the former modifies its search bias while the latter weakens its language bias. A search using RL invented predicates can be guided by an evaluation function modified by DEFT. This combination was tested along with each method individually on primary tasks for the King movement problem. A Knight task with 160 examples was used as a secondary task by RL to invent predicates. The same task was used by DEFT to construct a DFT using the $pred(P/N)$ and $arg(P/N, I, Const)$ descriptors. The base learner ALEPH was run four times on each primary task, once without any modifications, once using the invented predicates as background, once using an evaluation metric modified by the Knight DFT and once using both the invented predicates and modified metric. The performance of each approach was assessed using the same *balanced test accuracy* (BTA) measure as [7]. This is the mean of the true positive and true negative rate of a theory on the test set[5]. For each training size N, the BTA of each theory induced was averaged over the 20 datasets of size N. The results are presented in Table 2.

Table 2. Comparison of balanced test accuracy for the Base learner, DEFT, Repeat Learning (RL) and both DEFT and Repeat Learning (DEFT+RL) on the King movement problem. **Bold** entries are different from the Base entries at the 0.05 level of significance using a paired t-test. Entries for DEFT+RL with a R (resp. D) are significantly better than RL (resp. DEFT) alone.

	Training Size						
	10	20	30	40	60	80	160
Base	61.3 (1.1)	72.4 (1.4)	77.5 (1.0)	84.9 (1.1)	91.2 (1.3)	95.6 (1.0)	99.6 (0.2)
DEFT	**71.1 (1.4)**	**79.8 (1.6)**	**87.3 (0.9)**	**89.1 (1.1)**	**93.8 (1.0)**	96.3 (0.8)	99.3 (0.5)
RL	**66.3 (2.0)**	**77.8 (2.2)**	**83.7 (1.0)**	**92.0 (1.3)**	**95.5 (1.3)**	**98.9 (0.5)**	99.8 (0.2)
DEFT+RL	**72.3 (1.5)**^{R}	**80.8 (1.7)**	**88.6 (0.9)**^{R}	**90.5 (1.1)**	**96.5 (0.8)**^{D}	**98.5 (0.5)**^{D}	99.6 (0.2)

The results show that DEFT improves on the base learner to a greater degree than RL on very small datasets. To a lesser degree, this situation reverses when datasets become larger. The DFT used in these experiments has high β values (between 2 and 6) for descriptors $arg(P/3, 3, C)$ where P is rdiff or fdiff and C is $\pm 1, \pm 2$. Even when few negative examples are available, the modified evaluation metric prefers rules with those predicates whenever it does not harm their real true positive rate too much. This reduces the real false positive rate since the induced theories have several specific clauses rather then only a few over-general ones plus ground facts for the exceptions. On the other hand, the invented predicates used by RL are helpful when there are sufficient negative but too few positive examples as each rule using the extra predicates can cover what would require several small disjuncts without them. The two approaches therefore complement one another. RL compensates for missing positive examples when there are sufficient negative ones available, while DEFT compensates for missing negative examples. The accuracies for the combined approach reflect this.

---

[5] A preferable measure to standard accuracy since the positive to negative example ratio on the test set is 1:8.

4.3 Molecular Environment

This section reports the use of DEFT on a pair of benchmark ILP problems - mutagenesis [16] and carcinogenesis [17]. Both require the learner to predict cancer-related properties of organic molecules so it is reasonable to believe that one may act a useful bias for the other.

The background knowledge used by the problems to describe molecules can be partitioned into several groups concerning their atoms and bonds, chemical features, and three-dimensional structure. Only the atoms and bonds group is used here as its predicates (atm/5, bond/4, gteq/2, lteq/2, =/2) are common to both domains[6]. There are a total of 125 positive and 63 negative examples for the mutagenesis task and 182 positive and 148 negative for carcinogenesis. The carcinogenesis concept proved too difficult to learn using only this group as background (theories returned by the base learner and DEFT were no better than the majority class classifier) so we therefore focused on mutagenesis as the primary task. The complete mutagenesis and carcinogenesis datasets were used to construct two DFTs: Mut and $Carc$. Both types of descriptors, $pred(P/N)$ and $arg(P/N, I, Const)$ were used in the construction.[7]

Ten-fold cross-validation was used to determine generalisation accuracy for this task. Each fold holds out 10% of the data while the other 90% is used for training. In order to test DEFT's performance on small datasets in this domain, the 90% sets were randomly sub-sampled once on each fold to create example sets with 24 positive and 12 negative examples - roughly 20% of the original dataset. On both the 90% and 20% datasets, the base learner's minacc parameter was varied over the values 0.7, 0.8, 0.9 and 1.0 to assess the performance of the learner over a range of classification costs. The value for M was set to the training set size, $M = 36$ on the 20% tasks and $M = 162$ on the 90% tasks. The resulting ROC curves [19] on the two dataset sizes are shown in Fig. 6 for an unmodified base learner as well as a Mut-modified and $Carc$-modified learner. The test accuracies for each point in the figure are given in Table 3.

The use of the Mut DFT on the mutagenesis tasks is, in a sense, "cheating" as it indirectly gives the learner access to extra mutagenesis examples it otherwise would not have. The results in these best-case scenarios are not intended as proof of DEFT's effectiveness, but rather to remove possible explanations of the poor performance of DEFT when using the $Carc$ DFT. If no improvement was seen when using the Mut DFT for mutagenesis (where the primary and secondary tasks are decidedly similar) then fault would lie with the DEFT algorithms or the choice of descriptors. However, the improvement was significant when using the Mut DFT while none was seen when using the $Carc$ DFT, warranting a closer look at which rules are preferred in each case.

The Mut DFT has high β values (2200, 7100, 47, 55) for rules that mention an an atom of certain types (195, 28, 49, 51). The main improvement in the generalisation accuracy on the 20% task is due to an increase of the true positive

---

[6] These are called the M0 and C0 predicate groups in [19].

[7] One detail about the arg descriptors is pertinent here: the $Const$ parameter cannot take on floating point values. Descriptors with specific floats match very few rules.

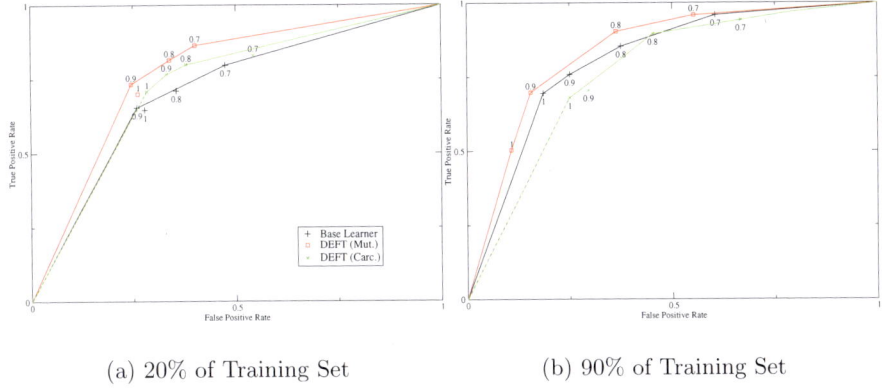

(a) 20% of Training Set   (b) 90% of Training Set

Fig. 6. ROC curves showing the performance of the base learner and DEFT on the mutagenesis domain for two training set sizes. Two DEFT curves are shown per graph, one using the *Mut* DFT and the other the *Carc* DFT .

rate. Like the chess tasks, this is due to the DFT-modified metric preferring many specific rules over a few general ones and several ground facts.

While there is also an improvement in the true positive rate when using the *Carc*-DFT, it comes as a trade-off for a higher false positive rate. This is because the *Carc*-modified evaluations also prefer rules over ground facts but the preferred rules generalise badly. The explanation is that the descriptors with high β values for the *Mut*-DFT either do not appear in the *Carc*-DFT (atom type $= 195, 28$) or are given indifferent scores (type $= 49, 51$ both have β around 1). Furthermore, some high β descriptors for *Carc* (type $= 94 : \beta = 6$) have low scores ($\beta = 0.5$) on *Mut*. The few descriptors both DFTs prefer (type $= 29, 52$) are responsible for the slight gains on the 20% task but cannot overcome their differences which have a detrimental effect when 162 virtual carcinogenesis examples are used with the 90% task.

The conclusion to be drawn from these results is that, as suggested by the *Mut* DFT results, DEFT could improve learning from small datasets in this domain. However, carcinogenesis appears to have a very different set of high performing clauses and so was not useful as a secondary task for mutagenesis.[8]

5 Related Work

The role of evaluation metrics in rule learning and the relationships between them has been a topic of interest recently [21,22,12]. Adding values to entries in a contingency table is a general way of parameterising evaluation metrics of which the Laplace and m-estimates [23] are special cases. The DEFT method of

---

[8] This is consistent with another researcher's attempt to exploit the apparent similarity between the domains. [20] notes "that the data were about such different sets of chemicals that this was not really the case".

Table 3. Test accuracies on the mutagenesis tasks for the base learner and DEFT using the *Mut* and *Carc* DFTs. **Bold** entries differ from the Base figures at a significance level of 0.05 using a paired t-test.

train size	20%				90%			
minacc	0.7	0.8	0.9	1.0	0.7	0.8	0.9	1.0
Base	70.6 (3.0)	68.5 (3.3)	68.0 (4.0)	66.8 (4.1)	77.1 (2.4)	77.6 (2.1)	75.5 (2.8)	73.4 (3.1)
Mut	75.2 (2.3)	**77.2 (2.3)**	**74.9 (2.7)**	**73.8 (2.3)**	78.8 (2.4)	**81.4 (2.5)**	74.6 (2.9)	63.3 (3.0)
Carc	68.5 (3.4)	72.9 (2.5)	71.1 (3.5)	70.0 (3.7)	73.9 (1.6)	77.7 (2.1)	70.4 (3.1)	70.3 (2.7)

learning those parameters can be seen as a special case of Bayesian approaches to learning to learn [24,25]. DEFT's use of priors for rules is similar to those in positive-only learning [13,26] and LIME [27]. Those systems randomly generate unlabelled examples (as opposed to using labelled examples from secondary tasks) to estimate the size of a rule's extension. This helps rule evaluation when negative examples are scarce or unavailable.

Unlike DEFT, other attempts at multitask learning in ILP have not considered learning evaluation bias. The MFOCL system [6] is similar to the Repeat Learning system [7] described in Section 4.2. Its "concept sharing" approach reuses rules and parts of rules from concepts learned on secondary tasks in the same manner as the invented predicates in RL. Since MFOCL's base learner performs a greedy search, the new predicates allow it to avoid local minima. This is also the motivation for the CLUSE/XFOIL system [8] in which CLUSE uses a "contextual least-general generalisation" procedure on secondary tasks to learn relational clichés. These combinations of literals expand the actions available to the greedy search used by its FOIL variant.

Descriptors are similar to first-order features used by systems to transform relational problems into propositional ones (e.g., [28]). The main difference is that the latter is a transformation on examples, allowing a search of propositional rules, whereas descriptors act on first-order rules and are used to improve their evaluation. However, it would be possible to apply DEFT to the propositional rule learners used in such systems to help their rule evaluation on limited data.

6 Conclusions and Future Work

Evaluating rules when there is only a small amount of data is an intrinsically difficult problem. It is also an important one, especially when classified data is expensive or difficult to obtain. DEFT, the multitask approach presented here, demonstrates how the evaluation of rules can be modified so as to take into account the performance of similar rules on secondary tasks. Rule descriptions are introduced as a general way to define rule similarity. This forms the basis of a simple Bayesian technique to calculate classification priors for rules. These are used to improve estimates of classification probabilities from small datasets. Evaluation metrics that are functions of the improved estimates provide more reliable assessments of rule quality.

DEFT was tested empirically on three environments. The first, a toy environment, confirmed that the approach can improve learning performance when the primary and secondary tasks are "intuitively" similar. This was the case again on the chess movement environment. Furthermore, DEFT was successfully combined with a different, predicate invention-based approach that had previously been used on the same tasks. Results on the third environment were less conclusive but strongly suggested that description-based evaluation could with help learning in biological domains.

Future work on the theoretical front will include a better characterisation of similarity in terms of descriptions and descriptor tables and investigate links with existing work on representation-based metrics, especially those using MML/MDL. Improvements to the current implementation of DEFT will include adding more sophisticated descriptors and statistical pruning techniques to manage larger DFTs more efficiently. The impact of these new descriptors will need to be thoroughly empirically tested, as will DEFT's sensitivity to its M parameter and the secondary tasks used to create DFTs.

Acknowledgements. The author thanks Ashwin Srinivasan for his help with ALEPH and discussions about the molecular datasets. Thanks also to Claude Sammut for his feedback on this paper. Suggestions from the anonymous reviewers were also valuable.

References

1. Srinivasan, A., King, R.D.: Feature construction with inductive logic programming: a study of quantative predictions of biological activity aided by structural attributes. Data Mining and Knowledge Discovery **3** (1999) 37–57
2. Caruana, R.: Multitask learning. Machine Learning **28** (1997) 41–75
3. Mitchell, T.M.: The need for biases in learning generalizations. Technical Report CBM-TR-117, Rutgers University, New Brunswick, New Jersey (1980)
4. Nédellec, C., Rouveirol, C., Adé, H., Bergadano, F., Tausend, B.: Declarative bias in ILP. In: Advances in ILP. Volume 32 of Frontiers in AI and Applications. IOS Press (1996) 82–103
5. Fürnkranz, J.: Separate-and-conquer rule learning. Artificial Intelligence Review **13** (1999) 3–54
6. Datta, P., Kibler, D.F.: Concept sharing: A means to improve multi-concept learning. In: Proc. of the 10th ICML. (1993) 89–96
7. Khan, K., Muggleton, S., Parson, R.: Repeat learning using predicate invention. In: Proc. of the 8th ILP, Springer (1998) 165–174
8. Morin, J.: Learning Relational Clichés with Contextual Generalization. PhD thesis, School of Information Technology and Engineering, University of Ottawa, Canada (1999)
9. Srinivasan, A.: ALEPH: A learning engine for proposing hypotheses. Prolog code (2001) http:// www.comlab.ox.ac.uk/ oucl/ research/ areas/ machlearn/ Aleph/.
10. Silver, D.: Selective Transfer of Neural network Task Knowledge. PhD thesis, Graduate Program in Computer Science, University of Western Ontario, London, Ontario, Canada (2000)

11. Good, I.J.: The Estimation of Probabilities: An Essay on Modern Bayesian Methods. MIT Press (1965)
12. Fürnkranz, J., Flach, P.A.: An analysis of rule evaluation metrics. In: Proc. of the 19th ICML, AAAI Press (2003) 202–209
13. Muggleton, S.H.: Inverse entailment and progol. New Generation Computing **13** (1995) 245–286
14. Srinivasan, A.: A study of two sampling methods for analysing large datasets with ILP. Data Mining and Knowledge Discovery **3** (1999) 95–123
15. De Raedt, L., Bruynhooghe, M.: Interactive concept-learning and constructive induction by analogy. Machine Learning **8** (1992) 107–150
16. Srinivasan, A., Muggleton, S., King, R.D., Sternberg, M.J.E.: Mutagenesis: ILP experiments in a non-determinate biological domain. In: Proc. of the 4th ILP. (1994)
17. Srinivasan, A., King, R.D., Muggleton, S., Sternberg, M.J.E.: Carcinogenesis predictions using ILP. In: Proc. of the 7th ILP. (1997) 273–287
18. Holte, R.C., Acker, L.E., Porter, B.W.: Concept learning and the problem of small disjuncts. In: Proc. of the 11th IJCAI. (1989) 813–818
19. Srinivasan, A.: Extracting context-sensitive models in inductive logic programming. Machine Learning **44** (2001) 301–324
20. Srinivasan, A.: Personal communication. Email regarding chemical data (2002)
21. Lavrač, N., Flach, P., Zupan, B.: Rule evaluation measures: A unifying view. In: Proc. of the 9th ILP, Springer (1999) 174–185
22. Vilalta, R., Oblinger, D.: A quantification of distance-bias between evaluation metrics in classification. In: Proc. of the 17th ICML. (2000) 1087–1094
23. Cestnik, B.: Estimating probabilities: A crucial task in machine learning. In: Proc. of the 9th European Conference on AI, Pitman (1990) 147–149
24. Baxter, J.: A model of inductive bias learning. Journal of Artificial Intelligence Research **12** (2000) 149–198
25. Heskes, T.: Empirical bayes for learning to learn. In: Proc. of the 17th ICML, Morgan Kaufmann (2000) 367–374
26. Cussens, J.: Using prior probabilities and density estimation for relational classification In: Proc. of the 8th ILP, Springer (1998) 106–115
27. McCreath, E., Sharma, A.: LIME: A system for learning relations. In: Proc. of the ALT-98. (1998) 336–374
28. Lavrač, N., Flach, P.A.: An extended transformation approach to inductive logic programming. ACM Trans. on Computational Logic (TOCL) **2** (2001) 458–494

A Experimental Settings

	clauselength	i	nodes	noise	minacc	sample_ex	sample_cl
Toy	4	2	200	0	-	40	100
Chess	6	3	200	0	-	40	100
Molecular	4	2	10000	-	0.67-1.0	100	50

Learning Logic Programs with Annotated Disjunctions

Fabrizio Riguzzi

Dipartimento di Ingegneria, Università di Ferrara, Via Saragat 1
44100 Ferrara, Italy,
friguzzi@ing.unife.it

Abstract. Logic Programs with Annotated Disjunctions (LPADs) provide a simple and elegant framework for integrating probabilistic reasoning and logic programming. In this paper we propose an algorithm for learning LPADs. The learning problem we consider consists in starting from a sets of interpretations annotated with their probability and finding one (or more) LPAD that assign to each interpretation the associated probability. The learning algorithm first finds all the disjunctive clauses that are true in all interpretations, then it assigns to each disjunct in the head a probability and finally decides how to combine the clauses to form an LPAD by solving a constraint satisfaction problem. We show that the learning algorithm is correct and complete.

1 Introduction

There has been recently a growing interest in the field of probabilistic logic programming: a number of works have appeared that combine logic programming or relational representations with probabilistic reasoning. Among these works, we cite: Probabilistic Logic Programs [14], Bayesian Logic Programs [9,10], Probabilistic Relational Models [7], Context-sensitive Probabilistic Knowledge Bases [15], Independent Choice Logic (ICL) [17] and Stochastic Logic Programs [13,3].

One of the most recent approaches is Logic Programs with Annotated Disjunctions (LPADs) presented in [22,21]. In this approach, the clauses of an LPAD can have a disjunction in the head and each disjunct is annotated with a probability. The sum of the probabilities for all the disjuncts in the head of a clause must be one. Clauses with disjunction in the head express a form of uncertain knowledge, for example the clause

$$heads(Coin) \vee tails(Coin) \leftarrow toss(Coin)$$

expresses the fact that, if a coin is tossed, it can land on heads or tails but we don't know which. By annotating the disjuncts with a probability, we can express probabilistic knowledge that we have regarding the facts in the head, for example the clause

$$(heads(Coin) : 0.5) \vee (tails(Coin) : 0.5) \leftarrow toss(Coin), \neg biased(Coin)$$

R. Camacho, R. King, A. Srinivasan (Eds.): ILP 2004, LNAI 3194, pp. 270–287, 2004.

expresses the fact that, if the coin is not biased, it has equal probability of landing on heads or on tails.

The semantics of LPADs is given in terms of a function π_P^* that, given an LPAD P, assigns a probability to each interpretation that is a subset of the Herbrand Base of P. Moreover, given the function π_P^*, a probability function for formulas can be defined.

This formalism is interesting for the intuitive reading of its formulae that makes the writing of LPADs simpler than other formalisms. Moreover, also the semantics is simple and elegant. The formalism that is closest to LPADs is ICL: in fact, in [21] the authors show that ICL programs can be translated into LPADs and acyclic LPADs can be translated into ICL programs. Therefore, ICL programs are equivalent to a large class of LPADs. However, ICL is more suited for representing problems where we must infer causes from effects, like diagnosis or theory revision problems, while LPADs are more suited for reasoning on the effects of certain actions.

In this paper we propose the algorithm LLPAD (Learning LPADs) that learns a large subclass of LPADs. We consider a learning problem where we are given a set of interpretations together with their probabilities and a language bias and we want to find an LPAD that assigns to each input interpretation its probability according to the semantics.

LLPAD is able to learn LPADs that are sound and such that a couple of clauses sharing a disjunct have mutually exclusive bodies, i. e., bodies that are never both true in an interpretation I that has a non-zero probability.

LLPAD exploits techniques from the learning from interpretations setting: it searches first for the definite clauses that are true in all the input interpretations and are true in a non-trivial way in at least one interpretation, i. e., they have the body true in the interpretation, and then it searches for disjunctive clauses that are true in all the input interpretations, are non-trivially true in at least one interpretations and have mutually exclusive disjuncts in the head. Once the disjunctive clauses have been found, the probability of each disjunct in the head is computed.

Finally, we must decide which of the found clauses belong to the target program. To this purpose, we assign to each annotated disjunctive clause a Boolean variable that represents the presence or absence of the clause in a solution. Then, for each input interpretation, we impose a constraint over the variables of the clauses that have the body true in the interpretation. The constraint is based on the semantics of LPADs and ensures that the probability assigned to the interpretation by the final program is the one given as input for that interpretation.

The paper is organized as follows. In section 2 we provide some preliminary notions regarding LPADs together with the semantics of LPADs as given in [22]. In section 3 we discuss two properties of LPADs that are exploited by LLPAD. In section 4 we introduce the learning problem we have defined and we describe LLPAD. In section 5 we discuss related works and finally in section 6 we conclude and present directions for future work.

2 LPADs

2.1 Preliminaries

A disjunctive logic program [12] is a set of disjunctive clauses. A disjunctive clause is a formula of the form

$$h_1 \vee h_2 \vee \ldots \vee h_n \leftarrow b_1, b_2, \ldots, b_m$$

where h_i are logical atoms and b_i are logical literals. The disjunction $h_1 \vee h_2 \vee \ldots \vee h_n$ is called the *head* of the clause and the conjunction $b_1 \wedge b_2 \wedge \ldots \wedge b_m$ is the called the *body*. Let us define the two functions $head(c)$ and $body(c)$ that, given a disjunctive clause c, return respectively the head and the body of c. In some cases, we will use the functions $head(c)$ and $body(c)$ to denote the set of the atoms in the head or of the literals of the body respectively. The meaning of $head(c)$ and $body(c)$ will be clear from the context.

The Herbrand base $H_B(P)$ of a disjunctive logic program P is the set of all the atoms constructed with the predicate, constant and functor symbols appearing in P. A Herbrand interpretation is a subset of $H_B(P)$. Let us denote the set of all Herbrand interpretations by $\mathcal{I}_P$. In this paper we will consider only Herbrand interpretations and in the following we will drop the word Herbrand. A disjunctive clause c is true in an interpretation I if for all grounding substitution θ of c: $body(c)\theta \subset I \rightarrow head(c)\theta \cap I \neq \emptyset$. As was observed by [4], the truth of a clause c in an interpretation I can be tested by running the query $? - body(c), not\ head(c)$ on a database containing I. If the query succeeds c is false in I. If the query finitely fails c is true in I. A clause c θ-subsumes a clause d if and only if there exists a substitution θ such that $c\theta \subseteq d$ and we write $c \geq_\theta d$.

A Logic Program with Annotated Disjunctions consists of a set of formulas of the form

$$(h_1 : p_1) \vee (h_2 : p_2) \vee \ldots \vee (h_n : p_n) \leftarrow b_1, b_2, \ldots b_m$$

called *annotated disjunctive clauses*. In such a clause the h_i are logical atoms, the b_i are logical literals and the p_i are real numbers in the interval $[0, 1]$ such that $\sum_{i=1}^{n} p_i = 1$. For a clause c of the form above, we define $head(c)$ as the set $\{(h_i : p_i) | 1 \leq i \leq n\}$ and $body(c)$ as the set $\{b_i | 1 \leq i \leq m\}$. If $head(c)$ contains a single element $(a : 1)$ we will simply denote the head as a. The set of all ground LPAD defined over a first order alphabet is denoted by $\mathcal{P}_\mathcal{G}$.

Let us see an example of LPAD taken from [22].

$$(heads(Coin) : 0.5) \vee (tails(Coin) : 0.5) \leftarrow toss(Coin), \neg biased(Coin).$$
$$(heads(Coin) : 0.6) \vee (tails(Coin) : 0.4) \leftarrow toss(Coin), biased(Coin).$$
$$(fair(Coin) : 0.9) \vee (biased(Coin) : 0.1).$$
$$toss(Coin).$$

2.2 Semantics of LPADs

The semantics of an LPAD was given in [22]. We report it here for the sake of completeness. It is given in terms of its grounding. Therefore we restrict our attention to ground LPADs, i.e., LPADs belonging to $\mathcal{P}_\mathcal{G}$. For example, the grounding of the LPAD given in the previous section is

$$(heads(coin) : 0.5) \vee (tails(coin) : 0.5) \leftarrow toss(coin), \neg biased(coin).$$
$$(heads(coin) : 0.6) \vee (tails(coin) : 0.4) \leftarrow toss(coin), biased(coin).$$
$$(fair(coin) : 0.9) \vee (biased(coin) : 0.1).$$
$$toss(coin).$$

Each annotated disjunctive clause represents a probabilistic choice between a number of non-disjunctive clauses. By choosing a head for each clause of an LPAD we get a normal logic program called an *instance* of the LPAD. For example, the LPAD above has $2 \cdot 2 \cdot 2 \cdot 1 = 8$ possible instances one of which is

$$heads(coin) \leftarrow toss(coin), \neg biased(coin).$$
$$heads(coin) \leftarrow toss(coin), biased(coin).$$
$$fair(coin).$$
$$toss(coin).$$

A probability is assigned to all instances by assuming independence between the choices made for each clause. Therefore, the probability of the instance above is $0.5 \cdot 0.6 \cdot 0.9 \cdot 1 = 0.27$.

An instance is identified by means of a selection function.

Definition 1 (Selection function). *Let P be a program in $\mathcal{P}_\mathcal{G}$. A selection σ is a function which selects one pair $(h : \alpha)$ from each rule of P, i.e. $\sigma : P \rightarrow (H_B(P) \times [0, 1])$ such that, for each r in P, $\sigma(r) \in head(r)$. For each rule r, we denote the atom h selected from this rule by $\sigma_{atom}(r)$ and the probability α selected by $\sigma_{prob}(r)$. Furthermore, we denote the set of all selections σ by $\mathcal{S}_P$.*

Let us now give the formal definition of an instance.

Definition 2 (Instance). *Let P be a program in $\mathcal{P}_\mathcal{G}$ and σ a selection in $\mathcal{S}_P$. The instance P_σ chosen by σ is obtained by keeping only the atom selected for r in the head of each rule $r \in P$, i.e. $P_\sigma = \{ \text{"}\sigma_{atom}(r) \leftarrow body(r)\text{"} | r \in P \}$.*

We now assign a probability to a selection function σ and therefore also to the associated program P_σ.

Definition 3 (Probability of a selection). *Let P be a program in $\mathcal{P}_\mathcal{G}$. The probability of a selection σ in $\mathcal{S}_P$ is the product of the the probability of the individual choices made by that selection, i.e.*

$$C_\sigma = \prod_{r \in P} \sigma_{prob}(r)$$

The instances of an LPAD P are normal logic program. Their semantics can be given by any of the semantics defined for normal logic programs (e.g. Clark's completion [2], Fitting semantics [5], stable models [6], well founded semantics [20]). In this paper we will consider only the well founded semantics, the most skeptical one. Since in LPAD the uncertainty is modeled by means of the annotated disjunctions, the instances of an LPAD should contain no uncertainty, i.e. they should have a single two-valued model. Therefore, given an instance P_σ, its semantics is given by its well founded model $WFM(P_\sigma)$ and we require that it is two-valued.

Definition 4 (Sound LPAD). *An LPAD P is called* sound *iff for each selection σ in S_P, the well founded model $WFM(P_\sigma)$ of the program P_σ chosen by σ is two-valued.*

For example, if the LPAD is acyclic (meaning that all its instances are acyclic) then the LPAD is sound. We denote with $P_\sigma \models_{WFM} F$ the fact that the formula F is true in the well founded model of P_σ.
  We now define the probability of interpretations.

Definition 5 (Probability of an interpretation). *Let P be a sound LPAD in $\mathcal{P}_G$. For each of its interpretations I in $\mathcal{I}_P$, the probability $\pi_P^*(I)$ assigned by P to I is the sum of the probabilities of all selections which lead to I, i.e. with $S(I)$ being the set of all selection σ for which $WFM(P_\sigma) = I$:*

$$\pi_P^*(I) = \sum_{\sigma \in S(I)} C_\sigma$$

For example, consider the interpretation $\{toss(coin), fair(coin), heads(coin)\}$. This interpretation is the well founded model of two instance of the example LPAD, one is the instance shown above and the other is the instance:

$$heads(coin) \leftarrow toss(coin), \neg biased(coin).$$
$$tails(coin) \leftarrow toss(coin), biased(coin).$$
$$fair(coin).$$
$$toss(coin).$$

The probability of this instance is $0.5 \cdot 0.4 \cdot 0.9 \cdot 1 = 0.18$. Therefore, the probability of the interpretation above is $0.5 \cdot 0.4 \cdot 0.9 \cdot 1 + 0.5 \cdot 0.6 \cdot 0.9 \cdot 1 = 0.5 \cdot (0.4 + 0.6) \cdot 0.9 \cdot 1 = 0.45$.

3 Properties of LPADs

We now give a definition and two theorems that will be useful in the following.
  The first theorem states that, under certain conditions, the probabilities of the head disjuncts of a rule can be computed from the probabilities of the interpretations. In particular, the probability of a disjunct h_i is given by the sum

of the probabilities of interpretations where the body of the clause and h_i are true divided by the sum of the probabilities of interpretations where the body is true.

The second theorem states that, given an interpretation, under certain conditions, all the selection σ in the set $S(I)$ agree on all the rules with the body true and that the probability of I can be computed by multiplying the probabilities of the head disjuncts selected by a $\sigma \in S(I)$ for all the clauses with the body true.

Definition 6 (Mutually exclusive bodies). *Clauses $H_1 \leftarrow B_1$ and $H_2 \leftarrow B_2$ have mutually exclusive bodies over a set of interpretations J if, $\forall I \in J$, B_1 and B_2 are not both true in I.*

Theorem 1. *Consider a sound LPAD P and a clause $c \in P$ of the form*

$$c = h_1 : p_1 \vee h_2 : p_2 \vee \ldots h_m : p_m \leftarrow B.$$

Suppose you are given the function π_P^* and suppose that all the couples of clauses of P that share an atom in the head have mutually exclusive bodies over the set of interpretations $J = \{I | \pi_\sigma^*(I) > 0\}$. The probabilities p_i can be computed with the following formula:

$$p_i = \frac{\sum_{I \in \mathcal{I}_P, I \models B, h_i} \pi_P^*(I)}{\sum_{I \in \mathcal{I}_P, I \models B} \pi_P^*(I)}$$

Proof. Let us first expand the numerator:

$$\sum_{I \in \mathcal{I}_P, I \models B, h_i} \pi_P^*(I) = \sum_{I \in J, I \models B, h_i} \sum_{\sigma \in S(I)} \prod_{r \in P} \sigma_{prob}(r)$$

A selection σ such that $WFM(P_\sigma) = I$ for an I such that $I \models B, h_i$ is a selection such that $P_\sigma \models_{WFM} B, h_i$. Therefore the above expression can be written as

$$\sum_{\sigma \in T} \prod_{r \in P} \sigma_{prob}(r)$$

where $T = \{\sigma | P_\sigma \models_{WFM} B, h_i\}$. Since clause c has a mutually exclusive body over the set of interpretations J with all the other clauses of P that contain h_i in the head, the truth of h_i in P_σ can be obtained only if $\sigma(c) = (h_i : p_i)$ for all $\sigma \in T$, therefore the numerator becomes

$$\sum_{\sigma \in T} p_i \prod_{r \in P \setminus \{c\}} \sigma_{prob}(r) = p_i \sum_{\sigma \in T} \prod_{r \in P \setminus \{c\}} \sigma_{prob}(r)$$

Let us expand the denominator in a similar way

$$\sum_{I \in \mathcal{I}_P, I \models B} \pi_P^*(I) = \sum_{\sigma \in Q} \prod_{r \in P} \sigma_{prob}(r)$$

where $Q = \{\sigma | P_\sigma \models_{WFM} B\}$. Clause c expresses the fact that, if B is true, then either $h_1, h_2, \ldots$ or h_m is true, i.e., these cases are exhaustive. Moreover, they are also exhaustive. Therefore we can write Q in the following way:

$$Q = \{\sigma | P_\sigma \models_{WFM} B, h_1\} \cup \{\sigma | P_\sigma \models_{WFM} B, h_2\} \cup \ldots \cup \{\sigma | P_\sigma \models_{WFM} B, h_m\}$$

Let $Q_j = \{\sigma | P_\sigma \models_{WFM} B, h_j\}$, then $Q_j \cap Q_k = \emptyset$ for all $j, k = 1, \ldots m, j \neq k$.

Since clause c has a mutually exclusive body over the set of interpretations J with all the other clauses of P, the truth of h_j in P_σ can be obtained only if $\sigma(c) = h_j : p_j$ for all $\sigma \in Q_j$, therefore the denominator becomes

$$\sum_{j=1}^{m} p_j \sum_{\sigma \in Q_j} \prod_{r \in P \setminus \{c\}} \sigma_{prob}(r)$$

Given a selection σ^T in T, consider a selection σ^{Q_j} that differs from σ^T only over clause c, i.e., $\sigma^T(c) = (h_i : p_i)$ while $\sigma^{Q_j}(c) = (h_j : p_j)$. From $P_{\sigma^T} \models_{WFM} B$ follows that $P_{\sigma^{Q_j}} \models_{WFM} B$ because B can not depend on the truth of literal h_i since otherwise there would be a loop and B would not be true in the well-founded model of P_{σ^T}. From $P_{\sigma^{Q_j}} \models_{WFM} B$ follows that $P_{\sigma^{Q_j}} \models_{WFM} B, h_j$ because B can not depend on $\neg h_j$ since otherwise there would be a loop through negation and the LPAD P would not be sound, in contradiction with the hypothesis. Therefore σ^{Q_j} is in Q_j. The same reasoning can be applied in the opposite direction. As a consequence

$$\sum_{\sigma \in T} \prod_{r \in P \setminus \{c\}} \sigma_{prob}(r) = \sum_{\sigma \in Q_j} \prod_{r \in P \setminus \{c\}} \sigma_{prob}(r)$$

for all $j = 1, \ldots, m$. Thus, the fraction becomes

$$\frac{p_i \sum_{\sigma \in T} \prod_{r \in P \setminus \{c\}} \sigma_{prob}(r)}{\left(\sum_{j=1}^{m} p_j\right) \sum_{\sigma \in T} \prod_{r \in P \setminus \{c\}} \sigma_{prob}(r)} = p_i$$

□

Theorem 2. *Consider an interpretation I and an LPAD P such that all the couples of clauses that share an atom in the head have mutually exclusive bodies with respect to the set of interpretations $\{I\}$. Then all the selection $\sigma \in S(I)$ agree on the clauses with body true in I and*

$$\pi_P^*(I) = \prod_{r \in P, I \models body(r)} \sigma_{prob}(r)$$

where σ is any element of $S(I)$.

Proof. We prove the theorem by induction on the number n of clauses with the body false in I.

Case $n = 0$. For each atom $A \in I$, there is only one clause c that has it in the head for the assumption of mutual exclusion. Therefore, for A to be in I, σ must select atom A for clause c. Moreover, all the clauses have the body true, therefore for each clause one atom in the head must be in I. Therefore there is a single σ in $S(I)$ and the theorem holds.

We assume that the theorem holds for a program P^{n-1} with $n-1$ clauses with the body false in I. We have to prove that the theorem holds for a program P^n obtained from P^{n-1} by adding a clause r_n with the body false. Suppose that the r_n is

$$h_1 : p_1 \vee h_2 : p_2 \vee \ldots \vee h_m : p_m \leftarrow B$$

Let $S_{n-1}(I)$ $(S_n(I))$ be the set of all selections σ such that $WFM(P_\sigma^{n-1}) = I$ $(WFM(P_\sigma^n = I))$. Moreover, let $S_{n-1}(I)$ be $\{\sigma^1, \sigma^2, \ldots, \sigma^k\}$.

Since B is false in I, any head disjunct in r_n can be selected and r_n will be true anyway in I. Therefore, for each $\sigma^i \in S_{n-1}(I)$, there are m $\sigma^{i,j}$ in $S_n(I)$. Each $\sigma^{i,j}$ agrees with σ^i on all the rules of P^{n-1}. $\sigma^{i,j}$ extends σ^i by selecting the jth disjunct in clause r_n, i.e $\sigma^{i,j}(r_n) = (h_j : p_j)$. We can write:

$$\pi_{P^n}^*(I) = \sum_{\sigma \in S_n(I)} \prod_{r \in P^n} \sigma_{prob}(r) =$$

$$= \sum_{\sigma \in S_n(I)} \prod_{r \in P^{n-1}} \sigma_{prob}(r)\sigma_{prob}(r_n) =$$

$$= \prod_{r \in P^{n-1}} \sigma_{prob}^{1,1}(r)p_1 + \prod_{r \in P^{n-1}} \sigma_{prob}^{1,2}(r)p_2 + \ldots + \prod_{r \in P^{n-1}} \sigma_{prob}^{1,m}(r)p_m +$$

$$+ \ldots$$

$$+ \prod_{r \in P^{n-1}} \sigma_{prob}^{k,1}(r)p_1 + \prod_{r \in P^{n-1}} \sigma_{prob}^{k,2}(r)p_2 + \ldots + \prod_{r \in P^{n-1}} \sigma_{prob}^{k,m}(r)p_m =$$

$$= p_1 \left(\prod_{r \in P^{n-1}} \sigma_{prob}^{1,1}(r) + \prod_{r \in P^{n-1}} \sigma_{prob}^{2,1}(r) + \ldots + \prod_{r \in P^{n-1}} \sigma_{prob}^{k,1}(r) \right) +$$

$$+ \ldots$$

$$+ p_m \left(\prod_{r \in P^{n-1}} \sigma_{prob}^{1,m}(r) + \prod_{r \in P^{n-1}} \sigma_{prob}^{2,m}(r) + \ldots + \prod_{r \in P^{n-1}} \sigma_{prob}^{k,m}(r) \right)$$

Since $\sigma^{i,j}$ extends σ^i only on clause r_n, then $\prod_{r \in P^{n-1}} \sigma_{prob}^{i,j}(r) = \prod_{r \in P^{n-1}} \sigma_{prob}^i(r)$. Therefore

$$\pi_{p^n}^*(I) = (p_1 + p_2 + \ldots + p_m) \times$$

$$\times \left(\prod_{r \in P^{n-1}} \sigma_{prob}^1(r) + \prod_{r \in P^{n-1}} \sigma_{prob}^2(r) + \ldots + \prod_{r \in P^{n-1}} \sigma_{prob}^k(r) \right) =$$

$$= \sum_{\sigma \in S_{n-1}(I)} \prod_{r \in P^{n-1}} \sigma_{prob}(r)$$

which, for the hypothesis for $n - 1$, becomes

$$\prod_{r \in P^n, I \models body(r)} \sigma_{prob}(r)$$

$\square$

The hypothesis of mutual exclusion of the bodies is fundamental for this theorem to hold. In fact, consider the following example:

$$P_1 = a : a_1 \vee b : b_1.$$
$$a : a_2 \vee b : b_2.$$

Then $\pi^*_{P_1}(\{a, b\}) = a_1 b_2 + a_2 b_1$.

One may think that is enough to have mutually exclusive bodies only when two clauses have the same disjunct in the head. But this is not true as the following example shows:

$$P_2 = a : a_1 \vee b : b_1 \vee c : c_1.$$
$$a : a_2 \vee c : c_2 \vee d : d_2.$$
$$a : a_3 \vee b : b_3 \vee d : d_3.$$

Then $\pi^*_{P_2}(\{a, b, c\}) = a_1 c_2 b_3 + b_1 c_2 a_3 + c_1 a_2 b_3$.

4 Learning LPADs

We consider a learning problem of the following form:

Given:

- a set E of examples that are couples $(I, Pr(I))$ where I is an interpretation and $Pr(I)$ is its associated probability
- a space of possible LPAD S (described by a language bias LB)

Find:

- an LPAD $P \in S$ such that $\forall (I, Pr(I)) \in E \ \ \pi^*_P(I) = Pr(I)$

Instead of a set of couples $(I, Pr(I))$, the input of the learning problem can be a multiset E' of interpretations. From this case we can obtain a learning problem of the form above by computing a probability for each interpretation in E'. The probability can be computed in the obvious way, by dividing the number of occurrences of the interpretation by the total number of interpretations in E'.

Before discussing the learning algorithm, let us first provide some preliminaries.

Definition 7 (Clause non-trivially true in an interpretation (adapted from [4])). *A clause c is* non-trivially true *in an interpretation I if c is true in I and there exist at least one grounding substitution θ of c such that both $body(c)\theta$ and $head(c)\theta$ are true in I.*

Definition 8 (Refinement of a body). *The* refinement of a body B *of a clause is a body* B' *such that* $B \geq_\theta B'$ *and there does not exist a body* B'' *such that* $B \geq_\theta B''$ *and* $B'' \geq_\theta B'$.

Refining the body of a clause c can make c non-trivially true in less interpretations.

Definition 9 (Refinement of a head). *The* refinement of a head H *of a clause is a head* H' *such that* $H' \geq_\theta H$ *and there does not exist a head* H'' *such that* $H' \geq_\theta H''$ *and* $H'' \geq_\theta H$.

Definition 10 (Mutually exclusive disjuncts). *The disjuncts in the head of a clause are mutually exclusive with respect to a set of interpretations* J *if there is no interpretation* $I \in J$ *such that two or more disjuncts are true in* I.

Let us suppose that the language bias LB is given in the form of set of couples (ALH, ALB) where ALH is the set of literals allowed in the head and ALB is the set of literals allowed in the body.

The algorithm (see figure 1) proceeds in three stages. In the first, it searches for all the definite clauses allowed by the language bias

- that are true in all interpretations,
- that are non-trivially true in at least one interpretation.

The reason for searching separately for definite clauses will be explained in the following.

In the second stage, the algorithm searches for all the non-annotated disjunctive clauses allowed by the language bias

- that are true in all interpretations,
- that are non-trivially true in at least one interpretation,
- whose disjuncts in the head are mutually exclusive.

When it finds one such clause, it annotates the head disjuncts with a probability.

In the third stage, a constraint satisfaction problem is solved in order to find subsets of the annotated disjunctive clauses that form programs that assign to each interpretation the associated probability.

The search for clauses in the first stage is repeated for each couple (ALH, ALB) in LB. For each literal L in ALH, a search is started from clause $L \leftarrow$ true (function Search_Definite, not shown for brevity). The body is refined until it is true in 0 interpretations, in which case the search stops, or in the case where the head is true in all the interpretations in which the body is true, in which case the clause is returned.

The search for clauses in the second stage is repeated for each couple (ALH, ALB) in LB. The search is performed by first searching breadth-first for bodies that are true in at least one interpretation (function Search_Body, see figure 2). Every time a body is true in at least one interpretation, the algorithm searches breadth-first for all the heads that are true in the interpretations where the body is true (set EB) and whose disjuncts are mutually exclusive with respect to EB (function Search_Head, see figure 3).

Search_Body is initially called with a body equal to true. Since such a body is true in all interpretations, the function Search_Head is called with an initial head $Head$ containing all the literals allowed by the bias (ALH). The clauses returned by Search_Head are then added to the current set of clauses and Search_Body is called recursively over all the refinements of true. This is done because different bodies may have different heads.

In Search_Head the head is tested to find out the interpretations of EB where the head is true. If the head is not true in all the interpretations of EB, the search is stopped and the empty set of clauses is returned because there is no way to refine the head in order to make the clause true. Instead, if the head is true in all the interpretations of EB, $Head$ is tested to see whether the disjuncts are mutually exclusive. If so, the head disjuncts that are false in all the interpretations are removed, the probabilities of the remaining head disjuncts are computed and the clause is returned by Search_Head. If the disjuncts are not mutually exclusive, all the refinements of $Head$ are considered and Search_Head is called recursively on each of them.

The probabilities of the disjuncts in the head are computed according to theorem 1: the probability of a disjunct is given by the sum of the probabilities of the interpretations in EB where the disjunct is true divided by the sum of probabilities of the interpretations in EB. The function Compute_Probabilities takes a disjunction of atoms and returns an annotated disjunction.

Example 1. Consider the coin problem presented in section 2.1. The set of couples $(I, Pr(I))$ is:

$$I_1 = \{heads(coin), toss(coin), fair(coin)\} \qquad Pr(I_1) = 0.45$$
$$I_2 = \{tails(coin), toss(coin), fair(coin)\} \qquad Pr(I_2) = 0.45$$
$$I_3 = \{heads(coin), toss(coin), biased(coin)\} \qquad Pr(I_3) = 0.06$$
$$I_4 = \{tails(coin), toss(coin), biased(coin)\} \qquad Pr(I_4) = 0.04$$

Given the above set E and the language bias $LB = \{(\{heads(coin), tails(coin),$ $toss(coin), biased(coin), \quad fair(coin)\}, \{toss(coin), biased(coin), fair(coin)\})\}$, the algorithm generates the following definite clause:

$$d_1 = toss.$$

and the following set of annotated disjunctive clauses SC:

$c_1 = biased(coin) : 0.1 \vee fair(coin) : 0.9.$

$c_2 = heads(coin) : 0.51 \vee tails(coin) : 0.49.$

$c_3 = biased(coin) : 0.1 \vee fair(coin) : 0.9 \leftarrow toss(coin).$

$c_4 = heads(coin) : 0.51 \vee tails(coin) : 0.49 \leftarrow toss(coin).$

$c_5 = heads(coin) : 0.6 \vee tails(coin) : 0.4 \leftarrow toss(coin), biased(coin).$

$c_6 = heads(coin) : 0.5 \vee tails(coin) : 0.5 \leftarrow toss(coin), fair(coin).$

$c_7 = heads(coin) : 0.6 \vee tails(coin) : 0.4 \leftarrow biased(coin).$

$c_8 = heads(coin) : 0.5 \vee tails(coin) : 0.5 \leftarrow fair(coin).$

function LLPAD(
    inputs : E : set of couples $(I, Pr(I))$,
        A language bias LB in the form of a set of couples (ALH, ALB),
        where ALH is a list of literals allowed in the head,
        and ALB is a list of literals allowed in the body)
    returns : SP : a set of learned LPAD

$SD := \emptyset$
$ES := \{(\emptyset, I) | (I, Pr(I)) \in E\}$
$ES' := \{(\emptyset, I, Pr(I)) | (I, Pr(I)) \in E\}$
for all couples (ALH, ALB) **do**
    for all literals L in ALH
        $SD := SD \cup$ Search_Definite($ALB, L \leftarrow$ true,ES)
    end for
end for
$SC := \emptyset$
for all couples (ALH, ALB) **do**
    $Body :=$true
    $SC := SC \cup$ Search_Body($ALH, ALB, Body, ES'$)
end for
for all $c_i \in SC$
    assert the constraint $x_i \in [0, 1]$
end for
for all couples (c_i, c_j) of clauses of SC
    if c_i and c_j do not have mutually exclusive bodies over
        the set of interpretations E **then**
        assert the constraint $x_i + x_l \leq 1$
    end if
end for
for all couples $(I, Pr(I)) \in E$
    assert the following constraint
        $\sum_{c_i \in SC(I)} x_i \log p_i = \log Pr(I)$
    where $SC(I)$ is the set of clauses of SC whose body is
    true in I and p_i is the probability associated with
    the head disjunct of c_i that is true in I
end for
$SP := \emptyset$
for all solutions of the resulting CSP
    let P be the LPAD that contains all the clauses c_i for which
        $x_i = 1$
    $SP := SP \cup \{P \cup SD\}$
end for
return SP

Fig. 1. Function LLPAD

```
function Search_Body(
    inputs : ALH : set of literals allowed in the head,
    ALB : set of literals allowed in the body,
    Body : current body,
    E: set of triples (Θ, I, Pr(I)))
    returns : SC : a set of disjunctive clauses

SC := ∅
Test Body over E
let EB be a set containing elements of the form (Θ, I, Pr(I)) where I is
    an interpretation where Body is true and Θ is the set of substitutions with
    which Body is true in I
if Body is true in 0 interpretations then
    return ∅
else
    Head := ALH
    SC := SC∪Search_Head(ALH, Head, Body, EB)
    for all refinements Body' of Body
        SC := SC∪Search_Body(ALH, ALB, Body', EB)
    end for
end if
return SC
```

Fig. 2. Function Search_Body

In the third stage, we have to partition the found disjunctive clauses in subsets that are solutions of the learning problem. This is done by assigning to each clause c_i found in the second stage a variable x_i that is 0 if the clause is absent from a solution P and is 1 if the clause is present in a solution. Then we must ensure that the couples of clauses that share a literal in the head have mutually exclusive bodies over the set of interpretations E. This is achieved by testing, for each couple of clauses, if they share a literal in the head and, if so, if the intersections of the two sets of interpretations where their body is true is non-empty. In this case, we must ensure that the two clauses are not both included in a solution. To this purpose, we assert the constraint $x_i + x_j \leq 1$ for all such couples of clauses (c_i, c_j). Finally we must ensure that P assigns the correct probability to each interpretation. For each interpretation we thus have the constraint:

$$\prod_{c_i \in SC(I)} p_i^{x_i} = Pr(I)$$

where $SC(I)$ is the subset of SC of all the disjunctive clauses whose body is true in I and p_i is the probability of the single head of c_i that is true in I. This constraint is based on theorem 2.

The definite clauses are not considered in the constraints because they would contribute only with a factor 1^{x_j} that has no effect on the constraint for any

```
function Search_Head(
    inputs : ALH : set of literals allowed in the head,
        Head : current head,
        Body : current body,
        E: set of triples (Θ, I, Pr(I)))
    returns : SC : a set of disjunctive clauses

SC := ∅
if Head and Body share one or more literals then
    % the clause is a tautology
    for all refinements Head' of Head
        SC := SC∪Search_Head(ALH, Head', Body, E)
    end for
    return SC
else
    test Head over E
    if, for all (Θ, I, Pr(I)) ∈ E, Head is true in I with every substitution θ ∈ Θ
        then
        if the disjuncts are mutually exclusive then
            % a good clause has been found
            obtain Head' by removing from Head all the literals that are
                false in all the interpretations
            Head'' :=Compute_Probabilities(Head', Body, EB)
            return {Head'' ← Body}
        else
            % Head has to be refined
            for all refinements Head' of Head
                SC := SC∪Search_Head(ALH, Head', Body, E)
            end for
            return SC
        end if
    else
        % Head is false in some interpretations
        return ∅
    end if
end if
```

Fig. 3. Function Search_Head

value of x_j. Therefore, for each assignment of the other variables, x_j can be either 0 or 1. This is the reason why we have learned the definite clauses separately.

If we take the logarithm of both members we get the following linear constraint:

$$\sum_{c_i \in SC(I)} x_i \log p_i = \log Pr(I)$$

We can thus find the solutions of the learning problem by solving the above constraint satisfaction problem.

Even if the variables have finite domains, it is not possible to use a CLP(FD) solver because the coefficients of the linear equations are irrational. Therefore we solve a relaxation of the above problem where the variables are real numbers belonging to the interval $[0, 1]$.

Example 2 (Continuation of example 1). In the third stage, we use the CLP(R) solver [8] of Sicstus Prolog and we obtain the following answer:

$$x_2 = 0, x_4 = 0, x_1 = 1 - x_3, x_5 = 1 - x_7, x_6 = 1 - x_8$$

meaning that c_2 and c_4 are absent, if c_1 is present c_3 must be absent and viceversa, if c_5 is present c_7 must be absent and viceversa and if c_6 is present c_8 must be absent and viceversa. By labeling the variables in all possible ways we get eight solutions, which is exactly the number that can be obtained by considering the three double choices. The original program is among the eight solutions.

We now show that the algorithm is correct and complete.

The algorithm is correct because all the disjunctive clauses that are found are true in all the interpretations, are non-trivially true in at at least one interpretation and have mutually exclusive disjuncts in the head. The probabilities of the head literals are correct because of theorem 1 and a solution of the constraint satisfaction problem is a program for which clauses which share a literal have mutually exclusive bodies for all the interpretations in E and that assigns to each interpretation in E the correct probability because of theorem 2.

The algorithm is also complete, i.e. if there is an LPAD in the language bias that satisfies the above conditions, then LLPAD will find it, since it searches the space of possible clauses in a breadth first way.

The algorithm can be made heuristic by relaxing some of the constraints imposed: for example, we can require that the clauses must be non-trivially true in more than one interpretation. In this way, we can prune a clause as soon as its bodies is true in less than the minimum number of interpretations. However, in this case the constraint satisfaction problem must not be solved in an exact way but rather in an approximate way.

5   Related Works

To the best of our knowledge, this paper is the first published attempt to learn LPADs. Therefore, the only works related to ours are those that deal with the learning of other forms of probabilistic models.

In [21] the authors compare LPAD with Bayesian Logic Programs (BLP) [9, 10]. They show that every BLP can be expressed as an LPAD with a semantics that matches that of the BLP. Moreover, they also show that a large subset of LPADs can be translated into BLPs in a way that preserves the semantics of the LPADs. Such a subset is the set of all ground LPADs that are acyclic and where each ground atom depends only on a finite number of atoms. Therefore, the techniques developed in [11] for learning BLPs can be used for learning this class of LPADs as well. However, the technique proposed in this paper are not based on a greedy algorithm as that in [11], therefore it should be less likely to incur in a local maxima.

In [7] the authors propose a formalism called Probabilistic Relational Models (PRM) that extends the formalism of Bayesian networks to be able to model domains that are described by a multi-table relational database. Each attribute of a table is considered as a random variable and its set of parents can contain other attributes of the same table or attributes of other tables connected to the attribute table by foreign key connections. The relationship between PRM and LPADs is not clear. For sure they have a non empty intersection: the PRM that do not contain attributes that depend on aggregate functions of attributes of other tables can be expressed as LPADs. Moreover, LPADs are not a subset of PRM since they can express partial knowledge regarding the dependence of an attribute from other attributes, in the sense that with LPADs it is possible to specify only a part of a conditional probability table. Therefore the learning techniques developed in [7] can not be used in substitution of the techniques proposed in this paper.

[1] and [18] propose two logic languages for encoding in a synthetic way complex Bayesian networks. They are both very much related to PRM. Differently from PRM they offer some of the advantages of logic programming: the combination of function symbols and recursion, non-determinism and the applicability of ILP techniques for learning. LPADs offer as well this features. Moreover, with LPADs partial decision tables can be encoded.

Stochastic Logic Programs (SLPs) [3,13] are another formalism integrating logic and probability. In [21] the authors have shown that a SLP can be translated in LPAD, while whether the opposite is possible is not known yet. Therefore, it is not clear at the moment whether the techniques used for learning SLPs can be used for learning LPADs.

PRISM [19] is a logic programming language in which a program is composed of a set of facts and a set of rules such that no atom in the set of facts appears in the head of a rule. In a PRISM program, each atom is seen as a random variable taking value true or false. A probability distribution for the atoms appearing in the head of rules is inferred from a given probability distribution for the set of facts. PRISM differs from LPADs because PRISM assigns a probability distribution to ground facts while LPADs assign a probability distribution to the literals in the head of rules. PRISM programs resemble programs of ICL, in the sense that PRISM facts can be seen as ICL abducibles. In [19] the author also proposes an algorithm for learning the parameters of the probability distribution of facts from a given probability distribution for the observable atoms (atoms in the head of rules). However, no algorithm for learning the rules of a PRISM program has been defined. Inferring the parameters of the distribution is performed in LLPAD analytically by means of theorem 1 rather than by means of the EM algorithm as in PRISM.

We have already observed that a large class of LPADs is equivalent to ICL, namely the class of acyclic LPADs. Another formalism very related to ICL and LPADs is Probabilistic Disjunctive Logic Programs (PDLP) [16]. PDLP are not required to be acyclic and therefore all LPADs can be translated into PDLP and all PDLP can be translated into an LPAD. However, it remains to be checked whether the transformation preserves the semantics. Moreover, in [16] the author does not propose an algorithm for learning PDLP.

6 Conclusion and Future Works

We have defined a problem of learning LPADs and an algorithm that is able to solve it by means of learning from interpretations and constraint solving techniques. The algorithm has been implemented in Sicstus Prolog 3.9.0 and is available on request from the author.

In the future we plan to adopt more sofisticated language bias, for example the $\mathcal{D}$LAB formalism or the mode predicates of Progol and Aleph. Moreover, we plan to use extra information in order to be able to select among the set of learned clauses. An example of this extra information is negative interpretations, i.e., interpretations where the clauses have to be false.

Acknowledgements. This work was partially funded by the IST programme of the EC, FET under the IST-2001-32530 SOCS project, within the Global Computing proactive initiative and by the Ministero dell'Istruzione, della Ricerca e dell'Università under the COFIN2003 project "La gestione e la negoziazione automatica dei diritti sulle opere dell'ingegno digitali: aspetti giuridici e informatici". The author would like to thank Evelina Lamma and Luìs Moniz Pereira for many interesting discussions on the topic of this paper.

References

1. Hendrik Blockeel. Prolog for first-order bayesian networks: A meta-intepreter approach. In *Multi-Relational Data Mining (MRDM03)*, 2003.
2. K. L. Clark. Negation as failure. In *Logic and Databases*. Plenum Press, 1978.
3. James Cussens. Stochastic logic programs: Sampling, inference and applications. In *Sixteenth Annual Conference on Uncertainty in Artificial Intelligence (UAI-2000)*, pages 115–122, San Francisco, CA, 2000. Morgan Kaufmann.
4. L. De Raedt and L. Dehaspe. Clausal discovery. *Machine Learning*, 26(2–3):99–146, 1997.
5. M. Fitting. A kripke-kleene semantics for logic programs. *Journal of Logic Programming*, 2(4):295–312, 1985.
6. M. Gelfond and V. Lifschitz. The stable model semantics for logic programming. In R. Kowalski and K. A. Bowen, editors, *Proceedings of the 5th Int. Conf. on Logic Programming*, pages 1070–1080. MIT Press, 1988.
7. L. Getoor, N. Friedman, D. Koller, and A. Pfeffer. Learning probabilistic relational models. In Saso Dzeroski and Nada Lavrac, editors, *Relational Data Mining*. Springer-Verlag, Berlin, 2001.

8. C. Holzbaur. OFAI clp(q,r) manual, edition 1.3.3. Technical Report TR-95-09, Austrian Research Institute for Artificial Intelligence, Vienna, 1995.

9. K. Kersting and L. De Raedt. Bayesian logic programs. In *Work in-Progress Reports of the Tenth International Conference on Inductive Logic Programming (ILP2000)*, London, UK, 2000.

10. K. Kersting and L. De Raedt. Bayesian logic programs. Technical Report 151, Institute for Computer Science, University of Freiburg, Freiburg, Germany, April 2001.

11. K. Kersting and L. De Raedt. Towards combining inductive logic programming and bayesian networks. In C. Rouveirol and M. Sebag, editors, *Eleventh International Conference on Inductive Logic Programming (ILP-2001)*, Strasbourg, France, September 2001, number 2157 in LNAI. Springer-Verlag, 2001.

12. J. Lobo, J. Minker, and A. Rajasekar. *Foundations of Disjunctive Logic Programming*. MIT Press, Cambridge, Massachusetts, 1992.

13. S. H. Muggleton. Learning stochastic logic programs. *Electronic Transactions in Artificial Intelligence*, 4(041), 2000.

14. R. T. Ng and V. S. Subrahmanian. Probabilistic logic programming. *Information and Computation*, 101(2):150–201, 1992.

15. L. Ngo and P. Haddaway. Answering queries from context-sensitive probabilistic knowledge bases. *Theoretical Computer Science*, 171(1–2):147–177, 1997.

16. Liem Ngo. Probabilistic disjunctive logic programming. In *Proceedings of the 12th Annual Conference on Uncertainty in Artificial Intelligence (UAI-96)*, pages 397–404, San Francisco, CA, 1996. Morgan Kaufmann Publishers.

17. D. Poole. The Independent Choice Logic for modelling multiple agents under uncertainty. *Artificial Intelligence*, 94(1–2):7–56, 1997.

18. V. Santos Costa, D. Page, M. Qazi, and J. Cussens. Clp($\mathcal{BN}$): Constraint logic programming for probabilistic knowledge. In *Uncertainty in Artificial Intelligence (UAI03)*, 2003.

19. T. Sato. A statistical learning method for logic programs with distribution semantics. In *12th International Conference on Logic Programming (ICLP95)*, pages 715–729, 1995.

20. A. Van Gelder, K. A. Ross, and J. S. Schlipf. The well-founded semantics for general logic programs. *Journal of the ACM*, 38(3):620–650, 1991.

21. J. Vennekens and S. Verbaeten. Logic programs with annotated disjunctions. Technical Report CW386, K. U. Leuven, 2003. http://www.cs.kuleuven.ac.be/~joost/techrep.ps.

22. J. Vennekens, S. Verbaeten, and M. Bruynooghe. Logic programs with annotated disjunctions. In *The 20th International Conference on Logic Programming (ICLP04)*, 2004.

A Simulated Annealing Framework for ILP

Mathieu Serrurier, Henri Prade, and Gilles Richard

IRIT - Université Paul Sabatier
118 route de Narbonne 31062 Toulouse FRANCE
{serrurie,prade,richard}@irit.fr

Abstract. In Inductive Logic Programming (ILP), algorithms which are purely of the *bottom-up* or *top-down* type encounter several problems in practice. Since a majority of them are greedy ones, these algorithms find clauses in local optima, according to the "quality" measure used for evaluating the results. Moreover, when learning clauses one by one, induced clauses become less interesting to cover few remaining examples. In this paper, we propose a simulated annealing framework to overcome these problems. Using a refinement operator, we define neighborhood relations on clauses and on hypotheses (i.e. sets of clauses). With these relations and appropriate quality measures, we show how to induce clauses (in a coverage approach), or to induce hypotheses directly by using simulated annealing algorithms. We discuss the necessary conditions on the refinement operators and the evaluation measures in order to increase the algorithm's effectivity. Implementations are described and experimentation results are presented.

1 Introduction

One of the main difficulties in ILP is to manage the size of the hypothesis space. For instance, as soon as we allow function symbols in the target clauses, the hypothesis space becomes infinite, even if we restrict ourselves to the induction of one clause with a maximum of l literals. In case of restriction to Horn clauses without function symbol, the hypothesis space still grows up exponentially with l. As a consequence, methods performing an exhaustive search are intractable. Most algorithms used in ILP [13,11,14] use deterministic heuristics based on *specialization* (*top-down* algorithms), or *generalization* (*bottom-up* algorithm) of clauses. Some of these algorithms are greedy ones [13,14]. For instance, the FOIL algorithm adds the best literal (according to a gain function) to a clause at each step of the induction process. It stops when there is no literal which increases the gain function, or when the confidence degree of the current literal is greater than a fixed threshold. But, as pointed out in [15], the separate addition of two different literals to a clause may decrease the gain, although when adding them simultaneously, the gain would be increased. A similar situation (the so-called "plateau problem"), rather frequent with relational databases, is encountered when the addition of a literal does not affect the gain but may be useful for finding "good" clauses (i.e. clauses having high support

R. Camacho, R. King, A. Srinivasan (Eds.): ILP 2004, LNAI 3194, pp. 288–304, 2004.

and confidence degrees). A large number of algorithms use a coverage approach. An hypothesis is obtained by inducing clauses, one by one, until all the examples are covered. Clauses with a large support, which are the most interesting ones, are found first. But when the number of examples to cover becomes small, the new added clauses tend to be marginal (because covering a few examples): then they are not very useful from an induction point of view. Moreover, the coverage approach tends to induce hypotheses with a large number of clauses. An algorithm for inducing hypotheses directly have been developed by Bratko [3], but it suffers from a very high computational complexity.

Meta-heuristics, in particular Genetic Algorithms (GAs), have already been used for solving ILP problems. The first contribution of GAs in ILP was implemented in GA-SMART [6], the individuals are fixed length binary strings encoding formulas. The size of an individual grows with the number of predicates appearing in it. REGAL [5] and DOGMA [8] follow the same principle by extending the representation to handle conjunctions of internally disjunctive predicates. A different kind of contribution of GAs to ILP lies in the propositionalization process [4]. Let us recalled that propositionalization is an effective method for reducing complexity of ILP process : a learning problem expressed in a first order formalism is rewriten with an attribute-value representation. This is done in two steps : in the first one, we have to find an "interesting" pattern and in the second step, we learn relevant constraints for this pattern. A new approach to this second step was proposed by [4], in which a search of variables partition is performed allowing to know which variables are identical. So, given an "interesting" pattern (i.e. a Horn clause where all the variables are distinct), possible propositionalizations of the set of variables are encoded by individuals and are clustered by a GA in order to find the most appropriate one. More recently, Tamaddoni-Nezhad et al. [19] have introduced a framework for the combination of GAs with ILP including a new binary representation for clauses and operators. In [20], they introduce a fast evaluation mechanism of genetic individuals representing clauses and they show how classical operations and evaluations can be done with simple bitwise operations.

A randomized search algorithm have been already developed in [22], but focusing on time efficiency only. Besides, simulated annealing techniques [9] have not yet been used in ILP (the ALEPH system proposes random search techniques based on the Metropolis algorithm, i.e. a special case of simulated annealing with a fixed 'temperature', but there is no available detailed documentation about it at this time), despite their well-known properties. Simulated annealing methods use topological notions (neighborhood and distance) for minimizing (or maximizing) a function. In this paper, we describe a simulated annealing framework for ILP. We describe two non deterministic algorithms that independently use generalization and specialization operations, and we show that they partially overcome the difficulties of greedy methods.

In section 2, we briefly recall the basic notions of simulated annealing and refinement operator. In section 3, starting from the notion of a refinement operator, we propose a definition of neighborhood for Horn clauses and for hypotheses. In section 4, we describe two general forms of algorithms using simulated annealing, one for a coverage approach and one for a straightforward induction of hypotheses. The needed properties of the quality measures and the tuning of the parameters are also discussed. Section 5 presents an implementation of the algorithms and several interesting results on the mutagenesis [1] database are pointed out.

2 Background

2.1 Simulated Annealing

Simulated annealing is a meta-heuristic method developed for optimization problems. The general form of simulated annealing algorithm is as in Alg. 1. This method is inspired from a well-known physical phenomenon, coming from metallurgy. Let us consider a function $F : s \mapsto \Re$ to be minimized, and representing the energy of a statistical mechanical system in a given state s. The probability for the system to go from the state s to the state s' at the temperature T is given by the Boltzman-Gibbs distribution $P(s) = e^{\frac{-(F(s')-F(s))}{kT}}$ where k is the Boltzmann constant (in Alg. 1. the constant k is merged with the parameter T). For high values of T, all states have a high probability to be

---

Alg. 1 Simulated annealing$(V, F, X_0, T_0, T_{min})$

1: $X = X_0$
2: $T = T_0$
3: **while** $T < T_{min}$ **do**
4:    $Y = $ random element in $V(X)$
5:    $dF = F(Y) - F(X)$
6:    **if** $dF > 0$ **then**
7:      $P = e^{-\frac{dF}{T}}$
8:      $A = $ random value in $[0, 1]$
9:      **if** $A < P$ **then**
10:        $X = Y$
11:      **end if**
12:    **else**
13:      $X = Y$
14:    **end if**
15:    decrease the value of T
16: **end while**
17: return X

---

[1] http://web.comlab.ox.ac.uk/oucl/research/areas/machlearn/mutagenesis.html

accepted. On the opposite side, when T is close to zero, only states improving the current minimization of the function will be accepted. The quality of the minima relies on the method used for decreasing temperature. It has been shown that it exists a value of K (depending on the problem) for which a logarithmic schedule of the form $T_t = \frac{K}{log(t)}$ insures the almost sure convergence of the algorithm to the global minimum. Given a minimal temperature T_{min}, the number of steps needed for reaching T_{min} with a logarithmic schedule will grow up exponentially when K decreases. So, for a low value of K, this method may be equivalent to an exhaustive search in the hypotheses space. Therefore, the most used method for scheduling temperature is to use geometric sequences. Given an initial temperature T_0, the temperature at step t of the algorithm is $T_t = r * T_{t-1}$ for $t \geq 1$ and $0 < r < 1$. With this method, we are not sure to find the global minimum, but we can expect to find at least a local one better than the one computed by a greedy algorithm. The values of temperatures T_0, T_{min}, and r are critical and depend on the problem we want to solve. The initial state can be chosen randomly, since a "good" initial state will be "forgotten" at a high temperature.

2.2 Refinement Operator

Stated in the general context of first-order logic, the task of *induction* [12] is to find a non-trivial set of formulas H such that $B \cup H \models E$ given a background theory B and a set of observations E (training set), where E, B and H here denote sets of clauses. A set of formulas is here, as usual, considered as the conjunction of its elements.

Shapiro [16] defines the notion of refinement operator (see [21] for a review) as a function computing a set of *specializations* of a clause. More generally, a *downward* refinement operator computes a set of specializations of a clause, and an *upward* refinement operator computes a set of generalizations of a clause. The formal definition is :

Definition 1. *Given $(G, \geq)$ a quasi-ordered set, a downward refinement operator (resp. upward refinement operator) for this set is a function ρ from G to 2^G, such that $\forall C \in G, \rho(C) \subseteq \{D | C \geq D\}$ (resp. $\forall C \in G, \rho(C) \subseteq \{D | C \leq D\}$) .*

Two standard quasi-orders are used : the *implication* order and the *subsumption* order. In practice, we expect some properties for the refinement operator. The first one is that the set of specializations is *finite* and computable. We also expect that every specialization of a clause to be reachable by a finite number of applications of the refinement operator. Finally, proper specializations of a clause are preferred. These requirements are formally expressed by :

Definition 2. *Given $(G, \geq)$ a quasi-ordered set and ρ a downward refinement operator :*

- *ρ is locally finite if for every $C \in G$, $\rho(C)$ is finite and computable;*
- *ρ is complete if for every $C, D \in G$, with $C > D$, there exists an $E \in \rho^*(C)$ such that $E \equiv D$;*

- ρ *is proper if* $\forall C \in G, \rho(C) \subseteq \{D | C > D\}$;
- ρ *is ideal if it is locally finite, complete, and proper.*

where ρ^* denotes the transitive closure of ρ and $\equiv$ is the equivalence relation associated to $\geq$. It has been proved that there does not exist any *ideal* refinement operator for the *subsumption* and *implication* orders over the set of first-order clauses. However, a lot of ILP algorithms use refinement operators for guiding the learning process, for instance FOIL [13], PROGOL [11], CLAUDIEN [14], despite their incompleteness. As for clauses, we can define refinement operators for hypotheses. We call HYP the set of all possible hypotheses. Quasi-orders on hypotheses can be derived from quasi-orders on clauses. Given a quasi-ordered set of clauses $(G, \geq)$, we can define the quasi-ordered set $(HYP, \geq)$ for hypotheses as follows : for all $H, H' \in HYP$, $H \geq H'$ if and only if $\forall C' \in H'$, $\exists C \in H$ such that $C \geq C'$. Definitions and properties of a refinement operator for hypotheses are similar to the one for clauses.

3 Neighborhood Definition

In order to use a simulated annealing technique for ILP, we need to define a notion of neighborhood for clauses and hypotheses .

3.1 Neighborhood for Clauses

Generally speaking, the neighborhood of a point corresponds to the idea of small variations around it. In the case of ILP, the hypotheses space is discrete. A natural notion of neighborhood of a clause C is made of the set of clauses which are within one step of specialization from C, together with the set of clauses of which C is within one step of specialization, according to the current refinement operator.

Definition 3. *Given a refinement operator ρ (downward or upward) on a quasi-ordered set $(G, \geq)$, the neighborhood V_ρ induced by ρ is a mapping from G to 2^G, defined for every $C \in G$ by :*

$$V_\rho(C) = \{D \in G | D \in \rho(C) \text{ or } C \in \rho(D)\}.$$

Therefore, we can construct a neighborhood from any downward or upward refinement operator. All of the above-mentioned properties of a refinement operator yet apply to the neighborhood.

Definition 4. *Given $(G, \geq)$ a quasi-ordered set and V_ρ a neighborhood :*

- V_ρ *is locally finite if for every $C \in G$, $V_\rho(C)$ is finite and computable;*
- V_ρ *is complete if for every $C, D \in G$, there exists an $E \in V_\rho^*(C)$ such that $E \equiv D$;*
- V_ρ *is proper if $\forall C \in G, C \notin V_\rho(C)$;*

- V_ρ is ideal if it is locally finite, complete, and proper.

Some properties are expected for a practical use of the neighborhood. It is required that the refinement operator be *locally finite*. If it is not the case, some elements of the neighborhood may be not computable and thus, not reachable by the algorithm. Moreover, the neighborhood of a clause may be an infinite set, making the choice for a random neighbor more tricky. Note that, even if ρ is locally finite, we should also require that ρ be such that $\{D|C \in \rho(D)\}$ is finite and computable.

The *properness* property is of no importance in the computation process that we shall propose. This differs from the case of greedy algorithms where a no *non-proper* operator can generate an infinite loop if the best choice in the refinement set is the same clause as the current one. In simulated annealing, if the current clause itself is chosen again by a random choice, this step of the process will have no effect. Fortunately, since the choices are randomized, this cannot happen repeatedly.

Another important property of the neighborhood for ensuring effectivity, is that, given a clause C, any clause D in the hypotheses space can be reachable from C in a finite number of applications of the neighborhood definition, i.e. the neighborhood is *complete*. This property allows the simulated annealing algorithm to potentially explore the whole hypotheses space. If the refinement operator is *complete* and $(G, \geq)$ has a top element $\top$ (for a downward refinement operator), the completeness of the neighborhood process follows immediately. *Complete* refinement operators are not so usual and require vast amounts of computation (e.g. the problem is NP hard for the case of the implication order on free-function Horn clauses). This is why we introduce the following definition [1] :

Definition 5. *Given* $(G, \geq)$ *a quasi-ordered set with a top element and ρ a downward refinement operator, ρ is weakly complete if and only if :*

$$\forall D \in G, D \in \rho^*(\top)$$

A *weakly complete* refinement operator allows us to reach all clauses from $\top$ by a finite repeated application of ρ. Obviously, this definition is weaker than the usual definition of completeness :

Proposition 1. *Given a weakly complete refinement operator ρ (downward or upward) on a quasi-ordered set $(G, \geq)$, V_ρ is complete and we have :*

$$\forall C, D \in G, D \in V_\rho^*(C).$$

Proof : Since ρ is weakly complete, $D \in \rho^*(\top)$ and $C \in \rho^*(\top)$. Then $\top \in V_\rho^*(C)$, then $D \in V_\rho^*(V_\rho^*(C)) = V_\rho^*(C)$ ∎.

Proposition 2. *Given a proper refinement operator ρ (downward or upward) on a quasi-ordered set $(G, \geq)$, V_ρ is proper.*

Proof : since ρ is *proper,* $\not\exists D \in \rho(C)$ such that $C \equiv D$ and $\not\exists D, C \in \rho(D)$ such that $C \equiv D$. Then $\not\exists D \in V_\rho(C)$ such that $C \equiv D$ ∎.

This result shows that a *weakly complete* refinement operator is sufficient for defining a *complete* neighborhood . Finally, the fact that there is no *ideal* refinement operator is not a drawback for our method, since ρ must only be *weakly complete, locally finite* and such that V_ρ is *locally finite* as well.

3.2   Neighborhood for Hypotheses

Neighborhood for hypotheses can also be derived from refinement operators over hypotheses. Refinement operators over hypotheses can be described from refinement operators over clauses in the spirit of [3,2] as follows :

Definition 6. *Given an hypothesis* $H = \{C_1, ..., C_n\}$ *(a set of n clauses), a refinement operator* ρ *(downward or upward) on clauses on a quasi-ordered set* $(G, \geq)$, *the refinement operator for hypothesis on a quasi-ordered set* $(HYP, \geq)$ ρ_hyp *is defined such as*

$$\rho\_hyp(H) = \{H - \{C_i\} \cup \{D\} | C_i \in H, D \in \rho(C_i)\}.$$

The refinement of an hypothesis H is the set of hypotheses for which we have changed a close C into one of its refinement. Then we can define a notion of neighborhood :

Definition 7. *Given an hypothesis* $H = \{C_1, ..., C_n\}$ *(a set of n clauses), a refinement operator for hypothesis* ρ_hyp *(downward or upward) on a quasi-ordered set* $(HYP, \geq)$, *the neighborhood for hypothesis* V_{ρ_hyp} *is defined as :*

$$V_{\rho\_hyp}(H) = \{H' | H' \in \rho\_hyp(H)\} \cup \{H' | H \in \rho\_hyp(H')\}.$$

This kind of neighborhood can be used for refining hypotheses that are found by a coverage algorithm in order to improve results. But, since we cannot add or remove clauses from the hypothesis, this kind of operators cannot be used for inducing an hypothesis in a straighforward manner from any starting hypothesis. Thus we extend this definition by adding the possibility to add or remove a clause in the hypothesis.

Definition 8. *Given an hypothesis* $H = \{C_1, ..., C_n\}$ *(a set of n clauses),* ρ *a refinement operator on clauses on* $(G, \geq)$ *a quasi-ordered set, the neighborhood operator extended for hypotheses for* ρ *on a quasi-ordered set* $(HYP, \geq)$ *is*

$$V_{\rho\_hyp\_ext}(H) = V_{\rho\_hyp}(H) \cup \{H - C_i | C_i \in H\} \cup \{H \cup \top\}$$

where $\top$ *is a top element for* $(G, \geq)$.

Thus, regardless of the kind of operators used (downward or upward), the neighborhood of an hypothesis H is obtained by changing a clause C in H into another clause in the neighborhood of C, or by adding the most general clause in H, or by removing a clause in H.

Proposition 3. *Given a weakly complete refinement operator ρ (downward or upward) on a quasi-ordered set $(G, \geq)$, $V_{\rho\_hyp\_ext}$ is a complete refinement operator for hypothesis and we have :*

$$\forall H, H' \in HYP, H' \in V_\rho^*(H).$$

Proof : Since we can remove a clause in H, there is an hypothesis $H'' \in V_\rho^*(H)$ such that H'' and H' contain the same number of clauses. According to Proposition 1, V_ρ is complete, so for all clauses $C' \in H'$, $\exists C''' \in H''$ such that $C' \in V_\rho^*(C'')$. Then $H' \in V_\rho^*(H'')$ and so $H' \in V_\rho^*(H)$ ∎.

Thus, if the refinement operator on clauses is *weakly complete*, all possible hypotheses with a finite set of clauses can be reached from another hypothesis with a finite application of the neighborhood. As in the previous case, using a *locally finite* refinement operator for clauses makes that $V_{\rho\_hyp\_ext}$ is *locally finite* as well.

4 Simulated Annealing Framework for ILP

4.1 General Algorithm

We now present two forms of algorithms using simulated annealing in ILP. The first one is a simulated version of a greedy algorithm (Alg. 2.) in a coverage approach. Given ρ, a refinement operator over clauses, we look for clauses that are good local optima of the quality measure by using simulated annealing. Rule are incrementally induced, until all examples are covered.

Alg. 2 SAILP$(B, E, \rho, F, T_0, T_{min})$

1: **while** $E \neq \emptyset$ **do**
2:   choose X a random clause
3:   Y=Simulated annealing$(V_\rho, F, X, T_0, T_{min})$
4:   **if** $H \cup Y$ has a better accuracy than H **then**
5:     $E = E/\{$ example covered by Y $\}$
6:     $H = H \cup Y$
7:   **else**
8:     break
9:   **end if**
10: **end while**
11: return H

Generalizations or specializations of a clause which do not change the evaluation measure are automatically accepted, and those decreasing the function can be accepted with a probability depending on the temperature. Thus, this algorithm can overcome the "plateau problem".

Simulated annealing can be used also in ILP for inducing hypotheses directly. In that case, we use the notion of neighborhood and quality measure over hypotheses in simulated annealing, leading to the second algorithm (Alg 3.).

Alg. 3 SAHILP$(B, E, \rho, F, T_0, T_{min})$

1: choose H a random hypothesis
2: H'=Simulated annealing$(V_{\rho\_hyp\_ext}, F, X, T_0, T_{min})$
3: return H'

As we see, the general algorithm is very simple and the whole set of examples is taken into account in each step. It allows us to overcome the problems of the coverage approach and to have hypotheses with less but more interesting clauses. As previously, the possibility to accept a worse hypothesis with respect to the quality measure allows us to overcome the "plateau problem" too. Finally, a *weakly complete*, *locally finite* refinement operator and an evaluating measure are sufficient for using our scheme in an ILP context. These algorithms are neither *top down* or *bottom up* since they use specialization and generalization independently. They are non-deterministic optimization algorithm, so they are not necessarily *correct* and *complete*.

4.2 Choosing a Quality Measure and Tuning Parameters

According to the previous algorithms, the accuracy is strongly related to the choice of the quality measure we want to maximize. This measure must favor the rules having a large support and confidence degrees because they have the most powerful predictive accuracy. With *top-down* algorithms, the measure used for selecting one clause among a set of refinements of a given clause C, usually relies on C and assumes that, at each specialization step, the number of examples covered by the clause decreases. With the previous definition of a neighborhood, the algorithm will indifferently use generalization or specialization at each step, so that we have no information on the evolution of the support (number of examples covered) and confidence degrees of the rule. So, we need to use an absolute measure (i.e. a measure which does not depend on the algorithm process). The quality measure on hypotheses must follow the empirical risk minimization principle i.e. it must favor hypotheses with a good accuracy on the sample set. Moreover, some other properties (having hypotheses with few clauses, with short clauses, etc..) may be interesting. Generally, having a quality measure bounded in $[-1, 1]$ allows an easier tuning of the parameters involved in the simulated annealing process as discussed below.

Nevertheless, the optimal tuning of the parameters for a simulated annealing algorithm is a hard problem. As pointed out in [17], the difficulty for validating a learning algorithm is related to the complexity of using it in terms of parameters to be tuned. The parameters to be tuned are, the minimum temperature, the starting temperature, the starting element and the ratio r of the geometric sequence describing the temperature evolution. A too high starting temperature has no incidence on the final result. On the contrary, a too small starting temperature will prevent the acceptation of "bad" results, and, thus, tends to make the algorithm equivalent to greedy ones. A too small minimal temperature will increase the execution time without providing better results. In fact, from some values of T, the algorithm converges to an optimum, global or local, and thus the result will not change. A too high minimal temperature tends to make the algorithm equivalent to a random choice procedure. A good experimental value for the starting temperature corresponds to a temperature where the probability to accept a bad element is equal to $\frac{1}{2}$. In the case of a measure bounded by $[-1, 1]$, the distance between two values cannot be less than 2 and a variation of 0.5 is considered as a high variation. So, the starting temperature is fixed to $-\frac{1}{\ln(\frac{1}{2})} = 0.8$ (in Alg. 1, the constant k is merged with T) in order to have a starting probability of $\frac{1}{2}$ to accept a new element which provides a diminution of 0.5 of the value of the measure. The minimum temperature is fixed at 0.0001 because variations of measure of this size are not very meaningful and this insures convergence. The choice of the starting clause or hypothesis does not change the result of the algorithm and can be a random clause or hypothesis as well as the most general clause or the empty hypothesis. In fact, after few iterations, the current element will be completely different from the starting one and since the probability of choosing a worse element is high, we cannot predict its form. The ratio of the geometric sequence will influence the quality of the result. The closer to 1 the ratio, the more effective (and the longer in terms of computational time) the algorithm. The relation between the quality of the result and the execution time is strongly related to the ratio r. So, it can be user-defined without making questionable the validation of the algorithms.

5 Testing the Algorithms

5.1 A Possible Implementation

Here, we present an implementation for each of our algorithms (SAILP and SAHILP). There exist many refinement operators and most of them are *locally finite* and *weakly complete*. For the sake of effectivity, we use an operator allowing easy computation of the neighborhood. So we use :

Definition 9. *FOIL refinement operator ρ_{FOIL}. Given a Horn clause C, $\rho_{FOIL}(C)$ is obtained by all the possible additions of a literal in the condition part of C.*

The FOIL refinement operator is downward and based on the implication order. It is *locally finite*, *weakly complete* and *proper* for Horn clauses without function symbol.

Proposition 4. $V_{\rho_{FOIL}}$ *is an ideal neighborhood for Horn clauses without function symbol under implication order.*

Proof : Without function symbol, up to the equivalence between variable names renaming, and taking into account only terms appearing in the domain described by B and E, the number of possible literals is finite and then ρ_{FOIL} is *locally finite*. Based on ρ_{FOIL}, the neightborhood of a Horn clause C is the set of Horn clauses obtained by adding or removing a literal in the condition part of C. Since we only consider Horn clauses with a finite number of literals, $V_{\rho_{FOIL}}$ is *locally finite* too. From the hypotheses space described by B and E, all clauses can be reached from $\top$ by a finite number of applications of ρ_{FOIL} by adding one of the missing literals at each step. ρ_{FOIL} is then *weakly complete* and according to Proposition 1, $V_{\rho_{FOIL}}$ is *complete*. It is obvious that ρ_{FOIL} is *proper*, so according to Proposition 2, $V_{\rho_{FOIL}}$ is *proper* too ∎.

The fact that the neighborhood based on FOIL refinement operator is *ideal* makes it theoretically well adapted to the simulated annealing method. Moreover, the random choice of a Horn clause in the neighborhood of another clause is very easy from a computation point of view.

There are many measures on clauses. As pointed out in the previous section, we need a measure which does not depend on the inductive process. In [10], Lavrac, Flach and Zupan propose a measure for Horn clauses which, according to experimental results, is maximal for the clauses that are preferred by experts. It is given by :

Definition 10. *Weighted relative accuracy.*

$$WRAcc(A \to B) = p(A) * (P(B|A)) - p(B))$$

where probabilities on first-order clauses can be computed by using domain probabilities [7] on the interpretation defined by B and E. This measure is well-suited for our SAILP algorithm because it does not depend on the process and the refinement operator which is chosen, the measure is bounded in the $[-1, 1]$ interval. Moreover, the clauses maximizing this measure are those ones having high support and confidence degrees.

So, having adequate refinement operator, measure and clause, we can use them in our SAILP algorithm. The starting rule is obtained by adding a random number of literals randomly chosen in the condition part of the most general clause. Numerical attributes are handled by using an extra-predicate indicating if a variable belongs to a given interval. In the neighborhood of a clause C containing such predicates, we add to the one described by the refinement operator, the clauses that differ from C only by changing the interval described into the concerned predicate by increasing it (generalization) or decreasing it (specialization).

For the SAHILP algorithm, we use the neighborhood on hypotheses described by the FOIL refinement operator. As proved by Propositions 2 and 4, this neighborhood operator is *complete*. We use the following measure, which is a normalized version of the one presented in [2] :

$$F(H) = \frac{pos(H) - neg(H) - |H|}{N}$$

where $pos(H)$ is the number of examples which are well classified, $neg(H)$ is the number of examples which are wrongly classified, N is the total number of examples and $|H|$ is the number of clauses in H. This measure will favor hypotheses with high accuracy and few clauses. At last, we consider the FOILWracc algorithm, a greedy algorithm using the coverage approach with the FOIL refinement operator and the WRAcc measure to be maximized.

5.2 Experiments

Our algorithms are written in Java and tests have been made on a 1,2 GHz personal computer. The results for the machine PROGOL are issued from [18] (we would need more recent results to get a more interesting comparison). In a first time, we will illustrate the efficectivity of the simulated annealing by comparing the capacity for finding rules which are good local optima for the WRAcc function of the SAILP and FOILwracc algorithms. We use the database named "document understanding" from UCI[2] that represents a classical problem of relational learning. It describes components of a document. There are 35 propositional attributes and 10 relational attributes to describe the relative places of components in the documents. We are interested in three different concepts which can be learnt in this database (Date, Rif and Sender). For each hypothesis found by the algorithms, we compare the average and the maximum values of the WRAcc for all clauses in the hypotheses. Results are presented in the table 1. SAILP1 and SAILP2 correspond to versions of SAILP, which are respectively speed oriented, with a ratio r equal to 0.995 and SAILP, ad which are quality oriented with a ratio r equal to 0.997. Since SAILP is a non-deterministic algorithm, the values shown below correspond to the average of the obtained results. Since we are mainly interested in the value of the WRAcc, the accuracy is just computed on the training set.

We see that SAILP is clearly the most effective algorithm. The extracted hypotheses have a better accuracy. Moreover, rules with high value of coverage and WRAcc are found only with SAILP. For effectively learning the three concepts, we need to use relational predicates. In this case, adding a relational predicate to the rules does not increase WRAcc, but the WRAcc grows up

---

[2] http://www.ics.uci.edu/ mlearn/MLRepository.html

Table 1. Comparison of results in terms of WRAcc on the document understanding database

Base: Document understanding Concept: Date					
machine	acc.	nbr rules	avg. WRAcc	max WRAcc	time
FOILwracc	0.80	5	0.14	0.52	1 s
SAILP1	0.93	3	0.29	0.72	11 s
SAILP2	1	3	0.30	0.75	19 s

Base: Document understanding Concept: Rif					
machine	acc.	nbr rules	avg. WRAcc	max WRAcc	time
FOILwracc	0.84	2	0.37	0.70	1 s
SAILP1	0.91	2	0.41	0.77	6 s
SAILP2	0.91	2	0.41	0.77	16 s

Base: Document understanding Concept: Sender					
machine	acc.	nbr rules	avg. WRAcc	max WRAcc	time
FOILwracc	0.92	4	0.22	0.67	1 s
SAILP1	1	2	0.45	0.87	6 s
SAILP2	1	2	0.46	0.88	15 s

rapidly by involving further information on new components by means of the relational predicates. As pointed out in the introduction, these rules are hard to find with greedy algorithms. Note that the quality of the improvement depends on the time passed in the induction of a rule (i.e. the ratio of the geometric sequence parameter). In some cases, taking more time for the induction does not improve the result, so it seems that the SAILP algorithm converges to an optimum which may be a global optimum.

In order to test the global effectivity of the algorithms, we test our approach on the database "mutagenesis" which is a standard benchmark for ILP. This database describes molecules. We use only the background knowledge corresponding to the predicate $atom$, $bond$, $lumo$, $logp$ and $I_{1,a}$, also name $B2$ in [18]. The target concept is the activity level of a molecule.

Figure 1 reports the evolution of the measure F with the temperature during the induction of an hypothesis by SAHILP. As can be seen, at the beginning, the value of F changes very quickly due to the high temperature. The measure F increases to a local optimum and, since poorer results are accepted, it decreases rapidly. Then, the temperature is such that only small decreases of the measure F are allowed. So, the measure F increases more regularly. Sometimes, we observe that a small decrease is needed to avoid being trapped in local maxima. Finally, temperature becomes too low for accepting a decrease of measure F and we converge to a local maximum. We can observe the same kinds of results with SAILP and the WRAcc for the induction of a clause (see fig. 2).

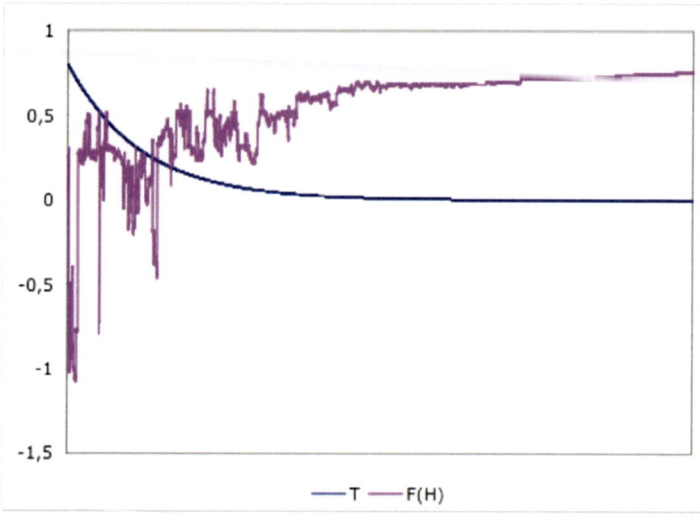

Fig. 1. Evolution of F(H) with the temperature in the induction of one hypothesis by SAHILP in the mutagenesis database.

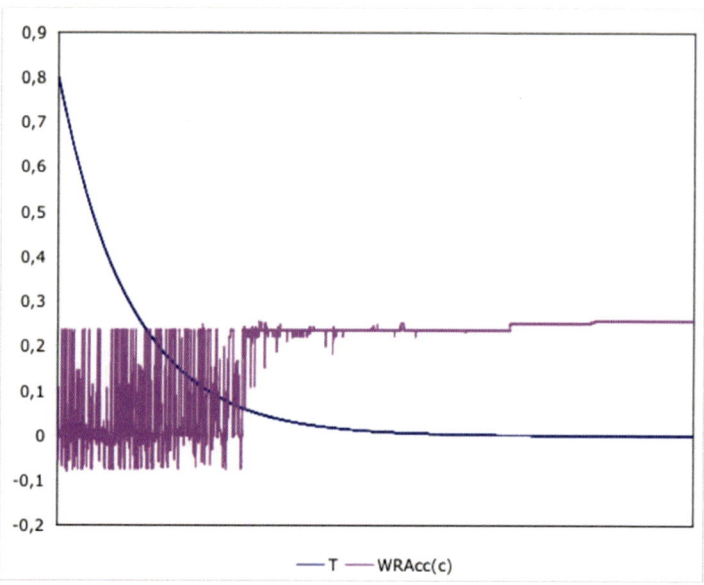

Fig. 2. Evolution of WRAcc with the temperature in the induction of one rule by SAILP in the mutagenesis database.

Table 2. Comparison of results on mutagenesis database

Alg.	accuracy	number of clauses	time (seconds)
FOILwracc	0.83[0.07]	12	4
PROGOL	0.86 [0.06]	11	4974
SAILP1	0.86 [0.09]	7	66
SAILP2	0.87[0.08]	9	140
SAHILP1	0.89[0.05]	3	97
SAHILP2	0.89[0.05]	3	167

In the table 2, we compare the algorithm with a 10-fold cross-validation. SAHILP1 and SAHILP2 correspond respectively to SAHILP, which is speed oriented, with a ratio r equal to 0.9995 and SAHILP, which is quality oriented with a ratio equal to 0.9998. Values between brackets correspond to standard deviations. Values for number of clauses are rounded to the closest integer. Results in terms of accuracy are globally better than the one of the greedy methods. The best results are obtained by the SAHILP algorithm. As expected, it finds less rules than the other algorithms and has the best accuracy. This is due to the fact that maximizing the function F insures that the hypothesis has a good accuracy and no redundancy. It confirms, according to the Occam principle, that the simpler the hypothesis, the more accurate it is. The fact that the results for SAHILP1 and SAHILP2 are identical on accuracy (although values of F for SAHILP2 are slightly greater than the one for SAHILP1) can be explained by the fact that, at a certain level, increasing measure F on training examples does not increase accuracy on the test examples. The FOILwracc is the most efficient in terms of execution speed. Since time measure for PROGOL has not be made in the same experimentation conditions, we cannot compare it with our algorithm but we can remark that the algorithms using simulated annealing keep acceptable execution time.

The following hypothesis have been found by the SAHILP algorithm on the whole mutagenesis dataset :

```
lumo(A,B), 1.742 ≤ B ≤ 3.768,
logp(A,C), 0.53 ≤ C ≤ 7.84 ->active(A)

lumo(A,B), 0.923 ≤ B ≤ 3.768,atom(A,C,D,E,F), 0.367 ≤ F ≤ 0.638,
ind1(A,1.0) -> active(A)

lumo(A,B), 1.293 ≤ B ≤ 1.34 -> active(A)
```

We notice that clauses are relatively simple but they show a very good ability for managing numerical attributes and particularly conjunction of numerical constraint for which "plateau problem" is very common. This shows that using random specialization or generalization of a numerical constraint may give good results. The hypothesis induced does not use relational predicates because numerical constraint are sufficient for maximizing the function F. Results on the document understanding database show that the algorithms manage very well the relational predicates too. The SAHILP algorithm finds shorter hypotheses for at least two reasons. First, the maximized function F favors hypothesis with few clauses and high accuracy. Thus, the clauses covering too few examples will not appear in the hypothesis and the algorithm tends to find non redundant clauses covering a large amount of examples. Secondly, at each step of the algorithm, all the examples are taken into account. This is a main difference with coverage algorithm where examples covered with the current hypothesis are removed.

6 Concluding Remarks and Further Works

In this paper, we propose a general framework for introducing simulated annealing methods in ILP. As pointed out by our experimental results, the method is really interesting from an accuracy viewpoint. We show that we can use simulated annealing for improving greedy algorithms. Moreover, our method seems to be an effective scheme, not only for overcoming the "plateau problem", but also for avoiding the coverage approach. The notions of neighborhood, introduced in this paper, allow us to explore the hypothesis space by using both generalization and specialization. Moreover, *ideal* neighborhood for clauses and hypotheses can be defined with a non complete refinement operator.

We think our algorithm could be improved in different ways :
- The difficulties with using neighborhood is that computation of the inverse image of a given refinement can be very hard in practice. It could be interesting to define neighborhood with two distinct operators, one for the specialization and one for the induction.
- The algorithm tends to often pass in the same places. We could force the probabilities of choosing a new place in the neighborhood to take into account previously visited places.
- Since the effectivity of the method crucially relies on the quality of the used measure, it should be interesting to test new measures, especially measures on hypotheses, which are more related to the accuracy on real data.

References

1. L. Badea. Refinement operator can be (weakly) perfect. In S. Dzeroski and editors P. Flach, editors, *Proc. of the 9 th International Conference of Inductive Logic Programming, ILP 1999*, number 1634 in LNAI, pages 21–32. Springer, 1999.
2. L. Badea. A refinement operator for theories. In C. Rouveirol and M. Sebag, editors, *Proceedings of the 11 th International Conference of Inductive Logic Programming, ILP 2001*, pages 1–14. Springer, 2001.
3. I. Bratko. Refining complete hyphotesys in ilp. In S. Dzeroski and editors P. Flach, editors, *Proc. of the 9 th International Conference of Inductive Logic Programming, ILP 1999*, number 1634 in LNAI, pages 44–55. Springer, 1999.
4. A. Braund and C. Vrain. A genetic algorithm for propositionalization. In C. Rouveirol and M. Sebag, editors, *Proceedings of the 11 th International Conference of Inductive Logic Programming, ILP 2001*, pages 27–40. Springer, 2001.

5. A. Giordana and F. Neri. Search-intensive concept induction. *Evolutionary computation*, 3(4):375–416, 1995.

6. A. Giordana and C. Sale. Learning Structured Concepts Using Genetic Algorithms. In D. Sleeman and P. Edwards, editors, *the 9th International Workshop on Machine Learning*. Morgan Kaufmann, 1992.

7. J. Halpern. An analysis of first-order logics of probability. *Artificial Intelligence*, 46:310–355, 1990.

8. J. Hekanaho. DOGMA : A GA-Based relational Learning. In *ILP98*, pages 205–214. Springer, 1998.

9. S. Kirkpatrick, C. D. Gelatt, and M. P. Vecchi. Optimization by simulated annealing. *Science*, 220:671–680, 1983.

10. N. Lavrac, P. Flach, and B. Zupan. Rule evaluation measures : a unifying view. In S. Dzeroski and editors P. Flach, editors, *Proc. of the 9 th International Conference of Inductive Logic Programming, ILP 1999*, number 1634 in LNAI, pages 174–185. Springer, 1999.

11. S.H. Muggleton. Inverse entailment and Progol. *New Generation Computing*, 13:245–286, 1995.

12. S.-H. Nienhuys-Cheng and R. de Wolf. *Foundations of Inductive Logic Programming*. Number 1228 in LNAI. Springer, 1997.

13. J. R. Quinlan. Learning logical definitions from relations. *Machine Learning*, 5:239–266, 1990.

14. L. De Raedt and M. Bruynooghe. A theory of clausal discovery. In R. Bajcsy, editor, *Proceedings of the 13th International Joint Conference on Artificial Intelligence (IJCAI-93)*, pages 1058–1063. Morgan Kaufmann, 1993.

15. B.L. Richards and R.J. Mooney. Learning relations by pathfinding. In *Proceedings of the AAAI conference, AAAI 1992*, pages 50–55, 1992.

16. E. Y. Shapiro. Inductive inference from facts. Research report 193, Yale university, 1981. Reprinted in *computational research*. J-L. Lassez and G. Plopkin, editors. MIT Press, MA, 1991.

17. T. Sheffer and R. Herbrich. Unbiased learning assessments of learning algorithms. In *Proc of the 15th International Joint Conference on Artificial Intelligence (IJCAI-97)*, pages 698–803, 1997.

18. A. Srinivasan, R. King, and S. Muggleton. The role of background knowledge : using a problem from chemistry to examine the performance of an ilp program. Technical Report PRG-TR-08-99, Oxford university Computing Laboratory, Oxford, 1999.

19. A. Tamaddoni-Nezhad and S.H. Muggleton. Searching the subsumption lattice by a genetic algorithm. In J. Cussens and A. Frish, editors, *Proceedings of the 10 th International Conference of Inductive Logic Programming, ILP 2000*, pages 243–252. Springer, 2000.

20. A. Tamaddoni-Nezhad and S.H. Muggleton. A genetic approach to ilp. In S. Matwin and C. Sammut, editors, *Proceedings of the 12 th International Conference of Inductive Logic Programming, ILP 2002*, pages 285–300. Springer, 2002.

21. P. R. J. van der Laag. *An Analysis of Refinement Operator in Inductive Logic Programming*. Ph.d. thesis, Erasmus University Rotterdam, 1995.

22. F. Zelezny, A. Srinivasan, and D. Page. Lattice-search runtime distributions may be heavy-tailed. In S. Matwin and C. Sammut, editors, *Proceedings of the 12 th International Conference of Inductive Logic Programming, ILP 2002*, pages 333–345. Springer, 2002.

Modelling Inhibition in Metabolic Pathways Through Abduction and Induction

Alireza Tamaddoni-Nezhad[1], Antonis Kakas[2],
Stephen Muggleton[1], and Florencio Pazos[3]

[1] Department of Computing,Imperial College London
180 Queen's Gate, London SW7 2BZ, UK
{atn,shm}@doc.ic.ac.uk
[2] Dept. of Computer Science, University of Cyprus
antonis@ucy.ac.cy
[3] Dept. of Biological Sciences, Imperial College London
f.pazos@imperial.ac.uk

Abstract. In this paper, we study how a logical form of scientific modelling that integrates together abduction and induction can be used to understand the functional class of unknown enzymes or inhibitors. We show how we can model, within Abductive Logic Programming (ALP), inhibition in metabolic pathways and use abduction to generate facts about inhibition of enzymes by a particular toxin (e.g. Hydrazine) given the underlying metabolic pathway and observations about the concentration of metabolites. These ground facts, together with biochemical background information, can then be generalised by ILP to generate rules about the inhibition by Hydrazine thus enriching further our model. In particular, using Progol 5.0 where the processes of abduction and inductive generalization are integrated enables us to learn such general rules. Experimental results on modelling in this way the effect of Hydrazine in a real metabolic pathway are presented.

1 Introduction

The combination of abduction and induction has recently been explored from a number of angles [5]. Moreover, theoretical issues related to completeness of this form of reasoning have also been discussed by various authors [33,13,11]. Some efficient implemented systems have been developed for combining abduction and induction [19] and others have recently been proposed [23]. There have also recently been demonstrations of the application of abduction/induction systems in the area of Systems Biology [35,36,18] though in these cases the generated hypotheses were ground. The authors know of no published work to date which provides a real-world demonstration and assessment of abduction/induction in which hypotheses are non-ground rules, though this is arguably the more interesting case. The present paper provides such a study.

The research reported in this paper is being conducted as part of the MetaLog project [32], which aims to build causal models of the actions of toxins from

R. Camacho, R. King, A. Srinivasan (Eds.): ILP 2004, LNAI 3194, pp. 305–322, 2004.

empirical data in the form of Nuclear Magnetic Resonance (NMR) data, together with information on networks of known metabolic reactions from the KEGG database [30]. The NMR spectra provide information concerning the flux of metabolite concentrations before, during and after administration of a toxin.

In our case, examples extracted from the NMR data consist of metabolite concentrations (up-down regulation patterns extracted from NMR spectra of urine from rats dosed with the toxin hydrazine). Background knowledge (from KEGG) consists of known metabolic networks and enzymes known to be inhibited by hydrazine. This background knowledge, which represents the present state of understanding, is incomplete. In order to overcome this incompleteness hypotheses are entertained which consist of a mixture of specific inhibitions of enzymes (ground facts) together with general rules which predict classes of enzymes likely to be inhibited by hydrazine (non-ground). Hypotheses about inhibition are built using Progol5.0 [19] and predictive accuracy is assessed for both the ground and the non-ground cases. It is shown that even with the restriction to ground hypotheses, predictive accuracy increases with the number of training examples and in all cases exceeds the default (majority class). Experimental results suggest that when non-ground hypotheses are allowed the predictive accuracy increases.

The paper is organised as follows. Chapter 2 introduces the biological problem. Background to logical modelling of scientific theories using abduction and induction is given in Chapter 3. The experiments of learning ground and non-ground hypotheses are then described in Chapter 4. Lastly, Chapter 5 concludes the paper.

2 Inhibition in Metabolic Pathways

The processes which sustain living systems are based on chemical (biochemical) reactions. These reactions provide the requirements of mass and energy for the cellular processes to take place . The complex set of interconnected reactions taking place in a given organism constitute its *metabolic network* [14,22,2].

Most biochemical reactions would never occur spontaneously. They require the intervention of chemical agents called catalysers. Catalysers of biochemical reactions - enzymes - are proteins tuned by millions of years of evolution to catalyse reactions with high efficiency and specificity. One additional role of enzymes in biochemical reactions is that they add "control points" to the metabolic network since the absence or presence of the enzyme and its concentration (both controlled mainly by the transcription of the corresponding gene) determine whether the corresponding reaction takes place or not and to which extent.

The assembly of full metabolic networks, made possible by data accumulated through years of research, is now stored and organized on metabolic databases and allows their study from a network perspective [21,1]. Even with the help of this new Systems Biology approach to metabolism, we are still far apart from understanding many of its properties. One of the less understood phenomena, specially from a network perspective, is *inhibition*. Some chemical compounds

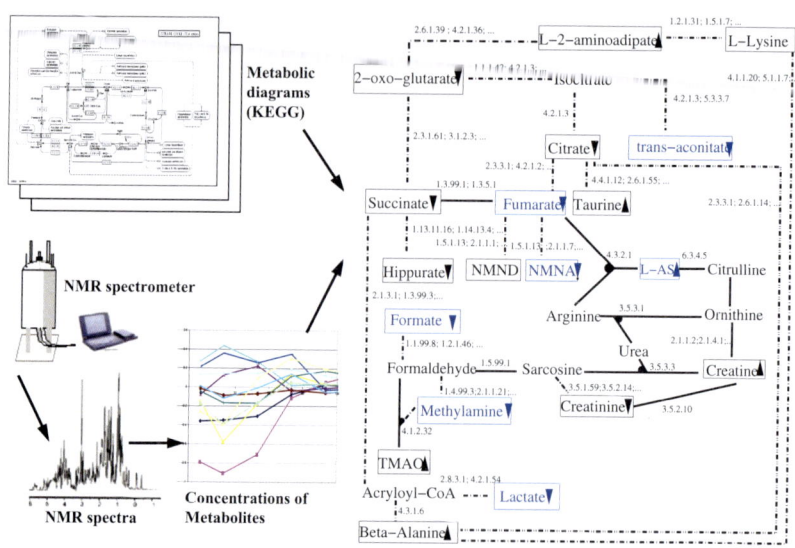

Fig. 1. A metabolic sub-network involving metabolites affected by hydrazine. Information on up/down changes in metabolite concentrations after hydrazine treatment is obtained from NMR spectra. This information is combined with KEGG metabolic diagrams, which contain information on the chemical reactions and associated enzymes.

can affect enzymes impeding them to carry out their functions, and hence affecting the normal flux in the metabolic network, which is in turn reflected in the accumulation or depletion of certain metabolites.

Inhibition is very important from the therapeutic point of view since many substances designed to be used as drugs against some diseases can eventually have an inhibitory side effect on other enzymes. Any system able to predict the inhibitory effect of substances on the metabolic network would be very useful in assessing the potential harmful side-effects of drugs.

In this work we use experimental data on the accumulation and depletion of metabolites to model the inhibitory effect of hydrazine (NH_2-NH_2) in the metabolic network of rats. Figure 1 shows the metabolic pathways sub-network of interest also indicating with "up" and "down" arrows, the observed effects of the hydrazine on the concentration of some of the metabolites involved.

This sub-network was manually built from the information contained in the KEGG metabolic database [30]. Starting from the set of chemical compounds for which there is information on up/down regulation after hydrazine treatment coming from the Nuclear Magnetic Resonance (NMR) experiments, we tried to construct the minimal network representing the biochemical links among them by taking the minimum pathway between each pair of compounds and collapsing all those pathways together through the shared chemical compounds. When there is more than one pathway of similar length (alternative pathways) all of them are included. Pathways involving "promiscuous" compounds (compounds involved in many chemical reactions) are excluded. KEGG contains a static representation of the metabolic network (reactions connecting metabolites). NMR data provides information on the concentrations of metabolites and their changes with time. These data represent the variation of the concentration of a number of chemical compounds during a period of time after hydrazine injection. The effect of hydrazine on the concentrations of chemical compounds is coded in a binary way. Only up/down changes (increasing/decreasing) in compound concentrations immediately after hydrazine injection are incorporated in the model. Quantitative information on absolute or relative concentrations, or fold changes are not used in the present model.

In this sub-network the relation between two compounds (edges in the network) can comprise a single chemical reaction (solid lines) or a linear pathway (dotted lines) of chemical reactions in the cases where the pathway between those compounds is composed by more than one reaction but not involving other compounds in the network (branching points). The directionality of the chemical reactions is not considered in this representation and in fact it is left deliberately open. Although metabolic reactions flow in a certain direction under normal conditions, this may not be the case in "unusual" conditions like the one we are modelling here (inhibition). Inhibition of a given reaction causes the substrates to accumulate what may cause an upstream enzyme to start working backwards in order to maintain its own substrate/product equilibrium.

The "one to many" relations (chemical reactions with more than one substrate or product) are indicated with a circle. The enzymes associated with the relations (single chemical reactions or linear pathways) are shown as a single enzyme or a list of enzymes.

3   Logical Modelling of Scientific Theories

Modelling a scientific domain is a continuous process of observing the phenomena, understanding these according to a currently chosen model and using this understanding, of an otherwise disperse collection of observations, to improve the current general model of the domain. In this process of development of a scientific model one starts with a relatively simple model which gets further improved and expanded as the process is iterated over. Any model of the phenomena at any stage of its development can be *incomplete* in its description. New information given to us by observations, O, can be used to complete this description. As proposed in [4,5], a logical approach to scientific modelling can then be set up by employing together the two *synthetic* forms of reasoning of *abduction* and *induction* in the process of assimilating the new information in the observations. Given the current model described by a theory, T, and the observations O both abduction and induction synthesize new knowledge, H, thus extending the model, T, to $T \cup H$, according to the same formal specification of: $T \cup H \models O$ and $T \cup H$ is consistent.

Abduction is typically applied on a model, T, in which we can separate two disjoint sets of predicates: the *observable* predicates and the *abducible* predicates. The basic assumption then is that our model T has reached a sufficient level of comprehension of the domain such that all the incompleteness of the model can be isolated (under some working hypotheses) in its abducible predicates. The observable predicates are assumed to be completely defined in T; any incompleteness in their representation comes from the incompleteness in the abducible predicates. In practice, observable predicates describe the scientific observations, and abducible predicates that describe underlying relations in our model that are not observable directly but can, through the model T, bring about observable information. We also have *background* predicates that are auxiliary relations that help us link observable and abducible information (e.g. they describe experimental conditions or known sub-processes of the phenomena).

Having isolated the incompleteness of our model in the abducible predicates, these will form the basis of *abductive explanations* for understanding, according to the model, the specific observations that we have of our scientific domain. Abduction generates in these explanations (typically) *extentional* knowledge that is specific to the particular state or scenario of the world pertaining to the observations explained. Adding an explanation to the theory then allows us to predict further observable information but again restricted essentially to the situation(s) of the given observations. On the other hand, inductive inference generates *intentional knowledge* in the form of general rules that are not restricted to the particular scenaria of the observations. The inductive hypothesis thus allows predictions to new, hitherto unseen, states of affairs or scenarios.

A *cycle of integration* of abduction and induction in the process of model development emerges. Abduction is first used to transform (and in some sense normalize) the observations to an extensional hypothesis on the abducible predicates. Then induction takes this as input (training data) and tries to generalize this extentional information to general rules for the abducible predicates. The cycle can then be repeated by adding the learned information on the abducibles back in the model as partial information now on these incomplete predicates.

As an example consider the integration of abduction and induction for modelling inhibition as shown in Figure 2. The purpose of the abduction process is to generate hypotheses about inhibited enzymes from the NMR observations of metabolite concentration. For this purpose we need a logic program which models how the concentration of metabolites (e.g. up-down regulations) is related to inhibition of enzymes (see Section 3.2 for such a model). The purpose of the induction process is to learn from the abduced facts, general rules about inhibition of enzymes in terms of chemical properties of the inhibitor, functional class of enzymes etc. Part of the information about inhibition required by the induction process can be obtained from databases such as BRENDA [29]. However, for many inhibitors the available data may not be enough to generate any general rule. The results of abduction, from the previous stage, then act as invaluable training examples for the induction process.

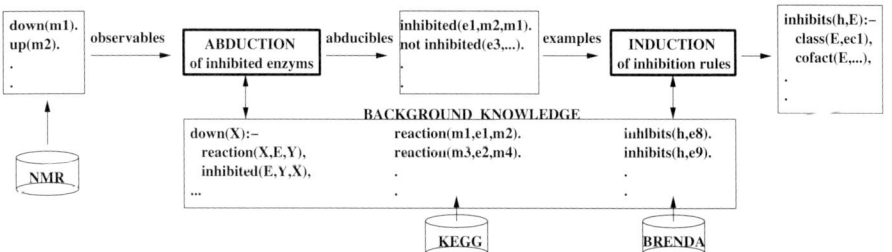

Fig. 2. An Abductive/Inductive framework for modelling inhibition.

In general, the integration of abduction and induction enhances the model development. Moreover, it provides a better opportunity to test the correctness of the generated hypotheses as this can increase the scope of testing. In a *tight integration* of abduction and induction the choice of an explanation in the first abductive phase of the cycle is linked to the second phase of how well the explanation generalizes through induction. Such frameworks of tight integration already exist, e.g. Progol 5.0 [19], ACL [17], SOLDR [34], CF-Induction [12], HAIL [23]. We will use Progol 5.0 to carry out the experiments in our study in this paper.

3.1 Modelling in Abductive Logic Programming

A framework that allows declarative representations of incomplete theories is that of Abductive Logic Programming (ALP) [16,15]. In this framework a model or a theory, T, is described in terms of a triple (P, A, IC) consisting of a logic program, P, a set of abducible predicates, A, and a set of classical logic formulas IC, called the *integrity constraints* of the theory. The program P contains *definitional knowledge* representing the general laws about our problem domain through a complete definition of a set of *observable predicates* in terms of each other, background predicates (which are again assumed to be completely specified in P) and a set of abducible predicates that are open. Abducible predicates appear only in the conditions of the program rules with no definition in P. The integrity constraints, IC, represent *assertional knowledge* that we may have about our domain, augmenting the model in P, but without defining any predicates.

Given such an ALP theory the inference of abduction (i.e. of abductive explanation) is then specialized accordingly in the following way:

Definition 1. *Given an abductive logic theory (P, A, IC), an abductive explanation for an observation O, is a set, Δ, of ground abducible atoms on the predicates A such that:*

- $P \cup \Delta \models_{LP} O$
- $P \cup \Delta \models_{LP} IC.$

where $\models_{LP}$ *denotes the logical entailment relation in Logic Programming*[1].

The abductive explanation Δ represents a hypothesis which when taken together with the model described in the theory T explains how a nonempty experimental observable O could hold. An abductive explanation partially completes the model as described in the theory T. The important role of the integrity constraints IC, is to impose *validity* requirements on the abducible hypotheses Δ. They are modularly stated in the theory, separately from the basic model captured in P, and they are used to augment this with any partial information that we may have on the abducible predicates or other particular requirements that we may want the abductively generated explanations of our observations to have. In most practical cases the integrity constraints are of the form of clausal rules: $B_1 \wedge ... \wedge B_n \to A_1 \vee ... \vee A_k$ where $A_1, ..., A_k$ and $B_1, ..., B_n$ are positive literals. In these constraints, k can be possibly zero (we will then write the conclusion as **false**) in which case the constraint is a denial prohibiting any set of abducibles that would imply the conjunction $B_1, ..., B_n$.

3.2 Modelling Inhibition in ALP

We will develop a model for analyzing (understanding and subsequently predicting) the effect of toxin substances on the concentration of metabolites. The ontology of our representation will use as *observable* predicates the single predicate:

$concentration(Metabolite, Level)$

where $Level$ can take (in the simplest case) the two values, *down* or *up*. In general, this would contain a third argument, namely the name of the toxin that we are examining but we will assume here for simplicity that we are studying only one toxin at a time and hence we can factor this out. *Background* predicates such as:

$reactionnode(Metabolites1, Enzymes, Metabolites2)$

describe the topology of the network of the metabolic pathways as depicted in figure1. For example, the statement

$reactionnode('l - 2 - aminoadipate',' 2.6.1.39',' 2 - oxo - glutarate')$

expresses the fact that there is a direct path (reaction) between the metabolites $l - 2 - aminoadipate$ and $2 - oxo - glutarate$ catalyzed by the enzyme 2.6.1.39. More generally, we can have a set of metabolites on each side of the reaction and a set of different enzymes that can catalyze the reaction.

Note also that these reactions are in general reversible, i.e. they can occur in either direction and indeed the presence of a toxin could result in some reactions

---

[1] For example, when the program P contains no negation as failure then this entailment is given by the minimal Herbrand model of the program and the truth of formulae in this model.

changing their direction in an attempt to compensate (re-balance) the effects of the toxin. The incompleteness of our model resides in the lack of knowledge of which metabolic reactions are adversely affected in the presence of the toxin. This is captured through the declaration of the *abducible* predicate:

$$inhibited(Enzyme, Metabolites1, Metabolites2)$$

capturing the hypothesis that the toxin inhibits the reaction from $Metabolites1$ to $Metabolites2$ through an adverse effect on the enzyme, $Enzyme$, that normally catalyzes this reaction. For example,

$$inhibited('2.6.1.39',' l - 2 - aminoadipate',' 2 - oxo - glutarate')$$

expresses the abducible hypothesis that the toxin inhibits the reaction from $l - 2 - aminoadipate$ to $2 - oxo - glutarate$ via the enzyme 2.6.1.39.

Hence the set of abducibles, A, in our ALP theory (P, A, IC), contains the only predicate *inhibited*/3. Completing this would complete the given model. The experimental observations of increased or reduced metabolite concentration will be accounted for in terms of hypotheses on the underlying and non-observable inhibitory effect of the toxin represented by this abducible predicate.

Given this ontology for our theory (P, A, IC), we now need to provide the program rules in P and the integrity constraints IC of our model representation. The rules in P describe an underlying mechanics of the effect of inhibition of a toxin by defining the observable *concentration*/2 predicate. This model is simple in the sense that it only describes at an appropriate high-level the possible inhibition effects of the toxin, abstracting away from the details of the complex biochemical reactions that occur. It sets out simple general laws under which the effect of the toxin can increase or reduce their concentration, Examples of these rules in P are:

    concentration(X,down):-
        reactionnode(X,Enz,Y),
        inhibited(Enz,Y,X).

    concentration(X,down):-
        reactionnode(X,Enz,Y),
        not inhibited(Enz,Y,X),
        concentration(Y,down).

The first rule expresses the fact that if the toxin inhibits a reaction producing metabolite X then this will cause down concentration of this metabolite. The second rule accounts for changes in the concentration through indirect effects where a metabolite X can have down concentration due to the fact that some other substrate metabolite, Y, that produces X was caused to have low concentration. Increased concentration is modelled analogously with rules for "up" concentration. For example we have

    concentration(X,up):-
        reactionnode(Y,Enz,X),
        inhibited(Enz,X,Y).

where the inhibition of the reaction from metabolite X to Y causes the concentration of X to go up as X is not consumed due to this inhibition.

Note that for a representation that does not involve negation as failure, as we would need when using the Progol 5.0 system, we could use instead the abducible predicate $inhibited(Enz, TruthValue, Y, X)$ where $TruthValue$ would take the two values $true$ and $false$. The underlying and simplifying working hypotheses of our model are:

(1) the primary effect of the toxin can be *localized* on the individual reactions of the metabolic pathways;
(2) the underlying network of the metabolic pathways is correct and complete;
(3) all the reactions of the metabolic pathways are a-priori equally likely to be affected by the toxin;
(4) inhibition in one reaction is sufficient to cause change in the concentration of the metabolites.

The above rules and working hypotheses give a relatively simple model but this is sufficient as a starting point. In a more elaborate model we could relax the fourth underlying hypothesis of the model and allow, for example, the possibility that the down concentration effect on a metabolite, due to the inhibition of one reaction leading to it, to be compensated by some increased flow of another reaction that also leads to it. We would then have more elaborated program P rules that express this. For example, the first rule above would be replaced by:

$concentration(X,down):-$
  $reactionnode(X,Enz,Y),$
  $inhibited(Enz,Y,X),$
  $not\ compensated(X,Enz).$

$compensated(X,Enz):-$
  $reactionnode(X,Enz1,Y),$
  $different(Enz1,Enz),$
  $increased(Enz1,Y,X).$

where now the set of abducible predicates A includes also the predicate $increased(Enzyme, Metabolites1, Metabolites2)$ that captures the assumption that the flow of the reaction from $Metabolites1$ to $Metabolites2$ has increased as a secondary effect of the presence of the toxin.

Validity requirements of the model. The abducible information of $inhibited/3$ is required to satisfy several *validity requirements* captured in the integrity constraints IC of the model. These are stated modularly in IC separately from the program P and can be changed without affecting the need to reconsider the underlying model of P. They typically involve general self-consistency requirements of the model such as:

$concentration(X, down), concentration(X, up) \rightarrow \textbf{\textit{false}}$

expressing the facts that the model should not entail that the concentration of any metabolite is at the same time down and up.

Example Explanations. Let us illustrate the use of our model and its possible development with an example. Given the pathways network in figure 1 and the experimental observation that:

$$concentration('2 - oxo - glutarate', down)$$

the following are some of its possible explanations

$$E_1 = \{inhibited(2.3.1.61,' succinate',' 2 - oxo - glutarate')\}$$
$$E_2 = \{inhibited(2.6.1.39,' l - 2 - aminoadipate',' 2 - oxo - glutarate')\}$$
$$E_3 = \{inhibited(1.1.1.42,' isocitrate',' 2 - oxo - glutarate')\}$$

Combining this observation with the additional observation that

$$concentration('isocitrate', down)$$

makes the third explanation E_3 inconsistent, as this would imply that the concentration of isocitrate is up. Now if we further suppose that we have observed

$$concentration('l - 2 - aminoadipate', up)$$

then the above explanation E_2 is able to account for all three observations with no added hypotheses needed. An alternative explanation would be

$$E_2' = \{inhibited(2.6.1.39,' l - 2 - aminoadipate',' 2 - oxo - glutarate'),$$
$$inhibited(1.2.1.31,' l - 2 - aminoadipate',' l - lysine')\}$$

Applying a principle of *minimality* of explanations or more generally of *maximal compression* we would prefer the explanation E_2 over E_2'.

Computing Explanations by ALP and ILP systems. There are several systems (e.g. [28,27]) for computing abductive explanations in ALP. Also some ILP systems, such as Progol 5, can compute abductive explanations as well as generalizations of these. Most ALP systems, unlike ILP systems, do not employ an automatic way of comparing different explanations at generation/search time and selecting from these those explanations that satisfy some criterium of compression or simplicity. On the other hand, ALP systems can operate on a richer representation language, e.g. that includes negation as failure. Hence although Progol 5 can provide compact and minimal explanations ALP systems can provide explanations that have a more complete form.

In particular, Progol 5 explanations are known to be restrictive [33,23], in that for a single observation/example they can not contain more than one abducible clause. Despite this in many domains where this single clause restriction is acceptable, as is the case in our present study of inhibition in metabolic networks, ground explanations of Progol 5 are closely related to (minimal) ALP explanations. ALP explanations may contain extra hypotheses that are generated from ensuring that the integrity constraints are satisfied. Such hypotheses are left implicit in Progol 5 explanations. This means that Progol 5 and ALP explanations have corresponding predictions, modulo any differences in their vocabularies of representation. For example, referring again to Figure 1, a Progol 5 explanation for the two observations for metabolites $l - 2 - aminoadipate$ and *succinate* would be:

$$E_{ILP} = \{inhibited(2.6.1.39, true,' l-2-aminoadipate','2-oxo-glutarate'),$$
$$inhibited(1.2.7.3, false,'2-oxo-glutarate','succinate')\}$$

This explanation does not carry any information on the rest of the network that is not directly connected with the observations and the abducible hypotheses that it contains. The corresponding ALP explanation(s) have the form:

$$E_{ALP} = \{inhibited(2.6.1.39,' l-2-aminoadipate','2-oxo-glutarate'),$$
$$not\ inhibited(1.2.7.3,'2-oxo-glutarate','succinate')\} \cup E_{Rest}$$

where E_{Rest} makes explicit further assumptions required for the satisfaction of the integrity constraints. In this example, if we are interested in the metabolite *isocitrate* then we could have two possibilities:

$$E_{Rest}^1 = \{not\ inhibited(1.1.1.42.,'2-oxo-glutarate','isocitrate'),$$
$$not\ inhibited(1.1.1.42.,'isocitrate','2-oxo-glutarate')$$

$$E_{Rest}^2 = \{not\ inhibited(1.1.1.42.,'2-oxo-glutarate','isocitrate'),$$
$$inhibited(1.1.1.42.,'isocitrate','2-oxo-glutarate')$$

These extra assumptions are left implicit in the ILP explanations as they have their emphasis on maximal compression. But the predictions that we get from the two types of ALP and ILP explanations are the same. Both types of explanations predict *concentration*('2-oxo-glutarate', down). For *isocitrate* the first ALP explanation predicts this to have down concentration whereas the second one predicts this to have up concentration. The non-committal corresponding ILP explanation will also give these two possibilities of prediction depending on how we further assume the flow of the reaction between $2-oxo-glutarate$ and *isocitrate*. In our experiments, reported in the following section, we could examine a-posteriori the possible ALP explanations and confirm this link between ground Progol 5 explanations with minimal ALP explanations.

4   Experiments

The purpose of the experiments in this section is to empirically evaluate the inhibition model, described in the previous section, on a real metabolic pathway and real NMR data.

4.1   Experiment 1: Learning Ground Hypotheses

In this experiment we evaluate ground hypotheses which are generated using the inhibition model given observations about concentration of some metabolites.

Materials. Progol 5.0[2] is used to generate ground hypotheses from observations and background knowledge. As a part of background knowledge, we use the relational representation of biochemical reactions involved in a metabolic pathway which is affected by hydrazine. The observable data is up-down regulation of metabolites obtained from NMR spectra. These background knowledge and observable data were explained in Section 2 and illustrated in Figure 1.

---

[2] Available from: http://www.doc.ic.ac.uk/~shm/Software/progol5.0/

```
for i=1 to 10 do
    Ts_i = m test example randomly sampled from E
    Tr_i = E − Ts_i
    for j in (2,4,6,8,10) do
        Tr_{ij} = j training example randomly sampled from Tr_i
    end
end
for i=1 to 10 do
    for j in (2,4,6,8,10) do
        H_{ij} = learned hypotheses using the training set Tr_{ij}
        A_{ij} = predictive accuracy of H_{ij} on the test set Ts_{ij}
    end
end
for j in (2,4,6,8,10) do
    Plot average and error bars of A_{ij} versus j (i ∈ [1..10])
```

Fig. 3. Experimental method used for Experiment 1. E is the set of all examples and in this experiment $m = 7$.

Methods. In the first attempt to evaluate the model we tried to predict the concentration of a set of metabolites which became available later during the Metalog project. Hence, we have used the previously available observations (shown in black arrows in Figure 1) as training data and the new observations (shown in blue arrows in Figure 1) as test data. According to our model, there are many possible hypotheses which can explain the up-regulation and down-regulation of the observed metabolites. However, Progol's search attempts to find the most compressive hypotheses. The following are examples of hypotheses returned by Progol:

```
inhibited('2.6.1.39',true,'1-2-aminoadipate','2-oxo-glutarate').
inhibited('2.3.1.61',false,'2-oxo-glutarate','succinate').
inhibited('1.13.11.16',false,'succinate','hippurate').
inhibited('2.6.1.-',true,'taurine','citrate').
inhibited('3.5.2.10',true,'creatine','creatinine').
inhibited('4.1.2.32',true,'tmao','formaldehyde').
inhibited('4.3.1.6',true,'beta-alanine','acryloyl-coA').
```

Using these ground hypotheses, the model can correctly predict the concentration of six out of the seven new metabolites. In order to evaluate the predictive accuracy of the model in a similar setting, we generate random test sets (with size equal to seven) and use the remaining examples for training. Figure 3 summarises the experimental method used for this purpose.

The model which has been used for evaluating the hypotheses generated by Progol explicates the Closed World Assumption (CWA). In other words, we are working under the assumption that a reaction is not inhibited unless we have a fact which says otherwise:

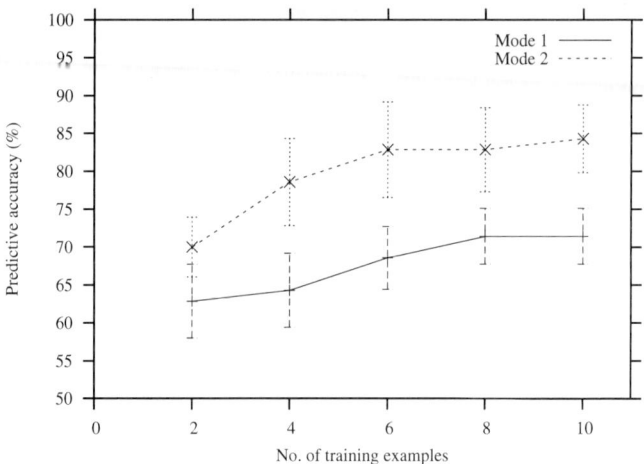

Fig. 4. Performance of the hypotheses generated by Progol in Experiment 1.

inhibited(Enz,false,X,Y):-
  reactionnode(Y,Enz,X),
  not(inhibited(Enz,true,_,_)).

When we include this we will call this evaluation, *mode 2*, and without it we will call the evaluation *mode 1*.

The predictor which we have used in our experiments converts the three class problem which we have ('up', 'down' and 'unknown') to a two class prediction with 'down' as the default class. For this purpose we use the following test predicate:

concentration1(X,up):-
  concentration(X,up),
  not(concentration(X,down)).
concentration1(X,down).

Results and discussion. The results of the experiments are shown in Figure 4. In this graph, the vertical axis shows the predictive accuracy and the horizontal axis shows the number of training examples. According to this graph, we have a better predictive accuracy when we use the closed world assumption (*Mode 2*) compared to the accuracy when we do not use this assumption (*Mode 1*). The reason for this is that the closed world assumption allows the rules of the model (as represented in Progol) have apply in more cases than without the assumption. According to the number of up and down regulations in the examples, the default accuracy is 64.7%. For both *Mode 1* and *Mode 2*, the overall accuracy is above the default accuracy and inreases with the number of training examples.

```
for i in (1,4,8,16) do
    for j=1 to n do
        Ts_{ij} = i test examples randomly sampled from E
        Tr_{ij} = E - Ts_{ij}
    end
end
for i in (1,4,8,16) do
    for j=1 to n do
        H_{ij} = learned hypotheses using the training set Tr_{ij}
        A_{ij} = predictive accuracy of H_{ij} on the test set Ts_{ij}
    end
end
for i in (1,4,8,16) do
    Plot average of A_{ij} versus j (j ∈ [1..n])
```

Fig. 5. Experimental method used for Experiment 2. E is the set of all examples and in this experiment $n = 17$.

4.2 Experiment 2: Learning Non-ground Hypotheses

As mentioned in the previous sections, abduction and induction can be combined to generate general rules about inhibition of enzymes. In this experiment we attempt to do this by further generalising the kind of ground hypotheses which were learned in Experiment 1.

Materials and Methods. Background knowledge required for this experiment can be obtained from databases such as BRENDA [29] and LIGAND [31]. This background information can include information about enzyme classes, cofactors etc. For example, information on the described inhibition by hydrazine and/or presence of the pyridoxal 5'-phosphate (PLP) group can be extracted from the BRENDA database when such information exists. In our experiments for learning non-ground hypotheses we include the possibility that a given chemical compound can be inhibiting a whole enzymatic class, since this situation is possible in non-competitive inhibition. For example, a very strong reducer or oxidant affecting many oxidoreductases (1.-.-.-). In our case, since the mechanism (competitive/non-competitive) of inhibition of hydrazine is unknown, we leave this possibility open. In this experiment we use all available observations and we apply a leave-out test strategy (randomly leave out 1, 4, 8 and 16 test examples and use the rest as training data). The experimental method is detailed in Figure 5.

Results and discussion. In this experiment Progol attempted to generate general rules for inhibition effectively trying to generalize from the ground facts in the abductive explanations. Among the rules that it had considered were:

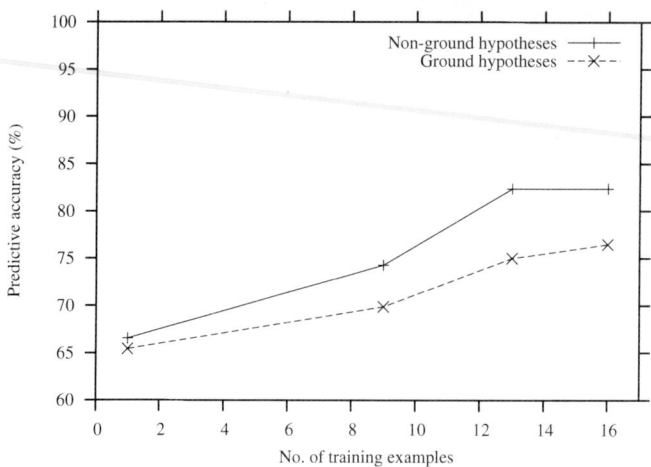

Fig. 6. Performance of ground and non-ground hypotheses generated by Progol using a leave-out test strategy as detailed in Figure 5.

$$inhibited(Enz, true, M1, M2) : \neg reactionnode(M2, Enz, M1), class(Enz, 2.6.1)$$
$$inhibited(Enz, true, M1, M2) : \neg reactionnode(M2, Enz, M1), class(Enz, 4.1.2)$$

expressing the information that reactions that are catalysed by enzymes in either of the two classes '2.6.1' and '4.1.2' are inhibited by Hydrazine. These rules had to be eventually rejected by the system as they are inconsistent with the given model. This is because they imply that these reactions are inhibited in both directions while the model assumes that any reaction at any particular time only flows in one direction and hence can only be inhibited in that direction. In fact, the available data is not sufficient for the learning method to distinguish the direction in which the reactions of the network flow. Moreover, it is not appropriate to learn such a relation as we know that metabolic pathways reactions are reversible and so depending on the circumstances they can flow in either direction (see Section 2). The problem therefore is a problem of representation where we simply want to express that these reactions are inhibited in the one direction that they flow whatever this direction might be.

Nevertheless it was instructive to accept these (seemingly overgeneral) rules into our model by adopting a default direction of the reactions of the network involved (i.e. whose enzymes fall in these two classes) and examine the effect of this generalization on the predictive accuracy of our new model compared with the case where the ground abductive explanations are added to the model. This comparison is shown in Figure 6 indicating that the predictive accuracy improves after generalization.

5 Conclusions

We have studied how to use abduction and induction in scientific modelling concentrating on the problem of inhibition of metabolic pathways. Our work has demonstrated the feasibility of a process of scientific model development through an integrated use of abduction and induction. This is to our knowledge the first time that abduction and induction are used together in an enhancing way on a real-life domain.

The abduction technique which is used in this paper can be compared with the one in the robot scientist project [18] where ASE-Progol was used to generate ground hypotheses about the function of genes. Abduction has been also used within a system, called GenePath [35,36], to find relations from experimental genetic data in order to facilitate the analysis of genetic networks. Bayesian networks are among the most successful techniques which have been used for modelling biological networks. In particular, gene expression data has been widely modelled using Bayes' net techniques [7,6,10]. On the MetaLog project Bayes' nets have also been used to model metabolic networks [24]. A key advantage of the logical modelling approach in the present paper compared with the Bayes' net approach is the ability to incorporate background knowledge of existing known biochemical pathways, together with information on enzyme classes and reaction chemistry. The logical modelling approach also produces explicit hypotheses concerning the inhibitory effects of toxins.

A number of classical mathematical approaches to metabolic pathway analysis and simulation exist. These can be divided into three main groups based around Biochemical Systems Theory (BST), Metabolic Control Analysis (MCA) and Flux Balance Analysis (FBA). BST and MCA are oriented toward dynamic simulation of cellular processes based on physicochemical laws [8,9,25]. However, progress towards the ultimate goal of complete simulation of cellular systems [25] has been impeded by the lack of kinetic information and attention in the last decade has been diverted to analysing the relative importance of metabolic events. FBA [26,3] unlike BST and MCA, does not require exact kinetic information to analyse the operative modes of metabolic systems. FBA, which includes the techniques of Elementary Flux Mode Analysis and Extreme Pathway Analysis, only requires stochiometric parameters (the quantitative relationship between reactants and products in a chemical reaction). However, by contrast with the approach taken in the present paper, BST, MCA and FBA are not machine learning approaches, and most importantly do not incorporate techniques for extending the structure of the model based on empirical data.

In the present study we used simple background knowledge concerning the class of enzymes to allow the construction of non-ground hypotheses. Despite this limited use of background knowledge we achieved an increase in predictive accuracy over the case in which hypothesis were restricted to be ground. In future work we hope to extend the representation to include structural descriptions of the reactions involved in a style similar to that described in [20].

Acknowledgements. We would like to thank the anonymous reviewers for their comments We also thank M. Sternberg, R. Chaleil and A. Amini for their useful discussions and advice, T. Ebbels and D Crockford for their help on preparing the NMR data and O. Ray for his help with the ALP system. This work was supported by the DTI project "MetaLog - Integrated Machine Learning of Metabolic Networks applied to Predictive Toxicology". The second author is grateful to the Dept. of Computing, Imperial College London for hosting him during the 2003/4 academic year.

References

1. R. Alves, R.A. Chaleil, and M.J. Sternberg. Evolution of enzymes in metabolism: a network perspective. *Mol. Biol.*, 320(4):751–70, 2002 Jul 19.
2. E. Alm E and A.P. Arkin. Biological networks. *Curr. Opin. Struct. Biol.*, 13(2):193–202, 2003 April.
3. J. S. Edwards, R. Ramakrishna, C. H. Schilling, and B. O. Palsson. Metabolic flux balance analysis. In S. Y. Lee and E. T. Papoutsakis, editors, *Metabolic Engineering*. Marcel Deker, 1999.
4. P. Flach and A.C. Kakas. Abductive and inductive reasoning: Background and issues. In P. A. Flach and A. C. Kakas, editors, *Abductive and Inductive Reasoning*, Pure and Applied Logic. Kluwer, 2000.
5. P. A. Flach and A. C. Kakas, editors. *Abductive and Inductive Reasoning*. Pure and Applied Logic. Kluwer, 200.
6. Nir Friedman, Michal Linial, Iftach Nachman, and Dana Pe'er. Using bayesian networks to analyze expression data. *J. of Comp. Bio.*, 7:601–620, 2000.
7. Nir Friedman, Kevin Murphy, and Stuart Russell. Learning the structure of dynamic probabilistic networks. In *Uncertainty in Artificial Intelligence: Proceedings of the Fourteenth Conference (UAI-1998)*, pages 139–147, San Francisco, CA, 1998. Morgan Kaufmann Publishers.
8. B.C. Goodwin. *Oscillatory organization in cells, a dynamic theory of cellular control processes*. Academic Press, New York, 1963.
9. B. Hess and A. Boiteux. Oscillatory organization in cells, a dynamic theory of cellular control processes. *Hoppe-Seylers Zeitschrift fur Physiologische Chemie*, 349:1567 – 1574, 1968.
10. S. Imoto, T. Goto, and S. Miyano. Estimation of genetic networks and functional structures between genes by using bayesian networks and nonparametric regression. In *Proceeding of Pacific Symposium on Biocomputing*, pages 175–186, 2002.
11. K. Inoue. Induction, abduction and consequence-finding. In C. Rouveirol and M. Sebag, editors, *Proceedings of the International Workshop on Inductive Logic Programming (ILP01)*, pages 65–79, Berlin, 2001. Springer-Verlag. LNAI 2157.
12. K. Inoue. Inverse entailment for full clausal theories. In *LICS-2001 Workshop on Logic and Learning*, 2001.
13. K. Ito and A. Yamamoto. Finding hypotheses from examples by computing the least generlisation of bottom clauses. In *Proceedings of Discovery Science '98*, pages 303–314. Springer, Berlin, 1998. LNAI 1532.
14. H. Jeong, B. Tombor, R. Albert, Z.N. Oltvai, and A.L. Barabasi. The large-scale organization of metabolic networks. *Nature*, 407(6804):651–654, 2000 Oct 5.

15. A. C. Kakas and M. Denecker. Abduction in logic programming. In A. C. Kakas and F. Sadri, editors, *Computational Logic: Logic Programming and Beyond. Part I*, number 2407, pages 402–436, 2002.

16. A. C. Kakas, R. A. Kowalski, and F. Toni. Abductive Logic Programming. *Journal of Logic and Computation*, 2(6):719–770, 1993.

17. A.C. Kakas and F. Riguzzi. Abductive concept learning. *New Generation Computing*, 18:243–294, 2000.

18. R.D. King, K.E. Whelan, F.M. Jones, P.K.G. Reiser, C.H. Bryant, S.H. Muggleton, D.B. Kell, and S.G. Oliver. Functional genomic hypothesis generation and experimentation by a robot scientist. *Nature*, 427:247–252, 2004.

19. S.H. Muggleton and C.H. Bryant. Theory completion using inverse entailment. In *Proc. of the 10th International Workshop on Inductive Logic Programming (ILP-00)*, pages 130–146, Berlin, 2000. Springer-Verlag.

20. S.H. Muggleton, A. Tamaddoni-Nezhad, and H. Watanabe. Induction of enzyme classes from biological databases. In *Proceedings of the 13th International Conference on Inductive Logic Programming*, pages 269–280. Springer-Verlag, 2003.

21. J.A. Papin, N.D. Price, S.J. Wiback, D.A. Fell, and B.O. Palsson. Metabolic pathways in the post-genome era. *Trends Biochem. Sci.*, 28(5):250–8, 2003 May.

22. E. Ravasz, A.L. Somera, D.A. Mongru, Z.N. Oltvai, and A.L. Barabasi. Hierarchical organization of modularity in metabolic networks. *Science*, 297(5586):1551–5, 2002.

23. O. Ray, K. Broda, and A. Russo. Hybrid Abductive Inductive Learning: a Generalisation of Progol. In *13th International Conference on Inductive Logic Programming*, volume 2835 of *LNAI*, pages 311–328. Springer Verlag, 2003.

24. A. Tamaddoni-Nezhad, S. Muggleton, and J. Bang. A bayesian model for metabolic pathways. In *International Joint Conference on Artificial Intelligence (IJCAI03) Workshop on Learning Statistical Models from Relational Data*, pages 50–57. IJ-CAI, 2003.

25. J.J. Tyson and H. G. Othmer. The dynamics of feedback control circuits in biochemical pathways. *Progress in Theoretical Biology*, 5:1–62, 1978.

26. A. Varma and B. O. Palsson. Metabolic flux balancing: Basic concepts, scientific and practical use. *Bio/Technology*, 12:994–998, 1994.

27. A-System Webpage:. http://www.cs.kuleuven.ac.be/~bertv/asystem/.

28. ALP-Systems Webpage:. http://www.doc.ic.ac.uk/ ~ or/abduction/alp.pl and http://www.cs.ucy.ac.cy/aclp/.

29. BRENDA Webpage:. http://www.brenda.uni-koeln.de/.

30. KEGG Webpage:. http://www.genome.ad.jp/kegg/.

31. LIGAND Webpage:. http://www.genome.ad.jp/ligand/.

32. MetaLog Webpage:. http://www.doc.ic.ac.uk/bioinformatics/metalog/.

33. A. Yamamoto. Which hypotheses can be found with inverse entailment? In *Proceedings of the Seventh International Workshop on Inductive Logic Programming*, pages 296–308. Berlin, 1997. LNAI 1297.

34. A. Yamamoto and B. Fronhöfer. Finding hypotheses by generalizing residues hypotheses. pages 107–118, September 2001.

35. B. Zupan, I. Bratko, J. Demsar, J. R. Beck, A. Kuspa, and G. Shaulsky. Abductive inference of genetic networks. *AIME*, pages 304–313, 2001.

36. B. Zupan, I. Bratko, J. Demsar, P. Juvan, J.A Halter, A. Kuspa, and G. Shaulsky. Genepath: a system for automated construction of genetic networks from mutant data. *Bioinformatics*, 19(3):383–389, 2003.

First Order Random Forests with Complex Aggregates

Celine Vens[1], Anneleen Van Assche[1], Hendrik Blockeel[1], and Sašo Džeroski[2]

[1] Department of Computer Science, Katholieke Universiteit Leuven,
Celestijnenlaan 200A, 3001 Leuven, Belgium
{celine,anneleen,hendrik}@cs.kuleuven.ac.be
[2] Department of Knowledge Technologies, Jozef Stefan Institute,
Jamova 39, 1000 Ljubljana, Slovenia
Saso.Dzeroski@ijs.si

Abstract. Random forest induction is a bagging method that randomly samples the feature set at each node in a decision tree. In propositional learning, the method has been shown to work well when lots of features are available. This certainly is the case in first order learning, especially when aggregate functions, combined with selection conditions on the set to be aggregated, are included in the feature space. In this paper, we introduce a random forest based approach to learning first order theories with aggregates. We experimentally validate and compare several variants: first order random forests without aggregates, with simple aggregates, and with complex aggregates in the feature set.

Keywords: Random forests, Aggregation, Decision Tree Learning

1 Introduction

Given the widespread use of multi-relational databases, relational learners are very important. Among the many approaches to relational learning that currently exist, an important distinction can be made with respect to how they handle one-to-many and many-to-many relationships. Whereas propositionalization approaches usually handle sets by aggregating over them, inductive logic programming (ILP) [20] techniques select specific elements. This imposes an undesirable bias on both kinds of learners [2].

In this paper we try to overcome this bias by introducing aggregate functions, possibly combined with selection conditions on specific elements, into an ILP setting. So far, this combination has been considered a difficult task, because the feature set grows quickly, and because the search space is less well-behaved due to non-monotonicity [16]. Our approach is based on random forests [8]. Random forest induction is a bagging method that builds decision trees using only a random subset of the feature set at each node.

The motivation for using random forests is based on two observations. First, because of the reduction of the feature space at each node and because of the search strategy used by decision trees, random forests seem to be very suitable to

R. Camacho, R. King, A. Srinivasan (Eds.): ILP 2004, LNAI 3194, pp. 323–340, 2004.
© Springer-Verlag Berlin Heidelberg 2004

tackle the problems mentioned above. Second, in propositional learning, random forest induction has been shown to work well when many features are available [8]. Because ILP typically deals with large feature sets, it seems worthwhile to investigate whether random forests perform well in this context.

The paper is organized as follows. In Sect. 2, random forests are discussed. Section 3 illustrates the problem of combining aggregates with selection conditions in ILP. Our method, which is a first order random forest with complex aggregates, is presented in Sect. 4. In Sect. 5, we experimentally evaluate our method both in structurally complex domains, and in a (highly non-determinate) business domain. Finally, we formulate conclusions and some ideas for future research in Sect. 6.

2   Random Forests

Random forest induction [8] is an ensemble method. An ensemble learning algorithm constructs a set of classifiers, and then classifies new data points by taking a vote of the predictions of each classifier. A necessary and sufficient condition for an ensemble of classifiers to be more accurate than any of its individual members, is that the classifiers are accurate and diverse [14]. An accurate classifier does better than random guessing on new examples. Two classifiers are diverse if they make different errors on new data points.

There are different ways for constructing ensembles: bagging [6] and boosting [13] for instance, introduce diversity by manipulating the training set. Several other approaches attempt to increase variability by manipulating the input features or the output targets, or by introducing randomness in the learning algorithm [10].

Random forests increase diversity among the classifiers by changing the feature sets over the different tree induction processes, and additionally by resampling the data. The exact procedure to build a forest with k trees is as follows:

- for $i = 1$ to k do:
  - build training set D_i by sampling (with replacement) from data set D
  - learn a decision tree T_i from D_i *using randomly restricted feature sets*
- make predictions according to the majority vote of the set of k trees

The part of the algorithm where random forests differ from the normal bagging procedure is emphasized. Normally, when inducing a decision tree, the best feature is selected from a fixed set of features F in each node. In bagging, this set of features does not vary over the different runs of the induction procedure. In random forests however, a different random subset of size $f(|F|)$ is considered at each node (e.g. $f(x) = 0.1x$ or $f(x) = \sqrt{x}$, ...), and the best feature from this subset is chosen. This obviously increases variability. Assume for instance that $f(x) = \sqrt{x}$, and that two tests t_1 and t_2 are both good features for the root of each tree, say t_1 is the best and t_2 is the second best feature on all the training bags considered. With a regular bagging approach t_1 is consistently selected for the root, whereas with random forests both t_1 and t_2 will occur in the root nodes of the different trees, with frequency $1/\sqrt{|F|}$ and $1/\sqrt{|F|} - 1/|F|$ respectively. Thus t_2 will occur with a frequency only slightly lower than t_1.

An advantage of using bagging is that out-of-bag estimates [7] can be used to estimate the generalization errors. This removes the need for a set aside test set or cross-validation. Out-of-bag estimation proceeds as follows: each tree is learned on a training set D_i, drawn with replacement from the original training set D. The trees vote over new examples to form the bagged classifier. For each example d in the original training set, the votes are aggregated only over those classifiers T_i for which D_i does not contain d. This is the out-of-bag classifier. The out-of-bag estimate is then the error rate of the out-of-bag classifier on the training set. Note that in each resampled training set, about one third of the instances are left out (actually $1/e$ in the limit). As a result, out-of-bag estimates are based on combining only about one third of the total number of classifiers in the ensemble. This means that they might overestimate the error rate, certainly when a small number of trees is used in the ensemble.

Random forests have some other interesting properties [8]. They are efficient since only a sample of $f(|F|)$ features needs to be tested in each node, instead of all features. They do not overfit as more trees are added. Furthermore, they are relatively robust to outliers and noise, and they are easily parallellized.

The efficiency gain makes random forests especially interesting for relational data mining, which typically has to deal with a large number of features, many of which are expensive to compute. On the other hand, relational data mining offers an interesting test suite for random forests, exactly because the advantage of random forests is expected to become more clear for very large feature spaces. In relational data mining, such data sets abound. Moreover, using random forests allows us to enlarge the feature set by including aggregate functions, possibly refined with selection conditions. We discuss this in the next section.

3   Aggregates and Selection in ILP

When considering multi-relational learning, sets (or more generally, bags) need to be handled. They are represented by one-to-many or many-to-many relationships in or between relations. Blockeel and Bruynooghe [2] categorize current approaches to relational learning with respect to how they handle sets. Whereas ILP [20] is biased towards selection of specific elements, other approaches, such as PRM's [17], or certain propositionalization approaches (e.g. the one by Krogel and Wrobel [18]) use aggregate functions, which summarize the set. The latter methods are optimized for highly non-determinate (business) domains, whereas ILP is geared more towards structurally complex domains, e.g. molecular biology, language learning,...

Perlich and Provost [23] present a hierarchy of relational concepts of increasing complexity, where the complexity depends on that of any aggregate functions used. They argue that ILP currently is the only approach that is able to explore concepts up to level four (out of five) in the hierarchy. However, until now, ILP-like feature construction and the use of aggregation features have mostly been combined in relatively restricted ways, e.g. without allowing complex conditions within the aggregation operator. The combination of both approaches is not a trivial task: the number of features grows quickly, and some issues with respect to monotonicity of aggregates arise. In the following, we present some related work on ILP systems that incorporate aggregate functions.

Krogel and Wrobel [18] present a system called RELAGGS (RELational AGGregationS), which builds on transformation-based approaches to ILP. RELAGGS computes several joins of the input tables according to their foreign key relationships. These joins are compressed using aggregate functions, specific to the data types of the table columns, such that there remains a single row for each example. The result is an appropriate input for conventional data mining algorithms, such as decision tree induction or support vector machines. However, the aggregation operators do not allow for complex selection conditions.

Relational Probability Trees (RPTs) [22] extend standard probability estimation trees to a relational setting. The algorithm for learning an RPT uses aggregation functions to dynamically propositionalize the data. However, as RPTs are not able to refer to a particular object throughout a series of conjunctions, again, no selection conditions can occur within the aggregate conditions.

We provide some definitions that are useful for our discussion [16]. An *aggregate condition* is a triple (f, o, v), where f is an aggregate function, o is a comparison operator, and v is a value of the domain of f. An aggregate condition is *monotone* if, given sets of records S and S', $S' \subseteq S$, $f(S') \; o \; v \Rightarrow f(S) \; o \; v$. In this paper, we denote the aggregate function f by a predicate with three arguments: the first one is the set to aggregate, the second one is the *aggregate query* that generates the set, and the third argument is the result of f. We illustrate the concepts with an example. Suppose we have the following query, which represents an aggregate condition on the *child* relation of a person X:

```
person(X), count(Y, child(X,Y), C), C>=2.
```

Adding a literal to the aggregate query gives

```
person(X), count(Y, (child(X,Y), female(Y)), C), C>=2,
```

which must have at most the same coverage (people with at least two daughters must be a subset of people with at least two children), so $(count, \geq, v)$ is a monotone aggregate condition. However, if we consider the following query

```
person(X), count(Y, child(X,Y), C), C<2,
```

and its refinement

```
person(X), count(Y, (child(X,Y), female(Y)), C), C<2,
```

then the examples covered by the refinement are a superset of the original set (people with less than two children certainly have less than two daughters, but people with less than two daughters may have more than two children), so $(count, <, v)$ is anti-monotone. The following aggregate conditions are monotone: $(count, \geq, v)$, $(max, \geq, v)$, $(min, \leq, v)$. By a *non-monotone* aggregate condition, we mean an aggregate condition that is not monotone, either because it is anti-monotone, or because it is neither monotone nor anti-monotone (such as $(mode, =, v)$, $(avg, \geq, v)$ or $(avg, \leq, v)$).

Knobbe et al. [16] present an approach to combining aggregates with reasonably complex selection conditions by generalizing their selection graph pattern language. Selection graphs are a graphical description of sets of objects in a multi-relational database. In order to have only refinements that reduce the coverage, they restrict refinement to monotone aggregate conditions.

In Sect. 4 we will discuss an approach that does not prohibit the refinement of non-monotone aggregate conditions.

4 First Order Random Forests with Complex Aggregates

This section discusses our approach, which is a first order random forest with (complex) aggregates in the feature space. The section is started by discussing first order decision trees (Sect. 4.1). We continue by explaining how (complex) aggregate conditions are added to the feature space (Sect. 4.2). Finally, we show how the first order decision tree was upgraded to a random forest (Sect. 4.3).

4.1 First Order Decision Trees

The base decision tree induction algorithm in our random forest is Tilde [4], which is included in the ACE data mining system [5]. Tilde is a relational top-down induction of decision trees (TDIDT) instantiation, and outputs a first order decision tree.

A first order decision tree [4] is a binary decision tree that contains conjunctions of first order literals in the internal nodes. Classification with a first order tree is similar to classification with a propositional decision tree: a new instance is sorted down the tree. If the conjunction in a given node succeeds (fails), the instance is propagated to the left (right) subtree. The predicted class corresponds to the label of the leaf node where the instance arrives.

A given node n of the tree may introduce variables that can be reused in the nodes of its left subtree, which contains the examples for which the conjunction in n succeeds (with certain bindings for these variables).

In Tilde, first order decision trees are learned with a divide and conquer algorithm similar to C4.5 [25]. The main point where it differs from propositional tree learners is the computation of the set of tests to be considered at a node. The algorithm to learn a first order decision tree is given in Fig. 1.

The OPTIMAL_SPLIT procedure returns a conjunction Q_b, which is selected from a set of candidates generated by the refinement operator ρ, using a heuristic such as information gain. The refinement operator typically generates candidates by extending the current query Q (the conjunction of all succeeding tests from the root to the leaf that is to be extended) with a number of new literals. The conjunction put in the node consists of $Q_b - Q$, i.e. the literals that have been added to Q in order to produce Q_b. In the left branch Q_b will be further refined, while in the right branch Q is to be refined.

procedure GROW_TREE (E: **set of examples**, Q: **query**):

$candidates := \rho(\leftarrow Q)$

$\leftarrow Q_b :=$ OPTIMAL_SPLIT$(candidates, E)$

if STOP_CRIT $(\leftarrow Q_b, E)$

then

   $K :=$ MOST_FREQUENT_CLASS(E)

   return leaf(K)

else

   $conj := Q_b - Q$

   $E_1 := \{e \in E | \leftarrow Q_b$ succeeds in $e \wedge B\}$

   $E_2 := \{e \in E | \leftarrow Q_b$ fails in $e \wedge B\}$

   $left :=$ GROW_TREE (E_1, Q_b)

   $right :=$ GROW_TREE (E_2, Q)

   return node$(conj, left, right)$

Fig. 1. Algorithm for first order logical decision tree induction [4]

4.2   First Order Decision Trees with Complex Aggregates

Tilde was modified to include (complex) aggregate conditions. We first discuss how these aggregates were added. Next, we focus on some issues regarding non-monotone aggregate conditions.

(Complex) Aggregate Conditions in Decision Trees. The feature set considered at each node in the tree was expanded to consist of the regular features, augmented with aggregate conditions (both simple and complex ones). By *complex* aggregate conditions, we mean aggregate conditions with selection conditions on the set to be aggregated. This results in aggregate queries having more than one literal. Of course, complex aggregate conditions could have been included by just declaring them as intentional background knowledge, but this presumes a large expertise in the problem domain. The main difficulty is that the aggregate query is itself the result of a search through some hypothesis space.

Our method works as follows. To include aggregates, the user needs to specify the basic ingredients in the language bias: the aggregate functions to be used as well as some sets to be aggregated, together with a query to generate them. The system then constructs simple aggregate conditions, using the components provided by the user, and using for example discretization [3] to obtain a number of values to compare the result with. The refinement operator ρ includes the aggregate conditions in the set of candidate queries it generates.

When also considering complex aggregates, a local search has to be conducted within the aggregate condition. Therefore, ρ constructs an inner refinement operator ρ_{inn}, which generates candidates by extending the current aggregate query, using only the regular features. Each candidate generated by ρ_{inn} is included in an aggregate condition, which is then considered as a candidate of ρ. There are two ways to use complex aggregate functions.

The first one is to refine a (simple or complex) aggregate condition, occurring in the current query Q. For example, if the current query at a given node n is

```
person(X), count(Y, child(X,Y), C), C>4,
```

then one of the refinements generated by ρ might for example be

```
person(X), count(Y, child(X,Y), C), C>4,
         count(Y', (child(X,Y'),female(Y')), C'), C'>4.
```

If the query above is chosen by the OPTIMAL_SPLIT procedure, then

```
count(Y', (child(X,Y'),female(Y')), C'), C'>4
```

is the conjunction added in the left childnode of n.

The second way to build complex aggregates is based on lookahead [3], a technique commonly used in ILP to make the learner look ahead in the refinement lattice. In most cases, the refinement operator ρ adds only one literal (i.e., the new node contains only one literal – not a conjunction). In some cases, however, it is interesting to add more literals at once, e.g. if the first literal yields no gain, but introduces interesting variables that can be used by other literals. If the refinement operator adds $k+1$ literals, one says that it performs a lookahead of depth k. We extend this mechanism to be directly applied to the aggregate query. When the aggregate lookahead setting is turned on in the language bias description, ρ_{inn} is called and aggregate queries are built with up to a predefined depth of literals. This way, the conjunction

```
count(Y', (child(X,Y'),female(Y')), C'), C'>4
```

could immediately be inserted, without having the conjunction

```
count(Y, child(X,Y), C), C>4
```

in one of its ancestor nodes. Obviously, this technique is computationally expensive, but it will turn out to yield significant improvements.

Non-monotone Aggregate Conditions in Decision Trees. Knobbe et al. [16] leave non-monotone aggregate conditions untouched, in order to have only refinements that reduce the coverage. In decision trees however, a refinement of a node that does not result in a specialization will never be chosen, since such a test will hold for all examples in the node and hence will not reduce entropy. Therefore, there is no need to explicitly restrict ourselves to monotone aggregate conditions. Moreover, allowing non-monotone aggregate conditions may lead to a number of meaningful refinements when adding selection conditions. We discuss three examples.

First, remark that in the propositional case, the set of objects to aggregate can only become smaller when a new conjunct is added. In relational learning however, this is not the case when the new conjunct is introducing a new relation in the aggregate query. In that case, the result is a bag instead of a set. In fact, the bag of objects is then generated by the cartesian product of the different relations in the aggregate query. This may change the outcome of certain aggregate functions, such as count and sum. Hence, the refinement of e.g. the anti-monotone $(count, <, v)$ may yield a specialization. For example, consider a node n with the following query:

```
person(X), count(Y, child(X,Y), C), C<5.
```

A possible refinement of this query would be obtained by introducing a new relation (e.g. *horse*) within the aggregate query. This could lead to the following conjunction being entered at the left child node of *n*:

```
count(Y', (child(X,Y'),horse(X,Z)), C'), C'<5.
```

The refinement results in the cartesian product of the relations *child*(X,Y) and *horse*(X,Z). The aggregate condition evaluates to true for the following examples: persons with three or four children and maximum one horse, persons with two children and maximum two horses, persons with one child and maximum four horses, and persons with zero children and any number of horses. Thus, the introduction of a new relation into the aggregate condition ($count, <, v$) yields a refinement that reduces the coverage.

Second, depending on the multiplicity of a relation, the set to be aggregated may be empty, i.e. the aggregate query generates no instantiations of the objects to be aggregated. This is naturally treated by aggregate functions such as count; however, other aggregate functions such as min, max and average, fail when dealing with an empty set. So in that case, examples with multiplicity 0 for that relation always end up in the right ("no") branch of the tree. This means that for these aggregate functions, although the aggregate condition is non-monotone, refinements can be found that reduce the coverage. For example, consider the following query in a certain node in the tree

```
person(X), max(A, (child(X,Y),age(Y,A)), M), M<12.
```

This node can then be refined by adding

```
max(A', (child(X,Y'),female(Y'),age(Y',A')), M'), M'<12
```

as a left-child, which is equivalent to adding a selection condition outside the aggregate condition:

```
child(X,Z), female(Z),
```

since both alternatives fail for all persons without daughters. Note that this kind of refinement can also occur with monotone aggregate conditions.

Third, the use of lookahead, in combination with anti-monotone aggregate conditions, allows to simulate a bottom-up search strategy included in our top-down decision tree induction method, which may lead to useful refinements. We illustrate this with an example. Say the maximum depth for lookahead is two. Assume that the following aggregate condition, which counts the number of blonde daughters of a person, occurs in a node of the tree:

```
person(X), count(Y, (child(X,Y),female(Y),blonde(Y)), C), C<4.
```

Since at each node all aggregate conditions with up to three conjuncts are in the feature set, the following conditions will be generated:

```
count(Y', child(X,Y'), C'), C'<4,
count(Y', (child(X,Y'),female(Y')), C'), C'<4,
count(Y', (child(X,Y'),blonde(Y')), C'), C'<4.
```

These conditions indeed reduce the coverage and hence, lead to valid refinements.

4.3 First Order Random Forests with Complex Aggregates

In order to upgrade Tilde with complex aggregates to a first order random forest, we proceeded as follows.

First, we built a wrapper around the algorithm in order to get bagging. We made some adaptations to get out-of-bag error estimates.

Next, we built in a filter that allows only a random subset of the tests to be considered at each node[1]. As a result, constructing a new node proceeds as follows: first all possible candidates $\rho(\leftarrow Q)$ are generated, then a random subset of approximate size $f(|candidates|)$ (where $f(x)$ is a function given by the user, e.g. $f(x) = 0.1x$ or $f(x) = \sqrt{x}$, ...) is chosen. For each query in this subset, a heuristic is computed and the optimal split is placed in the new node. Consequently, only a part of all generated queries need to be executed on the examples to calculate the heuristics, which obviously results in an efficiency gain.

Finally, we added another selection technique that could further increase diversity among the trees, and might improve the strength of the random forest. Instead of always selecting the optimal query at each node in a tree (out of the queries in the random sample), queries can be chosen according to a certain distribution. This way, even less good queries have a chance to be chosen; this chance being proportional to their quality.

To summarize, we provide an overview of the resulting algorithm in Fig. 2. The procedure GROW_FOREST takes the number of trees to grow as one of its input parameters (N). For each tree, it first builds a new set of examples, sampled with replacement from the original set E. Then the procedure GROW_TREE_2 is called, which is an adaptation of GROW_TREE (see Fig. 1). The refinement operator ρ includes (complex) aggregate conditions, as discussed in Sect. 4.2. The SUBSET procedure generates a random subset of the candidate set. Each candidate has probability P to be chosen. P can take any number between zero and one, it can also be $1/sqrt(|candidates|)$. The GET_SPLIT procedure either returns the optimal split, or returns a split with probability proportional to its quality, as explained above.

5 Experimental Results

In this section, we investigate the strength of first order random forests (FORF) in a setting where the feature set is expanded with aggregates, both simple and complex ones. We start by describing our experimental setup (Sect. 5.1). Next, we present results on three well-known data sets: Mutagenesis [26] (Sect. 5.2), Diterpenes [11] (Sect. 5.3), and Financial [1] (Sect. 5.4). The first two data sets contain complex structures and have been widely used as ILP benchmarks. The latter is a business domain data set with high degree of non-determinacy. Finally, we formulate some experimental conclusions (Sect. 5.5).

---

[1] This actually differs from the definition in [8] where a random subset of the attributes, instead of the tests, is chosen. Note that one attribute may yield different tests.

procedure GROW_FOREST (*N*: nb of trees, *P*: probability, *E*: set of examples):
  for $i = 1$ to N
    E_i := SAMPLE(E)
    T_i := GROW_TREE_2(E_i, *true*, *P*)
  return forest($T_1, T_2, ..., T_N$)

procedure GROW_TREE_2 (*E*: set of examples, *Q*: query, *P*: probability):
  candidates := $\rho(\leftarrow Q)$
  candidates_subset := SUBSET(*candidates*, *P*)
  $\leftarrow Q_b$:= GET_SPLIT(*candidates_subset*, *E*)
  if STOP_CRIT ($\leftarrow Q_b, E$)
  then
      K := MOST_FREQUENT_CLASS(E)
      return leaf(K)
  else
      conj := $Q_b - Q$
      E_1 := $\{e \in E | \leftarrow Q_b$ succeeds in $e \wedge B\}$
      E_2 := $\{e \in E | \leftarrow Q_b$ fails in $e \wedge B\}$
      left := GROW_TREE_2 (E_1, Q_b, P)
      right := GROW_TREE_2 (E_2, Q, P)
      return node(*conj*, *left*, *right*)

Fig. 2. Algorithm for first order random forest induction

5.1 Experimental Setup

All experiments with random forests were performed using out-of-bag estimation (unless otherwise stated) and were carried out five times, in order to obtain a more reliable estimate of the performance. The predictive performance is compared to that of Tilde, obtained by averaging five runs of tenfold cross-validation. We used the basic form of Tilde, i.e. without aggregate conditions.

Different parameters needed to be set. First of all, the number of random features in each node: we chose to consider random subsets of 100%, 75%, 50%, 25%, 10%, and the square root of the number of tests at each node in the trees. We have also examined the influence of the number of trees in the random forests, experimenting with 3, 11, and 33 trees.

To investigate the performance of first order random forests in the context of aggregation, we have performed experiments using different levels of aggregation. In the first level, we did not use any aggregates (afterwards, this setting is called FORF-NA). In the second level, simple aggregate conditions were introduced (FORF-SA). The third level includes refinement of aggregate queries (FORF-RA) and the fourth level allows lookahead up to depth 1 within the aggregate queries (FORF-LA). The aggregate functions used were *min*, *max* and *avg* for continuous attributes, *mode* for discrete attributes, and *count*.

If, for a certain data set, results are available for other systems, we also compared the performance of FORF to that of the other systems.

5.2 Mutagenesis

For our first experiment, we used the Mutagenesis data set. This ILP benchmark data set, introduced to the ILP community by Srinivasan et al. [26], consists of structural descriptions of 230 molecules that are to be classified as mutagenic (60%) or not. The description consists of the atoms and the bonds that make up the molecule. Since the data is not very non-determinate and does not contain many numerical attributes, we expected only a slight gain using aggregates.

Predictive accuracies are shown in Table 1. An example of a test that was frequently found at high levels in the different trees was the following aggregate condition (with the range of Mol bound to a molecule)

```
count(BId,(bond(BId,Mol,At1,At2,Tp)),C), C>28.
```

with the following conjunction in its left child

```
count(BId,(bond(BId,Mol,At1,At2,Tp),atom(Mol,At1,carbon)),C'), C'>28.
```

The first part of the example represents the set of all molecules that have at least 28 bonds. This aggregate was also found to be a good test by Knobbe et al. [16]. The refinement of the aggregate describes all molecules that have at least 28 bonds connected to an atom of type carbon. Unfortunately, we can not compare our results to those given by Knobbe et al. [16], since they only report predictive accuracies for one best rule, covering only a part of the positive examples.

Table 1. Accuracy results on the Mutagenesis data set. The rows indicate the sample ratio at each node. The columns compare predictive accuracies for FORF-LA, FORF-RA, FORF-SA, FORF-NA, and Tilde. The standard deviation is indicated between parentheses.

	FORF (33 trees)				Tilde
	LA	RA	SA	NA	NA
1	0.779 (0.008)	0.774 (0.014)	0.777 (0.011)	0.731 (0.010)	0.720 (0.007)
0.75	0.774 (0.013)	0.775 (0.010)	0.764 (0.017)	0.720 (0.015)	
0.50	0.777 (0.012)	0.781 (0.012)	0.789 (0.018)	0.747 (0.014)	
0.25	0.770 (0.013)	0.772 (0.016)	0.758 (0.011)	0.736 (0.014)	
0.10	0.790 (0.014)	0.765 (0.017)	0.761 (0.013)	0.653 (0.015)	
sqrt	0.785 (0.016)	0.752 (0.010)	0.743 (0.016)	0.690 (0.027)	

5.3 Diterpenes

In our second experiment, we used the Diterpenes data set [11]. The data contains information on 1503 diterpenes with known structure, stored in three relations. The *atom* relation specifies to which element an atom in a given compound belongs. The *bond* relation specifies which atoms are bound in a given compound. The *red* relation stores the measured NMR-Spectra. For each of the 20 carbon atoms in the diterpene skeleton, it contains the multiplicity and frequency. Additional unary predicates describe to which of the 25 classes a compound belongs.

Table 2 gives predictive accuracies of experiments using 33 trees. For efficiency reasons, we changed the minimal cases a leaf has to cover from 2 to 20.

Table 2. Accuracy results on the Diterpenes data set. The rows indicate the sample ratio at each node. The columns compare predictive accuracies for FORF-LA, FORF-RA, FORF-SA, FORF-NA, and Tilde. The standard deviation is indicated between parentheses.

	FORF (33 trees)				Tilde
	LA	RA	SA	NA	NA
1	0.859 (0.004)	0.829 (0.011)	0.849 (0.003)	0.768 (0.003)	0.737 (0.011)
0.75	0.859 (0.003)	0.840 (0.002)	0.849 (0.004)	0.769 (0.002)	
0.50	0.856 (0.006)	0.839 (0.004)	0.850 (0.001)	0.766 (0.004)	
0.25	0.856 (0.004)	0.849 (0.007)	0.847 (0.004)	0.763 (0.004)	
0.10	0.853 (0.004)	0.823 (0.012)	0.842 (0.002)	0.739 (0.007)	
sqrt	0.844 (0.005)	0.806 (0.004)	0.824 (0.006)	0.716 (0.004)	

The numbers in Table 2 do not compare favorably with earlier published results [11], but the experimental setting is also different; especially the minimal leaf size of 20 seems to have a detrimental effect. To allow a better comparison with published results, we performed a single experiment where, just like in [11], results of five runs of a tenfold cross-validation are averaged. The minimal leaf size of trees was reset to 2; and we used the FORF-SA setting with 33 trees and a sampling size of 25%, which, judging from our earlier results, are good parameter values. The result of this experiment is compared with published results for other systems in Table 3. FOIL [24] induces concept definitions represented as function-free Horn clauses, from relational data. RIBL [12] is a relational instance based learning algorithm. It generalizes the nearest neighbor method to a relational representation. The ICL system [9] uses exactly the same representation of training examples as Tilde, but induces rule sets instead of trees. It was already found that combining propositional (aggregate) features with relational information yielded the best results [11]. Comparing with those best results, we see that FORF is at least competitive with the best of the other approaches. (Unavailability of standard deviations for the published results makes it difficult to test the significance of the improvement of FORF-SA over RIBL.)

Table 3. Accuracy results on the Diterpenes data set compared to other systems. The results for FOIL, RIBL, and ICL are obtained from [11]. No standard deviations were given.

FORF-SA	FOIL	RIBL	ICL
0.928 (0.006)	0.783	0.912	0.860

5.4 Financial

Our last experiment deals with the Financial data set, originating from the discovery challenge organized at PKDD '99 and PKDD '00 [1]. This data set involves learning to classify bank loans into good and bad ones. Since 86% of the examples is positive, the data distribution is quite skewed. The data set consists of 8 relations. For each of the 234 loans, customer information and account information is provided. The account information includes permanent orders and several hundreds of transactions per account. This problem is thus a typical business data set which is highly non-determinate.

Predictive accuracies are shown in Table 4. In this case the square root of the number of tests is on average larger than 10%, so we switched these two rows.

Table 4. Accuracy results on the Financial data set. The rows indicate the sample ratio at each node. The columns compare predictive accuracies for FORF-LA, FORF-RA, FORF-SA, FORF-NA, and Tilde. The standard deviation is indicated between parentheses.

	FORF (33 trees)				Tilde
	LA	RA	SA	NA	NA
1	0.986 (0.009)	0.989 (0.005)	0.990 (0.005)	0.845 (0.005)	0.790 (0.027)
0.75	0.991 (0.005)	0.991 (0.005)	0.990 (0.002)	0.834 (0.010)	
0.50	0.991 (0.004)	0.992 (0.004)	0.992 (0.004)	0.846 (0.012)	
0.25	0.991 (0.006)	0.995 (0.006)	0.991 (0.002)	0.853 (0.011)	
sqrt	0.984 (0.010)	0.988 (0.004)	0.993 (0.009)	0.854 (0.004)	
0.10	0.975 (0.011)	0.972 (0.012)	0.964 (0.020)	0.864 (0.004)	

Table 5 shows predictive accuracies compared to other systems [18]. DINUS-C [19] is a propositionalisation technique using only determinate features and using C4.5 rules as propositional learner. RELAGGS [18] was discussed in Sect. 3. PROGOL [21] is an ILP learner capable of learning in structurally very complex domains. For our random forest, we used the SA setting, since neither LA nor RA yielded significantly better results for this data set. The forest contained 33 trees and a sampling size of 25%. For better comparisions, we averaged five runs of tenfold cross-validation instead of out-of-bag estimations.

Table 5. Accuracy results on the Financial data set compared to other systems. The results for DINUS-C, RELAGGS, and PROGOL are obtained from [18]. The standard deviation is indicated between parentheses.

FORF-SA	DINUS-C	RELAGGS	PROGOL
0.993 (0.005)	0.851 (0.103)	0.880 (0.065)	0.863 (0.071)

5.5 Experimental Conclusions

As can be seen from Tables 1, 2 and 4, the use of simple aggregates yields quite a large improvement on all data sets. As was expected, the gain is largest on the Financial data set (about 15%). Refinement of the aggregate conditions increased accuracy in some cases, while the use of lookahead within the aggregate query in general added another slight performance improvement.

We observe that for all experiments, using only a random part of the features (certainly down to 25%) to select the best test seems to be advisable, since there is no significant drop in accuracy (no significant gain either) and we profit from the efficiency gain by testing fewer features in each node. Breiman [8] on the other hand, obtained higher improvements with even much smaller proportions of features in the propositional case. This difference might be due to the fact that in our approach a random subset of tests is taken, while Breiman takes a random subset of the attributes, and selects the best test using these attributes. However, this remains to be investigated.

Random forests indeed seem to profit from a large feature space, which is certainly present when using lookahead in the aggregate queries. While for FORF-NA, FORF-SA and FORF-RA accuracy slightly tends to decrease when using smaller samples of features (an exception to that is the Financial data set, where for FORF-NA the accuracy tends to increase by decreasing the number of features due to the skewness of the data), this is less the case for FORF-LA.

As can be seen from Fig. 3, adding more trees to the forest clearly increased accuracy in all experiments. Of course more trees mean longer runtimes, so there is still a trade-off between efficiency and accuracy.

Concerning the complexity of the trees in the random forests, we found that both adding aggregate conditions and further refining them, strongly decreased the size of the trees for all experiments. For example, for the Financial data set FORF-NA produced trees with on average 17.65 nodes, while FORF-SA yielded trees with on average 4.72 nodes. Applying lookahead to the aggregate queries slightly increased the number of nodes in each tree, while still being much smaller than the number of nodes in each tree of FORF-NA.

While in general performing at least as well as bagging, random forests are computationally more efficient. If we compare random forests, consisting of 33 trees and using 25% of the features, with bagging using 33 trees, we found an efficiency gain of factor 1.3 to 2.6 over the different data sets. Again, this factor is smaller than in the propositional case, where there is no need to generate tests at each node, since the set of tests remains the same. On the Mutagenesis data and the Diterpenes data, computation times of FORF-NA, FORF-SA and FORF-RA are quite in the same range (i.e. a few minutes), on the Financial data on the other hand, computation times of FORF-NA and FORF-RA might differ up to a factor 5 (i.e. from seconds to minutes). As was expected, applying lookahead resulted in quite an explosion of features which couldn't be offset by the speed-up due to feature sampling. Comparing runtimes of FORF-RA and FORF-LA gives differences of factor 10 to 70 (i.e. from minutes to a few hours).

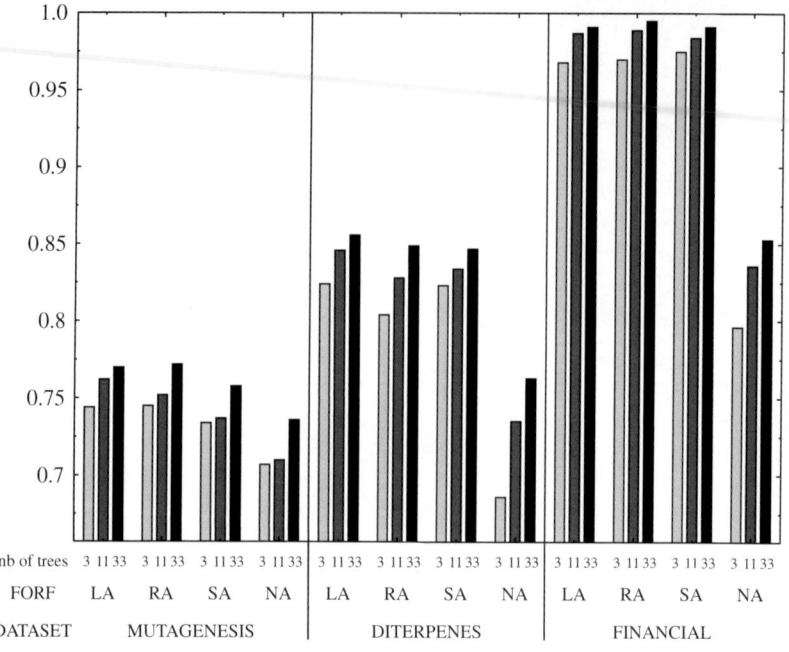

Fig. 3. Accuracy for random forests using 25% of the features. Results are shown for FORF-LA, FORF-RA, FORF-SA and FORF-NA on the three different data sets.

In order to compensate for these huge runtimes, we certainly need to reduce the time for generating the queries.

Another observation concerns the effect of proportional selection of a test in the GET_SPLIT procedure. We repeated our experiments using this mechanism. The difference in predictive accuracy between selecting the optimal test and proportionally selecting a test did not turn out to be statistically significant. Remark that when using aggregate functions, features may have several logical equivalent notations. Thus, when using a large set of features at each node (e.g. with a sample ratio of 1.0 or 0.75) it is likely that several equivalent versions of the best test are in the feature set. Consequently, even using proportional selection, this feature has a high chance to be chosen. When using only a small random sample of tests at each node, proportional selection did not seem to add any improvement over the randomization.

To conclude this discussion, we compared the results of FORF-SA to available results of a number of other systems that either include aggregates themselves or use a language bias with user predefined aggregate functions. FORF-SA clearly outperformed these systems on our chosen data sets (see Tables 3 and 5).

6 Conclusions and Future Work

In this paper we have presented a first order random forest induction algorithm. Random forest induction [8] is a bagging method that randomly samples the feature set at each node in a decision tree. In the propositional case, random forests have been shown to work well when lots of features are available. As this is often the case in relational learning, it seems worthwhile to investigate the strength of random forests in this context.

Moreover, using random forests, the feature space can be further enlarged by including aggregate conditions, possibly combined with selection conditions on the set to be aggregated. This combination can occur when refining an aggregate condition, or when applying a lookahead mechanism within the aggregate query. The resulting aggregate conditions are called complex ones.

The combination of aggregation and selection is not a trivial task, because the feature space grows quickly and because the search space is less well-behaved due to non-monotonicity of some aggregate conditions. However, the use of random forests overcomes these problems. First, the feature set considered at each node in a tree is reduced by the sampling procedure. Second, the divide and conquer approach used in decision tree induction algorithms allows to include non-monotone aggregate conditions, and as we showed, these can lead to some useful refinements. Moreover, non-monotone aggregate conditions can, in combination with lookahead, simulate a bottom-up search strategy included in the top down decision tree induction approach.

To implement the above ideas, we used Tilde [4] as a base first order decision tree induction algorithm. Tilde was upgraded to a first order random forest with complex aggregates in the feature space.

The strength of our first order random forest approach and the use of (complex) aggregates were experimentally validated. Our results show that, if we randomly decrease the feature set at each node in a tree down to a certain level, the classification performance is at least as good as bagging, thus we profit from the efficiency gain. In our data sets the optimal level turned out to be 25% of the features; below this threshold classification performance decreased. The benefit of including simple aggregate functions was clearly shown. Using complex aggregate functions yielded another small performance improvement. Furthermore, our approach clearly outperformed existing systems on our chosen data sets.

Now we focus on two possible directions for future work. The first and most important direction is to make the forest induction algorithm more efficient, in order to make it more generally applicable. Efficiency gain can be obtained by generating only a sample of all queries at each node. This could be done by using a probabilistic grammar to represent the language of possible tests. At each node in a tree, a random sample of the features from the probabilistic grammar could be taken. This way, features would be generated probabilistically, and runtimes would be further reduced. By doing this, we would move closer towards Breiman's approach [8], where attributes are selected instead of tests.

A second direction is to investigate the effect of degree disparity [15] in the context of random forests. Degree disparity occurs when the frequency of a relation is correlated with the values of the target variable. This can cause learning algorithms to be strongly biased toward certain features, when using aggregate functions. Consequently, this may influence the extent to which different trees in the forest are independent.

Acknowledgements. Celine Vens is supported by the GOA/2003/08(B0516) on Inductive Knowledge Bases. Anneleen Van Assche is supported by the Institute for the Promotion of Innovation by Science and Technology in Flanders (I.W.T.-Vlaanderen). Hendrik Blockeel is Postdoctoral Fellow of the Fund for Scientific Research - Flanders (Belgium) (F.W.O.-Vlaanderen).
We also would like to thank Maurice Bruynooghe, for some useful discussions that have led to a number of important improvements to the text.

References

1. P. Berka. Guide to the financial data set. In A. Siebes and P. Berka, editors, *The ECML/PKDD 2000 Discovery Challenge*, 2000.
2. H. Blockeel and M. Bruynooghe. Aggregation versus selection bias, and relational neural networks. In *IJCAI-2003 Workshop on Learning Statistical Models from Relational Data, SRL-2003, Acapulco, Mexico, August 11, 2003*, 2003.
3. H. Blockeel and L. De Raedt. Lookahead and discretization in ILP. In *Proceedings of the Seventh International Workshop on Inductive Logic Programming*, volume 1297 of *Lecture Notes in Artificial Intelligence*, pages 77–85. Springer-Verlag, 1997.
4. H. Blockeel and L. De Raedt. Top-down induction of first order logical decision trees. *Artificial Intelligence*, 101(1-2):285–297, June 1998.
5. H. Blockeel, L. Dehaspe, B. Demoen, G. Janssens, J. Ramon, and H. Vandecasteele. Improving the efficiency of inductive logic programming through the use of query packs. *Journal of Artificial Intelligence Research*, 16:135–166, 2002.
6. L. Breiman. Bagging predictors. *Machine Learning*, 24(2):123–140, 1996.
7. L. Breiman. Out-of-bag estimation. ftp.stat.berkeley.edu/pub/users/breiman/OOBestimation.ps, 1996.
8. L. Breiman. Random forests. *Machine Learning*, 45(1):5–32, 2001.
9. L. De Raedt and W. Van Laer. Inductive constraint logic. In K. P. Jantke, T. Shinohara, and T. Zeugmann, editors, *Proceedings of the Sixth International Workshop on Algorithmic Learning Theory*, volume 997 of *Lecture Notes in Artificial Intelligence*, pages 80–94. Springer-Verlag, 1995.
10. T. Dietterich. Ensemble methods in machine learning. In *Proceedings of the 1th International Workshop on Multiple Classifier Systems*, volume 1857 of *Lecture Notes in Computer Science*, pages 1–15, 2000.
11. S. Džeroski, S. Schulze-Kremer, K. R. Heidtke, K. Siems, D. Wettschereck, and H. Blockeel. Diterpene structure elucidation from ^{13}C NMR spectra with inductive logic programming. *Applied Artificial Intelligence*, 12(5):363–384, July-August 1998.
12. W. Emde and D. Wettschereck. Relational instance based learning. In *Proceedings of the 1995 Workshop of the GI Special Interest Group on Machine Learning*, 1995.
13. Y. Freund and R. E. Schapire. Experiments with a new boosting algorithm. In L. Saitta, editor, *Proceedings of the Thirteenth International Conference on Machine Learning*, pages 148–156. Morgan Kaufmann, 1996.

14. L. Hansen and P. Salamon. Neural network ensembles. *IEEE Transactions on Pattern Analysis and Machine Intelligence*, 12:993–1001, 1990.

15. D. Jensen, J. Neville, and M. Hay. Avoiding bias when aggregating relational data with degree disparity. In *Proceedings of the 20th International Conference on Machine Learning*, 2003.

16. A. Knobbe, A. Siebes, and B. Marseille. Involving aggregate functions in multi-relational search. In *Principles of Data Mining and Knowledge Discovery, Proceedings of the 6th European Conference*, pages 287–298. Springer-Verlag, August 2002.

17. D. Koller. Probabilistic relational models. In *Proceedings of the Ninth International Workshop on Inductive Logic Programming*, volume 1634 of *Lecture Notes in Artificial Intelligence*, pages 3–13. Springer-Verlag, 1999.

18. M.-A. Krogel and S. Wrobel. Transformation-based learning using multi-relational aggregation. In *Proceedings of the Eleventh International Conference on Inductive Logic Programming*, pages 142–155, 2001.

19. N. Lavrač and S. Džeroski. *Inductive Logic Programming: Techniques and Applications*. Ellis Horwood, 1994.

20. S. Muggleton, editor. *Inductive Logic Programming*. Academic Press, 1992.

21. S. Muggleton. Inverse entailment and Progol. *New Generation Computing, Special issue on Inductive Logic Programming*, 13(3-4):245–286, 1995.

22. J. Neville, D. Jensen, L. Friedland, and M. Hay. Learning relational probability trees. In *Proceedings of the 9th ACM SIGKDD International Conference on Knowledge Discovery and Data Mining*, 2003.

23. C. Perlich and F. Provost. Aggregation-based feature invention and relational concept classes. In *Proceedings of the ninth ACM SIGKDD international conference on Knowledge discovery and data mining*, pages 167–176. ACM Press, 2003.

24. J. Quinlan. Learning logical definitions from relations. *Machine Learning*, 5:239–266, 1990.

25. J. R. Quinlan. *C4.5: Programs for Machine Learning*. Morgan Kaufmann series in Machine Learning. Morgan Kaufmann, 1993.

26. A. Srinivasan, R. King, and D. Bristol. An assessment of ILP-assisted models for toxicology and the PTE-3 experiment. In *Proceedings of the Ninth International Workshop on Inductive Logic Programming*, volume 1634 of *Lecture Notes in Artificial Intelligence*, pages 291–302. Springer-Verlag, 1999.

A Monte Carlo Study of Randomised Restarted Search in ILP

Filip Železný[1], Ashwin Srinivasan[2], and David Page[3]

[1] Dept. of Cybernetics
School of Electrical Engineering
Czech Institute of Technology (ČVUT) in Prague
Karlovo Nám. 13, 121 35 Prague, Czech Republic
zelezny@fel.cvut.cz
[2] IBM India Research Laboratory
Block 1, Indian Institute of Technology
New Delhi 110 016, India
ashwin.srinivasan@in.ibm.com
[3] Dept. of Biostatistics and Medical Informatics and Dept. of Computer Science
University of Wisconsin
1300 University Ave., Rm 5795 Medical Sciences
Madison, WI 53706, USA
page@biostat.wisc.edu

Abstract. Recent statistical performance surveys of search algorithms in difficult combinatorial problems have demonstrated the benefits of randomising and restarting the search procedure. Specifically, it has been found that if the search cost distribution (SCD) of the non-restarted randomised search exhibits a slower-than-exponential decay (that is, a "heavy tail"), restarts can reduce the search cost expectation. Recently, this heavy tail phenomenon was observed in the SCD's of benchmark ILP problems. Following on this work, we report on an empirical study of randomised restarted search in ILP. Our experiments, conducted over a cluster of a few hundred computers, provide an extensive statistical performance sample of five search algorithms operating on two principally different ILP problems (artificially generated graph data and the well-known "mutagenesis" problem). The sample allows us to (1) estimate the conditional expected value of the search cost (measured by the total number of clauses explored) given the minimum clause score required and a "cutoff" value (the number of clauses examined before the search is restarted); and (2) compare the performance of randomised restarted search strategies to a deterministic non-restarted search. Our findings indicate that the cutoff value is significantly more important than the choice of (a) the specific refinement strategy; (b) the starting element of the search; and (c) the specific data domain. We find that the optimal value for the cutoff parameter remains roughly stable across variations of these three factors and that the mean search cost using this value in a randomised restarted search is up to three orders of magnitude (i.e. 1000 times) lower than that obtained with a deterministic non-restarted search.

R. Camacho, R. King, A. Srinivasan (Eds.): ILP 2004, LNAI 3194, pp. 341–358, 2004.
© Springer-Verlag Berlin Heidelberg 2004

1   Introduction

Computer programs now collectively termed "predictive Inductive Logic Programming" (predictive ILP) systems use domain-specific background information and pre-classified sample data to construct a set of first-order rules for predicting the classification labels of new data. Despite considerable diversity in the applications of ILP, (see [2] for an overview) successful implementations have been relatively uniform, namely, engines that repeatedly examine sets of candidate rules to find the "best" ones. Any one step of this sequence is an enumerative search—usually some approximation to the optimal branch-and-bound algorithm—through a space of possible rules. This choice of search method can critically affect the performance of an ILP system on non-trivial problems. Enumerative search methods, despite their attractive simplicity, are not *robust* in the sense of achieving a balance between efficiency and efficacy across different problems [3]. For many practical problems that engender very large spaces of discrete elements, enumerative search, however clever, becomes intractable and we are forced to take seriously Trefethen's Maxim No. 30 [10]: "If the state space is huge, the only reasonable way to explore it is at random." Recently, research into the development of efficient automatic model-checkers has led to the development of novel randomised search methods that abandon optimality in favour of "good" solutions. Prominent examples are the GSAT and WalkSat methods checking the satisfiability of propositional formulae [8], as randomised alternatives to the (enumerative) Davis-Putnam solver. In conjunction with this, there is now a vigorous line of research that investigates properties of large search spaces corresponding to difficult combinatorial problems [4]. Some intriguing properties have been identified, such as the high irregularity of the search spaces and "heavy-tailedness" of the cost distributions of search algorithms used. Such properties manifest themselves in a large collection of real-world problems and have been the inspiration for the design of randomised restarted search procedures. The basic idea of these procedures is simple: if each search trial has a small, but fixed probability of finding a good clause, then the probability of finding a good clause in a sequence of such trials can be made quite high very rapidly. Put differently, the SCD from the sequence has an exponential decay.

Previously, the heavy-tailed character of search cost distributions was reported in the context of the first-order rule search conducted in ILP [11]. There, a simple adaptation of a method known as Randomised Rapid Restarts [5] was shown to result in a considerable reduction of clause search cost. Here, we extend that investigation as follows:

1. We adapt a family of randomised restarted search strategies into an ILP system and present all of them as instantiations of a general algorithm.
2. We design and conduct an extensive Monte Carlo study that allows us to model the statistical relationships between the search cost, the score of the best clause and the number of clauses explored in each restart (called the "cutoff" value in the search algorithm).

Our experiments are conducted with data drawn from two domains: artificially generated, noise-free, graph problems, in which "target" theories can be modelled by a single, long clause (up to 10 literals in the body of the clause); and the well-known mutagenesis problem, which is typically modelled by multiple, relatively short clauses (typically up to 5 body literals) Although the natures of the problems are quite different to each other, the main statistical findings relate equally to both the domains.

The paper is organised as follows. In the next section we describe the clause search strategies considered and the performance metric used to evaluate the strategies. Details of the Monte Carlo study of these strategies and the dependence of their performance on some important parameters is in Section 3, where we also discuss our results and formulate questions requiring further investigation. Section 4 concludes the paper.

2 Search

We are principally concerned with performing a search in the clause subsumption lattice bounded at one end by a finite most specific ("bottom") clause derived using definitions in the background knowledge, a depth-bounded mode language, and a single positive example (the "saturant": see [7] for more details on the construction of this clause). For simplicity, we will assume the specification of the depth-bounded mode language to be part of the background knowledge.

2.1 Strategies

The five search strategies that we investigate in this paper are: (1) A deterministic general-to-specific search (DTD); (2) A randomised general-to-specific search (RTD); (3) A rapid random restart search (RRR); (4) A randomised search using the GSAT algorithm (GSAT); and (5) A randomised search using the WalkSAT algorithm (WSAT). All five strategies can be viewed as variations of a general search procedure shown in Fig. 1. Differences between the individual strategies arise from the implementation of the commands in bold-face (summarised in Table 1). All strategies include restarts (if γ is a finite value). Restarting DTD results in simply repeating the search.

As further clarification of the entries in Table 1, we note the following:

Saturant selection. A deterministic implementation ('D') of the first **Select** command (Step 3 in Fig. 1) results in the first positive example in the presented example sequence being chosen as the saturant. A randomised implementation ('R') results in all examples having a uniform probability of selection.

Start clause selection. A deterministic implementation ('D') of the second **Select** command (Step 4), results in the search commencing with the the the most general definite clause allowable. A randomised implementation ('R') results in a clause selected with uniform probability from the set of allowable clauses (see [11] for more details on how this is achieved).

$search(B, H, E, s^{suf}, c^{all}, \gamma)$: Given background knowledge B; a set of clauses H; a training sequence $E = E^{+}, E^{-}$ (i.e. positive and negative examples); a sufficient clause score s^{suf} $(-\infty \leq s^{suf} \leq \infty)$; the maximum number of clauses the algorithm can evaluate c^{all}, $(0 < c^{all} < \infty)$; and the maximum number of clauses evaluated on any single restart or the 'cutoff' value γ $(0 < \gamma \leq \infty)$, returns a clause D such that $B \cup H \cup \{D\}$ entails at least one element e of E^{+}. If fewer than c^{all} clauses are evaluated in the search, then the score of D is at least s^{suf}.

1. $S := -\infty$; $C := 0$; $N := 0$
2. repeat
3.   **Select** e^{sat} from E^{+}
4.   **Select** D_0 such that $D_0 \succeq_{\theta} \perp(e^{sat}, B)$
5. $Active = \emptyset$; $Ref = \{D_0\}$
6.   repeat
7. $S^{*} = \max_{D_i \in Ref} \underline{eval}_{B,H}(D_i)$; $D^{*} := \arg\max_{D_i \in Ref} \underline{eval}_{B,H}(D_i)$
8.   if $S^{*} > S$ then $S := S^{*}$; $D := D^{*}$
9. $N := N + |Ref|$
10. $Active := $ **UpdateActiveList**$(Active, Ref)$
11. $Prune := $ **Prune**$(Active, S^{*})$
12. $Active := Active \setminus Prune$
13.   **Select** D^{curr} from $Active$; $Active := Active \setminus D^{curr}$
14. $Ref := $ **Refine**$_{B,H,(\gamma-N)}(D^{curr})$
15.   until $S \geq s^{suf}$ or $C + N \geq c^{all}$ or $N = \gamma$
16. $C := C + N$; $N := 0$
17. until $S \geq s^{suf}$ or $C \geq c^{all}$
18. if $S = -\infty$ then return e^{sat} else return D^{*}.

Fig. 1. A general skeleton of a search procedure—possibly randomised and/or restarted—in the clause subsumption lattice bounded by the clause $\perp(e^{sat}, B)$. This clause is derived using the saturant e^{sat} and the background knowledge B. In Step 4, $\succeq_{\theta}$ denotes Plotkin's (theta) subsumption between a pair of Horn clauses. Individual strategies considered in this paper are obtained by different implementations of the bold-typed commands. Clauses are scored by a finite evaluation function $\underline{eval}$. Although in the formal notation in Step 7 the function appears twice, it is assumed that the 'max' and 'arg max' operators are computed simultaneously. In Step 11 **Prune** returns all elements of $Active$ that cannot possibly be refined to have a better score than S^{*}. If the number of refinements of the current clause is greater than $(\gamma - N)$, **Refine** returns only the first $(\gamma - N)$ computed refinements, to guarantee that no more than γ clauses are evaluated between restarts. The search is terminated when score s^{suf} is reached or c^{all} clauses have been evaluated, and restarted (from Step 3) when γ clauses have been evaluated since the last restart. If all **Select** commands are deterministic then restarting (setting $\gamma < c^{all}$) results in mere repetitions of the identical search.

Update active list. A greedy implementation ('G') of the **UpdateActiveList** function (Step 10) results in the active list containing only the newly explored nodes (elements of the Ref). A complete implementation ('C') results in $Active$ containing all elements (including elements of Ref).

Table 1. Implementation differences amongst the different search strategies. The entries are as follows: 'D' stands for 'deterministic', 'R' for 'randomised', 'G' for greedy, 'C' for complete, 'Y' to denote that pruning occurs, 'N' that pruning does not occur, 'U' for uni-directional refinement (specialisation only) and 'B' for bi-directional refinement (specialisation and generalisation). See text for more details on these entries.

Strategy → ↓ Step	DTD	RTD	RRR	GSAT	WSAT
Saturant selection (**Select** in Step 3)	D	R	R	R	R
Start clause selection (**Select** in Step 4)	D	D	R	R	R
Update active list (**UpdateActiveList** in Step 10)	C	C	C	G	G
Next clause selection (**Select** in Step 13)	D	R	D	D	R
Pruning (**Prune** in Step 11)	Y	Y	N	N	N
Refinement (**Refine** in Step 14)	U	U	B	B	B

Next clause selection. A deterministic implementation ('D') of the last **Select** command (Step 13) results in the clause with the highest score being chosen from the *Active* list (with ties being decided by the appearance order of clauses). A randomised implementation ('R') results in a random choice governed by the following prescription:

- With probability 0.5, select the clause with the highest score in the *Active* list.
- Otherwise, select a random clause in the *Active* list with probability proportional to its score.

Pruning. 'Y' denotes that pruning is performed, which results in a possibly non-empty set being returned by the **Prune** command (Step 11). A 'N' implementation means that an empty set is returned.

Refinement. The 'U' implementation of **Refine** command (Step 14) results in refinements that are guaranteed to be specialisations of the clause being refined. The 'B' implementation produces the (most general) specializations and (most specific) generalizations of the refined clause.

2.2 Evaluation

Informally, given some clause evaluation function, for each search strategy we ask:

How many clauses must be searched to achieve a desired clause score?

Here, we treat the number of clauses searched as representative of the 'search cost' and quantify this cost-score trade-off by the expected value of the smallest cost needed to achieve or exceed a desired score s^{suf} [1], given an upper bound

---

[1] At any stage of the search, the score value maintains the highest clause evaluation so far obtained in the search. In other words, within a particular search execution, the score value is a non-decreasing function of the cost (i.e. the number of clauses searched).

γ on the clauses searched on any single restart. Thus, for each strategy we wish to estimate:

$$cost(s^{suf}) \equiv E[C|s^{suf}, \gamma] \qquad (1)$$

The following points are evident, but worth restating:

1. Let us assume that strategy St_1 is found to achieve, on average, a desired score s^{suf} significantly faster than strategy St_2. Strictly speaking, even if the clauses added successively to a constructed theory do not reference each other, we cannot conclude that a set-covering algorithm employing St_1 will be more efficient than that using St_2. This is because in the cover algorithm, the individual clause search procedures are not statistically independent events (since one influences the following by removing a subset of the positive examples).[2]

2. We are only concerned here with the search cost in finding a clause with a given score on the training set. This does not, of course, translate to any statement about the performance of the clause found on new (test) data. It is certainly interesting and feasible to also investigate whether and how the generalization rate is statistically dependent on the procedure used to arrive at an acceptable clause, given a required score. This is, however, outside the scope of this study.

3. A search cost of immediate interest is the processor time occupied by a strategy. By adopting instead to measure the number of clauses searched, we are unable to quantify precisely the exact time taken by each strategy. Besides the obvious hardware dependence, research elsewhere [1] has shown that the cost of evaluating a clause can vary significantly depending on the nature of the problem addressed and formulation of the background knowledge. In this study we are concerned with obtaining some domain-independent insight into the five strategies.

4. Our evaluation of the strategies may have well been based on a different question, namely:
   What clause score is achieved given an allocated search cost?
   Here we would consider the expected score given an allocated cost c^{all}, that is $score(c^{all}) \equiv E[S|c^{all}, \gamma]$. Although the sample resulting from the Monte Carlo study can be used to evaluate the strategies in this way, space requirements confine this study to the former question, which we believe is of more immediate interest to practitioners of ILP.

3 Empirical Evaluation

3.1 Materials

Data. Experiments were conducted using two ILP benchmarks. The first data set describes a set of 5,000 directed graphs (containing in total 16,000 edges). Every node in a graph is coloured to red or black. Each graph is labelled positive

---

[2] The conclusion would however be correct for many other ruleset induction algorithms where the events are independent, such as CN2-like unordered rulesets, various other voting rulesets etc.

if and only if it contains a specific (coloured) subgraph which can be represented by a predefined clause of 10 body literals. Although this clause can be viewed as the target theory, there exist other clauses (subgraphs) in the search lattice that precisely separate the positive examples from the negatives. The second problem – mutagenesis prediction – has been discussed extensively in ILP literature and we use here one of the datasets described in our previous publication, namely the data pertaining to 188 "regression-friendly" compounds [9]. Table 2 describes the principal differences between the two data sets. The graph data set is available on request to the first author and the software for its generation can be obtained from the third author. The mutagenesis dataset can be obtained via anonymous ftp to ftp.comlab.ox.ac.uk in the directories pub/Packages/ILP/Datasets/mutagenesis/aleph.

Table 2. Differences between the experimental data sets.

Property	Graphs	Mutagenesis
Origin	Artificially generated	Biochemical literature
Noise	No	Yes
'Target' theory	Yes	No
'Good' theory	One long clause (10 lits)	Several short clauses (up to 5 body lits)
# pos/neg examples	20/20	125/63

Algorithm and Machines. All experiments use the ILP program Aleph. Aleph is available at: http://www.comlab.ox.ac.uk/oucl/research/areas/machlearn/Aleph/aleph.pl. Additional code implemented to Aleph for purposes of the empirical data collection can be obtained from the first author. The computation was distributed over the Condor computer cluster at the University of Wisconsin, Madison. All subsequent statistical analysis of the collected data was done by means of the R statistical package. The R procedures developed for this purpose can be obtained from the first author.

3.2   Method

Recall that we are interested in estimating the conditional expected cost value $E[C|s^{suf}, \gamma]$ for each of the five strategies in Section 2.1. A straightforward way to collect the required statistical sample needed to estimate the expected value for a given search strategy would thus be to run a number of instances of the algorithm in Fig. 1, each with a different setting of the sufficient score parameter s^{suf} and the restart cutoff parameter γ, each time recording the resulting value of C. This approach would however perform a lot of redundant computation. Instead we adopt the following method:

For each problem (5,000 graphs and 188 mutagenic chemicals)
   For each randomized strategy (RTD, RRR, GSAT, WSAT)

1. $\gamma = \infty$, $c^{all} = c_{max}$ (some large value: see notes below), $s^{suf} = s_{max}$ (the maximum possible clause score: see notes below)
2. for $i = 1$ to $\#Runs$
   a) Call $search(B, \emptyset, E, s^{suf}, c^{all}, \gamma)$ (see Fig. 1).
   b) Record the 'performance' vector $c_i = [c_i(0), \ldots, c_i(s_{max_i})]$ where $c_i(s)$ is the number of clauses evaluated before achieving (or exceeding) score s for the first time and s_{max_i} is the maximum score achieved on run i.
3. Compute the expected cost from the performance vectors recorded.

The following details are relevant:

1. The method assumes a finite, integer-valued scoring function. In the experiments we evaluate the score of a clause D as $P(D) - N(D)$ where $P(D)$ and $N(D)$ are the numbers of positive and negative examples 'covered' by D. That is, given positive and negative examples E^+, E^- let $E_p \subseteq E^+$ s.t. $B \cup \{D\} \models E_p$ and $E_n \subseteq E^-$ s.t. $B \cup \{D\} \models E_n$. Then $P(D) = |E_p|$ and $N(D) = |E_n|$. Rejecting all clauses for which $P(D) < N(D)$, the range of the score is $0 \ldots P$ where $P = |E^+|$. Thus in Step 1 $s_{max} = P$.
2. In these experiments c_{max} was set to 200,000 and $\#Runs$ was set to 6,000. Thus, the empirical sample after execution of Step 2 consists of 6,000 performance vectors. Each performance vector has at most $P = |E^+|$ elements (fewer elements are possible if score P was not achieved on a run).
3. Step 3 requires the computation of expected cost (i.e. the number of evaluated clauses) for any value of γ and s^{suf}. In Appendix A we describe how the sample of 6,000 performance vectors can be used to obtain an unbiased estimate of this value.

The method above does not refer to the non-restarted strategy DTD. DTD is deterministic and thus a single run (and corresponding single performance vector) should be sufficient to describe its performance. However, unlike the other strategies, DTD does not select the saturated example randomly, but it selects the first positive example for saturation. To avoid artifacts arising from any particular example ordering, we obtain instead an average conditional cost. That is, we thus perform Step 2a above $P = |E^+|$ times, each time selecting a different saturant. This results in P performance vectors: Appendix A shows how these performance vectors can be used to obtain a biased (lower bound) estimate of the expected cost for any value of s^{suf}.

3.3 Results

Figures 2–5 show diagrammatically the estimated expected number of evaluated clauses ('expected cost value') as a function of the restart cutoff parameter γ. Each graph has 2 kinds of plots: horizontal lines, representing (a lower bound on) the cost of the deterministic strategy DTD; and non-constant lines representing a randomised strategy. Each line is tagged with a number, which represents the sufficient clause score s^{suf}. Thus, in Fig. 2, for the plot labelled "Mutagenesis:

RTD", the horizontal line tagged "10" with a constant cost of 10,000 indicates that the expected number of clauses explored by DTD before finding a clause with score 10 is 10,000. The corresponding costs, for different values of the cutoff parameter γ for RTD are shown by the lowermost non-constant lines (each entry is tagged by "10"). Figures associated to the graphs domain contain 20 such plots (corresponding to all possible clause scores: some plots may overlay), figures belonging to the mutagenesis domain contain 7 plots (corresponding to $s^{suf} = 10, 20, \ldots 70$).[3] In all the diagrams, the highest vertical ($cost$) coordinate should be interpreted as: "c_{max} or higher" as all points corresponding to an expected cost in the interval $[c_{max}, \infty]$ are plotted with the vertical coordinate c_{max}.

Broadly, there are remarkable similarities in the plots from different strategies for a given problem domain, as well as from the same strategy for different problem domains. The principal trends are these:

1. The setting of the cutoff parameter γ has a very strong impact on the expected cost. A choice close to its optimal value may reduce the expected cost over DTD up to a 1,000 times for mutagenesis with RRR, GSAT or WSAT[4]. With RTD, the reduction is even higher for very low s^{suf}.
2. $\gamma \approx 100$ is a 'good' choice for all the investigated strategies in both domains. For the graph problems, the value is close to optimal (in the considered range of γ) for all strategies and for all of them it leads to similar expected costs, with the exception of WSAT where the costs are significantly higher[5] In mutagenesis, $\gamma \approx 100$ is a local minimum for all strategies (for RTD it is even the optimum) when $s^{suf} > 30$.
3. $\gamma < 10$ appears to be uniformly a 'bad' choice for all randomised strategies on the graph problems.
4. For a given domain, expected costs of the different restarted strategies are roughly similar, especially in the vicinity of $\gamma = 100$ (once again, WSAT on the graphs problem is the exception).
5. For both domains, other than very high values of s^{suf}, the costs of the restarted strategies are uniformly lower than that of the non-restarted strategy DTD for a wide range of γ ($100 \leq \gamma \leq 10,000$).

3.4   Discussion

For large intervals of the cutoff parameter γ, the restarted randomised search strategies (RTD, RRR, GSAT, WSAT) exhibit similar performance, outperforming the non-restarted deterministic clause search (DTD) in terms of the cost.

---

[3] We do not plot lines for further scores $s^{suf} = 80, 90 \ldots P$ since these were not achieved by any of the strategies in any of the runs.

[4] In mutagenesis, the high expected costs of DTD are due to several positive examples, whose saturation leads to an unfavorable search space.

[5] A tentative explanation of this may lie in the fact that the explored clause score is a particularly good heuristic for node selection in the noise-free graph problems. In these circumstances the randomization inherent in WSAT may be having a detrimental effect on the mean performance of WSAT.

Graphs: RTD

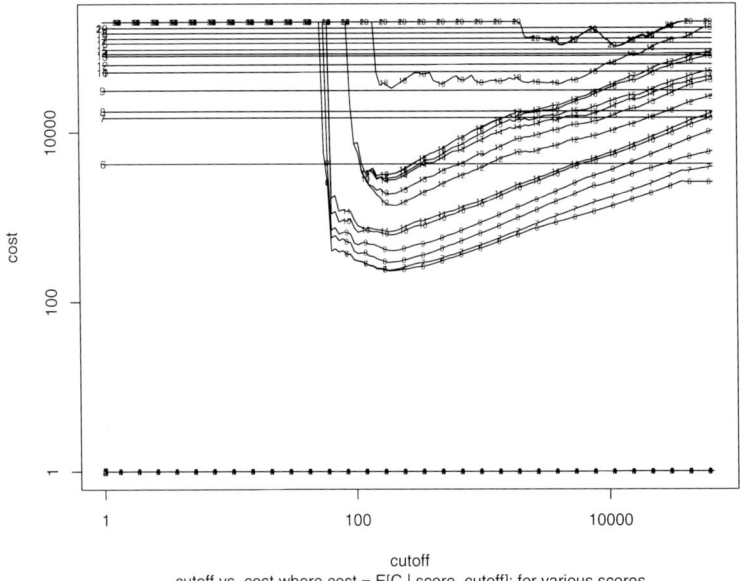

cutoff
cutoff vs. cost where cost = E[C | score, cutoff]; for various scores

Mutagenesis: RTD

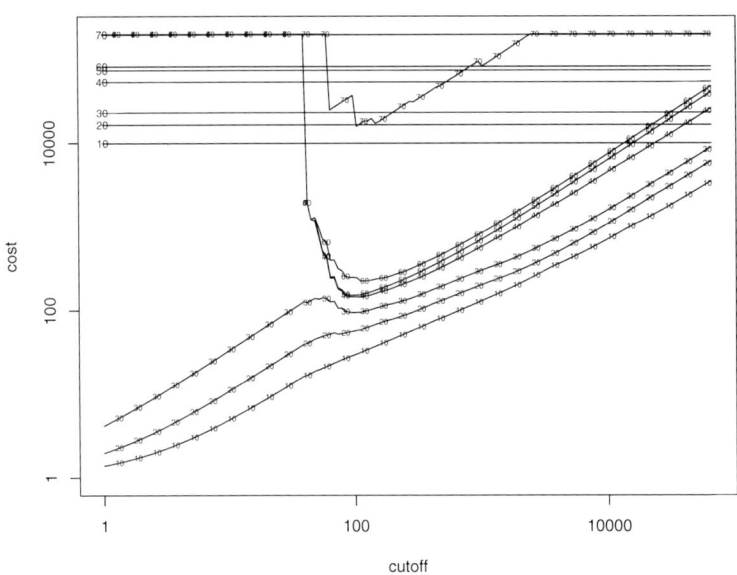

cutoff
cutoff vs. cost where cost = E[C | score, cutoff]; for various scores

Fig. 2. Randomised Top-Down vs. Deterministic Top-Down (horizontal lines) search

Graphs: RRR

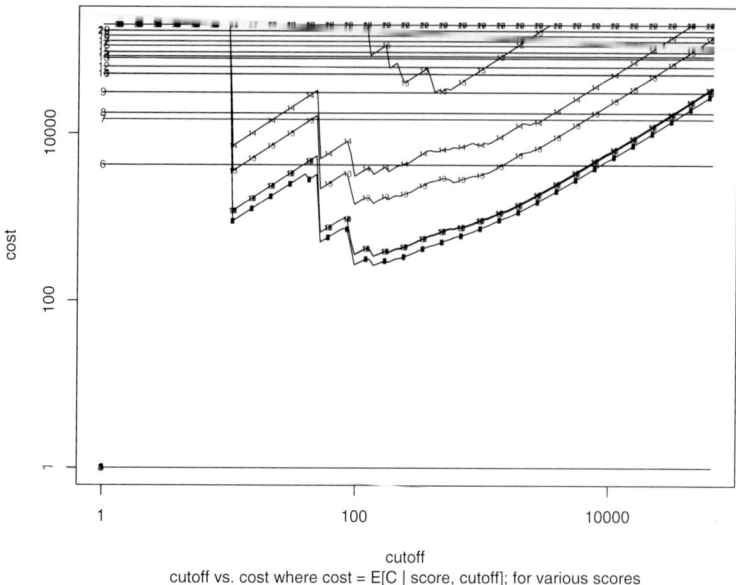

cutoff

cutoff vs. cost where cost = E[C | score, cutoff]; for various scores

Mutagenesis: RRR

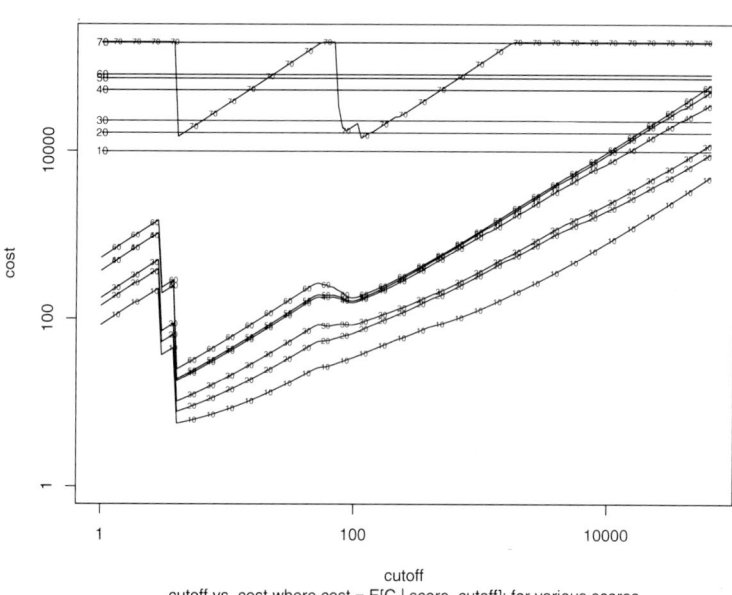

cutoff

cutoff vs. cost where cost = E[C | score, cutoff]; for various scores

Fig. 3. 'Randomised Rapid Restarts' vs. Deterministic Top-Down (horizontal lines) search

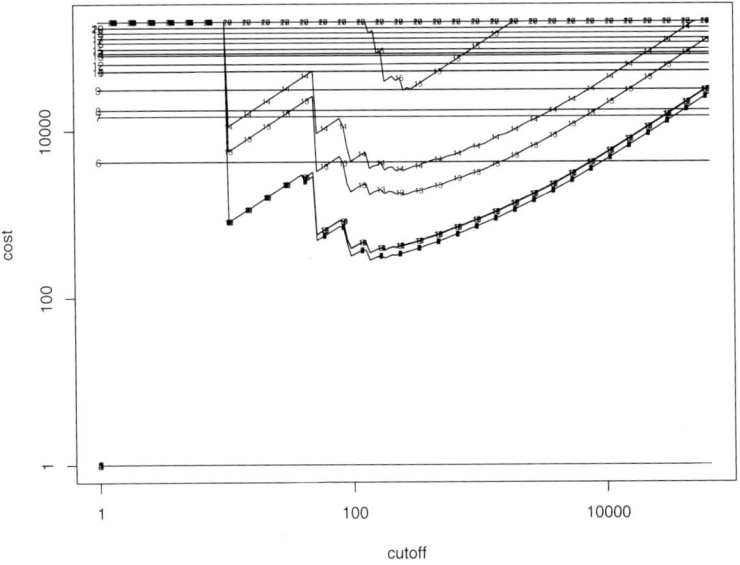

Graphs: GSAT

cutoff

cutoff vs. cost where cost = E[C | score, cutoff]; for various scores

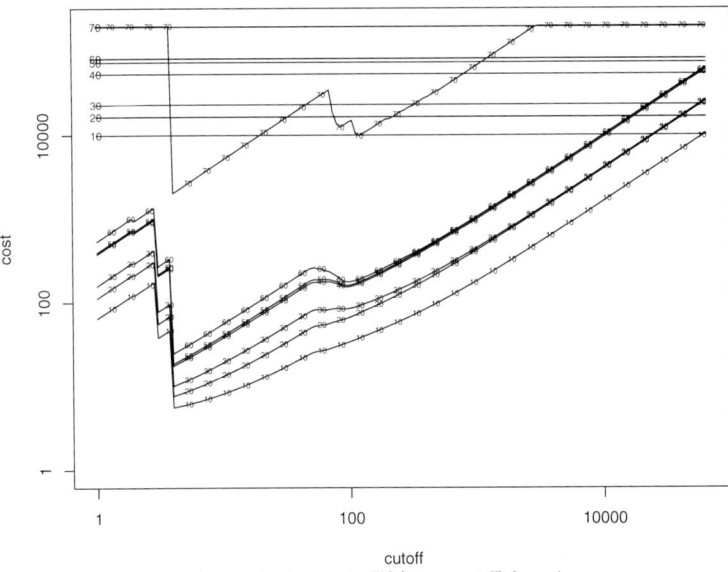

Mutagenesis: GSAT

cutoff

cutoff vs. cost where cost = E[C | score, cutoff]; for various scores

Fig. 4. GSAT vs. Deterministic Top-Down (horizontal lines) search

Graphs: WSAT

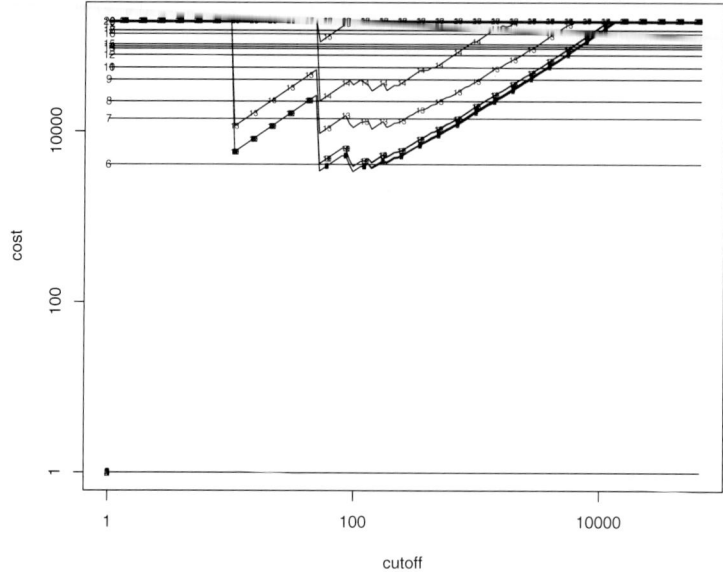

cutoff
cutoff vs. cost where cost = E[C | score, cutoff]; for various scores

Mutagenesis: WSAT

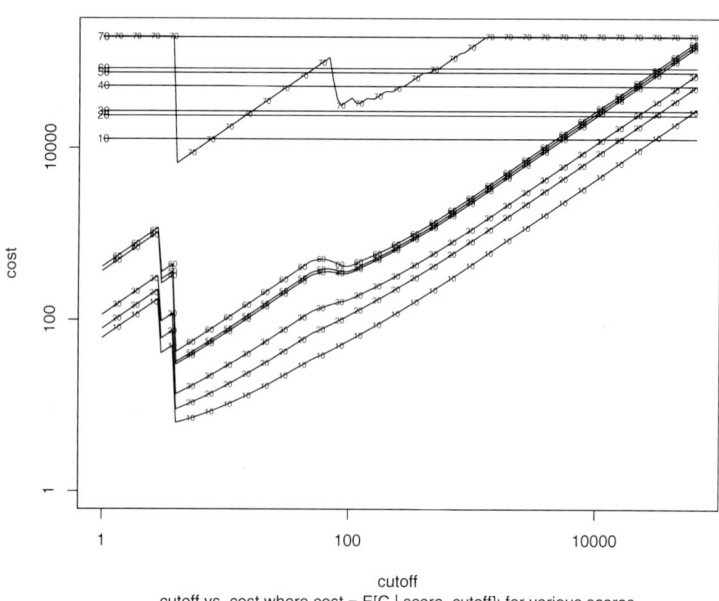

cutoff
cutoff vs. cost where cost = E[C | score, cutoff]; for various scores

Fig. 5. WSAT vs. Deterministic Top-Down (horizontal lines) search

However, two issues require further investigation before conclusions can be made concerning the ranking of the strategies. First, DTD (and RTD) always begins the search with the most general definite clause allowed by the language restriction. It is therefore biased towards evaluating shorter clauses than RRR, GSAT or WSAT which often means spending less total evaluation time for the same number of clauses scored. If processor time is assigned to the search cost, it is possible that both top-down strategies may improve their relative performance with respect to the restarted methods (of course, the empirical results suggest that the latter may evaluate far fewer clauses). Second, our measurement scheme does not assign any cost to the computation needed to construct a bottom clause for each restart. Clearly, the corresponding overhead time grows linearly with decreasing γ (there will be more restarts). As a result, when computation time is viewed as the search cost, the optimum value of γ is likely to shift to a higher value than that determined in our experiments, and the large performance superiority of the the restarted methods observed for small γ is likely to reduce.

It is encouraging that two apparently very different domains and all restarted strategies have yielded a similar range of 'good' values for the γ parameter. However, the plots, especially for the graphs domain, highlight a further aspect: there is quite a sharp increase in costs for values of γ that are just below the optimum. This suggests that it would thus be useful to consider a restarted algorithm that is less dependent on the location of the optimal γ. A solution may lie in a cutoff value gradually (for example, geometrically) growing with each restart. This idea of *dynamic* restarts has been considered before [6] and may result in a more robust search algorithm.

4   Concluding Remarks

Search is at the heart of all modern Inductive Logic Programming systems, and most have thus far employed well-known deterministic search methods. In other fields confronted with very large search spaces, there is now substantial evidence that the use of randomised restarted strategies yield far superior results to deterministic ones (often making the difference between getting a good solution, or none at all). Unfavourable conditions for deterministic search observed in those fields—the heavy-tailed character of search cost distributions—have also been reported in the context of the search conducted by many ILP systems [11]. In this paper, we have presented what appears to be the first systematic study of a number of randomised restarted search strategies for ILP. Specifically, we have adopted a Monte Carlo method to estimate the search cost—measured by the number of clauses explored before a 'good' clause is found—of these strategies on two quite different ILP problems. The result is encouraging: in each domain, for a wide range of values for a parameter γ controlling the number of restarts, randomised restarted methods have a lower search cost than a deterministic general-to-specific search.

The performance sample generated has also provided some useful insights into the randomised techniques. First, it appears that there may a 'good' value for γ that works adequately across many domains. Second, although they differ in the choice of the first element of the search and the refinement strategy employed, all randomised methods appear to perform similarly. Third, there may be some value in exploring a randomised restarted search strategy with a dynamically growing value of γ.

While accepting all the usual caveats that accompany an empirical study such as this, we believe the results here to be sufficiently encouraging for researchers to explore further the use of randomised restarted search methods in ILP, especially with other data domains and scoring functions; and on problems where the target hypotheses lie in 'difficult' locations identified by the research in [1].

A Calculating Expected Cost from Performance Vectors

We describe here a technique for estimating the conditional expected cost value $E[C|s^{suf}, \gamma]$ for each of the five strategies in Section 2.1. We exploit the fact that the expected cost for a strategy with arbitrarily set s^{suf} and γ parameters can be estimated from a sample of executions of the algorithm in Fig. 1 where $s^{suf} = P$ (where P is the maximum possible score) and $\gamma = \infty$. Since we require all trials terminate in a finite time, we let c^{all} equal to some large finite value c_{max} (for the experiments in the paper $c_{max} = 200,000$) for each of the random trials. As we shall see below, setting a finite c^{all} will bias the estimates for non-restarted strategies, but will still allow us to obtain unbiased estimates for restarted strategies for all values of $\gamma < c^{all}$.

Recall that executing the experimental method described in Section 3.2 results, for each strategy and problem, in a set of 'performance' vectors $c_i = [c_i(0), \ldots, c_i(s_{max_i})]$ where $1 \leq i \leq 6000$ for the randomised strategies RTD, RRR, GSAT and WSAT; and $1 \leq i \leq P = |E^+|$ for the deterministic strategy DTD. With each c_i $c_i(s)$ is the number of clauses evaluated before achieving (or exceeding) score s for the first time and s_{max_i} is the maximum score achieved on run i

For DTD, $E[C|s^{suf}, \gamma = \infty]$ is obtained by simply averaging the $c_i(s^{suf})$ over all i's. However, it is possible that in some of the trials i, the maximum score P is not achieved after evaluating c_{max} clauses. In such cases, there exist values $s^{suf} \leq P$ such that $c_i(s^{suf})$ is not defined. Here we set $c_i(s^{suf}) \equiv c_{max}+1$. Thus, the cost we associate to non-restarted strategies will represent *lower bounds* of their expected cost.

For the restarted searches RTD, RRR, GSAT and WSAT, let the sequence of steps 4–14 in Fig. 1 be called a *try*. The probability that s^{suf} is achieved in the t-th try (and not in tries $1 \ldots t - 1$), given the cutoff value γ, is

$$F(\gamma|s^{suf}) \left(1 - F_s(\gamma|s^{suf})\right)^{t-1} \qquad (2)$$

where the conditional cumulative distribution $F(x|s) = P(C \leq x|s)$ represents the probability of achieving or exceeding the score s having evaluated x of fewer clauses. It is estimated for a given score s from the empirical data as the fraction

$$F(x|s) \approx \frac{|\{c_i|c_i(s) \leq x\}|}{|\{c_i\}|} \qquad (3)$$

Note that the consequence of s not being achieved in a particular run i is simply that the condition $c_i(s) \leq x$ does not hold. That is, run i is counted as a realization of the random trial with an 'unsuccessful' outcome. Thus to estimate $F(x|s)$ we do not need to assign a value to $c_i(s)$ in such a case (as was done above for DTD) and the the the estimate remains unbiased.

The expected number of tries initiated before achieving s^{suf} is

$$E[T|s^{suf}, \gamma] = F(\gamma|s^{suf}) \sum_{t=1}^{\infty} t \left(1 - F(\gamma|s^{suf})\right)^{t-1} \tag{4}$$

It equals 1 for $F(\gamma|s^{suf}) = 1$ and for $F(\gamma|s^{suf}) = 0$ we set $E[T|s^{suf}, \gamma] = \infty$. If $0 < F(\gamma|s^{suf}) < 1$, it can be shown that Expression 4 converges to

$$E[T|s^{suf}, \gamma] = \frac{1}{F(\gamma|s^{suf})} \tag{5}$$

If we simply assumed that the algorithm evaluates exactly γ clauses in each try including the last, then the expected number of evaluated clauses would be

$$\bar{E}[C|s^{suf}, \gamma] = \gamma E[R|s^{suf}, \gamma] = \frac{\gamma}{F(\gamma|s^{suf})} \tag{6}$$

However, $\bar{E}[C|s^{suf}, \gamma]$ is imprecise because the algorithm may achieve s^{suf} evaluating fewer than γ clauses in the last try. The expected total number of clauses evaluated in all but the last try is

$$\gamma E[T - 1|s^{suf}, \gamma] = \gamma \left(\frac{1}{F(\gamma|s^{suf})} - 1 \right) \tag{7}$$

Due to the linearity of the expectation operator, we can determine the correct total expected cost by adding to the above value the expected number of clauses evaluated in the last try. For this purpose, consider the family of conditional probability distributions

$$D_t(n) = P(N = n|(t-1) * \gamma < C \leq t\gamma, s^{suf}, \gamma) \tag{8}$$

For $t = 1, 2, \ldots$, each D_t describes the probability distribution of the number of evaluated clauses in the t-th try under the specified parameters s^{suf}, γ, and *given* that the t-th try is the last in the search, ie. an acceptable clause is found therein. Since individual tries are mutually independent, the distributions D_t are identical for all t, that is, for an arbitrary t it holds $D_t(n) = D_1(n)$. Because in the first try it holds[6] that $N = C$, we can write

$$D_1(n) = P(C = n|C \leq \gamma, s^{suf}) \tag{9}$$

---

[6] Within the first try, the total number of evaluated clauses equals the number of clauses evaluated in the current try.

We did not include γ in the conditional part because its value does not affect the probability of the event $C = n$ given that $C \leq \gamma$, ie. given that no restart occurs. Applying basic probability algebra,

$$D_1(n) = \frac{P(C = n, C \leq \gamma | s^{suf})}{P(C \leq \gamma | s^{suf})} \tag{10}$$

If $n > \gamma$ then $D_1(n) = 0$. Otherwise, we can drop the $C \leq \gamma$ conjunct (implied by $C = n$) from the nominator expression:

$$D_1(n) = \frac{P(C = n | s^{suf})}{P(C \leq \gamma | s^{suf})} = \frac{F(n | s^{suf}) - F(n - 1 | s^{suf})}{F(\gamma | s^{suf})} \tag{11}$$

Now we can calculate the expected number $E[N|(t-1) * \gamma < C \leq r\gamma, s^{suf}, \gamma]$ of clauses evaluated in the last try as

$$\sum_{n=1}^{\infty} n D_t(n) = \sum_{n=1}^{\gamma} n D_1(n) = \sum_{n=1}^{\gamma} n \frac{F(n | s^{suf}) - F(n - 1 | s^{suf})}{F(\gamma | s^{suf})} \tag{12}$$

Summing up Eq. 7 with Eq. 12 we get the expected total number of evaluated clauses:

$$E[C | s^{suf}, \gamma] = \gamma \left(\frac{1}{F(\gamma | s^{suf})} - 1 \right) + \frac{\sum_{n=1}^{\gamma} n \left(F(n | s^{suf}) - F(n - 1 | s^{suf}) \right)}{F(\gamma | s^{suf})} \tag{13}$$

Recall that the conditional distribution $F(.|.)$ used above can be estimated from the performance vectors as described by Eq. 3.

Acknowledgements. The authors would like to thank the referees of this paper for their informative suggestions on future work. A.S. would like to acknowledge the generous support provided by the Computing Laboratory, Oxford University during the course of this work and for continuing to act as the primary source for the Aleph program. D.P. acknowledges the support of the U.S. Air Force grant F30602-01-2-0571. F.Z. is supported by the Czech Ministry of Education through the project MSM 212300013.

The Condor Software Program (Condor) was developed by the Condor Team at the Computer Sciences Department of the University of Wisconsin-Madison. All rights, title, and interest in Condor are owned by the Condor Team.

References

1. M. Botta, A. Giordana, L. Saitta, and M. Sebag. Relational learning as search in a critical region. *Journal of Machine Learning Research*, (4):431–463, 2003.
2. S. Dzeroski. Relational data mining applications: An overview. In *Relational Data Mining*, pages 339–364. Springer-Verlag, September 2001.
3. D. E. Goldberg. *Genetic Algorithms in Search, Optimization, and Machine Learning*. Addison-Wesley, 1989.

4. C. Gomes and B. Selman. On the fine structure of large search spaces. In *Proceedings the Eleventh International Conference on Tools with Artificial Intelligence ICTAI'99, Chicago, IL*, 1999.

5. C. P. Gomes, B. Selman, N. Crato, and H. A. Kautz. Heavy-tailed phenomena in satisfiability and constraint satisfaction problems. *Journal of Automated Reasoning*, 24(1/2):67–100, 2000.

6. H. Kautz, E. Horvitz, Y. Ruan, C. Gomes, and B. Selman. Dynamic restart policies. In *Proceedings of the Eighteenth national conference on Artificial intelligence (AAAI-02), Edmonton, Alberta, Canada*, 2002.

7. S. Muggleton. Inverse entailment and Progol. *New Generation Computing, Special issue on Inductive Logic Programming*, 13(3-4):245–286, 1995.

8. B. Selman, H. J. Levesque, and D. Mitchell. A new method for solving hard satisfiability problems. In Paul Rosenbloom and Peter Szolovits, editors, *Proceedings of the Tenth National Conference on Artificial Intelligence*, pages 440–446, Menlo Park, California, 1992. AAAI Press.

9. A. Srinivasan, S. Muggleton, M. J. E. Sternberg, and R. D. King. Theories for mutagenicity: A study in first-order and feature-based induction. *Artificial Intelligence*, 85(1-2):277–299, 1996.

10. N. Trefethen. Maxims about numerical mathematics, computers, science, and life. *SIAM News*, Jan/Feb, 1998.

11. F. Železný, A. Srinivasan, and D. Page. Lattice-search runtime distributions may be heavy-tailed. volume 2583, pages 333–345, 2003.

Learning, Logic, and Probability: A Unified View

Pedro Domingos

Department of Computer Science and Engineering
University of Washington
pedrod@cs.washington.edu

AI systems must be able to learn, reason logically, and handle uncertainty. While much research has focused on each of these goals individually, only recently have we begun to attempt to achieve all three at once. In this talk I will describe Markov logic, a representation that combines the full power of first-order logic and probabilistic graphical models, and algorithms for learning and inference in it. Syntactically, Markov logic is first-order logic augmented with a weight for each formula. Semantically, a set of Markov logic formulas represents a probability distribution over possible worlds, in the form of a Markov network with one feature per grounding of a formula in the set, with the corresponding weight. Formulas and weights are learned from relational databases using inductive logic programming and iterative optimization of a pseudo-likelihood measure. Inference is performed by Markov chain Monte Carlo over the minimal subset of the ground network required for answering the query. Experiments in a real-world university domain illustrate the promise of this approach.

(Joint work with Matt Richardson.)

R. Camacho, R. King, A. Srinivasan (Eds.): ILP 2004, LNAI 3194, p. 359, 2004.
© Springer-Verlag Berlin Heidelberg 2004

Author Index